D1596836

James Still

james still

A LIFE

CAROL BOGGESS

UNIVERSITY PRESS OF KENTUCKY

Support for the publication of this volume was generously provided by the Herman Lee and Nell Stuart Donovan Memorial Endowment at the University of Kentucky.

Editorial and Sales Offices: The University Press of Kentucky
663 South Limestone Street, Lexington, Kentucky 40508-4008
www.kentuckypress.com

Cataloging-in-Publication data available from the Library of Congress

 ISBN 978-0-8131-7418-1 (hardcover : alk. paper)
ISBN 978-0-8131-7420-4 (epub)
ISBN 978-0-8131-7419-8 (pdf)

This book is printed on acid-free paper meeting the requirements of the American National Standard for Permanence in Paper for Printed Library Materials.

Manufactured in the United States of America.

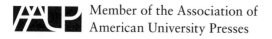 Member of the Association of
American University Presses

Until the leaf of my face withers,
Until my veins are blue as flying geese,
And the mossed shingles of my voice clatter
In winter wind, I shall be young and have my say.
I shall have my say and sing my songs,
I shall give words to rain and tongues to stones,
And the child in me shall speak his turn,
And the old, old man rattle his bones.
Until my blood purples like castor bean stalks,
I shall go singing, my words like hawks.

James Still, "I Shall Go Singing"

Contents

Illustrations follow page 218

Preface

When James Still turned eighty, Hindman Settlement School gave him a big party called "A Master Time." The obvious purpose was to celebrate a remarkable man and valued writer, but the hidden purpose was to explain what made the master "tick." Speakers included Appalachian notables Gurney Norman, Loyal Jones, John Stephenson, Wilma Dykeman, and Jim Wayne Miller. They all knew Still well, but they could not decide what kind of "fellar" he actually was. Still enjoyed the good-humored conjecture, no doubt smiling to himself when Miller quoted Robert Frost—"We dance round in a ring and suppose, / But the Secret sits in the middle and knows."

James Still was a mystery on his eightieth birthday and remained so until his death at the age of ninety-four. Wilma Dykeman ended her remarks that day by saying she would not try to figure out the man. She would simply enjoy discovering and rediscovering what he did "with blank paper and scratchings of words."[1] What Still did with words is the reason he is remembered. His publications began appearing in 1929 and continued throughout the twentieth century and into the twenty-first. His classic novel *River of Earth*—first published by Viking Press as a hardback in 1940, then released as a paperback by Popular Library in 1968, and finally republished by University Press of Kentucky in 1978—is currently available as a paperback, a web pdf, and an e-publication. Although he wrote in multiple genres, including poems, stories, novels, folklife collections, books for children of all ages, and autobiographical sketches, his work with the most enduring appeal is *River of Earth,* a book that does not go away. Still published twenty books between his first volume of poems in 1937, *Hounds on the Mountain,* and his collection of poems *From the Mountain, From the Valley* in 2001. After Still's death, scholar Ted Olson collected his stories and published them as *The Hills Remember* in 2012, and Silas

House edited one of Still's unpublished manuscripts and had it published as *Chinaberry* in 2011.

If we want to know the writer through his printed words, as Dykeman suggested, we have an adequate sample. But James Still is more than his writing. As Edward F. Prichard Jr. asserted at the seventy-sixth birthday celebration, Still's "personality and what it means is bigger than what he has written." He was a public figure, a legend in his time and place. The title most commonly attached to him, "Dean of Appalachian Literature," was conferred as much for his influence and personality as for his publications.

Why probe for the real James Still? Why write the biography of a "simple" man who often chose to be elusive and enigmatic? For one reason: learning about the writer's life gives readers a better context for understanding his work and art. Another is that his life illuminates the region where he chose to live—the hills of eastern Kentucky—a place, as his best-known poem says, he could not leave. Finally, reviewing his long career and his influence on younger writers leads to greater knowledge of Appalachia's rich literature. But he was a living person, not an entry in a literary study or a history book. The contradictions, the setbacks and successes, the mysteries of the man—all that is what interests us most.

In spite of his preference for a quiet, solitary life, James Still liked people; he freely communicated with them in letters and conversations. In a sense, he wanted people to know him; at occasions such as the birthday party in Hindman, he enjoyed their admiration and speculation. When he responded to an interviewer, or read a poem, or told stories after dinner, his eyes would sparkle, and his voice would cast a spell over his listeners. At such times, he revealed himself through the words he spoke. The autobiographical writing he published in his later years provides a map for exploring his life and a partly opened door that invites us on the journey.

How I met James Still and why I took on the project of writing his biography is a combination of planning and chance. I returned to graduate school when I was a faculty member in the English Department at Mars Hill College in western North Carolina. Thanks to the vision and generosity of the Appalachian College Association, then known as the Faculty Scholars Program, faculty from member institutions could receive research grants. I applied and, in 1992, arrived at the University of Kentucky with other scholars from Appalachia, some of whom were there thanks to a fellowship named for the writer James Still. Though my area of interest was American literature, I had not heard of Still. I would meet him on June 25 when the Faculty Scholars Program presented a luncheon and reading by Still at the Gratz Park Inn in Lexington. The special appeal of that day came from his words but also from the person. That eighty-six-year-old man possessed a quick wit, a mellow but confident voice, and the stamina to read and talk for an hour without a sign of fatigue.

That October, when a friend from Australia visited Lexington, I took her to hear James Still perform as part of a culture festival at the University of Kentucky. We made our way to a meeting room on the upper floor of the student center, where a large space had been partitioned into smaller rooms with little thought to acoustics or sound systems. Since the only empty seats were at the back, I felt sure this attempt at cultural sharing would be wasted on my Oxford-educated Australian friend. Waiting for the program to start, we observed the people in the audience: typical undergraduates, university staff, community people, and even a few children. The combination of Still's Southern accent, the inadequate sound system, and interference from voices in the hall meant that my friend caught few of his words, but she did absorb the spirit that filled the room. Magic spread across the audience when Still read *Jack and the Wonder Beans,* holding up the book as he turned each page. It did not matter that only the people in the first two rows could see the illustrations; his gestures held everyone's attention.

As we left, she was full of questions about this writer from eastern Kentucky. The more she probed, the more I realized how little I knew even though Southern literature was my field and Appalachia my home. She was witnessing James Still not through a different lens but through an imported camera, and she was intrigued. I soon read *River of Earth* and found even more than expected: the story of the Baldridge family told by a nameless boy, a time and place that are both particular and universal, themes of discovery that are mythic yet personal, words that are real and evocative, and a living writer with an intriguing persona. I had discovered *River of Earth,* a regional classic that had experienced a resurrection forty years after its national publication, and James Still, a man in the process of becoming a legend in his lifetime.

My dissertation topic was decided; three years later, the work was complete. Still had not resisted and had even granted me several interviews. With the support of my committee, especially my advisor, John Cawelti, and the generous help of the prominent Appalachian scholar and Still's personal friend Jim Wayne Miller, along with access to the

Still collections at the University of Kentucky and at Morehead State University, I enjoyed the entire venture. When that work, "Following *River of Earth* from Source to Destination," was complete, I returned to my teaching career at Mars Hill College. Soon I discovered that the project had not ended.

I became better acquainted with Still during the last six years of his life. In the summer of 1997, for example, I conducted an oral-history research project in Hindman to interview him and other residents. He never asked if I intended to write his biography, nor did he suggest that he wanted one written. I have since discovered in letters and papers from the last fifteen years of his life that he believed a number of people were engaged in writing his story. He never named these would-be Boswells, but I was not among them. In spite of an enduring interest and a nagging curiosity about the man's work and past, I did not have enough time for such a consuming project.

Then on April 28, 2001, James Still died. Three days later, people gathered in Hindman for the funeral. Mike Mullins, director of Hindman Settlement School, had asked me to give an overview of Still's life at the service. When Mullins introduced me as the person whom Still had chosen to be his biographer, I was surprised. Still had never voiced that expectation to me; now it had been openly stated on this most important occasion. But, "no matter," as Still would say, I would think about that later. At that moment, everyone was immersed in remembering and honoring the man, his work and words, his friends and family. Months later I began considering the challenge. I knew enough about his long life to anticipate the complexities but also feel the intrigue. At the publication of *From the Mountain, From the Valley*, edited by Ted Olson, it seemed that a biography would be appreciated. Several years later, Mars Hill College granted me a sabbatical, and the Appalachian College Association matched it with a research fellowship. The pieces were falling into place. Thus began my journey through the life of James Still, a travel experience that has been arduous, perplexing, and gratifying, but never boring.

I invite readers to take that journey, to experience Still's life in the hills he knew and loved. Those acquainted with James Still are already familiar with aspects of his personality and selected events of his life. Those who know him only through his prose and poetry will find a life story that sheds light on his work. Those who know nothing at all about him should prepare for an adventure that follows no previously charted map. Still's life was purposeful and accidental, premeditated and serendipitous, crafted and candid. He never presumed to tell others how to live, but we can gain wisdom from his experiences. Come along to learn of this man's quiet life of dignity and mystery, to explore his particular time and special place, and to meet his friends and family.

We begin with an invitation from James Still himself.

"Welcome, Somewhat, Despite the Disorder"

Come inside
Where I am—
I alone.

Nobody else
Is here,
Or ever
Has been.

Come in
Nevertheless;
Overlook this,
Blind eye to that.

Two rooms
Have I:
The Heaven Room,
The Hell Room.
I dwell in both.

Come inside
And discover
You live
Likewise.[2]

Part 1

A Southern Boyhood, 1906–1924

1

A Place to Begin

I had a happy childhood, surrounded by caring parents and other relatives.

—James Still

On Monday, July 16, 1906, a baby was born in a house on Double Branch Farm near LaFayette, Alabama.[1] Two days later, the weekly paper ran this announcement of a "Personal and General Nature": "Dr. Aleck [*sic*] Still arose early Monday morning with an old-time smile that extended from one side of his face to the other—all on account of a railing baby boy that made its appearance at his home Sunday night as a permanent member of the family" (*The Lafayette Sun*, July 18, 1906). The sixth child born to Alex and Lonie Still was special because he was their first boy. The proud parents gave him the father's name: James Alexander Still Jr.

His father was a farmer who also worked as a "horse doctor," a veterinarian with no official training. J. Alex, as he was formally known—or "Doc," as people called him—was acquainted with most of the animals in the area. By 1907, he was running weekly ads in the newspaper to make his practice known—"Dr. J.A. Still, Veterinary Surgeon, located 2 miles north of LaFayette. Calls answered day or night." He would raise his hat as he spoke to the horses he passed. He had helped them enter the world or doctored them after they arrived. He also made friends with his human neighbors. An honest and likable man with a sense of humor, Alex could drive a hard bargain. He was known to brag,

3

"I've never cheated anybody in my life, except in a horse trade. And that doesn't count. It's a game."[2] Alex was fair complexioned with reddish hair and eyes blue as a robin's egg—a handsome man who enjoyed mixing with people and who was never at a loss for words. The *Chambers County News* once described his talent for talk as a "rare uniqueness of expression" that, along with his ability to see "the interesting in the commonplace," always led to good conversation.[3]

One exasperated love letter from Alex to "his girl" on Valentine's Day 1892 shows that he did not hesitate to put his words on paper and that their courtship was not without trials. The young man wrote with passion:

> Darling Lonie you cannot realize the sadness of my heart.
> What you told me last Sunday evening was a mistake. . . . My
> heart is almost broken. You are the only Girl I ever loved.
> This is not the first time I have bloted [sic] your name with
> a tear. The love I have for you increases daily but you are
> liking someone else better than you like me and you must
> acknowledge that. I do not want you to answer this with
> flattery. But I want you to answer this with a true heart. You
> know that I have told you that I will not mix up [compete]
> with any other boy and if this does not suit you we will have
> to bust up. Oh how it would terrify my heart. But I hope that
> will never be. . . . I never will go back on you I never will love
> anyone else as long as I live. But if you want to bust up I will
> agree with a sad heart. Things must change with us right at
> once.
>
> Please answer this soon. Say darling, will you ever leave me or
> not?
> S. W. A. K. J.A.S.[4]

Alex made his case, and Lonie made the right choice. Their wedding came a year later on February 23, 1893, in her father's house. Though she was eighteen and he twenty-one, their youthful romance met adult reality when their first child arrived the following September. Two and a half years later, a second child was born; and within five years, they had three girls: Carrie Lois (1893), Elloree (1896), and Nixie (1898). Neither parent thought of attending college or receiving advanced training. They, like most young couples, would depend on their extended families and community church. Their intent was to benefit from their own hard work and hope for the best.

Lonie Lindsey Still was less of a public figure than her husband. She was quiet. In photographs, her hair was pulled back from her open face, and her eyes emitted a calm wisdom. In the letter above, his offer to let her have the last word on their future was only a suitor's gesture. He was the dominant personality. But they complemented each other and appeared to be well matched; the children heard no cross words between them. Lonie's married life was very busy. In addition to minding household chores, she worked in the fields. Even her pastimes were work—quilting, crocheting, embroidering, and tatting. Her one passion was her garden filled with vegetables and flowers. Lonie did not keep records of the children's babyhood; she was too busy bearing and raising them; growing, preserving, and cooking food; making and mending clothes; and cleaning everything. Her life of hard physical labor was more impressive because she was a slight woman who never weighed more than 110 pounds.[5]

Although they met and married in Chambers County, Alex and Lonie went to Texas early on as homesteaders and settled in Bell County, the area that is now Fort Hood military reservation. At least that was the story James Still told. The move was not officially recorded or even recalled by other family members, but the young couple could have lived there without entering into a formal homestead agreement. The Texas connection became part of the Still family mythology when it was included in Still's posthumous work, *Chinaberry*. Here, the boy narrator from Alabama is visiting Texas, a place that he knows about from his earliest memories: "Not only had my father spent three years farming near Killeen, Texas, but two of my uncles had followed on hearing about the rich earth where cotton virtually jumped out of the ground. And my Aunt Ada, just turned sixteen, had eloped with a widower, heading west, never to return even for a visit until the year of Grandpa's death, 1925. And as a coincidence, her sister—who was actually named Texas—followed."[6] Several of Alex's siblings did reside in Texas, and probably Alex and Lonie lived and worked with them for a few years. Although unsubstantiated, the Texas story is appealing and plausible. If the first two girls were born in Texas, the family would have been there at least until 1896.[7]

The Stills returned to Alabama for a visit, and while there, the third child, Nixie (1898–1901), died of scarlet fever and was buried in Rock Springs Church Cemetery. Because she had promised the baby she would stay with her, Lonie refused to leave the grave and return to Texas. The couple with their two girls then settled in Chambers County near their parents and began the struggle to forge a middle-class life in a rural crop-dependent economy. For a time, Alex worked at a drugstore, and in order to learn the Latin required by a pharmacy, they boarded the schoolmaster.[8] Two more babies were born. Ten years after they married, Alex and Lonie had five children, all girls, but no house or land of their own.

Their sixth child was James Jr. The new baby's world was filled with females. His oldest sister, Carrie Lois, was thirteen; Elloree was ten; Nixie was a memory; Lonie was six; and Inez, three. Aunt Fanny, the black nurse who helped his mother tend the children, also cared for and spoiled him. Diapering and washing diapers was her chief employment, along with quieting whines and rocking babies to sleep. When his mother had no time to cure a hurt or answer a question, Aunt Fanny did.

When James was two, a second boy was born, William Comer. The result, Still said, was that he was "kicked out of the cradle."[9] A short babyhood meant that young James learned to think for himself and be independent. As soon as he could walk, he would go to Fanny's house for sweet treats. One of his happiest memories was of sneaking off there to "sop syrup" out of a bucket lid. When his mother sent for him, he pretended to hide under the bed.[10] The image of running about and exploring suggests an early need to find his own way. Walking represented an adventurous spirit that Still exhibited fully in his late teens, but it began as soon as he could stand up. In the Still family, once a child could stand alone, he was treated as an adult.[11]

In later years, Still said he was born in a cotton patch. One of his earliest memories was of running about in the field, carrying a small sack his mother had made. The whole family worked together, and his mother would bring dinner for them to eat in the shade.[12] He recalled one special time when he was four. As he picked the odd bit, he chided his sisters to pick faster because his father was going to take him to the cotton gin in LaFayette when they finished for the day, and they could not stop until they had enough to make a bale (two thousand pounds). Finally, perched on the loaded cotton, he rode the wagon to the gin, then lost his cap up the suction tube drawing the cotton into the machine.[13]

Farming was the main occupation for the Still family. After hiring a neighbor to turn the soil, Alex got his children to help him plant the rows, cultivate the fields, and harvest the crops. They raised mostly cotton but also grew corn and soybeans, sorghum and sugar cane. Money was scarce, but the family got by. Working the land together meant they all developed a direct connection between the ground they lived on and the plants that grew in it. They were carrying on the life and work of their forebears and all the people in their extended families.

"Who we are, where we came from, what our ancestors did before us" was important to James Still.[14] Other than the family Bible, his parents kept no record of the family lines. Still never pursued a serious study of his genealogy; yet in later years, amateur genealogist and friend of the Still family L. F. Simpkins piqued Still's interest in his ancestry.[15] Still incorporated the research into the narrative of his family history. Being a natural storyteller, he had the license to occasionally twist facts or fill in blanks. His account went something like this. His forebears were of English stock on his father's side and of Scotch-Irish on his mother's. Both families had first settled in Virginia during pioneer days—the Lindseys near Berryville, and the Stills near Jonesville. These ancestors fought for the American Revolution and were rewarded with land—the Stills in eastern Alabama, and the Lindseys in northern Georgia. The ones who stayed in Virginia accounted for the connection that Still claimed to Andrew Taylor Still, the founder of osteopathic medicine, who has a roadside marker near Cumberland Gap.[16]

That Virginia connection to the Alabama Stills is not evident in genealogical records, but their origins can be traced back to Edgefield County, South Carolina, when in the middle of the eighteenth century John Still married Jane Jolly and had eleven children.[17] Their youngest was Still's great-great grandfather, Jolly James Still, who married Isabella Bean. Their son Abner (1810–1886) married Lonie Ann Quattlebaum (1813–1894) in 1830 and moved from South Carolina to eastern Alabama, settling in the Penton area of the newly created Chambers County. Abner was a successful farmer in Alabama, known for planting large vegetable crops, which he shared with anyone in need. The value of his holdings rose from $1,000 in 1850 to $4,000 in 1860. By the end of the Civil War, his real estate was reduced to its initial value. Lonie and Abner had twelve children. Their fifth son, William Watson, born in 1839, was Still's grandfather.[18] Still described him as a Civil War veteran, a handsome man, and a gentleman with his own special pew at Rock Springs Baptist Church. Still could not "imagine him hitting a lick of work" but knew he must have.[19]

William was wounded twice in the Civil War. One of the wounds he displayed like a badge—a Yankee bullet had shot off his index finger. Later, he fought in the battle of Corinth in Tennessee and was reported to have been captured at Newmarket. Still recalled his "Grandpa" talking with fellow veterans about the North's mining of the Confederate trenches at Petersburg.[20] William married Anna McLendon on May 5, 1861, in Chambers County. Their union resulted in seven children: Still's father plus four aunts and two uncles.[21]

The Civil War had also directly affected the Lindseys. Lonie's mother, Carrie Jackson (1843–1921), was first married to a man named Green, a Confederate soldier shot while attempting to head off Sherman's march through Georgia. Years later, Carrie told her grandchildren the story of finding her husband's emaciated body. He was near death when a fellow soldier delivered him to their house in Georgia, lifting him out of the wagon and leaning him against the fence at the edge of the property. Young Carrie picked him up and carried him into the house. Her take-charge attitude was her trademark, and Still remembered his grandmother as "a matriarch if ever there was one . . . the real brains in the family." She was also resourceful, and after her first husband's death, Carrie married a younger man, Still's grandfather James Benjamin Franklin Lindsey (1847–1930).[22]

Carrie Jackson was probably born in Franklin, Georgia, northeast of Chambers County. James Lindsey was born in Glenn, a small community close to the Alabama line and the birthplace of all nine of their children.[23] Still's mother, Barcelona Anadora (Lonie), was the fourth; her younger siblings, especially Uncle Luther, Uncle Eddie Boozer, and Aunt Carrie, made a clear impression on young Still, as did his grandfather, the star of "My Aunt Carrie." The poem tells of Carrie and Lonie's commiserating with each other about their father's squandering of their inheritance by paying $3,000 for an abandoned railroad station. They were sure that he had lost his mind, but they were proved wrong:

> When Grandpa sold the old station
> Three weeks later for nine thousand,
> Tripling his money,
> That was the last word we heard
> Of Grandpa going crazy and needing a guardian
> And throwing away the money coming to us
> The day he dies.
> Not a word.[24]

This man, James Lindsey, was an orphan. He was raised by an uncle who was reputed to have been a cruel slaveholder. As a boy, he had once been punished with a whip, and even into old age, his legs retained the scars. As a result of this strict upbringing, he became a devout church-man, and in 1886 he helped build a Primitive Baptist church near his home. If Edd, Lindsey's youngest son, was correct, his father's carpentry skills did not extend to the family house, where the kitchen floor was "beaten earth."[25] According to legend, Grandpa Lindsey mined enough gold on his Georgia farm to fill his teeth but certainly not enough to make him rich. A cyclone destroyed the Lindsey home, an incident that may have spurred the family's move to Alabama in 1890. Lonie was sixteen when they settled close to Roanoke, just north of Chambers County. At that time, her family lived about three miles, a good buggy ride, from the Still family, whose house was near Buffalo, a small community close to the county seat, LaFayette.

The Stills and Lindseys were typical middle-class white Alabama families at the turn of the century—owning land, working farms of less than one hundred acres, and remembering clearly the Civil War that had ended some forty years earlier. In 1900 the state had a population of 1.8 million, and only 200,000 lived in the towns and cities. More than 60 percent of the land was in farms, and cotton was the most valuable crop. On August 29, 1900, the LaFayette weekly newspaper proudly advertised the area as "the best average county in the state in point of agricultural resources, intelligence, and natural advantages." The community took care of its own, as evident by the paper's front page that, in addition to news of cotton prices and road improvements, frequently posted notices of family reunions and church functions alongside ads to sell a cow or to seek help in finding who shot a pig.

Both families owned and farmed land. Their property may have had the external look of the antebellum South, with big oak trees lining the driveways, but the life they lived was not one of luxury. An image that stuck in young Still's mind was of the two outdoor toilets at the Lindsey place. The one meant for guests had four holes, and the boy playfully imagined all of them being occupied at once. The large house was set in an oak grove. Still's memories evoke images of a plantation dwelling set in an air of romance: "the rambling house with more rooms than anybody could use, the parlor with glittering chandelier and an organ, the wide verandah with swing, the peach orchard, a vineyard yellow with scuppernongs in season, the red goblets to drink from."[26] The real place would have been less glamorous.

The Still family house, near Marcoot, was what might be called a planter's house, gray on the outside and surrounded by a wide veranda, the place where Confederate veterans would gather to reminisce about the war. Getting to the porch meant walking past high shrubs and a garden with fragrant flowers. The house was organized so that large rooms went off of a central hallway. The children never went into the parlor, though they were allowed an occasional look. The shades were pulled so the rugs would not fade, and an organ sat unplayed in the corner. A covered runway connected the house to a dining room and an old kitchen with a large fireplace for cooking.[27] Still described both of his grandfathers as patriarchs and landowners. They were respected citizens and leaders in their churches, but there is no evidence that they were part of the wealthy plantation-owning Southern tradition, and they did not pass any land on to Still's father and mother.

Where he came from and what his ancestors did before him influenced Still's life and writing. The roots of his family tree were deep in the Alabama soil. His descriptions embellished the origins of early relatives, just as he may have added the Texas interim to his parents' married life. He sometimes romanticized the houses of his grandparents. But the basic story is clear: he was born into a rural, agrarian culture of the deep South at a time when people remembered better days before the war as well as the tragedy of the war, but lived in a time when they worked hard and valued their families, neighbors, and churches. Alex Still and Lonie Lindsey were part of that tradition, and like most couples in the early twentieth century, they must have been pleased when a son was born to them, a boy who could carry on the family name.

What Alex and Lonie may have lacked in material wealth, they made up in kinfolk. Still boasted that he had "barrels of relatives, dozens of cousins."[28] The Stills had seven children; the Lindseys had ten. Altogether, James had fifteen aunts and uncles, many of whom made a lasting impression on him. He memorialized several in his poem "Those I Want in Heaven with Me (Should There Be Such a Place)." His Aunt Enoree, "too good for this world," was his father's older sister. Uncle Edd, his mother's younger brother, "had devils dancing in his eyes." Another two of his mother's brothers were Luther, "who laughed so loud in the churchyard he had to apologize to the congregation," and Joe, who saved all the money he ever earned. Aunt Carrie, his mother's youngest sister, was stingy with compliments and kept James informed, "Too bad you're not good looking like your daddy." Grandpa Lindsey would bite his ears, and Grandpa Still could not remember his name because there were so many children at every gathering. Though it was not published until 1991, the poem's good-humored portrait of his relatives began to take shape in his earliest memories. He was a quiet, independent, observant child who enjoyed visiting his kin.[29]

Most recreation for the Still children depended on family activities, especially socializing on Sundays after church. James's own family was not pious, though regular church attendance was a must.[30] He described them as "wearing their religion lightly: no one smoked, no alcoholics, no divorces."[31] The older generation had a more serious commitment to religious practice. Both sets of grandparents thought Baptist was the only denomination, but they came from different traditions. The Lindsey family was Primitive Baptist and went to the Macedonia Church; the Stills were Missionary Baptist and went to Rock Springs Baptist. The children thought that Grandpa Still owned the church because he had a special seat and was often called on to pray. Not far away, Grandpa Lindsey was an elder in his church and was finally buried in the cemetery under a tombstone that read, "An honest man is the handiwork of God."[32] James's family belonged to Rock Springs, but they attended both churches. Because each congregation worshipped only one weekend a month (Macedonia on the second Sunday and Rock Springs on the third), it was possible for Alex and Lonie to alternate attendance and satisfy both families.[33]

After church, family members would visit one another, riding the distances in their buggies. Everyone would eat a big meal; then the adults would relax on the porch while the children played in the yard. There was always plenty of talk and laughter. One of his father's jokes conveys the flavor of these Sunday afternoons: "Passing through LaFayette on a Sunday [Papa] heard the Baptist congregation singing 'Will there Be Any Stars in My Crown?' and the Methodist simultaneously, 'No, Not One.'"[34] His father liked a good joke, and so did his uncles. When they all got together, "they'd start telling things and you could hear them a half mile. They'd whoop and holler, and laugh and shout."[35]

The young child's life was filled with happiness but also moments of great sadness. The loss of his dog stayed with him his whole life. Still told the story to Randy Wilson in 1988: "We called him Jack. I don't know how we got him but I was a little boy, no more than six. And one day somebody came to the house who wanted the dog and asked Papa to give it to him. And he did. Anybody wanted anything Papa had, he'd give it to them. . . . When I came home, the dog was gone. . . ." Jack has a place of honor in the poem "Those I Want in Heaven." He is mentioned in the first line and again in the second stanza:

First, I want my dog Jack,
Granted that Mama and Papa are there,
And my nine brothers and sisters,

. . . .
I want my dog Jack nipping at my heels,
Who was my boon companion,
 Suddenly gone when I was six. . . .[36]

Another memorable but strange incident of early childhood was the boy's visit to the neighboring farm, which was a settlement for the county's indigent old men. He memorialized the place in his poem "On Double Creek."

I was born on Double Creek, on a forty-acre hill;
North was the Buckalew Ridge, south at our land's end
The county poor farm with hungry fields
And furrows as crooked as an adder's track.

James went there only once, and that was to have a man take a wart off his finger. He remembered sitting by the fireplace where a pot of beans was boiling. The procedure must have been painless because he never recalled any stress on his part. But the wart came off. He did remember that the ghostly neighbors were mysterious. The poem goes on to describe them with words like "plodding," "worn," shapeless," then closes with the haunting line "I can remember the dark swift martins in their eyes."[37]

Young James was four or five when the family moved from the house on Double Creek to Grandpa Still's house. When his mother died suddenly in 1910, Alex took his wife and children to live with his father and maiden sister, Enoree. That farm was located between Pigeon Roost and Hootlocka Creek near the small community of Marcoot. Still's memories of his grandfather's house included large rooms, an attic full of relics from the past, and the fragrance of gardenias near the porch when water was thrown on them.[38] The same year they moved, James gained a second brother, Thomas Watson, who was born on January 13, 1911. Even a large house must have seemed a little crowded with eight children and four adults.

When James was six, the family moved again, this time to the Carlisle place on the Buffalo Road, a few miles southeast of Marcoot. They purchased acreage and built their new house on a typical plan: "roomy, hall down the middle, veranda halfway round, a frosted pane distinguishing the front door." Still always thought of this place as home because it was there that he "came to awareness." Again, the whole Still family was involved in farming. Alex would hire a man to plow in the spring, but after that the children did most of the work in the fields. The peak work season was May to September. His sisters were careful to shield themselves from the sun and from passersby. They covered their exposed skin with cream, donned stockings on their hands and arms and wide-brimmed hats on their heads, and refused to work close to the road. Being only six, James kept busy picking off boll weevils and dropping them in a kerosene can. He also picked potato bugs and rooted out nut grass. Resourceful even then, young James recognized that the bulbs of the grass tasted like coconut. He would pull and eat them.[39] When the crop was ready, everyone picked cotton.

The boy was a careful observer and good listener. "All ears," his mother used to say, referring to his habits as well as his features. All the Still boys tended to have protruding ears. But his mother thought his stuck out a bit farther than necessary, so she put a band around his head to flatten them until they assumed an acceptable position.[40] If her "cure" made any difference at all, it certainly did not dampen his curiosity or hinder his attention to detail.

One day while hoeing in the fields, James listened as Inez began a story that lasted for what seemed like hours to the child. At first he thought the incident she related was true but eventually realized his sister was making everything up as she went along. This was to be Still's first lesson in storytelling. "From that moment my horizon expanded into the imaginary. I could make my own tales and did."[41] But that was not the full extent of his sisters' influence. They taught him to "read" by reading to him over and over a little book on Eskimos. It was about a boy, a dog, and a sled. Rather than reading the actual words on the page, young James memorized the sentences then recited them as the pages turned.

He also walked to school with his sisters, even before he was officially old enough to enroll. He enjoyed the adventure and wanted to go every day. When asked by a teacher why he did not come to school more often, he answered, "I would wust [wouldst] Mama would let me."[42] From an infant who crawled early to a would-be school boy, he was a quiet, observant child who sought adventure and found it in short journeys, visits to family, stories he heard, or trips to school.

In Still's stories, learning and growing is often associated with walking and traveling. Nowhere is the connection more apparent than at the end of Still's last chapter of *Sporty Creek*, when the young narrator and his brother, Dan, are headed for school at Hindman. This journey marks the end of their protected childhood and the beginning of their life outside of home. The narrator calls to mind the day Little Jolly, the baby of the family, took his first step: "He had risen up, put a foot forward, and toppled. Up he stood again, brave and certain, heading for the door, going from us." A walking baby leads to a growing child, and the story's final scene shows the two brothers near the end of their journey. Somewhat timid and skeptical about going to school, they hold hands and walk on.[43]

2

Old Enough to Go Traipsing

I was nine years old, old enough to go traipsing, to look abroad upon the world.

—Narrator, "On Quicksand Creek"

Like most children of his day, James (now called Jimmie) started to school when he was seven, and he walked. Along with his sisters, he attended the "college" in LaFayette, two miles south of their house on the Buffalo Road. When he first began making the trip, his sisters would carry him if he got tired.[1] But soon he could carry his own weight. The large building with its clock and bell tower on the edge of town must have been daunting to the little boy. The original school building, a two-story rectangular brick construction, first opened in 1885. There was no electricity, and a fireplace or stove in each room provided heat. An addition was built in 1907, when the total enrollment was 266, including all students from grammar school through two years of post–high school study, hence the name "college." LaFayette was proud of the institution; the newspaper, the *LaFayette Sun,* had declared it "second to none" on September 26, 1900. Because it offered all the grades and was the pride of the town, it had more resources than the one-room rural schools. Even so, Still never recalled brilliant or inspiring teachers except for Miss Porterfield, his first-grade teacher.[2]

She provided a positive first impression when, on the opening day of school, she taught Jimmie how to write. With a piece of chalk, Miss

Porterfield wrote his name on the desk, then gave him an ear of corn so that he could break off the kernels and use them to outline the letters she had written. By the time he went home, he knew the look and feel of his name. Before long, he was writing. One early example was a note to his mother who had gone to visit relatives for a week: "Mama, come home. Lois is baking the biscuits too big!"[3] As the year progressed, the class engaged in more hands-on activities. One was an introduction to agriculture. The students planted corn seeds in pots and tended the growing plants.[4] Another experience was the required recitation. When the class acted out *Hiawatha*, Jimmie was the squirrel, Adjidaumo. That role suited him because he was small for his age, the only student who "had to stand on a box to reach the blackboard."[5]

Jimmie enjoyed the attention of an audience. More than seventy years after the event, Still told of a recitation that made him momentarily famous. In this, his "first public appearance," he "brought down the house."

> Every grade had its day to perform in chapel—and Miss Porterfield taught me a verse by Robert Louis Stevenson as my contribution. Our class of first graders marched onto the stage, the principal at one end of the platform, the teacher on the other, we children seated between. Proud parents and students made up the audience.
>
> My turn came. I marched and began. Hardly had I spoken "birdie with a yellow bill hopped upon a windowstill" [sic]. Then squeals and squalls of glee broke loose in the audience, followed by general pandemonium. The principal jumped to his feet—mystified. But Miss Porterfield guessed the cause and dragged me into the wings. I was unbuttoned![6]

Another memorable school experience involved visits from local Civil War veterans. The war had been over for fifty years, and the soldiers who fought it, like Still's grandfathers, would have been in their seventies, but they tried to instill in the younger generation an appreciation for their efforts and the region's heritage. Jimmie would listen to war stories told over and over when the old men gathered on his grandpa's veranda. On Confederate Memorial Day (April 30), the children would gather in chapel to hear veterans talk about the war; then they would march to the cemeteries to decorate the graves of fallen heroes with Confederate flags, all the while singing, "The Bonny Blue Flag."

Still admitted that the children did not understand what the war had been about, but they were convinced that if it were fought again, they would win.[7]

Jimmie was a skeptical and curious child, not easily deceived. One time at school he heard that rabbits laid eggs on Easter. While wanting to believe, he had doubts. The local tradition was for families to make holes in the field and put flowers around them. On Easter the rabbits would come and lay eggs in the holes so the children could find them. Jimmie designed a test for the Easter rabbit; he dug his hole and marked it without telling anyone, so the grownups did not know to put the egg in. In another case, his doubts were proven wrong. Going to school in town was an education in itself for the children from country farms. One of the town boys, Clyde McLendon, bragged about having two spigots at his house—one for cold water and one for hot. His friends, including Jimmie, were appropriately skeptical that such a marvel could exist and eagerly accompanied Clyde home one day to call his bluff. The spigots, which were on the back porch, worked just as Clyde had claimed.

Jimmie made friends both in school and out. Looking at a photo of his first-grade class, Still once pointed out to Jim Wayne Miller a little girl named Amy Wellington, whom he said he would surely have married if he had stayed in Alabama.[8] Of course, he did not stay, and Miss Wellington was not heard of again. About this same time, Jimmie privately became friends with a black boy. It was possible then to live very near African Americans in the county without having much interaction unless they worked for your family. A black family lived on Uncle Luther Lindsey's place, within walking distance of Jim's house. Nearby was a swimming hole that both boys liked to visit. They would swim together. He and Jimmie became friends without telling anyone. Maybe his parents would not have objected to the boys' playing together, but Jimmie never gave them the opportunity. Another common sport for young boys was wrestling, but he did not wrestle with this friend. He knew without being told that while playing with a black boy might be tolerated, physical contact would not be.[9]

Though Jimmie did not come in contact with many other black children, he did know a few adults in the town. One was a barber named Green Appleby, who served only white clients, and another was "Old Black Joe," the school janitor. Jimmie especially liked the janitor of the courthouse in LaFayette, "Puss" Irwin, who would lift little children so they could drink ice-cold water from the fountain reserved for "Whites

Only."[10] Assistant to Mr. Irwin was Munroe "Mun" Barrow, father of Joe Louis, the world-champion heavyweight boxer who put Chambers County on the sports map.[11]

When children were not in school or exploring the town or woods on their own, they worked with their parents in the fields. Jimmie never thought of work as unpleasant and even seemed to enjoy the opportunity for interactions. People never felt they HAD to work; it was something they just did.[12] Some jobs belonged exclusively to him. When he was eight, he started milking the family cow, a chore with trials and rewards. He recalled going out barefoot early in the morning and having the cow step on his foot. But before he began to collect the milk in the bucket, he would take a swallow himself or aim a squirt at the cat's mouth to give it a special treat.[13] The afternoon milking ritual started with hunting the cows in the big pasture or, on hot days, in the cool woods. He would roust them out by calling, "Sooke."[14]

Still prepared another cow story called "The Crippled Cow" to use on a spot for National Public Radio. Being a vet in a cash-strapped economy, his father was sometimes paid for services in cattle, but not the pick of the lot. One particular cow that Alex brought home was a good milker but had one leg smaller than the others, and "no amount of food or grain could fatten her." The boy's job was to lead the miserable beast to be dipped in an insecticide at the county vat. There was a law that all cows had to be dipped in an effort to control an insect called "wools." "I was urging this cow, so painfully crippled along the road, and so slowly, and being passed by other boys pressing on with fine Holsteins and shapely Guernseys. At the county dipping vats— all the observers—all eyes on my miserably appearing beast. Well, I was ashamed of this cow. But, foremost, and overriding this emotion I was *ashamed* of being ashamed."[15] This story shows the boy's self-consciousness and his sensitivity toward living creatures. It also shows a degree of introspection not often seen in children.

Jimmie turned eight in 1914, an eventful year for the world. When World War I began, he became interested in trying to read the newspapers. He remembered soldiers coming to the school to talk to the children.[16] It was also an eventful time for the Still family. His third brother, Alfred, was born in March. The family temporarily moved from the Carlisle place into town, where they lived in a residence called the Judge Norman house owned by distant kin. His memories of that house in town seemed very "Old South." He described it as one of the fine antebellum structures in LaFayette on a spacious lawn with crepe myrtle and magnolias. "We could also smell the cottonseed oil being processed in a nearby plant, and we could hear the laughter and singing coming from the black quarters, where we were told the people were carefree and content."[17] Still remembered the Judge Norman house as having a chandelier and a great hall; even though the house they moved from was spacious, this one was so large that his family did not have enough furniture to fill it.[18] Not much else is known about this interim life in town. Why they moved and how long they stayed is unclear, but it was a forced move, probably related to the decline of cotton. In 1909 the boll weevil had come to Alabama, and cotton production fell by 36 percent in the decade beginning in 1910. Whatever the reason for leaving, the Stills wanted to return to the Carlisle place and did so in 1915, remaining there for only three years before having the mortgage foreclosed.

His memories of the Carlisle place include a childhood game of danger and excitement related to a big hornet nest in the ground near a patch of sunflowers. The house was so large that one whole room served as storage for his mother's quilt boxes and a big spare bed. Jim and his friends would take bottles out to the sunflowers and gather bumblebees, then go into the spare room, get under the bedcovers, and release the bees in the room. They enjoyed the excitement of scrambling around under the covers to dodge the attacking bees. He never said how many stings the children got before the bees were back in the bottle or out the window.[19]

Another incident associated with the Carlisle place shows that his father set some rigid expectations for Jimmie. Still wrote the story for truth and stored it with notes associated with a short piece called "Beside the Plow."[20]

> When I was ten I'd been struck by my father with the flat of his hand on my face, the only time he was ever to touch me in anger, and for a reason entirely incomprehensible. Papa, with help of two carpenters were building our new house at the Carlisle Place. . . . arriving home from school I climbed a ladder where the work was in progress on the roof, and I thought I would show off a little. I began to sing a ditty which I'd just learned from my cousin, Mitchell: "Everybody's doing it / Doing it, Doing it. / Everybody's doing it now."

Alex, like most parents, had a double standard. The boy was intruding into a world of working men. It was okay for adults, especially men, to be a little bawdy, but even hints were unacceptable from children. The Still family appreciated humor. An example Still told was the time when "Grandpa Lindsey accused Papa's bulls in an adjoining pasture of 'demoralizing' his cows."[21] Laughter was always welcome unless it came from a smart-aleck kid who had very little knowledge of double meaning until his father pointed it out to him.

The big event for the children each year was Christmas when Santa would leave the young ones an apple or orange, a couple of peppermint sticks, or a handful of nuts. Jimmie felt lucky one holiday when he got a toy pistol. Later, when the family moved to town, the factory presented children with Christmas treats—every child got a bag "brimming with a variety of fruits, nuts, candy, and a toy."[22] But Still never expressed regret that he had grown up on a farm outside of town.

Country life was balanced by the occasional trip to LaFayette for entertainment and culture. He described a few childhood excursions: "With a ticket provided by a teacher I attended Chautauqua—a classical guitar performance and a lecture which I choose to believe was the famed 'Acres of Diamonds.' Jean Webster read from *Daddy Long Legs* at the school. William Jennings Bryan came to town. The warden of Sing Sing Prison lectured. Papa pulled me through a crowd to have me shake hands with Governor Comer. A circus came to town and our class learned to spell *elephant, lion,* and *tiger.*"[23]

Jimmie saw the first movie to come to LaFayette, *Daemon and Pythias*. Because there was no theater building, the movie was shown in the back of the store where someone had put up a screen. It was very flickery, and he remembered most vividly his curiosity as to how it was being done at all.[24] A little later he saw another film; this time his circumstances of entry and the movie itself stuck with him, not the technology. *The Kaiser, the Beast of Berlin* was made during World War I and released in March 1918. The intent of the film was to give people a dramatic presentation of Kaiser Wilhelm II and the crimes against humanity committed under his rule. Still remembered it well, a propaganda film that showed Germans cutting off the hands of children in Belgium. The film was upstairs in the opera house of LaFayette. He went with only fifteen cents, but the movie cost twenty-five—a lot at that time. When he looked as though he would cry, the staff let him in for a reduced rate.

One Sunday, Jimmie's family drove in their Model T Ford to visit Uncle John Lindsey and Aunt Claudia, who lived with their eight children twenty-five miles away in West Point, a town on the river separating Alabama from Georgia. Theirs was a big two-story house with lofty ceilings and a porch all the way around, supported in front by square columns. After dinner, they heard a sound coming from the southeast and went out on the porch. Though the sky was cloudy, there was no threat of rain. Only the dull roar disturbed the ominous silence. Suddenly, a tornado was upon them, and shingles began to fly like leaves. In seconds, the top story of the house was torn away, the porch was ripped off, and the house lifted momentarily. He remembered vividly a picture on the wall swinging out over his head, and his father struggling to hold the door shut. When the wind died, they went outside to find that the barn and the outlying kitchen had not been touched. A nearby tenant house had been blown away. On their way home, they stopped to help people who needed a hand.[25] For years after that, when a black cloud appeared on the horizon, the boy became fearful. He repeated a little prayer to himself when a peal of thunder disturbed the sky: "Lord preserve me . . . preserve me . . . preserve me."[26]

Leaving a less traumatic but deeper impression on Jimmie during his early school years was his encounter with books and magazines. His family owned only four books: the Bible; *The Anatomy of the Horse*, which was useful to his father; *Palaces of Sin; or, The Devil in Society*, which must have been intended to prepare the children to avoid temptation; and a large book called *The Cyclopedia of Universal Knowledge*, his favorite. His description of the book to Elisabeth Beattie in an interview eighty-five years after reading it shows that the pages etched his memory and fired his imagination:

> It had a little of everything in it you could imagine, and some things you can't. It had some short history of every country. It had social correspondence, it had business correspondence. It had samples of maybe ten or twenty or twenty-five words of several foreign languages, and how to pronounce them. I'm sure that I was the only person in that state, or child, who knew twenty-five words of Arabic. Then there was a section of poetry—Byron, Shelley, Keats, great poetry—and Shakespeare. I memorized them. It was my first introduction to poetry.[27]

Still was so fond of telling about the influence that book had on him that he let the narrator describe it in *Chinaberry*: "*The Cyclopedia of Universal Knowledge* was my chief instrument. What did a child know of the world in those days? Only what he could hear, or observe in the fields and at the barn and the meager knowledge gained from school-books. What I knew of the world came from *The Cyclopedia*."[28] From this eclectic work, Jimmie learned about everything from the language of flowers to instructions on how to prune a fruit tree. But most of all, he learned the power of knowledge and the pleasure of reading.

His family also subscribed to several papers and magazines: the *Tri-Weekly Constitution,* a Georgia newspaper; a veterinary journal; *Farm & Fireside;* and *Southern Cultivator.*[29] From the newspaper, he read enough about the war consuming Europe that it became a life-long interest. At school one day Jim came across the January 1917 issue of *National Geographic,* and one article about a volcanic erup-tion in Alaska made a lasting impression. "The Valley of Ten Thousand Smokes" was responsible for inspiring in him a love of travel. As he read the story of the journey to photograph the crater of the volcano, he could not wait to grow up so he could go there.[30]

His fifth-grade schoolteacher, Miss Almond, read stories to the class from a children's magazine called *The Youth's Companion,* and that may have been the spark Jim needed to begin his own little magazine. His sister Elloree was his only subscriber; each issue was written on two pages of folded stationery, and he would fill the eight small pages with very short stories and poems. This was not Jim's only effort at writing.[31] He wrote a story on a tablet. Miss Almond had read the class a story about the Kentucky mountains. It, along with other stories he heard, inspired "The Gold Nugget," his first attempt at a novel.[32] Many years later when he found the tablet, he could barely read the faded handwrit-ing. When asked if he saw promise in the story, he responded, "I saw my future in it. Everything I was to do and be was right there. I saw it between the lines."[33] Around that same time, he wrote his first poem, which he described as stilted and formal. But writing it was an adven-ture. He made a tent out of sacks in his yard, then got inside to compose the poem.

Whether in *The Cyclopedia, National Geographic,* or *The Youth's Companion,* articles and stories held a strong attraction for Still. Reading was always his passion. One time, it was also a source of embarrassment. He was going with his father in a buggy ride to visit his grandparents.[34] At the end of his journey, he needed to go to the bathroom and expected a lengthy stay. So he took along a bunch of papers to read. As he was carrying this parcel across the yard to the outhouse, everyone saw him. They had a good laugh, and his father made him return the papers. But no amount of teasing could discourage the reader in the boy.

From an early age he was a reader and a storyteller. Jimmie had a lot in common with the eight-year-old narrator in *River of Earth*. Both enjoyed exploring, learning, and "tale-telling." They both walked to school with their older sisters and had younger brothers who followed them around. Their lives in rural Kentucky and in Chambers County, Alabama, were also similar. Children grew up in large supportive families but were rarely pampered. Everyone worked. People had little money, but that never seemed to bother the children. Because of ties to the land, geography was central in people's lives. When times got tough, families would move to another place not far away and start again. That was the case with the Stills. During his childhood, they had moved five times. As he approached his teen years, they would move again, east to the Chattahoochee Valley, which was growing cotton mills like mushrooms.

3

The Model Scout

When I was a boy we never travelled much and seldom left the county. One time I went with my scout troop to Atlanta. . . . I heard the trains blowing in the night, and I yearned to go where they were going.

—James Still

World War I ended. Kaiser Wilhelm II abdicated on October 9. The armistice went into effect on November 11. The Treaty of Versailles was signed on June 28, 1919. The flu epidemic was ongoing. None of these major events touched Jim, who was twelve when the war ended. He did remember the day of celebration: "A truck loaded with celebrants passed, shouting 'The war is over! The war is over!'"[1] But that was all. He was more concerned with moving from the country to town.

The farm at the Carlisle place was mortgaged, and when, toward the end of the war, cotton prices fell, the mortgage was foreclosed. The family then moved about twenty-five miles east into the Chattahoochee Valley, to a town on the river called Shawmut (the Indian name for "Living Springs"). Shawmut was a mill village for West Point Manufacturing, and the people living there needed a veterinarian. Alex Still saw the opportunity to switch from treating cattle, horses, and mules in the country to caring for the milk cows and dogs that people kept in their yards in town.[2] At the same time he could move his family from the farming area, which was in decline, to the manufacturing area, which was growing. Six children were living at home: James plus two of his older sisters and three younger brothers. Their house was on Lanier Avenue, commonly known as "Boss Row," near the Chattahoochee River.[3]

The economic roar of the 1920s was gearing up in eastern Alabama. One newspaper reporter, Ewell Coffee, brought the good feeling pervading the nation closer to home for his local readers when he began a description of Valley, Alabama, "The skies hold many bright beacon lights for those who are looking for optimistic signs in the business world." The area was enjoying an increase in road and street work, more building and improvements to existing structures, and a general expansion. The economy was shifting from agriculture to manufacturing. By December 1921, the West Point Manufacturing Company (located in Shawmut, Fairfax, and Langdale) employed a total of four thousand workers with a weekly payroll of $75,000. The Still family's relocation from farm to town was a balance of escaping hardship and following opportunity.

With the move, Jim immediately became involved in playing basketball, and early in 1921 he was a forward on the Shawmut boys' team, but not a starter. Later in the season the newspaper published the scores for the area tournament. Still's total of eight points placed him in the middle of the list of nineteen tournament forwards, but the top scorer was also from Shawmut, and he scored forty-nine points in the tournament.[4] Still once described his interest in basketball, showing a little bitterness in his implication that the tournament participation was "arranged" by the local management. "I got caught up in the game of basketball. Often played from school's end until dark. Our team was invited to the state tournament at Birmingham. Only one member of the team was taken along, the other players being 'ringers' recruited from the factory. They attended classes a half-day to qualify. We were joyful when they were roundly defeated their first game, probably by another team of ringers."[5] As it turned out, basketball would not be Jim's main interest in Shawmut, nor would his subjects at school. His teenage world centered on his old love of reading and his new involvement in scouting.

When he moved to town, Jim began to visit the small Chattahoochee Valley library, which he described as the corner of a recreation hall holding about two hundred books, all of which the elderly librarian guarded with a vengeance.[6] He later described an interaction with that librarian, which became his initiation into literature:

She would never let you touch the books; she would go bring you one. And one day she kept bringing books and I didn't want to read them—I didn't like them—so she told me to go look for myself. So I went back, and I found a book called *Father Goriot* by Balzac—I'd never heard of him. It had no pictures in it and had very small print and looked very unpromising, but I took it home. And that night I read this book. I don't know that I read all night, but I read a long time. That was my first approach to literature. And I never turned back.[7]

Balzac was a new discovery, but *Treasure Island,* which he had read when younger, was a favorite. The subject of his early attempt at writing was sailing boats and whales, though he had never seen the sea and was unfamiliar with boats. The topic could not sustain his interest, so he abandoned the project.[8] Like most serious young readers, he liked to try adult books, but he could not turn down a good adventure story. At that time, Tarzan was the popular hero for boys, and Jim borrowed the books from his friends. They inspired him to try out a few of the jungle stunts from a neighbor's barn.[9]

One summer Jim kept a diary to log his daily activities. He remembered writing about baseball and berry picking and fishing in the river, the things that boys did in the lazy days of summer. More creative or daring than some of his friends, he tried his hand at writing dramas for neighborhood children to perform. One of his plays required a volcano, perhaps inspired by the *National Geographic* article, and he tried making one as a prop, or at least the smoke to suggest an eruption.[10]

Though his plays went up in smoke, his novel lost momentum, and his diary buried itself in dreary detail, he was successful with an essay that he submitted to the *Birmingham News* contest. Even at this young age, he had the makings of an organic farmer. The essay topic was insect control; his recommendation was to use birds. He won second prize, while the winner of the first prize had advocated insecticide.[11] Here is the essay as reprinted on the front page of the *Chattahoochee Valley Times* on July 26, 1922, under the headline "James Still Wins Prize in News Essay Contest":

Harmful insects that trouble the gardeners and farmers have alarmed the agricultural world and the people have set their forces together to exterminate them. Poisons have been used successfully, but to my opinion our native insect destroying

birds have been more helpful to the farmers and gardeners than any other agency.

Birds aid mankind by making insects a greater part of their food. The house wren, blue bird, and mocking bird are the farmers' and gardeners' most useful friend. They rid the gardens and fields of cutworms, spiders, weevils, grasshoppers, potato bugs, beetles, ants and many other plant-destroying insects.

Because of the rapid extermination of our native birds by thoughtless hunters the insects have begun to ravage our fields by eating, killing, and destroying the plants that are essential to the life of man.

The government is doing everything it can to protect the birds, but until they get the hearty aid of the farmers and gardeners, the birds will keep on getting smaller in population and will finally disappear. I write this article with the hope that the growers will wake up to the fact that birds are one of their own most valuable friends.[12]

The high school Jim attended at Shawmut was brand new, but the teachers were like the ones he had experienced during most of his school years. After Miss Porterfield, they had run together in a blend of mediocrity. At Shawmut and later at Fairfax, the teachers were reputed to be better than those in the county school because they were chosen by the textile mill officials, but he did not remember them as special.[13] He did recall one teacher from Shawmut, Mr. Carl Lappert. He was also the principal, and he ruled the school "with a hickory stick." He, unlike Porterfield, was a successful teacher because he maintained a level of fear that served to keep students in line and on task. Jim also related to a geometry teacher, Miss Jeanette Garrett, who was, by his own admission, a good teacher but was not successful in teaching him because he always proved himself "a dumbbell in math."[14]

His interest in writing continued. In the summer of 1921 the young man, who was turning fifteen and preparing to enter tenth grade, had written to the U.S. senator from Alabama, Thomas E. Watson. His precise reason for writing is unknown, but the senator's short response reveals that Jim had probably asked about programs in journalism. "I would suggest that any school or college, giving literary degrees, could give you such training as would be necessary to enable you to become a newspaper correspondent. Yours very truly, Thomas E. Watson."[15] While dreaming of a future in journalism, Jim was living in a mill town.

In the summer of 1921 or 1922 he worked in the textile mill owned by the West Point Manufacturing Company. He did it just because he wanted to, "on a lark," so he claimed. Other boys were working there, and he decided to try it too. He twisted bands on the spinning machinery. Though he worked several different stints in the mills, the work never kept his attention, and he never intended to make it his long-term job.[16]

When he was in high school, the family moved again, this time to Jarrett Station, where they lived about a mile from the school in Fairfax.[17] Jim's report card indicates that he attended school through December 1922 at Shawmut High School then shifted in January 1923 to Fairfax High School, which had a total enrollment of 661. He stayed there for half of his junior year and all of his senior year, graduating along with thirteen other students on May 16, 1924. At Fairfax his best subjects were history (where he earned an A), reading or classics (A-), literature (B+), and French (B). He also made strong marks in "Deportment." Less impressive but still respectable were his marks in science and geometry.[18]

In high school English class, Jim memorized "The Village Blacksmith." He was named the school poet of Fairfax High School in the fall of 1923 and was noted in the *Chattahoochee Valley Times* on September 26, 1923, for writing an essay about "The Value of High School," an essay that did not win him any prizes. Maybe he was too honest for the paper's readers. After all, he later stated, "My high school was not much. I don't ever recall being assigned to read a book." The students never worried about the tests because everybody passed. His parents did not emphasize homework or stress academic achievement; they were satisfied. Maybe he was too. He remembered carrying dull textbooks home every night but never opening them.[19]

His least favorite class at Shawmut was algebra. The textbook, *Elementary Algebra* by Walter R. Marsh, enjoyed the distinction of being the only book that Still ever hated. The extant copy not only gives evidence of his disdain for the book and the subject but also shows how he passed his time in a class that did not interest him. His outlet for frustration and boredom was words and humor. On the title page, he wrote in his characteristic handwriting:

Walter R. Marsh.
Headmaster at the school of Saint Paul
I wish he lived in Gaul.

This the 27 day of April do here by undersign my name that
I never could and never will work algebra, as it is so full of
nutty nonsense. Jim A. Still

And on the facing page was an original ditty:

Walter R. Marsh
Ain't got no sense by gosh.
He wrote crazy lines
for me to work all the time
If he were near and could be seen.
I'd crock him on the bean.[20]

In the pages of the book, Still amused himself by creating a scavenger
hunt that takes the gullible reader from page 1 to 89 to 181 to 263 to
273 to 305 to 230 to 144 and back to page 1, with the final message,
"You're a nut for looking." Elsewhere in the book he wrote a truth more
appropriate to him: "Orators are made but poets are born."

Perhaps he was already recognizing his birthright as a poet, but he
also noted other interests in the book: names of thirteen friends and
classmates and a list of five knots.[21] The importance of knots at this
point in Jim's life did not relate to his brain's attempting to unravel
mathematics but to the beginnings of his life as a Boy Scout. He first
joined the scouts in Shawmut and went to his first summer scout camp
in 1922. He became even more serious when he moved to Troop 1 in
Fairfax at the beginning of 1923. There he worked to reach his goal
of Eagle Scout. A new scoutmaster, W. A. Dobson, took charge of the
area's scouting program on March 21, 1923, and began a regular column in the *Chattahoochee Valley Times* called "Scout Trail Tracks."
Mr. Dobson was a strong, idealistic leader who expressed his confidence in their lofty mission: "Boy Scout leaders are producing for the
nation with greatest speed, men of character trained for citizenship." In
a subsequent essay, Dobson was eloquent in his praises of scouting as a
way to strengthen comradeship between father and son.[22]

In July 1922 Camp George Lanier opened at Pine Mountain about
twenty-five miles to the east in Georgia and was a big success. The camp
allowed boys to relate to forests and lakes rather than towns and fields.
Jim never wanted to sit around; he wanted to go out in the woods. The
scout program claimed that the camp taught a boy self-reliance and
improved his character at the same time that it gave him "an opportu-

nity to satisfy his savage instinct by camping out, and learning the ways of the woods." Jim was among the first boys to spend a week at Camp Lanier; while there he rose from Second Class to First Class and earned a merit badge in swimming. He was one of only four boys to win the prestigious "emblem" of Scout Signal Flags.[23]

Jim's connection with scouting activities inspired him to write. He kept a diary during his first summer-camp experience, a week at the end of June 1922.[24] Here is an excerpt:

June 26 Monday. Awoke this morning in high hopes. Could do nothing but think about going. Left Shawmut for the camp at one thirty on the truck and arrived after a fourteen mile ride at the camp (which is an ideal camping site). Went in washing [swimming] twice, river very swift and water about neck deep.

Packed cots with oats straw and Jim W. and I bunked together.

Roll call at 5.30 then supper which consists of eggs, bacon, pie, buns and sweet milk. After nightfall we went to the bridge and sang for a while then came back to camp and was intertained [*sic*] by some other campers and especially a small darky (Roy Johnson) who danced, shimmied, and spoke. Turned in at 8.30.

June 27 Tuesday. Rolled out at six, washed, and ate breakfast. Took exercise for about 40 minutes then filed to the woods and sudied [*sic*] snake bites, sprains, cuts. We returned at ten and went in the river to cool off. We had a dinner of sweet milk, corn on the cob and many other good things. The evening was spent in playing rook and checkers. . . . Our show was a hit tonight including plays, comic saying by our boys. Turned in at 9.30.

June 28 Wednesday. Breakfast, exercise then off for a seven mile hick [*sic*]. We marched three miles and a half to Abbortsford then ran and walked back making the last 3½ in 30 minutes. Had a show tonight. . . . Turned in at 8.30. . . .

June 29 Thursday. Went in washing, played games, sang and did a multitude of things today not mentioned. Mr Standby was sick last night and went to Shawmut.

June 30 Friday. This is our last day at camp and we all packed up. Then went in washing. Made candy. Papa and the family came and staid [*sic*] about an hr. Came home on the truck about 3.30 and we unloaded the cots in West Point and came on home. . . .

Not a gripping account of a week at Boy Scout camp, but his starting the diary while there set him on a path of record keeping. Another value of the camp experience for Still's later career was the brief article he wrote for the newspaper the next summer—early practice for his journalism skills. The purpose was to honor the donor as the title states, "Boys Appreciate Opportunities at Camp": "The Pine Mountain Lake built at Camp George Lanier was donated by Mr. George H. Lanier, of West Point, Ga. The appreciation for this lake has been highly shown in Scout circles—not only as a means of recreation, but as a method of instruction toward swimming and life saving. . . . The Boy Scouts of the McIntosh Council feel greatly indebted to Mr. George Lanier for his fellowship, and for his consideration of the Boy Scouts. James Still, Jr., B.S.A. July 18, 1923."[25]

Whether as a result of this news piece or because he volunteered, Jim had become the official scribe for his troop by the following spring. Less than a month before his high school graduation, another of his scouting reports announced the upcoming field event. "A great interest is being shown by all the Scouts in the coming field event. Our wall has been built at last and we are ready for some real practice. . . . Look out for Troop 1, we are bound to win the field meet. JAS. STILL, Scribe."[26] The field day for which the troop was preparing took place on Saturday, May 24, at the Lanett baseball park, just a week after the high school graduation. The invitation to everyone conveys the enthusiastic public spirit that pervaded the program and influenced the boys. Spectators were promised a "revelation" of scouting and told that they would go away with a stronger love for their community. Young Still wrote the lyrics for a campfire song for all to sing at the celebration:

All around the campfire at the set of sun,
Watching flick'ring embers as the day is done,
Though the scouts be weary, tired of work and play,
Still to them at nightfall comes the end of day,
Comes the welcome end of day.[27]

The Chattahoochee Council of the Boy Scouts of America had been started only two years earlier, but by the spring of 1924, it was strong and visible throughout the area. Jim Still was involved in the whole range of programs. He attained the rank of Eagle Scout and earned a total of twenty-three merit badges. He wrote one of his earliest poems, "A Burned Tree Speaks," while in high school and published it in *Boys' Life*, the scout magazine, in 1931. For young Still, scouting was a means rather than an end. He was searching for a new identity—a town boy with a spirit of adventure and a love for learning that was not being satisfied in school. The program offered interesting activities like adventures in the woods, the field day in town, and a week at Pine Mountain Camp. Physical strength and personal assertiveness were not required for most scout projects. The merit-badge system appreciated and rewarded Jim's intelligence, determination, and attention to detail. The opportunities offered by the Boy Scouts provided a safe way to leave home and family without really going anywhere. Progress was measured and rewarded in small increments so that a determined boy could go from Tenderfoot to Eagle Scout in a predictable way. That kind of security and challenge was exactly what Jim needed as he adjusted to adolescence and his new environment. But he grew beyond the controlled environment and the basic ideals of scouting. By the time he graduated from high school, his horizons had broadened.

In his 1928 reference letter, the energetic and successful Scout Executive described Jim Still as a scoutmaster's dream: "Mr. Still is one of the most outstanding Scouts I have ever known. He made a splendid record. . . . By advancing to the Eagle Rank, the highest, and by his willingness to help younger boys advance in the program, [he] drew the attention of the leading men of his community who co-operated in making it possible for him to receive a college education."[28] Here Dobson was showing that Chambers County was proud of this exemplary young man. But it is hard to verify his statement that leading men helped Jim in his transition from high school to college. What help he got from the community was moral, not financial, support.

Alex Still had no spare resources to give his eldest son, and no experience with travel or higher education himself. Given the choice, his father would have wanted Jim to become a lawyer or politician. Alex was a gregarious, friendly man with aspirations for political office. According to Still, his father "heard William Jennings Bryan once and could never forget it. From the day I could walk I was taken into the offices of lawyers and judges. And when the governor visited our community I was pushed forward to shake his hand."[29] But Jim was not to fulfill his father's dream of law and politics or his more practical expectation—a job in the textile mill. Jim did work in the factory office the summer before he left for college, and he found there was not much to do but sit in a little room and read until someone brought a message for him to deliver to another office. An industrious young man could move up in the mill step by step just as a boy could work to earn the rank of Eagle Scout. By building on his start as an office boy, Jim could have avoided assembly-line work and moved directly into management. The opportunity was there, but Jim was not interested.

The young man did not know what his future would be, but he did know that it would not be in the Chattahoochee Valley. He wanted something different, somewhere else. The one thing he insisted on, "like a bull-dog ahold of a pants leg, was going on to college." His grandfather Lindsey thought he should go to work and "help out" his parents. The Baptist minister had the same idea and sat with him in a church pew one Sunday morning, trying to influence his decision. On his mother's side, he was the first to graduate from high school. On his father's side, two or three had managed to graduate from normal school, but higher education was not a priority for his parents or their parents. Everyone expected him to stay in Alabama and get a job. But he could not "fulfill the expectations of society. . . . The world was too big, too beautiful, too exciting to merely sit down in it and while it away."[30] He wanted to experience the world. To do that, he had to leave home.

Just as *The LaFayette Sun* had announced his birth in July 1906, the *Chattahoochee Valley Times* announced his departure without fanfare on September 24, 1924: "James Still left Monday for Cumberland Gap, Tennessee to enter Lincoln Memorial University."

Part 2

College Years
Searching and Learning, 1924–1930

4

Working His Way

First Years at Lincoln Memorial University

> "I ought ne'er thought to be a scholar," Lark said. His voice
> was small and tight. . . .
> We started down the ridge, picking our way through stony
> dark.
>
> —From "Journey to the Forks"

In his 1941 story collection, *On Troublesome Creek,* James Still tells a tale
of two boys, the twelve-year-old narrator and his younger brother, walking six miles to begin their schooling at the forks. By the time he wrote the
story, education had become a way of life for Still, but the apprehension
sustained throughout the narrative likely was rooted in Still's experience
of leaving Alabama to begin college in Tennessee. The narrator says to
his brother, "They never was a puore [*sic*] scholar amongst all our folks.
Never a one went all the way through the books and come out yon side.
I've got a notion doing it."[1] Going to college was a major departure for a
Still child. Going as far as Tennessee was dramatic.

Still never claimed his reason for going to college was to be the first
in his family to graduate, but he always liked a challenge, and he did not
want to be in Chambers County, Alabama. Many years later, he told
about selecting and adjusting to Lincoln Memorial University (LMU) in
Harrogate, Tennessee.

> The college . . . flourishes to this day and is in a natural set-
> ting probably unequaled in America. The opportunity to work

my way through was the draw. In the fall of 1924, with sixty dollars earned as an office boy at the factory and as a door-to-door delivery boy of *The Atlanta Constitution,* I set off for this school of some eight hundred students drawn mainly from the mountain areas of the three adjoining states. I had made a genealogical circle. Up the road in Virginia was the site of the Stills' pioneer home.[2]

Any connection the Alabama Stills had to the Virginia Stills is vague. The amount of money he took with him to college and its source cannot be verified. Yet he did go, with little encouragement or modest financial support from his family. Though he respected his parents, the young man did not want to live the life they had. College promised something different.

In the *Heritage* interview, Still recalled that a teacher at his high school had come from Tennessee and was the son of the dean of LMU. The man put an LMU catalog on the desk and invited students to look through it.[3] Still would have seen a description something like this: "Lincoln Memorial University, a co-educational, non-sectarian but distinctly Christian institution . . . has been steadily increasing its circle of usefulness for twenty-eight years. Its purpose . . . is 'to make education possible for the children of the humble, common people of America.'"[4] The opportunity for students to "earn while they learn" was one selling point; another was that graduates would be able "to secure immediate and profitable employment" and rise quickly in their chosen profession. The college recruited in the "neglected regions of the states of the Upland South" and emphasized "Christian character, good citizenship, and industrial type training."[5]

Reflecting on the institution two years after he graduated, Still wrote but never published an essay describing Lincoln Memorial. His picture differed from the image projected by the college catalog. He described 1924 as a "lean year": the institution's endowment was diminishing; its football team was not paying off. The year before, the community had suffered a typhoid epidemic. The basic problem, he noted, was that during the twenty-seven-year life of the institution, the majority of its students were unable to meet even minimum expenses and were academically ill-prepared. The faculty was underpaid but valiantly struggling to overcome obstacles. While the ten-page, double-spaced manuscript is neither a well-documented analysis of LMU in the 1920s nor a nostalgic walk down memory lane, it does show that Still wanted to understand and assess the institution that had furnished him his first college degree.[6]

Still shared few impressions of his own early LMU experiences except to say that because he was very small for his age, the administration attempted to enroll him in the Academy, a private high school associated with the college.[7] Since there is no evidence that Jim was unusually small, this self-description probably referred to how he felt—insignificant and alone. The first year was difficult because he was far from home and the physical work was taxing. But he had to pay his way. By current standards, the charges for tuition and board seem modest, but to Still, they were daunting. The cost of attending for three quarters in an academic year was approximately $230 excluding travel, clothes, and incidentals.[8] But most students paid in work rather than money. Approximately 75 percent of the student body was dependent entirely on the school for their room, board, tuition, and books.[9]

The school operated on the principle that many young people lacked the means or opportunity to extend their education, so it kept expenses affordable. Like most, Still held a work scholarship that made it possible for the institution to pay for his "valuable but non-productive labor."[10] Since Still was not large or muscular, it is surprising that he was assigned the rock quarry instead of the farm, the hatchery, or the dairy—all areas of his experience—but such is his claim. "I pried limestone croppings out of a pasture and sometimes operated a rock crusher. One Christmas vacation, lacking a ticket home, one nickel in my pocket, I shoveled gravel onto roads and crosswalks."[11]

As compensation for breaking limestone on the rock pile or driving steel with a sledgehammer, students received twenty cents per hour in the form of credit toward tuition. Presuming they worked four hours each afternoon and five on Saturday, healthy individuals could earn five dollars worth of credit per week, or sixty dollars per quarter. If the cost was seventy-six dollars per student per quarter, the college was losing money even if student labor had yielded cash. Perhaps hard work was increasing their strength and endurance and solidifying values or building dignity, but it did not seem to improve their learning. Still observed, "Even to many of the most hardened mountain youth this labor was so exhausting that it was practically impossible to do efficient study at night. An afternoon spent heaping frozen rock, ofttimes without gloves and insufficiently clad for the weather, was too strenuous to be followed by worthwhile concentration."[12] After the assignment to the rock pile, Still worked at less-demanding jobs including mixing concrete, raking leaves, mending roofs, and painting houses before he landed the job of his dreams in his junior year, janitor of the library.

Still's adjustment to college and to Harrogate was slow. A few people from home offered him encouragement and moral support. One was Jeb Martin, a supervisor at West Point Manufacturing in Fairfax. Still had written to him about the particular pressures he was facing. Martin must have been a former factory boss because his return letter was upbeat and encouraging, as a mentor would try to be. In addition to his advice that "Jimmie" should go to church and teach Sunday school, he warned against paying attention to the college "FLAPPERS," his term for alluring and forward young women. If the advice was not enough, Martin promised to send him some Fairfax bath towels.

His family tried to be supportive by writing often. Occasionally, his parents included a dollar bill for haircuts, or in one case for postage so that he could send his unused trousers home to his brothers. His sister Inez mailed him a box containing a cake, some homemade peanut fudge, and a half-pound of English walnuts.[13] His mother was the most faithful letter-writer, and she would gently scold him for not writing back. She filled her letters with news of the family and details of her busy days. Health issues were always a concern, as were money shortages because his father could not keep regular work. But most importantly, his mother wanted to stay in contact with her oldest son. Excerpts from two letters illustrate her frustration at not having him close: "I wish you were here to help me sure do miss you." "Dear Son, What is the mater [sic] that you don't write some oftener been nearly two weeks since we heard from you . . . you should know how it worries us when you don't write."[14]

Still did not make a distinguishing mark as a freshman, yet he began to show personal traits that would become stronger with time: determination, resourcefulness, shyness, sensitivity, independence, and pride. Some of those qualities were mentioned in a description that appeared in the 1938 publication at LMU, the *Lincoln Herald*: Still "came with forty dollars in his pocket and made a trembling, hesitant appeal . . . for a chance to work out his expenses. He did not make any dominant impression with his personality, for he was not a large chap, and he had a retiring disposition. With an inflexible will and unfailing determination he set to work on the business of getting an education."[15] In a 1991 interview, Still attributed his lackluster early performance to the required work: "My grades were poor the first year because I was so tired. You went to school in the morning, worked in a rock quarry in the afternoon. . . . I was too tired to study. I wanted to sleep."[16]

Whether because the tight budget meant smaller portions at the table or because the physical work increased the need for calories, Still's memory of those first years was fatigue and hunger.[17] The diet consisted of beans and potatoes as a staple, meat once a day, and ice cream and cake only at Sunday dinner. The Sunday supper was scant indeed: "a glass of milk, a spoonful of jam, and an exceedingly thin piece of cheese."[18] He didn't mind combing the hillsides for nuts and fruit, yet he adamantly resisted any sign of charity. "The president of Lincoln Memorial spirited me into his house to try on a suit he could spare, and it fit perfectly. I broke into tears when he presented it to me—not from joy, as reported, but from humiliation. I never wore it."[19] Still was not alone in wanting to avoid the appearance of need. The college had friends who regularly sent secondhand clothes to be distributed among those who could use them, yet it was common for students to refuse these hand-me-downs. "The odor of charity was too strong, and besides much silent disapproval was felt toward anyone who would accept clothing from the 'missionary barrel.'"[20]

Although never outgoing or widely popular, Still did begin to make friends; his closest and longest lasting was Dare Redmond, whose background was similar to Still's. After attending high school in his hometown of Leicester, North Carolina, Redmond had worked on his family farm, then on a dairy farm near Gastonia. The fourteen-hour workday convinced him that he would not get anywhere as a farmer. He wrote to Lincoln Memorial, asking for a summer job with the intent of beginning college in the fall quarter. With encouragement from the dean, Redmond set out for Harrogate. In his autobiography, Redmond told about meeting Jim, an encounter that reveals the typical freshman's need to find a kindred spirit. Yet without Redmond's persistence, this friendship might not have happened. Redmond arrived at LMU in the summer of 1924 and began working happily. Then:

> After school started in the fall, it was a different story. I was saddled with too many hard courses, since I had to work every afternoon and all day Saturday. . . . I knew I had to drop something so decided to drop Latin. There was another boy in Latin class named Thad Brown. He decided to drop Latin too. I didn't know him very well, having had only one class session

with him. A few days later I met a boy in the hallway whom I thought was Thad Brown.

"Hello, Thad," I said.

The boy said, "That's not my name."

A day or two later I met him on the stairs and said, "Hello, Thad. Are you glad you dropped Latin?"

He replied, "You called me that before. My name's not Thad."

A few days later I was in the Cashier's office when the boy I had mistakenly called Thad walked in. We started talking about my calling him Thad. We left the office together, and became close friends. We graduated together and went to the University of Illinois together. His name was James Still, and he is the closest friend I have ever had, except for relatives.[21]

Between working, making all the adjustments required of freshmen, and establishing a few friendships, Still had little time or energy for extracurricular activities. But he did join the Grant-Lee Literary Society.[22] His academic record during his first year was adequate, not stellar. His courses spanned three quarters and were all at the introductory level: English, history, French, sociology, and economics. He earned grades of Bs and Cs. The record in his sophomore year showed no improvement—Cs dominated.[23] One exception was that he did earn his first A in the second quarter of the course that should have been his nemesis: College Algebra. The first quarter he made a C, and the third quarter, a D.[24] What could explain this anomaly—an A in his least favorite subject? Maybe it was a special girl, a math genius.[25]

Mayme Brown was only fifteen when she enrolled at Lincoln Memorial in the fall of 1925, Jim Still's sophomore year. She was young, small, and very bright. She came from Well Springs, Tennessee, not far from Harrogate, and when she entered the university, she roomed with her older sister Mattie, who was also a freshman. It is not known how Mayme and Jim became friends, but sitting together in class was the most likely scenario. Mayme's niece, Betty Brown Whitney, says that the family lore supposes that Mayme tutored Still in math. A handwritten note in her memory book shows that he wished to accompany her to at least one school function: "Mayme—May I have a date with you for the math picnic? R.S.V.P. James Still."[26] If she had not cared to accept his invitation, she likely would not have kept the paper on which he had written it. Suppose they did go and that they became better friends—

suppose she did tutor him in math. What better way to learn a subject? If the grades are any indication of the intensity of their friendship, what does it mean that his second quarter A dropped to a D in the third quarter? Probably that they hit a snag.

As an adult, Still rarely alluded to this relationship except in the poem "Those I Want in Heaven with Me Should There Be Such a Place," and when he signed a copy of a book for Mayme's brother with the inscription "For Milburn Brown, brother of my *first* sweetheart." Still could keep the whole affair, if there was one, muted or spin it his own way because during her sophomore year (1926–1927), Jim was not at LMU. When he returned for the summer quarter in 1927, Mayme was at home in Well Springs. He was not to see her again. In early August 1927 Mayme became seriously ill with what was probably typhoid fever and lived only four weeks. The campus had fewer than two hundred students, so everyone felt the loss. The 1928 yearbook, *The Railsplitter,* devoted a page to her with a photo and the following words:

> In memory of one who was our friend and classmate. She was loved by all who were so fortunate as to know her. Her presence was sunshine and joy. Her smile meant happiness. Her influence has so saturated the atmosphere with kindness, friendship, love and obedience. . . . It was difficult and heartbreaking for us to part with one who has been our classmate so long, but we comfort ourselves with the thought that the *One* who called her forth from our number knoweth best and that *He* has made it possible for us to meet in that Great Beyond where parting and sorrow are unknown.[27]

James Still's heaven is a place where sorrow is unknown. According to his poem, he wants with him there—along with others from his youth—his "first sweetheart, who died at sixteen." In spite of, or because of, the tragic ending, the relationship between Jim Still and Mayme Brown makes a romantic story, especially with the testimony of the Brown family that James Still was known to visit and lay flowers on Mayme's grave with some regularity, even in his old age. Also, the fact that he never married might imply that this attraction was both powerful and long-lasting. Yet he rarely spoke of Mayme Brown when recalling his years at LMU. And while he was taking a year off in Fairfax, his few references to her were not complimentary.

Mayme was not the only mystery of his first years in Tennessee.

After his sophomore year, which concluded in the spring of 1926, Still went home to Alabama for the summer quarter and did not return to Harrogate for three quarters. His reason was unclear. In recounting his days at LMU, he made only one reference to taking time off, claiming it was because of financial hardship.[28] He maintained he did not have the train fare to return to Tennessee or money for clothes. Then he followed with Depression imagery to describe his experiences.

> That year I hunted work in several states over the South. The unemployed were everywhere. I walked. I thumbed on the highway. I sometimes rode the rails. One box car I crawled into was occupied by war veterans heading for D.C. to join the bonus army. I rode out to Texas with some fellows and picked cotton for a while. We were in the fields at daylight and until dark. We baked in one hundred degree sun. My bed was a cotton sack on the floor. The drinking water was alkaline. It was too much. I hitchhiked and rode freights to Georgia. . . .

But the country was not in an economic depression in 1926–1927, when Still stayed home. Possibly the confusion was accidental. But he sometimes exercised his writer's license to misplace an incident or dramatize a description. Still did wander around looking for work during the Depression, and he did travel some during his year off from school. He made a trip to Texas, for example, but he did not hop boxcars to get there.

Even his explanation for why he took the year off is suspect. He had a work scholarship that had not been revoked, so if he had wanted to return, he could have used his summer earnings for transportation, or he could have hitchhiked back to Tennessee, taken up his scholarship, and resumed his studies. In addition to his college work, he had received a "gift" scholarship in May 1925, which he could have applied to the next academic year's expenses. This letter from the business manager informed him of the award: "In recognition of your earnest efforts to gain an education and for your loyalty to the University, Dr. Matthews has awarded you a gift scholarship of $25.00. We sincerely hope you will show your appreciation of this award by continuing your efforts to make the very best of yourself, and by protecting the property and good name of the University."[29] Apparently, the school was happy to have him return even though his grades in his sophomore year had not been as strong as those of his freshman year. Did his parents need him at home and block his return? Was he suffering from burnout? Did he want to try his hand at working?

One clue to his motivation for staying home showed up in a letter he wrote to Dare Redmond, who was at LMU at the beginning of the term. Still, who was having second thoughts about his decision not to return, missed his friend. On September 15, 1926, he wrote:

> Dear Governor—It is a sad reality to know that it will be impossible for me to continue my college course during the next year. I could come back to L.M.U. but I'm determined to change so in that case I must stay out a year. I would like to be back there this year and enjoy your companionship during another year—as I have had the pleasure and good fortune to do. Too bad that I can't–but I aim to see you at least in a years [sic] time. Please write me a long letter and tell me about who all has come back to school. . . . Any little piece of news will be greatly welcomed. . . .
>
> Even if I can't attend school, I'm not going to "draw in my shell" mentally. I'm going to do a great deal of reading. . . . I solemnly promise to answer every letter you write me. I'll write long ones too, so as to make up for my "laziness" during the summer.
>
> Yours 'till gnats wear sunbonnets and elephants don lavender pajamas.
>
> Your affectionate friend and well wisher, Jimmie[30]

Still's declaration that he was "determined to change" is adamant but ambiguous. Did he mean that he intended to change himself and his behavior, or did he mean that he wanted to transfer schools? Of course, knowing his youthful pride, the real reason he did not return could have been financial need, but he had no intention of sharing that with his friend. The most romantic and farfetched explanation was that he had been rebuffed by Mayme Brown. In a letter dated March 28, 1927, Jim teased Red: "You never mention your girl these days. You haven't let any of those sorrel-types beat your time have you?" Then he followed with this question: "Who is rushing out poor, inno-cent, sweet little, petite Mamie [sic] Brown?" Again, the ambiguous tone.

The sarcasm is even clearer in the letter dated September 27, 1926, in which his response to Redmond referenced both Mayme and her sister, Mattie. Red also had an interest in the sisters. Jim's comment: "Do you think Mattie Brown is the best looking? I agree with you, for once. You would like to know my reason. At any rate Mattie is a much nicer girl than Mammie [*sic*] . . . [his ellipsis] I speak with authority of experience."[31] Was his friendship with Mayme short-lived, one-sided, or merely undergoing the ups and downs of a first romance? Still was only nineteen when he met her, and she only fifteen. If Mayme had not died an early death, her part in his life might have been larger. Her death certainly added drama to the story.[32]

The mystery of young Mayme remains unsolved. Yet it is unlikely Still would have laid out of school as a result of being rebuffed by a girl. It is more likely that he was having second thoughts about his decision to go to college and to go so far away to a place where he had to work harder out of the classroom than in. It is also likely that he had been too sensitive to his peers and had overreacted to their teasing, chiding, or criticism. One comment to Red implied that the change he was demanding of himself was related to getting along with people: "For the last two years at school I have got into several silly, childish and unreasonable 'fusses.' In fact I was to blame for most of it. I'm mighty sorry now—but it isn't too late to reform. I've made up my mind to be more congenial for as Shaw says 'keep yourself clean and bright for you are the mirror through which you see the world.'"[33]

Whatever the reason, he left the college in the spring of 1926, looking for a change. His intent at the beginning of the summer was to work in the "book business," but his plans hit a snag when he did not prove physically up to the task. He had agreed to sell bibles for Nashville's Southwestern Publishers in Lee County, Mississippi. After an enjoyable week of training in Nashville, he was sent to work the sales field in Tupelo, Mississippi, and found that "the sun was hell itself."[34] He was determined not to give up until he got sick with what the doctor diagnosed as sunstroke. On the doctor's written recommendation to the company, he was relieved from his contract. He returned to Fairfax and took it easy until fully recovered. Then he became a driver for his father in his political campaign, which Alex did not win.[35]

Toward the end of the summer, Still made a trip to Texas, the itinerary of which he outlined in a letter to Redmond written on September 27, 1926. He did not include the names of his fellow travelers nor the purpose of their trip, but later he recalled going to Texas with his father and brothers when he was twenty to visit relatives.[36] Details were conspicuously absent from his description to Redmond as if, with his return to Alabama, Jim was consciously erasing the particulars and recounting only the framework and highlights.

He and his travel companions had left Fairfax early on the last day of August and set out on the Dixie Overland Route, which is now U.S. Route 80 and Interstate 20. When they reached Meridian, Mississippi, they slept a few hours, then drove on to Jackson. They stopped in Vicksburg to visit the National Military Park, then crossed the Mississippi River as the sun was setting on the water. Still described that moment: "Music was playing on the boat and naturally it makes one feel romantic. Its [sic] been a long time since I've had another thrill that could equal that." They went on to Tallulah, Louisiana, and spent the night, sleeping on a lumber pile in the fairgrounds.

The next day they saw the oil refineries at Shreveport, finally arriving near Marshall, Texas, where they spent that night. They had traveled about five hundred miles since leaving Fairfax. Moving on, they drove to Dallas and spent the night in a tourist camp in Fort Worth. The remainder of the first week Still described this way: "Went through the museum and art gallery there. Saw some friends at Palo Pinto; visited Lovers Retreat (a mirical [sic] of nature). From there to Ranger, and saw the famous oil-field; thence to Cisco and to winters [sic] where we spent a half day. Spent the night at a tourist camp at Abilene. Went to Anson the next day and spent the week-end with an uncle. I've got some fine cousins too. Real westerners."[37]

The second week necessitated backtracking to Fort Worth, then going 150 miles south to Temple and west to Killeen, on the southern edge of what is now Fort Hood, where they visited another uncle. Then to Bruceville, where they stayed three days and picked a bale of cotton for a fellow. They pushed on to Waco and saw Baylor. The trip back to Alabama was mostly riding, stopping only to sleep at Palestine "near a Catholic grave-yard." The night before reaching home they spent in a Mississippi churchyard and finally arrived back in Fairfax at midnight on Tuesday, September 14.

Much of the travel and many of the experiences Still described as part of his job search during the Depression actually had roots in this 1926 summer travel. It also contributed to his creation of the Texas manuscript, which became the publication *Chinaberry*. This Texas trip may, in fact, be the only visit that Still made to the state in his childhood and youth. In the *Heritage* interview, Still told Judi Jennings, "I had many relatives out there [in Texas], many. But I never went back until let's see. We went when I was twenty. We visited that farm and relatives or the spot where it had been. And the graves of some relatives are still there. I can see my father pulling up the weeds off the graves."[38]

When Still returned to Alabama, he was depressed to think that the fall semester was beginning at LMU and that he would not be a part of it. While indulging in a "fantasy of loneliness," he enjoyed the lazy days of Indian summer but wondered with some apprehension what the approaching winter would bring. He kept busy taking a troop of Boy Scouts to Pine Mountain Camp for the weekend and affectionately described their activities to Redmond: "The mill truck carried us over and we had a most wonderful time. We swam in the lake, hunted wild grapes, muscadines, and sugar-berries, went canoe-riding on the grand old Chattahoochee, and too, told the 'ghostest' tales at night."[39] He also visited his sister in Rome, Georgia, where the countryside reminded him of the Cumberland Gap. He was homesick for college, and the feeling worsened when he worked as an apprentice at the Fairfax Towel Mill. He was not assigned a particular job; the management simply wanted him to become acquainted with the business by observing what was going on. He learned all the styles of towels, the numbers and names. Most important, he learned that the job was not for him.[40] He stayed just until he had enough money to get back to college.

Though Jim had not been miserable during his year at home, he discovered what Thomas Wolfe would say in 1940: "You can't go home again." Life in Alabama was too tame and familiar for the young man, the work too boring. He was also beginning to witness the difficulties of finding and keeping gainful employment. The year in Chambers County felt familiar, yet he came to realize that he was more at home at Lincoln Memorial. In March 1927 Redmond received poor results in chemistry and was feeling down on college. Still, on the other hand, was missing the place even more than he had the previous fall. He summarized their attitudes: "I am thinking just now how happy I would be if I were back at L.M.U. and you are disgusted with being there!"[41]

His first two years of college had triggered a break from childhood, perhaps no more traumatic than what most college students feel. But now his experience of home fueled his desire to go back to a challenging place that promised more stimulation and a better future. He returned to Tennessee with greater maturity and a clearer purpose.

5

Mentors, Friends, and Patron

Finishing at LMU

For Iris Grannis and Guy Loomis
— Dedication in *The Run for the Elbertas*

When James Still turned twenty-one in July 1927, he had already returned to Lincoln Memorial and was taking three summer classes. Harrogate was where he belonged, but his last two years at LMU would be different from the first two. The determination "to change" that he expressed to Red in September 1926 had become a reality. He did not change schools, nor did he consciously change himself, except in attitude, but his situation was better.

Still claimed to have had three excellent classes at LMU, all of them in his last two years: one in biology, one in history, and one in literature.[1] He described the challenge of classical literature in a letter to his parents: "It's a real pain. I like [Professor Moore] and his method of teaching but he doesn't seem to know when to stop assigning a lesson. On today's lesson we had 53 pages of fine print about Sophocles, Euripides and other ancient characters and their participation in the tragic competition at Olympus."[2]

This long letter is filled with details, probably more than his family could absorb, but it shows clearly that Still was engaged in college life in a way that he had not been before. He was busy but spending less energy on heavy work. His letters home, which were now frequent and newsy, related his daily activities on campus: studying, cleaning his dorm room in preparation for a visit from the girls' dorm, attending basketball games, reporting those games for the newspaper, driving visiting dignitaries around the town, attending banquets, and so forth.[3] He never mentioned being physically tired, insatiably hungry, or hopelessly bored.

He also became interested in the life of the area. He began absorbing the surroundings, the stories of family quarrels, the isolated life of the hill people. He even made plans with two faculty members to take some books to a remote part of the county and wrote the news to his parents: "Mrs. Grannis, Dr. Danforth, and I were contemplating a trip back up in the mountains last Wednesday to visit an isolated school and carry some books and magazines. . . . It is a long way from here and I was to drive the car. We'll have to go before the winter rains set in or we can't make it at all this season." Though it was not an excursion of interest to the typical college junior, Still was looking forward to it. He ended with a quick thanks for the books, clothes, and two dollars they had sent.[4]

In his last two years, Still appreciated the value of a small college—the kind of school he needed—and the place where it was set. The faculty was filled not with scholars like those he came to know later but with dedicated teachers, who took a personal interest in students. One supporter was Lucia Danforth, the French professor. Several years after graduating, Still requested a reference from her. The letter she sent back described him as "gentlemanly and thoughtful of others" and "keenly interested in the best things in literature."[5] The attention that he received from teachers like Danforth built Still's confidence and provided him emotional support. He had not discovered those qualities at LMU or in himself earlier, but now he was open to a different, fuller experience. Another change Still made involved curriculum. In the fall of 1927 he enrolled in a course called "Introduction to Teaching." During the summer quarter of 1928 he took six courses, four of them related to education. He did not earn a teaching license, but this practical coursework showed his increasing interest in preparing himself for a job. The career he would eventually follow—librarian—was related more to his work-study position than to his academic work.

James Still's final success at LMU revolved around one place on campus, the library, and a few people with whom he had close relationships. While his friendship with Dare Redmond continued to strengthen, he met two other students who would become lifelong friends, Jesse Stuart and Don West. More important at the time, he established links with a couple who became his surrogate parents—Frank and Iris Grannis. Frank taught biology, and Iris was an English teacher and librarian. His most important financial association, which began when he was a senior, was with the elderly gentleman Guy Loomis, who became his patron.

Redmond was Still's strongest connection to LMU when he was at home in Alabama. Their enjoyment of each other is evident from their correspondence. Still's letters were filled with questions about the place and people, with news of his daily life, and with speculation on the college sports of the day, particularly football. His March 27, 1927, letter ended with the charge "Be yo self, Boy, be yo age—'an give 'em particular hell!"[6] Redmond was being himself and finding himself. In particular, he was discovering that hard manual labor did not mix well with classes and studying. Like Still, he changed jobs several times, moving from the rock quarry where he ran an "old-time twelve horse power gasoline engine," to the woodwork shop, the farm, the laundry, and the grounds and garden crew. Finally, when Still returned and settled into his own work, he told Red, "I can get you a job working in the library if you want it." He did want it, so Still put in a good word. Red got the job and worked there until he graduated.[7]

Iris Grannis arranged and supervised all of the library's student workers. That meant she was the overseer for Still's most significant opportunity at LMU: his job in the library. "What Lincoln Memorial did for me," he often said, "was the library. I discovered the publishing world, all these magazines, and I discovered, no thanks to any teachers, the writer Thomas Hardy. . . . I lived there. I just went mad."[8] Beginning late in his sophomore year and continuing through his last two, Still was a janitor for the library. He would arrive about nine o'clock each night and, soon after, lock the doors. Then he toured the building, emptying the wastebaskets, sweeping the floor, and polishing the tables. After completing those tasks, he had the place to himself. He described his state as a kind of ecstasy. He hardly knew what to read first. Though he discovered several authors who were to become favorites, the periodicals were of particular interest and importance. There he found *The Atlantic Monthly,* which was to be a key publisher of his stories over the next ten years. He especially enjoyed the project of adding missing issues of periodicals to the library collection because it yielded him free reading material. When the library received past issues of a journal, he checked the files, removed the ones they needed, and was told to "dump the rest into the furnace." Instead, he sent issues to Alabama; when the Great Depression was in full swing, he read every story, poem, and essay.[9]

His library job was prophetic in several ways. Besides giving him work and future connections, the building became a haven, a source for a complete and self-directed education. Books began to play a more prominent role in Still's life. On a practical level, the library would become a link to his future career. He began as janitor, but Iris Grannis soon promoted him to the position of her assistant and set him the task of creating a cataloging system for the library's Lincoln Collection.[10] Her influence continued even after he graduated. When the Depression made job searching a chore, he followed her suggestion to go to library school and took advantage of his patron's generosity to enter the University of Illinois, where he earned a bachelor's degree in library science. But that is getting ahead of the story.

Though he had met Frank and Iris Grannis earlier, Still came to know them well in 1927. One of Still's favorite classes was the biology course taught by Mr. Grannis, which he took in the summer of his return. Grannis held a bachelor's degree in agriculture and a master's in agriculture and biology from the University of Illinois. He had been on the faculty at LMU for six years. Although Still never described the course in detail, he later worked for Grannis in his science lab and developed a lifelong love for growing things, a penchant that may have had its beginnings in the cotton fields of Alabama but was further cultivated by these field and lab experiences. Iris Grannis held a joint appointment as English instructor and librarian. She was also involved in advancement or fund-raising for the institution. Still described her as a striking beauty, a wealthy woman (inherited wealth) who had good taste in furniture, food, and music as well as an impressive collection of classical records. When Henry Ford and his wife came to LMU, Mrs. Grannis was his hostess. Even all her charm could not convince Ford to make a substantial and needed donation to the school, but he did give her a Ford car. As a result, James Still got the use of the Grannis' old car.[11]

When working in the library, Still became closer to Mr. and Mrs. Grannis. Evidence of their changing relationship involved a young dog named "Grannis." The couple gave James a male German Shepherd puppy, gray with fawn and black markings, born on August 10, 1927, and "sold" to Still on March 10, 1928.[12] Still could not keep Grannis with him at college but was fond enough of the dog to go to the trouble and "stupendous" expense of shipping him home to Alabama. A letter to his folks written that spring indicated that the dog had arrived. At the end of his traumatic journey, Grannis had exhibited strange behavior, and Still was attempting to assure his parents that he really was not vicious and only required a lot of petting and coaxing.[13] Little else is heard about that dog, aside from brief references from his mother.[14] Apparently, Grannis adapted to Alabama because ten months later, she reported that they also had one of his pups.

Mr. and Mrs. Grannis and their dogs were not uniformly popular in the LMU community. In 1927, for example, Jesse Stuart, while doing some gardening for Iris Grannis, was bitten by her German shepherd. He walked off the job when she dismissed the incident with, "Oh, it didn't hurt much."[15] Stuart was not a fan of Frank Grannis either, referring to him as "the protozoology professor who 'lacked feeling for life.'"[16] Stuart's antipathy was partly related to the rivalry Iris had with Stuart's mentor Harry Harrison Kroll. Kroll referred to her as the strong-willed editor of the campus magazine, for which he served as associate editor, "a woman eaten out with vanity and self importance."[17] Kroll claimed that in the fall of 1928 Mrs. Grannis had tried to seduce him; when he declined, she turned on him.[18] To him she was "a striking, raven-haired patrician woman. Her primary professional qualification was her skill at intrigue. She held a stranglehold over campus administration and politics."[19] Since the community was small, it is not surprising that students would have taken sides, especially when the characters in the drama were so striking. What Stuart remembered was a woman who was troublesome, even antagonistic to his favorite professor. What Still remembered was a beautiful woman who was attentive, helpful, and encouraging to him.

Personal conflict between colleagues is evident in this story of Grannis and Kroll. But the tension was more than personal; the arrival of Kroll at LMU marked a shift in the campus approach to pedagogy and to literary study. Kroll came to Harrogate in the fall of 1926, the year that Still was in Alabama. He had been a public-school English teacher before receiving his master of arts degree at Peabody College in Nashville. More important, he was a published writer with fifty stories to his credit when he arrived at LMU. He taught every English class at the college in 1926–1927 and became "a defining influence" on the students. He was a practicing writer with a casual classroom style. He took a populist approach to literature and praised students for their raw but candid efforts, encouraging them to write about what they knew, their own culture. Jesse Stuart, quite naturally, joined the Kroll camp.[20] Stuart's view was that Kroll became "a force of nature on campus, attracting students who responded to his market-driven literary ethos with such enthusiasm they took to meeting with him at night under street lamps."[21] When Still returned the next year, he took up where he had left off, in the company of two people he knew and liked, Lucia Danforth and Iris Grannis. Their approach to just about everything seemed to differ from Kroll's.

Dr. Danforth was the only faculty member at the time holding a doctorate; she taught French and was fluent in several languages as well as being an active member of the Modern Language Association. Elizabeth Lamont described her house on the campus as "an art-and-music-filled cottage" that served as "an idyllic literary retreat" for students. Kroll's streetlight meetings and Danforth's cottage hideaway offered LMU students a diversity of literary theory and practice.[22] To say that Kroll and Danforth maintained a rivalry is overstating, but they were different. She introduced students to a traditional study of literary classics and appreciation of their aesthetic value, while Kroll promoted the production of large quantities of material that would appeal to the popular press. She was a scholar, while he was a maverick writing teacher. In addition to teaching, Kroll served as associate editor for the alumni/development magazine, the *Mountain Herald*. The editor was Iris Grannis; Danforth was copyeditor. Whether Kroll avoided the work or Grannis excluded him from it, the publication was primarily her own. In one issue she described Mr. Kroll's contribution by saying that he was "busy writing articles to sell, so he can only contribute something every now and then."[23]

He was busy writing and, while teaching at LMU, produced his first novel, *The Mountainy Singer*. He wrote it fast and sent the manuscript to potential publishers in the summer after his first year. William Morrow & Co. accepted it, releasing it on September 22, 1928, just two years after his arrival at LMU. Kroll was thrilled, and the institution was proud. This was the first book ever published by a faculty member. Soon his accomplishment turned into calamity. As Kroll's biographer, Richard Saunders, put it: "Kroll naively miscalculated that the book's mere existence would trump its colorful elements for his conservative and religious administrators and colleagues." The plot hinted at infidelity and incest and included more description of physical affection than was seemly. His local audience found it tasteless, even crude. Jesse Stuart wanted to blame Danforth for encouraging the negative response, but according to Saunders, "Kroll's book was a brickbat against him in an already divided faculty."[24] The result was his dismissal. He exited

LMU in the middle of the term (October 1928: Still's senior year) but not without leaving a strong impression and some vocal student followers. He and all that happened around him had changed the atmosphere of the place.

Years later, when Still was asked about his experience at LMU, his response led to comments about Kroll:

> We had a professor there named Harry Harrison Kroll, who was writing and published a novel, which I never read. I tried it once. And Stuart claims he was a great influence. But not with me. I had two courses with him [Kroll]. One was poetry, which amounted to nothing and the other was the teaching of composition. And we did write compositions everyday; that's all we did. And he would choose one and read it to the class. I don't remember any criticism of them. . . . He was a very unusual man. Not a gifted teacher. . . . But he had something to give, and I'm not sure what it was.[25]

One thing that Kroll gave to students was a less-traditional approach to writing and publishing—he saw stories and books as a commodity that could be produced quickly and marketed widely. Also less traditional was his choice of subject matter; Kroll wrote about ordinary people engaged in ordinary life. There was nothing highbrow about Harry Kroll. Finally, he encouraged students to write about their own world, to embrace and promote their local culture. It is possible that Still did not know Kroll personally at LMU and that he was not directly influenced by Kroll's classes. Yet Still did display throughout his writing this last principle—he always wrote about the world and culture in which he lived. What else did Kroll give? He energized the small mountain college campus and drew the students' attention to a living literature.

In 1929 a noteworthy coincidence occurred. Three young men, who would become major twentieth-century voices of the Appalachian region, all graduated from Lincoln Memorial University—Jesse Stuart, James Still, and Don West.[26] Harrison Kroll cannot be credited with leading them to their academic or career choices, but the atmosphere on the campus when he was there became part of their experience. Their backgrounds are impressively similar; their personalities, very different. The three were all born in the summer of 1906, and they shared an upbringing as eldest sons of farmers. All three boys were the first in their families to go to college, and they represented the kind of student that LMU wanted to serve: hard-working individuals who did not have money or opportunity readily available.

Although the same age, they did not enter LMU in the same quarter. Still matriculated in September 1924, but Stuart and West began two years later, when Still had stayed in Alabama. The earliest they all could have met was the summer of 1927. While Still had a rough start at LMU, Stuart and West began college with flair. What Still lacked in physical prowess, Stuart had in abundance. And West was endowed with a gift that Still had not yet developed: social skills.

Stuart embraced the hard work that scholarship students were obligated to perform. Initially, he was in the fields where he dug potatoes, cut corn, and raked leaves. He laid a waterline through frozen earth, "dynamited rocks in the quarry, swung a sledgehammer and beat the rocks into smaller rocks so he could feed them into a pulverizer, and wheeled the stones in Irish-buggies."[27] Stuart was a large man used to manual labor. His competitive nature made him try to outwork his fellow students. Don West was also willing and able to work.[28] His assignments included helping on the campus farm, digging ditches, and serving as a general laborer.[29] So while the three young men ate little and worked hard, West and Stuart were physically better able than Still to handle the strain.[30] By sometime in their second year, Stuart was working in the cafeteria, where he could scrounge extra helpings; West was in the campus laundry; and Still was janitor in the library.

Stuart became involved in campus life. He was athletic, though his competitive impulse was not limited to organized sports. He loved to engage in theatrical combat that ended with his physically dominating his opponent. An example is the mock-heroic battle that took place in a hayfield where one of his classmates played the part of a possessed animal. Jesse's role was to correct his problem, and he did it dramatically by whacking him with the backside of a pitchfork.[31] Stuart was also editor of the campus newspaper, *The Blue and Gray,* for three years. He participated in the debate club, went on hiking parties, and played in the Student Volunteer Band. He always seemed to be pursuing girls and picking fights, which sometimes related to the girls. At graduation, the faculty selected him as the "most original" student, and he shared honors for being the "most rebellious."[32] Perhaps Stuart's most impressive achievement at LMU was his large volume of writing. He was both inspired and encouraged by Kroll. Stuart published at least fifteen poems before he graduated, some in the paper he edited.[33]

Like Stuart, Don West was a big man about campus from the

moment he arrived, and he became a leader by the time he graduated. He served as class president and as president of the YMCA and the Student Volunteer Band. His active involvement is revealed in the December 1928 issue of the student newspaper, where his name appears in four articles: as a leader in establishing a new literary society, as the student welcoming a guest evangelist, as the president of the Harrogate YMCA, and as a star member of the basketball and the track relay teams. If all that, along with his work and studies, were not enough to keep him occupied, he ran a laundry business in town. Many of his activities were connected with the community and included charitable work organizing Red Cross drives, starting Sunday schools in isolated areas, and carrying food to indigent people. At graduation, his classmates voted him as second in the list of seniors who had "Done [the] Most for LMU."[34] He also began writing poetry while at LMU. As a staff writer for *The Blue and Gray,* he worked for Stuart, and the paper published several of his poems.[35]

Although the campus was small, Stuart and Still did not travel in the same circles. Their descriptions in the 1929 college yearbook make it clear that others saw them as different: Still was described as reserved and dignified, having "a genial, affectionate, and generous nature." Stuart was an "aspiring, determined man" who "conquers adversity with the same zeal he enjoys prosperity."[36] Still had more in common with West because they were both interested in Boy Scout work. In the summer of 1928 the *Mountain Herald* noted that the Lincoln Memorial Boy Scout patrols were under the leadership of two assistant scoutmasters: one was Don West. The groups all met together on Fridays with scoutmaster James Still. One weekend they camped out at Nash's Mill, "where they swam, played games, enjoyed contests and cooked their meals."[37] This work would have appealed to both young men because it offered the camaraderie and opportunity to help others that West craved and the contact with the outdoors plus the connection with scouting that Still enjoyed.

Another venture they shared was the establishment of a new literary club. Still had been a member of the Grant-Lee Literary Society during his first two years but became disenchanted as a junior, probably because it was becoming too much like a Greek social fraternity. It was West who took the initiative in their last year, but he had fifteen other young men who joined him; Still was one and became the treasurer.[38] The new organization was called, in honor of LMU's founder, the O. O. Howard Literary Society.

This working relationship that West and Still shared did not include Stuart. It is possible that Stuart became aware of Still only when he began winning essay prizes. After all, Still was his foil: nonathletic, shy, somewhat introverted; neither aggressive and outwardly competitive nor openly ambitious, and certainly not a ladies' man. Still was not in Kroll's group and did not publicly display his poetry, if he was writing any. But because Stuart was editor of the student newspaper, he would have known this quiet man who was on the honor roll and consistently winning prizes. *The Blue and Gray* ran a May 1929 article about James Still's play *Nancy Hanks*, which had been chosen to represent Kentucky in a national contest.[39] After describing the winning performance, the article described the playwright:

> Still is that modest quiet type of lad who is remote to men. He lives his life as a student almost in seclusion. But he has that rare type of intellect that not many youths are gifted with having. No one knows how much he writes, or what he writes until it appears. But one finds Still's room a very interesting place— filled with odd and interesting books—the most modern, some just off the press and others old as the ages. You will also find files of manuscripts and queer paints usually oriental [*sic*].

The article has no named writer; its several errors might indicate it was done quickly. Whether he wrote or edited it, Stuart would have seen the piece and been aware that James Still was a man worthy of notice.

It was only in their last term that the two became friends. In a 1933 letter to Still, Stuart described an evening walk in the countryside that highlighted the LMU phase of their friendship: "I remember that evening we walked over those sacred hills in east Tennessee together—I remember that walk very distinctly with you—I remember the moon in a clear sky and the mountains covered with deep green foliage—the wind a rustling the leaves—you, and your voice. . . . Those days were fine we spent together there."[40]

Stuart, Still, and West all began writing while in Harrogate: poems, plays, newspaper articles, essays for class, or articles for LMU publications. And they established a three-way friendship that lasted for years. Still's memory never idealized the time he had there nor the friends he made; quite the contrary, he played the experience down. A few years later, in a letter to Red, he sarcastically proposed that they organize a writers' association called the Harrogate Group. It would include such persons as H. H. Kroll, Roland Carter, Don West, D. V. Redmond, and Jesse Stuart. A better name would be "O god the Hills! school of writers."[41] Whether reflections on those times were sentimental or silly, there is no doubt that LMU, in the late 1920s, inspired young writers.

Another important person to young Still was Guy Loomis, a wealthy man from Brooklyn, who sponsored scholarships for students at the college. Iris Grannis was largely responsible for Still's opportunity to meet Mr. Loomis, and that meeting developed into a long-term financial commitment to Still's future. Loomis had been giving money for awards, sponsoring work scholarships, and providing support in a general way to needy students at LMU and several other Southern colleges.[42] The connection between Mrs. Grannis and Mr. Loomis was established through her position as secretary of the Nancy Hanks Memorial Association, which cultivated donors for the college. He would occasionally make visits to campus, but the students never saw him. On one visit, he observed that some of the young men were not well dressed, so he left money for twelve of them to have new suits. He had money to give, and he had found a place that needed and appreciated his gifts. Why did Still stand out for special treatment?

According to stories Still told years later, Guy Loomis was an elderly gentleman—around eighty when they first met—and heir to a sash-and-blind fortune; he wanted to give away some of his money, and having no children himself, he sought out college students who needed help. Mrs. Grannis was handling the arrangements for his gifts to LMU. Still went to her one day after receiving a new suit of clothes and said that he wanted to write a thank-you letter to the donor. She told him correspondence was not expected or necessary, but Still insisted that he write a simple note that she could mail. She agreed. Still was the first student to contact Loomis. Later, Still wrote again and invited the old gentleman to attend the commencement exercises to be held on June 4, 1929.

Guy Loomis did come from New York in his chauffeured Cadillac limousine. He stayed several days, perhaps a week, attending classes and commencement functions. As Still told the story, when Loomis exited the ceremony, he stopped the young graduate on the sidewalk and offered, there and then, to send him to graduate school at the college of his choice, as long as it was in the South. But not wanting him to go alone, he asked if Still knew of another young man who had good grades and needed help. Still responded immediately that Dare Redmond was a good candidate. Loomis agreed without having met Redmond.

Was Loomis desperate to give away money or was he, on this their first meeting, so impressed with Still that he knew he wanted to sponsor this young man's promising future? In fact, he already knew of Still's potential for becoming a successful writer. Still's honors—all writing contests—had caught the attention of the old man. Still claimed that he had "swiped all the literary prizes except one."[43] The LMU catalog for 1929–1930 listed the prizes for the previous year, and James Still was the winner of three:

- Rush Strong Medal, awarded for the prize essay on "The Value of Truth," from the Rush Strong Fund, University of Tennessee, Knoxville.[44]
- Ten dollars in cash for the best essay written by a college student on "Man and His Fellow Creatures." Donor, Miss Alice Morgan Wright, New York City.
- Third prize of $20.00 for best essay on "Science and Religion." Donor, Hugh Gordon Miller, New York City.

In his recounting, Still made Loomis seem impulsive as well as generous. However, like any savvy donor, the old gentleman had done his homework. Correspondence shows that he knew of Still's abilities long before the June graduation and had written the young man a letter in September 1928 complimenting his essay "The Value of Truth." Here is an excerpt from the letter that came to Still at the beginning of his senior year:

Dear Jimmy:

I was reading your paper on "The Value of Truth," a copy of which Mrs. Grannis sent me, and I want to congratulate you on the way it is written and assure you that if you will follow the precepts and principles laid out in your article, you certainly will have little to regret.

It may be hard at times, but in the long run you will win out . . . it doesn't make so much difference whether we win out or lose out, but if we play the game as it should be played, we certainly will retain the respect of all who know us.[45]

This first letter from Guy Loomis foreshadowed all those to come. He was continually offering encouragement—a sentiment that would be much needed during the 1930s—but he was practical and down-to-earth. He never advised the young man to seek a handout, but he was always ready to help him pursue his dreams.

One year after receiving this letter from Loomis and three months after graduating from LMU, Still experienced a piece of that dream when Loomis invited him to visit Brooklyn. He wrote his parents about the trip.[46] First he took the train to Grand Central Station; then in a bit of free time, he spent the afternoon in the New York Public Library, visiting the Charles Dickens and Washington Irving manuscript exhibition. Another highlight was taking the subway to Brooklyn, then a taxi to Loomis's home in the Hotel Bossert, which overlooked New York Harbor. They dined in the roof garden amid the "dancers and the honky-tonk of a jazz band." Afterward retiring to Loomis's suite of rooms, they viewed a movie of the LMU graduation, which must have involved state-of-the-art home viewing for the time. Still stayed in a fine room in the hotel, courtesy of Loomis. All his expenses had been covered. It was an excellent introduction to a world far away from Harrogate, Tennessee, and Fairfax, Alabama.

Still's talent for writing at this time was best revealed not through essays or articles but through letters. His interest in the surrounding region, his folk-research technique of observing and noting, and his narrative style of selective reporting are evident in one undated letter he wrote to his parents probably in October 1927. It shows his tendency to observe the local people and participate in events, then create a story from his experience. In this letter, he described an old-time fiddlers' convention where he had heard mountain ballads. He also told of a trip he was planning to make into the hills where "mountain people are shut-off from the outside world. Occasionally the men tramp into town after supplies but the women and children must stay at home and eke out a miserable existence." Without any introduction, he continued as though writing sections of a book:

Chapter II (Containing other foolish relations)

I learned something new yesterday. This county auctions off their poor each April at the County seat for 75 cents per day. Anybody who wants one of these derelicts to work for them can bid. . . .

Mrs. Grannis once received a long distance telephone call from Knoxville and was told the following "We have an old negro man here, and he belongs to you. What must we do with him?" She was greatly puzzled until she found that they meant that the negro belonged to the county. The associated charities were trying to get him back to his home county.

Chapter III (A tragedy without a moral)

The culmination of an ancient grudge was revenged at Pineville a month ago. Many years ago (about 1900) a mountaineer shot another fellow to death at Cumberland Gap. The son of the deceased man was brought up by his mother with the impression that he must avenge his father. Last month at a carnival at the Gap this boy met up with the man, but bystanders sensed the situation and sent one off in one direction and the other another way. The man called back—"I keeled your daddy, and I'll kill you yet." The next day the boy walked calmly into the railroad station at Pineville and got his man, boarded the 8.30 train and went home. He wasn't even arrested. Everybody thought he was justified in killing the murderer of his father.

Following another page of loosely connected thoughts, Still concluded, "I find time to enjoy life and the interesting country around here."[47] Still's Alabama family had mixed feelings about his experiences in Tennessee. As he was beginning his last winter quarter, he received a wish-you-were-here letter from his mother: "Sure will be glad when you get thru college so you can be making some money people hear cant [sic] understand how you can stay up there so long and dad not making much they think we are sending you money and I wish we could." She ends with her hope that they can come to Harrogate for his graduation and see the place he has "talked so much about."[48] In the end, they could not go. On May 19, just three weeks before the special day, she wrote:

When are you coming home I would like to know, have you got a new suit to wear to graduation. I sure wish Dad and myself could be there . . . it hurts me because I can't come. But am glad for you that you are finishing this time. Are you still planning on going to Duke's [sic] university I heard you were going to Harvard College another year and what studies are you going to specialize on I have read the Herald but could not tell what subject you were going to take say you must treat Mr. Loomis as nice when he comes down there you can thank Mr and Mrs Grannis for the interest they have taken [in] you while you were at LMU we certainly appreciate it.[49]

As he contemplated graduation, he assumed the role of the eldest brother, the pioneer of the family who had set out to get a college education. In a letter to Tom, he expressed his confidence that the Still brothers would make good in the world. They all had the "stuff" in them to put the name "Still on the map."[50] Perhaps his family did not understand or share his accomplishments, but that did not diminish his achievement. As his college years at LMU were ending, he was finding success in the classroom and confidence in himself.

His success was due partly to his growing independence, but more likely because he had established a surrogate family there and had found a patron in Guy Loomis. Still's adventure at LMU had begun when he was eighteen and concluded five years later on June 4, 1929, a month short of his twenty-third birthday. The place had been good for him; the close friends he made would stay with him for years; and the interests he had developed would serve him for a lifetime.

His graduation occurred just four months before the stock market crash that marked the beginning of the Great Depression. But for Still and his family and friends, the pre-Depression years had already been a time of financial hardship. It was a condition that he had learned to live with and one that he had seen as a personal challenge. Had he been able to acquire a satisfactory job immediately after graduation, he might have chosen to take it, but an opportunity did not present itself. During his time at LMU the young man had taken a lesson from Mr. Lincoln himself who said, "I will prepare and someday my chance will come." With the help of friends and supporters, Still was preparing himself. In the summer of 1929 he was looking forward to the future though still unsure of the shape it would take.

6

The Scholar's Tale

Vanderbilt

James Still is one fellow who was not destroyed by a college education.

—Harrison Kroll

Selecting which graduate school to attend was complicated. Still did not settle on his choice until the end of the summer he graduated from LMU. As if on a fishing expedition, he put his hook in the water and waited. Both he and Redmond had thought they would continue studying with the support of Guy Loomis, who had made the offer at the LMU commencement. Their plan had been to earn a practical degree, a second bachelor's in library science from the University of Illinois. This did eventually happen but not in the fall of 1929. Illinois had offered them "unclassified" status because LMU was not accredited.[1] Rather than make up undergraduate credits for a library-science degree, they each decided to try for a master's. As the academic year began, they went in different directions—Red to the University of North Carolina and Still to Vanderbilt—both entering as graduate students in English.

Why Still chose Vanderbilt is not entirely clear. There were at least two other fish in the river. He had an opportunity to attend Duke University, which was establishing itself on a new campus in Durham. In addition to supporting the university with the Duke family name, Benjamin Duke had donated a substantial sum of money to LMU for the construction of the Duke Hall of Citizenship, which was opened for the

1929 commencement. Though the elder Duke was too feeble to attend the dedication, members of his family did. Still assumed that they read of his accomplishments in the *Lincoln Herald,* and as a result Duke University invited him to interview and ultimately offered him a scholarship. Mrs. Grannis was even sent money to take Still to Durham to visit the new campus. They made the trip in the summer of 1929, stayed in a hotel, and had a meal at the faculty club.[2]

On the way back to Tennessee they visited the nearby University of North Carolina (UNC) at Chapel Hill, a much older campus, and in his words, Still "fell in love with the place."[3] Because of this immediate attraction and because Redmond planned to go there, UNC would have been the logical choice for Still. In spite of such invitations and connections to North Carolina universities, Still chose Vanderbilt. Perhaps he felt it had a more established reputation.[4] Throughout his years at LMU, Still had dreamed of attending a more prestigious institution. In the summer of 1928, for example, he had submitted an application to transfer from LMU to Yale but did not complete the request until a year later.[5] That application arrived three weeks after the deadline and was for undergraduate admission. Two letters of recommendation followed under separate cover, one written by Iris Grannis. The response to her from the board of admissions stated that the application was received late and added that since Still now had a degree from LMU, he should apply as a graduate student. He did not follow up with Yale, and he may not have been serious about it to start with, but this incident underscored his hit-and-miss approach to finding the right school while indicating that he was setting his heights high.

He was also getting advice and help, too much of both, from Iris Grannis. Soon after he began at Vanderbilt, he wrote to his LMU friend Ralph Shanks, imploring him not to condemn his choice of Vanderbilt, as some people had. He declared it had been his own choice: "I came here [to Nashville] with the Grannis curse upon my head for doing so. No matter I'm here, I like it, I know better than most people what's best for me, I'm tired of being dragged and directed." He might have thought of Vanderbilt as more prestigious than the North Carolina universities, but his declaration to Shanks implies that he was rebelling against his surrogate parents, especially Mrs. Grannis. He wanted to "start over again uncommitted." A Tennessee university would have been more familiar to him because a number of graduates from LMU were there. At that time, Vanderbilt was not a surprising choice. Years later, however, he described the decision as a conundrum.[6]

Still occupied himself during the summer of 1929 by traveling in the East and Northeast. In addition to his trip to North Carolina, he went to New England with the Grannises.[7] Frank Grannis was pursuing a doctorate at Yale and had been in New Haven for the academic year 1928–1929. Still and Iris went there during the summers, and he got to know some people in the biology labs.[8] In spite of all this traveling, he did not visit Vanderbilt that summer. In fact, he did not receive word of his acceptance until the end of August, two weeks after he had received a check for $2.55 from the Christian Board of Education for his story "Johnny Appleseed." A modest sum, but it was the first money he had made from his writing. Competing with that news was the telegram from Nashville on August 29, 1929, saying that admission had been granted.[9]

Within the month, he and Redmond would embark on their graduate-school adventures. Red's first letter from Chapel Hill to Jim in Nashville indicated that he missed his friend:

> It seems an age since I saw you the last time. Wonder what
> you are doing now. Wish you had come to Chapel Hill.
> I registered in the graduate school yesterday without any
> trouble. Don't know what the result will be but think I can get
> by pretty well. . . . Write to me soon and let me know where
> you are and what you are doing. I will need lots of inspiration
> to keep up under the work I have to do.
>
> Your Old Pal, Redmond

Only two weeks passed before Red wrote another letter conveying the apprehension of a schoolboy entering a big academic world: "Certainly was glad to get your letter, but I was sorry to hear that you are in the same condition that I am in. Gee, but we had an easy time during our college days. . . . with all my classes to keep up with, how can I do it?"[10]

Still's early situation in Nashville was also far from easy. He had admitted to Ralph Shanks soon after he settled in that he was "blue" from having to leave everything "dear at LMU." He described himself as alone and "feeling very humble, weak and forsaken."[11] Harrogate was small like Still's Alabama environment. Nashville was not. His description of his housing arrangements sounds as though he were living in a Poe short story or a murder-mystery film.

> I lived in the home of a widow [Mrs. Marlin], 1913 Broad
> Street, the only roomer in a house of heavy mahogany furni-
> ture and drawn curtains and silence. Her children were adults,
> rarely seen. The son operated a night club on the river; the
> daughter, probably in her late 20's had some sort of night work,
> presumably at the Club. The few times I passed her in the hall
> she was swathed in mink and silk and her Night in Paris per-
> fume lingered after. She never spoke. The night club burned in
> March, the son in it. Arson and murder presumed. My landlady
> considered it an aberration that I insisted on a hot bath every
> day. I blew the speckles of soot from the rail road yards off my
> pillow at night.

But, he concluded, "there was learning to be had at 1913 Broad Street"
just as there was in the classroom building, Calhoun Hall.[12]

His sense of intimidation came not from the cosmopolitan atmosphere of the city but from his graduate courses and demanding professors. This was his first encounter with known scholars and possibly
the first genuine academic challenge of his life. Many years later Still
referred to his experience at Vanderbilt as "hell" and to Calhoun Hall
as the place where he "suffered greatly."[13] He enrolled at Vanderbilt in
September 1929 and was awarded his master's degree in June 1930.
Professor Edwin Mims, Still's advisor, signed him up for four three-
credit-hour classes.

> English 15 Literature of Our Own Age taught by John Crowe
>   Ransom
> English 23 American Literature, John Donald Wade
> English 21 Chaucer, Walter Clyde Curry
> History 11 Renaissance and Reformation, Wilfred Walker

This course load earned him a major in English and a minor in history.[14]
But before he was fully into the courses, he had to become accustomed
to communicating with professors like Mims.

Critical to Still's situation was the Vanderbilt English department,
especially its chairman in 1929. Dr. Edwin Mims was fifty-seven years
old when Still began as a graduate student. His trim mustache and goa-
tee were accentuated with oiled hair on either side of a center part, a
stiff white collar, black tie, and dark suit. He had earned both his bachelor's and master's at Vanderbilt, then had gone to Cornell for his doc-

torate. In the early 1900s he had taught at Trinity College (later Duke) and UNC before returning to Vanderbilt in 1912 as chair, at which time he began to build the department, emphasizing the graduate program.[15]

From Still's retrospective description, Mims was an interesting mixture of stern advisor, popular lecturer, and cavalier approver of master's theses. Still referred to him as "a famous man of the times." It was one of Mims's addresses in a Nashville church that introduced Still to the first serious support of Darwin's revolutionary theory just five years after the Scopes Trial in Dayton, Tennessee. Still also noted the man's reputation with students: "His office door was always cracked open [because] he had kind of a bad reputation with his girl students. I was glad I wasn't in his class because he was a terror. Hard."[16] The most detailed account of Still's Vanderbilt memories appeared in a letter Still wrote to H. R. Stoneback in 1985. There, Still recalled his advisor who "picked the courses for me, which did not include one of his own. He was the spit image of my Grandpa Lindsey down in Buffalo Wallow, Alabama. When at term's end I presented a thesis for his approval and signature he said he'd sign after Curry and Ransom affixed theirs. And he did, without riffling a page."[17]

One section of Mims's history of Vanderbilt, written in 1946, described the other members of the English department who were key figures when Still was there. John Crowe Ransom joined the department in 1914. He had graduated in the first Vanderbilt class (1909) then gone to Oxford as a Rhodes Scholar. By 1927 he had published four volumes of poetry, and for three years he was a member of the Fugitive group. He taught creative writing at Vanderbilt for a decade.[18] Mims praised Ransom's "Literature of Our Own Age," a course Still took, as an important contribution that inspired many students.[19]

Still remembered Ransom's literary and scholarly reputation to be more impressive than his teaching style. He was admired at Vanderbilt, but not because of a dynamic classroom presence. In fact, claimed Still, "he did not spend time teaching the subject. Instead he talked about when he was in Oxford and traveling in Europe. The students just listened to him then studied the textbook on their own. Ransom seemed very shy. When he came in the room he would give the impression that he wondered if he was in the right place."[20] Still described him as a kindly Southern gentleman of the old school—a professor who did not entertain students in his classes but who did "stretch their imaginations beyond the subject at hand."[21]

Based on four of the essays that Still wrote for Ransom's class, he also had a knack for succinctly conveying to students how they should improve their essay-writing skills. Few editorial comments were scattered throughout the essays, but each one had a summary evaluation.[22] The following list includes the essay title, date, grade, and Ransom's comment:

a) Ways of Escape. November 23, 1929. Grade B *It's not about literature—it's too general and verbose, rather—it's difficult and obscure—*

b) Hester Prynne and the Witch. December 12, 1929. No grade. *A nice piece of imagination.*

c) The Inestimable Mr. Darcy: A Character Study from Jane Austin's "Pride and Prejudice." No date. Grade: B *Nice writing—a bit unproductive—a sort of gentle presentation of the characters and situation—the technical questions indicated at the end should have occurred to you. You should elaborate [the last point]: it's the main body of your article—Show in detail this "absolute realism" and "elision of sentiment."*

d) Dona Rita: A Character Study from Joseph Conrad's "Arrow of Gold." Date 1930. Grade: B+ *You don't quite establish her inscrutability, the fact of her getting out of hand after Allegre's death—but your writing is greatly improved.*

Even if Ransom did not "teach" the subject to the students, it is obvious by comparing the opening of the first essay with the opening of the last one that Still's expository writing grew from the vague pretentious ramblings of a novice graduate student to the expository style of the critical essay more in line with the expectations of New Criticism, which Ransom helped pioneer. Note that his complaint about the first essay was that it is not about literature. The paper on Dona Rita is all about the text and is more clearly expressed. A comparison of the respective first paragraphs show why Ransom thought Still's writing had "greatly improved":

First essay opening, Ways of Escape: The growing complexity of human life and its attendant urge to keep pace with its spasmodic shiftings and in the goose-step of pseudo-progress is causing confusion and disgust among those who balk at having such an unwelcomed trend of life forced upon them.

Ransom's comment in the margin: *"a might hard sentence"*

Last essay opening, Dona Rita: One may be certain that no mere reader ever becomes so well acquainted with Dona Rita as to feel that he confidently understands her. It is to be doubted whether Conrad understood her in spite of his realistic portraits. As the author, he appears as reporter, bewildered with the rest at his own creation and equally as astounded at her incomprehensible actions as Monsieur George and the parsimonious sister Therese.

Still, as a young graduate student, did not know all of Ransom's accomplishments, nor was he aware of the project that concerned Ransom and eleven of his colleagues in 1929—the well-known collection of essays *I'll Take My Stand: The South and the Agrarian Tradition.* At the time, Still had no idea that he was in the middle of a movement, nor did he ever acknowledge that the movement directly influenced his life choices or his writings. Years later he recalled that the Southern Agrarians were there: "I didn't know anything about them then. Nobody else knew. But I had John Crowe Ransom and John Donald Wade, both of whom contributed to *I'll Take My Stand,* the book they published the year after I was there. They read their chapters to us. . . . It was my first encounter with scholars, and important ones."[23]

John Donald Wade was another professor that left a mark on the young scholar.[24] When Still began at Vanderbilt, Wade was fairly new, having arrived in 1928, but he was already an accomplished scholar with a bachelor's from the University of Georgia, a master's from Harvard, and a doctorate from Columbia; he was as well a recipient of a Guggenheim fellowship to research his biography on John Wesley. Wade was the son of a country doctor and had grown up in a small Georgia town, about one hundred miles southeast of Still's hometown. But Still was probably not aware of that personal connection. The special bond between professor and student formed when Still, who knew no one and was unknown himself, excelled on a pretest for Wade's history of American literature course. Still enjoyed telling the story. Wade had said to the class at the beginning of the semester:

"I want to give you a little test. No grades will be recorded. I just want to get some idea of what you already know about American literature." So he handed us out a card and we numbered 10 on each side, and then he said "I've done this every year and nobody ever passes so don't worry about it." So he read one sentence from writings, authors from the Civil War period to that day. . . . Well, nobody did pass except me and I made a perfect score. Well, I was nobody that day. Next day, I was famous.[25]

This instant fame must have given the young man a needed boost. Dr. Wade called him to the office and said, "You don't have time to bother with my class. Just drop in once in a while and learn what we're up to." Still claimed that he took advantage of the offer and "skipped every other class." He liked the course because Wade let the students talk. The class members were collecting essays on American writers throughout literary history; Still's contribution was the chapter on Cotton and Increase Mather.[26] In all three grading terms of 1929–1930, James Still earned straight Bs in all classes, except for one A in Wade's class.[27]

If Ransom was the professor who "stretched" his imagination and Wade the one who built his self-esteem, Walter Clyde Curry was his inspiration and the man who set him the greatest challenge. Curry, who joined the department in 1915, had received his doctorate from Stanford University. In 1926 he published his book *Chaucer and the Mediaeval Sciences,* making him, according to Mims, "one of the most distinguished scholars in his field."[28]

Still's most rewarding class and the one that required the most time was Professor Curry's course on Chaucer. He described it as a "horse" and calculated that he spent seventeen hours in preparation for each class meeting. But he took great pride in what Professor Curry told him at the end: "From where you started, you have made more progress than anybody in the class."[29] He enjoyed the challenge of this "marvelous and punishing" course and the rigor of the professor whose final compliment propelled the shy young man to greater effort. But more importantly, Still felt an affinity for the subject matter: "Chaucer happens to be the only author that I totally relate to. I feel that I knew him. I sometimes feel that I am Chaucer."[30]

Though his master's thesis was not about Chaucer, the idea for the topic came from the course. He reflected on the experience of learning to read Middle English very quickly and wading through 106 volumes of the Early English Text Society. But about the work itself, he said, "I can't believe that I wrote [this thesis]. It's not bad at all. It was written in blood I assure you."[31] His title was "The Functions of Dreams and Visions in the Middle English Romances," and his faculty director was Walter Clyde Curry. The introduction states the purpose: "To deal with the dream as a literary device in the Middle English Romances, to define the various dream-types and to reach some conclusions as to their function." Curry read the sections of the thesis as Still presented them. He apparently gave little feedback as the project progressed, but he must have been honored that Still relied heavily on his own scholarship in *Chaucer and the Mediaeval Sciences*. Curry and Ransom signed and approved the thesis in June 1930.[32]

Still was not asked to make an oral defense of his work. The thesis was never published, and he never again wrote about Middle English romances. While he was at Vanderbilt, he did publish two short articles in *American Speech*, which he had originally written as essays in an LMU English course—"Place Names in the Cumberland Mountains" (1929) and "Christian Names in the Cumberlands" (1930).[33] In spite of his affinity for Chaucer, it was the culture of the mountain region that was pulling his heartstrings.

Still remembered his year at Vanderbilt as "tough." But his academic success made his effort worthwhile. He had come as a young student from a small unaccredited college where only one faculty member had a doctorate and only one had published a book, to a known university that was fast building its reputation as a graduate school, especially in English, and had a number of its known faculty engaged in a regional and national discussion about a cultural revolution—the agrarian past and industrial future of the South.[34] These men and some of their students were in the process of taking a stand that would be a major factor in the Southern Literary Renaissance. Here Still found scholars and thinkers the likes of whom he had not met before, except in books. At the time, Still had little interest in or context for the intellectual contribution of the Southern Agrarians. Ironically, his own life was later to become a test of some of their most important principles. The fact that the "Agrarians" were not farmers themselves but only theorized about a farming economy and its effect on society did not slip Still's attention. With characteristic wit, he once described the situation at Vanderbilt as "professors who didn't have any turnips in the backyard talking about agriculture."[35]

The reason to pursue graduate study is for the course content, the intellectual stimulation, and the diploma. Still gained these, but equally interesting were his life adventures that critical year. Guy Loomis, the man financing his experience, had said from the start, "I'm going to make graduate school possible, not easy." The total charge for tuition and fees was $150, which adjusted for inflation in 2014 would have been $2,100. Through an additional allowance, Loomis had provided him with two meals a day, which "consisted of a ten-cent bowl of cereal in the morning and a thirty-five cent supper at a boardinghouse. Slim rations for a growing boy tackling Middle English."[36] At another time, Still claimed he ate only one meal a day until Loomis made a trip to Nashville around Christmas when on his way to Florida. "And he had me come up and have a meal with him in a hotel. It was rainy, drizzling. I didn't have a raincoat and I was a little damp. He said 'Don't you have a raincoat?' I said 'No.' He said, 'I will buy you one,' and I said 'Remember you said you would make it possible, not easy.' He didn't buy the coat."[37] At the beginning of 1930 Loomis raised his allowance modestly, but Still did not change his living conditions.

His rate of correspondence suggests that he had little time for anything but studies while at Vanderbilt; he did not go home to Alabama for the holidays. In fact, he traveled very little except in the area surrounding Nashville. He did experience one memorable adventure. Don West had been a fellow student at LMU, but they became much better acquainted when they were both at Vanderbilt, where West was studying religion. Their friendship consisted mostly of wandering about Nashville on Sundays and listening to street-corner preachers. But they took a longer jaunt together when West persuaded Still to accompany him to a coal mine at Wilder, Tennessee, on a mission to distribute food and clothing to the striking miners. The predicament of the people impressed Still, and he told the story with emotion:

We found the people drawn and pale from malnourishment, although their resolve was strong and unshaken. They were held together by their common misery. The town was divided, the scabs living in the camp houses on one side, the strikers on the other. There was a "dead line," and a person crossed it at his peril. On the strikers' side, the water and electricity were cut off. It was my first inkling that folk could starve to death in the United States of America in plain view of a largely indifferent populace. . . .

I lodged in the home of Jim Crownover, president of the union that year. . . . We attended a gathering at one of the homes after dark, blowing out the light before leaving to avoid providing a ready target for a sharpshooter. Arriving men deposited pistols, rifles, and shotguns on a bed. The conversation was as gloomy as the light shed by a coal-oil lamp. When the meeting was over a banjo-picker provided music for a bit of square dancing.[38]

Although Still never wrote stories of striking coal miners, both the social difficulties and the human will to endure that he witnessed on that trip became part of his life experience and transferred to his writing.

In addition to the rigors of study and the joys of spring, the month of April brought other ups and downs. Still's maternal grandfather, Grandpa Lindsey, died on April 12, 1930, at the age of eighty-three. He had been declining physically for two years, but in his last week he "did suffer a great deal," reported Still's mother. As he died on a Saturday morning and was buried the next day, Still did not go home for the funeral. In hindsight, he probably wished that he had gone, more for his mother than for his grandfather. The suffering evident in her letter of April 14 was a premonition of her own decline: "My mouth is so sore I cant [sic] hardly eat anything yet I been this way for last five weeks they are fever blisters under my plate [sic]."[39] A month later, Still wrote a long letter to his folks and did not refer to his mother's troubles but offered advice about the difficulty that had arisen over his grandfather's will. He decisively told his mother, "Stay as completely out of the affair as it is humanly possible. Have nothing to say pro or con, and most especially avoid discussing it with the Uncles and Aunts. Let them think you are unconcerned."[40] The old man had fathered nine children, and it seemed that several of them were contesting the division of his property, small as it was. Still would have been glad for his parents to get enough to buy a little land of their own, but he wanted his uncles to do the challenging work. He thought his mother had a better chance if she stayed out of the fuss.

In the same letter, along with his advice on family litigation, Still described in great detail his most recent adventure—a weekend journey to the fifty-sixth running of the Kentucky Derby. Here is an excerpt from his play-by-play:

> Crowds gathered from all parts of the world; over two hundred and ten special trains that had come from all parts of the U.S. bringing people. . . . Very wisely we planned on a meeting place after the races for in ten minutes after mixing with eighty thousand people we had lost one another. Hundreds of people were asleep on the grass in front of the track, doubtless having been there since early morning, and many of whom had not slept

the night before as hotel accommodations were absolutely out of the question. Being quite tired I found a spot big enough to lay my carcass and in spite of the mob, the noise, and of people constantly stepping on and over me I managed to get a few winks of sleep before the first race.

Four races transpired before the derby. Just before the horses went to the post I crossed the track and hung over the fence right beside the starting forms. I could almost reach out and touch the nearest horse. To the winner of this race a $56,000 prize is awarded, besides a gold trophy, and eternal fame for the horse. The finest horse-flesh pranced out before me, then suddenly as a battery of moving-picture cameras were grinding away from all points and even from aeroplanes overhead, the line sprung and like a blaze of lightning the horses sped down the track.

A mighty cry rose from the excited mob . . . "They're off!" . . . then for a second there was silence with everybody straining to see which horse was forging a-head out of the huddle. As the best horses sprung in the lead the crowd went wild. People cried, jumped up and down, screamed to the top of their voice, and went completely mad. Hundreds of them had every cent they had on a horse. Many of them saw thousands of dollars melt away as their favorite slipped behind. . . . As the horses came around the second time, thirty-two flying hoofs covered me with a shower of mud, and the moment they passed I jumped onto the track and rushed madly toward the judges stand.[41]

Young Still observed that the famous radio announcer Graham McNamee "was there telling the world about it over the radio." Still's audience was smaller, but his enthusiasm must have equaled or surpassed McNamee's.

After three typed pages, Still finally gets to the immediate question: "By the way, are you all going to find it possible to come up here for commencement. The exercises take place on June 11th." He promised to be ready to leave later that night so that he could go home with them. He reported that Guy Loomis would try to come, but he had not invited the Grannises. He had three tickets for his parents and his patron. But he downplayed any possibility of spectacle: "If there's anything as dumb as a graduation exercise it's a funeral conducted by the Masons. Nothing else approaches it. Still I wanted you all to be here if possible as this will be the only time you will get to see me have a college degree poked at me."

He expressed his strong wish to have his parents come in a letter to his brother Comer: "Get papa to see what Mr. Chambers would charge to bring them. Maybe he'd bring them for the gas. Let me know right away. Mama will not have to worry about anything to wear to the exercises because here in the city nobody pays any attention to anybody else. Any kind of dark dress will do. I have a suit of clothes I am going to give papa so he'll be fitted out."[42] His appeals were unsuccessful. His parents did not go to Nashville. His mother's failing health was likely the cause. When it was clear that she could not come, he wrote a note to her, describing himself in his cap and gown as looking "strikingly like an Augustine monk."[43]

Vanderbilt University held its fifty-fifth commencement in Neely Memorial Auditorium on Wednesday, June 11, 1930, at ten o'clock in the morning. The university granted forty-six master of arts degrees; twelve of them were in English. Still was one of five graduates from Alabama and the only one who had graduated from LMU.

His year-long excursion to Nashville had been a pilgrimage. He had met his first real scholars as well as his first academic challenge. He had moved beyond the kinds of books he had read in the library at LMU. Most importantly, he found an affinity for Chaucer that later would inspire his wit and storytelling. But Nashville was a detour, not his final destination. After graduation, he rejoined Dare Redmond in their plans to attend the University of Illinois.

7

A Practical Degree

The University of Illinois

> What can my sorrows be
> For having dreamed gloriously
> Life's short hour?
>
> —From "Dreams"

By the time of the Vanderbilt commencement, James Still was thinking about his next step: first summer, then more education. In 1930
any graduate would have been fortunate to find a job, particularly one
whose master's had been in English or history.[1] Still did not even look
because he and Dare Redmond expected to follow through on their
plan to attend the University of Illinois together and earn a practical
degree—a bachelor's in library science. Mrs. Grannis had encouraged
them, and Guy Loomis would finance them. But first, there was summer. His postgraduation break in 1930 had much in common with the
one in 1929. He visited friends here and there, spending several weeks
with Redmond in Chapel Hill; he traveled with Iris Grannis, staying a
while with the couple in Amherst; he also went to Alabama to visit his
family for a month. The difference this summer was that his mother
was not well.

In early May, Guy Loomis had written to Still, congratulating him
on the likelihood of his June completion, enclosing one hundred dollars as a graduation gift. It had been, he said, a "joy" to help the young
man "make good." He wrote again later with fatherly advice to rest and

eat well, showing his concern about the hard work that Still was doing to complete his master's by June 11. If it turned out he was not able to finish, Loomis offered to continue the financial help. In either case, he would not be coming to Nashville for the commencement. When Still took too long to respond to his letter, Loomis gently reprimanded him. A short handwritten note in July asked if he were "asleep at the switch." He had heard from Mrs. Grannis that Still had gone to Chapel Hill to help Dare Redmond finish his thesis.[2] Loomis wanted to be in touch with Still, or at least be informed of his intentions by the young man himself.

He was not the only supporter feeling disconnected. His parents, especially his mother, wrote frequently. A letter after his graduation from LMU a year earlier shows her declining health and increasing need for attention: "Im feeling some better but Im might tired and lonesome Dad and I are by ourself . . . Comer gave me $5.26 to buy me some dresses said he would send me more this week to get me a pair of slippers I sure do need them as I am just pass going any whear I have not went to church but once this year on that account . . . I am ansious to see you comeing on home cant hardly wait . . . write more oftener."[3] His mother had never tried to keep James at home. On the contrary, she had encouraged him to take advantage of opportunities and support from friends and mentors, but she longed for his presence as she became weaker. In May 1930 she wrote that sores in her mouth were keeping her from eating. If this news was distressing, Still did not show it, reacting instead with a mix of denial and unconcern. Busy with his thesis, he had no time to think about Alabama. He assumed that her sores were the type that would either respond to antibiotics or clear up on their own. His next letter was the long exciting one that described his day at the Kentucky Derby.

His mother hoped he would come home when the Vanderbilt commencement festivities were over; instead, he went to LMU for two weeks. Then he told her that he wanted to take a couple of short courses at UNC that could count toward a doctorate; after that he planned to come home.[4] His story to Loomis and Grannis was that he was going to Chapel Hill to help Redmond, who needed to finish his thesis before leaving for Illinois. Still did not take any courses, nor did he help Red. What he really did there was enjoy a brief holiday while providing diversion for his friend. Years later, Still remembered that interlude:

> He [Red] was working on Pocahontas. . . . He wouldn't even let me see [the thesis]. He had a room on Elizabeth Street. And

there was another cot. He told the landlady that we were half-brothers, some excuse for me to stay there. She didn't much believe it and every time we would come in she would ask questions and we had to get our tales together. I had hair then. Sitting on the cots right against the wall—we used something called Staycomb; it was something to make your hair stay where it was supposed to. Well, it was greasy—I made a grease spot on the wall in back of my cot.[5]

To pass the time, Still surreptitiously sat in on a Chaucer class. Perhaps he wanted to test his own knowledge against that of the professor, or maybe he was just entertaining himself while his friend slogged away in the library. When the professor started calling on students, Still quit attending before he was discovered as unregistered. It was a very hot summer. In the evenings, he and Red would walk through the arboretum to keep cool. The heat was hard to avoid in the daytime because nothing was air conditioned. The local movie theater had big fans, so he went there to see the movie about Admiral Richard Byrd's South Pole adventure.[6]

Had Still been mindful of his mother's health condition, he might not have made a side trip to Harrogate to catch up with friends or a visit with Red in Chapel Hill. His letter dated June 28 implied that he would be coming to Alabama and that he would send details when he got to Atlanta. That news plus a recent visit to her doctor roused his mother to be more direct. She had been hinting about her problem for a year, but it was not until July 1, 1930, that her message was painfully clear:

Dear Son,

Received your letter and sure glad to here from you and that
you were settled long enough to get one letter in edge ways
anyway. All are well except myself and don't guess I will ever
be any more. I have been writing you for some time about my
mouth it is pretty bad and don't get any better it pain me so
bad at times it nearly ran me crazy Im just killing myself at
work to get it off of my mind the more the Dr. do it get worse
it is getting larger every day. Dr. Hunt sent me to Dr. Norman
in West Point Monday was a week ago he said he could not
do anything for me but told me to go to Atlanta at once to
Grady Hospitle and take the Radium treatment he said I could

not stand any other treatment it being in my mouth they told
me it was a cancer it sure worrie me haven't got any money
to have anything done for me. I was in hope you would come
home and spend the summer with me. You may not have the
chance to do so don't come home on my account stay . . . I
was somewhat disappointed today when I got your letter that
you were staying longer.[7]

That letter spurred him to abandon his fun with Red. But he did not
head home immediately. Perhaps he believed her case was not as serious as the doctors were saying. On July 3, he wrote to express sympathy, then added, "Let us hope that it is not as bad as the doctors think."
He followed with an explanation for why he could not leave for Fairfax at once. It related to the "mental health situation" of his friend and
LMU roommate, Ralph Williams, from Harlan, Kentucky. After one
sentence sympathizing with his mother, Still took three long paragraphs
to describe the problems facing Ralph—he was "losing his mind." The
complexity and severity facing his friend was offered as an explanation
for his not coming home right away:

> [Ralph's] father is of moderate means and can't do so much for
> him in that respect. Besides Ralph is beyond the aid of medi-
> cine or surgery and only a psychologist can do anything with
> his case. In view of the fact that I am his friend and that for over
> a year I was with him nearly all the time and that I am more
> intimate terms with him than anybody else it is expected that I
> may be of help to him. If I can do anything for him, naturally I
> shall be glad to but in the case I am called to come to Kentucky
> I shall not be there more than a week or two at the most and
> will hurry home and spend the rest of the summer. At least I
> will be home by the sixteenth.[8]

Possibly, Still was overstating Ralph's difficulties to help put his mother's in perspective. Or perhaps he could not admit to himself that she
really was sick. In any case, he made the detour to Harlan. He left Chapel Hill and Redmond on July 5 and finally arrived in Alabama around
the fifteenth.

When word of the mother's illness got to Loomis, he responded
with sympathy, then commended his protégé. Still had given the impression that he went home to help his mother discover that her case was

not as serious as she had thought. Loomis wrote, "While I had heard that your mother was threatened with some cancerous condition I did not know that it had proved to be a false alarm, and I am very glad. It certainly was a wonderful thing for her that you got down there and took the matter in hand, otherwise the infected condition might have developed into cancer."[9] In spite of efforts to downplay her situation or lift her spirits, his mother was deteriorating. Her "infected" condition was indeed cancerous, and she had little time left. Still remained at home for only a month. There is no record of her progress during that time and no evidence that he was taking her to doctors for treatment or consultation.

As described in a letter to another friend, Ralph Shanks, his summer visit to Alabama was uneventful. His mother, father, brother Alfred, and the dog, "Grannis," met him at West Point. Only the dog, he claimed, was joyful to see him. His whole stay was uneventful and boring: "Fairfax is much the same as it has ever been. Dullness pursues dullness, monotony heaps upon monotony. Most of the conversation I hear is bitter patter that bores me stiff. . . . Not more than a couple hundred people have asked me what I was going to do next year. . . . I have been alone around the house." Both he and Red were looking forward to Illinois. By August 20, Red was trying to make plans about how they should get there. He suggested they hitchhike. But they still had a month to go, time for Red to finish up and time for Still to kill.[10]

Their next adventure was something to look forward to, but Still was thinking of the immediate future. A way out of Fairfax and assurances for the coming year arrived in a letter from Guy Loomis, dated August 19.

Mrs. Grannis may bring you north with her so that you may have a change, and I have sent her a check for $50.00 to help out with your expenses. You know she will likely leave Harrogate for good very shortly and it will be necessary to handle your finances in some other way. When you started in I thought that you might get through in one year, though there was nothing certain about it, so I planned to stand back of you for another year, that is until June, 1931, but after that time it will be up to you to make your own plans for any further college work. . . . I asked Mrs. Grannis how much she thought it would take to put you through this year and she said $1,000 payable in ten monthly installments of $100.00

each, and I will stand back of you to this amount and send the checks on monthly as soon as you locate. You seem to have gotten along mighty well so far and I sincerely hope that you will keep up the good work and finish with flying colors and thus make me proud that I have been able to help you out.[11]

Alabama was a dead end for Still; travel was a diversion, but school was his future. So by the end of August he was, thanks to Loomis, off again. On the twenty-ninth he wrote his mother from a hotel in Morristown, Tennessee. He had left Atlanta four days earlier, gone to Knoxville for a night at the YMCA, then driven to Harrogate. There, Iris Grannis was packing to leave LMU for good, and Still was to be her co-driver and assistant as she moved possessions to Asheville and then made her way north to Yale where Frank was. Still labeled the upcoming adventure a "trek." As soon as he left Fairfax, his spirits lifted. In his next letter home, he told of the fun that he and Mrs. G were having as they drove north to Amherst. They stopped in Washington and saw all the sites—the Washington Monument, the Lincoln Memorial, the Capitol, the White House, the Smithsonian. He had few worries now, having convinced himself that his mother's health problems would pass. While in Amherst, he received a note from Nella Chambers, a family friend who was caring for his mother, reporting that the patient seemed a little better. That news on September 10 gave him some assurance that his assessment had been correct. But a letter from Comer the next day indicated things were not good, and a follow up from Nella informed him that the radium treatments had been halted but that they were giving his mother "dope" to keep her quiet. She was growing worse fast.[12]

The semester at the University of Illinois began on September 22; a week before, Still and Red had arrived in Champaign to settle into their rented room. On September 17, Nella wrote an urgent letter to Amherst, which was forwarded to Champaign:

Your mother is much worse. She continually begs for you. For a day or two she has been begging us to send for you. I don't think she can last more than a week if that. Of course Jim, we may be wrong, for it is hard to tell anything about her. She can hardly swallow at all. She sings all she says and does it continually. . . . you may judge what is best to do. If you *can*, come. I understand how things are and if it is necessary go on

to your school and then come here. There is really nothing you
can do, but she has raged and begged for you so much.[13]

At that point, he did go to Alabama and stayed a week. He seemed
to be the family member to take charge at this difficult time. A number
of people were there, but only Nella Chambers was keeping the world
balanced for everyone. Redmond notified the professors of the reason
for Still's absences, then wrote Still that everyone would try to help
when he returned. It would "be easy to catch up with classification, and
cataloging, book selection," reported Red, but the others would take
more time. Time seemed to be what no one had. Red was busy getting
the semester started and had undertaken to inform Loomis and Grannis of Still's family problem. Jim was trying to manage the situation at
home while needing to be involved in his new classes. And Lonie Still
had less time than anyone. Still left Alabama to return to Champaign
on October 5; Nella wrote him again the next day, indicating that she
was trying to carry out his instructions. She had understood his ambivalent feelings and behaviors when he left, and she included a list of visitors coming to the house so that he would feel part of the gathering.
Everyone seemed to be on hand, except Still. They all, she added, asked
about him but did not criticize him for going back to school. A true
friend and helper, Nella understood the emotional and logistical difficulties that everyone faced.

His mother died on October 7, 1930.[14]

Still did not return to Alabama for the funeral. Nor did he go home
at Christmas.[15] He did return eventually, but it would never be the same
for him. His mother was not there, and the following year his father
remarried a much younger woman. His mother was only fifty-five years
old when she died, but her life had not been easy. She had given birth
to nine children, raising eight of them to adulthood. She had worked in
the fields and later in the mills. Money was scarce, especially in the last
years of her life. She had not had extra to give her son for his education,
but she had never stood in his way. In a January 1928 letter, after saying
he should write more often and that she had sent him "every cent" she
could, she included a dollar for his next haircut. Then in January 1929
she had written that she wanted him to be through college so that he
could get a job. She saw his adventures in higher education as the practical road to a better life.

Though she could not support him financially, Lonie wanted to
make sure that her oldest son was grateful to the people who were "help-

ing" him. One time when she displayed gratitude involved the dogs. She and Alex agreed to take them from Frank and Iris Grannis. The first one, "Grannis," was a gift to Jim, but the second, "Yale," was a dog that the couple needed to find a home for when they were moving away from LMU. Still's mother accepted and cared for them, but they did cause her some trouble and expense. After Grannis arrived, she reported that his father had said to tell Jim that he should not accept presents unless he could put them in his pocket. It costs a lot to feed him because, unlike farm dogs, he would not eat bread. When Yale arrived, she wrote that he was sick and that she had no money from Mrs. Grannis to do anything for him. Yet her "mother" instinct took over. When the dog was getting "poor," they brought him in the house to lie by the fire.[16]

She missed having her son near; she wanted him to stay in touch and visit. She needed him when she became ill. It is hard to know what she thought of her highly educated son, but she appreciated the nearness to learning that he provided. In a letter to Still at Vanderbilt, she said, "I [would] give anything if I had half the education you [have] I would be satisfied but it is late now."[17] Lonie had given her life to her family. Of all her children, the only one to get a college degree was James. At the time of her death, he was beginning work on his third degree.

The semester had begun on September 22, just two weeks before her death. Had he been a less-experienced student, this rough start might have discouraged him, but his attitude was that both life and the study of library science must go on. Perhaps the coursework was a welcome distraction. He received letters of sympathy from several friends; the longest and most touching was from Don West. The fourteen-page letter West wrote on October 25, 1930, began with words of condolence:

Dear Friend Jim:

Was more than delighted to hear from you again after such a long interlude. Let me also right here make an attempt to express appreciation for your recent and deep sorrow. Of course I cannot sympathize with you having never had a similar experience, but Old boy, I surely do "feel" for you. I know it has taken the best part of your manhood to meet this crisis, but after all it is just a part of living. . . . We all need to live as long as we can serve. But whenever death visits we can always rest assured that God has decreed it. I am sure your mother must have been happy. She could but be proud and

happy over a son such as you were. She had always dreamed
you would be a real man. Nothing you may ever do will go
beyond her expectations for you. She saw you as a big man, a
man using your talents and abilities to uplift, to serve. So you
have a job ahead, you have a real task if you hope to live up to
your mother's ideal of what her son should do.[18]

West continued with thoughts on service and courage; with statements
of faith, hope, and determination; and with observations of the mountains and people of eastern Kentucky, where he was surveying rural
churches for his thesis. He concluded with an apology for his jumbled
letter: "I'm glad to have a friend that will excuse such jumpy incoher-
ent writing. . . . Those days in Vanderbilt meant much more to me, were
made richer because you were there. I don't believe I'll ever find another
friend that I'd rather be with and talk with than you."[19]

Red and Still lived in an apartment at 313 E. Green Street in Champaign; the cost was thirty dollars per month.[20] It was a private dorm
called the "One Hundred," arranged as suites, each with a screened-in
porch. Just below their place was a dancehall that had a live band every
Saturday night.[21] When recalling Illinois later, Still condensed his experiences into that one image of the dancehall but alluded to other memories of the place.[22] He went to lectures sponsored by various departments
almost every day. It was there that he heard Admiral Byrd lecture before
his second trip to Antarctica. Without recalling a word he said, Still did
remember Byrd as a little man dressed in a naval uniform. He also had
a memory of an African American man, Walter Williams, from Alabama, who was a fellow student in the library program. He had earned
a doctorate from Williams College in Massachusetts and was teaching
at Tuskegee. When the librarian retired, they sent Walter to Illinois to
gain qualifications so that he could take over as head librarian. Still got
to know him and acknowledged that he was the only black man he had
ever gone to school with. Later, he visited him at Tuskegee.[23]

The experience at Illinois was valuable because it expanded Still's
exposure to people he had not known before and places he had not
been. He had made short trips from Nashville when at Vanderbilt, but
they were within the state or region, a location that Still had come to
know at Lincoln Memorial. While in Champaign, he and Red made
at least four trips to Chicago, and they went on "an inspection trip
through Wisconsin, which was wonderful. The school work, though,
was tedious and boring" and the instructors uninspiring.[24]

Still never commented in any detail on the courses he took at Illinois or the professors who taught them. The classwork was very different from that at Vanderbilt. His transcript shows that he took six courses each semester—the first semester earning four Cs and two Bs but reversing that in the second semester with four Bs and two Cs, for a total of thirty-one credit hours. The course titles convey a sense of the subject matter: "Reference," "Cataloging," "Selection of Books," "History of Libraries," "Ordering and Accessions," "Library Administration," and so on. Most of the course materials that Still saved were mimeographed lecture notes. "Selection of Books" was one class he liked because it involved reading and choosing books.

For one assignment in that class, he wrote a review of Edwin Mims's *The Advancing South,* published in 1926. He started with a brief identification, which pointed out that Mims had taught at Duke and UNC but was currently head of the English Department at Vanderbilt and was closely connected with the Fugitive group. The assignment then required a discussion of the subject and scope of the text, its strengths and weaknesses, and finally a comparison to a similar book. For that last part, Still compared *The Advancing South* with another notable book of the Vanderbilt faculty, the recently published symposium:

> "I'll take my stand" cannot rightfully be called a similar book either in style, treatment or attitude but due to the fact that it was written by twelve men, ten of whom are either teaching in his department or else are his friends the point of view taken by this work is interesting to note. Dr. Mims represents the industrialists while "I'll take my stand" is a plea for the return of agrarian in the South. Dr. Mims takes a calm unruffled stand, the twelve authors of "I'll take my stand" take a vehement viewpoint.[25]

Still seemed more aware of and interested in the works of his Vanderbilt professors after he left Nashville than he was when a student there.

Coursework at the University of Illinois did not fill all of Still's free time. In addition to writing about his Vanderbilt professors, he also wrote an essay about LMU, probably for no reason other than it was on his mind. His alma mater was experiencing growing pains and internal conflict. The situation was so problematic that Iris Grannis and Lucia

Danforth had left.[26] Still's essay did not explore the entire history of the institution and never mentioned the difficulties that had surfaced the year after he graduated, but the situation concerned him.[27] And working on it connected him to his past experiences, as did the paper on the Vanderbilt professors.

His library-degree work at the University of Illinois was not especially demanding, and his life in Champaign-Urbana was not especially transforming. But his goal in pursuing this degree was intended to be practical and lead to a job. On June 17, 1931, both he and Redmond were granted bachelor's degrees in library science. Later, when Still wrote or spoke of his educational career, he rarely gave details of his Illinois experience. He always implied that he would not have chosen to study library science except that it was the Depression and "library work was something to do." For his effort he earned one more diploma, and he had, as he was fond of saying, "graduated three times in the same pair of shoes." [28]

More important than what he gained during his year at Illinois was what he lost—his mother. Still had a fondness and respect for her, but he never spoke of a strong emotional bond between them. Rena Niles wrote a feature article about Still in 1939 and conveyed his feeling of loss at his mother's death. According to Niles, he remembered his mother as "the person to whom he owes the most. . . . she alone read his stories; she alone read the poems when they first were published. . . . It is indeed ironical that the one person in his family who would have gloried in his success, as she encouraged him in his obscurity, lies buried under Alabama sod—his mother: Lonie Lindsey Still."[29] The claim exaggerated her appreciation of her son's published writing because before the spring of 1931, Still had not published any poems or stories.[30] But his mother's letters give ample evidence that, in her simple way, she supported and encouraged him as he left Alabama and pursued his education at three different institutions. When she died at the age of fifty-five, James was twenty-five. Though he missed her, the loss did not slow him down. He continued to pursue his dreams, both the practical and the grand ones.

A simple slab marks his mother's resting place. She had always wanted a marble slab over her grave, and Still saw that she got it in 1938—"the proceeds from *Hounds On the Mountain* paid for it." His mother's death in the fall of 1930 is surely connected to the sentiment and images of his first poem published in *Arcadian Magazine* in April 1931, two months before he graduated from the University of Illinois.

Dreams

Daring to dream of that which cannot be,
I have plucked my roots from earthly ways
For a cloisonne vase of unreality,
And a cup of water for my share of days.

What can my sorrows be
For having dreamed gloriously
Life's short hour?[31]

Part 3

Early Work

Finding a Place and a Purpose, 1931–1941

8

"19-Dirty-one"

Choosing Hell to Limbo, I have come back.
—Letter from Still to Redmond

When James Still graduated from the University of Illinois in June 1931 with his third degree in as many years, he had no job and no prospects. As for being jobless, he was not alone. Many Americans faced unemployment and unprecedented hardship. One option for the young man about to turn twenty-five would have been to return home to Alabama, live with his family, and begin a serious search for work. But Still felt that he could not go home again. His mother had died the previous October, and four months later his father remarried a much younger woman, Fannie Mae Bailey. His youngest brother, Alfred, was now seventeen years old. The family, as he had known it, no longer existed.

His patron's advice underscored Still's own inclination: "[I] would certainly think it foolish for you to go home with no brighter outlook than a ten hour day in the fields under the hot sun. Would almost think it suicidal. If you wanted at anytime to get away from a confining job to get out in the open and do hard labor I might say O.K. to the plan, but now my advice is positively NO."[1] The extent to which Loomis was giving his protégés spending money in addition to strong advice is unclear, but he did maintain contact with both Still and Red. The young men would remind each other not to keep Loomis fully informed of their activities because he might disapprove.[2] Their plans were tentative and shifting, while their patron liked stability and predictability.

Still did make a trip to Alabama but without intending to stay. Without the anchor of home, Still fell back on his "adopted" family from LMU, which included Red and the Grannises. By the end of June, Still was in Gadsden, Alabama, writing to Red, who would return to Chapel Hill to complete requirements for his master's in English. In the meantime, Red was at his family's home in Tryon, North Carolina; coincidentally, that is near where Still would be staying with Iris Grannis. Still's first letter to Red is a spoof on the type of exercise they had survived during their library-science courses, but it sets a serious undertone for the next few months:

Dear Red:

1. Identify the language this letter is written in? (Any available aids may be used)
   2. How many degrees hotter than hell is Gadsden?
   3. What is to be done for amusement when you've already seen every movie in town?
   4. What is to be done when you stay one mile from the center of town and there are no streetcars or bus lines in this direction and to set out walking would mean a sunstroke? . . . Toward the end of this week perhaps I am returning to Tryon. I want you to be there. We will drive up after you and you can write Mrs. G and arrange the place and time to meet you. . . .
   Write me immediately . . . Gotta job for fall yet. I ain't!

Intentionally, J.[3]

Still had written to Iris Grannis even before his graduation to inquire about the possibility of spending time with her and Frank during the summer. She responded from Lake Lure, near Tryon, to confirm their plans. She was being treated by a physician for a condition that she insisted was not serious but that had somewhat incapacitated her. For recuperation, she had rented a "rather deluxe" log cabin at Tryon for the summer. But she looked forward to sharing with Still a simple, quiet life of reading, writing, and enjoying the outdoors. She had already begun a book about the mountains and had decided that they should continue it together.[4]

By the middle of July, Still was in Tryon, living with Mrs. Grannis. Together they were writing the book, which, in Still's mind, was not a good one.[5] But it kept them occupied. On July 19, he wrote Red to report that they had finished about sixty pages, or a third, of the "pretty rotten" book. They were engrossed in it but had taken off Thursday, July 16, for his twenty-fifth birthday. The celebration consisted of a trip to Bryson City via Asheville.[6] Still was embarking on a life journey that, over the next few years, would be something like the trip he made that day—wild, lonely, forsaken, and dotted with the unexpected. He described it to Red:

> While there we went to the Indian reservation [Cherokee]. I suppose I expected to see them encamped in little teepee's. They were living in houses like anybody else.
>
> On the way back we cut across from Waynesville to Brevort [Brevard] and saw some of the wildest country imaginable. For thirty miles we didn't see one living soul except a forest ranger. The road was terrible and the poor car got so hot and bothered that it stopped dead for a while. We emerged into the Pisgah forest and travelled ten more miles without seeing anyone.

Still's next letter to Red, dated July 24, 1931, provided insight into his living conditions at Tryon. Frank Grannis, who was still in Amherst, Massachusetts, wired frequently that he was about to join them in North Carolina. Meanwhile, Still and Iris continued to write the book that he felt sure would never be published. By this time they had completed 107 pages. They did not quarrel much but did "talk a blue streak." He washed the dishes and was becoming quite a proficient cook. One of the most interesting bits from this letter related to his sleeping arrangements, which he had recently changed for the sake of privacy and modesty. He must have been sleeping in the general living area where drapes did not keep out the sun. He told Red that he could not guarantee his nightshirt would stay put around his ankles; it had a way of crawling up. Admitting his suspicion that his "nude body is not particularly inspiring to the females of the species," he made a decisive move to the back room of the house. It was just what he wanted—a nice, private room "with a reading lamp attached to the bed."[7]

Right after Still's light-hearted description of his body, he told Red of a visit he and Mrs. Grannis had made to a young man who was suffering from tuberculosis. His thin, sickly body and his large blue eyes made a distinct impression on Still. The man was living in a secluded camp house and had been in bed for two years. His emaciated body and his courageous spirit had touched Still. Another piece of sad news concerned his brother Tom and his wife who had lost their two-day-old baby girl. But Still did not dwell on the loss. The letter marched on through four typed pages, as if the writer were refusing to be overcome with sadness or misfortune.

Like the letter as a whole, the surface of Still's life appeared calm and controlled during the early summer after graduation. Yet he was, on a deeper level, very concerned about his future, the state of the economy, and the lack of jobs. In closing, he expressed that concern to his friend: "well red I get mighty despondent at times. what with three university degrees i am worth less of a damn each succeeding day. at least if i hadn't gone to college i could work in a filling station. . . . i am determined to keep my chin up whatever the weather and come smiling through to whatever the fates may have in store."[8]

In addition to worries of unemployment, Still's relationship with Mrs. Grannis was becoming strained. By the end of July, he described an adventure that appeared humorous but showed the early stages of his disintegrating connection to Frank and Iris Grannis. Still's words reveal his disappointment and growing frustration:[9]

Last Saturday we received a telegram from F.C.G. [Frank Grannis] that he was "shot to pieces" and so was his new car at Mt. Jackson, Virginia about one hundred forty miles north of Lexington [NC]. We set out at 4 pm to his rescue or succor (as the case may be) and reached Winston-Salem that night at 12m after having one blow-out, a flat and a rattle that had to be fixed. We had to buy two new tires.

Leaving W-S early next morning we drove on all day at about 50 mi. per. At noon we had an excellent dinner at some place or other. Mrs. G. got mad for some reason and began to make herself exceedingly unpleasant. (I do not think you have ever seen her at her worse.) Eventually I went off the handle too and used such words as "hell," "damn" etc., with such effectiveness that she decided that crying would be a better method of subjection.

After dark we reached Mt. Jackson and found F.C.G. at the Shenandoah Lodge and put up there ourselves. Eventually it (the car) was fixed and we started for home at 7 p.m. Monday evening. I drove the Essex alone to Harrisonburgh. I changed to the Nash then changed back at Staunton. I got ahead and was going along at a good rate when I decided that I should drink a coke to insure my not going asleep at the wheel as I did over a week ago. While stopped unbeknownst to me or the G's they passed by.

I ambled along thinking they were behind and they sped on thinking I was ahead and with the intention of catching me. I reached Lexington about 10:30 but they were not there and I couldn't believe that they would go on as they knew positively I only had one dollar and that was already spent for gas. At any rate they did go on and kept going on until they reached here some eighteen hours later. After waiting for them at Lexington until about 12m I started out for Roanoke thinking surely they would wait for me there. I kept the car on about 60 all the way reaching there at 2 a.m. but couldn't locate them. I called all the hotels and drove up and down the streets and looked at all the cars and in all the possible places. My gas was running low and I knew it was best to be stranded in the city than along the roadside and decided to wait. Surely they would come back for me when they discovered I was not ahead.

I pulled my car up to a parking space where they couldn't miss seeing it if they came back and slept until morning. After waiting several hours not knowing exactly what to do it occurred to me to wire you for funds. I received your answer at six p.m. and set out. I reached W-S about nine that night. I struck out for Shelby but got so sleepy I couldn't go along any more and pulled up by the road and took a nap. After an hour a car sped by and woke me up.

I managed to get into Salisbury and went to a hotel. Next morning . . . I drove on home reaching here about 4 p.m.

I asked why they left me knowing that I was broke and that there was a possibility that the car had broken down. Their solution was that I had either a) struck up with some girl and was spooning somewhere, or b) I had "ditched" them and set out for Chapel Hill to visit you.

Both of them sounded like mighty thin excuses.[10]

Such an adventure must have intensified his search for a job that would free him from dependence on the Grannises.

By mid-August, Red was finishing his summer course at UNC and spending more time trying to line up work. The most interesting discovery he made was the opportunity to take two government exams for librarians, but the applications were due soon. He wrote again, saying that he wanted to see Still about the civil-service exams because "that is the only chance now."[11] On August 16 Still responded, "I f-i-r-m-l-y agree with you that the Govt. exams is our last forlorn chance." They decided to meet in Tryon to cram but to keep their plans a secret in case they should fail. Still urged Red to bring materials to review. Still now had free time to study because the book he was writing with Mrs. Grannis had been sent to Scribners. He reiterated that he did not expect it to be published and asserted that if it were, his confidence in the profession would be lowered. Their preparation for the civil service did not work as they expected. Still received a form letter dated September 17, 1931, notifying him that his application was incomplete and therefore disapproved.[12] They did not mention the civil service in their subsequent correspondence. This, like so many job searches, had come to nothing.

At summer's end, the Grannises left Tryon, and Still returned to Alabama, after a side trip to Florida, which included the first of many visits he would make to Rollins College in Winter Park. The purpose of this one was to contact the assistant librarian; perhaps he was exploring job possibilities. Back in West Point, Georgia, while staying with his sister, he wrote Red about his isolation and poverty: "Daniel Boone never felt more removed from civilization that [sic] I do. I have to walk over a mile to borrow a Sunday paper to see the football scores. . . . Wouldn't it be great to see the Ga.-Tulane game this week end? I could go for ten dollars but ten dollars is ten dollars, which is 9.95 more than I have." To pass the time, he was writing poetry. And he was publishing. His second poem, "A Burned Tree Speaks," appeared in *Boys' Life* in October. That small accomplishment helped keep his spirits up. In spite of being stuck at home again and without funds, the tone of Still's letter was witty: "I am particularly attracted to the sonnet of late, and have been wisely, as never before, counting syllables, and sticking to rhyme schemes . . . I have no money to take out poetic license this year."[13]

Like Still, Red was passing time at home, reading books, keeping up with football scores, and feeling lonely. Few of their friends had landed jobs. A number were living at home; some had gone back to graduate school, adding to debt already accumulated. They estimated that only a third of the graduates from the library school now had jobs. In addition to writing poetry to pass the time, Still was collecting letters of reference. When one teacher agency gave him a lead, he "bombarded them with testimonials and recommendation," but he wasn't even lucky enough to get a polite refusal.[14]

His stash of references included a professional recommendation letter dated October 30, 1931, from Iris Grannis, in which she described Still as having a "charming personality" and being "agreeable to work with."[15] He also had a letter from Dr. Lucia Danforth, the French teacher who had moved from LMU to Iowa Wesleyan College. On November 1, 1931, she wrote a cordial letter to Still that included a supportive recommendation describing him as "gentlemanly," "thoughtful," and "exceptionally valuable."[16] One other connection that he had with LMU at this time was that his brother, Comer, enrolled there as a freshman. With Still's encouragement but without his financial assistance, Comer entered on September 25, 1931, but stayed only one quarter. It is safe to presume that Comer was following his brother's lead in choosing LMU, but his scholarship package was based on sports—playing on the football team and possibly basketball and baseball.[17] Still recalled that brief college experience years later when he quoted Comer as saying, "I'm proud to be your brother, but I'm damn tired of being nothing else."[18] If he went to LMU under Still's influence, he left under his shadow.

Still went home to Fairfax but quickly became, as usual, anxious to leave. To get away, he fell back on his LMU connections. Either he had forgotten about the difficulties at Tryon or he had simply become more desperate, but sometime between mid-November and the end of 1931 he once again hooked up with Frank and Iris Grannis and was able to leave his father's house. Frank had found a job as a science teacher at the relatively new Austin Peay Normal School in Clarksville, Tennessee.[19] It was January 1932 before Still reported to Red about his latest move and new employment:

Have been here since the last day of 19-Dirty-one. Came as the result of two telegrams and two special delivery letters, and the desire to prove to my beloved neighbors that I had not come back to Ballybama to live forever and aye. And my folks, too incidentally. Great must have been the relief of Mrs. Still (Pop's No. 2) when I rolled out of sight. And I don't blame her for I am a great burden.

Thus and so, choosing Hell to Limbo, I have come back. Am earning my board and keep by working (the-rail-thang) for Mr. G. Help him with laboratory sections. Teach his classes for him sometimes, grade all papers and drawings for Biology, Bacteriology and Human Psyiology [*sic*], as well as prepare media and grow bacteria, protozoa, and other micro-organisms for class use.[20]

Some time later Still typed out a short description of that winter in Clarksville on a scrap of paper. It paints a bleak picture in a dark time:

> I lived that winter through on the concrete floor of the labo-ratory, growing amoeba and protozoa and feeding them with beef concentrate and agar-agar, and sometime I read the chap-ter in Cambridge Natural History on death, remembering now the sentence that the moment of death had no pain but rather was a withdrawal from pain. I got a curious comfort from those words, though I was twenty-five, and yet young, and wanted much to live. I think it was hunger that made me feel the fragil-ity of life, and it being a time of uncertainty when people were wanting in the midst of plenty, and the smoky, cold damp of the weather made me feel the world was dying.[21]

Much later, Still recalled the experience by saying that he slept on a cot in the lab and that he was paid script instead of money.[22] Though he never saw this as a good situation, it must have seemed better than the limbo he had been experiencing at his father's house.

In the same January letter to Red, he described the continuing men-tal and physical deterioration of Mrs. Grannis. When he arrived in Clarksville, he had found her in the hospital with a few scratches on her chin because she had fallen out of a car. Three days later she was out again, "steaming around like a Cadillac," eating heartily, and "mak-ing everybody miserable." She was not paying attention to Still except to criticize him. He must have seemed like a servant who would be expected to drive her here and there as the whim struck. Still described her instability:

> Then, she decided to go to Florida again. I was to drive her down. She wavered back and forth on the idea hourly for over two weeks, and decided to go last Monday. Monday came, we were all packed and ready to get into the car and hie away, and she said we should wait until Tuesday; Tuesday, ready again, and again another reason why we should wait until Wednes-day; Wednesday, ready to step in car and she is still undecided.

I waited from 6:30 to 10:30 for her to get ready. At the latter hour she came in and asked me if we should go that day. Sez I: "Hell naw!" and unpacked my things.

That was sufficient to make her think she needed hospitalization again and Mr. G's. took her an hour later.

Iris Grannis did have particular difficulty, which affected the people around her, but Still's letter also alludes to the general troubles that were affecting everyone. He passed on news he had heard of Champaign-Urbana: banks closed, hundreds of students losing their savings, stores closing for long stretches. And, he concluded, he had not the "slightest intimation of a job" anywhere or beginning any time.[23]

The "dirty" year closed with his having earned a third college degree but continuing his dependence on others. In the very beginning of the decade, 1,300 banks had failed; in 1931, another 1,000 had failed; and at the end of that year, on December 7, people marched on Washington to demonstrate their dire situation, their hunger. By comparison, Still was in good shape. Though he had no "real" job or interesting prospects, he did have friends who stuck by him: Red, Frank and Iris Grannis, and Guy Loomis. And he had published two poems.

9

To the Jumping-off Place

It happened. I didn't plan it.

—James Still

The year 1932 began just as 1931 had ended, with Still at loose ends but not losing heart. Despite lacking security, he liked not being tied down. Whenever he was not in Clarksville assisting Frank Grannis, he was moving around the Southeast and enjoying his relative "freedom." He wrote a friend from the Illinois library program, Anna Roberts, sometime in late February. Her long, friendly response, on March 7, 1932, opened with her appreciation for his lifestyle:

> Your wandering career—maybe that isn't the correct expression—sounds rather attractive to a confirmed (for the time being) stay-at-home. You see, a three month's diet of I.O.U's. instead of salary checks does much toward influencing our tastes. You may be sure, however, that I read with interest of your jaunts. Somehow I hate to think of your having to settle down to a job and have always thought it quite fortunate that you had your seventy year old guardian angel to stand by while you tried out your wings. . . . By the way, I am still looking forward to reading that novel that you refused to even let me peek at.[1]

Anna's words weave together three important threads of Still's life: his tendency to wander, whether out of choice or by necessity; his mentors' continued support, which freed him from the confines of a menial job; and finally, his interest in writing a novel. What she referred to was probably the fiction that Still was co-writing with Iris Grannis, a piece he had not allowed her to read because it was a poor attempt. Later in her letter, Anna concluded her own quaint account of going to the Tennessee mountains with the comment "I am depending upon you to furnish my vicarious experiences in your mountain novels." Continued reliance on his friends of the past and a premonition of writing about the place where he would soon choose to settle were the themes that guided him through the year in which he turned twenty-six. But his journey was neither focused nor direct.

While traveling that winter, he enthusiastically told Red about his living situation. In February he wrote from Hollywood Beach, Florida, where he was staying for a month in an apartment with the Grannises. He was swimming, attending lectures, reading, and trying to avoid "bridge invitations and social intricacies." He had bought himself a pair of plus fours (knickers), a grayish-greenish jacket, and a black French beret. In case Loomis might think he was enjoying himself too much, he shared this concern with Red: "I don't know what Mr. Loomis would say if he knew I was here. Perhaps I should say nothing about it for a while and wait anyway until he writes me."[2] He wanted to keep the trip a secret from Guy Loomis because a couple of months earlier he had received a letter in which Loomis asked why he was "running around so much and didn't it cost money and please explain." Still admitted to Red that it was "a difficult situation."[3]

When Loomis wrote to Still later in February, he had already begun sending checks and promised more to come, but he also included advice on job hunting:

Glad my check came in so opportunely. While, like the majority, my income has been cut it is still big enough to let me lend a helping hand in a moderate way so if you do get up against again and need a little to help you keep out of the poorhouse drop me a line and I will respond even tho it be in a small way. But keep your eyes open and grab the first job that shows up even tho the pay be small so that you will get the experience and be in shape to grab a good one when the chance offers.[4]

Early in 1932 Still's job search involved keeping options open and connections current. In late February he wrote Red that he would drive Mrs. Grannis from Florida to Tryon before returning to Clarksville. In that same letter he mentioned that Don West was back at Vanderbilt and that Jesse Stuart was at Peabody, adding, "Will see them when I pass through Nashville."[5]

The actual date of Still's rendezvous with the friends is uncertain, but he did see West sometime that spring—a meeting that was critical to his future. The seeds of Still's connection with Don West and Hindman, Kentucky, had been planted earlier. They had been close friends at Vanderbilt, but when Still left for the University of Illinois, they saw less of each other. In 1930, right after Still's mother died, West had written him about his fieldwork in Hindman. The description of the boys he was teaching took second place to his passion: "service, giving yourself for others," and the opportunity to suffer. West believed that it "takes a big soul to suffer, be unpopular, be criticized, and then keep up the game." He felt that nothing was worth doing unless it involved suffering. Though Still sometimes "suffered" at his studies or while looking for work, he saw no virtue in it; his "cause" was different—he wanted a job. In an earlier letter to West, he had shown some interest in the natural environment around Hindman. The response from West was that while the streams and mountains were clean, "the people were not." He found them to be unhealthy and degenerate.[6]

In the winter of 1930–1931 West was touring Knott County to survey rural churches for his thesis. He reiterated his desire to improve and control conditions for the people whom he described as "selfishly destroying themselves." The situation inspired him to work harder because "it is the sick that need the doctor."[7] In March West ended a letter with a story that portends Still's future life in Knott County. Don wished that Jim could visit Hindman to find material for his writing. "Every time I see a real character, have an experience, or something that would be writable, my mind runs to you and wishes you were here to get the thing."

Still did not visit West at Hindman in 1931, but a seed had been planted. Sometime in the spring or early summer of 1932—possibly on his way back to Clarksville—Still met his friend in Nashville. At this point West presented Still with the option of summer work at Hindman. Still did not take the offer right away, and he received a letter from West dated May 13 that showed impatience, even fury, that Still was silent "like the hills" in making his Hindman plans known.[8] Still's undated

response to West apologized and said that he "could not know instanta-
neously if [he] could break away from home" but that now he was ready
anytime to set out.[9]

The actual details of what took place between Still and West during
the summer meeting are unclear, but Still recounted the story in 1994 of
how he first got to Hindman:

> It happened. I didn't plan it. I went to school with Don West . . .
> I went to Vanderbilt and he was there. . . . Then I went on to U
> of I. On the way back I stopped in Nashville and he was still in
> school, but he was working in a settlement house somewhere in
> Nashville. I went out to the settlement house. He was not there,
> but he was expected any minute. I waited quite a while. Finally,
> I saw a clock on the wall and I thought "I'll give you five min-
> utes, then I'll leave." And he came in that five minutes.
>
> He wanted me to go to Knott County, Kentucky, where he
> and his wife had taught. . . . His brother-in-law, Jack Adams,
> would also be there. And we organized Boy Scouts . . . we
> played ball all summer, and camped, and so on.
>
> Then down at the Settlement School, the librarian resigned
> and they hired me.[10]

This "official" but shortened account of how Still first went to Hindman
shows his decision as simple, inevitable, and a work of destiny. If West
had not shown up within the five-minute limit, would James Still have
chosen another path? He was trying to keep his options open; a future
with Mr. and Mrs. Grannis was undesirable, and a return to his family
home in Alabama was impossible. So when Don West invited him to help
with the summer program, Still took the offer.[11] What he does not say in
retelling the story is that the job was on a volunteer basis. Guy Loomis
was planning to pay his board at Hindman, evident when he wrote, "Let
me know as soon as you find out what the board will cost at Hindman
and I will send you a check for it. Remember that with your experience
you should be of great help to the boys you will meet there."[12]

By the summer, Still was settled in Hindman, and he described the
job and the place in a letter to Red on June 28, 1932:

> I am working for the Congregational Board of Education here
> this summer. I have charge of two baseball teams, a boys' club,
> a community club of adults, am superintendent of the Sunday

School at Mill Creek, etc. Am also part-time librarian here at the Settlement School.

The Settlement School is really a remarkable place. There are 16 buildings and seems to be a little world of its own run by old maids who have incidentally done well with it in spite of their sex.

The county has only 12 miles of graded roads. The meanest boys in America reside here and it is with them that I do my work. As yet I have had no trouble although several of the old heads around here have predicted I would be either dead or crazy before the summer is over.

People here either walk or ride mule back. Troublesome and Mill creeks are the main highways into town. Red Cross days, and Court days are big events.

I can honestly say that I have never enjoyed being any place any more than here.[13]

His positive feelings for the place are evident. The comments about the "old maids" would today seem sexist and derogatory, but in 1932 for one young single male to admit to another that women could operate a "remarkable place" rather well while they themselves could not find a job was a high compliment.

Still also wrote of his summer work to Loomis, who responded that it would give him a "different slant on life." He congratulated and encouraged the young man: "Keep up your courage; do your best to handle the boys; educate them as to what is right for them to do, and it may lead to a permanent job for you—if not there, then elsewhere." In his August 10 letter Loomis included an offer of more board money should Still need it and some advice about the continuing job search. "If you cannot get a position as Librarian somewhere, it would seem to me you might connect up out there with some settlement school and thus do wonderful work with the mountain kids."[14]

Still was attracted to both the school and the community from the first, but the Hindman that he experienced in the summer of 1932 was not his permanent haven yet. His work with West and the boys did not lead directly to a library position at the school. When he wrote Katherine Pettit, a cofounder of the Settlement School, to inquire about work opportunities, she did not bother to respond herself but passed his query to Robert Stapleton, who was looking for a young man to work for a nearby community.[15] Undoubtedly, Stapleton's letter discouraged

Still because they were seeking a volunteer who would teach the local boys music and conduct an orchestra.[16] Still was not a musician.

A salary, even if small, was his goal. Seeing no prospects in Hindman, he continued to look for other opportunities, using a scattershot approach. Some of the applications were for temporary work, such as his enquiry to the Waco Chamber of Commerce to ask if Texas was seeking cotton pickers for later in the summer. The response was that they already had an excess. Other efforts were directed at long-term employment. A draft of a letter to the president of Bowdon College in Georgia shows that he was seriously looking for a library position to follow his summer job and to that end was exaggerating his experience:

> I am a young man, twenty-six years of age, a librarian by profession and am particularly interested in locating in a college library. I hold an M.A. from Vanderbilt University, and a B.S. in L.S. from the University of Illinois Library School. As an undergraduate I was first assistant in the college library for two years and have had experience in cataloging, classifying, reference work, and bibliography. During the summer of 1931 I did considerable cataloging for the Lanier Library, Tryon, North Carolina. Last summer I opened the library of the Hindman Settlement School to the village and county people.[17]

Even if he never sent this application to Bowdon College, merely drafting it shows that he was intensifying and configuring his job search.

In the meantime, his work with the boys at Hindman continued. Plus, he was finding time for a social life. Still's friend at LMU, Ralph Williams, was from nearby Harlan.[18] Still developed a friendship with Ralph's sister Irene. She was a lively young woman who enjoyed "social" gatherings. In early August she had been to Hindman, then she invited Still to Harlan, promising to organize a hayride in his honor. Terms of affection thread through her remarks, but the tone is more an overture than a love letter.[19] Though Still did enjoy times with the people his age in Hindman, he did not take Irene's bait.

Still was feeling "at home"—busy with the boys and the job, making friends in nearby towns, spending time in the Settlement School library. Though details are unclear, Still accepted a job at Caney Creek Junior College, precursor to Alice Lloyd College, approximately ten miles from Hindman. In an interesting letter, Alice Lloyd herself made an offer to Still to become head of the English department.[20] The person they had employed, she said, could not be in Kentucky until December, thus the job would be his for nine months or more beginning in September. She requested his immediate response and warned him to "keep his word." Apparently, Don West had telegraphed an acceptance but then changed his mind without informing her.[21] After this August 8 letter, the plans were official enough that Still received a letter of congratulations from LMU for his appointment as head of the English department at Caney Creek Junior College.[22] Friends were addressing letters to him at Caney Creek.[23] Why Still never took the position is unknown, but he did not refuse it for a more lucrative offer.

The mystery of the Caney Creek offer deepened when a letter from Lucy Furman to James Still, dated August 13, 1933, implied that something "dishonorable" had taken place.[24] Furman had visited an old friend in Hindman and heard of a "very disagreeable experience" that Still had had with Caney Creek Community Center.[25] Either a lack of knowledge or a sense of decorum prevented Furman from being specific, but she alluded to the situation in this way: "You [Still] would be expected to do things which you considered dishonorable and which you refused to do." Furman then asked Still to write down the details of what Lloyd had demanded he do because she was collecting evidence of the "crooked proceedings" she suspected were part of doing business at Caney Creek. Since an ongoing conflict had existed between the Settlement School and Lloyd's organization since 1917, Furman's seeking information to establish a case against proceedings at Caney would not have been surprising.[26] In fact, Still may have exaggerated his unpleasant encounter with Lloyd because he believed doing so might aid him in acquiring a job at the Settlement School. Apparently, Still did not respond to Furman's request, and he never explained to anyone the details of his negotiations with Lloyd and Caney Creek.

The most interesting reference to these plans for the fall of 1932 came from someone who should have known his whereabouts: Iris Grannis. In September she wrote, "By this time you are in your situation [at Caney Creek] and probably have met your classes. I am all eagerness to hear about the work. . . . I am anxious to hear more about Mrs. Loyde [sic]."[27] The letter, which was addressed to "Professor James A. Still Caney Junior College," is a rich source of inference and speculation. In addition to showing that Still intended to take a job at the college, it indicates that he must have ended his summer work in mid-August, then joined Iris and Frank in Tryon for a short visit before returning to take up his post at Caney Creek. She opened her letter by describing his leav-

ing and not sending word of his safe arrival. Although her words could
be taken as those of an overprotective mother, her tone is more that of
an abandoned lover.

> My dear;
>
> It is a week since you left us and I have been worried about
> you and have wondered about you and have thought about
> you almost constantly. I suppose of course you got there and
> that you had a nice week-end with your Harlan friends and
> that all was well for you. However I thought of you being
> mashed up somewhere on the mountains or shot in the back
> up in Harlan or some terrible thing happening to you. I am
> the typical old hen with a duckling who swims out and away
> from me. . . . I was heart broken when you left that day. I did
> not see how I could live until Christmas without seeing you.

After much disconnected news, her salutation ended, "Do write dar-
ling. I am your devoted slave." [28] Yet at the end of this long and emotional correspondence, she included no signature of any sort. The mental
health and emotional stability of Iris Grannis had been in decline for
some time, so perhaps this response to Still's absence reflected nothing more than her shaky state of mind. Yet her writing and mailing of
the letter raises questions about their relationship, at least her view of
it. She was too old to be a potential lover, too young to be his surrogate mother, too needy to be a close friend, and too self-centered to be
a generous patron. But she might have fulfilled pieces of all these roles.
Whether consciously or unconsciously, the young man was continually
looking for ways to disconnect himself from this complicated relationship. Plus, he was looking for a job.

Even Red never received an explanation of why the Caney Creek
opportunity did not work out; in October Red expressed his sympathy
but tried to keep his chin up as he looked forward to the upcoming presidential election and closed his letter to Still: "This life is worse than
Hell! But we are getting a change they say, under Roosevelt."[29] In spite
of promises of future change, the fall found Still and Redmond back
where they had been in the spring of 1932—bouncing around looking
for work.

Still could not have felt much satisfaction when he slipped back into
his role as companion and driver to Iris Grannis. On October 19 he

received in Gadsden an urgent telegram from Frank Grannis asking him to pick up his wife in Chattanooga and take her to Florida.[30] Still did meet and take her to Florida, and he stayed with her. By November 21, Still wrote Red a letter from Gadsden where he had gone after leaving Florida. His tone was remarkably positive, probably the result of a sense of freedom gained by, once again, giving up his role as assistant to Mrs. Grannis. Still began, "Am just back from a month stay in Florida. It is so warm and beautiful there I hated to leave. I put up with the madame as long as I could then came back. There seemed to be no work there of any description, although a card just forwarded to me from an ad I answered offered me a job in a fish-grill. Oh yeah!"[31]

The letter went on to say that he believed they were on to "something hot"—another job lead in Tennessee—and encouraged Red to write immediately and inquire.[32] Perhaps Still's good humor could be attributed to that prospect or perhaps to the visit he had with Jack Adams at the Berry School in Rome, Georgia. Further along in the letter came the most likely source of his renewed energy. He had sold an article, "Horse Swapping Court," to the magazine *Our Dumb Animals*.[33] And his poem "A Burned Tree Speaks," which had been published in *Boys' Life,* was to be printed in a grammar-school textbook.

Almost six months passed before Still heard again from Red. In the meantime, he was receiving letters from Don West, who desperately wanted him to put aside his casual attitude and take up the cause, any cause. West had become involved with Myles Horton and the founding of the Highlander Folk School in Monteagle, Tennessee. In early September he invited Still to write an article about the school for a publication called *The Cumberland Empire*.[34] When he had not heard back by September 18, West wrote again, asking, "What in the devil has become of you?" and urging him to hurry up with the article. At that point West believed that Still was at Caney Creek, but by the next note he simply wanted a confirmation of the correct address. Upon receiving that, he followed with a long typed letter vacillating between words of admiration for his friend and chastisement for his not being more concerned about injustice. West was becoming more radical without apology. His final paragraph begins with a word about Jack Adams, then trails off into a tirade:

> I think Jack is about to go 100% socialist at Berry. If he does I hope he gets expelled. Berry, Berea, and other such mountain mission schools are damnable abominations to the cause

of human justice. They are smoke screens thrown out by the
church and capitalism to cover up their rotten filth. But they
want [sic] stand. Capitalism is now in its last throes of death
agony, and it is going to die a bloody death. . . . But you have
no understanding of what I mean. You who have come from the
proletariat have tried to rise to the bourgeois class which has
lived and still lives on the life's blood of your people.[35]

Still did not share his stand and certainly would not have been persuaded by such a letter. However, he was interested enough, or desperate enough, to keep the possibilities open with West. In December
Guy Loomis wrote Still in Gadsden, saying he hoped there would be a
chance for Still and West to work together even if there were no pay:
"If you can get your board and lodging, and the work appeals to you, I
should suggest your taking it without hesitation." Loomis closed with
the words of support that were customary by this time: "If the 'Gloom
Boys' get on your trail and you get up against it, I will stand behind you
until the skies clear."[36]

A following letter from West to Still dated March 16, 1933, shows
that Still had not shut the door on the possibility of working with West.
The upbeat feeling here overshadows the reality that money would be
hard to come by:

Jim, boy, You are a great soul!

I surely appreciate your interest and cooperation, or
willingness to cooperate. It certainly gives a fellow a lot of
encouragement to have a fellow like you believing in what he
is doing, and that he's not altogether a fool. It's the opinion of
folk like you that really count anyhow. . . . I have no illusions
about the difficulty of getting on with no funds in this work.
That's why its [sic] so important to have friends like you and
others. Damn you, you are going to help!

West closed with information about an article that Still was planning to
write for the Atlanta paper. His final comment implies that Still's interest in the project was monetary: "Just remember that the Atlanta papers
are capitalist and conservative. They like stuff about Georgia Mts. And
will probably give you ten dollars if you do a good story."[37] Several
months later Still wrote to Red about his interchange with West: "Don

West, fanatic, writes concerning his drive for 'mass justice' like this: 'Damn you, you are going to help. You know this thing is right and you are going to contribute.' Oh yeah! . . . [his ellipsis takes up three lines of typing] so let the dragon roar!"[38] Still did not sympathize with West and his causes, yet he maintained the contact.

This particular letter to Red shows that while Still was trying to keep all his options open, he was experiencing frustration and fragmentation. He was writing from his father's house in Fairfax, Alabama, and the letter admitted in an obtuse literary way that he had been forced to return to the shelter of family, against his will: "Still this side of Jordan, believing . . . [his ellipsis] the Progressive Era is as dead as a . . . [his ellipsis] Chuzzlewit, I have put away my Vanity Fair and returned to The Fortress where meat and bread is plentiful to lead the Sheltered Life until such time that I can go Faraway. Sons usually return to the Fathers of Their People when the Man Wants But Little and hasn't even that."

His next paragraph began, "I hear everything, know nothing, read little," followed with an eclectic list of the books he had recently read: Willa Cather's *Obscure Destinies,* Rollo Walter Brown's *Dean Briggs,* Butler's *The Way of All Flesh,* Thoreau's *Walden* and *Maine Woods,* Alec Waugh's *Hot Countries,* Sherwood Anderson's *Beyond Desire,* William Faulkner's *Light in August,* and H. G. Wells's *The World of William Clissold.*[39] He was reading for information and enjoyment but also to escape his situation or surroundings and pass the time.

He had been writing too, though not publishing. He bragged to Red that he was now the "proud owner of rejection slips from *Harper's* and *Atlantic.*" The letter never settled into a sustained narrative, but toward the end his tone turned somber when he said that he was farming with his father and fishing on the Chattahoochee but finding no one in town (Fairfax, Alabama) with whom he could talk without getting into a "hopeless argument." He closed with a folksy story to convey the sad reality that his dog had died: "He chewed up two bulldogs simultaneously, skeeted them through his teeth, and came home dying from overheat." The dark humor gave way to a concluding comment that his brother Tom was "off to rejoin the circus. He runs a merry-go-round."[40]

Another image that captures Still's progress over the year occurred in a letter from Jesse Stuart who wanted to know where he had drifted and why. Still had not thought of himself as adrift, and the thought made him feel like a raft.[41] A year earlier, Anna Roberts had referred to Still's "wandering career" with longing, but by May 1933, he seemed weary of what must have felt like a life without purpose. With the exception of the summer of 1932 when he was in Hindman, the time between July 1931 and August 1933 had involved plenty of movement but little forward progress. Living in Alabama with his father or his sister Inez and his one-year-old half brother Don was not acceptable. He had enjoyed some of his time with Inez in Gadsden, but he had pursued no jobs there. Working for Don West, though the possibility had been raised, was not a good alternative.[42] He had been with Frank and Iris Grannis in both Florida and Clarksville, but that relationship was intolerable. Guy Loomis was still willing to help but had no concrete suggestions. Still was drifting without an oar.

The only constants during this time were friends like Red and supporters like Loomis, his habit of reading and desire to write, and the attraction of eastern Kentucky, where he had spent the summer in 1932. A year later Still was planning a walking tour of western North Carolina and had invited Jesse Stuart to join him. On August 21 Stuart wrote that he could not take part in the venture because he was too busy finishing his book of poetry before he began the school year.[43] Though Stuart and West were going in opposite directions, they were both busy with living. Still and Red were marking time, at least until the end of July, when Still received a letter from Hindman asking about his credentials for the librarian job at the school. He quickly gave up his plans for the walking tour to pursue this lead.

Still must have sent a query letter to the school in July because on August 1 he received a response from May Stone, the secretary-treasurer of the school's executive committee, asking about his qualifications. In this letter she outlined the parameters of the job: "We cannot afford to pay any salary for this work, except room, board, laundry and traveling expenses. I shall be glad to have an answer from you as soon as possible as time is short and we must settle this position very soon. School opens Sept. 4 and all our workers must be here by Sept. 1."[44] He welcomed this news—feeling relief at any possibility of working, even without a salary, and pleasure at the thought of returning to Hindman, a place he wanted to be. He sent May Stone convincing evidence that his library credentials more than met the requirements. Still's acceptance of the position reached her on August 7, and she immediately responded that the school was pleased that he would join them. They expected him to arrive by bus or train on Friday, the first day of September 1933.

More than two years after he had completed his library-science degree at the University of Illinois, the twenty-seven-year-old was embarking on his first real job. It would not bring a salary since he was volunteering, but it would mean independence. Many years later, Still conflated all this wandering, searching time into a few weeks or months as he described his connection to Hindman beginning with his summer experience and folding seamlessly into his job at the Settlement School. The transition was not easy, but an optimistic spirit like Still's could endure the trials in favor of the rewards. Work at Hindman Settlement School was worth the wait.

One notable firsthand account of Still's move to Hindman appears in the interview beginning *The Wolfpen Notebooks:*

> While in Knott county [summer 1932], I stayed a week at the Hindman Settlement School, and when I returned home they sent a letter offering a job as a volunteer worker. They would shelter and feed me but couldn't pay me. I was willing having no other prospects. The school was located at the county seat at the forks of Troublesome Creek. The hardtop road stopped dead in town, and a rutted wagon road took over. The bridge had washed out. You walked a plank, waded, or used a jumping pole. Or rode a high-water horse. I had come to the jumping-off place.

10

Hindman Becomes a Haven

In the dark hours I have heard your questing words
Creep out of nowhere in the mountain silence
                              —From "Child in the Hills"

James Still had a love affair with Hindman, Kentucky. Knott County served as his home base for the sixty-eight years between 1933 and his death in 2001. He spoke of the town with humorous affection in one off-hand comment: "Hindman was surely the only place you could cash a check at four in the morning and call for your mail at midnight . . . the cashier was an early riser, the postmaster an insomniac."[1] He was even proud of being assigned post office box 13. He wrote of his bond to the landscape in his signature poem "Heritage": "I cannot leave. I cannot go away / . . . Being of these hills, I cannot pass beyond." He seemed to feel an immediate and unequivocal attachment to it. His familiar label "the jumping-off place" implied that life, when he arrived at Hindman, had taken an inevitable turn that he could not undo.

Since leaving his parents' Alabama home for college, Still had been to Harrogate and Nashville, Tennessee, and to Champaign, Illinois, to earn degrees; and he had wandered through the South seeking work and adventure. He had come to the end of his journey. If his college years were a time of searching and learning for Still, the period that began with his work in Hindman in 1933 and continued until he was drafted into the army in 1942 showed a commitment to stability, community, and a simple agrarian way of life that allowed him time to write. But in September 1933 he could not have known that this little town would be anything other than a temporary haven.

What later seemed like destiny was, at the time it happened, more like a convenience. The move to Hindman was a big step, but his alternatives were almost nonexistent and certainly unattractive. He no longer wanted to stay with Frank and Iris Grannis, and he did not want to live with his father in Alabama or his sisters in Georgia or Florida. His relationship with Don West was inconsistent, and West's future uncertain. Traveling around might have satisfied him, but Guy Loomis would not continue to support a man who had no job or home base. Even without the promise of a salary at the Settlement School, Still would have something to do there, a place to live, and food to eat. Besides, he liked it more than any place he had ever been. Knott County held a familiarity for him; it was rural like Chambers County, Alabama, and mountainous like the area around LMU in Tennessee and Tryon in western North Carolina.

What did Hindman, Kentucky, look and feel like in the early 1930s? As implied in his description of the washed-out bridge, roads were primitive. There were very few cars until the late 1920s, and even when they began to show up, they had trouble getting far because of the condition of the dirt roads. Supplies were brought in by horse and wagon, and what commerce there was depended heavily on mail order. People rarely went anywhere. As one older resident recalled, going to nearby Hazard was like going to New York. In the late 1920s "modern conveniences" were rare; moonshine and pistols were more common than electricity and telephones.[2]

In 1932 the U.S. Department of Agriculture labeled Knott County a "typical creek bottom settlement of the Kentucky mountain area" and conducted studies that concluded the obvious: subsistence farming supplied people with the products they needed at home. Because the average farm had less than 3.5 acres of level land, commercial farming was impractical. In addition, the county's isolation, lack of a railroad, and poor road conditions meant that transporting crops would have been impossible. The typical family did farm but also worked at other jobs. Though the region is now associated with coal mining, at that time there were only eight locally owned coal operations in the county, and most of that coal was mined for home use. Other industries in the county included sawmilling, grist milling, blacksmithing, stone quarrying, weaving, and basket and furniture making.[3] The entire county had just over fifteen thousand people according to the 1930 census. Hindman itself was small enough that its population was recorded as part of District #1, which included the lower Troublesome Creek area. The district had 2,500 people, and approximately 400 of them lived in the town itself. About five thousand of the county's residents were of school age. These young people and the business of educating them were the concern of Hindman Settlement School and, in turn, of James Still when he came there in September 1933.

While working for the Congregational Church Extension Board the summer before, he had learned about the Settlement School's set up and programs and something of its mission. When he joined the staff, the school had already been in operation for thirty years and was the first rural social settlement school in the United States. It was begun in the context of the social-reform movement of the late nineteenth century when settlement houses were established in major cities to improve living conditions in urban slums. A good example was Chicago's Hull House, founded in 1889 by Jane Addams, who was an inspiration to many young women at the turn of the twentieth century. Two such women were Katherine Pettit of Lexington and May Stone of Louisville, reformers who saw education as the key to improving mountain society.

They began their work in eastern Kentucky in the 1890s. The Kentucky Federation of Women's Clubs sponsored three summer camps, and it was at the first, held near Hazard in 1899, that Pettit began to work with Stone.[4] As the story goes, a patriarch of the area, Soloman Everidge—"Uncle Sol"—walked all the way from Hindman to Hazard to encourage the two women to hold a camp for his kin. On June 14, 1900, they located the second summer camp at Hindman. Two years later they began the permanent school and settlement, which consisted of a schoolhouse and a rented cottage on three acres of land. Over the next decade, the school grew to comprise ten buildings on seventy acres of land and had become the county's high school. By the 1920s it had 345 acres and 20 buildings. Through this growth it remained faithful to its purpose: "To provide an educational opportunity for the youth of the mountains and keep them mindful of their heritage."[5] The program taught students how to read and write effectively and equipped them with good habits and practical training. The founders and teachers valued the culture of the mountains and wished to strengthen and preserve it. Pettit and Stone knew that the school's success depended upon how well it adapted its teaching to local needs. They realized that students might never pursue education at a higher level but wanted them to return to their communities with better habits and more effective ways of living.[6] However, many of the students did pursue further education. By 1928 the school had 124 total graduates, three-quarters of whom went on to other institutions and about a third of whom worked as teachers in the mountain region. A survey in 1937 showed that 84 percent of the Settlement School's graduates had returned to the mountains to work as teachers, doctors, lawyers, and businesspeople.[7]

The growth and success of the school was not continuous nor assured. The most serious problem the school faced from 1915 through the Depression was a long, unsuccessful quest for financial stability. Fund-raising was important, but another approach to the problem was to keep costs down by recruiting volunteer staff or paying very small salaries. A number of the teachers remained at the school for many years, but to supplement this core, younger teachers were recruited through the College Settlement Association, which was active on campuses of women's colleges in the East. These women came to support the cause of social justice but usually stayed just a few years before leaving to marry or pursue a career.[8] In most cases they were semivolunteers, meaning they received only room and board from the school. Any funding crisis took a toll on those teachers and staff who were dependent on their paychecks.

James Still began working at Hindman as one of these semivolunteers. His only source of income was Guy Loomis, who was willing to pay him a small salary (twenty-five dollars per month) if he would return to Hindman, where he could resume working with the children and pursue his writing. So Still exchanged his work for room and board. The exact details of the arrangement are unknown, but in the introduction to *The Wolfpen Notebooks*, Still recounts his first work experience as six years with the Settlement School library (1933–1939): the first three for no pay, and the last three for a modest salary beginning at fifteen dollars per month.[9] He figured that the money the school paid him over the six-year period averaged out to six cents per day.[10] He did not anticipate accumulating riches or fame through this work at the Settlement School, but neither was he there out of a sense of social concern. He needed a job and a place to stay.

The jobs of everyone at the school were multifaceted, and the work never stopped. Teachers taught all day and then tutored every evening in the dormitories, where two-hour study halls were nightly events. Though Still was not primarily a teacher, he did live in the dormitory,

Eastover Hall, with the boys; he would have been "on call" much of the time. Everyone's goal was to help students learn while being alert to all their needs. The staff was always on duty. Still drew from his memory when in 1994 he described the operations of the school at his arrival:

> They ran a very tight ship—100 or 105 students. The students got to go home only twice each school year. They had a dairy and an enormous garden. The girls cooked and kept everything very clean. For example I used to ask them not to scrub my floor because it wasn't dirty. It was said in that county in the area, if you passed a mountain home—if that child had gone to Hindman Settlement School, you would know it by the grounds. When I asked about the scrubbing, they said we're trying to get into the children's heads the idea of keeping the home. Overdoing it a little bit is not too bad. That was the idea there.
>
> While it was not church related, on Sunday they had a little choral reading, and the children were expected to go to the church downtown. They didn't check on them. But the children were so glad to get away. They couldn't go to town, although we were right in town. They were strict about that. They remained strict, even the teachers didn't go. It wasn't safe. After all, we had killings down there.
>
> When I first went there they had a little boys' house, Lucy Furman lived in it. At the start they had mostly orphans, little children. Then they had 8th graders and then the high school—the only one in the county. And it was a remarkable school. What high school in the state, even today, has such a staff as that? Highly dedicated people who came, given no salary, from Smith, Mt Holyoke, Vassar.[11]

From his first year at Hindman, Still felt attached to the place and the people. He became interested in several of the boys at the school and their family situations.[12] One he especially liked was Robert Miller, who wrote him a few letters. Their attachment was short but strong enough that Still recalled the boy many years later:

> Cotton Miller. There are two boys rolled into one. He was a mischievous little boy. They called him cotton because his hair, white hair, and blue-eyed, skinny [sic]. He fought somebody everyday. He never got mad, he just fought everyday. He [was]

expelled for something (it was easy to get expelled there) and
then I went to the director and pled with her to let him come
back. In fact, I told her I would buy his books. So she let him
come back and then in about 6 months he got in some more
mischief. . . . [13]

Even more significant than his growing connection to the boys was
the establishment of a surrogate family. He was transferring his attachment from Iris and Frank Grannis to the man who would become his
Hindman "guardian" and loyal friend for many years—Jethro Amburgey. Jethro had attended Hindman Settlement School as a boy and was
the second of the school's graduates to return as a teacher after World
War I. In addition to being the area's respected dulcimer maker, he had
been teaching manual training and coaching basketball at the school
for twelve years when he first met James Still, who was ten years his
junior.[14] Since there were few male teachers at the school, Amburgey
and Still naturally gravitated to each other. Jethro had a wife and young
son plus a large extended family, of which Still eventually became an
honorary member. From the start, Still latched on to Jethro.

As late as May 15 of his first school year, Still had no idea where the
wind would take him that summer. But before long he went with Jethro
and his wife and boy to the Chicago World's Fair: the Century of Progress.[15] They could not have stayed long because by June 11, Still was back
in Richmond, Kentucky, where he had arranged to work in the library
of Eastern State Teachers College. He had driven with the Amburgeys
to Chicago; then as they went south, they dropped Still off in Memphis
where he caught a bus, then a train, to get back to Kentucky. On June 14
he wrote Jethro, who was now in Judkins, Texas, that he liked the work,
which consisted of cataloging $2,000 worth of new books and hoped to
have the entire job done in a month. The letter included an interesting
aside that involved Irene Williams, the girl that he had met in Harlan
two summers earlier. She was an avid partier and wanted Still to join her
when possible. He described the "fun": two girls visiting from Harlan
on Monday "were driving an airflow Desoto. They picked up another
girl and two boys and we went up to Joyland Park at Lexington, dancing
there until 1:00 in the morning. No more of this night life for me. I can't
stand it and work too. Incidentally there was whiskey in the crowd but I
didn't touch a drop."[16] Was his renunciation of late-night fun and whiskey for Jethro's benefit, or was it a resolution that needed strengthening?
Either way, he was finding Richmond friendly.

On June 18 he wrote Jethro another letter from Richmond, which ended with a request: "I have been thinking about a little project for next year and would like to have your opinion of it. Am anxious to talk it over with you." When he finished his summer work at the college, he went to Judkins, Texas, to drive Jethro, Ranie, and Morris home to Kentucky. Presumably, they discussed the project on the long trip. Still was thinking of setting conditions on his return to the Settlement School, and he wanted to discuss those demands with Jethro. He needed a salary but had little experience making demands. He valued Jethro's experiences with the school's frugal administration.

Still did communicate with May Stone in July, saying he did not plan to return to Hindman unless they would give him a salaried position. Stone replied on July 13: "We should all like very much to have you return, but feel that the matter of even a small salary would make this hard on us while money is still hard to get."[17] When they successfully hired another candidate who was willing to "volunteer," Still quickly changed his demand and agreed to work under "Miss Spriggs," the new librarian, for food and lodging. So as not to appear that he had retracted his salary request entirely, the young man inserted into the negotiations his desire for time to write. In a letter drafted in late July 1934, Still explained his new offer by saying that his friend (Loomis) had generously offered to pay him a small salary if he would return to the school. Then he added, "For some years I have been interested in writing though I have had so little time to devote to it. Recent encouraging letters from the editors of the *Atlantic Monthly* and the *Virginia Quarterly Review* have led me to feel that I should give it more attention than I have done in the past."[18]

In case Stone did not care about his having time to write, Still sweetened his offer by describing additional work he would do for the school library: cataloging the entire juvenile library, creating a shelf list, and reworking the card catalog. He was "willing to work under Miss Spriggs in bringing about these needed changes. The work could be carried on in the 'book room' and would in no way interfere with the study halls, or regular service of the library." He was willing to help in other ways as well:

Serving as a sort of "utility man" I could be of help wherever needed. I have had office experience and touch typing. If I could help in any way at the Hillside office I would be glad to. I would expect to carry on the recreational work with the boys as I did last year. . . . I trust that I am not being presumptuous in this offer, and that you feel I am making it in the spirit of helpfulness. I am interested in work with the people of that section and want to continue to be connected with educational work in the Kentucky mountains.

Stone received his letter on July 23 and responded three days later that the school was pleased with his generous offer. "I think your suggestion of doing all that extra library work a good one. . . . It is also good to have someone with the Kentucky certificate who could substitute or replace a teacher if one should be called away."[19] She did not acknowledge his desire for time to write. Her only difficulty would be finding a place for him to live, but that must have been easily taken care of because he was back in Hindman on Friday, September 7, ready to begin the term. During this second year (1934–1935), he was a more permanent staff member.

He was also becoming a more serious writer. Though his bibliography shows no publications in 1934, the correspondence indicates that he had submitted at least sixteen poems to seven different journals. Three letters were acceptances, and seven were rejections. In 1935 his acceptance-to-rejection rate was level—ten yes, ten no—and in 1936 he had seventeen acceptance notices and only nine rejections.[20] Perhaps his poems were improving; more likely he was learning which periodicals favored which poems. Several letters came from the same editor, showing that he was becoming known as a poet from the mountains who was, if nothing else, persistent.

The year 1934 ended with Still busy in the Settlement School library, modestly supported by Guy Loomis, befriended by the Amburgey family, and pursuing a course to become a poet. In January 1935 he caught up with Red with apologies for not being a faithful correspondent. Still reacted to Red's news of writing a children's novel with his own efforts. "I diddle and dabble a bit myself but to no effect until lately." The *Virginia Quarterly Review* had accepted one poem; the *Sewanee Review,* two; and Harriet Monroe had accepted three for *Poetry: A Magazine of Verse.* Another positive for the year's end was that he had become proud owner of two Amburgey dulcimers; he bragged to Red that he was "making the air hideous with perpetual strumming."[21]

The next year began much as 1934 had ended, with Still writing and submitting poems when he could. The difference was that they were appearing in journals. Among the first was "Mountain Dulcimer," which the *Virginia Quarterly Review* had accepted in October 1934 and published in July 1935.[22] What is most interesting about this poem and much of his early work is what was left out. It has nothing of the town, the school, the people, the local economy; it seems not to draw on his actual experience of living and working in Knott County. But it does echo the sounds of nature—both wild and domesticated: the music of hounds, the turkey's treble, the creak of saddlebags, the lambs' crying—and it illustrates Still's strengthening link to the dulcimer maker, very real in his life but unnamed in the poem.

A letter to Red on April 12, 1935, shows that he was busy and mildly discouraged. He was in Louisville for a meeting of the Kentucky Educational Association but barred from attending because he was suffering with measles. While stuck in his hotel room, he wrote to his friend about publishers' reactions to his recent submissions. The *Saturday Review of Literature* had accepted a poem.[23] But Still was more concerned about the mixed response he had received from the editor of *The Atlantic Monthly,* who told him that his verse "lacked emotional appeal" yet said his descriptions were "magical." He ended with a cryptic comment about "*The* Jesse Stuart" being at the conference. They had not met, however. Perhaps Stuart was basking in responses to his own mammoth book of sonnets, *Man with a Bull-Tongue Plow,* and Still wished to avoid encountering any perceived or imagined swagger from the competitor he could not bring himself to acknowledge.[24]

Whether driven by Stuart's success or responding to comments from magazine editors, Still was sending out poems at an increased rate. In the last six months of 1935 he published ten. Finally in September 1935 *The Atlantic* accepted Still's poem "Child in the Hills," with the comment that its "calm quiet beauty . . . had gone home to us all in this office."[25] This poem apparently had emotional appeal as well as magical description. Much of the inspiration for work going forward can be attributed to the experience that Still had in Knott County during the summer of 1935, when the Depression was gaining strength.

Verna Mae Slone, a lifelong resident of Knott County who was only a few years younger than Still, claimed that the economic troubles brought on by the Depression did not begin as early or become as severe in eastern Kentucky as in the big cities of the nation. Because the people of the area had been self-sufficient for generations, she said, they knew the meaning of "make do" and "do without." As for money, no one ever had much, so having a little less did not make a big difference.[26] The people did, however, take advantage of the recovery programs of the New Deal. Sloane, her family, and their neighbors worked hard in those jobs created by the CCC (Civilian Conservation Corps) and the WPA (Works Progress Administration). The Depression may not have brought an immediate, recognizable change to the region's economy, but over time the agrarian economy based on self-sufficient farming would diminish, and wage-earning, whether from a government program or from industry, would become the norm for families in eastern Kentucky.[27] In 1935 James Still saw firsthand the beginning of this trend. What opened doors for him was his experience as a FERA worker, and it fired his creative juices.

By the summer, Still had worked for two full school years in Hindman, but he was to learn more about life in the region during one month in 1935 than he had in all the time he had been a librarian. He worked as a social worker in Knott County for the New Deal's Federal Emergency Relief Administration (FERA) program.[28] His territory was lower Knott County, and his task was to visit homes by invitation in order to inventory their belongings; observe their gardens, crops, and livestock; and estimate the health of the family members. The data he collected would be used to evaluate the need for government assistance. He penciled notes in school copybooks, which he later claimed furnished some of the background for *River of Earth*. He reported having worked the whole summer, but his notes recorded visits only from June 20 to July 5. He described that experience in the *Heritage* tape interview: "Miles of walking so all summer I walked . . . [and] visited families who invited me that wanted help. I would go to their homes and look in their meal barrels and see how many chickens they had and how many eggs they got and look at their gardens and see what the general situation was in the family and I put this down in composition books."

The notes indicate, just as Still remembered, that he went in homes and recorded what the families had, what state the house was in, and how they were faring. The following verbatim entries provide a sample:

Thursday June 20, 1935

Charley Perkins (Montgomery). Crops looking good. 7 or 8 acres of corn in and working on 2 others at present. About an acre of Irish potatoes; some now mature. Garden vegetables ready for eating. Plenty milk and butter for family. About 60 chickens hatched out. Son Dorsey there about half the time. No income for flour, land etc. except Ethel's sewing center.

Troy at home working. About 35 bu. corn left, will last until new corn comes in—one horse, pigs to feed. Milk 1 cow.

Coon Gayheart. Mr. Gayheart lives alone with small boy. No livestock—no mills—1 can berries—no meat—live solely on vouchers. Helps Mrs. Charley Perkins work in garden occasionally for vegetables. Arm broken 2 years ago, bone now misplaced and gives out easily when washing etc. Small garden—veg not ready. Home clean. 24 cans—no rubber or lids

June 24, 1935

Hiram Hicks. Mr. Hicks working in field. 6–7 acres corn. No old corn or meat. Planted 1½ bu. Potato slips. Fair garden—eating veg out of garden. Have to buy all household necessities. 3 hens—no cow—no milk—no fruit jars—no orchard—no pigs.

Beds, cornshucks in burley sacks—need mattresses badly. Piteable condition—no furniture in room with exception of 2 d. beds.

Mr. H probably has T.B. Seems to be working hard to get a start farming. This is first year they have farmed. No lard or meat in house, a little meal. Are trying to get along until the next relief cheque. Elizabeth Hicks and child, sister to Hiram is staying with them for the present. May stay on indefinitely.

July 5, 1935

Nelson Prater. Mrs. P. gave birth to child last Sat. Child and mother getting along fine. Wants to know if relief can pay midwife service of $5.00. Claims he is absolutely unable to pay. Crop: 2½ acres corn, 2½ bu i [Irish] potatoes, 700 slips s [sweet] potatoes.

Good garden—intends looking into garden. Cow 4 qts. 1 pig; 40 chickens

House fairly clean, yard in bad shape, pig rooting in the yard.

Food supplies on hand: 4 lbs. lard 10 lbs. meat Vegetables ready in garden.

July 6, 1935

    Rufus Ritchie. Family in good health. House clean also
children. Rufus working for stove mill, logging since last
Wednesday cross-cut. Don't know how long will work.
Expecting to have only few days work—claims only temporary work. $1.60 day. Crop: 4 acres corn, 3 bu i-pot, 125
slips. Cow: 1, 1 pig, 22 chickens. Supplies on hand: 4 lbs meal
5 lbs flour.

The existing composition books, which are available in the James
Still room at MSU, include notes on thirteen visits to different house-
holds in Knott County. Some families were barely surviving; others were
getting by. He probably made more visits than these, but regardless of
the number of homes he saw or the number of days he did the job, Still's
experience in the summer of 1935 set the stage for the stories and the
novel he was to create over the next four years. The FERA work gave
him the opportunity to get a detailed inside look at the daily lives of the
people. He absorbed their situations and attitudes. His role as a FERA
volunteer was largely as an objective observer and recorder. Still wrote
one short story, "Sunstroke on Clabber Creek," that reflects a particularly difficult day of interviews; though never published in his lifetime,
it is now available in *The Hills Remember.* Even that depressing story
does not pass judgment. The narrator, who is the "furrin" government
visitor, just observes and collects facts and tries to eat a meal with the
family. The story trails off with the narrator's going into an ambiguous
mental and emotional state as a result of either the poverty he witnesses
or the sun's beating down on him.
    Except for that story, Still's use of the FERA experience was indi-
rect. *River of Earth* takes on a similar objective tone when the young
narrator recounts his life without placing value or passing judgment.
Direct contact with the people of the local communities provided Still
with the raw material that would be the basis of all of his stories, poems,
and notebooks. He was becoming intricately tied to the life and place
that fed his writing.[29]
    Another way Still got into the countryside and closer to the lives
of the people was through his role as the "book boy," a walking bookmobile. Working at the school library, he quickly saw a need for books
in the surrounding area and began taking reading material to different
schools. He later told of this project as his own undertaking. The chil-

dren welcomed his arrival with the cry "Here comes the book boy."[30] Reports of the number of schools he visited and the quantity of books he carried vary from one account to another.[31] One important and possibly more objective version comes from the pen of an observer and supervisor. Elizabeth Watts, executive director of Hindman Settlement School, praised the project in a letter of appreciation she wrote to Still's father in June 1936: "If you ever come to Kentucky, we should very much like to have you visit the Settlement and see for yourself the work your son is doing with the library and in other ways. You would be particularly interested in the work he has done with 'travelling libraries,' carrying twenty books on his shoulders, and often walking as many as sixteen miles in a day in order to take books into communities where there are very few if any."[32]

Walking through the county familiarized Still with the local geography, customs, and people. No doubt it also helped the closed mountain communities to accept him, but that acceptance did not come easily and sometimes not at all. For example, one official prevented Still from bringing "them old books" into his school on the grounds that they were taking the children's minds off their studies.[33] Nevertheless, Still persisted and reached many remote schools. This "traveling" job took him into the surroundings, but his knowledge of the people was intensified as he got to know the children and, through them, their families. In the library, he assumed a role as reader for the primary grades' story hour. He would hold books up and read to the children. Sometimes they would act out the stories. The older children would come to the library once a week to choose books, and he enjoyed making suggestions.[34]

Still never set out to write about actual people in his stories and novels. But his fictional characters were sometimes rooted in real personalities, just as some of the incidents reflected real-life happenings.[35] The language of the characters also derived from words and expressions that people used. An example of one child who greatly inspired Still was William Lee Parks, the prototype for the narrator in *River of Earth*. Still described him as a delightful child, about ten years old, who came from a fine family in Letcher County. The boy would ask the housemother for permission to come to Still's room and visit. Still seemed to be his surrogate father. "One day I was sitting at the typewriter and he came in and started telling me the time he like to got killed. He had many narrow accidents, like a log rolled over him once. As he told it, I just typed it." Later, Still published that boy's tale in a short piece for the *Courier-Journal* titled "I Likta Got Killed."[36] Most of his writing was not based on stories related to him by people he met, but they did inspire him.

The key to Still's prose was his talent for observing and listening. All of his exposure to the surroundings, the people, and their lives was becoming material for his fiction. But in 1935 he was more successful at publishing poems than stories.[37] A letter he wrote Red from Fairfax, where he had gone after the school year ended, showed how determined he was to make writing the center of his life. "Reckon I could write a short story if I busted two or three guts trying? Well, during this month I'm going to burn up my typewriter writing even if nothing ever comes of it."[38]

In making the move to Hindman, Still had found his place to live and had begun to make good friends. The landscape was inspiring the emerging poet. His walks through the county were contributing experiences from which he would draw his fiction; so too was his contact with the children at the school and his summer work with FERA. Being a librarian was important to him because the work provided room and board plus a sense of stability. The Settlement School gave him a home that he had not known since leaving Alabama, a place he could put down roots. But something more important to his career was happening in the mid-1930s. In answer to the question why he stayed at the Settlement School library for six years for so little pay, he said, "No amount of money could have substituted for the joy I felt from 1932 to 1939."[39]

11

Beyond the Hills, 1935–1940

The wind-drawn manes
And supple knees of the stallions fly the gate
Of hills to smooth meadows beyond the mountain wall;
And the strong mares drink in quivering haste
From the limestone waters, turning their anxious heads
Toward greener shores of grass, toward clattering passings
Of the fleet and proud. . . .

—From "Journey Beyond the Hills"

In February 1936 *The Atlantic Monthly* published the poem Still called his first major publication, "Child in the Hills."[1] Six months and twelve poems later, "Journey Beyond the Hills" appeared in the *Yale Review*. These two works provide insight into Still's early career. The stability that Hindman offered him in 1933 was welcome and necessary. The job gave him a home in Knott County. The landscape drew him like a magnet. The staff and children at the Settlement School welcomed him into the life of the place.

Still had been in the area for two years when *The Atlantic* accepted "Child in the Hills" in September 1935. The poem evokes a spirit of innocence that is secure and comfortable in routine. It ends by foreshadowing the child's growth and separation, but the final phrase, "the child did not go," shows an unbreakable bond. "Journey Beyond the Hills" embraces, even celebrates, the idea of leaving. The powerful image of the stallion racing down the mountainside contrasts with men who are imprisoned in the hills but have set "their hearts upon this journey never made." Together, these two poems illustrate a dilemma that Still faced soon after he immersed himself in the place that was to be his permanent home. He had become part of his surroundings; he appreciated its heritage and was comfortable in its spirit. Yet in 1935 he was already seeking "greener shores of grass." He did not intend to be a prisoner of the hills. He had set his heart on the journey beyond.

Still left Hindman when school was not in session. The first few years, he traveled to Alabama, Georgia, or Florida to visit family. But he aimed his sights higher than stopovers with relatives. For example, in August 1935, after he had completed the FERA assignment, he was off to Fairfax. He left Little Carr in Knott County on a Sunday afternoon and got to Alabama on Monday evening. The next day, "seized with a fit of wanderlust," he "caught the first bus going South." He went to Mobile, then across the Mississippi to New Orleans. His description to Red of the remarkable city quickly led to a report on his writing: "New Orleans was fried and par-boiled hell. No city I had ever seen quite prepared me for N'Orleans. . . . Got back here [Fairfax] today in time to crack out a poem called 'Fox Hunt on Defeated Creek' which I like very well."[2]

In the mid-1930s the two activities he enjoyed most were going places and writing poetry.[3] Gradually, through the latter half of the decade, he made personal literary contacts beyond Knott County, which he maintained for years. They were friends, mentors, teachers, agents, and editors who believed in his talent. One part of this wider world was entirely new to him, the world of writing colonies—"literary watering holes" he called them. Between 1936 and 1940 Still attended four different workshops: Blowing Rock School of English in North Carolina, Bread Loaf Writers' Conference at Middlebury College in Vermont, MacDowell Colony in New Hampshire, and Yaddo, an artists' community in Saratoga Springs, New York. At these places he found people who encouraged and inspired him plus experiences that challenged and stretched him. His relationships with several of those people are worth tracing.

During the 1935 Christmas vacation, Still made a trip to Rollins College in Florida at the invitation of his Settlement School coworker Frances Grover. Her father, Edwin Grover, was the librarian at Rollins College and the director of the Blowing Rock School of English, a summer school in the mountains of North Carolina.[4] Grover liked discovering young writing talent, and he had a wide network of literary connections. One of his many friendly contacts was Theda Kenyon, who was on the executive board of the Poetry Society of America. She was also a friend of Guy Loomis.

Late in 1935, Loomis and Kenyon had dined together in Brooklyn. When Loomis told her of Still, she immediately requested copies of his published poetry; she then nominated Still to the Poetry Society of America and related her discovery to Grover with these words: "We may look to James Still for *big things*."[5] Even before Still went with Frances to Florida for the Christmas holiday, Grover and his houseguests, one of whom was Kenyon, eagerly anticipated the visit. Seeing this opportunity as the break his young protégé needed, Loomis sent him money for the trip plus these words of encouragement: "Best of luck . . . anxious to hear how you came out and if it helped you any."[6]

At Grover's house, Still met a range of people, all of them interested in literature. On returning to Hindman, he wrote Redmond:

> Had a nice visit with Jesse Rittenhouse who said very kind things about my verse and read aloud to me from them. . . . Edwin Granberry (O. Henry Memorial short story winner several years ago with his "Trip to Czardis") was an interesting fellow. I let him see my short story No. 1. . . . He's going to write me a letter with the whole-truth-and-nothing-but-the-truth concerning it and my ability (if any) to command the short story. So my fate hangs in the balance. And I'm not particularly giving a damn.[7]

That trip to Winter Park was pivotal to Still's career. It showed that important literary figures would take an interest in him even though he had published only a handful of poems—ten, to be exact. It also showed him that living in Hindman did not mean he had to be isolated from writers. A less direct lesson, but valuable in the long run, was the hint that short stories sold better than poems.

His words may have claimed that he cared nothing about his fate as a writer, but his actions indicated otherwise. He was making plans. At that holiday meeting, Grover invited Still to attend the 1936 summer program in North Carolina. Noted professors would lead the classes and would be supported by distinguished lecturers, including Marjorie Kinnan Rawlings. Still agreed. Grover, however, did not wait until the summer to begin creating a bond with the young man. As the two corresponded during the first months of 1936, Grover gained trust and respect for Still because on May 4 he proposed that Still enroll in Granberry's summer class for four weeks, then take over as teacher when Granberry left early to lead a course at the University of Florida. In exchange, Grover would give him a tuition scholarship of seventy dollars. The only expense to Still would be the room and board of thirteen dollars per week.

There is no indication that Still took Grover's offer to replace Granberry, but he did go to the Blowing Rock School of English in the summer of 1936. A flyer lists the teachers: Granberry, Kenyon, and Grover himself, plus distinguished lecturers Rawlings, author of *South Moon Under* and *Golden Apples;* Dr. Bertha Wright, professor of American literature at the University of London, England; Herschel Brickell, literary editor of the *New York Evening Post;* and Kathleen Morehouse, author of *Rain on the Just.* A special visitor was Margaret Mitchell.[8] Considering that by July 1936 Still had published only twenty-three poems and two short stories, he probably felt out of his league in such company. He was relatively young and not socially outgoing. Grover had described him to one literary agent as "a very modest and rather shy fellow."[9]

His public shyness is not evident in a description of the summer experience that Still preserved in this brief, rough manuscript:

> The author of a "bucolic hill-billy" book of poetry found himself in the lofty mountain coolness of Blowing Rock, North Carolina. There was something called the "Blowing Rock School of English" holding sessions there, and though connected only in the most casual way, the poet found himself there at the invitation of the director, whose daughter he knew. . . . He lived in a rustic cabin of a tourist camp, built of rough slabs of lumber, ate at the country table with the summer-permanent guests of the camps. There he spent his evenings with three beauty parlor operators who operated in a Miami hotel in winter, in Blowing Rock in summer. They imparted to him their wisdom of resort life, gave him manicures, pedicures, buttermilk massage, worked to restore circulation and hair to his already balding head. By night they were three plain girls . . . by day dolls in high heels, sheer hose, neat and tucked and pinned. . . .
>
> And the poet, sitting in on the class held by the then secretary

of the Poetry Society of America [Theda Kenyon], was told that he was "a flash in the pan." An autograph party was arranged at the seasonal bookshop, but on the day was informed that the books ordered had not arrived, clearly meaning that those desiring autographed copies would also not arrive. He attended with an author and his wife a cocktail party, sans cocktails. The guests sat glumly in the parlor sipping ginger ale. But he and his companions were spirited into the kitchen and surreptitiously served a jigger of Old Crow. . . . And at the "school" on being introduced to someone was informed, "Oh, I know about you. From the person who corrects your poetry." The poet was nonplussed.[10]

This first workshop experience was a trial for Still. His oblique allusion to having been considered a poet in need of tutoring is the closest he came to relating the incident that disturbed him most. Kenyon, who thought of Still as her own discovery, shifted roles; instead of his mentor, she became his teacher. Still resisted and was so offended that he left Blowing Rock early. His reaction resulted in one of the most important friendships of Still's career: Rawlings took note of the young man's early departure.[11]

The story developed this way: Kenyon, in her poetry class, had informed the young man that he needed to learn more about metrics before he could be a competent poet. Still strongly resisted her advice and was insulted that she would offer it. The first letter Still received from Rawlings shows that she understood the situation and sympathized with Still. More importantly, she recognized his talent and potential, as evident in this excerpt:

My dear James Still,

I cannot tell you how wise I consider you to turn away from all formal training, particularly in your poetry. When I first told you that your own critical judgment was sufficient for your purposes, I did not dream that exactly the opposite advice had been given you by others. I was shocked when Mr. Granberry told me that Miss Kenyon had told you that you "must" take her course—learn metrics and what-not. . . .

Your lessons, James, are in your Kentucky hills. They are in the waters of Troublesome Creek. They are in the strange minds and destinies of your mountain people. They are most of all in your own innate good taste in writing—and in your own heart, sensitive and raw.

What would Walt Whitman have done with "metrics"? He was a poet, and he sang. . . . I beg you, go on writing from your deeper well of beauty. . . .

You have a gift that, at its best, satisfies and stirs me exactly as does the best of Wordsworth, of Whitman, of Keats and Shelley. I am not afraid to tell you this, because your natural modesty and humility make you immune from any of the dangers of praise. You will always, I am sure, accept from praise only that encouragement, that stimulation, that incentive to go on working.[12]

On July 31 Still responded to Rawlings with sincere gratitude for her words of encouragement. With uncharacteristic overstatement, he assured her that he was serious about writing, "as serious as death." Then he alluded to the incident and concluded with a delightful country image showing that he was over the problem: "Your letter helped me to see the other side and now I am sufficiently contrite to forgive everybody, all the way around. . . . It was no more than a landslide in a doddle-bugs cone."[13]

This incident initiated a correspondence between Still and Rawlings that included more than thirty letters over twelve years. At times the exchange was almost confessional, describing the difficulty that one or the other was having in writing a story. For example, as Still was moving from poetry to prose, he expressed doubts to Rawlings: "It goes along like a mountain road. I never know what is around the next curve, and feel I do not want to know. . . . Prose is a strange nag for me to ride. I am aware that my writing too often has the austerity of poetry. This may be a dark fault. Or it may have some advantages. . . . I am not sure of anything in this novel. I am writing it out of my heart."[14] Rawlings responded, "I warn you, there is not the peculiar satisfaction in doing fiction that there is in poetry. The poetry is so very personal, that when you have said the special thing you wanted to say, you are relieved. Fiction is more objective, and there is in it the pain of detachment."[15]

She opened that letter with a humorous command that Still was fond of quoting: "I told Frances Grover to give you my very best and to tell you I had loved the things you had been doing, and to be sure and tell you to go to hell for not having stopped to see me at Christmas time." Still's response began with good news: "I did go to hell as you suggested. Have been in it all week facing a deadline. The Viking Press is to bring out *Hounds on the Mountain* [his first book] early in June."[16] A year later Rawlings wrote about the gift copy of *Hounds* she had received: "I have treasured and given it to others, and read aloud from it whenever I thought I had an audience that would appreciate it. Robert Frost was in Gainesville this winter, and we spoke of your verse. He liked it immensely . . . after we had talked of another poet, Wallace Stevens . . . and I had said that he had a great gift, Frost said, 'Well, give me James Still.'"[17]

That first workshop in 1936 gave Still this special friendship with Rawlings, but it also introduced him to the importance of networking, self-promotion, and prioritizing time to write. In spite of the setback he experienced at the tongue of Kenyon, he continued to correspond with Grover and accept his help. The following Christmas he once again visited Winter Park. At this point he was trying to publish a volume of poems. His most promising conversations were with Marshall Best at Viking Press, who seemed to be stringing him along. Best had written to the young man, "I have read and liked your poems a great deal, and others have read them with admiration also. They are worthy of publication as a book and they would be a credit to any publishing list which included them." About the novel that Still was working on, Best wrote, "The language is always right, sometimes extremely beautiful. Your feeling for the setting and for the people in their setting seems perfect. You manage to achieve a reconstruction within a narrow frame which has the authentic color in every detail, and yet escapes becoming academic, as a genre painting is apt to do. Instead it remains warmly felt and alive throughout." The concern that Best expressed was the danger for Still in writing a longer work and keeping "the quiet pitch" without being monotonous. He would need to develop the story so as to change the tempo along the way.[18]

Still internalized the critique and suggestions. Unlike Kenyon, Best had not said that Still should take a class in prose or novel writing, but the message was clear that his prose would prove itself only when he wrote a novel. Also, Best put Still's name forward as a candidate for Bread Loaf. By March 10, 1937, Viking Press had accepted *Hounds on the Mountain* for publication. By late June, Still was back at the Blowing Rock School of English, this time as a published poet. Later that summer (August 18–September 1) he went to Bread Loaf Writers' Conference in Vermont, as one of seven fellows attending. There he roomed with Robert Francis.

Francis was only five years older than Still, so he was not a mentor like Grover or a model like Rawlings. The two men were peers and friends. Francis had lived in Amherst, Massachusetts, since 1926 when he went there to teach high-school English. A year later he gave up teaching to write full time and moved to an isolated spot in the countryside to find the peace and time to do so. He described that life as "obscure and happy-go-lucky," but he did not "drop altogether out of sight."[19] When they met at Bread Loaf, Francis had recently published his first book of poetry.[20] The fellowship to the conference, he believed, was his reward.

In his autobiography, Francis said that the highlight of his 1937 Bread Loaf experience was having James Still as his roommate:

> Full of earthy tales of the Kentucky hills, he was wonderful company, once I had got to know him beneath his protective shell of shyness and taciturnity. . . . It was my first experience of being with a fellow-writer at work. In those years I used to start work on a poem with pencil or pen, and move to the typewriter when I began to feel anything permanent in what I was doing. But Still, I think, composed at the typewriter. It was all very much a matter of sentence by sentence with him. He would work on a sentence or short group of sentences until it satisfied him, then tear off the strip of paper and add it to a little pile of sentences already written. Someone was writing prose with as much attention to detail as I was trying to write poetry. What was less obvious was how every detail in his stories was functional, no matter how casual it appeared. He had to point this out to me time and again. What was easiest to appreciate and relish was the delicious speech of his Kentucky mountain people.[21]

These observations about Still's personality and his method of work offer insight into how others saw him at the time—a quiet young man from the Kentucky hills who enjoyed telling stories to a willing listener, a poet who wrote prose with care and intensity.

Although Robert Francis was the most important connection Still made that summer in Vermont, he came in contact with a number of known literary figures there, including Paul Green, James T. Farrell,

Archibald MacLeish, Louis Untermeyer, the director Theodore Morrison, and Frost. Still did not return to Bread Loaf as a fellow, but he did visit again in 1940 when the fellows included John Ciardi, Carson McCullers, and Eudora Welty. It was that year that he met W. H. Auden and Katherine Anne Porter.[22]

The following summer, 1938, Still attended MacDowell Colony in Peterborough, New Hampshire. He began the application process in January with an appeal to Grover who, in turn, asked some of his connections to put in a good word for him. By then, Still had more than sixty publications, including ten short stories. On April 27, 1938, Grover wrote that Still's application to MacDowell had been approved. When Still answered, he was filled with appreciation for Grover's help and full of pride in his most recent success. The *Saturday Evening Post* had accepted a short story, "paying a sizeable chunk of the U.S. Mint for it. $500." Even more impressive than the payment was Still's refusal to change the story when the editor complained that the hero got killed in the last paragraph. Still told Grover that the editor wanted right to triumph over wrong; he wanted sweetness and light to reign. "He asked me to change it, and sent the story back. I refused. So he asked for it back, and accepted it."[23] Considering that Hindman Settlement School paid James Still only $83.86 per month, or a total of $754.74 per year between 1936 and 1938, $500 for one story must have seemed like a pot of gold. Plus he had kept his ending and thus his artistic integrity; this news was momentous coming from the shy Kentucky writer.

Still was in New Hampshire between June 15 and August 13; at least part of that time, he had a fellowship.[24] Once there, Still wrote to Frances Grover, describing his accommodations at MacDowell:

> My studio is the Youngstown. It sits in a clearing of a great pine forest where the wind goes woo-oo-oo the day long. And as the enormous grounds of the MacDowell Association are also a bird and game sanctuary, many little creatures wander about. Yesterday a deer walked blandly across my yard. The hermit thrush—the first ones I've seen—sing all hours.
>
> My studio is one large room. A huge red rug covers the floor. There's a table twelve feet long, and for once in a lifetime, there is room to spread everything out. The fireplace is also twelve feet from one end to the other, and on the porch is an abundance of wood, ready to burn. The room has eight large French windows, four small ones. A bed, heaped with pillows. Two

rocking chairs. Two straight ones. A small dining table. On the wall hangs an autograph-board, bearing the names of those who've worked in this house. To list a few, beginning 1913: Willa Cather, Thornton Wilder, William Rose Benet, etc. . . .

At meals, breakfast and dinner, we have a pleasant social time. (Lunch is delivered at the studio). After supper, Cowboy Pool, or Croquet. The mallets for mine. Poets, novelists, composers, artists—all knocking balls on the grass.[25]

The description Still wrote to Red in July was less detailed and complimentary but much livelier. He objected to the prevalence of the New England Republicans and described them as "loud of mouth, Hoover-loving, Landon-worshipping, Roosevelt-hating." He pointed out "three Russian-reds on these here grounds to leven [sic] the dough." Plus Swedes and Germans, "a various assortment of fotched-on Jews from across the waters, and even a thin scattering of Americans."[26] It was quite a scene for the young man from the hills of Kentucky.

Still did accomplish work at MacDowell. As he told Red, he "knocked off a 5550-word short story the first two weeks." But he also felt homesick. Though he met a lot of people, the only friend he made that summer was John Gould Fletcher, who wrote to Jim sometime after he left the colony. Fletcher's complimentary description affords a look into how others saw Still.

Your personality, with its blend of complete integrity and love for your own local background, is not a common kind of thing in America. I believe that you are going to do fine things— perhaps in prose rather than in poetry, for your temperament seems to be deliberating and reflective, rather than emotional and lyrical. But you will always find it hard to satisfy yourself, and you are by nature so sensitive as to be almost unable to protect yourself from the world by means of warding off things that upset you.

I am very sorry that I upset you on the last night we were together. I can only apologize and say that I was under a strain at the time.[27]

How Fletcher upset the young man is unknown, but reference to this incident shows that Still was very sensitive. By his own admission, he felt alone at MacDowell and sent a short letter to Robert Francis, insisting that he come visit. He described himself as "homesick here in this far green corner of the earth" and urged his friend to hurry.[28] Francis did visit him for a few hours in the cabin in the woods. They exchanged thoughts on one another's current work and shared the meager lunch that was delivered at Still's door.[29]

The place held to traditions of generosity. Mrs. Edward MacDowell herself invited each colonist to tea. On his way to his obligatory visit, Still mistakenly entered at the rear of her house. The staff had to take him to the hallway leading to her study. The floor was freshly waxed and polished; he slipped on a throw rug, fell to the floor, and cracked his head. Mrs. MacDowell graciously assisted him and attempted to comfort his embarrassment by relating a story of a memorable fall she once had. When she stumbled down the grand staircase of the Paris Opera House, her dignity was restored only when a handsome officer helped her up, then walked her in to be seated. Her gallant escort had been Archduke Franz Ferdinand of Austria.[30]

Another more lively and younger lady that Still met that summer was Joy Davidman, who later married C. S. Lewis. Soon after leaving MacDowell, she wrote Still a letter full of memories of "the Colony," as she called it. She stayed on for two weeks after Still had left and spent the time finishing a play and improving her beer-drinking. She mentioned several of their mutual friends. Finally, she told him of the biggest news of the season: one morning Jeff Levy sprinted to breakfast, slipped on a pebble, wrenched his arm, and broke his ankle—becoming "an interesting invalid." The energy and flair in her newsy letter illustrated the drastic difference between herself and Still. She complimented his *Post* story for its "quiet strength and precision of detail" while she described her own style as splashing colors about.[31]

Later, Still wrote to Grover that he liked the MacDowell Colony experience and "found the place mighty stimulating—maybe a bit too much so." But the stimulation meant that his writing was finding success. His horizons were expanding, and he requested that Grover act as a reference for a Guggenheim Fellowship application.[32] By April 1939, Still was again thinking of summer. He considered returning to MacDowell, but the great New England hurricane of September 1938 had damaged the place so extensively that the 1939 session was canceled.[33] As a result, he applied to Yaddo in Saratoga Springs, New York.[34] He knew little about Yaddo except that some people at MacDowell had recommended it. The more critical information for Still, however, was that Yaddo gave fellowships to everyone accepted.

Still's stay at Yaddo began on August 5 and lasted until September 20, 1939.[35] There he met Delmore Schwartz. Until this point, most writers Still had befriended were older than he. This man was seven years younger. Also, he was from New York, Jewish, married, and a serious drinker.[36] If Schwartz caught Still's attention, the opposite was also true. In a letter to Mark Van Doren, Schwartz described the Yaddo participants of 1939.[37] He set Still apart from the group:

> A generalization about writers drawn from the writers who have been here [at Yaddo] this summer . . . makes me sick with the idea of how, as a class, writers are self-indulgent, full of self-pity, forever seeking reassurance, constantly occupied with what they consider the proper conditions of work, and the next thing to invalids in their demands upon life. One fine exception was a Kentucky poet and fiction writer named James Still, who had recently refused to allow *The Saturday Evening Post* to change the ending of a story for which they offered him $600 when changed, a refusal which seems to amaze some of the other people here.

Defying the request of the *Post* concerning "Bat Flight" was a story that Still enjoyed telling, and it had made an impression on Schwartz. This retelling added to the drama and showed Still as exceptional.

By September 1939, Still was in the last phase of putting his novel *River of Earth* together. He had so much confidence in Schwartz's assessment that he left the manuscript with him when he departed from Yaddo. Schwartz took the task seriously and wrote a two-page typed response to Still on September 29. He began, "The book is pretty nearly perfect. All the episodes ring true, all the characters come to life, and it is moving just when you want it to be so. Best of all, it has a rhythm, in the style of the prose, which is very beautiful and which makes the whole thing like one big prose poem." His major objection was the title, which he found too "poetic sounding." He thought it should be "a little more like the language and the style of the book."[38] Just as Still did not change the ending of the story for the *Post*, he did not change the title of the book to suit his new friend.

The last extant letter from Schwartz to Still shows that they had acquaintances in common. At the Modern Language Association (MLA) conference in New Orleans, Schwartz had visited with Cleanth Brooks, John Crowe Ransom, and Allen Tate. By then, Schwartz felt as if he had a stake in Still's novel, so he had mentioned it to these people and had even solicited a promise from Ransom that he would try to review it in the *Kenyon Review*. Still was reciprocating. In his closing, Schwartz commented that he was receiving letters from various publishers thanks to Still's putting in a good word for him. He was impressed that a writer from the Kentucky hills could know so many: "How in Heaven's name do you happen to be corresponding with all these people when your own publisher is Viking and you live two thousand miles away?"[39]

Though the distance is exaggerated, the question is valid—how could James Still be in communication with so many professional people, how could he know personally so many writers, when he lived in almost complete isolation from the literary world? The answer is that between 1935 and 1941 he lived in two worlds, one of them the Hindman Settlement School and the other a wide world of writers' workshops in the Northeast plus a network of connections sustained by friends in Florida and New York. His journeys out of eastern Kentucky were expanding his personal experiences and strengthening his professional connections. As long as he could afford to travel, why would he not?

In the summer of 1940 Still once again attended Yaddo. This trip yielded him the most special literary friend of his career—Katherine Anne Porter. Though considerably older than Still, Porter was young at heart, a passionate and outgoing person. Before devoting herself to serious writing, she had worked as an actress, singer, secretary, and journalist.[40] Though her major awards came late in her career, the stories she was writing in the 1930s illustrated the close attention she paid to every word and the perfection of form she achieved. Still certainly enjoyed reading and praising them. In an early letter, he described two stories as evidence of her genius: "Only K.A.P. could have written them."[41]

Although sixteen years older than Still, Porter never acted as his teacher or mentor. Yet her craftsmanship influenced his developing prose style. He also had an influence on her, which was more about life choices than literary techniques. He inspired in her an appreciation for place. Unlike Still, Rawlings, and Francis, Porter was not strongly attached to a specific house or region. She was born in Texas but lived many places, including Chicago, Greenwich Village, Denver, California, and Mexico. At the time they met, Still's attachment to place, to Knott County, was strong and becoming stronger.

Porter's first letter to Still is reminiscent of his initial exchange with

Rawlings when he had abruptly left Blowing Rock. Still had left Yaddo early, but not before giving Porter copies of his poetry book and his novel.

Dear James Still:

You disappeared, in your habit, suddenly and no doubt rightly; but I did not know this until my note to you thanking you for your lovely books was returned to me. . . .

In the South, at least, the poets write the best prose, too. It seems hardly fair, but there it is. Your novel is superb, quietly and deeply glorious; I have read it twice, for pure pleasure. It is an extension of the poems, as the poems are the further comment on the experience which made the novel. I love the evenness and unity. . . . I am so grateful to you for giving me these books; they should be read together. . . . [42]

Still's respectful response on October 21 explained his early departure and expressed gratitude for her comments. "How happy and grateful I was for your message, and for all your generous words. I left Yaddo because I couldn't keep looking at my typewriter day after day with nothing happening. Knew suddenly I had to leave. Perhaps the atmosphere was too stimulating. So I came back to my Kentucky corner."[43]

Still regained his peace of mind by working in his garden and tending chickens on Dead Mare Branch. The farming activities suited him and helped his writing. Porter's next letter showed that she too was seeking a homeplace; she was planning to buy a piece of property with an old house typical of upstate New York: "Georgian style, pegged together, with a great old fire place and bake oven in one big square room . . . small barns, and good fertile fields. . . . Someday I hope you will visit me here, and that I may see your house, too. I remember what you told me about it."[44] Still's response was joyful: "By your letter I know you have longed for this home of your very own. This upstate New York farm has been in store for you, mellowing, weathering, tree-growing, getting lived in, and it is for you now. Your PROMISED LAND." He followed with details of his own trees and plants and promised to send her special seeds and a handmade dulcimer.[45]

These summer workshops between 1935 and 1940 gave Still the opportunity to travel, to reach beyond the mountains, to meet people that would be important to him personally and to his career. During that time, when Still was living in a quiet corner of Kentucky, his local connections were growing stronger. Yet he needed the inspiration and stimulation of the outside world to help him define his subject matter. In 1935 the emerging writer required guidance from mentors like Edwin Grover; by 1941 the established writer of three books had a multitude of acquaintances and a handful of close writing friends. Most of his connections came from beyond the hills, but he also made a few literary friends closer to home. Three very important ones were the Kentucky writer Elizabeth Madox Roberts and the writing couple James Stokely from east Tennessee and Wilma Dykeman from western North Carolina.

Elizabeth Madox Roberts and James Still had much in common, though she was twenty-five years his senior. She lived in the small town of Springfield, Kentucky, in the hill country on the edge of the bluegrass. Her first book was a small volume of poetry, *Under the Tree.* Over the next two decades she published two more volumes of poetry, two collections of stories, and seven novels, among them the bestseller *The Time of Man.* In addition to sharing the same general setting for their works, Roberts and Still shared the same editor and publisher, Marshall Best at Viking Press.

How he first contacted her is not known, but on April 17, 1937, Still made the 160-mile trip from Hindman to Springfield and visited Roberts at her house, Elenores. He took away a signed copy of her 1932 short story collection, *The Haunted Mirror,* with the following inscription: "To James Still—Who spent a morning with me in Ellen Chesser's country and brought me much pleasure—Elizabeth Madox Roberts." Since Still was not a man to exaggerate, his account of that visit to Edwin Grover shows just how memorable it had been: "Had a wonderful visit with Elizabeth Madox Roberts recently. We drove out into the country around Springfield, scene of 'Time of Man' and she told me about her original idea for the book. She gave me one of her books with a nice message inside. She has been sick a long time, and she looked very thin and worn. But my morning with her was one of the best things that ever happened to me."[46] The first letter from Roberts to Still ends, "Your call with me was the bright spot in a week of difficulties. I am glad that you liked being here and I hope that you will come here again." Her praise for *Hounds on the Mountain* must have been especially valuable: "I find the verses beautiful, contemplative, a personal record that mirrors the hills themselves—the reflection being in the impression more than in the mere physical descriptive picture." A year later, her letter referenced two of Still's short stories—"So Large a Thing as Seven" and "Mole Bane"—which she jokingly suggested were inspired by the troublesome moles on her property. That letter closed with this compliment: "What a gift of story-telling you have, the emphases shifted and delicately adjusted to the needs of the theme."[47]

How directly Roberts influenced Still's writing is hard to know, but he certainly valued her friendship. Years later, when Jerry Williamson asked him about their literary connection, Still responded that he was her friend and he treasured her letters. He thought *The Time of Man* an exceptional work. Roberts, he said, was "a genius of sorts and her books could only have been written by a woman of great literary and intuitive powers."[48] The letters that he treasured were only eight because Roberts was already in poor health when they met; she died in March 1941.[49]

Two other writer-friends who valued and helped promote James Still were James Stokely and his wife, Wilma Dykeman.[50] Stokely was seven years younger than Still, had grown up in Newport, Tennessee, and was educated at the University of Tennessee. To Still, Stokely must have been a combination of Jesse Stuart and Dare Redmond. He was thoughtful, perceptive, and fun loving but was also outgoing and prone to the dramatic, as seen when he invited Still to visit: "If you like a football game, why don't you blindfold yourself and truckle with me to feel Alabama's red heart's blood spilled on the breast of the Volunteers. There is nothing like a good old-fashioned bullfight." In September 1940 he wrote with zest in describing his "mountain lass," Wilma, and invited Still to their wedding: "We are to be married Saturday, October the Twelfth, [in Asheville] and our happiness will be complete if we can persuade the Hermit of Noback Hollow to give up his quite honorable job of writing for a weekend."[51] Stokely and Dykeman enjoyed a happy marriage and coauthored a number of books about the region. As the 1930s closed, they shared with Still a growing friendship, a common dedication to the region, and a passion for writing. They remained friends for life.

By 1940, the year *River of Earth* was published, James Still had achieved the balance he needed—a juxtaposition of rootedness in his place with intermittent journeys out in order to keep his creative juices flowing. He was making connections and friends from far and near. He was busy, he was productive, and he was gaining a reputation.

12

A Man Singing to Himself

The literary juices were flowing.

—James Still

Still was not a man who needed an active social life. Whether attending writers' workshops or working in the Settlement School library, he kept his distance from people. That may account for his tendency to be oversensitive, or perhaps that sensitivity led to his shyness. More than once Still acknowledged that the summer workshop atmosphere was too stimulating for him. At least twice he left earlier than expected. His introverted nature kept him from being entirely comfortable with groups. Plus he needed the familiarity of his surroundings, the quietness of his own place, and time to think and work. The remote little town of Hindman was where he was finding his material and himself. In the last years of the 1930s Still was a homing pigeon—he looked forward to the lofty heights and unfamiliar territory of a world beyond the hills, but his ultimate aim was always to get back home.[1]

The years between 1935 and 1941 were the most productive in James Still's writing career. His publications included a total of fifty-nine poems and twenty-five short stories in twenty-seven different periodicals, plus three books with Viking in three different genres: *Hounds on the Mountain* (poetry), *River of Earth* (novel), and *On Troublesome Creek* (short stories).[2] When he negotiated with May Stone to stay on at Hindman a second year without a salary because he wanted to write, he could not have foreseen the level of productivity he would achieve before 1940. Some combination of the living arrangements and the job responsibilities at Hindman, along with support from patrons like Guy Loomis and mentors like Edwin Grover, had made that happen. But another important element was the young man's determination. He had devoted time to writing and to maintaining professional connections. His efforts were paying off.

Hindman was an ideal setting for the mental and emotional state he needed to be productive. After returning from an active summer, he wrote to Red: "Back to the hills, the Settlement School, the library. I fall into a routine like wagon wheels into a rut."[3] Later in his life, Still was fond of telling about his work at Hindman School, as he does in "A Man Singing to Himself": "I remained at the Hindman Settlement School for six years [1933–1939]. The library was excellent, the students were eager, and the staff was highly motivated. . . . My first three years at the Hindman Settlement School I received no salary; however, the Depression waning, the school paid me a few dollars for the next three years. Averaged out, I worked six years for six cents a day."[4] Sixty years after the experience, Still, not surprisingly, romanticized his description of his early work at Hindman. He made the job seem more attractive than it probably was and the salary less than it actually was.

His letters to Red at the time show the work as trying but not difficult. The following excerpts reveal typical frustrations accompanying any job as an educator: "Jan. 14, 1936: My library assistant (student) didn't return after Christmas so they are now in the process of providing me with another. But it's taking a mighty long damn time for them to do it. Meantime I do all the work. But I have drawn the line at sweeping the floor. . . . Dec. 3, 1936: the school days roll by. Have been doing double work this week as one of the teachers is sick."[5] He was also frustrated at what he considered the miserly administration of the place. Elizabeth Watts, for example, would not give him even ten cents for a pack of index cards needed for cataloging. But, he confessed, high ethics and practicality backed the school's frugality: "Every penny that came in here went to the right place."[6] He also liked that the administrators did not tell him how to do his job; nor did they interfere in the classroom. The job was neither stimulating nor stressful. It brought him satisfaction, stability, free room and board, and a little travel money.

The compensation was never high or even adequate, but it is easy to refute his claim that for the first six years his salary averaged six cents per day.[7] The first two years he was a volunteer. Hindman began paying him a salary in that third year. Loomis opened his letter to Still on August 14, 1935, with these words: "Glad to hear the Settlement has awakened to your value to them and will arrange for a salary." Clara Standish had come to the school the same year as Still, 1933. When she took a job back home in 1935, she wrote to Still, congratulating him on "getting fat, having so many poems accepted, inheriting my room, and receiving a $75 salary."[8] Although his exact salary is impossible to determine, it averaged a good bit more than six cents per day. His tax return for 1938, his last year working there, shows his Hindman Settlement School income as $675.00 for nine months, or $75 per month.[9] If he received that much for four years, his average would have been at least $1.25 per day. Add on room and board, travel money, and the help provided by Loomis, and the deal was not bad. Beginning in 1936, he was also adding money to his budget from magazine payments and later from book royalties. It was not a way to get rich, but that was never his goal.

Nor was it his goal to become involved in the public life of Hindman. Since the school was directly adjacent, the town could not be avoided. No doubt he had invitations to join churches and community groups, but he was not inclined. He described Hindman to Red: "Our little frontier town is fast civilizing itself. We now have a Lion's Club and the Boy Scouts. What is civilization more than this? I have refused to join the Lion's Club, branding myself as a most peculiar and antisocial person."[10] Perhaps his retiring nature kept him from becoming involved in civic activities, but he was also protecting his time.

He had the full-time job at the school library. He got along with his colleagues, but even at school he did not socialize. Jess Stoddart in *The Story of Hindman Settlement School* reported that in those years, Still probably felt excluded from the social life of the female teachers. But in a similar way, the middle-aged female staff would have felt "uncomfortable having a young man in his twenties at their tea parties, waffle suppers, and such."[11] He was friendly with Clara Standish and Frances Grover, but his social interaction consisted mainly of corresponding with people related to his writing, especially those he met at summer workshops. When he first came to Hindman, he had spent time with Jethro Amburgey and his family, but in 1936 Amburgey went to Morehead State Teachers College to pursue a degree in manual training. They wrote each other but rarely visited during those years.

Though a loner, James Still was not cut off from the outside world, which was available to him through the post office. He used the mail like many people use electronic messaging today.[12] He wrote letters every day. Those that survive show the personal relationships he was initiating or maintaining. That correspondence also reveals his emerging connections with editors of periodicals, literary agents, and publishers.

In later years, Still talked about publishing as though it were as natural as breathing. One familiar comment conveys his casual approach: "If an editor returns a manuscript, I don't feel upset about it. They're not buying turnips today. Maybe next year."[13] When Still began sending manuscripts out, a lot of people were not buying turnips. But he kept sending. At first he submitted poems to the magazines that he had read when he was at LMU. Rejections came. Bits from response letters give the flavor:[14]

> October 26, 1934 I am accepting "Mountain Dulcimer" on one condition: if you send me something better in the next six months. Lambert Davis *The Virginia Quarterly Review*
>
> May 31, 1935 . . . we couldn't use this poem. Malcolm Cowley *The New Republic*
>
> July 15, 1935 I am returning your poems with regret that we cannot find a place for them. . . . They show a great deal of power, and I hope that you will let us see more. Cleanth Brooks *The Southern Review*
>
> October 26, 1935 There is a great deal about these poems which we admire, but as a group they do not measure up. Robert Penn Warren *The Southern Review*

Six months into 1935, Still's efforts began to pay off; poems began to appear in the *Virginia Quarterly Review,* the *Saturday Review of Literature, Poetry,* the *Sewanee Review,* and *The New Republic.* By the fall, Still received the letter from Edward Weeks praising "Child in the Hills" for its "authentic folk feeling, and for a diction which will appeal to readers far removed from your own hills." The most heartening message Still took from Weeks's letter was assurance that *The Atlantic* looked forward to reading more of his work.[15]

Even as the poems appeared, Edwin Grover urged Still to write stories. Prose was what publishers wanted because it sold better than poetry. He had sent Grover the manuscript of "On Defeated Creek" after he left Florida in December 1935. Grover gave the story to Granberry, who declared that Still had a "real story-teller's gift, a personal and dramatic style, and a rich fund of materials from which stories are made." Grover liked the story too but recommended that Still "at once begin planning for a novel." Still seemed genuinely surprised and appreciative that Grover had been "willing to spend so much time and energy" reading it.[16]

In early February Grover wrote Still news of another protégé, Maxeda Hess, whom he had connected with a literary agent: Carol Hill in New York City. Grover strongly suggested that Still send "On Defeated Creek" to Hill to see what kind of interest she could find.[17] Aside from those of Grover and Granberry, the reactions to the story were not positive. Still received a letter from Hill, dated May 27, 1936, which returned the story and gave the bleak news that she had sent it to six magazines, and all of them had rejected it.[18] Those rejections would not have made much difference to Still because in the interim he had had a story accepted by his choice magazine, *The Atlantic Monthly.*

His second publication in *The Atlantic* appeared in June 1936. He had sent them two stories, one of which met with a warm reception in a letter from Edward Weeks:

> *The Atlantic* has always had a soft spot in its heart for the Old Primitives, and your mountaineering sketches come to fill a place which has not been well occupied since Lucy Furman last turned our way. Of your two brief narratives, our preference is strongly in favor of "All their Ways are Dark." The atmosphere is almost perfectly transcribed, and the scene will have a certain bearing upon those many households which have been overcrowded in these lean years. I am happy to accept it for *The Atlantic,* and hope that it argues well for other contributions to come our way.

By the time Still received this letter, he knew his "literary juices were flowing." On April 27 Still wrote to Grover, casually including a copy of the acceptance letter from Weeks, and mentioning that he would be making a quick trip to New York on May 8. The invitation to the city had come from Loomis via Kenyon, who began, "There is a matter of real importance, and I hope joy, of which Mr. Loomis and I wish to talk to you." The plan was for him to take the night train on Friday, May 8, and return on Sunday. Of course, Loomis would pay for the trip.[19]

Still asked Grover for the names of people he should meet in the city. Grover answered immediately, overjoyed at both *The Atlantic*'s decision and the planned trip. The contrast between Still's letter telling the news and Grover's reaction to it was striking; Still was calm and understated, while Grover was exuberant. He attached a list of eleven contacts that Still should make. He even wrote to a number of those, including Viking Press; Macmillan Company; and Dodd, Mead & Company. Since Still was in New York only Saturday and Sunday, he was able to make few connections.[20]

Meanwhile, *The Atlantic*'s acceptance of "All Their Ways Are Dark" showed that both his poems and his stories could reach a national audience through a respected journal. A letter from Weeks followed in August, accepting "Job's Tears" with praise: it is "the longest specimen of your prose that has yet come my way, has the delicious dialect and the aspect of misery which seem to go hand in hand in the mountains. But it also has an underlying vitality and a fillip [*sic*] at the close which gives your sketch additional taste and color."[21] Weeks did not accept every story Still sent; for example, he found "The Egg Tree" too grim. However, between September 1935 and November 1939 the magazine published two of Still's poems and five short stories.[22]

The Atlantic Monthly was also launching a book department, and by the end of 1936 it was clear that they wanted Still, if he published a book of narratives, to do so with them. Paul Hoffman, assistant to Weeks, wrote at the end of 1936, taking credit for discovering Still by picking "Child in the Hills" from the "daily influx of manuscripts." He had been transferred to the book department and was trying to solicit promising writers. "Having only yesterday read the manuscript of *Job's Tears* and reread *All Their Ways Are Dark,* I am wondering whether you have ever seriously considered incorporating some of your fine material in the larger pattern of a book." If so, he goes on, be sure to send the manuscript to the Atlantic Monthly Press.[23] In fact, Still had been considering a book.

By July 1936, Still was pursuing book publication with Viking Press. Apparently, he had written to Marshall Best and sent him *The Atlantic* story. Best was eager to see his novel, which he did not yet have. Still must have asked about publishing a volume of poetry, but Best was hesitant. He hinted that he might consider the poetry if a novel were on the way. His next letter was more direct: "I have read and liked your poems a great deal. . . . They are worthy of publication as a book. . . . Unfortunately, however, there is almost no chance for a book of lyrics to pay its own way. . . . If we could be sure that you had a novel coming which we would want to publish, there would be no hesitation about our taking the poems."[24] By mid-February, Still drafted a letter to Best that would force his own hand. He expressed understanding of the press's desire to hold off on the poems until they could see parts of the novel. He then announced that, under separate cover, he had sent two chapters that would present the essence of the novel "because they best show the two extremes in the lives of the Baldridges—starvation and abundance. It is a first person story. I have tried to keep it quiet and honest, and ture [sic] to the social structure of mountain life."[25]

Marshall Best responded on February 24:

> The two chapters from your novel confirm our admiration for your work and our feeling that the Viking Press will want to be your publisher. You speak of this as a rough draft; yet the language is always right, sometimes extremely beautiful. Your feeling for the setting and for the people in their setting seems perfect. You manage to achieve a reconstruction within a narrow frame which has the authentic color in every detail, and yet escapes becoming academic, as a genre painting is apt to do. Instead it remains warmly felt and alive throughout.[26]

Best requested a timeline for publication and a plan for the whole novel that would show where these chapters fit. If Still expected to have the novel completed by June 1937, he said Viking would publish the poems in the summer and bring out the novel in the spring of 1938. Still must have satisfied Best because on March 5 Best sent a formal agreement along with explanations of contracts and royalties. The press expected the complete manuscript in early April. In the letters that followed, they discussed details, including the formality of writing to the magazines that had published the poems for permission to reprint.

This permission request would have shown *The Atlantic Monthly* that Still had not chosen them as his book publisher. Weeks sent tempered and professional congratulations to Still in March:

> I am delighted to hear, both from Marshall Best and you of the association which you have formed with the Viking Press. And yet I should be less than candid if I did not admit at the same time a feeling of regret that, rather than entrust the publication of your future books to the Atlantic Monthly Press, you have taken the path to their door. . . . You see, then, why there is a tinge of disappointment in your congratulations.
>
> This, you understand, will make no difference in our genu-

ine enjoyment of your work and in our wish to print as much of it as possible in the columns of the Atlantic.[27]

In April Still received the final typescript and the galley proofs, which he corrected and returned to Viking. *Hounds on the Mountain* included thirty-five poems over the span of fifty-five pages. Not surprisingly, "Child in the Hills" was the opening poem. By June 4, 1937, the finished book had arrived at Viking and ten copies were on their way to Still. The first edition was limited to 750 numbered copies and priced at two dollars. It was dedicated to "G. L." (Guy Loomis) and "Jethro" (Amburgey), both important and supportive friends. Still felt proud and gratified. Not only had he written the poems and had them collected by a major New York publisher, but he had managed the whole process himself. There is no evidence that Edwin Grover or Carol Hill had played a part in the transactions beyond their initial encouragement. Interestingly, when he finally told Grover the publication date of the book, his words implied trepidation: "Wish I could work up some enthusiasm (e.g. optimism) over this book. I feel only dread and distrust."[28]

In a follow-up letter, Still sent Grover the press's description of the volume:

> The poems of James Still have one quality, among others, which sets them apart and earns them a distinguished rank—they spring from a single locale and evoke a world of their own. The poet writes only of the Kentucky hills—of Troublesome Creek, along which he has lived, the sycamores and elms, the meadow flowers, the rabbits and the foxes that haunt its banks. His poetry is of an unusually pure and uncomplicated beauty. His vocabulary is enriched by the mountain speech, which probably retains more Elizabethan English than will be found anywhere else in the world today. Like the work of Robert Frost, it speaks its own authentic language. In ten years the Viking Press has published just six new American poets: two who later won Pulitzer Prizes. . . . We now add James Still to this list with the same conviction that his book is worthy in its own right, will become a collector's item, and will introduce a notable literary career.[29]

Still followed this quote with a mildly sarcastic correction— "Incidentally, no rabbits, no elm trees, no meadow flowers, etc. are mentioned in my book"—and closed with the overly modest prediction "I'm beginning to think a hundred copies of my book may be sold before it goes definitely out of print."

Reviews of *Hounds on the Mountain* were good. One reviewer practically shouted his prediction in 1937: "There seems to me not the slightest doubt that he [Still] is at the outset of a distinguished career. . . . You'll be hearing of this young man or I shall give up prophecy." Before the end of June, Still wrote Red to express amazement at these words from Hershell Brickell. Also, he reported, "William Rose Benet gave it a good sendoff in the *Saturday Review of Literature.*" *Kirkus Reviews* described the collection as having "purity of diction, a certain force and power in its very simplicity." The poems blended "beauty with a certain homespun quality, a primitiveness." Although sales of the book were "not rapid," they were, according to Best, "entirely satisfactory." Best even nominated it for a Pulitzer Prize, though he admitted that it was too much to hope for.[30]

What was not satisfactory was the length of time Still was taking to submit the first full draft of the novel, which the press had wanted in the fall of 1937. He continued to write and publish stories, but he was not sending Viking a manuscript.[31] On April 8, 1938, Best wrote Still that he was glad to know the novel was growing. But he ended with the question "Is it too soon to predict any sort of date for its completion?"[32] Finally, in February 1939, two years after he had sent the press the first two chapters, he followed with part one of the novel, the first twenty-five thousand words, and predicted that it would take him until August to complete the work.

Best responded to the first section with glowing words and great appreciation. "It is everything that I expected it to be and there is not the slightest doubt in my mind about our wanting to publish it." His only concern was the lack of overall structure, though he sensed that the threads were there to create a plot. He was confident that Still would "work it out satisfactorily in the succeeding sections." His comments concluded, "I cannot tell you how delighted I am with the atmosphere and tone of the whole work thus far. It is a distinguished piece of writing with a marvelous sureness of perception and without a single false note." He then offered Still an advance on royalties, which Still did not take.[33] By June, Best had received the second part of the novel and delighted in the grandmother's character and in memorable Uncle Jolly. Even though Still was by then meeting his scheduled deadlines, the press had decided to postpone the publication until Best had the entire manuscript. The book did not come out until the spring of 1940.[34]

Not surprisingly, Best found the work to be more a series of episodes than one continuous story. Still was constructing many of the chapters as free-standing short stories. For example, of the twenty-one chapters in the first two parts of the novel, nine had been previously published. Whether the novel was built around the already existing stories or whether Still excerpted the individual chapters from the overall work, we cannot know. We do know that he was working toward a novel as early as 1937, and that a common way for novelists to increase their income in the early twentieth century was to have much of their work appear in magazines before being published as a book.[35] The fact that approximately half of the total pages appeared in magazines before the novel's publication would indicate that Still was collecting income from the parts in order to complete the whole.

Years later, Still talked as though he had had no intention of getting the highest dollar for his efforts. He implied that everything about the novel happened more or less by accident. One of his accounts casually folded his early efforts into his workday at the Hindman library: "I began to take writing seriously rather suddenly. . . . I recall distinctly the Saturday morning I began writing a novel in the storeroom of the high school. I always retreated there for my one-hour break during the school day and on Saturdays when my duties allowed. The principal was to remark, 'He goes in, bolts the door, and only God knows what he does in there.' I began writing *River of Earth*."[36]

In the interview that opens *The Wolfpen Notebooks,* Still claimed that his only purpose for writing *River of Earth* was to "tell the story." He did not realize that he was starting a novel and recalled that *The Atlantic* accepted the first piece he sent them ("All Their Ways") but published it as an article instead of a short story. Then "it became the first section of a novel. When the editor at Viking asked if I was writing a novel, I said yes I am. He wanted to see some of it. . . . They sent a contract."[37]

This casual attitude was typical of Still when reflecting on his career. But the correspondence shows that his motivation was serious and his decisions deliberate. He admitted that money was something of an issue when he said Viking asked him to take a year off and proposed to put him on a salary. That description of the offer is exaggerated; they offered an advance, not a year's salary. In any case, Still once said to Jim Wayne Miller that his pride would not allow him to accept money for something that was unfinished. "Then I had the luck to have *The Satur-day Evening Post* take a story . . . they paid very well indeed—actually, fabulous prices for those days. So after that I just wrote one story a year for them."[38] He did publish two sections of the novel as stories for the *Saturday Evening Post:* "Bat Flight" in September 1938 and "Two Eyes, Two Pennies" in April 1939. It was fairly easy money; from those two stories, his total income of $1,000 compared favorably to the advance of $250.00 that Viking finally did provide.[39]

Best never expressed concern that the book was appearing in pieces before its publication. In fact, he seemed to applaud the exposure that the stories would provide to the future publication. In one letter he congratulated Still on the O. Henry Prize for "Bat Flight" with the comment, "This will be an added bit of publicity for the book."[40] Reviewers were not critical either; the practice was common, and the stories appeared in a variety of magazines over a four-year period. In fact, few reviewers even noticed. What concerned Best was the time it was taking; he wanted a completed novel. In order to achieve that goal, Still needed more time to write, which involved extricating himself from the work at Hindman Settlement School.

The job provided a source of writing material as well as a personal haven. Still never said that his library and teaching duties were too demanding or time consuming, but after six years at the school and with the help of his increasing publications and his friend, Jethro Amburgey, he made a move. His life-changing decision was to quit his job, go to "the backside of Nowhere and sit down and finish *River of Earth.*"[41] In a letter to Grover on April 17, 1939, Still proposed his plan and asked advice: "Have asked for a fifteen-month leave of absence. But the matter is still unsettled. I've managed to save a few dollars to keep door from wolf. . . . Six years have I labored and toiled (after a fashion) in this school, and on the seventh I want to do as I please. Wander, write, read, a lot of just doing nothing at all. Do you think it's a good idea?"[42]

Still had begun discussing with the school the possibility of taking a temporary leave in the spring of 1939, but the administrators urged his staying on because he was such a valuable member of the faculty.[43] That was not what Still wanted, but he was unable to tell them directly. Instead, he sent his message by simply extending his summer break. When he was at Yaddo that summer, he wrote to Frances Grover, asking that she appeal to Elizabeth Watts and May Stone on his behalf. They agreed to his terms but let him know that they expected him back by September 18, the third week of school.[44] Soon after he returned, he gathered his courage and told them his plans. By October they managed to find a replacement for him as a typing teacher. He was to train this next person, Mrs. Dixon, before he left, and they paid him $18.40 for the few days he stayed to help out. Although he had moved to the Amburgey log house on Dead Mare Branch earlier in June, he did not live there full time until October. In February 1940 Watts wrote another letter to Still, asking if he would definitely be returning in the fall, showing that the school was still counting on him. She and Stone had considered his absence a leave. Now that one book was published and he was committed to several more, he had no intention of returning to work at the school.

Watts and Stone recognized the value of Still's endorsement. The stories were bringing them excellent publicity. For example, in the May 1938 letter requesting donations, they had built their appeal around the story "Journey to the Settlement," which had appeared in *Mountain Life and Work* a year earlier, and they included a reprint of the story with the letter. It described the applicants to the school as children just like the boy Lark in the story. They wanted to help many children, and to do so they needed financial support from donors. The Settlement School would miss Still's increasing visibility as a writer as well as his work as a librarian. In her last letter, Watts asked that he do them a favor and give his opinion on the plans for the new library. He had become a mainstay of the staff at the school as well as a friend. When Watts got the final word that he would not return, she responded, "I like to picture you in the 'lonesome place' you have chosen. I felt the charm very keenly in the little while I was there last fall. We continue to miss you at Hindman and are sorry you aren't returning. I wish you'd come to see us sometimes."[45]

Still had known he was ready to leave Hindman, but it was not until Amburgey offered him a house that he knew where he would live. In *The Wolfpen Notebooks*, Still quotes Amburgey's comment about his childhood home: "I was born in this log house and I'll never sell it; I might give it away." He did give it away, to James Still, not as an outright gift but to live in for his lifetime.[46] Finding the house was probably more critical to Still's life and career in 1939 than were the contract offers from Viking. Located eleven miles from Hindman—nine miles over a wagon road and two miles up a creek bed—the two-story log house had been built by German immigrants in 1837 and had been Amburgey's birthplace and his family home. The friendship between

Still and Amburgey had grown from when they met in 1933.[47] Several times Still had accompanied his friend to the log house on visits to his mother. After her death, Amburgey wanted the place occupied and offered it to his friend for a summer. At first, Still had planned to stay only a few weeks in June, but the house quickly became his home, and he never gave it up. This move from Hindman to Wolfpen Creek, specifically Dead Mare Branch, represented a retreat from the working world to a personal world of writing, a change from living in a student dormitory to an independent existence in an isolated setting.

In a 1960 article by Joe Creason of the *Courier-Journal,* Still denied that the move was based on a philosophical commitment. Rather, he said simply, "I wasn't satisfied with the place where I was living. Then one day I saw this place and knew it was what I had been looking for all my life—remote, picturesque and quiet." Still's verbal descriptions often focused on the location of the house with respect to the surrounding land and water: the dwelling faced east, with Dead Mare Branch running on one side and Wolfpen Creek on the other. Tree-covered mountains rose in front of and behind the house. He continued, "Mine was to be a domain of thirty-one acres, once a farm, now long lain fallow. I [had] found a home. I marked the day by an observation in a notebook: 'A pair of black-and-white warblers teetered along the banks of Dead Mare and minnows riffled the glassy pools. Partridges called in the water meadow, and from a cove sounded an occasional *e-olee* of a wood thrush. A rabbit flashed a tail in the wild flax.'"[48]

The move to Dead Mare embodied a symbolic commitment to both a lifestyle and a vocation. He had settled in a place "certain and enduring," to use the mother's words in *River of Earth.* One section of "A Man Singing" includes a detailed description of his early years in his log home. In addition to writing, farming, and gardening, he experimented with wild strawberries and violets; studied a tiny insect, the leaf miner; and spent his evenings reading by lamplight.[49] He was happy and productive. Some of the locals called him a hermit, and he became known as "the man in the bushes," but his quiet life was not isolated and friendless. In fact, he may have been more social when living there than when he lived at the school. He began to attend community happenings and associate with local residents. He soon became acquainted with all of Amburgey's five brothers, who were his neighbors, and he frequently ate supper with the Melvin Amburgey family.[50]

He was becoming a part of the local community, and they accepted him as a neighbor. Yet as indicated in the title of Rena Niles's article,

"Obscurity Begins Back Home for Kentucky's James Still," the people of the area, even of the state, did not know and appreciate the young writer: "James Still is not as well known in Kentucky as he deserves to be—but in Hindman he is practically unknown; unknown as a writer and a poet. To the people of his community he is a hard-working school teacher . . . and James Still would be the last one to want things changed." Niles had written Still in January 1938 to request an interview that would lead to her feature article on him as part of the Kentucky Profiles section in the Sunday *Courier-Journal*. She noted that Still's lack of publicity was not a result of his snubbing the press but of his "insurmountable shyness and a patient willingness to let time take its course and bring him either fame—or the lack of it—as destiny ordains."[51]

His goal was neither fame nor riches. He shunned publicity. Between 1939 and 1942 Still wanted, most of all, the time and peace to write. He moved to his log home with the intent of finishing the novel, and he did so in 1939. In the same way that he recalled the moment the characters came alive for him at Hindman, he remembered details of the day he completed the manuscript in his own house: "Not having a suitable table, I perched the typewriter on two steamer trunks, one atop the other. I had expected to write an additional chapter, had it clearly in mind, so clearly that I could produce it today, but when I wrote the last sentence of the book as it now stands I realized I had ended the journey. In my relief I jumped to my feet and ran around the stacked trunks a couple of times."[52]

Before exploring how neighbors, readers, and critics received the novel in 1940, a brief review of its structure and characters will be helpful. The narrator of *River of Earth* is a young unnamed mountain boy who recounts his family's experiences over a three-year period. The collection of related episodes begins with the six-year-old running barefoot on the floor of their small house. His father, Brack Baldridge, is a coal miner, but the opening sentence tells us that the mines closed in March. As the boy and his brother and sister grow, the family struggles to have food, work, and a place of their own. The overall story follows a cyclical pattern, like the seasons. It ends in early spring in the same general area, with the family facing the same question—what to do now that the mines are closing, again. The novel follows the boy's growth and is presented in three parts: life with his family at their farm on Little Carr; life at Lean Neck where he comes to know Grandma and Uncle Jolly; then life again with his family in the coal camp Blackjack. On one level, the book is the boy's personal coming-of-age story. On another, it is the story of his family and the whole mountain society transitioning from an agrarian to an industrial economy. Beyond that, it is the human story of spiritual questioning that rises above any particular setting or problem. As the preacher asks in his sermon near the end of part 1, "Where air we going on this mighty river of earth, a-borning, begetting, and a-dying." In the final scene of the book, the grandmother has died, Jolly has chosen to settle on the land, Brack is preparing to move his family to another coal camp, and the mother, Alpha, has given birth. The narrator's closing words—that last sentence Still celebrated by running around the stacked trunks—"A baby was crying in the far room."[53]

River of Earth was not written for the local people, Still's friends and neighbors on Wolfpen Creek. Most of them were not aware of what he was writing, or even that he was a writer. He, however, was critically aware of them. One story that he actually lived took place on February 5, 1940—the day *River of Earth* was published. Still was awaiting a late train in a railway station at Jackson when a deputy sheriff was shot down in front of him. He boarded the train and wrote a letter to *Time,* thanking the editors for their kind words on the forthcoming novel but also describing the shooting incident he had just witnessed in Breathitt County. He concluded, "Long have I looked to this day [because of the publication of his novel], but I've got no pleasure out of it. I have seen a man die."[54] When *Time* published the letter as "Bloody Breathitt," the citizens of Jackson were furious at Still because, as he said, "I had given a local matter national attention."[55] Giving local life national attention is exactly what *River of Earth* did, but the people of the area were undisturbed by this publicity, perhaps because they remained essentially unaware of the book, or perhaps because those who did read it recognized its picture of mountain life as both realistic and sympathetic.

In a letter to Grover, Still expressed serious reservations about the book just after he had mailed the proofs to Viking. He was convinced it would not sell. "It has none of the come-hither, the who-done-it, of domestic best sellers. Nor does it provide vicarious identification of reader with characters. No warm and fed and comforted reader would want to be one of my characters. It will be a grim volume. It lacks dramatic happening." The only strength he saw was that it was one of a kind for novels about the region. "It strikes below the mountain-sentimentality belt, it ought to knock chips off shoulders of professional literary mountaineers."[56]

His fears were unfulfilled, but his prediction of the novel's place in literary history was accurate—it opened a new genre, Appalachian realism. The novel's publication in 1940 marked the height of Still's early writing career. The positive book reviews gave him much-needed national exposure, and his career was off to a successful start: he had displayed versatility, control, and appeal in his writing and persistence in the pursuit of his goals. Viking's prepublication press release described *River of Earth* as follows:

> A first novel by a young poet of Kentucky, this enchanting story brings a rare delight and introduces a strong new talent in fiction. Through the bright eyes and tingling ears of a boy of about Tom Sawyer's age, James Still unfolds the lovely, smoky, peaceful yet exciting world of the Kentucky mountain country. Mr. Still calls his book fiction, but the youngster who rides proudly on the bony rump of his father's mule, smokes bats out of the schoolhouse roof, keeps his uncle company in the local jail, and ever finds himself an animated participant in the social and business events of his family, must be close kin to the author's own boyhood.
>
> Mr. Still's country is the land where ballads are still sung, where school children are called "scholars," where the memory of feuds is still green, and the special flavor of that land flows onto every page of his book. Readers in quest of comparisons will search far and long for a story of the American scene as moving and yet as gay as *River of Earth*. Perhaps the best way to indicate its special quality is to prophesy that Elizabeth Madox Roberts, John Steinbeck, and Marjorie Rawlings should all have a fellow-feeling for its author.

This same description appeared, with slight variation, on the dust jacket of the book itself, with this addition: "*River of Earth* captures the imagination by its poetry, holds the interest through the honesty, vitality, and humor of its people. Tender but not sentimental, realistic without being sordid, gay, youthful, but understanding the depths of life, it can scarcely fail to convince its readers that in James Still they have discovered a strong new voice in American fiction." The qualities noted in these descriptions—first novel, enchanting story, boy narrator, Kentucky country, and a style characterized by poetry, honesty, vitality, humor, realism, and understanding—are the same as those admired by early reviewers.

Best had also sent advance copies to Viking's book club of amateur readers, called The Preview Associates.[57] Their job was to report on books from a lay reader's point of view. Best reported that most of them liked the book very much but wanted to know the narrator's name—hardly the rave response afforded a potential best seller. The book did not become a major seller; after two months had passed, Best offered some consolation and explanation: "On the book I cannot report as cheerfully as I should like, but then one rarely is satisfied with the sale of a much-liked book. It has really had a very gratifying run for a first novel. I am sure that only its lack of concentrated story interest has prevented it from becoming a real best-seller. . . . I hope you are as pleased as we have been with its general reception and not too disappointed at its not following more closely in the footsteps of 'Gone With the Wind.'"[58] Of course, Viking might have wished for a blockbuster such as Macmillan and MGM had found in Margaret Mitchell's work. Yet everyone must have been satisfied with this first novel, this "much-liked book" by a little-known Kentucky author. For the most part, the reviews were positive; the few that were negative seemed to want the book to be something it was not. First, *River of Earth* was not historical romance or social melodrama destined for sweeping success at bookstores or box offices—not a *Riders of the Purple Sage* (1912) nor a *Gone with the Wind* (1936). Although it exposed social injustice, it was not a national or racial protest novel along the lines of *The Grapes of Wrath* (1939) or *Native Son* (1940), nor a farcical satire of poor whites like *Tobacco Road* (1932). *River of Earth* was not a sensation.

Most reviewers noted the book's feature of loosely connected chapters, but only a few found that a weakness. Ann Springer in the *Boston Transcript* had a mixed reaction; she observed that Still contented himself with episodes of family life and had written a "beautiful book, almost perfect of its kind, deft in the writing, sharply realized in characters, setting and speech." Her objection was that the book lacked protest, which she equated with plot: a novel "ought to move, it ought to have some fight and back-talk, it ought in a word, to have plot." Her review concluded, "Surely the 'river of earth' is not a creek."

The river of earth in eastern Kentucky may very well have been a creek, and many readers considered the work an example of a regional novel. The model such readers were using was local color fiction and provincial works of the late nineteenth and early twentieth centuries.[59] As such, it was an excellent example. Faithful rendering, stylistic control, authentic voice, seductive simplicity—these are the characteristics of the book that the reviewers uniformly praised. According to *Time* magazine, Still achieved "the sense of what is fitting" and produced a "work of art." The *New York Times* called it "a little Kentucky masterpiece." *The Atlantic Monthly,* reviewing it as one of the "Novels That Are Different," described it as a beautifully phrased story of the "homespun mountain people and their hard lives." The *New York Times Book Review* said "homespun" was not a good label for *River of Earth* and assigned it "special excellence as a regional document." May Cameron ended her *Post* article by recommending *River of Earth* "for a first-hand picture of a world far removed from that in which most of us live."

Two reviewers emphasized the work's potential for broader appeal. The first, Edwin Granberry, concluded, "Its fame, we think, will be sure and widespread, placing Mr. Still in the front rank of younger American novelists."[60] The second, Dayton Kohler, demonstrated critical perception in his praise of the novel's broad scope. Kohler reviewed *River of Earth* for the *Southern Literary Messenger* in March 1940. He found beneath the novel's regional feeling a sense of social injustice that was never directly articulated because it lay outside the boy's knowledge of life. Kohler also praised Still's choice of boy narrator and the dramatic structure that conveyed youthful sensitivity. *River of Earth,* observed Kohler, is "more than a novel of local color. It is a picture of life in our time."[61]

The first critical study of Still's work appeared in *College English* in 1942 and was also by Kohler. One objective of this article was to reveal Still's ability to tap human nature, but Kohler's overall concern was to redefine regionalists. Kohler saw both Still and Stuart as a new type of "mountain regionalists." When they wrote from a sense of identity with place and people, their stories, he claimed, were *of* the place, not *about* it. Kohler's attempt to review the book in a larger human context ended with his effort to prove just how successful Still was in artistically portraying his own region and having it speak a more general truth.[62]

In addition to positive reviews and critical studies, Still's writing was being honored. Even as he was hearing about the reception of his novel, he received a major award for his poetry. He was chosen as the Phi Beta Kappa poet and invited to receive the honor at Columbia University's commencement exercises scheduled for June 3, 1940. Best was very pleased and strongly encouraged him to accept and attend. One of Still's fellow Viking authors, Irwin Edman, had been instrumental in getting Still named. Best noted that the award committee would pay fifty dollars toward Still's expenses and added that Viking would supplement that amount if he needed more.[63] Still was hesitant to accept, and on April 8 he received a telegram from Edman at Columbia asking if he could respond. Still had had a bad case of the flu in late March, but there was no reason he would not be perfectly fit by June. In a letter dated April 9 he wrote to tell Kohler that he had been in an automobile wreck at Prestonburg and was thrown through the windshield. He ended that letter with the news that he had been chosen Phi Beta Kappa poet and the comment "Don't think I will accept." It is hard to know why Still did not go to Columbia. Perhaps he thought he would be uncomfortable in such a rarified environment, especially since he himself was not a member of Phi Beta Kappa. In later years he seemed greatly honored by the invitation, but he was also quick to say that he did not go and that Robert Lowell was honored instead.[64] Sometimes his excuse was that he did not have money for a suit—unlikely since both Viking and Loomis would have been willing to give him money for such an event. At other times, he said that he was sick. More likely, his refusal was an example of his oversensitivity and shyness.[65]

River of Earth did more than the poetry volume to establish Still's reputation before a national audience, even if his position was as a regionalist. Ironically, he was not well known in his own region, but he was gaining readers from a variety of places. The most prestigious prize awarded to the novel was the Southern Author Award for the most distinguished book of the year by a Southern author on a Southern subject. In fact, Thomas Wolfe won the prize for *You Can't Go Home Again,* published posthumously in 1940, and James Still was the runner-up. Since the prize money of one hundred dollars had to be given to a living author, Still received the cash award and the honor. His first response was to decline the award and the invitation to go to New York to receive it, but Best appealed to him strongly, offering to pay any costs that the modest travel allowance of thirty dollars did not cover.[66] Possibly, Still regretted having turned down the previous poetry honor and thought better of snubbing the fiction prize. Whatever the reason, he did go, and he enjoyed it.

Years later, he told a story about meeting Wolfe's sister, Mabel Wolfe Wheaton, at the award luncheon. She was there to receive the honor for her brother; he was there to receive the prize money. The *New York Times* of Sunday reported that "Mrs. Wheaton described her brother as she had known him, expressing the thought 'that he had always seemed like a younger brother' and never a successful author."[67] Still must have felt right at home with Wheaton since any of his sisters could have described him in the same way. He even described her as a big, tall woman who reminded him of his older sister.

After the ceremony, Still went with Wheaton to a party with university professors and people who worked for Columbia broadcasting and radio. They left the party in a taxi and were talking in the back seat when the taxi stopped and the driver got out to argue with someone about a traffic incident. Still described their reactions: "I started to get out of the car and Mabel pulled me back in and said that's none of your business." As a result, he stayed in the taxi.[68] He yielded to that command, but when she wanted him to go to the apartment where she was staying, he said it was too late. Wheaton told the same story, but with a different outcome, to Wilma Dykeman, and Dykeman retold it years later: "We [Jim and Mabel] were in the taxi together going to receive this award and the taxi happened to pull out just a little bit and a bus hit it. It didn't hurt the bus or the taxi, but the bus driver and a policeman came out just attacking this poor taxi driver. James Still was out of that taxi just like a shot and he made such a compelling case that they didn't say anymore."[69] It would seem that Wheaton remembered Still as the hero of the situation, while Still remembered her as the boss.

By mid-June 1940, Still had approached Best with the idea of publishing a collection of short stories. Best responded that Viking wanted to consider the stories and added, "If you have a book that ought to be published at all, it ought to be published by us." He did warn that stories were not a good commercial venture.[70] On November 18, 1940, Still mailed Best the manuscript of *On Troublesome Creek*, which included ten stories. The response was respectful but less than enthusiastic. His concern was that the book was not substantial and that the dialect was too dominant: "You have developed a trick of style in some of these stories which surprised me and I must say disappointed me. I am referring to you elimination of articles and possessive pronouns. I can see that in moderation this device might have the desirable effect of making your style seem economical and clean. Used to such an extreme, however, it strikes the reader as a self-conscious mannerism which becomes rather annoying."[71] The critique must have inspired Still because he worked on the manuscript for eight more months and brought the total number of stories to eleven. In August, Viking sent a formal agreement for publication and offered an advance of up to $250. Best remained unenthusiastic about the sales potential, but he was much more complimentary of the stories than he had been earlier, expressing his conviction that the book would advance Still's "standing as a writer." One factor that might have helped change his attitude was that the story "The Proud Walkers" had been published in the May 10 *Saturday Evening Post* and was chosen to be included in the O. Henry Story Collection. *On Troublesome Creek* was released on October 13, 1941. A month later, Best reported that the book "had some beautiful reviews," but like most short-story volumes it was facing tough competition from the best-selling fiction.[72]

Marjorie Kinnan Rawlings wrote the most cherished review of the collection for the *Chicago Daily News* Christmas section. The *News* literary editor, Sterling North, found the review stunning and complimented Rawlings for it. She, in turn, complimented Still, saying he "would write well and beautifully, in whatever milieu he found himself. He is not dependent on any chance quaintness for his writing, for its source is within his own heart and humor, his own love and knowledge of human beings."[73] As North predicted, Still was "overwhelmed" by the review. Still wrote to Rawlings on December 11, congratulating her on her recent marriage to her long-time friend Norton Baskin. The main part of his letter, however, reacted not to her marriage but to her review and ended simply, "Marjorie, . . . Thank you for this generosity."[74]

Still's third volume was in the hands of readers by the end of 1941, and although he could not have known it at the time, that marked the end of his most productive period. Since 1935 he had published three books in three different genres. Four of his stories had been selected as O. Henry Memorial Prize Stories.[75] As a result of his success, Still was awarded a Guggenheim Fellowship for research and creative work in 1941. His writing had won him more than acclaim. He had attended prestigious writing workshops for five summers in a row and made numerous friends among the people he met there.

Another notable accomplishment was that Still had held a steady, rewarding job, though not lucrative, for six years while establishing himself as a writer. He had put down roots in Hindman. He had saved enough money to quit—or as he put it, "I was so rich I retired."[76] So he left his salaried job and moved to the house of his dreams in a remote area of the county; there he began to make the house a home and himself a farmer-gardener and horticulturalist. The move from Hindman to Dead Mare Branch was the inspiration for his story "The Proud Walkers," which Still must have drafted soon after situating himself in the log house.

The story tells about a family's moving from Houndshell mine camp to a home place that the father of the family was building on Shoal Creek. As is typical for Still's fictional families, the people are on the move, this time going from the town to the country, just as Still was doing. The mother is concerned about the state that the house is in; the children are worried that they won't have any friends in the new strange place; the father is feeling pressure to plant the garden and to finish essential parts of the construction, especially the windows and chimney. There is a strong sense that the parents do not agree about the priorities or even the move itself. The tension created by all these concerns mounts when silhouettes appear walking on the ridges. It is the Crownover family, first thought to be a strange lot with peculiar habits. The story ends in a positive spirit. The Crownovers, a proud and honorable family, have been using a cave on the property for food storage. Now they are quietly emptying it out, so as not to be trespassers. Allaying all concerns, the Crownovers turn out to be helpful and neighborly—they haul windows to the house and come to start the garden. So within a dozen pages the trauma of the move is resolved. The tension between the mother and father becomes friendly bantering. The family has made a successful transition.

Still described his own transition to life on Dead Mare in "A Man Singing to Himself":

> Save for three broken chairs and a small table, the house was bereft of furniture. The back door was painted green to ward off witches. I slept on an army cot and cooked on a two-burner coal-oil stove until I could gather other furnishings. . . . The second week in June was late to start a garden and plant a field of corn; moreover, the signs of the zodiac were not auspicious. I planted nevertheless, and, as hard frosts held off until the middle of October, I had vegetables aplenty, both to eat and to store for winter. . . .
>
> Log houses are not as warm as reputed. Not mine at least. My first winter there, a February blizzard dipped many degrees below zero. I pushed my bed as close to the fire as I dared; I heated a rock, wrapped it in a towel, put it at my feet. I wondered how my neighbors fared, many of them in less sheltered quarters. Spring came, and there they were, without complaint.[77]

Although his house was more habitable than the one in the story, he was experiencing some of the same frustrations. Instead of strange neighbors, he was the strange one, this "man in the bushes." He was reported to be "ancient with a two-foot beard. A hermit shunning human contact." It did not take long, though, for the neighbors to accept him. He called for his mail once a week at Bern Smith's store, at the foot of Little Carr Creek. His surroundings were becoming more familiar and comfortable, but mail was his lifeline to the outside world, the world to which he sent his writing.

By the end of 1941, James Still had a house and land and garden, a writing career, and a network of friends. Yet he was missing a wife and family. He was a man singing alone.

13

Jolly in a Courting Mood

I've got me a young mule, new ground cleared, and soon to
have a doughbeater fair as ever drew breath.
—Jolly to Brack in *River of Earth*

By 1941, James Still had established professional connections, yet personally he was alone. Though shy and retiring, he liked people and made friends with a variety of them. He was not a passionate man who wanted to marry early, like his friend Don West. He was not a ladies' man who was in love with a different girl every few months, like Jesse Stuart. He was not even like his closest friend, Dare Redmond, who took his time to find the right woman but eventually married her in 1939. James Stokely met and married Wilma Dykeman in a span of six weeks. Almost everyone Still knew was married. His three younger brothers—Comer, Tom, and Alfred—all married between 1930 and 1935; two of them had children. Even his father had remarried twice since Still's mother had died in 1930. At the age of thirty-five, Still seemed no closer to marriage than he had been when he graduated from college.

Years later, Still led people to believe that he had loved Mayme Brown when he was at LMU, the girl in the poem "who died at sixteen, / Before she got around to saying 'Yes.'" He purposely created a mystery about this early love. Possibly, he wanted people to think that because her death caused him such heartbreak, he never again considered marriage.[1] If he was permanently smitten with love for this girl, there is no clear evidence in his correspondence of that time or in his storytelling of later years. Their "romance," if it happened at all, was short lived. The tragedy of Mayme's death, Still's memory of her, and the lines of the poem that immortalize her all resonate with the tone of romantic poetry. But was there real romance in James Still's adult life?

Still seemed to avoid amorous encounters in his own life as well as in the lives of his characters. His story "Uncle Jolly" appeared in *The Atlantic* in July 1938, and on August 23, Edward Weeks wrote to him that Jolly is "an Atlantic natural," adding, "We want him in our midst whenever possible." The story had Jolly serving two weeks in the county jail for roughing Les Honeycutt. Jolly was always a spitfire of the best sort, a delightful fellow who got into trouble as easily as breathing, a trickster with a good heart. Since every energetic young man needs a woman, at least for a spell, Weeks asked Still, "Might it not be possible for you to show us Jolly in one of his courting moods? If you could match him with a girl of spirit, it would be something to see— even if, as I suspect, Jolly would somehow dodge the altar."[2] Whether or not Still was taking the advice of his editor, Jolly made plans to marry. We never see him courting and never eavesdrop on his conversations with his girl, but we do hear of his intent to settle when, in the final pages of *River of Earth,* he says to Brack, "Ever hear o' that pretty girl I fit Les Honeycutt over? Tina Sawyers? I writ I'd be at her homeplace next Sunday, fotching Sim Mobberly [preacher] and a license. . . . I aim to settle. I've got me a young mule, new ground cleared, and soon to have a doughbeater fair as ever drew breath."[3] Still himself must have felt the clock ticking; he had already settled, and he was meeting women who were interested in him.

Since he never talked about any courtships, the question can be explored only through his correspondence with women or with his other friends about women. During the years between Still's moving to Hindman and his going to World War II, he showed an interest in four women, all of whom he met during summer travels or through friends he made while on those travels. The first was Regina Codey.

Still and Robert Francis met Codey at Bread Loaf in the summer of 1937. The letter Francis wrote to Still on November 28, 1937, devoted a paragraph to her. "A little over a month ago I drove out to Millbrook, New York, to see Regina Codey. I found the same sensitive, magical person we knew at Bread Loaf. You and I are lucky to have her for a friend. She asked if I had heard from you." From this reference, it seems that Francis was closer to her than Still was. He told Still of a serious illness she had in February 1939. After recovering in a New York hospital, she went to Florida. Still wrote to Edwin Grover on April 17, requesting that he visit her:

> Would you mind meeting, and comforting, a young lady friend of mine at 800 Pulsifer Circle, Winter Park. She's there convalescing from a recent illness. Up and about, however, not bedfast. Regina Codey is her name. She's an actress, and a remarkable person in many ways. I first met her in Vermont, at Bread Loaf. I think you'll find her a rare person, with great talent. A little bit of a body though, and gentle—and colorful. . . . Will be interested to know your reaction to her. Give her my best wishes.[4]

Still's admiration of Codey did not seem to go further, but they continued corresponding until 1945.

Another potential affair that never developed beyond letters was with a young woman Still met in the summer of 1938 at MacDowell Colony. Joy Davidman, nine years younger than Still, was a middle-class Jewish girl from New York. She had earned a master's in English literature from Columbia in 1935. Like Still, she wrote poetry and published her first novel in 1940. It is unknown how many letters Still wrote to her, but she wrote three to him, all of which he highly valued. The first came soon after she left MacDowell that summer—he had left two weeks earlier. In it she reported that she had read and liked "Bat Flight" in the *Saturday Evening Post*: "I expected you to write like that, with that admirable trick of understatement and quiet strength and precision of detail. I understand now what you meant, when you described the time you spent over each sentence. There wasn't a bit of casual description in the story you hadn't . . . made a part of the whole. I wish I could do so much with so few words; I'm apt to splash colors about like an impressionist painter."[5]

Joy Davidman always made an impression. She was endearing, insightful, witty, and bright. She was perhaps careless, but she made an impact on every place she went and on every person she met. She ended that first letter with apologies for the hurried writing: "Good Lord, Jim! What awful prose style I've used in this letter! I should adopt your carefulness—only I am so lazy that then I'd never write letters at all. Send me an answer, anyhow!"

Her next letter was from Beverly Hills and on Metro-Goldwyn-

Mayer letterhead. She claimed to hate life in California and yearn for New York City or upstate or, better still, the quiet of Kentucky. These excerpts convey her homesickness:

> Look at where I am! It's horrible. I'm a New Yorker, used to crowds, strangers, loud noises and sudden explosions—but not to this. I should like to hide in your rhubarb patch. . . . You are growing beans and corn; I am entangled in a nest of cement. . . . I wish you'd write me more. I'm homesick for the peace and quiet of the subway in this horrible flat city full of pink and green stucco and frowsy palms. I wish I could be in New York to see you. . . . How I would like a log house deep in the hills just now, and a chance to work at my own work. I've finished a new book of poems though. . . . I've been following your short stories; the one about the little school teacher who was shot (Bat Flight, isn't it) will stay with me all my life.[6]

The last letter from Joy is full of joy because she was fired as a screenwriter, which allowed her to return to New York. Her headstrong, independent ways are not unlike Still's, though he was never so vocal. "The film business fired me with many compliments two months ago; the consensus of opinion was that I didn't take kindly to 'consultation.' Once, in a moment of emotion, I said No to a producer, so they were right. I'm too much of an egoist to listen to anyone tell me how to write. I rushed home howling with joy, and have been kissing skyscrapers and subway trains ever since." That letter ended with the news that her own novel would be published by Macmillan—then a long glowing report on *River of Earth:* "Your novel is taking New York by storm. Everybody's talking about it, even an aunt of mine who usually never hears about a book till someone hits her over the head with it. I've seen enthusiastic reviews, even in the New York Sun, which is Morgan's paper and officially disapproves of Grapes of Wrath and Abraham Lincoln. I've just got my social Security money and I'm going downtown to buy it. . . . I'll write you again as soon as I've read the novel. . . . Yours, Joy"[7]

There is no evidence that she wrote Still again. She went on to marry William Gresham in 1942, a marriage that gave her two sons and a lot of grief. After ten years, Joy Davidman met the love of her life, C. S. Lewis. They were married on March 21, 1957, when she was on her hospital bed. She died in 1960. Given that she disliked her own experience in Hollywood, it is ironic that the story of her love life and early death should be the subject of the popular 1993 movie *Shadowlands,* staring Anthony Hopkins as Lewis and Debra Winger as his wife. Was Still romantically involved with Joy? Probably not, but she certainly intrigued and charmed him. When he saw the movie, his reaction was that Winger had captured her outgoing and outspoken qualities but that she had not captured the essence of the person. Still knew Joy David-man well enough to be attracted by that essence, her joyful spirit.

In 1940 Still made special friends with two more women: Pan Ster-ling and Dorothy Thomas. Both were a little older than Still and unmar-ried. He met Sterling at Yaddo, and through her he met Thomas. They lived in New York City at the time. Sterling was frequently looking for work; her friend had sufficient income for a beautiful three-room apart-ment on 76th Street. Pan wrote lovely, newsy letters to Still, sometimes telling him of interesting people she had met in New York, sometimes remembering moments at Yaddo. She addressed him as a dear friend, but their relationship did not include romantic attraction. He described his house to her and told her about people he liked and stories he was writing.

One of her letter from January 1941 showed that he had been tell-ing her about "Mrs. Razor," the real little girl around whom he built the story by that name.[8] Pan encouraged him to bring the girl to New York for a visit. That letter also included her reaction to photos of his house: "Seems proper and dignified, with smiles breaking over it—almost unsmiled smiles—waiting for you or Timothy [the cat] or the rain or for Mrs. Razor's mother with a great pan of cornbread. It's like you too, alone and un-alone, and real. I like it. Is the tree a willow or a cut-leaf weeping birch? Are the bushes barberry? Yes, and is the tree beside the kitchen door a plum?" Still must have loved her reference to his cat and trees, since they were favorites of his. He cherished her many letters and kept forty of them, dating from 1940 to 1964.

Pan was a good friend to Still, but her friend could have been his intimate friend. Dorothy Thomas was born in Kansas in 1898, making her eight years older than James. Like him, she was the sixth child of ten. Unlike him, she came from a family of artists and writers. When she was seven, her family moved to Alberta, Canada, to homestead. After her father died, the mother and children moved to Lincoln, Nebraska. She was engaged to a young farmer in 1934, but they never married because her mother objected. In 1928 Dorothy took the bold step of choosing to be a writer, which she described in this way: "Sink or swim, I would risk everything, work at whatever jobs I could get, and write for my life and my living." She succeeded and supported her family throughout the 1930s. By 1935, she had two novels published by Knopf. That year she attended Yaddo, where she enjoyed and benefited from her association with other artists. She also fell in love with a prominent writer, Leonard Ehrlich, whom she expected to marry. When the romance ended, she was emotionally devastated and wrote to her mother, "I never before had torn ligaments in my personality."[9]

Although Still and Thomas came from different backgrounds and lived in different areas of the country, they shared similarities. They had both committed themselves to writing for a living. She had chosen that path earlier in life than Still, and it could be that her success appealed to him. She published stories in magazines just as Still did, and she won praise for them.[10] Her novels, *Ma Jeeter's Girls* (1931) and *The Home Place* (1936), were more like loosely connected short stories than thickly plotted novels, and she wrote about remote or obscure areas of the country. She had attended Yaddo in 1935, where she had come to know Pan Sterling. Like Still, she kept in touch with her many friends and acquaintances through letters. A major difference in their personalities was that Thomas was an extrovert who enjoyed being with people, socializing and collaborating with them. She lived happily in the hustle and bustle of Manhattan. Still, on the other hand, leaned toward introversion and worked well when solitary, even isolated in his eastern Kentucky home.

Still instigated their correspondence in 1940 when he wrote a "fan" letter to Thomas. She replied on July 30, while taking a breather from what she called "a good spell of work" to answer a few special letters—she made it seem that Still's was the most special in the stack. She filled three single-spaced typed pages in this first letter. Feeling pleased with his comments on her stories, she reciprocated: "Long have I followed your stories too, with admiration and real enjoyment, and with always the wish [to] see what your next story will be. I read River of Earth too, and like it much. I think the story I like best is the one about the little boy plowing for the first time." From reading the contributors' notes, she knew that he lived near Hindman and that he worked at the Settlement School. She assumed from the realism in his stories that he had grown up there and that his family still lived there. His stories were written, she noted, "from the inside out with honesty and dignity, and sympathy and real human understanding."[11]

They exchanged letters over the next several months. By April 1941, they were on a first-name basis, and she wanted to visit him in Kentucky. But, she added, she could not leave New York until July without interrupting the psychoanalysis that was helping her solve some problems and making her "a better and happier person." By her own admission, this need for help was something that she did not share with many friends, but she wanted him to know. That newsy, five-page letter revealed her sensitivity and compassion as well as her growing trust in him. Obviously, she related to the peaks and valleys of her friends' lives. She talked with sympathy of personal difficulties that Pan was experiencing in one paragraph and, in the next, was full of genuine congratulations to Still for having been awarded a Guggenheim: "Now you can go right on working in your own way, there in your home, can't you, and not have to be anxious?"

Her letter of May 19 touched on a topic that was just below the surface for everyone but conspicuously absent from most of the correspondence Still was receiving at the time—the war in Europe. After a good day spent visiting friends in the country and then an afternoon of rearranging furniture in her living room, Dorothy settled down to listen to the news.

> I find myself very tired and more than a little sad, and deeply in need of talking to a friend and there's no friend I want to call and wake at this hour of night. It is the news that is most saddening, for I've just heard a man tell, at length, the reasons he believes England will surely fall before the summer is done, and how, even now, not twenty percent of the American people believe it possible that that could happen, or that we should help with more than food and aid "short of war." . . . Surely tomorrow will be a better day![12]

With optimism reminiscent of Scarlett O'Hara's, her brushing the impending war under the rug and rationalizing the angst it was causing were typical in America before the bombing of Pearl Harbor, which was still seven months away.

By June her letters became even more frequent and intimate. Without formally dating them, she simply recorded the day and time at the top (e.g., "Friday morning, early"). Still was writing her regularly too, although his letters have not survived. Their relationship was becoming deeper and showed the possibility of intimacy. The Guggenheim offered him support and allowed him freedom to travel. He had written her of his plans to make a trip west in the summer and invited her to join him for part of that trip. Her acceptance was guarded because she considered this a big step in their friendship:

> Many times, these busy, pleasant days, I've thought of your good letter and of your friendly wish that I might share the trip you have planned with you, and of my answer, wondering whether that wish was one you would really like to see come true and whether my saying it might, if it suited you, dismayed or pleased you. Possibly the idea seems, in reality, too unconventional, with too much of a responsibility toward another person and her having a good time, to be right. So long as it was all right to you and to me, as I think it surely would be, it would *be* all right, wouldn't it?[13]

She continued by expressing her desire to know him much better. He had visited her and Pan in New York twice, but since her friend was always in the picture, Dorothy felt that they had not had a good chance to get to know each other. She wished for some unhurried time when they would have the opportunity to "really get acquainted, with hours free from obligation for either of us toward other friends, and freedom, for me, from any need to feel that I was being selfish or unkind toward a friend I love by wanting as much of your interest and talk as I naturally would like."

Though not a passionate love letter, this did show that Dorothy, even at the beginning of their relationship, wanted to spend time with Jim and share his life. While today an unmarried couple traveling together across the country would not raise an eyebrow, it would have been unconventional and rare in 1941. The only clue to her family's reaction came in a letter that Margeurite Lewis, one of the family friends they met on their travels, wrote to both Dorothy and Jim: "Regarding this excursion your mother told me over the phone that she felt you and Jim both came home rather fearfully, wondering how Mama would like it." When Marguerite asked how she did like it, Dorothy's mother said, "If Dorothy isn't old enough to take care of herself by now, I don't know what I could do about it!"[14] Indeed, in her early forties, Dorothy could take care of herself. But her mother was conservative, and Dorothy did not like to cross her. All this shows that even before the trip began, she and Still were serious enough about their friendship to be willing to ruffle feathers. Reading between the lines, it seems that she hoped this adventure would be the beginning of an intimate love affair. It is more difficult to judge what Still wanted from it, but he could not have missed the message her letters were conveying. At the least, he was curious about the potential for love between them.

While they were planning the trip, several letters followed in quick succession. Still made it clear that they must travel "on a shoe string." She accepted that because she did not yet know the fate of a "big" story she had submitted. If it did not sell before they left, she would also be economizing. She was very accommodating of all his ideas about the trip; she wanted him to do the arranging. Finally, by Saturday evening, she wrote a touching acceptance of his offer:

> Jim, are you quite serious, and speaking from a wish that you would really like to have come true when you say "I wish you could take part of this trip with me. It would do us both good"? For if you really wish it, I think I could go then, and I don't see why I shouldn't. The world is so unsure, and I am sure you are right in believing it would do us both good to look on places enduring. I should like to be beside you when you see for the first time our prairies and the Rocky Mountains, and I'd like you by me, and hold my hand when I first see Yellowstone.[15]

Much of 1941 had been emotionally difficult for Still. His brother Alfred had been shot in a hunting accident in mid-February. Still went home to Fairfax to stay with him and did not return to Dead Mare Branch until May. He described the hard recovery to Katherine Anne Porter: "For seven weeks his life was uncertain. Three operations were performed, many transfusions administered, and there were days on days of cruel suffering. Thanks to his courage, to his will-to-live, to sulfanilamide and 1941 surgery, he has come through."[16] He also thanked Porter for the recommendation she had written to support his Guggenheim Fellowship application, which had been successful. In March he had received word that he would be granted a stipend of $1,200 for the year. That was sufficient for his needs, but he had not counted on the major interruption, and his funds were dwindling.

He had also intended to concentrate on writing the entire year, but his brother's slow recovery made it difficult for him to regain a level of creative productivity. His frustration lasted into late spring. Dorothy tried to encourage him when she wrote, "Jim, I don't like you to be feeling a need to say of your work, of any part of your work, 'I am unhappy about it all.' I know how it is to feel like that, and lonely it is!" Always supportive and optimistic, she concluded, "It is good work, Jim, wonderfully good. Surely a way will open."[17]

If he was showing signs of depression, she was the opposite. The very thought of the trip was lifting her up. She reported that she had gone to town to buy two books and a red wool jacket. She had always wanted a red jacket, but she was finally inspired to get one when she read the chapter in *River of Earth* in which the grandmother pulled the small red coat out of the trunk and put it on the boy. Dorothy was somehow molding her life in New York City to fit Still's quiet world of Kentucky stories. She ended that letter with one more positive expectation about their upcoming trip: "I'm still tasting the surprise and pleasure of your thinking of this for us to enjoy together, Jim."[18] By mid-June, they were still making and adjusting plans. Now she was talking of their writing a story or a whole book together and was busy coming up with ideas for it. She wondered if they should take a typewriter with them on the trip. She was all packed except for putting her dresses in her suitcase. But again they experienced a setback. Still was working on the manuscript of his story collection *On Troublesome Creek*, which he needed to get to Viking before they left, and he was having some eye problems that were slowing his work. Thomas was all sympathy and encouragement, just like an attentive girlfriend or wife would be. She did not rush him. The tentative plans had been to meet in Chicago around June 26.

It is impossible to say what exactly happened on their extended trip, but she outlined their itinerary in a letter she later wrote to Pan. Jim and Dorothy rendezvoused in Chicago on Sunday, July 28, where they met her brother Macklin, who seemed to get along well with Still. Then the couple took the train to Lincoln and arrived at 2:00 a.m. He stayed at the Cornhusker, a hotel in downtown Lincoln; she stayed with her mother. The next day they visited Marguerite and in the evening saw the state capitol. From Lincoln they took the train to Billings, Montana, and got hotel rooms there. They spent several days seeing Yellowstone and the Grand Tetons and spent one night at Jackson Hole Lodge near Old Faithful. Then they proceeded to Salt Lake City and finally to Denver, where they went their separate ways—she to Santa Fe and he to Kentucky. This separation was not in their original plans.

Only two weeks after they had met in Chicago to embark on their adventure, Thomas wrote Still a short letter with birthday greetings. She seemed sad but resolved: "I waited, just out of the rain, those minutes before your zypher [train] went so suddenly, my good wishes went up to you, there beyond the steel and the glass. I was glad to see your face, in the moment of going. . . . Bless you, dear Jim, and may this new year of your life be a good one."[19] With this short note, she sent him copies of two letters, the one that Marguerite had written to the two of them and a second that she herself had written to Pan. Together those give a clue to the outcome of the trip. Marguerite expressed great sadness to learn that Dorothy had had to finish the trip alone. She was also sorry that her friend would not get to see Jim again in Lincoln as planned.

Dorothy's long, descriptive letter to Sterling captured the spirit of their travels until they unexpectedly separated:

> It was good to meet Jim in Chicago, to hear his Kentucky voice answering, when I phoned him at the hotel from the station "That you Dor'thy?" he looked just the same. We went first to have lunch with Macklin and I was pleased to have them like one another. . . . From the beginning it seemed such a holiday. We walked by Lake Michigan and watched the boats and rested under the trees, along with other Sundaying people. We were so pleased in the evening to get on the Zypher for Lincoln, though the only places for us were in the cocktail lounge. The car was full of very young soldier boys and vacationists. . . . After we left Chicago, he said, with that air of joy in discovery that is his that he felt the world leveling out, in the darkness. We got into Lincoln at two ten in the morning. . . .
>
> After we left Lincoln we were twenty-four hours on a slow train to Billings, riding coach, to save Pullman fare, with not even the length of a seat to stretch out in. . . . We talked and laughed much, Jim with what seemed to me, unused laughter, holiday laughter, and slept when and as best we could. We were both very weary when we got into Billings, and very glad to find rooms and beds.
>
> We entered Yellowstone by way of Cody, and went up into the mountains in a hard rain, by bus of course. . . . We started in the dawn and drove up to the mountain height and saw the sunrise over all that part of the world, and it was awesome. The park abounds in animals: elk, moose, Grisley [sic] and black bear, antelope and deer, and we saw them all and walked a few feet from a moose stag, grazing near the road. . . . Jim was most interested in the thermol [sic] activities to be seen, and found it

hard to come away from boiling, spouting pits. Best, to me were
mountains mirrored in water, and mountain flowers. . . . That
second morning there [in the Grand Teton country] was especially happy in that way looking into a room is, when the door
is to be closed, at any moment. I was sorry to have to leave for
the trip out to Salt Lake.

I'm not sorry we went to Salt Lake and will always be glad
we saw it . . . but it was hot there, and seemed a strange country,
though people were nice, and interesting, and I felt heart-light-
ened when we left the place. The organ recital was impressive.
It made me cry when the organist played Lead Kindly Light, it
being a hymn of my father's, that they sang when he was put
in his grave, and I had no hanky in my pocketbook, and so
turned my head away, and lifted tears from my cheeks with my
program, hoping Jim would not see them—he has self-control
equal to his depth of feeling, and I think would not let tears
come, in a church. I was sad, that day, any way. I felt very much
a stranger in a strange land. Sometimes one can feel very close
to Jim, and sometimes very far, beside him. On the whole he is a
good companion, and there is so much we shared, in looking on
beautiful places, in listening, in talk, and in simple untried-for
understanding that is as good to remember as to have known.
Jim, I found in those days we spent together, is as individual a
person as he is an artist, and as fine a one, and I am happy to
have found we could be friends.

That was all she wrote to Pan. Her comment about "looking in a room
when a door is to be closed, at any moment," her description of him as
an individual person, her sense of being close to him some times and
far away at others—all these hint at a strained relationship. She felt "a
stranger in a strange land." Since Dorothy always strove to be optimistic and happy, she certainly would not describe negative details to a person who was close to both of them, especially since she intended to send
a carbon copy of the letter to Jim. A week later she wrote again and sent
snapshots of their travels. She brushed over any troubles and talked of
the story they had planned together. She was intending to write it soon
but expressed doubt that she could use a man's point of view. Instead,
she would start again and tell it from a woman's. That is the only hint
in the letter that they had not seen eye to eye.

Four months later, in November, she wrote Still another letter and included one more photo. She had remained in Santa Fe and seemed generally happy and productive in spite of her recent bout with the flu. After the polite formalities, she wrote a long passage criticizing him for remaining silent. Herein lies the clue to the emotional turmoil of the trip:

> Surely there is enough that is good to remember of our trip, and of one another as we came to know, respect and truly like one another through our stories and your poems and through letters before we came to really know each other, and through our talk on the trip while there was still a good, natural, kind and open-hearted comradery [*sic*] between us, before weariness from the hard journey and things said by each of us that had better have been left unsaid, hurt us and put us at odds, enough that is good to remember and enough that is good in our work when we read it, to make it possible and still enjoyable for us to write, as friends. If you are silent through carrying some grudge, it is unworthy of you, Jim, and unworthy of the friendship we shared.
>
> I, because I am a woman, because I treasure my friendships and hold to them, because I'm older and want not to be proud in ways that harm, because I do forgive you for things you did and said that hurt me so, and expect you to forgive me too for anything I did that you still resent, and because I like you Jim, hold out my hand, in friendliness.[20]

It is not clear if he took her outstretched hand. She did write him a few letters after that, but the spark and joy were gone. The last letter he received from her was dated January 11, 1948. She had sold the house in Santa Fe that she had bought after they parted on that fateful trip and had moved back to the New York City area. By then she had adopted a foster child, Deanna, who was ten, and went on to adopt another child in the 1950s. In 1959 she married John Buickerood and lived happily with him until they both died in 1990.[21] In the meantime, she had had a successful writing career, although by the late 1930s her stories shifted from literary, edgy, and bold to comfortable, entertaining, and popular.

Since the relationship between Dorothy and Jim was told almost exclusively from her point of view, it is impossible to know what his feelings were toward her. But the pattern of breaking suddenly from people with whom he was very close did become more obvious as he aged. James Still could hold a grudge, and perhaps he was doing that with her, but what upset him is not known because he never spoke or wrote to anyone about her or about the trip.[22] He did keep her letters and a photograph.

In 1941 Still turned thirty-five. He had put down roots in a place that he could now call his own. He had a house and thirty acres, supportive neighbors, and a satisfying profession. Just like Jolly at the end of *River of Earth,* he had a stand of bees. But unlike Jolly, he did not have a fair woman to be his wife. Brack wonders about Jolly's motives and planning, and he questions whether Jolly is really certain about his future wife: "What if this Sawyers girl says no?" Jolly replied: "She said yes a'ready. Just never said when. . . . A man's the master. I write that letter saying when." Then, in typical Jolly fashion, he confesses that he put sneeze powder in the proposal letter. And he enjoys the joke more than anyone. That is the full extent of Jolly's courting. There is not much romance in his story and very little seriousness. To answer Marshall Best's question, Still could not get proper courting into Jolly's life, and quite probably he had little success in his own. But the lack of romance did not seem to bother either of them.

Part 4

Army Life

To the War and Back Again, 1942–1946

14

Joining Up and Shipping Out

Weather and time, time and weather
Shriveled the wall, crumbled and chinking,
Raised the top log, the lower sinking,
Opening a space between upper and nether,
Making a crack for inside to look out
And outside to peer wonderingly in;
Peer wonderingly in where I am sleeping,
Trouble the dark, harry and flout
Slumberer from sleep, cricket from neeping.
But who on an evening at a quarter past seven
Stared from dusk and weight of heaven?
Mars hung bright in the Wolfpen sky
And glared and met me eye to eye.
Mars looked in and routed me out.

—On Being Drafted into the U.S. Army
from My Log Home in March 1942

After returning to Kentucky from the West, Still wrote Edwin Grover about his struggle to get back into writing. "Every new story is as difficult as the first one I ever wrote. I have learned nothing. I am still the rankest of amateurs; I am a blind man with a stick, trying to tap out a road going I know not where."[1] His frustration and despair had no specific origin. Simply put, life was not going well for Still in 1941. It should have been an excellent year because he was situated in his log house and had adequate funding from the Guggenheim. He also had a

183

specific task—revision and resubmission of the collection of stories *On Troublesome Creek,* which Viking was soon to publish. Yet he had set aside that task, he told Katherine Anne Porter, to work on a "project novel" that was promising to take a long time.[2] Its eventual completion was doubtful. When he turned his attention back to the stories, he grappled with them as well. When *On Troublesome Creek* was finally released, it met with muted enthusiasm and low sales. Early in the year, his brother Alfred had been at the point of death for weeks and out of work for months. In addition, his trip West with Dorothy Thomas had not been entirely happy or relaxing.

Another problem, which he shared with Guy Loomis, was also bothering Still. He was anticipating criticism that he had used his Guggenheim money to go on an extended vacation and to pay for his brother's medical bills. Maybe someone had questioned his use of the money, or more likely, he was pressuring himself for receiving funding without producing more writing. Whatever the case, Loomis tried to allay Still's self-doubt: "You know the world is full of jealous people who cannot stand the prosperity of any one else. . . . You are sticking close to the requirements of the Guggenheim award and have played fair with them. You said they granted you a months [*sic*] vacation and you took it to see your own country. . . . They put no strings on the money and if you wanted to use it to save your brothers [*sic*] life that was your privilege. And they would commend you for doing it."[3] Another part of the letter addressed Still's concern about his lack of progress with writing; again Loomis tried to be encouraging. "It is only by hearing from both admirers and critics that one can get at the real meat on any subject. . . . You know best the type of writing you are adapted to so why not follow along the lines you pick out." Such advice was meant to reassure his protégé, but the effect seemed minimal.

Still's discontent influenced his decision to join the army, a decision that changed his life. He later described the transformation simply: "I really didn't know myself till I got in the army."[4] A search for self, however, was not the reason he enlisted. His decision had little to do with patriotism and nothing to do with a desire to fight. He was not a pacifist like his brother Comer, nor was he a wartime soldier like his brother Tom, who joined the infantry.[5] Still did not think much about the war until late in 1941 when oblique references to the deteriorating situation began to appear in his correspondence.[6]

He later implied that enlisting was not really a choice because he knew he would be drafted. He was thirty-five, the upper end of the age

range for men who could be called. Also, he had no family and no political pull to keep him at home. "Parents did everything in the world," he
said, "to keep their boys out of the army, and I had nobody to do this for
me. In fact, I didn't want anybody to try." He did not want to join, but
neither did he want someone else taking his place. He tells of a woman
in the enlistment office determined "to get her son off," who made her
attitude clear when she blurted out, "Let them that want to go go, and
them's that want to stay stay." A person who overheard her responded:
"Well, we couldn't fight much of a war if we did that."[7] So he went.

That is how Still recounted his enlistment, but the actual story was
more complicated and less colorful. Jethro Amburgey wrote Still a letter
on December 6, the day before the attack on Pearl Harbor occurred. The
winter was extremely cold; the temperature in Hindman was six below
zero, and Amburgey was concerned that Still would be even colder in the
log house on Wolfpen. More threatening even than the weather was the
impending draft. He warned Still that the draft board was reclassifying
men from the age of twenty-eight to thirty-five and that Still's number
could be called by March.[8] Still went south for Christmas, but he had
returned to Kentucky by January 22, 1942, when Amburgey wrote him
a second letter, saying that Still would need to go to Hazard for a physical on February 23. Ten days after that, he could expect to be called.
That timeline came to pass, and Still offered no resistance.

Part of his motivation to join up was that, like millions of Americans, he was caught up in a wave of inevitability. In "On Being Drafted,"
his only war poem, Mars, the planet named for the Roman god of war,
found him sleeping peacefully in his log house and routed him out. His
sanctuary in remote eastern Kentucky could not remain a refuge in such
uncertain times. It was not the same place to him as it had been a few
years earlier; issues of the world had invaded. Whether called "enlisting" or "being drafted," entering the army was a function of his being
a healthy male member of the adult population. At home he was feeling
anxious, left out, and unproductive. By joining the war effort, he was
doing something useful with his life, at least for the time being.

Still enlisted on Tuesday, March 10, 1942, then spent one week
at Fort Thomas, Kentucky, where he took an IQ test. His high score
allowed him to choose the army air force.[9] From there, he was sent with
the 8th Air Depot Group to Duncan Field, Texas (near San Antonio).
He was immediately put to work in the main headquarters so did not
undergo basic training after the first day. His record needed to show
that he had been to the rifle range, so he spent a day at Fort Sam Hous-

ton on the firing line. Along the way, someone made the observation
that he was the exception to the rule that all Kentuckians were good
shots. That challenged him to get better, and he did. "If I'm the worst
I'm gonna be the best," he vowed. At the end of his instruction, he was
much improved. He described the outcome: "I didn't have any skin on
my rear-end, my knees or ankles . . . you had to fire from all positions
. . . I learned to handle the rifle just like a Marine."[10]

Still must have been cooperative and helpful in the office because in
less than six months he was promoted three times; the first was to private first class. He explained the impetus for that promotion: "As a private, I would have to line up in a long line, and it would take a long time
for me to get in, get something to eat, and then get back to the office.
So . . . [the sergeant-major] immediately made me a private first-class,
got a stripe so I could be in another line, in another dining room where
it couldn't take so long."[11] Then on June 19 he was made corporal, and
on July 1, sergeant. His group, most of them from Texas, was staged at
Fort Dix in New Jersey. They took the train to Jersey City and loaded
into barges on the Jersey shore.[12]

In an early letter to his father, Still gave a humorous and pitiful
description of himself as a soldier learning to carry all his equipment in
preparation for leaving the United States:

On the night we left our country we took a train from our station. Every man was loaded with equipment. I am frank to say
it was *more* than I could carry, but I did carry it somehow. My
field pack was strapped to my back jambed with personal articles like soap, razor, towels, raincoat, messkit, etc and under
the flap was a blanket tightly rolled. I had an ammunition belt
snapped around my middle, and to it was snapped first aid kit
and canteen filled with water. The field pack is held on by a
maze of straps, and is snapped onto the ammunition belt. Just
the above was a nice little load. Next my gas mask is swung at
my left side, with a strap going over the shoulder, and another
going around the body. Next my Springfield rifle, with strap
slackened so it will hang to the left shoulder. Along with the
above I was dressed in O.D. (wool) from head to toe; and I wore
leggings. The above mentioned items make a good load, but it
isn't too heavy if you don't have to walk too far, and if all the
buckles and snaps are fastened correctly, and all the straps are
given proper slack or drawn tight in the right places.

However, what actually happens (in my particular case) is that after I have gone a couple of hundred yards the ammunition belt begins to slide in the general direction of my neck, and the iron snaps of the pack slip off the protecting straps and begin to eat meat out of my shoulders, and the strap under my arms begin to pinch. However, on that day we left I had things fairly well adjusted. I had learned to put folded handkerchiefs on my shoulders under my shirts where two particularly offending iron snaps had to rest. Now comes the biggest load: the barracks bag. Mine and all the others, were packed to bursting with Army paraphernalia, personal supplies of all sorts, clothes, hundreds of razor blades . . . the things we thought would be lacking.[13]

All this was carried by a man who described himself as slight.[14] In the practices leading up to the final maneuvers, Private Still hurt his arm. The doctor told him complete rest was needed, but of course, that was impossible. Instead, he became determined that he would carry that bag or "bust"! He repacked, eliminating all but the essentials, and through sheer willpower made it onto the train with the other men. He described getting from the train to the ship:

As we rode along [on the train] I wasn't particularly caring about leaving America or anything of that sort. I thought of a long up-hill gangplank I had to climb at the last moment, and then I would have to go up like a soldier. We got off the train somewhere. We started marching; we stopped, started again. Well, it was tough going for me. Late at night we reached the pier, came off the thing we were riding, lined up in an enormous building. There was the ship, no lights showing outside, there was the gangplank looking like the climb to Mt Everest. There I discovered that both arms and shoulders were numb, and when I picked that bag up again I felt nothing. I went up the gangplank as painlessly as if I'd been in a balloon.[15]

He continued up several flights of stairs and threw his bags on a top bunk in a compartment amidships. He put the rifle in the bed with him and went to sleep within three minutes.[16] The next morning when he awoke, the boat was moving and America was disappearing behind.

There was a dreamlike quality to the experience, but nothing particularly patriotic or inspiring.

Although he did not reveal the identity of the ship in letters, he later acknowledged that the overseas venture was on the *Aquitania*. Still and the *Aquitania* left America at 10:00 p.m. on September 21, 1942. Still had very little experience with ships, none with ocean liners. The RMS *Aquitania*, Britain's largest vessel, was built by the Cunard Line and launched in April 1914. Still was proud of having traveled on this massive cruise ship—nine decks and space for three thousand passengers—even though the journey was anything but luxurious. She had been pressed into service in World War I, where her speed of 23 knots and ability to zigzag through submarine-infested waters made her an excellent transport for men and supplies. Again in World War II, she carried 384,586 servicemen to and from battle.[17] Still was one of those soldiers, and he claims there were ten thousand on board with him as they slowly traveled to Africa.

The account of leaving New York in a piece he wrote for the Louisville *Courier-Journal* in 1986 is very different from the description he sent to his father in the letter. The early version told of arriving on board, hurrying to a bunk, and laying exhausted until morning, at which time he noticed America fading in the distance behind the ship. The published account told of leaving America's shores with profound feelings, but without a touch of weariness. Here is another version Still related to George Zachry in the mid-1990s.

> As we left Jersey, packed together in a manner familiar to sardines, the men began to sing a bawdy song, a not uncommon practice. Running without lights we entered New York harbor. The towers of Manhattan were lost in mist. Suddenly the mist parted and there bathed in moonlight stood the Statue of Liberty, the base hidden, floating in air as it were. The singing stopped and only the breathing of hundreds of men and the slapping of waves against the hull could be heard. It was a solemn moment. With hand in air Miss Liberty seemed to be waving farewell. For some it was the last view of America forever. The singing began again, and the song was "Shall We Gather at the River?"[18]

Colored by time and memory, this version is touching and uplifting, whereas the original account was sarcastic and exhausting.

Although he had taken all the superfluous stuff out of his baggage in order to reduce the weight, he did not take out a small paperback copy of Thoreau's *Walden,* which Frances Grover had given him in June 1940. Why pack *Walden?* Perhaps he saw himself as a kind of Thoreau and Dead Mare Branch as Walden Pond, or perhaps it was a small, light volume that would remind him of home. In any case, he used that copy of *Walden* as a diary to record the first part of the trip overseas. He wrote all over the first few pages, then filled up the top and bottom margins of the first third of the book. Here is an edited account of the trip Still made on the *Aquitania.*[19]

Diary in *Walden* September 21—October 11, 1942

21 Sept: Sailed 4:30 am. Breakfast. Seasick. No lunch. Supper. Planes and blimp overhead all day. Boat drills. Heavy seas.

22 Sept: Ship alone in heavy seas, pitching. Hundreds seasick. Noon reported off coast NC. Air raid and boat drills. Bunk fatigue most of day. Afternoon, calmer seas. Flying fish. Very warm. Sun breaks through. Supper: cheers, coffee, bread, cold meats. Soldiers grousing. Water lines form. Boat beginning to stink. Reported 25 knots. I dropped "no cookies." Mess Officer: "We're going to have better food if we have to cook Limeys." Boys mocking English speech. Young English sailor: "I'm getting on a smaller boat. Too much red tape, too much class distinction." Already water precious.

23 Sept: No butterflies in my stomach now. Ate 1st big meal. Sea calm. Changing courses every 7 minutes, zigzagging South. Most dangerous night for submarines, it's said. Black out 5:45 pm. Have come by several books. Water short. Long lines at fountains, waiting for taps to be turned on. Gunner practice 10:45.

24 Sept: Gunners practice again today. Fire and boat drill. On break most of the day. Picked up 8 books.

25 Sept: Reading. Calm seas. Much "bitching" about food, the British.

26 Sept: Bath in saltwater. Spent day on deck. Reading E. M. Roberts "A Buried Treasure."

27 Sept: Crossed equator. Glassy sea. Reading.

28, 29, 30 Sept: Haven't sighted land since sailing. Getting used to food. I lost morning Report. A new one had to be made.

Setting clocks forward 30 minutes daily. Physical exams: crabs and jock itch in plenty.

1 Oct: Set clock 30 minutes. Boat drill. Good breakfast: coffee (bad) boiled eggs, bacon, cereal, brandy figs. Reading Undset's "Madame Dorthea." Over loudspeaker 5:45 pm: "Blackout regulations are now in force. No lights will show externally until 5:10 AM. Clocks will be retarded—I repeat, retarded, 30 minutes at midnight. Thank you." Down to canteen after supper. Talked to Al Wilhelm on deck until 10:00 PM.

2 Oct: 1:30 PM Fire siren. Awaked, (naked), put on clothes, stayed on bunk. Officer rushed among us: "Below. This is no practice. A raider has been sighted." We didn't move. Bell rings for boat stations. We file out quietly, line up by rails, "wings" touch wings. Officer, "If you have to jump, swim like hell if you can, or rafts will be thrown down on you." I feel calm. I am only concerned for the mass fear that seems just under control in those about me. To Starboard there's a light flashing over the water. Presently skipper over loudspeaker tells us to return to quarters.

Breakfast. Will reach Rio De Janeiro tomorrow. Water on all day. Washed my dirty clothes in my helmet. Shaved. Put on clean khaki. Ship news says Stalingrad still holds. Saw school of Porpoises. Two big fish. Fly fish rise in flocks. Water rougher. Boat tosses and pitches. Zigzagging.

3 Oct: On deck at daybreak to see entrance into Rio. Mountain rising sheer out of water. Sugar Loaf Mt. with cables. The city against high dark mountains. Beautiful harbor. Many boats. An old battleship. A U.S. Destroyer. City a half moon about harbor. In the distance, on a mountain top, a cross rising above the clouds. Boat anchors. I watch all day. Not allowed to go ashore. All are shaven, and in Class A. Uniforms. "Some day I shall come back to Rio," I said. Many said the same. Crude Oil tanker on all day. Boats pump in water. To bed in a bunk, perfectly still. (Supplies taken on in the night)

4 Oct: On deck most of day, watching, studying Rio, building after building, mountain after mountain. Oil pumped in from boats all day. Guard craft go up and down. Ferry crowds shout as they go by, hold up fingers in V symbol. (We are under Union Jack. All wish American Flag waved overhead.) Planes fly over. No lighting restrictions while in harbor. Dark, low-hanging clouds most of day. Sunday—quiet.

5 Oct: Sunshine on Rio. A convoy moves out. Watch cable cars go across to Sugar Loaf. On deck most of day. Reading S. T. Warner's "Lollywillows." Gun inspection. Lost cap, dropped into harbor. Ships crew swim about. Oil and water boats alongside all day pumping. Red sails of our lifeboats spread to dry. I have memorized the water, mountains, buildings. Night, boys singing "America," "God Bless America." Rio lighted at night. No blackout in Brazil. Hot, smothering night.

6 Oct: Felt boat moving 5:45 AM sprang from berth, rushed to deck. No convoy. Sun rose out of sea. Past the forts, the circular city, Sugar Loaf. Goodbye Rio! Boat drill 6:30 AM. Cool, spray flying. By now cold wind and spray has driven most to our bunks. Announcements: Shorter rations; greater light precautions.

7 Oct: Cold wind, blowing spray. Visibility low. Field jackets out. Reading Hamsun's "Shallow Soul." Afternoon in bunk. Shaved. Few on deck. Boat drill. Singing in our bunks before going to sleep.

8 Oct: All waked by 1st Sgt for breakfast: eggs, bacon, figs, coffee. Formation 1 hour long on deck 10am. Clear sunny day—cool.

9–10 Oct: Cold. Few on deck during day. Boat drill. New Orders: "Don't jump if boat is torpedoed." Physical exams: I have caught "jock itch." Told to report to R.A. P #2 for treatment. There, told no treatments 'till Monday. Reading Melville's "Typee." Ocean slightly rough. Food better. Took salt baths. Exercise daily 2:00 pm.

11 Oct: Cold. Weak sunshine. On deck all AM chilled. No formation 10 AM Sunday. More "Typee" 1:15 pm. Boat zigzagged wildly. German radio announced Aquitania sunk last week loss 18,000 men. Afternoon while I'm taking bath men called on deck, told 5 ships sunk off Cape Town during past 2 days. We are to wear belts, canteens, overcoats etc. on deck. Two destroyers are to meet us at noon tomorrow, convoy us into Cape Town. Men uneasy. Everywhere discussion of the danger we're in, in latrine, on bunks etc. Men quieter, intense. 4:00 pm. Ship making wild zigzags. Most men have dressed, ready for boat stations in case of emergency.

The diary entries, which ended with October 11, show that Still had spent his first month feeling seasick, bored, occasionally anxious, usually grimy, and sometimes miserable. His primary pastime was reading books from the ship's library. Rio seems to be the only attractive part of the trip, but the soldiers were not allowed to set foot on shore. There is, however, a structure to the day, and there is always an abundance of men leading a collective life without really knowing much about what that life is and what it will bring. The next stage of the journey took the soldiers from Rio to Cape Town, though they were not told their destination. Since the ship traveled without protection, it continued to zigzag. As they neared the continent, destroyers came to escort them.[20]

At Cape Town the men were moved to a Norwegian ship, the *Antenor,* with a British captain and a Chinese crew.[21] They landed on the west coast of Africa at Freetown in Sierra Leone. "Every soldier aboard will remember the hour we awaited the signal to board the landing craft. Each of us a walking arsenal. The order rang out, 'Let's go men!'" We were excited but I think not afraid. We went. We hit the beach and nobody was there. We'd half-expected the Vichy French. We had no inkling of the vast movement of men investing the horn of Africa that day."[22] Still's outfit was ultimately headed for the Gold Coast of Africa. In the poem, Mars routed him out, but the U.S. Army Air Force took him in and transported him to another continent, a different world.

15

Somewhere in Africa

> A good New Year to you. It's almost bound to be an improve-
> ment over the one just past, wouldn't you think?
>
> —Katherine Anne Porter

Two months after arriving on the African continent, Still sent home postcards with Christmas greetings. The one to Katherine Anne Porter pictures an African woman carrying a tray of bananas on her head and a baby strapped to her back. On the other side, a cryptic message: "Merry Christmas; James Still, Somewhere in Africa, December 1942."[1] His terseness was met with her flood of words covering two single-spaced typed pages. Writing to him on Christmas Day 1942, she told a wonderful story of a truck "floundering through the snow" and up her driveway to bring roses from her publisher. Throughout, the letter attempted to move his mind away from the trials of military life and back to the world that he had known—a world of home and writing. Her philosophy was to go on with work because not to do so would be to lose faith and thus to add to the confusion and pointlessness. She struggled to lift him up in her closing paragraph.

> If all this seems very far away to you now, still it is the life you knew, that you will know again, when all our so strange and so varied experiences of now will have been absorbed and become part of our growth. Speaking only of those people I

know, I have never seen them so positive, so energetic, and so cool headed as I see them now. The men are simply off to the army and navy without a backward look, the women are taking hold at whatever they have to do, the capacity of human beings to rise to an emergency is always astonishing and admirable. You know of course that we have news and news, and stories and stories, and in the main we are as well informed as is possible, but it would be nonsense to pretend we can know all that is happening, and really there is no need. What I most want is an occasional word from my friends and my family—so, when you can, let me hear from you. . . . Yours, Katherine Anne[2]

The world she described must have seemed far away and long ago to Still. The year, 1943, would not be much of an improvement, but it did offer him more excitement. To friends and family in the States, he could not reveal his exact whereabouts. "Somewhere in Africa" was an acceptable description but also intriguing, as were his experiences. More often than not, his desk job was boring, but his health woes resulting from malaria and dysentery were exotic and only sporadically debilitating. It was his travel away from base that he remembered best. From the end of 1942 through the spring of 1945, Still was situated on the Gold Coast of Africa, a British Crown colony that gained its independence in 1957 to become Ghana.

The coastline was low and sandy; the central and eastern part of the country was tropical rainforest. The 8th Air Depot was a ten-square-mile cleared area near Accra on the Gulf of Guinea. The jungle began about five miles beyond the base. Ocean breezes moderated the near-equator conditions. Daytime temperatures averaged eighty degrees and remained fairly constant throughout the year. The depot was designed to make major overhauls to engines and aircraft; the airfield served as a storage area for C-47 transport planes. The base was identified only by an entrance sign that read, "U.S. Army Air Force 8th Air Depot Group"; from it hung a crest of a Roc, a giant mythical bird of the Arabian Nights, so mighty that it held an airplane hangar in one claw and in the other a banner with the motto "We Take the Rocky Road."

The air base was originally a Pan American Airways (Pan Am) operation. In 1941 the United States was technically neutral but wanted to support Britain. One way to do that was to use a civilian business to cover military aims. Pan Am already had an air route through Central Africa to India and was expanding routes in South America. When asked by the military to extend service to and across Africa, the company gladly did so, with advanced funding from the government. One of the building projects was the airport at Accra. Airfields in Africa had to be close together so that fighter planes could hop across the continent to the North African front.[3] According to a staff correspondent of the army weekly magazine *YANK,* "Pan American Airlines did a pioneer job in establishing airbases, training men to fill necessary jobs, hacking airfields from the jungle tangle, tactfully encouraging natives to work for them." When the United States entered the war, the army air force took over the airfields and the Pan Am planes. Pilots became part of the Army Air Transport Command. The first army personnel arrived at Accra air base in August 1941; Still's group arrived there approximately fifteen months later.[4]

Still sent his father impressions of the people he was meeting in Africa. His group was associated with a British camp. When he first saw British soldiers drill, he was amused by how fancy the performance looked—"the heel clicking on coming to attention, the way they swung their arms front and rear, their modified goose-step, their knee-lifting and stomping to do an about-face."[5] But he described the Americans as also looking a little strange; a South African soldier told him that the Yankee helmets made them look like Jerries. All the Americans, he reported, were called "Yanks," even the Southerners. The local people, whom Still identified as "black" because he was not allowed to name them by nationality, addressed every soldier as "Joe." His effort to distinguish groups of people by some feature that would be relevant to his father showed his own need to place himself in this new world.

Still rarely wrote or spoke about his everyday work and life in Accra. Perhaps he quickly found it routine and boring. However, not every soldier was so reticent; one veteran, Wade Johnson, an eighteen-year-old soldier at the time, provided a picture of the typical soldier's life there.[6] They carried out repair work on aircraft that were active in Italy and Germany. Supplies came through the area on the way to the front, and damaged planes were brought to Accra for repair. The runway was less than a mile long, which limited the types of planes that could take off and land. Some British pilots would "get to the end of the runway and just pick the gear up and be out over the ocean."[7]

Accra had open sewers, a six-foot-deep ditch that ran alongside the paved road. Soldiers did not visit the town often because of the smell, but there was a hotel with an upstairs balcony, which enjoyed a breeze that freshened the air. Since it was a British colony, many local people spoke English, and some worked for the soldiers. The military hired locals for carpentry projects and to fetch parts and equipment in their red Radio Flyer wagons. Still employed a local, named Bamfo, to work in the office and described him to Jethro Amburgey: "He does the dirty work. He is clean almost to the point of being finicky, dresses in freshly starched white shorts that practically rattle when he walks. He is intelligent, does his work so quietly he is hardly noticed, speaks English in a clipped British manner."[8] Other than employing them for minor service jobs, the soldiers had little interaction with the local people.

Johnson described the PX (post exchange) on the base as the place where the men shopped for the things that were not provided, such as shaving cream, cigarettes, underwear, candy, and 3.2-percent beer. The PX was also the place where the payroll was dispersed from a little cubbyhole once a month. Still was in charge of payroll, but his job was finished before the actual distribution and cashing of the checks. The base also had a movie house, which showed films on Friday and Saturday nights. Johnson told of a "skinny little fellow named Frank Sinatra" who came to entertain them one night. Still never reported hearing Sinatra, but he did often report on his favorite recreation, going to the nearby beach.

In a July 1943 letter to Marjorie Rawlings, Still described the beach on a day when the waves were rough. Instead of swimming, he walked along the sand, reading inscriptions on the native boats; his favorite was "I will try and see." He also walked in the edge of the nearby grasslands and wrote that she would like the tropical flowers and exotic birds. "We will all buy and take home things from this continent, but we cannot take the blue African sky, or the birdlife that looks freshly painted, or the way the wind goes through the palms, or the wild look of vast savannahs, or the great biological mastodon that is the jungle."[9]

The camp, which housed about one thousand men, was located approximately one mile from the airfield and contained hundreds of fourteen-foot-square plywood huts with screen windows on all sides. Each hut had four or five canvas cots with mosquito netting to shield sleepers from the malaria-carrying mosquitoes, which were a major problem. For protection, soldiers were supposed to take Atabrine tablets (an antimalarial drug—synthetic quinine), which turned their skin yellow. Either the drug did not work for Still or he failed to take it regularly because he suffered several bouts of malaria. In April 1944, after being released from the hospital, Still wrote Amburgey about his most recent episode: "Must still report to dispensary daily for 6 green catty-cornered pills of ferrous sulphide. Glad to stop taking atebrine [sic] as I'm yellow as a sunflower from being so chuck full. Feel a bit weak yet, and am not quite up to former self. . . . Here's hoping I have established an immunity to malaria." He did not develop the immunity he wished for and suffered another bout in May or June, also resulting in hospitalization. The men also suffered from the "beastly" heat, which Still described to Amburgey as "the hottest weather we've experienced. So long as there's a breeze it is bearable. But about bedtime when the breeze dies and the mosquito nets must be down the huts are like ovens. Yet it is not so torrid in my hut as it was in the hospital. There my pillow would get sopping wet every night."[10]

To contrast with the miserable living arrangements, the men created strong bonds within small groups. Two of Still's hut mates were Horace Forest and Charles Krull. Also in the hut were two canaries, Little Joe and Little Moe, tame enough to eat peanuts out of their hands.[11] He never thought of the men as close friends, but he got to know and like many of them. The five men in a hut would do things together and "become like a family. When somebody got a box from home, it was always shared; we'd scrounge for each other. Everything about it was good." The men were not allowed to have cameras, but somehow somebody got one and took a picture of him asleep in the nude.[12] Obviously, a playful camaraderie existed among hut mates.

On one occasion, Still was surprised and delighted to meet a man from Knott County who was passing through Accra. He described the chance encounter to Amburgey: "Yesterday a team of U.S. Sailors came to play our soft-ball nine. This morning as I ate breakfast at the mess hall I looked up to find Seaman Paul Johnson, (Mitchel Johnson's boy from Mousie, KY) standing beside me. At first I thought I had been in Africa just one day too long—but it was Paul." Still introduced him to the officers, and they arranged for the sailors to stay on another day. They all attended a USO show that night.[13] Locally organized social events also occurred. For example, they marked their first anniversary in Accra with a barbeque. Then on September 21, 1944, the 8th Air Depot Group celebrated its second year with "a day-long holiday and a carnival complete with American hamburgers, ice cream, beer, music, and various events culminating in a lottery at night in which $3,000 in prizes are to be given to G.I.'s holding the lucky tickets."[14]

One piece of memorabilia that Still sent Guy Loomis in 1943 was a mimeographed Christmas program. It listed a Christmas Eve service of scripture reading, choir performance, and the regimental band plus

African dancers. The carol singing ended with a joint salute: "The Star-Spangled Banner" followed by "God Save the King." The menu for Christmas dinner on the following day included avocado and oranges, cream of tomato soup with croutons, turkey with fillings, cranberry sauce, mashed potatoes, green beans, corn on the cob, coleslaw with dressing, apple fruit cake and ice cream, coffee, bread and butter, pickles and chow, cigarettes, and candy and gum—a true feast.

The men did create a social microcosm in Accra, yet their day-to-day life was hard work, not fun or celebratory. The *YANK* article "Wings over Africa" reminded readers that "behind every plane that roars from the ground of Africa are hundreds of men doing ordinary duties. The 8th Air Depot deserves great credit in keeping the ships of CAFW in the air. Most of the men have been in Africa many months without recognition. Their only job, seeing planes take off on schedule, has been their reward and their reason for existence."[15] There was always work to do even for those not directly connected to the planes.

Men throughout the organization had to be maintained, fed, paid, and granted sick leave or furloughs. The continual stream of complaints had too few personnel clerks to handle them. Though not physically demanding, Still's work was detailed, tedious, stressful, and often boring. The military description of his position, included in his discharge papers, read, "Administrative Non Commissioned Officer: Supervised personnel clerks in maintaining service records, and qualification cards of individual soldiers. Directed the make up of pay rolls for the unit, and all other clerical duties involved, handling personnel."[16] In later years, Still described his job as keeping records of everything that was requisitioned, especially food. Plus he was in charge of the bank and provided information to the accountants. Since soldiers had only the PX and the town in which to spend money, they kept most of their pay in the bank.

"The main problem with the Army," said Still, "was boredom. Day in, day out, trying to figure out what to do with all these young men."[17] Then there were days when the tension mounted. He described how once he had the feeling he wanted to break windows out. To control himself he merely kicked a wire basket full of papers.[18] In September 1944, two and a half years after leaving home for the army, Still wrote this description of his job to Amburgey

I have been Personnel Sergeant Major for nearly ten months. In some ways I had no gifts for such a job, in others I was cut out for it. No slackening of work in my department; it seems to come on forever. We are short-handed at the moment. . . . The detail is immense. The two soldiers who had this job before me were edgy-tempered, loud-mouthed bastards—and I understand now how they got that way. On the whole I have kept my temper and blown-my-top seldom. For one thing I decided long ago not to worry. On rare occasions when I think my head is going to explode I just walk out, put on my bathing suit and head for the beach. An hour's swim usually clears up all problems. But I do like this job, and am a little bit proud to have it. In this outfit there are jobs far more important perhaps, but there are none I would find more interesting, more diverse. There's none other which would fit the contrary human being that I am.

He reassured his friend that he did not want to return home as long as the European war was in progress. It was partly a matter of commitment, perhaps of honor. But the letter ends with a hint that it was also a matter of choice. "I don't want to get out of the Army at any time soon. In some ways, as the common G.I. saying goes, 'I never had it so good!'"[19]

One good thing about living in Africa was that he found time to read. How he found the books is a mystery. Rawlings offered to send him some, but he declined, explaining that they would take too long to arrive. His eclectic taste meant he covered a range of titles. The list he sent to Rawlings included Nathaniel Hawthorne's *The House of the Seven Gables,* Sigrid Undset's *Return to the Future,* Van Wyck Brooks's *New England: Indian Summer,* William H. Hudson's *Green Mansions,* and Daniel Defoe's *Robinson Crusoe.*[20] In 1944 he suffered a case of dysentery so serious that he was checked into the British hospital. While recovering, he read all seven hundred plus pages of the unabridged version of T. E. Lawrence's *Seven Pillars of Wisdom.*[21]

He liked certain challenges of the job, and he liked the beach. However, the best aspect of military life for Still was the possibility for travel. He loved it—the adventure, the risk even. For a wandering soul, this was the opportunity of a lifetime, and he took full advantage. Still did not keep a detailed travel journal while there, but he did keep highlights of the trips he made in his memory. Much later, he reflected on his exploration but in a fairly disorganized way. It is difficult to recount or even count his trips. He described one of them in a letter to his father that was published in a local Alabama paper under the headline "Staff Sergeant James Still Tells of Trip to Holy Land." This twenty-eight–day trip probably took place in December 1944 and was part of an eight thousand–mile junket by air.

> During the seven days in the Holy Land it rained a little nearly every day; my tent leaked, my cot got wet. I wore ODs [warm olive drab uniform] for the first time in two years, and was chilly a good bit of the time. Two years in the tropics has thinned my blood to the consistency of water. But during the seven days I worked hard at seeing the land of Canaan—Judea, Samaria, Ballilee [Gallilee]. Travelled mostly by GI truck.
>
> Jerusalem is a beautiful city, and I was surprised to find it so. Seen from afar, it is a kind of dream in stone. A closer view destroys this illusion partially, though not altogether. New Jerusalem is modern; old Jerusalem is much as it was in ancient times. Judaism, Christianity and Islam claim this as their "Holy City." For a thousand years the various sects have scrambled to control the Holy Places. . . . The key to the Church of the Holy Sepulcher is kept by the Moslems—a curious fact.
>
> I walked the Via Dolorosa to Calvary; I entered King Solomon's quarry, a cave under the city, where milk white marble is still mined, as in ancient times; I went to the Mount of Olives, the Garden of Gethsemane; I saw Zion, the Valley of Jehoshaphat, Valley of Kedron [Kidron], Tyropoeon Valley, Mount Moriah, Mount Scopias [Scopus], and went in and out of the various gates, the Damascus Gate, Golden Gate, Jaffa Gate, Herod Gate, Dung Gate. . . .
>
> Bethlehem, northernmost city of Judea, was as I had imagined it; below spread the field of the Shepherds, all about the hills of Judea where David watched his flock, and I thought of Goliath, Jonathan and Saul. . . . Over the spot where Jesus is thought to have been born stands the oldest Christian church in the world. . . .
>
> On another day I traveled with a group through the Province of Samaria to Galilee. We stopped in the Plain of Esdraelon and our guide informed us that in a special sense this plain was the Key to the World. No other place has had so many decisive conflicts. . . .
>
> We drove on to the old Roman city of Tiberius, on the Sea of

Galilee. A retired missionary led us to his porch over-hanging
the sea and pointed out the places of interest. Somewhere there-
about Jesus walked on the water, and there he fed the five thousand, there were the cliffs before us where the Gadarene swine
plunged into the sea, there rose the "Mount of Beatitudes." . . .

At the end of seven days, I enplaned for Egypt, and checked
in at the casual section of an Army camp in the desert—a camp
of tents, sand, more sand, and at night, stars.[22]

He continued with a description of staying in a desert army camp at
night and in Cairo during the day. He visited the pyramids and the
Museum of Egyptian Antiquities. He described with feeling the Christmas Day visit that 750 Yugoslav refugee children made to the camp,
where the GIs presented them with gifts from their own holiday boxes.[23]

This description is beautifully detailed, and the letter has the sound
of a well-written travel document, appropriate for an American audience at the Christmas season during wartime. Since the original letter
has been lost, it is impossible to see if it was edited for the newspaper, but a good guess is that Still knew when he wrote the letter to his
dad that it would be published, so the paper probably printed it word
for word. Accounts of other adventures are not so carefully structured;
they tend to be confusing and impressionistic; however, the result can
seem more authentic. Certain motifs emerge from the collection of stories he told: foremost, a sense of danger and risks; also a marginally
acceptable level of insubordination on his part, irritation on the part of
his peers, but tolerance on the part of officers; a strong element of curiosity and his need to take advantage of the moment; also pervasive illness, weakness, and discomfort.

Here is the same trip just described in the "published" letter to his
dad, but this version is one he told at the age of ninety-two. His remarkable memory was surpassed only by his ability to "spin a yarn."

The second time I went to Cairo, I wrote the orders. The adju-
tant didn't want me to go. And he had good reason; he didn't
have a replacement. If anything went wrong it was his problem.
But I wrote the orders, and he let me go. "Ten days on arrival
4,200 miles from Cairo and if you're not back here, you'll be
AWOL." The colonel standing nearby said "I'll probably have
some business up there. I'll see that he gets back." So I had the
right to stay as long as I wanted to.

The colonel said "Who's going with you?" I said "I'm going alone." Colonel said "Cairo's a dangerous place nowadays. You can't go alone. Get somebody to go with you, whoever you want." Here was this fellow James Hakes, had been a movie actor. I didn't know him well. But I knew he had travelled in Europe on a bicycle. I could leave him somewhere. So I chose him. When he came, we had to wait for a plane.

I was sick. Malaria. It got me down. I couldn't go. Oh, he got excited. He went and somewhere found a beer and I couldn't drink it. One night I got a little better and he got me in a jeep and took me to an area not far away. And I stayed there in bed for a week. The natives didn't know what I was doing there. They would bring me food. They thought I ought to be in the hospital. Finally, I got better and I said "I can go now." We got on the first plane transport. This plane was going to Cairo. . . . I lay down all the way.

When we got there we didn't check in. They put us there on the sand in a double tent. It was supposed to keep sand out, but it didn't work. A huge tent with another one inside with two flaps. You'd burn up in the day time and freeze to death at night. I mean freeze. They would give us two candles a day. One night it was so cold we lit all our candles to keep warm. . . . And I started going into Cairo everyday to the YMCA. I was freezing to death. I'd get in a hot shower and just stay there.

Alright, eventually, we wanted to go to Jerusalem. One day I went in the headquarters in Cairo. That's the only place we saw WACS over there. I went up to the transportation desk, and a woman was sitting there. I had my orders here, but I didn't have orders to go out of that territory. I said "When is the next plane we can catch up to Tel Aviv?" She saw the order but she didn't look at them. She was supposed to but she didn't. I was counting on that. She said "8:00 in the morning is the first."

So to do that we had to come in to Cairo and we stayed in a hotel that was just one floor of the building, run by a Russian immigrant. There were children in the streets, in the gutters looking for food. We got to the airport—it wasn't in Tel Aviv but was a field. . . . We got on the plane and flew into Dalaman airport [Turkey]. They took us to the camp. My tent leaked and my mattress was wet. And I thought if I live to daylight, I'll turn myself in to the medics. I couldn't eat, keep anything down. I'd drink a cup of coffee.

The Red Cross would take people to Jerusalem and Bethlehem. And so I went with them. It was so slow, poking around. So me and James went and asked permission to go back just ourselves. It was dangerous. And I'll never forget that long argument. We talked them into it. We went and the minute we got there, here were all these guides that wanted us to choose them. Ours turned out to be a Roman Catholic. Well, we went to Bethlehem and all those places. We went to where Christ was born in a cave.

Then Hakes took off. I wanted to go to Alexandria. It was maybe 75 miles more. Then I learned that an Army truck went there every day from a certain point. This fellow said just get in the back of the truck, so I did. . . . Some places had roads and some didn't. And some places were supposed to be mined. In places where Italians had been shot down there was a grave with a cross and the helmet was hanging on the cross. We went into Cairo—it had been bombed. We couldn't find a place to stay. A man had a little buggy and he took us some place. I was alone.

That was the day I went to the catacombs. . . . I got back to Cairo and I decided I had better go back to base. I signed in. They knew very well I had been there a month. But they couldn't prove it, so they punished me. I sat there every day, day-in-day-out through Christmas, waiting to be called to get a plane.

One day there were a lot of planes; they were about two hours apart coming from the United States, filled with soldiers going to India. They had been sitting on that plane maybe 15 hours. Well, they'd get off and come in and sit down. Then we heard the announcement: "the Red Cross is waiting outside with trucks. You have permission of your commanding officer to go see the Sphinx and the Great Pyramids. You'll be accompanied so you can be back in time for your plane." There were 60 people there but only 8 or 10 went.[24]

Of course, Still went. He was so anxious to experience everything available to him that he expressed frustration at the lack of interest shown by the young soldiers. He blamed their poor education in American elementary schools. Or it might be that they were weary and insecure. Their youth led them to more familiar recreational pursuits. For example, the young soldier, Wade Johnson, explained that he once made a trip to Asmara in Eritrea. He was supposed to go on to the Holy Land, but he got sidetracked and stayed in the city instead. He got a friend to write out an order for rib eye steak, French fries, and salad. When he would go into a restaurant, he would show the waiter the list, and he ate steak, salad, and fries three times a day for three weeks. Perhaps Johnson is exaggerating, but the point is clear that some soldiers wanted to recreate the comforts of home when they were on furlough, and others, like Still, wanted to experience the wonders of the wider world.

To continue the story as Still told it in 1998: Finally, he and Hakes got on a plane to go back to Accra. On this leg of the trip they came very close to disaster.

We were on this plane going down the Nile and all of a sudden—it was a C-46 [Curtiss C-46 Commando], a two-engine plane—and one of the motors stalled. We started falling. You don't have any pressurized cabin and you know it. You think your heart's going to burst. The radio boy came out and he looked scared. Here came the copilot and the pilot. They were white as sheets.

Well, anyway they said the radio instructions told them not to turn back. We went on one hour and 35 minutes. I had a watch on, so I know. We saw Khartoum, the airport. And there were two runways, and we saw the ambulances running to keep up with us as we came down. We didn't have the power to come around and land on the runway. We just went across. We put blankets over our heads in case of explosion. I was relieved when we saw the ground.

I'll never forget. I was sort of proud of myself. I knew I was going to die and what I thought about. I can remember everything about it. I tried to speak to this lieutenant next to me, he looked so terrible. I tried to speak to him and I couldn't get my mouth open. But it wasn't fear. I accepted it.

All right. I didn't remember a thing about the landing. The next thing I knew there was an MP. And he was holding me by the arm and he was feeding me. I don't know what happened, and the next thing I knew we were sitting in a room. There were five of us. And we didn't have broken bones or

anything. They brought us coffee. We couldn't have told you
our names. I'd had a concussion is what I'd had. And maybe
they had too, I don't know. I didn't know where I was. Then
they put us in a carrier and took us to the hospital which was
a warehouse with cots in it. We went in. It was the afternoon.
Then a British doctor came after a while and he spoke to each
of us. He told us not to talk. In the night somebody came in
with a flashlight and called my name and this fellow's name.
Told us to dress. We did. Took us to the airport and we went
west and we went back to the base. And that's all we ever
knew.[25]

Other than this story, which he related some fifty years after the
event, the only reference to the crash-landing was a short piece published in the *Hindman Herald* on January 26, 1945: "A letter recently
from T-Sgt. James Still tells of his special missions he made to different countries of Europe. Sergeant Still almost met with a fatal accident
on his return trip from Asia to his base on the Gold Coast of Africa,
because the two motors of his plane went bad."[26] It seems that the missions were part of his duties and that they had taken him to Europe,
where the war was in full force. The article goes on to quote a commendation that Still had received on January 6. He did receive such a
commendation, but it was merely an unsigned form letter commending
him for performing his duties in a "superior and reliable manner" and
for "improving the efficiency of this organization, and the morale of its
personnel."[27] The public presentation of Still's war experience differed
from the actual life he remembered. Even the army apparently did not
realize his tendency to buck authority, and the people at home could
not know the difference between what he did for the cause and what he
did for himself. Comparing the newspaper account of the time with his
oral version from much later shows how he could meet the needs of an
audience as well as how his memory would embellish and his storytelling remake the event.

Another of his interesting African adventures is preserved in two
forms that invite comparison. He noted the incident as it was happening, and he recounted it years later when telling war stories. First, the
factual account. The James Still Room at Morehead State University
(MSU) has two small notebooks that Still used in Africa. One of them
contains notes like those he collected in Knott County to record sayings, words, or observations. The other contains only four pages of a

personal log recording a trip he began in Accra. The following is his written account of the incident at the time:

Accra Nov. 4 43

I am to ride [in the] plexiglass nose. Climbed in. Krull in behind, with the baggage. As we taxied down runway saw Mal and Al waving. Rough take-off, plane (A-30) turned toward hangers [sic], rose sideways, but we made it (I decided we had a 50–50 chance) I felt a slight, momentary unease, but had no fear. . . .

We are in convoy. Gulf of Guinea on one side, below the moist, water-strewn coast. Below white egrets are flying. Far inland Mountains are a purple streak.

Keta Lagoon ahead, and Keta. Water freckled with shadows of clouds. Turned over water now, flying almost into sun. I sit in a glass ball, floating through the air. Only the instruments about me give this an air of reality—of actuality. The Volta River

Home, Togoland below, in a forest of coconut palms. The grey somber church spire, white line of waves breaking on beach. The orderly streets

Over Dahomey [now Benin] Nigerian Niger River twisting like a great brown snake between green banks.

(Down) Ikeja, Nigeria. [air strip near Lagos]

All planes landed except mine. We circled several times, finally came in for perfect landing on a landing strip in the jungle-Ikeja. It began to appear there wasn't enough of the strip to halt upon but by strenuous application of brakes we made it.

I saw the pilot for first time, talked to him.

2nd day (in air). Took off 1311 fairly good take off, but far from perfect. We were catty-corner of the runway when ship lifted through clouds, circling, waiting for other ships to join us—170 mph, 1100 alt. Lagos [Nigeria] in the distance, seen through a cloud break. Niger River muddy below—All ships are up. On our way. Clear heaven ahead, the storm falling behind us. I check mph, alt, time frequently—Cruising 180 mph, alt 1900

Jungle below. Occasional opening for village. Clouds playing out. . . .

I think I see Cain in an opposite "nose." I call. No response.
I guess it's the navigator.

Jungle gives way. Fairly open country with belts of forests.
Passed two cities, many villages. Clouds gone. Blue haze. Visibility getting low. Ikirun below. 3 mt ranges to the right

    1402 hours—195 mph
    Over tops of bare rock mts—mulberry color stone.
    1405 hrs—200 mph.
    1411—mts ahead, sun breaking through overcast
    1418—no villages, no sign of human habitation
    Alt is making me very sleepy can hardly keep eyes open.
    Niger River ahead, pronged
    Villages—rusty and dead-looking.
    1500 hrs. 200 mph 5900
    Getting cold—feet chilly.

This event, recorded in objective detail while sitting in the Plexiglass nose of the A-30 bomber, is the raw material that he turned into the following narration in 1998:

The British were using a plane called A-30s. . . . they were very
short winged therefore very dangerous taking off and landing
but very maneuverable in the air. They carried one bomb and
they had a nose gunner in front and they had a belly gunner
down below.

American pilots flew them down to South America and they
put belly tanks on and flew them on to our base. So I learned
they were doing it, and I put in for it. There again they let me
go. It was all the colonel's doing. Everybody knew these planes
were dangerous. Some fellow said we thought you had good
sense. You'll get killed in that plane.

I'm in the nose. I can't get back in the plane. I'm sitting on a
parachute and also supplies, a hatchet, water, food and so on.
And I had the instructions about parachutes. We took off. The
way these planes go, you have to get up to 138 miles an hour
and lift the wheels before it'll take off.

You can't see the end of the runway. It goes into a mirage
. . . you have two knobs you pull back at the same time. One
of them slipped, sure enough, just as we got off the ground.

We dipped and that would have been death for me. We went straight for the barracks. The fellows working around the barracks just flopped on the ground. He just shot that thing straight up. I believe that's the worst thing that ever happened to me.

It nearly killed me. I swear it was terrible.[28]

If the original account was accurate, the takeoff gave him momentary unease but was not "terrible." The notebook does not refer to the trip in the A-30 again, but Still went on to tell an elaborate story including a Greek captain, a stay in Ikeja, and a serendipitous meeting with some GIs in a unit that was under his personnel jurisdiction. His 1998 telling of the story continued:

Alright, we flew down to Nigeria, Ikeja was the name of the village. It had one runway and a little base in the jungle. We got stuck there for about a week, bad weather. We didn't have anything to eat except biscuits and crackers. While we were there, there was a Greek captain who had escaped from Greece and joined with them. He paid no attention to the flight leader. Here I was an American. He didn't like the British. He took me in to Lagos one night. There were Greeks everywhere. He had connections. They threw a party—drinking, breaking dishes, throwing them. Wildest party you ever saw.

Then the weather got right and we took off. What did this fellow do? The tarmac was about as wide as a road. Then there's grass, then the jungle. And by gum if he didn't run off the tarmac into the grass. And as I tell it, I could have picked bananas as he went through the trees.

He landed at a place called Ikeja, with three palm trees and a runway and two or three buildings. But as we got near, there was an American flag flying and several buildings. It looked like 300 to 400 yards, but it must have been a mile. So as soon as we landed, an American soldier came out of the place and said "Why don't you stay with us?" I asked the flight leader and he wouldn't give me permission. That night the moon was full, just like daylight. I could see the trucks out there so I left [on foot]. And I thought I never would get there. When I did, they had already had supper, but they cooked steaks for me.

There were 12 men. Talking about coincidences—I requisitioned everybody's food as sergeant major. First, I did a report on troop strength; then food was ordered according to that. And we had units in places we didn't even know about. This was a group attached to us. They put up a sheet and showed a movie. Then I walked back to the barracks.[29]

A little later in his story he told of a time when he thought he might have to bail out of a plane. At one point, the pilot passed a note to him that said, "We are running out of gas. If we do not sight a runway in 10 minutes, you must jump." They must have found a runway because he never told a story of jumping out of a plane.

These "tales of near-misses" are reminiscent of Still's only publication between October 1941 and the spring of 1945.[30] A month after he entered the army, the Louisville Courier-Journal Roto-Magazine published a short humorous article "Hit Like to 'a Killed Me," which begins with a brief introduction in which Still says the idea of having a mountain boy narrate River of Earth came from hearing an eight-year-old Leslie County boy recount his adventures.[31] Still claims to have set down the words exactly as the boy spoke them. This rambling yarn about near misses has the same flavor as many of the war stories he told in the 1990s about himself. Perhaps it is coincidence that the boy's opening thoughts—"Some fellers don't never get growed up. They get killed down."—embody an attitude appropriate to the unpredictable dangers of war and the circumstances accompanying an adventuresome spirit.

This short piece was not the only one that Still published while he was stationed in Africa, but it was one of only a few.[32] Time to write was scarce. His job was consuming, and when he was not working, he was occupied with travel and adventure. Even if he could have written, communication with publishers would have been slow and difficult. Most importantly, the setting and situation were not conducive to the kind of stories and poems he had always written. Yet he did maintain a semblance of his former writing habits. For example, he kept a notebook to record the life going on around him, just as he did in Knott County. It included:

Provocative quotations he came across while reading, such as "The new deed is yet a part of life—remains for a time immersed in our unconscious life. In some contemplative hour, it detaches itself like a ripe fruit, to become a thought of the mind," from Emerson's The American Scholar.

Short dialogues he overheard:

Lt. Cohn: "I'll never get through regretting this war."

Lt. Johnson: "Why keep harping on what can't be helped. Nothing ever comes of regretting the past."

Lt. Cohn: "You never regret the past merely when you regret war. You are also regretting the future. Wars keep happening, over and over."

Interesting occurrences in the town: "An insane girl, about 16, dancing on street corner in Accra, naked. Crowd gathered around. She danced with closed eyes, a stick in hand. Occasionally would open her eyes and rush at crowd with raised stick. The crowd pushed back, shouting. A native said to me: 'You take picture?' No, I said and went on."

Comments of fellow soldiers such as this GI's candid sentiment: "My grandmother is a gossip and trouble-maker and keeps my folks always torn-up, but I love the old hag." Still observed life going on around him but did little more than collect bits and pieces. He might have been playing with ideas for stories from Africa, but they never materialized.[33]

His publishing was reduced to the submission of a few poems. Edward Weeks at *The Atlantic* politely rejected two of them in March 1944.[34] Still sent Rawlings a poem but had not kept a copy himself. When he requested that she send a copy back to him, she responded, "I have put your poem so carefully away that it will take me a hell of a long time to find it. I have an envelop [sic] marked 'Keep' that I bury in all sorts of places. When I find it, I'll send it on. But what a fiendish thing for a poet to do—send a lady a verse, keep no copy, and then later demand it!"[35]

Early in 1943 Still sent "School Butter" to *The New Yorker*. The story tells of Uncle Jolly's clever shenanigans to get the country school to rid itself of the old, outdated textbooks so the children could have new ones. The magazine rejected it as "too regional in content and tone."[36] James Still had never had a story in the classy city magazine, so he could not have been surprised. What is surprising about William Maxwell's February 1943 letter was his offer to send the manuscript directly to other magazines so that Still would not have to do so from Africa. Ten months later, Maxwell was still sending it around, going out of his way to accommodate the soldier because he was eager to receive a write up of "some incident" from Still's army experience "that would work out for *The New Yorker*."[37] That never worked out for Still, however.

The only real success Still had with publication while he was in

Africa came early in 1945, with this short letter from Weeks: "Your portrait of Mrs. Razor, as eerie as it is touching, is certainly one for the *Atlantic,* and unless I miss my guess, one for the anthologies later. I am delighted to have it for our spring schedule: it is a pleasure to us all to know that your pen still finds its voice despite your other duties." On March 18, he received a two-hundred-dollar payment for "Mrs. Razor." He returned the proofs by May with the request that the story be published without any military connotation. It appeared in *The Atlantic Monthly* in July 1945. Weeks had been correct in projecting that it would be reprinted in anthologies. It was a popular story—delightful and captivating, set as much in a magical world as in a typical mountain family of Troublesome Creek. It had no flavor of war or military life.

If this story was so well received, Still should have written more in Africa. But a question remains about how much of the story he actually wrote there. In a 1946 letter, he described the circumstances of generating "Mrs. Razor" in October 1944 while in Accra:

> One evening I climbed behind a pile of cots in a storage hut and wrote the first half of the narrative, and on the following evening completed the whole. Those nights under the hump of Africa were torrid. The faint breeze usually moving off the Gulf of Guinea had struck a dead calm. My hideaway would have glazed bricks—almost. I bandaged my wrists, like a tennis player, to keep the paper dry. The second evening I shed my khaki and worked in a fog of insecticide. . . . I hauled the manuscript to the Middle East, in a hip-pocket, folded, buttoned-in; for three months it skipped from one pair of breeches to another. The story went to you early the next year, and proofs arrived a few hours prior to my sailing by air for America. I had been away thirty-one months. Over the South Atlantic I discovered my hip-pocket was empty. The proofs had vanished.[38]

In spite of this engaging account of the origins of "Mrs. Razor," the story was not fully written in Africa. He had the idea for it as early as 1940. He wrote to his friend Pan Sterling about the real child he nicknamed Mrs. Razor and also about her story that he was in the process of writing. He must have taken the idea and probably a draft manuscript to Africa, where he completed and mailed it.[39]

In his romanticized account of writing through a fog of insecticide and losing the manuscript over the Atlantic, Still was reflecting on what could have been. The reality was that he published little and wrote even less between 1943 and 1945. In spite of his limited creative output, Still had extraordinary experiences as a soldier. They tested him and taught him, thrilled him and sickened him. As he said later, he became acquainted with himself during the war. It was the experience of his lifetime. When Rawlings first knew that Still was in Africa somewhere, she wrote to him to express her hope and belief that he would ultimately incorporate all his varied experiences into his writing: "If you were not a realist as well as a poet, I should be suffering about you, but as it is I rather rejoice in the experiences you must be having, which, for all the pain and hardship, you will assimilate and return again in a creative form. I don't mean that you will write war poems or war books, but only that everything that happens to you goes into the deep reserve pool from which you draw."[40]

His friend was right. He did incorporate all the experiences from Africa into his reservoir. He never wrote a story or poem set "somewhere in Africa," but the place had become part of him and would figure large in his future storytelling.

16

Coming Home Again

Life has had two distinct phases: before World War II and after
World War II. It rearranged my thinking.
                    —James Still in letter to George Zachry

James Still did return from Africa, as Rawlings had known he would,
but it took him a long time "to assimilate" and even longer to find "his
creative form." He was still a soldier when he left Africa in early April
1945 and would remain so for five months. His army time in the United
States was more unsettled and varied than it had been in Africa, but
not as exotic or interesting. His primary goal was to get himself out of
the army and back home to eastern Kentucky. A step toward that goal
was to renew connections from his past and tie them to his recent experiences. He had maintained correspondence with a number of people,
yet genuine communication had been sparse.[1] Now that he was back on
U.S. soil, he felt the need to see people.

His journey to the Gold Coast had been a slow ship voyage, but his
return to the United States was by air. Leaving Accra on April 3 at 11:25
in the morning, the flight stopped first in Ascension Island, then made
stops in Natal, Brazil, and in Georgetown, Guyana, and finally landed
in Miami on the afternoon of April 5. Once stateside, he began visiting
friends and family. One of those was Iris Grannis, who by now was suffering from loss of youth, health, money, and her husband. She had been
living alone in Miami, and when her protégé showed up at her door,

she was so surprised that she forgot to ask him about his plans for the future. Her follow-up letter of April 11 was filled with questions about his next step. He knew almost nothing about what would follow.[2] He was still in the army, and everything beyond that was uncertain.

From Miami, he went to his sister's house in Alabama. He remembered being there when a phone call came on April 12, saying that Franklin Roosevelt had died in Warm Springs, Georgia, about forty miles away. That event was the topic of national conversation, but the circumstances of Still's brother Tom was the family's major concern. Tom, age thirty, had been drafted into the army the same year James had left for Africa. Tom began his training at Camp White in Oregon as an "acting" noncommissioned officer and spent evenings taking classes so that he could be a "real" officer before being shipped overseas. He was proud to be in the 91st Division—"the toughest in the army."[3] While James was stuck in Accra and exploring the Middle East, his brother was fighting at the front in Italy.

Thomas Watson Still was in the Florence-Bologna offensive, where his infantry regiment was part of the 91st "Powder River" Division. An article clipped from a local Alabama paper described the July 4, 1944, encounter as one of its roughest battles: "A battalion of the 363rd captured Hill 634, southwest of Chianni, and repelled a number of savage enemy counterattacks in hand-to-hand fighting. The rockiness of the hill made it impossible for the doughboys to dig in sufficiently to withstand a highly concentrated artillery and mortar assault that followed, but, after withdrawing slightly, the outfit returned and retook the hill."[4] This report illustrates how completely different Tom's fighting experience was from his brother's deskwork. Tom survived that offensive, but on September 13, 1944, he was seriously wounded. He wrote his brother on October 18 with the confession that his situation was much worse than he had reported. He had told the family that he had been wounded only in his right arm when, in fact, both legs were also damaged. For six months he suffered with his knees, periodically having bits of shrapnel surgically removed. He asked James not to give away his secret because "Papa will worry enough as it is."[5] From the fall of 1944, he was in limited service in Italy. The fighting had been so heavy that two-thirds of the men in his company were killed. Tom's bravery and suffering earned him the Medal of Honor, the Purple Heart, and two battle stars on his company ribbon. By 1945, he was transferred to the air corps's air technical service command, yet he yearned for action.

The last letter Tom wrote James from Italy reflected on the day he was wounded—eleven men from his company had been with him. By the time he was writing that letter, only five of them were still alive.[6] When James returned to his sister's house in Alabama, Tom was in Italy. He had survived and was regaining the use of his arm and legs, but he must have been a constant reminder to his older brother that the war had many facets, most characterized by violence and sacrifice. While James was lucky not to see combat, Tom had been lucky to survive it.

After the family visit, Still had a week of R&R. Men were being sent to either Wilmington, North Carolina, if they were single or to Miami if they were married. He claimed to be married, so off he went to Miami. When he got there, he told the authorities that his wife was on her way. Though he was not booked into the "Cadillac" hotel where the couples were, he ended up in a nice suite in the hotel next door.[7] A week in Miami surely improved his morale.

Still had returned to the United States a short time before his outfit arrived at Morrison Army Airfield in West Palm Beach. When he joined them, he discovered that his records had been lost. The process of making new ones meant that he had to follow the steps of a new recruit, which involved retaking the IQ test. Having administered such tests himself, he had developed a strategy. He rushed through the easy parts, saving the hardest math problems: "I don't think I got it quite all when time was up. Then [the test administrator] grabbed the papers and graded them right there. He graded mine three times. He said, 'I've been here three years, done this test a thousand times.' It was the highest grade ever recorded."[8] Still was proud of his ability to work the military system to his own advantage. Scoring high and impressing the soldier was an example. It gave him a feeling of power.

He also enjoyed challenging officers to do him favors. One example occurred when he was separated from his outfit; rather than rejoin them, he requested a transfer. The verbal exchange between Still and his major went like this:

"I've been overseas two and a half years and I have had medical problems. Do you have the authority to send me somewhere else?"
"I certainly do."
"Well, I'd like to see you exercise it."
"OK, where do you want to go?"
"I want to go as close to home as I can."[9]

As a result, he was sent to Bowman Field in Louisville. On the trip, he was in charge of a group of soldiers. When his superiors were generous to him, he showed his generosity to those in his charge. One of the boys came to him as they approached Somerset, Kentucky, and said he had a girlfriend there that he had not seen in three years. He asked permission to get off. Still told him that he did not have the authority to give him permission and said, "If you get off, it will be real hell for me when I get there, but it's up to you." The boy got off, and Still simply responded, when asked, that he did not know where the soldier was. No serious repercussions.

Through age and experience, Still had developed the confidence to state his preferences when he had the chance. In Louisville he was ordered to write articles for the air force magazine, but that was not something he wanted to do. When he said he knew nothing about airplanes, the response was that they would furnish the information and he could just write. His response:

> "No, I'm a creative writer and I've never written anything on orders in my life." And by gum, they saw that I was the author of three books, and this fellow sent me to talk to the brigadier general. The higher you go, the easier it is. But you had better know what you want. He was very kindly and talked about where I'd been and all. Then he said, "Well, what do you want to do? Where do you want to be transferred?" [My answer] "As far away from the equator as possible."[10]

As a result, he was sent to Plattsburgh Barracks in New York, just south of Montreal. At that time the base housed an army air force convalescent hospital. The general's orders had been deliberately ambiguous because Still did not know what he could do there. Two officers claimed him, and neither would give him up, so he had a desk in each area: "I would sit a little while in one and go to the other and then I would go to the PX." The hospital there was for soldiers getting well enough to be discharged; the psychiatric unit appealed to Still, and he wanted to get out of his current situation. Again, he went to the person in charge and explained how he was expected to serve two officers and was "catching hell from both sides." He was soon put to work in the psychiatric unit. The soldiers would lie on couches and talk; Still would sit on the other side of a screen and listen.

He was sent to New York City for training in August 1945.[11] He had no reason to take the training seriously, having chosen Plattsburgh only because of its location and weather. He was simply biding his time, but being in Manhattan would give him the opportunity for adventure. One trip he "arranged" was inspired by a book he was reading about a warden at Sing Sing prison.[12] On the day that the army heard Japan announce the intention to surrender, August 15, everyone in the office, except Still, took the day off. He stayed to answer the phones. His own personal celebration came the next day when he was off to Sing Sing, located on the Hudson River in Ossining, New York, about an hour's train ride from Manhattan. Of course, he joked, he only visited the outside.

Another time, a movie star came into the training office at Number 2 Park Avenue.[13] Still did not recognize the person, but others were so excited that he knew little would be accomplished that day. He walked out and went to Brooklyn to visit Guy Loomis, who by then was elderly and housebound. Throughout the war, Loomis had written to Still with advice, friendly support, Christmas packages, and genuine good wishes. This homecoming visit from his protégé was special for the old man. In his suite of apartments, he had a private secretary, Dorothy Mount, and an extensive collection of clocks. On that day, Loomis requested that Still not "leave until the chiming of the hour—cuckoos and everything ringing all at once." This quick trip to Brooklyn was the last time Still saw his patron. They continued to correspond until Loomis died in November 1946. For years, he had given "Jimmie" money when he needed it, encouragement when he asked for it, health advice whether requested or not, connections in New York, and frequent "fatherly" attention. He had also given him special gifts such as an early Hamilton pocket watch.[14] In his will, Loomis instructed Mount to send Still a final gift of money.[15]

When Still returned to the personnel school office in Manhattan after visiting Loomis, the sergeant was annoyed that he had left the day before. Still quietly said that the sergeant did not need to reassign him—he wanted to be discharged from the army. The New York Times had stated that morning that everyone over the age of thirty-five was to be discharged automatically. The officer on duty concurred and gave instructions to discharge Still and send him back to where he came from. His next destination was Bowman Field, again. The supervising officer there welcomed him because he wanted Still, who was experienced with personnel paperwork, to help discharge other soldiers. Still speculated that the man was really looking for someone to take over so that he could make a smooth exit himself. This called for another maneuver:

I worked several days there. Sometimes we would have to do night work. We'd work up records; then we would have a list that we'd send by telegram to Indianapolis. Back would come approval for some of them. One night he told me to come back to work, but I didn't. Next day, he said "Too bad you didn't come. We might have put your name in." I said, "Really?" That gave me an idea. When I typed up a telegram, I put my name in. And the next day, there was my name. Boy, was he angry! After he cooled off, he admitted "Pretty nice trick."[16]

Still's final army destination was Indianapolis, for discharge. Once there, he met up with Corporal Charles Jones from Dothan, Alabama, who was also waiting for discharge. Exactly when they had met or how much time they had spent together is uncertain, but Still described him as a great friend.[17] Still spent one night in the barracks with Charles and some other guys—it was to be his last night in the army. The next day was September 3, the day after Japan had formally surrendered on the battleship USS *Missouri*. In a chapel at the separation center of Camp Atterbury, the military personnel followed protocol for the discharge. Still had one last opportunity to put his individual touch on the military experience: "This fellow came out and said to us 'You are no longer soldiers. You are not required to salute this officer. But as a courtesy, I suggest you do.' By gum, mine was the first name called. I went up and took my discharge paper out of his hands, did an about-face, and didn't salute. And nobody else did either."[18]

Jones had been there too; together they took the train south. Still got off in Winchester, Kentucky. The transition gave him a jolt, even though his friend Jim Stokely, in a letter six months earlier, had accurately described the world that Still was reentering. Jim and his wife had driven through Still's county on April 7, 1945, on their way to Berea. They had met William Hale, on the Hindman road. Stokely related the story:

Hale stopped his team and plow to talk: Yes, he knew Jimmy Still, had known him since he was a boy—indeed a fine lad who was too still and quiet and full of sense to ever get married; he had a yard full of blossom-bushes somewhere up on dead man's branch. Sometime ago heard he was printing some books. Never read any of them himself but knew they must be good books if Jimmy Still was printing them. He was somewhere in Africee now but hoped he would come back home soon.[19]

*"We dance round in
a ring and suppose
But the Secret sits in the
middle and knows."*

-Frost

"A Master Time"—photo montage of speakers at James Still's eightieth birthday celebration at Hindman Settlement School (created by Kristie Hollifield at Mars Hill University with photos from the Hindman Settlement School files). *Clockwise from top:* Wilma Dykeman, Jim Wayne Miller, Wade Hall, John Stephenson, Herb E. Smith, Loyal Jones, and Gurney Norman. *Center:* James Still (courtesy Tom Eblen).

Still's parents, J. Alex and Lonie Still. (MSU)

Chambers County Court House, La Fayette, Ala.

Early postcard of the courthouse in Lafayette, Alabama. (Still storage)

Young James
with his dog,
Jack, at home in
Alabama. (UK
Box 3 #2)

Alfred Still (1914–1965). Years
later Still said of this photo,
"My baby brother Alfred—a
very gifted human being."
(MSU)

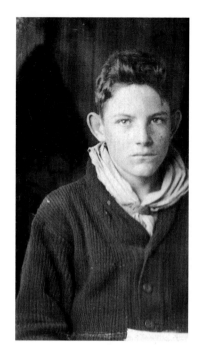

James Still, schoolboy. (MSU)

James Still, young man.
(UK Box 3 #3)

Mayme Brown "Brownie" (1910–1927). This photo appeared with her memorial in the *Mountain Herald* at LMU, October 1927. (MSU)

Still in Odessa, Texas, c. 1926, during the term he did not return to LMU. (MSU)

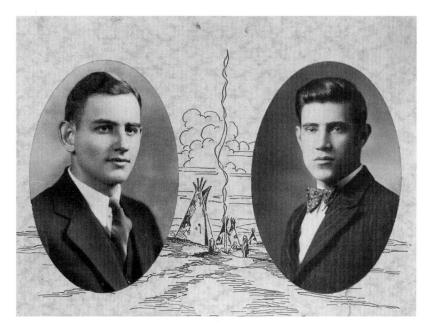

James Still and Jesse Stuart featured on a page of the 1929 LMU yearbook. The last sentence in Still's senior statement was "Men at some time are masters of their fates." Stuart signed Still's yearbook with these words: "I shall remember you as being remote from men. Therefore, apply yourself, and no doubt you will be master of your fate." (The photographs were originally made by Charley Cargille Studio; this copy is from UK Box 3 #14.)

Guy Loomis, c. 1930. Loomis was Still's patron from LMU days until his death in 1946. (Still storage)

James Still and Elizabeth Watts at Hindman Settlement School. (HSS)

Still, "the book boy," in Knott County. Elizabeth Watts once described him as walking sixteen miles with a box on his shoulder to take books to remote communities. (UK Box 3 #2)

Jethro Amburgey beside the well at his family's log house on Dead Mare
Branch. (MSU)

Front view of the log house on Dead Mare Branch, c. 1940. (UK Box 5 #2)

A sample of Still's writing notebooks. (Still storage)

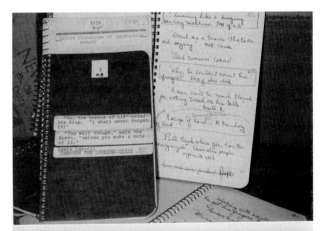

Still with Dorothy Thomas in Yellowstone in 1941. (MSU)

James Still and Dorothy Thomas in matching souvenir photos. (MSU)

Still in military uniform. (MSU)

Relaxing at
Duncan Field,
Texas, before
leaving for Africa.
(MSU)

First page of
the diary Still
kept in his
copy of *Walden*
while on his
way to Africa.
(Paperback at
MSU)

Military life in the Gold Coast in Africa and travels in Egypt.

Entrance to the U.S. Army Air Force 8th Air Depot Group near Accra. (UK Box 4)

Relaxing on the beach. (MSU)

"The Personnel Gang," May 1943; names and nicknames are written on the back of the original photo; T/Sgt Still ("Lucky") is in the second row on the right. (UK Box 4)

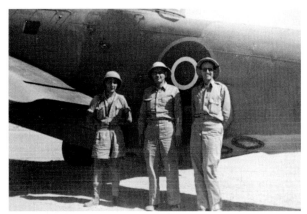

Forest Cain,
Still, and Charles
Krull. (UK Box 4)

Still with fellow soldiers at the Sphinx.
(UK Box 4)

Riding camels in Egypt. (UK Box 4)

Still in his garden near the log house. (MSU)

The front of Still's log house in December 1959. (Photo by Dean Cadle; UK Box 5 #3)

Reading to children at the Hindman Settlement School library in 1955. (HSS)

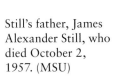

Still's father, James Alexander Still, who died October 2, 1957. (MSU)

Still with Monroe Amburgey in Whitesburg, early 1980s. They were friends for forty years, and especially close between 1945 and 1955. (UK Box 4 #19)

Still with Jethro Amburgey at the Hindman Settlement School workshop, c. 1955. (HSS)

Still with Dean Cadle in 1977. (Photo courtesy Dean Cadle)

Still reading to Teresa Lynn Perry in 1977. (Photo by Dean Cadle, UK Box 4 #18)

Still with Robert Penn Warren, preparing to enter the Letcher County coal mine in May 1976. (Photo courtesy Loyal Jones)

Weatherford Award ceremony at Berea College, 1977. Pictured with Still are Gurney Norman, Laura Shakelford, Al Perrin, Gordon McKinney, and Bill Weinberg. (HSS)

James Still washing dishes in the old kitchen of the May Stone Building at
Hindman Settlement School in 1978. (HSS)

Still's seventy-fifth birthday celebration in Hindman, 1981. Sharing cake with him are Helen Earp and Brenda and Cassie Mullins. (Photo by Frieda Mullins, HSS)

Still with Kentucky governor Martha Layne Collins and writer Harriette Arnow, early 1980s. (Still storage)

Still at his typewriter in his log house, 1982. (Photos by Warren Brunner, UK Box 4 #4)

Still receiving his fifth honorary degree, this one from President Charles Shearer at Transylvania University, on May 29, 1983. (MSU)

Still in Mexico, 1989. (Courtesy Sam McKinney)

Still at Chichén
Itza, 1989.
(Courtesy Sam
McKinney)

Still and Sam McKinney on the steps of Hemingway's Finca Vigía outside Havana, March 12, 1989. (Courtesy Sam McKinney)

Still in England, late 1980s. (Still storage)

Still with Randy Wilson performing their "dog and pony show" at the Campbell House in Lexington, July 1994. (Courtesy Molly Bundy)

Still "giving away" Teresa at her wedding, though he told her at the time, "I will never give you away." (MSU)

Thomas Clark and James Still celebrating birthdays together. (HSS)

Still holding Kaila, age twenty-two months. (Still storage)

Still holding Jacob, age three years.

Still at the gate to his house on Wolfpen Creek, 1982. (Courtesy Warren Brunner)

James Still at the well. (n.d.; UK Box 4 #10)

James Still with cat. (Courtesy Brunner Studio)

James Still's grave. The inscription reads, "The range of the mountains is his pasture, and he searcheth after every green thing. Job 38.8." (Courtesy Dobree Adams)

Still at the door of his log house. (Courtesy Brunner Studio)

Hale obviously knew of Still, but the incorrect details show that he did not know him well. The flavor of this brief encounter could have been a premonition of how Still's community would receive him when he returned from the war. If they had not really known him when he was among them, how would they think of him now? He would find himself a stranger in his own small world.

At last, forty-two months after he had left, he was home again on Dead Mare Branch. He must have felt satisfaction, but he also experienced a great letdown and a sense of despair, though he could not put a name to it at the time. He later described himself as not coping, just sitting in the door of his house, staring out. He had problems: could not keep food down, could not focus on work around the place or on writing. Possibly he was suffering a recurrence of malaria, but his difficulty seemed more general. A month after discharge, he wrote Katherine Anne Porter, describing his rough transition back to civilian life.

> The Army has discharged me after three and one-half years, and I am back on my land between Dead Mare Branch and Wolfpen Creek trying to establish contact with reality. It has been a long time. Coming back to peace has been infinitely harder than expected. America seems so quiet and self-bemused, so curiously untouched by the War.
>
> Weather and time have ravaged my log house. The front steps rotted down. The roof leaks. The well needs cleaning-out. My stove is out of whack and all cooking must be done on the fire place. The days are chilly. I keep a fire the day long. My service in the dead tropics has thinned my blood to the consistency of water, so I'll not attempt to stay here during the cruel months. . . . [20]

She responded a week later, on October 21, 1945: "What a scene to come back to, James, your little house and all around it gone to pieces; and those three and a half years gone, which could have been spent in it, keeping it pleasant and getting your work done. We have all lost those years. I wonder if what seems to you self-bemusement is just the lassitude after long strain."[21]

Was his situation the result of "lassitude after long strain"? Did his lethargy result from "thinned blood," which was another way of saying poor health? He was not suffering from "shell shock," the term of that time, nor from "post-traumatic stress syndrome," a more contemporary description. Still had witnessed no frontline shelling or trauma of battle. His condition was a result of moving quickly from interaction with people, opportunities for travel, and plenty of structured work to the quiet isolation and solitude of Dead Mare Branch, his beloved place that had suffered from neglect. The sudden lack of stress and structure plus the sense of being trapped in a setting that was both familiar and strange was the source of his disorientation.

His letter to Porter continued, "Overseas I had no time for creative writing. . . . But now I don't know when I can settle to writing again. I must get rested; I must dig up a little faith."[22] With strained optimism, she invited him to come to California where he could have warm weather and medical attention and finally concluded, "When you are able to write again, you will find your life returning to you."

The process of life's returning to normal did not begin for months. At first, nothing helped pull him out of his malaise. One event made him feel even worse. Not planning to stay in the log house during the winter, he left sometime in the fall for his sister's house in Alabama.

Charles Jones was living in Enterprise, Alabama, near Dothan, and was working in a School Daze Peanut Butter factory where Still remembered visiting him. The experience of this brief encounter was very negative for Still. He recalled staying in a hotel nearby and hearing a woman in the next room screaming as her husband was suffering a heart attack. That was enough to rattle his frayed nerves, but the next day Jones brought his wife to the hotel to meet Still. He described their meeting: "Charles was a short fellow. His wife was tall. She wasn't nice to me. She shook hands with me but that's about all. And then she said 'All Charles does is talk about you. He thinks more of you than he does of me.'"[23] This unfortunate exchange showed a strained relationship between Jones and his wife and may have had little to do with the friendship between the two soldiers. Still happened to be the object of her frustration, but because he was feeling displaced and vulnerable himself, her indictment was enough to cut all ties with the only man that he described as a good friend in the army. He left Enterprise and never saw Jones again.

"Go to Guinea" is an expression Still remembered from childhood as a polite version of a more common admonition. He had been there and was now back. In spite of the difficulties of Africa, Still had been more alive and engaged there than he was back in eastern Kentucky. Many years later, Jim Wayne Miller shared tidbits collected from Still, one concerning his experience in the rmy: "It seemed there never had been anything else, never would be anything else."[24] Yet if he was to go on living after returning home, there had to be something else.

He set about to discover the source of his difficulty. One possibility was physical health. He had suffered intermittent health problems. He had been hospitalized for malaria (blackwater fever) twice in 1944 and once for acute diarrhea in a British hospital in Eritrea. He had also experienced frequent attacks of lumbago or back pain between 1943 and 1945. From time to time he had suffered dizziness and nausea but had not sought treatment.[25] He claimed he was thin, but his recorded weight at discharge of 165 pounds would have been normal for a man of 5 feet 8 inches.

More significant than physical health was the dramatic change in the pace of daily life and the opportunity for social interaction. With the possible exception of Jones, Still did not create close friendships with his army buddies. Many of them he did not even like. He despised one officer, Major Nolan (named by Still "Major Nothing"), so much that soldiers taught his pet parrot to say, "Go to hell, you son of a bitch." In the army, groups of people were ever present. Even if Still did not become close to them, they had enjoyed a special sense of kinship. Being in charge of personnel, he knew a great deal about the men in his outfit, and he was acquainted with many of them. Something was always going on; someone needed help or just wanted to talk. There was a military hierarchy, of course, but little sense of competition except with the enemy.

Studs Terkel introduced his oral history of World War II, *The Good War,* with the insight that soldiers were not thinking of women, politics, family, or even God. They were thinking of food. Since Still's role for his group was requisitioning food, he enjoyed some standing with the men. The dominant themes for soldiers, wherever they were and whatever their jobs, were food, fear, comradeship, and confusion.[26] Still could add to that list excitement and adventure. The war, his years in the army, had been good. After victory, the boys—men now—came back to resume their normal lives. Yet, as Terkel pointed out, "it was a different country from the one they had left."[27] Still echoed this observation when years later he wrote that life had two distinct phases, before the war and after.

Ken Burns's documentary *The War* addresses the change that all returning soldiers felt. In the fall of 1945, 750,000 military personnel were returning every month. Redeployment and readjustment became an enormous issue for the nation and for individual soldiers. In the film,

Quentin Aanenson of Minnesota expressed the strangeness of being home when he said, "We all changed. We went out as a bunch of kids and were fought by kids. And we came back. Looked maybe the same but inside we were so different. They [Americans at home] thought we were just odd, I guess. What's happened? What's wrong? Nobody knows, nobody understands." Still's situation was not unique: his body was on Dead Mare Branch, but his mind was not. Civilian life seemed strange; something was missing. The common advice to soldiers feeling disoriented was to act normal; then they would feel normal.

This is exactly the advice that Still received when he finally went to the doctor at the clinic in Lexington in May 1946, eight months after he had been discharged. Years later, he remembered the diagnosis: "Dr. Kirkpatrick at the clinic said, 'You have a better heart than I have. You're like a clock that's wound too tight. Do the things you used to do.'"[28] It must have felt abnormal to force himself to be normal, but he did. Still took the doctor's advice literally and tried to continue his life as though the war had not interrupted it. He spent all but the coldest months in his log house; he had no car, so he walked or caught a ride if he needed to go places; he ate dinner with neighbors, hung out with men in the vicinity, went to a stock sale with his neighbor Mal Gibson, and jotted down interesting observations and sayings in his notebooks. He corresponded with friends and family. The mail arrived on horseback from the nearby post office at Bath, about two miles from his house. He spent so much time at the post office that he was dubbed the "unappointed mayor of Bath." He received a few letters from army associates but not enough to indicate that he had acquired an important new group of correspondents from his military days. The post office was his lifeline because it linked him to publishers.

He needed to resume the most important part of his life, his writing. Porter had correctly told him that when he could write again, he would find life returning. He did begin to write and brought his submission level back almost to the rate it had been ten years earlier. For example, in 1946, letters from magazine editors show that he submitted twenty pieces, most of them stories; in 1937 he had submitted twenty-seven pieces, most of which were poems.[29] He was approaching the business aspect of writing in the same manner as well, even sending pieces to the same journals and magazines. The difference was their acceptance of his submissions. In 1937 he enjoyed a 63 percent acceptance rate; in 1946 the rate declined to 30 percent.

James Still was not a stranger to rejection notices, and his attitude toward them appeared to be nonchalant. If the first "buyer" did not accept, he would try another. The submission history of one story of the period must have made him question that casual approach and may have caused him further self-doubt. He wrote "The Nest," his haunting tale of a lost girl, late in 1945 and began by showing it to Weeks at *The Atlantic*, who according to Still shuddered and said, "Alas and alas."[30] Next he submitted it to *The New Yorker*. When it was rejected there, he sent it to *American Mercury*, then to *Mademoiselle, Story, Common Ground, Ladies Home Journal*, and *Good Housekeeping*. They all rejected it. Finally, in the spring of 1948, it was published in *Prairie Schooner*, a regional nonpaying magazine based in Lincoln, Nebraska. Why did so many magazines turn down "The Nest"? Was it not good enough? Or was it too good, too real and disturbing? Years later, when a reader complained that the story distressed her, Still responded that it bothered him too—that was why he wrote it, to get it out of his mind.

That may have been the impetus for the story, but beneath the surface Still was expressing his own disorientation in surroundings that should have been familiar to him, just as Nezzie Hargis, the young protagonist, was lost and desperately searching for comfort and security—a nest. Still's attachment to the story could be one reason why he continued to submit it again and again. Part of his personal search was to return to his familiar life that balanced the solitude of work, the companionship of neighbors, and the place that inspired his creativity. When he could achieve that balance on a regular basis, he would be readjusted, and productivity would return. His seeking a publisher for "The Nest" was an expression of his determination to "do the things he used to do."

This evocative story contrasts sharply with his other story of this time, "Mrs. Razor." Both are set in a place like Wolfpen; both were inspired by real people and events; and both are about young girls in unsupportive homes—Mrs. Razor's difficult situation is imaginary, while Nezzie's is real. Still finished "Mrs. Razor" while in Africa and submitted it to *The Atlantic*, which snapped it up and predicted its bright future. The story did have an excellent run—the best of any of his stories. Anthologies that selected it for inclusion in the 1940s were *The Pocket Atlantic; The Best American Short Stories of 1946;* a college textbook of short fiction; and an anthology of stories called *The Wings of Madness,* which purported to illustrate "the literary mind at work on psychiatric material."[31]

The delightful and exasperating six-year-old Elvy—aka Mrs.

Razor—imagines that she is married to a "lazy shuck of a husband," who has abandoned her and their three children. Elvy's real father begins the story wanting "to do something about that child." Instead of following his first line of thought and giving her "a small thrashing," he plays along, loading his family into the wagon and taking them to the imaginary Biggety Creek to hunt for Razor. It was his way of indulging her fantasy while leading her back to actuality. That situation could be the subject of a psychiatric study, but it also shows the power of the creative imagination. Does Mrs. Razor exit her invented world and return to a reality that is drab but supportive? The story does not say, but the real family turns back toward home as Elvy dozes.

Unlike Elvy's situation, Nezzie's father is not trying to help. He is unaware and unconcerned. He wants rid of the child so that he can get on with his business, which is to adore his baby son and placate his wife, Nezzie's stepmother. He instructs his six-year-old to cross the mountain to her aunt's house for the night, then sweetens the deal with "I'll bring you a pretty." Nezzie's journey is gripping and tragic. The winter weather and her fragile emotions make her trip lonely, harsh, confusing. She loses her way and her grasp on reality. Like Elvy's, Nezzie's story ends with her falling asleep, but not in a wagon surrounded by her family. She gives way to the overwhelming need to bury herself in a soft comfortable home, a clump of broomsage. It was like a rabbit's bed, a nest.

Both stories are beautifully rendered but with differing effects. Elvy's tale is charming; Nezzie's is disturbing. When considered together, they reveal something about James Still in 1945–1946. Still had the idea of Mrs. Razor and possibly even a draft before he left for Africa. He completed it there, so not surprisingly, it is infused with the spirit of Still's war experience. She is not happy about her lout of a husband at Biggety Creek or the situation he has put her in, but she is persistent in duty and determined that she can fix the problem. With group support, she sets out to do so. The imagined adventure becomes real in the telling. She is a victim, but her situation is not hopeless.

The completion date of "The Nest" is unknown, but Still's search for a publisher did not begin until several months after he returned from the war. Nezzie is alone; she is determined to do what she is told to do, but through no fault of her own, she is controlled by forces much bigger than she. In spite of her best effort, she is not up to the task, and she has no help. She is lost even as the sun begins to rise and life returns to the world. The story reveals something of Still's state of mind when he returned home. He retreated to the place where he had once found comfort, but for a good while he found no renewal there. Perhaps he did write the story, as he said, to get rid of it. Through the writing he began to feel himself again.

It is not hard to account for America's love for "Mrs. Razor" and the corresponding rejection of "The Nest." The country wanted to feel as if they, all together, had visited Biggety Creek and solved the problem. A story of a persistent and delightful young girl, one who is wise beyond her years and who has at least the imagination to triumph over adversity, is just the sort of character Americans needed. Why would they embrace a story about a lost and abandoned child who curled up to die in a rabbit's nest in the woods just as the sun was rising and the world was waking up to a new day? No one wanted to read about a poor mountain girl overcome by forces beyond her control. World War II had rearranged everyone's life and thinking.

Part 5

Middle Work
Making a Living, Living a Life, 1947–1974

17

On Dead Mare Branch

I haven't found the woman yet who's willing to play second fiddle to a typewriter.

—James Still

Although everything was different after the war, Still tried hard to make it the same. In 1946 he was partly successful. He reconnected with friends and made repairs on his house. He was able to renew the Guggenheim Fellowship, which provided him living expenses plus a little money to give his youngest brother, Alfred, who was in financial trouble. Still even became involved in professional outreach when he agreed to serve on the editorial board of *Mountain Life and Work*.[1]

His writing and publication were slowly resuming also. While trying to find a buyer for "The Nest," he published four other stories. The most interesting, "Cedar of Lebanon" (later titled "The Sharp Tack"), reveals something about Still's frame of mind in his first year home. The story consists of six letters written between March 2 and April 17 by Jerb Powell, a preacher who prides himself on "snatching souls from the Devil's paws," to Mr. Talt Evarts, a soldier back from the war who claims to have visited the Holy Land.[2] The letters start with the literal, closed-minded Powell accusing the soldier of blasphemy; then he gradually begins to understand that going to the Holy Land does not mean ascending to heaven and that a place on earth can share a name with the place "Up Yonder." The reader never sees responses from Evarts but can imagine the soldier's amusement and irritation. The preacher has as little experience with the war as with geography. But the more troubling aspect of the story is the insinuation that the soldier had not been serious about fighting: "While soldiering how did you get to traipse all over creation? Why weren't you forever in the battle, chastising the enemy? Upon my word and honor I believe you hung back."[3]

When everything is finally resolved to the preacher's satisfaction, he offers the soldier his metaphorical olive branch—advice on how to keep the cedar alive: "Shovel barnyard dirt to it." And he withdraws his accusation: "You were a brave soldier by all my hears. You held your ground square in the whiskers of the foe." Evart's only response is to send the preacher a sprig of the cedar, his own peace sign. The final letter shows that the preacher's mind and his world have broadened. He wants to meet the soldier for he has "a host of questions to ask."[4] What saves the preacher from the reader's scorn is his humor more than his conversion. Other characters in the story are not so backward and literal-minded. The postmaster and the teacher are willing to tolerate the preacher's stupidity and arrogance because of the soldier's tolerance and goodwill. In the end, people accept one another. But this fictional glimpse into the life on Wolfpen presents a dilemma: would Still see his community as a place from which he might interact with the outside world or as a place where he might escape from it?

While writing the story, Still was perusing nursery catalogs. The original version of the story included this accusation from the preacher: "They say you've got [the sprig] fenced against people stealing a limb, in the same way that they surrounded the sire of the Golden Delicious apple in West Virginia." This allusion to the apple variety that originated on the West Virginia farm of Anderson Mullins was intentional. Still must have gotten the idea from reading the 1946 catalog in which Stark Brothers advertised itself as the oldest and largest nursery in the world and proudly stated they had purchased the rights to the Mullins apple in 1916, which they renamed the Golden Delicious. Not only did Still use the name in the story, he also wrote to Stark Brothers (March 5, 1946) telling them he had done so. They promptly ordered a copy of the issue of *American Mercury* and sent Still a box of apples![5] The advertising manager may have been disappointed to find that, aside from this passing reference, the story had nothing to do with fruit.

"Cedar of Lebanon" yielded more than a box of apples; it renewed Still's correspondence with Robert Francis, who wrote him as soon as he read the "flavorsome" story. After serving in the army for only five months, Francis taught English at Mount Holyoke College and had found occasion to use Still's writing as a model for students: "One day last year I took your *River of Earth* to my Freshman English classes and read a part of it aloud as an illustration of its beautiful organization of details. I challenged them to pick out a single detail that was not functional in the story."[6] He ended his letter with an invitation to New England. Still responded that it was good to be back from Africa—"back to frost, snow and ice," back to his first spring since 1941. But, he added emphatically, he would not be able to visit in the summer. No reason given, just the phrase "Must stay home."[7] For the next few years, that was his mantra and his practice.

The Amburgey log house that he had moved to in 1940 became the center of his world. It was a good house for the time and place—one big room with two windows and a door on the main floor and one room above it accessed by a straight-up, built-in ladder. An oil lamp lighted the darkness until the house was wired in 1947, and the only heat was from a log fireplace, which was later fitted with a gas heater. A small kitchen was attached to the back of the main room, and water was fetched from the well in the front yard. The outhouse stood about fifty feet outside the back door. Albert Stewart, who visited the house several times in the 1940s, described the interior as orderly and simple: "The log walls were left natural, the walnut bed and dresser were as near the natural wood as simple preservative would manage. The Van Gogh or Cezanne prints, the pictures of master tomatoes, peaches or apples from seed catalogs, or the occasional carving or gourd, seemed chosen."[8] Dean Cadle's description of his first visit in 1946 was similar. He recalled two dulcimers hanging on the wall and a string of red peppers, plus some hats. Still's writing table was in the corner, and on the wall above it was a trailing vine that had grown through a crack in the mortar. Cardboard boxes filled with jars of canned fruits and vegetables lined the floor near the fireplace. Upstairs, correspondence and copies of magazines were spread over the floor near a trunk filled with manuscripts.[9]

Still had no car or horse. The Bath post office was a walk along the creek bed, and the nearest town was miles away. He was fairly isolated unless people came to visit him or he caught a ride to town. He managed a comfortable life on Dead Mare Branch, but over the next few years he remained relatively solitary and only marginally productive. Off and on between 1947 and 1950 he kept a journal, which allows a glimpse into his very private world.[10] The following is pieced together

from the 1947 journal and edited to feature descriptions of his environment, his interactions with his neighbors, and his work routine, which
was dominated by writing and gardening.

Dead Mare Branch 1947

January 1: The first snow of winter lies on the world and
seems to have brought the hills nearer. The physiogomony [sic]
of the mountains stand out like human faces in their wintry
whiteness. A rain fell on the snow before daylight. My steps are
a slide. . . . I've put out a double handful of sunflower seeds on a
board propped in the crabtree. Titmice, chickadees, cardinals,
and Carolina wrens busy feeding. With the snow for a background the pale pink spots under the titmouse wings are notice-
able. The cardinal's sweeping flight is like a ball of flame across
the whiteness. In time of snow all things that are unfinished or
ugly or malformed take on the beauty of completion and wonder and service. My old broken fence, posts leaning askew, wire
a rusty trammel, has become a work of perfection—the wires
are glazed with ice, each post wears a white peaked cap and in
their idle slants and slopes points as true as a compass. . . . On
the mountain across the way the stooping trees are marked by
their weight of snow—the straight-standing ones shed it as it
fell. Afar, the Raven Rock seems an artificial snow scene, out
of Currier and Ives. . . . Looking far beyond Big Hollow I can
see under the very sky a hump of mountain never seen by me
before.

January 2: Rain fell upon the snow all night and is dripping
thinly this morning. At 8:30 AM clouds are breaking up and a
bit of blue showing in spots. . . . A gun shot. Drip, drip, drip. A
dog barks far off. Bird squeaks about the mound of sunflower
seeds. Two shots—shotguns this time—followed by explosive
reverberations in the valley. The dry rattle of fire in the grate.[11]

January 3: Warm as wet May weather. Rained all night,
melting the snow. A few small handkerchiefs of snow are yet
spread upon the ground. Last evening, going to supper, I had
to keep to the hillside on the right bank of Wolfpen and hold
to bushes and trees to support every step. Halloed Alonzo out
of their house and had him throw across a scantling to help me
walk their si-goggling footlog. When the log was split long ago

it spiraled, and walking it is much like negotiating the edge of a razor blade. On returning after dark Melvin held a flashlight on the bank and hardly had I begun when I slipped . . . .

January 4: Warm, no frost, snow clouds overhead, smoky valley, and scarcely a twig trembles in the breathless air. The last few days have been loud with flooded streams. Rapidly melting snow made them roar. Wolfpen roared; Dead Mare roared; Little Carr thundered. . . .

At Melvin's last night they had soupbeans for supper, a rarity. In past years they were forever on the table. M [Melvin] said they couldn't afford to eat many beans this winter at 25 cents a pound. Yesterday afternoon Elmer came down to re-ditch a path for Dead Mare. The stream keeps reaching toward my fence, eating away ground—this was no concern of his. He's only concerned about a truck-way to get his mine-props out to the highway. M. skinned the willow trunks there last spring so to make them die, and at various times, ditches have been dug to try to train the waters leftward; but Dead Mare is a hard-headed stream and re-orders all our plans. . . .

January 6: Old Christmas (Twelfth Night). Temp. 26 F. Grew colder in the night. Put the typewriter to the fire to warm the metal parts. Quietest of mornings, the world seemed a vacuum. Birdless, soundless. Only the fire laughs in the grate. Cooked two rashers of bacon, ate with molasses, which poured mighty slow on such a freezy morning. This week I must begin to prepare for going to Alabama and a word check run on "Master Occasion.". . .

January 7: Moderately warm, a bit above freezing. . . got four pages along in 4th draft of MO ["Master Occasion"]. A good number of word substitutions, a few sentences deleted—all, it seems, toward making the piece one long flow of conversational speech unmarred by asides and extraneous matter.

January 8: Frostless, spring-like, sunny morning. Spears of jonquils are an inch above ground under the apple trees. A hollyhock by the back door hadn't died completely all winter in spite of many freezings. . . .

I am dismayed at the slowness of the 4th draft of MO. Six pages managed only after a many-houred struggle yesterday. Extraneous material keeps falling out of it and I have a feeling it might become too compact . . . .

In the middle of the night, going into the kitchen for a moment where all was pitchy dark, I saw the yellow square of light which was the cat-hole lighted by the full moon outside. I looked out upon the cold and calm serenity of the full moon riding high, far away and impersonal. One of the beautiful nights of the world.

January 9: Much cooler, and the air sharpening. Weather in state of change. . . . Dexter Combs was visiting at the 'Burgeys, and we talked Army & Navy a couple of hours . . . Seed and nursery stock catalogs are beginning to arrive. . . .[12]

March 7: [Returning from Alabama, Still walked from Littcarr to his home.]

When I got to the gate I said, "Thank God I have this place!" Home! Built a roaring fire. Put on his army clothes for the wool, the warmth. . . . Mail heaped up at Melvin's. To bed at eight. Razor Roy [his cat] had come home with me, and slept on my feet atop the cover. I waked several times in the night, drugged with sleep and comfort and gratefulness that I had got back.

March 8: As I got a drink of water after daylight I noticed a cuff of snow at the cat hole. Throwing open the door I found a great snow had fallen in the night, silently, secretly—perhaps six inches deep. It had come like the benediction of nature. . . .

March 9: . . . Transported most of my mail back with B-3 bag. . . . Today, five years ago I started off to the Army. . .

March 11–13: Cold. Pale sunshine. Though melted everywhere, the snow yet holds around my house and up the hill. How old the ancient apple trees look in these last weeks before must awake. . . . This was an almost fruitless day of writing. I feel handcuffed and tongue-tied. I kept casting about trying to get started on a piece. . . Should I try to begin this? Or that? Or what? Finally, I got to work on re-writing The Rusty chapter. I was dismayed to find the first draft in such a rustic condition. . . .

March 14, 17, 19: Spent Thursday afternoon straightening papers and sorting books, and make out [sic] a seed order. . . . Still casting about, trying to get writing again. . . . a moderately good day's work, shaking off the lethargy caused by long absence from the typewriter. . . .

Planted lettuce, radishes, sweet peas, and cut back honeysuckle that was taking over.

March 23: Went down-creek at noon. . . . Talked to Kell and Sam Stamper at Ob's store. Kell asked, "Just how many hours a day do you work on your writing?" I replied, "Listen, I'll do anything to get out of work." Went along to John M's place to get items his mother has promised to me: a sack of potato onions, a regal lily bulb, a perennial sweet pea; and John walked home with me to get "swap" plants for his mother: flowering almond, settings of two unidentified plants sent from Alabama.

March 24: Guy Fugate, the electrician, came back with a hangover pallor. I gave him a small stone I picked up out of the edge of the Sea of Galilee. "My wife'll be tickled," he said. He put it in his breeches pocket; and present [sic] got it out again and put it into his jacket pocket all by itself and buttoned it. "There—that'll keep it from losing." They finished at noon— 27 man-hours of work; total charge $55. . . . Final check from John Simon Guggenheim Memorial Foundation; fellowhip [sic] terminates April 30th. . . . Letter from Van Wyck Brooks: "It gives me great pleasure to inform you that the American Academy of Arts and Letters and the National Institute of Arts and Letters have awarded you a Gran [sic] of $1,000 in recognition of your creative work in literature and to further your efforts in that direction."

April 15: A bright sunny day. The wheedle-dees were liquefying the valley with their melody. Went to Hazard, returned with an electric Philco radio-phonograph. Brought it upcreek on my back. It was raining slightly and the carton began to melt and tear away and my burden grew more unmanageable by the yard . . . Viking wrote me last week that RIVER OF EARTH is to be remaindered at 20 cents per copy—and did I want a few copies? I ordered 100 copies. I felt momentarily abandoned and rejected on getting the notice from Viking. But it was selling only ten copies or so a year. In these days of million copy printings, etc. ROE sold slightly more than 5,000 copies in six years. And this the book Time called "a work of Art," and Elizabeth Madox Roberts, Marjorie Kinnan Rawlings, John Gould Fletcher, and others went to bat for; a book whose reviews were almost whole complimentary. I am sad that ROE could find no more readers than it did . . .

During the last half of April he welcomed the spring and planted peas before the rain. He noted all the blooms: the Service trees on the hills, the Narcissi that had joined the daffodils. The forsythia as a maze of yellow. During that time of new spring life, Still picked up the pace of his writing but found it hard to concentrate on any one project. Initiatives and ideas he described in the journal include:

1. Notes on a chapter for TWM [The Wild Man] called "Morning Glory Hell: Trials of a Wolfpen Gardener."[13]
2. Initial efforts on a running recollection for *Alabama, Alabama*.[14]
3. A novel telling the story of Andersonville prison.[15] As he walked along the creek one day, he began to think of this work, *Blood of Hundreds*. He described it as his "gift to humanity . . . to show man's inhumanity to man, the beast in the heart of all of us, and to guard against it for all future time we must first recognize it. Before Dachau, and other places of death in this century there was Andersonville. This book will try to be an explanation, not an incitement. How could it happen here? To us?"
4. Revision of the third draft of the first section of *The Rusties*. He had spent two days on the first paragraph. He wanted it to be clean and honest and could not let go until it was. His self criticism read: "There was enormous superficiality in the first draft, much branch water in the second, and my business with the third is to make it at last *come true*. . . . I am astounded at the snail's pace of my work."
5. The idea for a novel called *Cane Ridge,* which would attempt to present the mob psychology of the camp meeting at Cane Ridge, Kentucky, in 1800 or 1801. One day he recorded that he felt great excitement, made himself a cup of coffee, and walked up and down.

None of these writing projects ever came to fruition. His only publications in 1947 were two poems: "Apples" in *The Atlantic* and "The Broken Ibis" in the *Virginia Quarterly Review*. He even gave up journal writing during the summer and fall, spending his time, instead, in his garden. He continued to draft and revise, but the work proceeded at a "snail's pace." One habit that never slowed was his eclectic reading. Among the books he found engaging were Emery Neff's *Edwin*

Arlington Robinson, Ellery Sedgwick's *The Happy Profession,* Tennessee Williams's *A Streetcar Named Desire,* and Samuel Eliot Morrison's *Admiral of the Ocean Sea.*

Still had succeeded in returning to the place he wanted to be and to the life he was living before the war, but something was different. He put in as many hours at his typewriter, but the publication rate did not compare to that of the years between 1935 and 1941. In 1947 he was receiving some of the accolades that he had become accustomed to before joining the army. For example, in addition to the Guggenheim, he won an award from the American Academy of Arts and Letters.[16] Yet his signature work, *River of Earth,* had been remaindered. The novel's disappearance reflected a shift in Still's readership. After seven years, he was writing not the same stories but the same themes and settings. Yet the post–World War II readers had shifted. Still was choosing to live essentially the same life that rural Knott County had provided its inhabitants for more than one hundred years, with the addition of a typewriter and, finally, electric lights. But the nation had moved much further. Its concerns and interests had changed.

Still was a loner during this period. His stories were not irrelevant or unappealing, but his subject matter seemed out of synch with mainstream taste. "The Nest," published in the spring of 1948, for example, was ahead of its time, frightening and depressing; while "A Master Time," published in January 1949, could have been considered old-fashioned. Compare those two stories to a few known titles of 1949 and 1950: Arthur Miller's *Death of a Salesman,* Shirley Jackson's "The Lottery," Anne Frank's *Tales from a Secret Annex,* J. D. Salinger's *Catcher in the Rye,* Ray Bradbury's *Fahrenheit 451,* or George Orwell's *1984.* As Still said years later in an interview for the *Iron Mountain Review,* "Writing is a pretty lonely profession." During his middle years on Dead Mare Branch, he was living out that truth. He was not a hermit, he had friends and neighbors, but he existed in a small sphere.

Later, Still resumed his journal. The entries from December 1947 are narrative and lyrical. The tone is dark, quiet, and lonely. Yet as Christmas approached, that wintry quality is punctuated with the motif of children. Could this indicate a latent need to feel part of a family? He seemed to be weighing the burden of dependents against the pleasure companionship could bring.

December 14: An inch of ice on the water bucket—a fair, blue, cold day. In early afternoon I walked up to Bath Post Office.

Perry was grinding meal in a shed. He asked presently, "Want to get into the post-office?" I said, "Yes, but I'm in no hurry." Perry said, "It's dinner-time. Won't you eat with us." I said, "No thank you, I've eaten." He went into the house and I heard his voice "Jim Still wants in the post-office." He came out with a bunch of keys, saying, "I'll try to wait on you." I bought a dollars worth of stamps. Making talk I said, or rather blurted, "Perry, I hear you've sold your mine." He said "Yes." – nothing more. I put the stamps into an envelope and into my pocket. I said, "Thank you, Perry." He said nothing. We came out of the store, he pausing to lock the door, and as I moved off I said, "Well, thank you very much for letting me in." (That is, for bothering you on Sunday at dinner-time.) He said nothing, and then with abrupt dismissal, "It's all right."

I could hear children, many children; I could see them through the glass panel of the door. The house seemed bursting with children.

December 16: A dark, dark day—but not a gloomy day, gloom being a product of the mind not of the weather. Wind in the night, and soot blew down. Windy and minuscule pellets of snow or sleet. Cornstalks shake in the fields and the shredded fodder blades flow back like dirty ribbons. The wind it seems had blown off the sparrows and chickadees. The yard was empty, bird-less. The wind was flowing like a swollen stream.

December 24: Moderately cold. Christmas Eve. Put on my red-checkered shirt and walked down to the Foot. Met nobody on the road, how forlorn and empty Littcarr looked at a distance. The road down had bad stretches of mud. In the storehouse Bern and Ob are alone, and being a gloomy day, it's darksome inside. The little stove drew noisily.

Williard Collins came in, weighed down with a poke of Christmas stuff for his children. He'd had a "bunch o'drinks" and, rare for him, was glib. Says he to me, "You don't know what you're missing. You're missing everything." Ought to be in my shoes."(Meaning implied that he was fortunately married and had several chaps to play Santa Claus for.) "You ought to be in my shoes." (His shoes—he lived miserably in a one-room log cabin with wife, three children, and his father. The room was incredibly packed. The nest of a packrat or the nest of a magpie would not be more crammed with oddments.) I replied, "Williard, your shoes wouldn't fit me. Wrong size."

Pretty soon in came Maryland Collins also warm and talky from drink. But Maryland is sad. His wages have been garnished. His son, Astor, has requested a mouth harp and he hadn't been able to find one. His other children request [sic] various things and he has no money to buy them all. In his talk he implies that his family had him flat on his back and jumping in his face. Suddenly he says to me, "Jim, you're the only one of us here who feels like a man! Beholden to nobody!" . . .

I went alone up the creek, and the road was empty. It seemed everybody had gone out of the world. . . . After dark I walked down to the neighbor's house, Whit Thornsberry's. I took a candle along, and as the lamps were not lighted—they had no oil—and as the fire burnt low—they had little fuel—I asked for a saucer and stuck the candle onto it and set it burning onto the mantel. The little children seemed fascinated by the candle. Back home and to bed by 9:30 PM.

December 25: Christmas Day. A clear, cool day. A knock on my door before I got out of bed. Two of Thornsberry's little boys had come to bring me a gift of fresh meat— they had killed a hog Christmas Eve. One of the boys brought an apple to me. I gave them oranges.

This journal, like many of his short stories, is simply written and poignant. Throughout, his motive is clear: Still wanted to preserve his independence, to be beholding to no one. But the cost of that freedom was isolation and absence of family. He was now in his forties. People in the community were asking why he did not marry. As he hinted in the journal, there were women he could have had for the asking, but he did not know any that he wanted to spend his life with. He never addressed the matter directly, but his story "A Master Time," published in January 1949, reflects one aspect of his situation at the end of the decade. There is no evidence that Still participated in a family hog kill like the one in the story, but it would have been possible since work was often combined with fun, and families joined with friends to share both. His neighbors frequently included Still in their activities.

This fictional hog kill took place on the eve of Old Christmas. A group of young married couples gathered at the house of Ulysses Jarrett, and the narrator was invited to join them for a good time, a "master" time. Though their work is serious, the spirit of the story is playful. Preparing the meat is background for drinking moonshine, bantering with the old midwife, Aunt Besh, and throwing snowballs at one another. The narrator was welcomed at the house, yet he remained on the periphery for two reasons: first, he had not been "fotched" by Aunt Besh, meaning he was not a native of Logan Creek, and second, he was not married. He witnessed a good time and told about it, but he was not one of them.

Soon after the publication of "A Master Time," Still received a letter from Pauline Amburgey,[17] a niece of Jethro and Ranie, a young woman who had known and "loved" him for a long time. She had come across the story and read it aloud to her parents, who "died with laughter." That was the ostensible reason for her writing, but the real reason was to confess that she had always loved Still—though earlier it had been "puppy love." She had just disengaged from an entangling alliance, and although she did not presume Still would take that man's place, she implied that she would not resist any relationship he might want to pursue. She ends the letter, "After the passing of years I still think you are a very wonderful guy and I hope you don't mind this bit of sentimentality."[18] Still was somewhat receptive because they did write for several years after that. But like his other potential romances, this one did not develop beyond a friendly correspondence.

Part of Still's interest in family may have come from seeing his brothers and sisters all married with many children. At the start of 1947 his youngest brother, Alfred, had welcomed twin boys, who, along with his other five children, made a large group that illustrated to Still the condition of being trapped by responsibility. His longtime friend, Dare Redmond, had married in 1945 and had a baby boy in 1947.[19] Around the same time, Still heard from Dorothy Thomas, his first letter from her in a long while. She had moved back to New York and had doubled her family. She had not found a husband, but she had adopted an eight-year-old girl named Deanna, who was "the joy of her life."[20] Still felt no such joy.

Still's journal writing in 1948 was spotty. But he noted on March 21, Palm Sunday, that he and Melvin Amburgey went up Big Hollow to Williard Collins's house. This is the same man who the Christmas Eve before had chided Still to join the ranks of family men. Here is Still's description of their visit: "Up and up the winding sledpath, and there sat his house on a foot-starved spot. We sat in chairs in the sketch of a backyard and the sour washplace smell was strong. The earth seemed to have died about the house."[21] Amburgey joked with Collins's father, Valentine, about his estranged wife and how much he missed her. The men spent the afternoon swapping stories and smoking Rum and Maple Tobacco. They shared a good time, but the visit showed Still that Williard's "shoes" definitely did not fit him.

During the winter of 1948–1949 Still accepted an invitation to visit California. He was searching for a respite from the cold and from loneliness and isolation. Jim Hakes was the army friend who had been his travel partner on the trip to Cairo and the pyramids four years earlier. The two had not communicated since the end of the war, but Still wrote him a letter, to which he responded on October 10, 1948. Hakes had been married but was now divorced, living alone in an apartment in Santa Monica and managing his own small bookstore in Los Angeles.

> I have had a lot of things to prove to myself since becoming a bachelor and have discovered that I do have a capacity for enjoying life and accomplishing certain things without leaning on another's personality and ability. I have worked very hard, also to prove something to myself, and the store as a result is one of the very few that has held its own. . . . I am officially inviting you to stay with me if you can come to Cal. this winter. How about it? I don't have a lot of room, but I am gone all day and you would have a chance to work if you wished.[22]

Still did go to California and stayed with Hakes from early December 1948 through February 1949.[23] He would have stayed longer, but he came down with some illness, which he took to be the resurgence of malaria. Still never talked about this three-month visit to California, but from the update Hakes wrote his friend in March, it seems that Still's time there had involved much socializing with several female friends: going to the race track, attending plays, discussing books. Hakes was learning to fly an airplane and was perfecting his ice skating. He had always been an avid hiker and outdoorsman. Probably these activities or the level to which Hakes pursued them was too intense for Still, who was perfectly happy watching his plants grow and talking to his cat.[24]

Back on Dead Mare Branch, the days passed in a predictable routine, but his publication rate was declining even further. He published nothing new in 1950. His only consolation was the honor of having "A Master Time" chosen as one of the Best American Short Stories of the year. Also Ethel Glenn Hier set one of Still's poems, "Epitaph for Uncle

Ira Combs, Mountain Preacher," to music, and it was performed in New York City.[25] In the summer of 1950 he returned to Yaddo. While trying to retrieve his old level of productivity, he thought that the environment of the artists' colony would help. It did not.

One new acquaintance from that year at Yaddo was poet May Swenson, who wrote him after returning to New York: "I picture you [in your little house in the hollow] as a sort of combination of Huck Finn and Rip Van Winkle. Your ability to get along in this world without handling money is something that impressed me very much. Betty Smith and I had some interesting interpretive discussions about your poetry—In fact your reputation 'lived after you' and Still was still at Yaddo long after you'd gone."[26] This relationship is reminiscent of his earlier stays there. Writers and artists who came to know Still typically associated him with his isolated mountain home. They found him interesting and his writing compelling, but they did not develop close friendships.

How he financed his visit to Yaddo is unclear, but an invitation was an award and usually meant the artist would cover modest expenses. Still, at that time, had few major costs—he paid no rent, grew most of his own food, did not own a car, and was generally frugal. Somehow he met the expenses and went to Yaddo that summer and again in February 1951. One "lonesome Sunday" he penned a letter to another artist he had come to know there, sculptor and painter Eugenie Gershoy. This report shows that in spite of getting work done, he felt himself on the fringe of the group:

Dear Eugenie:

Decided utterly and beyond all recall not to return to Yaddo this winter. So here I am. . . . Day I arrived, February 10th, temperature was ten below zero. Warmer since, the snow is languishing, the roads an unwalkable glaze. . . . I live at West House, first floor, east end. Working, too, and that's something I couldn't manage last summer.
Present guests: Katherine Ann Porter, Elizabeth Bishop, Kit and Ilse Barker, Calvin Kentfield, Eleanor Clark, Alexei Haieff, William Goyen. . . . [27] We dine in Garage Building, elbow to elbow, breathing down each other's necks. Much too snug for my comfort. At least the immense dining room in the Mansion absorbed some of the hostility last summer. Nobody

likes me here now. Most any remark of mine gets a snide
rejoinder. Of course [several] are real people. The others?
Phooey. . . . [28]

A letter that he later received from poet Elizabeth Bishop showed his
attempt to reach out to her with a special gesture, which she had unin-
tentionally ignored. It also indicated that he left Yaddo earlier than he
had expected on the pretense that a neighbor in Kentucky had an accident. The letter from Bishop shows no hostility and includes not the
slightest hint of a snide rejoinder.

> Ever since Polly wrote me that you had actually gone down to
> the Saratoga station to say good-bye to me and I think took
> some flowers, I have been meaning to write to thank you, but I
> just got your address the other day. It's a wonderful address and
> pray what is a "wolf pen"? It was awfully kind of you to think
> of seeing me off. . . .
>   It must be spring where you are and I envy you—you're
> probably gardening right this minute. You know I don't believe
> I've ever read anything you've written except that story "Mr.
> Razor" [sic] in Mary Lou Aswell's anthology. I liked that very
> much. I had lunch with her yesterday and she was asking all
> about you—unfortunately I had to tell her that I was sorry but
> I really didn't get to see much of you at Yaddo. [29]

Many years later, Still described that Yaddo winter experience to
Jim Wayne Miller. His memory of it was different from his account at
the time, warmer and more optimistic.

> I met [Katherine Anne Porter, Elizabeth Bishop, and Eleanor
> Clark] at Yaddo. I was with them a great deal, especially in
> the winter of 1951 when we were frozen in. This was our
> company. . . . We'd sit at breakfast for hours. After all, the
> snow was very deep and it never melted. We just had some
> more snow. We lived within a very small perimeter there. So
> we used to talk. And that's pretty good company. I remember
> for a long time it was just we four. And Yaddo being what it
> is, we had four people and four cooks, so we ate most of the
> time. And played ping-pong. Katherine Anne was a very poor
> loser. [30]

In fact, his 1950 and 1951 stays at Yaddo did not yield publications and did not result in any new intimate or long-lasting friendships.[31] But his going there was part of his effort to resume his life as a writer, the life that had been so full and relatively profitable before the war. Yaddo was far from Dead Mare Branch, which was the place he was most comfortable as the 1950s began.

18

Back to Hindman

You've got to make a living somehow. In my case, I taught
school.

—James Still

His log house on Dead Mare Branch was a refuge that offered him a satisfying, simple, and old-fashioned life. He kept busy with writing, gardening, and chores. In the introduction to *The Wolfpen Notebooks,* he
described attending community activities: "Depending on the season,
bean stringing and corn shucking and molasses making and hog kill-
ings. In the fall the pie suppers at the Wolfpen school. . . . The fourth
Sundays in the month I attended the Old Regular Baptist meetings."[1]
He often hung out with three other men: John M., Sam Stamper, and
Shorty Smith. The four were known as the Littcarr Gang.[2] According
to Still, they "ran together," which included visiting cemeteries and old
homesites, fishing with cane poles, hunting ginseng or pawpaws, and
attending stock sales. In spite of close friends and varied activities, he
experienced periods of loneliness. His ambivalent longing for a family
resulted finally in a compromise. Instead of having his own, he adopted
the families of others, especially those of the Amburgey clan.

The extended family provided Still with friends and neighbors.
Jethro and Ranie had one son, Morris. Jethro's brother Woodrow and
his wife, Armita, had seven children. Melvin and Isabell had six; one
of their younger daughters was the prototype for Mrs. Razor. Still fre-

quently ate meals at Melvin's house. He paid them an allowance for the food, but the major exchange was that while Isabell prepared the meals, Still talked with the children, offering them an education that they would not otherwise receive. It also offered Still direct contact with their everyday life. As he says of the meals, "When the cow went dry we sometimes had homemade 'beer seed beer' a non-alcoholic drink. When the dried apples came up short we ate vinegar pie."[3]

The member of the extended family with whom Still was the closest was Monroe, the parent and sole caretaker for seven children: one girl and six boys. Monroe Amburgey became very special to James Still.[4] He was seven years older than Still and had married in 1930; his wife, Frances Combs Amburgey, had died in 1945 when their youngest child was only two. Monroe did not remarry because he wanted to devote himself entirely to his children. Still once quoted him as saying, "People say I ought to get married again. I wouldn't throw my children away for no woman. . . . I think more of my children than I do anybody."[5] The two had probably known each other since Still moved to Wolfpen because Monroe was a cousin to Jethro, but ten years passed before they became close friends. In 1950 Monroe's youngest child was seven, and the oldest would leave home by 1952. Their house on Big Doubles was not far from Still's on Dead Mare, maybe a mile as the crow flies, but by the road or the creek bed it was just over two miles. They had to make an effort to visit each other, and they did that frequently.

The oldest child, Berta, was a surrogate mother to the boys until she married and had a baby of her own.[6] The fifth child, Jasper, had serious health problems in the late 1950s and spent almost a year in and out of hospitals in Louisville and Lexington. Still helped with caring for him and paying medical expenses associated with his rheumatic fever. The two youngest children needed the most parenting. The baby, Earl, was only seven in 1950 when Still entered their family circle, but he was more independent than the next oldest, Lausie, who seemed almost too gentle for his own good. He is the only one of the children Still described in *The Wolfpen Notebooks*. There he quoted Monroe's telling of the boy's way with animals: "Lausie has everything about the place too petted up. The other day he tried to go squirrel hunting and when he started the cats followed. Six of them. At the upper end of the barn lot our three dogs took after him. And at the end of the pasture gate the heifer came running. Hardly had he got into the woods than he heard the mule making for him. He just come back to the house."[7]

Sometimes Still would spend the weekend on Big Doubles and take the younger boys fishing. At other times, Monroe would come to his house so they could enjoy a quiet meal without the children. At one point they made plans to go into business together raising chickens, but nothing came of it except for the hours that Still spent looking at poultry catalogs. Monroe worked at manual jobs—carpenter, stone-mason, road worker among them.[8] When they began hanging around together, he was working on a county road crew. Still frequently caught rides with Monroe to get from place to place. The two men were mutu-ally helpful. Monroe brought Still companionship and a house full of children, while Still provided Monroe a devoted friend and helpmate. Both were private individuals, so few people in the county realized how close they were for more than thirty years. Monroe died in 1988 and is buried next to his wife in Carr Fork Cemetery. Much later, Mike Mul-lins described their friendship: "Monroe was a kind and gentle man. In many ways he became closer to Mr. Still than any other person. I remember seeing Monroe on several occasions at functions where Mr. Still was being honored. He didn't have much to say but his presence told everyone, especially Mr. Still, how much he cared for him. It was a sad day for Mr. Still when Monroe passed away [January 29, 1988] because there was no one to take his place."[9]

All the Amburgey families filled a void in Still's life. While their company did not provide him the intellectual stimulation of a place like Yaddo, the conversation was more to his liking and gave him both inspiration and material for his writing. The life on Dead Mare Branch offered Still much of what he wanted but not an adequate source of income. If he had been publishing more stories in popular magazines, he might have gotten by since he lived modestly. In 1951 he published only one story, and in 1952 he had no publications at all. He began to need a salary. He was not actively looking, but when opportunities came up, he paid attention. For years he had participated in writing workshops or attended artists' colonies like Bread Loaf and Yaddo, but never as a teacher. In the summer of 1951 his role shifted due to the persistence and discretion of one man, James McConkey.

When McConkey, who was from the Midwest, joined the English department faculty at Morehead State College (MSC) in 1950, he had not read anything by James Still. One of his students told him about *On Troublesome Creek*. That introduction made him want Still on the staff of the new summer writers' workshop, which he was direct-ing. The invitation he sent Still got no response, so he turned to people who might know the reclusive writer of eastern Kentucky.[10] It was suggested that Still might respond more readily if approached in person. So McConkey and his wife made a trip to the hills. Here is his description:

> From the sketchy directions I'd been given, I knew I was to turn off the paved highway at a hamlet (a store, mainly) not far from Hindman to take a rutted dirt road that paralleled Little Carr Creek. I remember passing decrepit barns with muddy pastures that held small wagons not with wheels but with runners—sleds, as if we were going back in time.[11] There were no mailboxes with street addresses. I'd been told to look for a dry creek bed with a path either in it or next to it that led uphill past a bean field to a log house probably invisible from the dirt road. Unsuccessful in finding anything like that, we returned to the store, which seemed to be a community gathering place; there were five or six people there, who stopped talking when Gladys and I came in. I asked the proprietor if he could tell us how to find James Still's house. He told us that Still wasn't home yet, having gone to the cattle auction in Knott County with others; but that if we'd stand outside, in about ten minutes we'd see a yellow Studebaker pickup truck with three men in the front seat. I should gesture for the driver to stop, and ask for Still, one of the passengers.
>
> And so ten minutes later Still stepped down from the pickup truck; it was as if he had been expecting us to be there. We talked for a few moments. . . . I liked him at once. He must have agreed to be on the writing staff for the two weeks of the summer writers workshop. I know that I promised to pick him up the day before the conference and return him to his log house. He got in our car to direct me and a few minutes later we were walking up the dried creek bed. . . . What I remember from my brief visit in the house was the sharp contrast between the muddy rural world outside and the literary world inside: the bookcase nearest me held book after book.[12]

The May 1, 1952, *Hindman News* carried a front-page story about the July workshop at MSC, including a photo of Still taken ten years earlier.[13] This story showed how proud the community was that he was a published writer and living in the county. McConkey sent a letter to Still before the workshop, apologizing for not mailing manuscripts ahead of time. The workshop was to have thirty-five participants, he said, with ten of them "showing more than average promise."[14] Still was scheduled to participate only during the second week, and he was not required to speak publicly. Because Still had no car, McConkey returned to the log house on Sunday, July 20, to take him to Morehead. "I waited in his log house while he cut the large vine that had come through the open kitchen window. He really liked the vine as a living decoration; but to avoid vandalism he had to shut and lock the window. And then he told me he had to visit all his nearby neighbors, to tell them he was leaving for a spell and to say goodbye. . . . He got along well with his neighbors, and didn't want anything that would disturb the relationship."

The leaving ritual shows how connected Still was with the place where he lived. The private dormitory room where he stayed during the week of the workshop must have seemed stark and ordinary by comparison. That summer, as in subsequent workshops, Still was not included in the evening lectures. His role was to read and critique manuscripts by talking to individual participants or in small-group sessions. According to McConkey, he was sought after as a teacher and critic. He liked to talk to students one-on-one. His conference schedule filled quickly because he was known for his helpful responses. And, added McConkey, he was well liked by other writers on the staff, joining them and students at mealtimes in the college cafeteria.

Several workshop participants from that first summer wrote Still thank-you letters.[15] At least one became a loyal friend: Temple Baker from Portsmouth, Ohio. She and her husband, Charley, first came to Morehead in the summer of 1952. They befriended Still while there, and he visited them the following September. They returned the visit in October. The following January, Baker wrote him a long letter that is worth reprinting because it reveals Still's tendency toward introversion. She began by saying that she was writing with mixed feelings. There were several reasons why she believed she must, and the letter set out to explore each one. Her task was both an analysis of Still's failure to respond and an explanation of her need to connect:

> First: You said that you answered the first letter which I wrote you, but you didn't send it. That lets me know that it is difficult for you to trust your words to paper . . . fear of being misunderstood. . . . You must know that my interest in you is in your writing which is so good and is not receiving the recognition which it should have. . . .
>
> Second: As I read [*River of Earth*] again, I am impressed by

the beauty of its simplicity and I am provoked that so few people know about it. By the way, the autograph in the book . . .
shows creative ability, friendliness, but not tension and inhibi-
tion, not even the characteristics of an introvert. *You* said you
were an introvert, remember?

Last: and I believe the most important reason for writing
you. I have read and re-read "Ride on the Short Dog." It is,
as I expected, a good story and expertly written. But I hated
the symbolism. I can't feel that the symbolism was intentional
while you were writing it. But I had trouble reading it. . . .

I realize that I have imposed, but if it is ever possible and if
you want to come to visit us, I wish you would. On the other
hand, if you want to cross off our friendship as a peculiar experience, I will understand.[16]

After writing this letter, she waited a few days before mailing it. Her
hesitation was justified. She was testing a new friendship. The previous
summer she had been a student writer under Still's mentorship. Perhaps
she was willing to delve into Still's psyche and situation simply because
she was bold. Or maybe she trusted her instinct that some elusive connection existed between them. Whatever the case, this letter marked the
beginning of a correspondence that lasted forty-five years and consisted
of more than fifty letters from Baker to Still.

Her observations provide a look into Still's life and personality during the period when he was considered a "hermit." Was he an introvert
as he had claimed? Why would he not promote himself? Why did he not
write and publish more during the 1950s? Was he making progress on
his writing? He did not promote himself because at that time he was not
a self-promoter. He didn't "believe in it." He was naturally modest, and
he enjoyed, in some way, being an unknown. It made him feel more a
part of his place and the people who lived there. When he was at Yaddo
in 1951, he had felt ignored or scorned. Back home on Troublesome, he
was accepted by his neighbors. He was one of them. Yet something was
still missing.

The story Baker had not liked, "A Ride on the Short Dog," was first
published in *The Atlantic* in July 1951, just as Still turned forty-four. It
represented a departure in his fiction. The boy characters are teenagers
and troublemakers who engage in bullying as a sport. The gang of three
boards the bus on its way to Roscoe and immediately causes problems
for the driver, the passengers, and one another. Godey Spurlock makes

his debut in this story. Baker acknowledged that the story was well written, but she did not like its hidden meaning. The narrator, she felt, was Still himself. Godey was another Still, a big, boisterous character. And Mal was the boy that the narrator wanted to trust but could not. To her, the ending was unresolved, and the story was filled with a "bitterness that no man should ever feel. At least no man who has so much talent and goodness to share."

Baker's reaction was justified. The story did reveal a fictional world that was new to Still, one filled with hurt, petty violence, and a sense of frustration, even desperation. He was not consciously writing his own world, but the story projects uneasiness. He had lost his confidence and direction. Part of his frustration must have been that he was not publishing at the rate he once had and consequently could not earn enough to sustain himself, in spite of his modest lifestyle. Also, his social interaction with people was limited, especially when compared with his life in the army. Whether as a result of financial or personal needs, Still made a change that would alter his workday and enlarge his world to include more people.

Since leaving Hindman Settlement School in 1939, Still had kept up with the school's news and his friends there. May 1952 marked the fiftieth anniversary of the founding of the school. The local newspaper published a bonus issue on May 1, detailing the history of the school and outlining dreams for its future. It announced a big celebration complete with a picnic for alums and a pageant for everyone.[17] One of the articles in that issue talked about the retirement of Clara Standish, the woman who served as librarian after James Still. Meanwhile, Still was negotiating to return to Hindman as the librarian. In the summer he made a donation to the school to start a marker fund. Elizabeth Watts responded to this pleasant surprise on August 12, saying that she and Ann Cobb would see about getting a piece of land where they could place the marker. She closed her letter with kind words showing that their negotiations were completed: "I hope you realize how very happy we are that you are to be with us again as librarian for this coming year."[18]

Still was returning to his past. He knew Hindman Settlement School, and he was familiar with the work he would be doing there. But the world had changed since the late 1930s, and so had the school. As Jess Stoddart points out in her history, the early Depression years created a financial strain for the Settlement School, but the public works projects of the later 1930s helped the county and the school by open-

ing the region and integrating it better into the state and nation. World
War II created another major transformation: out-migration. Still said
in the Wolfpen interview that war gave people a glimpse of the world:
"Especially during World War II a lot of folk here about dug potatoes
in Maine, threshed peas in Wisconsin, or picked tomatoes in Indiana. They went up to the factories in Detroit and Chicago and Cincinnati and remained."[19] The postwar period witnessed a continuation of
out-migration and more automation in coal mining, which led to less
employment for miners. Ensuing financial problems made it harder for
the Settlement School to serve the community. Public agencies began to
take over some of the work that the school had done. Financial support
began to diminish. Still was rejoining the faculty at a precarious time,
so it is not surprising that his salary was modest.

Before three years had passed, he was doing the same job, but his
employer had shifted from Hindman Settlement School to Knott County
and Hindman High School. The library building was on the Settlement School property that was adjacent to the public school. When the
high school was built in 1930, the library was housed there, but it grew
to eleven thousand volumes, which was too large for the high-school
building. Around the time of Still's leaving in 1939, May Stone and Elizabeth Watts constructed a new public library. The building was special
to Watts because its plan was that of her own family home. The downstairs had a large reading room for adults and a small one for children.
Upstairs were two bedrooms, a kitchen, and bath. Still moved into that
building in 1953. He worked downstairs and, during the week, slept
upstairs.[20] On Friday afternoons he took the bus to Dead Mare Branch,
then caught a ride back to Hindman on Monday mornings.

While considering his return to the Settlement School, Still was
writing "The Fun Fox," which was published in the September 1953
issue of *Woman's Day*. This story provides an interesting contrast to "A
Ride on the Short Dog." It is also about a well-known trickster, Mace
Crownover. The setting is not a bus but a schoolhouse, Keg Branch
School. The narrator is the new teacher who from his first day is overwhelmed by mischievous children. Unlike "Short Dog," this story has
a happy ending: Crownover tricks the local landowner into donating
property to the school so the children can have a playground, and he
gets the citizens to donate their small change to pay for equipment.
His courage to initiate the trick helps him make a place for himself in
the community. Presumably, the new playground will give the young-
sters the space to work out their energy, so they will spend class time

learning lessons rather than harassing the teacher. As the title suggests, the story is fun, but it includes tension and suspense. The narrator has reservations about teaching, about rambunctious children, about inadequate facilities, about an unsupportive, even hostile, community. All those doubts are resolved by the last line when he says, "It turned out that I taught through the entire session on Keg Branch—and two more besides."

Still did not write in order to work out personal issues, but these two stories do reflect his private concerns in the 1950s. The narrator of "Short Dog" is filled with hurt and suppressed anger stemming from the need to establish himself in the clique, while in "The Fun Fox" the narrator begins as an outside observer but finally joins the whole community in a positive endeavor.

His statement "You've got to make a living somehow" expresses Still's basic attitude toward earning money. His reason for returning to Hindman was not for altruism but for salary. His budget notes show that in 1953–1954 the Settlement School was paying him $150 each month.[21] In the next school year, the amount increased to $200 per month. Beginning in September 1956, Knott County began paying his salary, which was $364 per month, but after taxes only $280. To put these numbers in perspective, he earned from his work at Hindman about $1,700 in 1953 and $4,800 in 1960.[22] This salary was his main source of income but not the only one; he was also paid for the Morehead summer workshop and for publishing rights to stories.

If Still had been working only for money, the reward would not have matched his effort. But he was doing more than cataloging library books; he was interacting with young people and encouraging them to become readers. He believed in learning, and the school system, with the help of the Settlement School, was achieving its goal in the mid-1950s, especially if that goal could be measured by the number of high school graduates who went to college. In 1957 Knott County had 52 percent of its students enter college, the highest percentage of all 120 counties in Kentucky. Jesse Stuart, always active in the state's public education, was so impressed by the statistic that he wrote an article for the Louisville newspaper asking, "Why does Knott County Send the Largest Ratio of Graduates to College?" His speculative, philosophical answer began with a significant nod to his friend:

Maybe James Still, novelist, short story writer, poet and teacher, has been influential. He has been in Knott County many years.

Being a classmate of Still at Lincoln Memorial University and
at Vanderbilt University, I know he is a builder of youth. . . .
The first Bookmobile in the state of Kentucky was operated
in Knott County. . . . Where this Knott County Bookmobile
couldn't operate, didn't Jimmie Still carry books on his back?
How much of this basic foundation of education can be accredited to Hindman Settlement School, which has inspired youth
to go to Caney, Berea, Union, Eastern, Lindsey Wilson and Lincoln Memorial?[23]

Stuart concluded by giving final credit for the success to the large, hard-
working families in the county. The children learned early how to get
along with others and how to struggle for success, said Stuart. Finally,
he pointed to the Kentucky-born Abraham Lincoln, the world's model
of integrity and fortitude. We might wonder at Stuart's bookending his
article with the humble librarian James Still and the giant hero Abe
Lincoln. Yet the part of Still dedicated to education would have been
pleased and proud to know that Knott County was leading the state in
high-school graduates going to college.

The young people of Hindman collected a variety of memories of
Still at this time. Bob Young, a student at the high school, remembered
him as helpful to students but not overly friendly. He was very willing to
recommend books to those who asked, and he took a particular interest in young people who liked to read. Hiram Bradley, another Knott
County teen during the late fifties, described Still as a grouchy librarian. During study hall, Hiram would go to the library. One day Still
"chewed him out" for "walking heavy" on the library floor.[24] Still was
not always popular with large groups of students, but over time he made
friends with individuals. One of his favorites was James Perry.[25] On
an isolated page of typed notes, Still recorded his first encounter with
Perry, a young man who would become an important part of his life:

As I pulled into the school lot at Hindman late in the day along
came James Perry. James has one good eye, reads regularly
five or six adult books a week—"I'll read anything you'll tell
me to"–aged sixteen. Said I, "What are you doing away down
here." "Ay, just running. I run about six miles a day. Some days
lately I run twelve, on Sundays, say when I can. All I do when
I'm not in school is run and read." Then, "Say! You want to
go up in the mountains on Bill Dee Branch and see where the

plane fell? Some Sunday? The plane that fell last year with that man and woman and child in it they couldn't find for a couple of weeks. My aunt's the one who found it."[26]

Still was attracted to Perry's reading habits but also to his level of activity and his insatiable curiosity. Perhaps Still knew a number of young people like him during this time, but he befriended only a few.

Not much is known about the day-to-day work Still did for the library in the 1950s. The most interesting description comes from Gurney Norman, a former graduate of Hazard High School, who in 1958 was a journalism student at the University of Kentucky. His summer job was working for his hometown newspaper. In his October 1958 article for the *Hazard Herald,* he described the Hindman library: "Mr. Still puts in full days to maintaining the high state of efficiency which so characterizes his library. The building is a neat one built of native stone, and books from generous doners [sic] pour daily into the library, from which Mr. Still uses his experienced eye to select the best reading for Hindman students."[27]

The article was respectable, coming from a novice reporter. But even more interesting and revealing is his visit that led to the article—Norman met Still in the summer of 1958. He related the story in his tribute to Still at the Hindman Writers' Workshop in July 2002:

I was working as a reporter and feature writer for my hometown weekly newspaper. The great thing about my job was that I got to choose my own stories. There I was a college senior being paid $40/week, going out in the county looking for interesting stories. I had James Still on my mind all summer, but it took me until late July to work up the courage to call him. I asked him if I could come to Hindman and interview him for a story. I could tell through the telephone line that he wasn't exactly grinning for my proposal. But he said, "I don't ordinarily do that kind of thing, but since you're local, come on over."

My appointment was for 1:00 pm, but naturally I showed up 20 minutes early. Mr. Still had said that I would find him in the library. I looked around the main room but didn't see a soul. I didn't mind waiting. It was as quiet as a church in there. The only light came through the windows. I guess I made a noise because all of a sudden a man sat up on one of the reading tables in the far corner. It was Mr. Still. My early arrival had interrupted his nap.

"You're early," he said, rubbing his eyes.

But he didn't punish me for it. He showed me around the library and asked some questions about myself. I told him I had grown up around there in Perry County and Letcher County and that I had been reading his works since high school.

I had no idea of how to have a literary conversation. But I did manage to ask him a few journalist questions: Where were you born? Why do you write?

He told me on the phone that we would be going out to his house on Dead Mare Branch. So about 3:00 we set out in his car. It was possible to relax around this man, he wasn't nearly as odd as I'd been led to believe, and he was as interested in ordinary things around us as he was in literature.

We sat a while in his home and talked about writing. He told me about his many seasons as a resident at Yaddo. I think that he appreciated that I was familiar with the work of most of the writers he mentioned. He could tell that I was interested in literature, not just a journalist looking for a story.

I loved his log house—its musty antique smell and the quality of light inside. It was an environment of old wood, the walls, the floor and old furniture. It was the most literary place I had ever been, the home and workplace of a true practicing writer of poetry and fiction. Seeing his books on the rough shelves caused me to realize that I could build a library too.

Mr. Still was an active gardener in those days. In addition to the vegetables, he cultivated the prettiest roses I had ever seen. The arrangement of the shrubs and smaller trees, the grass was under control but showed no signs of the military haircut that suburban lawns are expected to have. His garden had his own sense of form and content, a unique gardening style.

From the well in front of the house we got water and we each drank from the dipper. I had brought my professional camera with me, one of those late 50s Polaroid cameras that weighed about 4 pounds. I said I would like to take a picture of him by the well if he would oblige me. It wasn't easy to oblige a Polaroid photographer in those days, especially an inexperienced photographer. I had to put poor Jim Still through the procedure three times.

It was about 5:00 pm when we set out for Hindman. We were talking easy by now. The visit was a success. It was only when I got out of the car that I had a shocking realization. I had left my camera sitting on his well.

He was utterly calm and generous about it. "Let's go get it."

Norman's account of their first meeting reveals Still as welcoming and talkative. He was interested in the young man from Hazard and openly shared with him his workplace, his log house, and his time. Norman had a rare glimpse into the private world of James Still during a phase when his reputation was as a solitary, even odd, man.

Still was aware of his reputation as distant and retiring. Ironically, his effort to dispel that perception may have helped perpetuate it. For example, in 1954 he contributed to a regular feature of *Mountain Life and Work* called "This Is My Best." The story he selected for reprint was "Mrs. Razor." The most interesting part of the article is the introduction, which Still either wrote or heavily edited. He was described as "an easy-going and soft-spoken countryman who values the ways of his own people and who never calls attention to himself. His voice seldom is raised, but his smile is always on the point of flashing wide in a salute of friendliness." This affable image was an attempt to counter the "cloak of distinction" placed on him by "well-meaning friends" who thought a writer must be "different" and have an "artistic temperament." In trying to alter his temperamental image, the introduction reinforced it:

> Somehow [this smiling friendly man] does not fit the picture of what some of his admirers think a nationally honored author ought to be, so statements are often made that "James doesn't like visitors," or that he "won't talk to groups," or that he "absolutely refuses to have his picture taken." The truth is that he is not concerned about seeking publicity, and he shares the general mountain feeling against "showing off." He is more concerned about writing the best short stories that it is possible for him to write than he is about being an "Author" . . . this unaffected normality makes him the writer he is.[28]

If Still had been a total recluse, he would not have invited Norman to Hindman and certainly would not have taken the young man to his log home or posed for photographs. Yet Norman knew Still's reputation as a private man was for a reason. In his late forties, Still was shy and wanted to avoid the limelight. "Recluse" is too strong, but he was not outgoing. He was more comfortable staying in the shadows.

McConkey at MSC would not let Still live in the shadows, at least not during the summers. He continued to involve Still in the Morehead Writers' Workshop and made the trip to Dead Mare Branch to fetch him each July until 1956.[29] That year McConkey's letter saying when he would arrive also contained the news that he would be leaving MSC after the workshop because the large class size and teaching load meant he had no time for his own writing. He had accepted an offer at Cornell University. Albert Stewart had been appointed to fill his position, including the yearly task of organizing the writers' workshop.[30]

As McConkey predicted, Stewart took over the position of creative writing teacher and director of the Morehead workshop. In a 1957 letter to Still, Stewart seemed to be overwhelmed by the work and responsibility, but he did keep the workshop going, and he kept Still involved. In fact, the first year Stewart was organizer, he invited Still's friend Robert Francis from Massachusetts. That led to a cordial reunion for Still and Francis, who had not seen each other since 1948. They stayed together in a dorm room on campus. The following note from Francis, written on August 24, shows that they shared some special hours: "I have just waked up, and glancing over with half an eye at the bed where you are I see you lying flat on your back, wrapped like a mummy (part in sheet and part in pajama) your arms wide spread. And then it happens. You speak. The first words of the day. 'Oh, world I cannot hold thee close enough.' That was worth going to Kentucky to hear and see."[31]

If you do not count publications, and he claimed he did not, the 1950s were good for Still. He published only four poems, fours stories, and three short articles during the decade, but he had reoriented himself to post–World War II life in Knott County; he had returned to Hindman to make a living; and he was connecting with old and new friends. One of the poems, "Apple Trip," appeared in the *New York Times* on June 17, 1958. The last stanza expresses the same *joie de vivre* as his greeting to the day that Francis cherished.

> That trip I hauled home two hundred bushels
> Of melt-in-your-mouth, of swallow-your-tongue—
> Two hundred bushels of tooth-ticklers and grin-busters,
> Two hundred measures of World Wonders and Sweet Rusters,
> And O the trip was a sight to the world,
> The journey a worldly wonder.[32]

19

Family Loss and Brotherly Love

The cliff gave way and the slope shifted ground,
The oaks rode upright and possessed the road
And what had been hanging changed its abode,
And to get beyond was to go around.
                                        —From "The Trees in the Road"

Nineteen fifty-seven was a watershed year for James Still. Not because the Soviets launched Sputnik or because winter floods ravaged eastern Kentucky. The importance of that year for Still's life was private and profound. He turned fifty, and his father, James Alexander Still, died at the age of eighty-five. His father's death was a deep loss that left him feeling as if part of himself had passed away.

Family was important to Still, yet he and his father had never been close. Their personalities were different. Alex was an outgoing, public man. In his later years he took an interest in local politics and ran for office several times. He was also a consummate family man, having married three women and fathered ten children. A 1939 article in the local Alabama newspaper, *The Chambers County News,* showed that J. Alex was a well-liked citizen and claimed that the father and son shared powers of observation and storytelling. "[Alex] has a talent for seeing the interesting in the commonplace. A boy, or a dog, a cow, a horse, a politician, a peddler will almost certainly create an interesting train of thoughts in the mind of the elder Still. . . . He didn't give his boy great riches, but he has given him something far more priceless."[1]

After his mother died in 1930, Still and his father corresponded regularly. The father's letters were full of family news and questions about when James would visit. Still did see him on trips south but usually stayed with one of his sisters, either Inez Barnes in Gadsden or Elloree Sharpe in Florida. According to his niece, Barbara Sue Barnes Harris, Still's sisters catered to his every whim. As the first boy after four girls, Still had enjoyed special treatment. When Uncle James came to Alabama, her mother would have everything planned, and the family patiently awaited his arrival, which was usually later than scheduled. Inez liked to cook for him and enjoyed washing and ironing his clothes. A clean bathrobe was hanging in the bedroom, and a special china cup was ready at the table.[2]

One reason for such care was that they felt their oldest brother had no one, except his sisters, to look after him. Although he soaked up their attention, visiting family put him in a different environment; their homes were filled with activity, while his was quiet. A family reunion could involve more than forty people: Alex, his wife, eight adult children and their spouses, as many as two dozen grandchildren, and a few great grandchildren. James had no woods or creeks for escape. He once described a time in 1955 when he was in Alabama for the funeral of his oldest sister, Lois. Her daughter-in-law, Mary, helped him out of a minor predicament. Lois had two sons—James Allen and Wilfred, whom Still described as the wittiest person he had ever known. Mary, the wife of James Allen, was constantly teased. "Poor little ignorant Mary," Wilfred would say. Still took up for Mary; he appreciated her cooking and her wit, as demonstrated in this anecdote: "I liked her. Mary was a wonderful cook, made delicious asparagus casseroles. I remember when my sister died, I was there at the house and needed to change clothes. There were so many people around. I needed to change clothes somewhere and Mary said, 'My mother, she's blind. Let's go where she is.'"[3]

Still's stories of Alabama conveyed the sense of many people in small houses, a large extended family around a table piled with food or sitting together and talking on the porch.[4] In spite of his sisters' attention, he did not feel appreciated for his accomplishments. Later in life he stated, without animosity, that as far as he knew, no one in his family had ever read a single one of his books. In some ways, he felt himself an outsider among his own kin. His closest sister, Inez, was only two years older. Being a tomboy, she had spent a lot of childhood time with her brother. Still once quoted Inez as having said, "Jim, I don't understand you," meaning she did not know what he was thinking.[5] Still was quick to punctuate such stories with the observation that there was no disagreement in the home.

Sometime in the 1930s it became clear to all his relatives that James Jr. would not be moving back to Alabama. His first disconnect was when he left for Lincoln Memorial University in 1924, but he continued to think of his parents' house as his. The death of his mother in 1930 changed that permanently, and Still emotionally disconnected himself from Alabama. Less than a year passed before his father remarried a much younger woman, Fannie Mae Bailey, who died a year later in childbirth. Lonie looked after the child, Still's half brother, who died of dengue fever when only two years old. Then in 1935 Alex married Fannie Will Lee, who already had an eighteen-year-old son.

Even when there was no chance of his moving closer to the family, Still was a source of pride for his father and siblings. He was well educated and a "success" in their eyes. Inez thought of him as "a famous man." They appreciated that he was a respected writer even if they did not read his books. To them, he was brother James. Although they stayed in touch through letters, it was during a family predicament that Still paid particular attention. For example, in 1941 his brother Alfred, at the age of twenty-seven, suffered a gunshot wound in a hunting accident; Still spent several weeks in Alabama, helping care for him and taking charge of the expenses. That became a pattern. When facing a medical crisis, members of the family would contribute as they could, but usually Still would manage the bills, and if others could not pay their share, he would take up the slack.

In March 1955 his oldest sister, Carrie Lois, died of cancer at the age of sixty-two. Two years later, their father began to fail. Alfred wrote to James that the old man was in the Valley hospital in West Point. He was weak and losing weight, but after three and a half weeks in the hospital, he was showing improvement and would come home.[6] The bill amounted to more than $400. The costs could be shared, but the burden of home care fell on Lonie, the sister who lived in Fairfax. She was, by her own admission, unable to manage. At some point in the spring of 1957 Alex called his estranged wife, Fannie Will, who was living in California, and asked her to return to Alabama. She did.

None of the children welcomed this decision, but James was particularly unhappy. Alex had been a reasonably healthy man, but as he began to decline in the early 1950s, Fannie Will had left and moved to California with her son. When it became clear that Alex would not live long, she returned. Still was angered because he saw her not as a woman who cared for his father but as an opportunist out to get whatever inheritance was left. Still let his sisters know that the turn of events was unacceptable to him. Several of their letters show that they were more accepting of the situation. They, after all, were hoping for some relief from the nursing responsibility.

In June 1957 Inez wrote that on Mother's Day she had seen their father at Lonie's house: "Papa was looking good he says he feels good and had gain weight. Fannie Will had aged since I saw her last she seemed to be real glad to see us."[7] Later in June, Lonie wrote to Still, anticipating his summer visit. She was looking forward to having him there but wanted to prepare him:

> Our dady was real sick a few day last week. but he seem to be some better. They went to Rock Spring church today. I think you will be sorry what you said about Fannie Will. You would not put up the way papa was living
>
> You will agree with me when I tell you true story When you come home. Its more like home than it ever has been in a long time. Go to see them first.
>
> I think that what the matter with papa he think you are mad with him because he call Fannie Will to come back home. He need her to wait on him for I wasn't able to see after him. We see you in a few day.[8]

Lonie's perception and directness compensated for her lack of writing skills.

Details of the family drama surrounding the father's death are unknowable, but the events left a mark on Still. He always claimed that his parents did not display affection easily, but neither did they have open disagreements. He had "never heard an unkind word exchanged" between them.[9] The situation with Fannie Will was an anomaly. Still was never reconciled to her return, despite Lonie's explanation and justification. After Alex died in October, it seemed as though James's suspicions were fulfilled. Two letters to Still from Alfred described the behavior that Still had feared:

> (Oct. 6) I went by to get Papa's tools but Fannie Will would not give them to me. She thinks they can be sold. They are not any

good. They are not worth any money, but to me they are worth a lot. . . . She told Mike she was going to get the shot gun back. But I am mailing it to Comer. Papa told me he wanted Comer to have his gun. Lucky for Comer it was out here. . . . (Oct. 11) I went by and asked F.W. for Papa's tools. She refused to let me have them. She also told Mike that he had to give her the gun. I told her it belonged to Comer. She raised hell, saying she was going to get it.[10]

Still took few items with him when he left Alabama after his father's funeral. But his niece, Barbara Sue, remembered that he drove his father's old black Model T Ford back to Kentucky. When asked who inherited the items in the house, she responded that the family was poor enough that there was not much to inherit. What interesting furniture they had owned was destroyed in a fire, so there was not much of value in the house where he died—only his car. She remembered how funny it was watching her dad and others trying to teach Uncle James to drive that car. But they succeeded because he called her mother when he got safely back to Hindman.[11]

Another thing that Still took away from the funeral was hospital bills. He did not pay them all but divided the expenses among the siblings who were able to pay. He managed the accounts. Elloree, his sister in Florida, sent James the news that the final charge from the hospital would be $1,763, or about $252 each. Then she asked if anything would be left over from the sale of the place once the mortgage had been paid. By December 1957, Fannie Will had left Alabama. While Elloree was prepared to pay her share, she made it very clear that she would not cover any bills that Fannie Will might "hatch up."[12]

By the end of February 1958, the First National Bank of West Point, Georgia, published a foreclosure notice in the local paper concerning failure to pay the mortgage on the house belonging to J. Alex Still and wife. If Fannie Will had come back to collect what was rightfully hers, she had not gotten much other than trouble. She had caused trouble too. Still never forgave her.

In this cryptic note to his brother Tom, Still referred to a difficult encounter that was his last with Fannie Will. "Of the unpleasantness that happened to me on the night of July 12 in the Valley, I don't know what to say. I was deeply wounded. Nothing was gained, much was lost. . . . But let us forget about all this. It is not worth the effort of thinking about it or burning about it. It is already behind me."[13] Along with this note was an up-to-date account of the hospital and doctor payments. It is doubtful that the family was able to put it all behind them. Later, when describing the experience of his father's death, Still acknowledged that the time was highly significant for him, but he never discussed bill payment or unpleasant details related to his stepmother.

The heart of his description was the personal, mystical aspect of his loss. In 1997 he described his epiphany resulting from his father's death:[14]

> My father died. Doctor said "just a matter of a few days. Nothing could be done. If we wanted to take him home, it would be fine." He was unconscious. I had never seen him stripped, his body. I was astonished. He wasn't a big man. I'm shaped somewhat like him. About the same height. He was red headed. By then he was gray, but he had red hair on his arms. We were all born red-headed.
>
> We were taking turns staying with him. I was at my sister's about a mile away. All the business about the funeral; there was no closure for me. There was this woman he had married, his third wife, who hated my guts. She was always as unpleasant as she could be. That's a long story.
>
> Anyway, I came home but I couldn't give him up. It went on a long time. One day I was here in this room [on Dead Mare Branch] and all of a sudden I had the feeling that I had become my own father. At that moment I had a feeling of peace. There was a closure. It happened rather suddenly, a realization. I had assumed his role. We had become one, in a sense. I don't know how to explain it, but that's what happened, several months after the funeral.

He never tried to write of that experience. Yet his poem "The Trees in the Road" relates his coming to terms with the loss.[15] The poem was not published until 1968, but it was probably drafted ten years earlier. Comments he made in the 1986 video *Conversations with James Still* indicate that the poem was inspired by the experience in Alabama as well as a specific tree falling near his Kentucky house:[16]

> One day the mountain slid down, covered that road up—just slid pretty as you ever saw, trees still standing up where they were. Except for one tree, which fell. We used to go up that way

to the post office. You'd have to go under it or over it, and it was difficult either way. You had to get down and crawl. . . . I wrote a poem called "The Trees in the Road," which is really a memorial to my father. I didn't know it at the time I was writing it, but I realized later I was saying something about him. Although he came down, nothing really changed.

In some ways nothing did change after the tree fell and the man died. The path was blocked or altered, just as Still's life shifted. Yet it was possible to get around the tree, or under it, or over it. Eventually, it decayed and became part of its environment. New travelers would hardly notice it. Just so, as time went on, the passing of J. Alex Still became part of his son's world. And James took his place.

Eleven months after his father's death, Still's brother Thomas Watson, at the age of forty-nine, suffered a sudden heart attack and died three days later.[17] Having survived combat in Italy and recovered from his war injuries, Tom, or "Watt" as his wife called him, was the strength of the family living in Fairfax, Alabama. That loss was a shock, but the prolonged illness of Still's youngest brother, Alfred, was an even greater strain.

Alfred had married when he was twenty-one, and by the time he was forty-three he had seven boys to support. The family lived in New Orleans. Alfred returned to Alabama for the funeral of his sister Lois in 1955. When he got back from the cemetery, he received the tragic news that his wife had died suddenly in New Orleans. After recovering from the shock, he faced his major challenge—the care of his children. He did not make enough money to hire a helper; in fact, his work was low-paying and sporadic. Finally, his wife's mother took four of the boys, and he brought two of them to Alabama; the oldest joined the army. The youngest boy lived with Alfred's nephew Wilfred Johnson and his wife, Ophelia. The third, Michael, aged twelve, stayed with Alfred.[18]

Alfred's life had not been easy, but after his father's death it became even harder. He had been seriously wounded as a teen by a gunshot. Then he experienced the loss of his wife and the challenges of being a single parent. Finally, his own health problems led to long suffering and early death. He needed a helping hand, and he got it from his older brother James. More than any of his other siblings, Alfred was drawn to writing and creative storytelling, and Still once described him as having "a potentially gifted imagination."[19] Still took a special interest in Alfred.

In 1957 Alfred's letters were mostly about the family situation in the Valley. After their father died, he was concerned with the settlement of their father's affairs, then with his own future: the way he would make a living and the place where he would live. Even before his health problems surfaced, he had money problems. In December 1957 Alfred wrote to James about his latest plan. He and Wilfred (Lois's second son) would go into business in LaFayette. They planned to take over a chain-saw dealership. To do that, Alfred needed $1,000, and he was writing Still with a request to borrow money. By all indications, Still did not grant that request, but he did help in another way. He began to support Alfred's youngest son, Michael.

Still was giving his nephew an allowance as long as he stayed in school and made good grades. That seemed to be the incentive the young man needed. He wrote his uncle several letters toward the end of 1957, reporting his "B" in science, better than he expected. The rest of his news revolved around hunting (he had killed three rabbits and two squirrels that season) and football (their team had set a new record). At some point, Michael went from living with his father to living on the farm with his cousin Wilfred. During that time, serious school problems arose. He was doing so poorly that Wilfred decided he should quit school and help full time on the farm. Alfred, who retained some power over the decisions, insisted that he would not farm but enter the navy.

All of this happened within six months of Alex's death and before all the bills had been settled. On the last day of March 1958 Alfred wrote to James, assuring him that Michael would repay all the money his Uncle James had sent.[20] On April 3 Ophelia wrote Still with her suspicions that the few good grades Michael got in high school had resulted from cheating. She had intended to send his report card to Still but assumed that Michael had torn it up. Her summary: "He made C- on conduct (chewing gum) he said. He made Ds on most everything except one D-. I am sure if he had tried he could have done better and I am very sorry that he didn't."[21] This news was distressing to Still. He had every reason to expect better from Michael.

By June, Alfred was in better spirits when he shared the news that Michael would soon be home for a visit. Another source of excitement resulted from his own effort—his first attempt at writing, which he sent to his brother. "Tell me what you think of it [the manuscript]. If you think it alright, tell me where to try sending it. Or send it off for me. I would like that. . . . The name I will use is part of my own: TED STILL.

I do not care to be known too soon. . . . you can give the return address: c/o Still Chain Saw Co.—Gen. Del. LaFayette, Alabama."[22]

There is no further mention of Alfred's story, of Still's efforts to find a publisher, or his advice on how to improve it. Letters show that Alfred was not a practiced or polished writer. The next letter, however, revealed his direct way with words. He seemed encouraged by Michael's visit. The young man had gingerly approached the topic of getting a tattoo. His father responded:

> "Michael. I'm the son of James Alex Still. Also your dad. I know because I was there when you were born. I know that my daddy did not approve of everything I ever did, but he still loved me as a son. I do not approve of everything you have done. And may not, of everything you do in the future. But, I am a proud man.
>
> "A tattoo is not a mark or picture that means that the feller with one, is a man or can ever be one. But it is a sign telling everyone who sees it, that this person was very weak at one time. Because he has marked his body for life. He cannot hope to be a leader, he is a follow the leader guy. Our 'Uncle Sam' spends plenty of money each year trying to erase tattoos from young fellers and men who become wiser and did not want that mark anymore. A man that comes out of the NAVY without a tattoo, I think, is a real man. If he was my son, I would be very proud of him."
>
> Little Michael came home and was very proud to show me that his body was unmarked. I have found out that, by just being honest with myself, "TRUTH" is a very powerful weapon.[23]

This excerpt shows that Alfred had convictions and confidence in expressing them. But it also indicates a need to convince his older brother that he could be a wise mentor to his own son. Alfred's struggle to keep his life together became more difficult over the next few years.

During the 1950s James Still had experienced the loss of close friends and family: Iris Grannis died in 1952, Marjorie Kinnan Rawlings in 1953, his oldest sister in 1955, his father in 1957, his brother Tom in 1958, and in 1959 his neighbor Ruby Amburgey. Ruby was Woodrow's daughter and a person Still had known since she was a child on Wolfpen. His telegram with the news to Temple Baker generated a response from Baker that must have reflected Still's feeling: "Losing a friend is like cutting a guy wire that holds us in place. The breaking of each tie makes us more conscious and grateful for those left us."[24] A few days later Still wrote to Baker, saying, "We buried Ruby beside her father in the Amburgey plot above my plot on Dead Mare Branch. I helped to carry her up that hill, that part-way to the sky."[25]

Helping carry the burden of debt, sickness, and death was a chore for Still over the next six years. He became the caretaker, provider, and advisor to Alfred in 1960 and maintained that role until Alfred's death from emphysema on April 3, 1965. The close relationship that grew between the brothers in those years reveals as much about Still's choices as it does about his compassion. Helping Alfred was his top priority.

When he moved back to Alabama from New Orleans, Alfred tried to be more involved with his brothers and sisters, but the situation was unfamiliar to him. By the spring of 1960 he was verging on despair. The chainsaw-repair shop, which Wilfred had opened with Alfred as a helper, was not going well. It was "dead," and Alfred didn't know "what he was going to do."[26] Making a reasonable salary over a period of time was difficult, but in the summer his finances were not the only problem. In August he received the first of many reports indicating that he had emphysema and would never be healthy again. The doctor, according to Alfred, had said that he had enough lungs left to move around with but not enough to work.[27]

Still visited in July and found his brother thin and generally debilitated. He moved him to live with a couple who would give him room, board, and some attention for a monthly cost, which Still himself would pay. For the next few months, Alfred's letters showed a shift between forced optimism and deep despair. He could do very little; even walking to the outside toilet wore him out. One short letter dated August 29 illustrates his physical and psychological difficulty: "I called James Johnson and ask him to take me to Langdale to see my doctor. He said he did not have time. I do not have any money or any way to get the medicine I need. I ask Wilfred to get it for me, but he said he was not able. Since last week, this has been one long nightmare. There is not any need to go to the doctor if I can't get any med. I do not know how long I can last like this. Answer soon."[28] He had no one to turn to, except his brother. The only thing Still could do from a distance was send advice, money, and books. Reading, sleeping, and fretting were Alfred's major pastimes.

Having little money to spare, Still solicited Alfred's adult sons. Charles and Phillip, the two oldest, agreed to send a small amount each month. Efforts to contact Michael ended in additional heartache.

Michael was in the brig. He had gone AWOL; his punishment was five months in military prison and loss of his pay, seventy dollars per month. His letter informing his uncle of the situation is matter-of-fact. He did add, "I guess you think Dad raised some pretty sorry sons, well maybe he did, but I won't go into that. All I can say is, I'm sorry things are turning out the way they are."[29]

By January 1961 Alfred had again been in the hospital. He received some relief for his financial situation when Social Security began paying disability. He also noted that his four underage boys would be receiving small payments. At some point they had been moved from his mother-in-law's into a church orphanage in Clinton, South Carolina.[30] The displacement of the boys was distressing, but Still's January 20 letter to Alfred was beautifully constructed, touching on the weather, his library work, the bills that needed paying, and the writing he was trying or wanting to do. The letter is full of life, not despair:

> Today is a day that January has stolen from April. The sun is shining, and it is cold but not unpleasantly so, and if the wind is a bit icy it has in it a threat of spring. What a week we had last week? And the week before. Snow, bitter cold. . . . And so we have a sky-blue (if nippy) day and I begin to think about farming when this happens. But not today. Too busy. About 600 brand spanking new books are here for processing before being put on Library Shelves. . . .
>
> The way I found out about you being in the hospital was by letter from Mr. Stedham, administrator of the hospital. As you know, the bill is large indeed, and according to him nothing has been paid on it. Could you pay at the least $25.00 a month on this bill from your Social Security income? I am standing with considerable awe at the hospital bill which at this time comes to nearly $2,500. Of course I have never seen that much money at any one time in my life. It would probably take me the rest of my life to pay it—in the only way I can, on a monthly basis.
>
> No matter what else I do or am compelled to think about, one thing is paramount in my mind: the novel I am writing. . . . When it can be finished I do not know. I can't see that far ahead although I know in a general way what is to come in the remaining fifteen or so chapters. Writing is the thing that makes life for me an ever-recurring pleasure. It has its agonies, its disappointments, but the act of creation outweighs them.[31]

This friendly attempt to share his life with his brother also reveals Still's goals and conflicts. In springlike weather he wanted to farm, but there was time only for work in the library. He wanted to help with the hospital bills, but they seemed insurmountable. What he really wanted to do was write, but his progress toward that goal was slow indeed.[32] He needed to be engaged in the act of creation but was consumed by the act of rescue.

As the year went on, James stayed busy while Alfred lost ground. At Thanksgiving, Still visited the family in Alabama. On his return to Hindman, he found his obligations mounting. He knew he needed more money because he could see that Alfred would need more care. Still remained optimistic. In February the president at Morehead State College had approached him about teaching during the summer-school session from June to mid-August. He wrote Alfred, "It pains my gizzard to think of working a whole year through without a vacation. But I may do it." He ended that letter with his latest idea for the farm: "A beegum—the old-fashioned type, a hollow log. Will order a mess of bees from Sears, Roebuck when the weather opens up. . . . It's not the honey they might make that interests me. When I go to my back door on hot summer days I want to be able to smell bees and/or honey or bee-bread, whatever it is that is so nose-tickling in a beelot."[33]

A month later Still had spring on his mind when he reported the air was "snappy and pungent," the trees "expectant." He told Alfred of his notebook devoted to spring, a place where he could keep up with the changes from day to day until mid-April when there would be "an explosion of spring" and he would "bog down in detail."[34] At the end of April, Still realized his plan to bring bees to his farm and described the special day to Alfred:

> A note from the post-office Wednesday said "Bees in the PO." But when I went down and asked at the counter, "Bees, please," there were no bees in the building. They had set them outside, saying some had got out and they were afraid of them. But none had got out. All the way from Sylvester, Georgia the two cages had collected visiting bees. Over to Dead Mare Branch I went with them, fetched down Monroe Amburgey, local bee-expert, from Lick Branch of the Big Doubles and we hived them without a sting. Very friendly bees. They swarmed about our heads. Let's hope they stay that way. Plenty of bloom now for them to get right into production.[35]

Alfred had been moved into the nursing home in Lineville, Alabama. His letters to Still dropped off during 1962, but Still's to him increased. They were optimistic without being falsely upbeat. By November, Still wrote to an administrator of the nursing home, expressing appreciation for her concern about his brother. He ended, "I'll write to Alfred soon. I often wonder why he never nowadays replies to any of my letters. This is, I suppose, the reason I don't write him more often. But he has his reasons I judge, and whatever they are they are good enough for me. I accept them."[36]

He was in a mode of acceptance; he must have known that his youngest brother would not live many more years—but he was never tempted to abandon or neglect him. On November 28 Alfred did write and began with this appreciation: "This Thanksgiving I have more to be thankful for, than anyone I know. High on the list is your being my brother." For Christmas, Still gave himself a gift: rather than go to Alabama, he spent the holiday at his farm. And as he told Alfred, he had stocked up on a twelve-pound ham to avoid having to drive during the predicted snowstorm.[37]

The financial effort of supporting Alfred was a burden for Still. He was always behind with payments to the doctors, the nursing home, and the pharmacy. A letter he drafted in September 1962 attempted to explain his difficulty to the Lineville Clinic. It is clearly a draft because he struck through sections and added words in the margins. Nevertheless, it provides a summary of his financial predicament:

> Your bill has arrived and I will send you a check for as much of it as I can when I am paid by the local school board at the end of this month. In fact, if I can manage to borrow it on top of what I already owe I'll pay the whole bill. What bothers me is next month, and all the months after. . . .
>
> Considering that all the money I earn above my basic and unavoidable expenses will probably be going to you and the Nursing Home from now on I think you should understand something about me and my financial condition. To sum up briefly:
>
> I own no property, save an automobile which is a necessity to transport me to my work.
>
> I owe approximately $500 from past borrowing to help my brother and am repaying that.
>
> I have no income outside the salary I receive for teaching in the local school.

I have at present medical problems of my own.[38]

There is nobody in my family who can help me pay my brother's bills. My three sisters are retired under social security. My other brother faces probable retirement from chronic arthritis.

I have lived close to the bone for a long time. I'm fairly used to it. In August 1955 I began to contribute toward the care of my aged father, and this continued through his illness which lasted two years and which involved three long periods in the hospital, doctors, medicines. Often his drugs alone were costing more than I was earning. After his passing at age 85 there were the expenses of the funeral and a number of bills of which I was not previously aware. Less than 5% of these amounts were paid by others. By using *all* my savings and disposing of some mutual stock I owned, I came through. By April 1959 I had paid them all! Then, almost immediately, I had to come to the aid of my brother, Alfred, who is now under your care. For the three years prior to his coming to the Nursing Home at Lineville practically everything I made outside of my bare living went toward his upkeep, his drugs, his doctors, his hospital bills. I accept this. I accept the responsibility of being my brothers [sic] keeper. Dr. John Horton Smith of the Langdale Clinic told me that anybody who takes responsibility for a patient with emphysema will end with nothing, broke, bankrupt. By the time I started helping my brother I was already broke.[39]

Beginning with the spring term of 1961, Still taught as a visiting writer-in-residence at Morehead. By 1963 he was a full-time faculty member in the department of English. It did mean more money, but it also meant he would be paying for his own room and board, which Hindman Settlement School had been providing during the week. It also meant he needed to keep his car well maintained because he would be driving more. He stayed at Morehead during the week, and when weather permitted, he drove three and a half hours to get himself home to Dead Mare Branch. His support continued, but his letters to Alfred became less frequent and took on the tone of a parent giving strong advice and much-needed guidance to a wayward child. In December 1963 he responded to a letter that Alfred had had a nurse write for him:

From the letter that was written for you to me I had some difficulty in understanding your problem. I think you know that
living in a nursing home is a built-in problem in itself. I have
counted on you coping with whatever comes up. You know,
or ought to know, my commitments here. I teach every day. It
would be practically impossible for me to get away except for
an emergency. The business of hopping around from one nursing home to another is unpromising. You are already in the
best one I know anything about. The thing for you to do is to
cooperate with them to the best of your ability. Don't become a
problem patient to them. And to me.

In the letter that was written for you the writer said "she
(the nurse) suggested that his people take him some place else
where may be some doctor would understand his case." I think
your case is well understood. You understand it too. Medicines
are not the final answer. In fact I have been under the impression you were being plied with too much of them.

Still went on to describe the two people he knew who suffered from
emphysema. The only drug they took was a decongestant to clear
phlegm from the throat and, when absolutely necessary, supplemental
oxygen. Both of these people, he noted, were chain-smokers like Alfred.
Rather than taking drugs, Alfred needed to change his expectations and
behavior. "So I recommend a change of attitude. The nurse spoken of in
the letter is a human being. She has her own problems. She has to deal
daily and hourly with people who make great demands on her physically, mentally and emotionally. Try to understand her problem. Try to
be the kind of patient they appreciate instead of recommending they go
elsewhere. Nothing whatsoever is gained by being unpleasant, chip-on-
the-shoulder, demanding. Nothing. So, I ask you to *Cope*."[40]

Coping is exactly what Still was struggling to do. Still was bus-
ier and Alfred was sicker, but the financial support continued when he
took a full-time teaching position at MSC. Less than two years later,
on April 3, 1965, Alfred died. Still never talked about the burial except
to say that one of his own suits was Alfred's final dress. Still made
one of his few comments about Alfred's death to Jim Wayne Miller in
1986 when Still recalled his brother's last days.[41] Getting to him, Still
said, "Alfred, I'm here." Those words and his older brother's presence
relaxed the dying man, who never spoke again and died fourteen hours
later. After the burial, Still took a few items of Alfred's clothing to his

sons. The only memento he kept was an oxygen tank. Years later when a recording was made of Still's comments about a set of photos, he came to one of Alfred at age five and said: "My baby brother Alfred—a very gifted human being. We loved him so much. He died a tragic death caused by emphysema. He had more potential than all the rest of us put together."[42] Alfred did leave seven sons, most of whom eventually disconnected from the family. And he inspired in his older brother this simple poem: [43]

On the Passing of My Brother Alfred

After this death it will
Be easier
To pass beyond, to go
Where he went,
Out of this light into
A greater light.

20

On to Morehead

What I am trying to do at Morehead State College is conduct reading courses . . . in which students with genuine creative talent might discover themselves.

—James Still

The year after Still's father died, Gurney Norman published his article in *The Hazard Herald*. Though the paper's distribution was narrow and the interviewer inexperienced, the story revealed a theme central to Still's creative life: he wrote because it made him happy. In February 1960 Joe Creason, a staff writer for the *Louisville Courier-Journal*, explored the same theme. Creason's article "Some things a man does just for himself" covered three full pages in the magazine section and featured six photographs showing Still engaged in a variety of activities: flipping through manuscripts in an open trunk, filling a bird feeder, helping a student in the library, distributing books from the bookmobile, typing at his desk, and pruning bushes in front of his log house. Creason's original idea had been to write about the Hindman library.[1] When they had first met at a Morehead Writers' Workshop, Creason thought the bookmobile would make an interesting topic and serve as a reminder that the state should provide more money for books and libraries. He wanted to feature Still as the librarian.

The published article devotes only a couple of sentences to the bookmobile. It is all about James Still, the man and writer, complete with hyperbole and special emphasis on how different he is from the "typical successful creative writer." He does not make speeches, nor attend autograph parties, nor submit to publicity tricks. He does have manuscripts he has never submitted for publication, and he is practically indifferent to the payment he receives from the ones that are published. According to the article, Still was "a compulsive writer that writes because he must, not because it is a shortcut to gold and glory."[2] The title comes from Still's declaration "There are some things a man does just for himself and nobody else." This notion of a private pursuit and secluded lifestyle led Creason to label Still "a literary hermit." The article helped establish the early persona that would become a major feature of Still's personality and values later in his career. Still never thought of himself as a literary hermit and sometimes recoiled at the description, yet that was the person he had projected to Creason.

The article led to numerous "fan" letters. One was from Frank Gulledge, president of the Bank of St. Helens in Shively, Kentucky. He had been acquainted with Still years earlier when he was an office boy in the Fairfax mill. "Knowing you at that time and reading [Creason's] story yesterday, I don't think you have changed a bit." The article generated several letters to the editor, and at least one reader, Polly Bing, was inspired to write directly to Still. She thanked him for letting Creason do the piece then gently reminded him that it is fine not to seek acclaim or money, but people should know more about him and his writing. Elizabeth Watts at Hindman Settlement School said something similar. Her congratulations carried the sentiment of many readers: "I do hate to think how much we are missing by not being able to read the stories that are shut up in the trunk!" She went on to say that any honor to him reflected well on Hindman; his working there was a tribute to the school, and the library was fortunate to have him. She did not say that if he were not working there, he might publish more.[3]

Dean Cadle, the man who was to become Still's close friend and promoter, also responded.[4] On February 15, just four days after reading the paper, he wrote that he planned to visit over the coming weekend. Then he described the article as "rather a good job." Its strength, however, he attributed to Still, not Creason. "You are something different from the various costume and historical writers, the gentleman farmer writers, the publicity-seeking writers, the self-admitted money-making writers, the past-time writers, and all the others clambering toward some vague heaven that the Magazine section has been featuring over a period of years."[5] Cadle ended with the advice that if another article was to be done, it should appear in a more important publication. He was thinking how to "sell" the writer who did not seek publicity and how to sell himself as the writer's promoter.

While Creason drew a compelling portrait, it was not entirely accurate. Before World War II, Still had been actively engaged in efforts to publish. Since 1945 he had produced less and published very little. The implication was that he had continued to write but had not submitted material. Evidence shows that he did submit and resubmit one manuscript, *Way Down Yonder: Riddles and Antics from Troublesome Creek*. He sent it to Houghton Mifflin for their juvenile collection on March 8, 1956. The response was that "the majority of the riddles were too local in significance to be appealing to the general reader."[6] Three months later Still sent the manuscript to his agent Toni Strassman with a detailed letter warning her that it might be difficult to place because he had already received rejections from Houghton Mifflin and two other publishers: Viking, which responded that it did not fit into their small list, and Atlantic Monthly Press, which said, "It is quite fascinating material for a collector of folklore, but . . . obscure [for] young readers."[7]

Still encouraged his agent by saying that these responses should not be the final word: "Moonbeams and fodder seed are hard to peddle in any season." He had rid the manuscript of "obscure items" and had removed some of the too-local riddles. He suggested approaching Oxford University Press and then Macmillan. Three years later, Strassman returned his manuscript with apologies; she had sent it to seventeen different places and received the same negative reaction and general prediction that the book would not have a broad enough market.[8]

Still's efforts to publish were meeting with little success. So when something was accepted, he was pleased and energized. In July 1959 he hit a winner: *The Atlantic* published "The Run for the Elbertas," his first story to appear since October 1956. His excitement led him to type out the letter from Edward Weeks and mail it to Temple Baker. Weeks had called it powerful, "one of the finest narratives we have published in a long, long time, and I take great pleasure in sending you this extra dividend which you deserve in view of its extra length. Thank you again for writing so well, and do please turn our way when next the spirit moves you." An attached note indicated that the "dividend" was $100, a supplement to the original payment of $400. Baker wrote back, "Thanks for the note and the copy of Mr. Week's letter. Now, will you believe how good you are? It was a wonderfully complimentary letter.

... I am more eager than ever to read 'Peaches' (my name for the story) since seeing his comments."[9] Early in July Still wrote Baker again, this time detailing how he was spending his money:

> Thank you a cattle truck full for kind words, the grace to say them. . . .
>
> From proceeds of above-mentioned narrative I'm having a small house built—two rooms. One for hoes, rakes, washtubs, etc. The second a cogitating room—maybe to write in—maybe to sleep in when you and Charlie are occupying the bed in the big house. I'm calling it Peach House. . . .
>
> I'm scheduled to lecture and/or read from *Hounds on the Mountain* at Morehead some fair July afternoon. Don't buy tickets for this occasion as I'm the sort of cad who stands up an audience when not consulted on his own appearances upon a public platform. Anyhow, at that time I'll probably be chin-deep in Elberta ice cream at the drug store—with lady friends naturally. . . .
>
> I'm looking forward to the peach ice cream at Morehead nevertheless and anyhow and just because and how do you do.[10]

High spirited and mischievous, Still assumed the tone of a grown-up Godey Spurlock in "The Run for the Elbertas." Similar to "A Ride on the Short Dog," the story Baker had not liked, this one tells of two young men going on a trip more for fun than for gain. They accompany Riar Thomas on a run to South Carolina to pick up a truckload of peaches, which he plans to bring back to Kentucky and sell for a big profit. A major difference between the stories is that an omniscient narrator tells "Run," thus keeping readers from feeling firsthand the hurt inflicted by the pranksters. Also the two sixteen-year-olds play tricks on Thomas, who is not an innocent bystander; he deserves their treatment for being so miserly. Besides, he plays the last trick on them—dumping peach fuzz down their shirt collars. The story ends with balanced justice and illustrates the cockiness and wit of the characters and the writer.

Still did not build on the enthusiasm *The Atlantic* showed for "Run" in 1959 by promptly submitting more or longer works. An early 1961 note from Marshall Best gently reminded him that Viking was hoping for a novel manuscript. To avoid placing too much pressure, Best simply closed with "I'd love to know how you are coming along." If Still was coming along, he did not let his editor know because seven years later, Best was still "longing" for a novel.[11] The image of Still as a writer who worked only for himself continued over the next decade. His publication rate reflected a change in his approach to writing. The spontaneity he exhibited in the late 1930s had changed to purposeful deliberation.

Being organized and disciplined, Still recorded his work hours every year from the mid-1950s through the late 1960s. These small notebook pages included no details about what manuscript he was writing, but "work" meant drafting or revising. During the fourteen years that he kept records, the highest number of work hours was in 1959 and the lowest in 1965. The numbers indicate that Still was writing even when he was not publishing, and that he spent more time writing in the years before he became enmeshed in teaching at Morehead. In addition to numbers in a grid, the pages include quotations or short phrases that hint about what he was reading, thinking, or feeling. The following lists a selection of these entries and the year he made each:

> "For I have promises to keep . . ." Frost 1956
>
> "And miles to go before I sleep." Frost 1959
>
> "The things of a man for which we visit him are done in the dark and the cold." Emerson 1960
>
> "The only way to resume is to resume. It is the only way. To resume." Gertrude Stein 1960
>
> "What saves a man is to take a step. Then another step. It is always the same step, but you have to take it." Saint-Exupery 1961
>
> "Work and to hell with everything else." Chekhov 1963
>
> "Constant effort is the law of art . . ." Balzac 1966
>
> "Inconsistency, timidity, laziness, weakness—these are my enemies." Tolstoy 1966

While seeking inspiration from the greats, Still was writing motivational messages to himself: "Work, relax, don't think" 1962; "Silent and alone" 1965; and "Finish it" 1969.[12]

"The Run for the Elbertas" was a product of this time when Still was keeping such meticulous records. The tone and fictional situation of the story marks a departure, but the manuscripts also show that his writing process had changed. He wrote at least seven full drafts, the earliest dated 1956 and the final dated May 1958. All are typed on flimsy brown paper and most include handwritten revisions. These drafts, which contain many more markings than earlier stories, show that he very consciously crafted this one. When asked about his approach to writing "Run," Still responded, "I was becoming more self-conscious. There were certain natural little tests I'd run after the manuscript was written. I wanted to know where all the adjectives were and I would circle them, say with a red pen. And I wanted to know where the adverbs were and also I wanted to check on certain words that I had a tendency to repeat."[13] This consciousness partially accounts for his slower publication rate. It simply took longer to get a manuscript to meet his high expectations. Yet the story moves quickly, displays a carefree quality, and conveys local dialect and humor. The tale is stamped with the personality of Godey Spurlock.

Still was showing another side of Godey in his own life. The boy was a bargain-maker who knew just how far he could push Riar Thomas and still get what he wanted. Plus he used his friend, Mal, as an accomplice. In Still's case, he needed a better-paying job, and his friend Albert Stewart was willing to help. A successful, well-received story in July jump-started negotiations with Morehead State College. Still had been participating in the summer workshops; the summer of 1959 was his eighth.[14] Stewart saw great potential coming from Still's connection to Morehead State, and he wanted the college to take him on as a writer-in-residence. A month after "Run" appeared in *The Atlantic,* Stewart had a letter on the college president's desk, outlining the possibilities for hiring Still full-time. His strategy was to show President Adron Doran that Still had other suitors, and if Morehead did not move quickly and decisively, he would take a position elsewhere. Still was not actively pursuing any positions anywhere. On the contrary, he was committed to Hindman Settlement School through the 1959–1960 school year. But Stewart was aiming high for his friend, so he proposed to Doran that the college offer Still a good salary (at least $7,000) for the academic year. In addition, Stewart was negotiating for an ideal teaching schedule: "We must not in any way vitiate or misuse . . . his special intelligence and abilities. There are hundreds of people who can be trained to do a reasonably good job with freshmen English. There is only one James Still."[15]

A week later, Doran's guarded response informed Stewart that he did not want to bid against other colleges for Still's services but that he was "ready to deal" if Still would make his terms clear.[16] Stewart's follow-up to Doran showed signs of retreat. He had discovered, he said, that Still could not get a replacement at Hindman and so could not negotiate an agreement for any part of that academic year. He backed away from the notion of bidding and closed the letter by acknowledging that Doran had made an appropriate effort. "I am in favor of letting the situation ride until he [Still] makes the move in our direction and makes it definitely enough and early enough so that something can be done about it."[17] Maybe Still's wishes were hard to read, but Stewart's delicate balancing act was clear. He wanted Still at Morehead State because it would be a boon to the college, because Still was his friend, and because he believed that Still would be better off in terms of money and writing if he taught at Morehead than if he stayed in Hindman. On the other hand, Stewart had to be sensitive to the position of the president because he was a junior, nontenured member of the faculty.

Stewart was not successful in bringing Still to Morehead in 1959, but he was allowed to engage in negotiations that would place Still's papers in the college library, which was prepared to dedicate a space for them.[18] Stewart began his October 12, 1960, letter to Still with this admission: "I wrote Dr. Doran Sunday night and talked with him nearly two hours this morning. I am acting now in two capacities: his emissary and your friend. This is somewhat difficult." The first part of Stewart's progress report involved the James Still Room, which would be a space to hold his papers. Doran and the librarian, Miss Chapman, wanted Still to be perfectly satisfied with all the arrangements, and Still needed to discuss the archive with them in person before October 22. The college was hoping to have the dedication in November even if all the materials were not on site.

The second part of Stewart's report related to Still's coming as writer-in-residence for one semester. The requested salary had been $5,000, an amount that could not be reached because division heads received only $9,000 for twelve months. The compromise "deal" that Doran offered was $4,000 plus a free college apartment and meals in the cafeteria. Still's responsibilities would include teaching two night classes in literature and working with the library staff to set up the James Still Room. Still's lukewarm commitment to academic life was evident when he wanted assurance that acting as writer-in-residence for one semester would not obligate him to become a regular faculty member in the Department of Language and Literature.[19] He did eventually become a full-time faculty member, but in 1960 and 1961 his commitment remained tentative.

An official letter dated November 15, 1960, from Doran spelled out the terms. First, the college accepted his manuscripts for the "Jim Still

Collection" and designated a space for them in the Camden Library. Second, he would serve as writer-in-residence for the spring semester beginning February 1, 1961, at a salary of $4,000. Ten days later, Still accepted the offer in a telegram then followed up with a letter in which he spelled out his refusal to be a publicity agent for the college: "As you well know, I am far from being a 'public' personality. I can't make speeches, abhor platforms—not, I judge, much of a catch in the way of a writer-in-residence. However, I'll try to do the solid work of encouraging budding authors and future teachers of literature at Morehead." That response could not have surprised Doran, but the closing of the letter must have frustrated him. Still claimed he could not come to campus to discuss the James Still Room. Doran felt that establishing the guidelines for the collection was "exceedingly important" because he wanted to announce the dedication of the room prior to Still's arrival.[20]

It was almost a year later when the room was publicly dedicated. Still served as writer-in-residence for the spring semester of 1961, but the next fall he was back in Hindman working at the Hindman High School library. The dedication of the James Still Room took place on October 12, 1961. A week before, Doran wrote to Still, again thanking him for the manuscripts and looking forward to the time when he could join the faculty on a permanent basis. The letter ended with an explanation of why he would not be present at the dedication and assurances that his absence did not in any way reflect "a lack of interest and appreciation" for Still and his work.[21]

The dedication took place without Doran and without Still.[22] A scheduled conference in Somerset kept Doran away. It is unclear what prevented Still from attending. Perhaps his absence was a display of his reluctance to become a public figure for the college. He used the excuse of having to visit his sick brother, but he did not make a trip to Alabama. Instead, he wrote Alfred three times about the event, including newspaper clippings and a report on people who drove long distances to attend. The postscript to the second letter read, "I've been much-too-much in the newspapers this week—the dedication of the room at State College being the reason. I think I sent you a couple of clippings. They've come in from all over this section—Ohio, Va., West Va. To me this is painful. I've been threatening to leave the state. Of course I don't mean it." A third letter to Alfred reported that the governor of Kentucky, Bert Combs, had sent Still a personal letter of congratulations on the dedication at Morehead.[23] Such references to the recognition and his comments on his uneasiness indicate that he really enjoyed it. Still would face this paradox often as he transitioned from being a solitary man to a public figure who appreciated awards and publicity.

The change occurred gradually. The first step was going from Hindman to Morehead in the spring of 1961. He returned to Hindman for the following school year but was once again in Morehead for the summer of 1962 as both a professor in summer school and a teacher at the writers' workshop. His primary motivation was the increasing financial demands for his brother's care. His letter to Alfred outlining his plans showed both trepidation and interest:

> I'll teach a course in origins and development of the modern short story—the course I taught there last spring. This offers no particular problems. The other course will be a survey of English and American Literature, the textbook . . . is a whopper, thick, wide, 2-column pages. When I first looked at it my heart sank. But on examining it I decided its heft and inclusiveness an advantage. My students will nearly all be high school teachers taking summer school, a group already psychologically beaten and battered by a school-year. . . . But, as Jung says, "Nobody comes to consciousness without pain."[24]

Any pain that Still endured at Morehead was not related to his pay, not when compared to what he was making at Hindman. His last year at the high school (1962–1963), he earned a total annual salary of $4,842.[25] By contrast, his appointment letter from Doran indicated that his rank would be associate professor and his annual salary would be $9,400.[26] His first year of full-time teaching was 1963. The college newspaper, *Trail Blazer,* announced his arrival in the July 9 issue: "James Still, nationally acclaimed poet, novelist, and short story writer, has been named to the Morehead State College English faculty as a permanent writer in residence." Doran's words about Still were quoted in the article—"one of the nation's outstanding writers. We are exceedingly pleased that a man of Jim's stature has joined our faculty. He adds great strength to the Division of Languages and Literature."[27]

Doran believed Still would help raise the institution's profile. Still did not relish the opportunity, but he accepted it as inevitable. Perhaps it was his way of coping, as he had urged Alfred to do. He would make more money, but the trade-off was commuting each weekend from Morehead to Knott County. He told Alfred, "I am not giving up my house on Dead Mare Branch and will go home every weekend the

weather permits. It's a 3½ hour drive each way. Good roads—concrete
and blacktop—but crooked." He closed with arrangements to pick
up Alfred in Lineville at the nursing home and take him to the family
reunion in Gadsden on July 12.[28] The forces pulling on Still were palpable—Alfred needed him, he needed money, the college needed a known
writer, but that writer needed to stay intimately connected to the place
that was his anchor and inspiration.

Many years later Still recalled his experiences at Morehead. Details
had faded, but the general outline remained: the president offered him
a job, and he accepted on the condition that he did not have to teach
freshman English. After he worked there for five years, he was given
tenure instantly. He regularly taught sophomore literature. He also
recalled some of the people he invited to campus under the visiting-
writer program. He did not remember associating much with the people
at Morehead.[29] That might have been because he was there only during the workweek. But he did make friends, and he maintained correspondence with several of his English department colleagues including
Carlyle Cross, Betty Jean Wells, Joyce LeMaster, and M. K. Thomas.[30]

Still was probably closest to Dr. Thomas, who was originally from
Kerala, India. Thomas had attended Princeton Seminary then earned
a doctorate in English in Oklahoma. He joined the English faculty in
1964, a year after Still. He was also unmarried and lived in an apartment near Still's. The large complex, Lakewood Terrace, was designated
for married students and faculty members at nominal rent.[31] Since Still
was on campus only four nights a week, having a trustworthy neighbor
was important. They soon became friends. Thomas's academic special-
ties were the Bible as literature and the history of language. Not surprisingly, their favorite activity was talking about the books they were
reading. Sometimes they attended events or performances on campus
and frequently spent time driving around country roads.[32]

Still's primary responsibility at Morehead was teaching. Thomas
reported that Still had the reputation of being a hard grader, but he was
also very helpful to students.[33] Still acknowledged that he taught sophomore literature thirty-two times at Morehead and always "tried to give
students something beyond the text."[34] He would not have been "popular" with students looking for an easy A. In 1967 one mother was so
surprised at her daughter's failure in English 290, taught by Still, that
she wrote him to request an explanation. The chairman of the department, Gary Harmon, consulted with Still and responded to the mother,
including precise details of the young woman's less-than-adequate per-

formance in the course. Still's grading records were in excellent order; he had even kept her final exam. He was not a slack instructor or generous grader; his standards appeared reasonable and his responses thoughtful and fair.[35]

Letters from former students express appreciation. In September 1964 senior Johnny Greene wrote a friendly letter to Still, thanking him for the short-story class he had taken the previous summer.

> I had been dreading taking my literature requirement as I am a Chemistry major and have thought of literature as being dry. In your class . . . I realized a deeper insight into life was gained both by reading and writing fiction. So I wrote a story last summer while class was going on purely for my own benefit with no idea of ever getting it published. This came about from something you said in class about having a trunk full of stories you never intended to have published. Since then I have on the spur of the moment when thinking of some phase of life, written some letters to an imaginary character. It seems to help set things straight and gives me kind of a viewpoint to look at life with. You may not understand what I am talking about, but it seems to me some way that if anybody would understand this feeling you would. I am drifting away from the purpose of this letter. I meant only to tell you what a wonderful experience your class has been for me.[36]

Still would have understood just what the young man was talking about, and he would have appreciated the sentiment as much as any compliment from a peer or publisher.

Another letter Still saved was from a student who had taken his advanced composition course, Karen Bussey O'Rourke. While in the class, she had respected and feared him. But she had worked harder in his class than in any other, and two years after graduation she was an English teacher herself. Her note ends, "You are the kind of teacher one never forgets. I can hope that in the future I will be remembered by one of my students. Somehow it makes teaching seem worthwhile."[37] Though Still was never effusive about the rewards of teaching, he did find satisfaction in his work at Morehead. Yet he continued to think of Knott County as home.

In the 1950s few "outsiders" visited him on Dead Mare Branch. When he went to Morehead, some of his new acquaintances became intrigued by his remote homesite. He invited a few for short visits. At least three guests wrote short pieces describing their experiences.[38] Their accounts all feature leaving Morehead and entering the remote setting of Dead Mare Branch. Whether their imagery denoted a retreat, a haven, or a sea of green, the feeling on arrival was of being "at home after a long, long trip." The descriptions include the sound of the katydids and screech owls, the fragrance of flowers and honeybees, the feel of the breeze rustling in the trees. Still would quietly lead his guests through a welcoming ritual. First-time visitors entered through the front door. It was a "custom," he told Marshall Porter. He explained in more detail to Pat and Jane that coming through the large wooden door without harm meant that they were not witches. It had been painted green two hundred years earlier to ward off evil spirits. Only a little of the color remained, but it was enough, Still said. That opening ritual may not have brought comfort to guests, but the inside of the house made up for their unease. Next was a meal, prepared by Still, which typically included steak or ham, fried potatoes, tomatoes or other garden vegetables, pickled peaches, sweet pepper jelly, and honey for the store-bought biscuits. After dinner and washing up came conversation. If the guests were to stay the night, they would sleep in the big four-poster bed made by Jethro Amburgey, and Still would sleep on a cot in the kitchen or in the rafter room upstairs.

His personal life centered on Dead Mare Branch, but early in that period he spent the workweek in Morehead where he had ample opportunity to be with writers and would-be writers as well as undergraduates. For years he had been making friends at the writers' workshop, and some of them were also connected to the college (renamed university in 1966). Though he rarely sought out new acquaintances, his circle of friends and his sphere of influence were gradually expanding. After serving as writer-in-residence and teacher for several years, he added to his duties the coordination of an initiative to invite more publishing writers to Morehead to take part in a lecture series. Thanks to his reputation and connections, he had a set of people from which he could draw. Among those who came were Caroline Gordon, wife of Allen Tate, as well as Wilma Dykeman and James Stokely in 1965; Fred Wolfe, Robert Francis, and Harriette Arnow in 1966; and James T. Farrell in 1967.

The most memorable visits were also the most challenging to organize. Wolfe, brother of Thomas Wolfe, and Farrell, well-known novelist, were Still's contemporaries, but he did not know either of them before issuing the invitations.[39] He arranged for Wolfe to come on April 5 and expected him to talk the next day at four o'clock in the Combs Classroom Building. The general topic was personal memories of his brother and of *Look Homeward, Angel*. Still's effort to be well organized met with limited success because, as he described it, Wolfe was anything but prompt and reliable. "He had this thing about time. I started about an hour ahead. I just barely got him there in time." Still did credit him with delivering an "altogether sensible" talk.[40] The two men established a casual friendship in Morehead, and Still later visited him in Spartanburg, South Carolina.

Farrell's visit was a more dramatic story. Farrell had grown up in Chicago but lived in New York City; eastern Kentucky was a foreign land to him. Still once described Farrell as "the last of the giants of the American Naturalistic or Realistic tradition." Of his forty novels, the *Studs Lonigan* trilogy, written in the 1930s, was the most highly acclaimed. Since he was a sought-after speaker, Still set the plan in motion in October 1966 by writing to Cleo Paturis, Farrell's assistant. After much arranging, Farrell arrived early on the morning of February 23, 1967. Paturis's specific instructions about changes that had to be made to his train ticket revealed some eccentricities. He required that the roomette be changed to a bedroom because he was a restless man. He slept in stretches of three or four hours and could not be confined. Obviously, Paturis was accustomed to explaining his special needs. She closed her letter to Still, "I tell you all this so that you, personally, can be prepared for him. He is not a vain person—there is an ego, the ego of a master, but this is directly involved with his work. In your day to day conversations with him, he is always willing to listen."[41] She was trying hard to present Farrell as a "normal," friendly person. He and Still did not become friends. The salient feature Still recalled was his beret.[42]

The problems came later when expenses were submitted. The university failed to pay promptly, so Still found himself in the middle of a conversation about reimbursement. Seven months later, he wrote a two-page single-spaced letter to an administrator, trying to clear up any misunderstanding and politely demanding that the university pay. The letter concluded with Still's questioning the entire initiative of visiting writers with these words: "Our status as an institution has changed considerably since I was assigned the duty of bringing writers of achievement. . . . If I am to continue, how much leeway do I have regarding amounts to be paid a lecturer?"[43] Farrell was paid, but the project did not continue, at least not with Still in control. It is surprising that Still ever agreed to coordinate the series because he was not the managerial type.

Of all the notable or curious events that happened to him in Morehead, the one Still remembered most vividly was personal and involved a young man from Hindman. The care that he had heaped on Alfred ended with his brother's death in 1965. But taking care of others was in Still's nature and was not limited to his own family. He had long been a supporter of people, especially children.[44] While in Morehead, Still turned his caring nature on full force when James Perry and his family needed help.

Still met Perry in the Hindman Settlement School parking lot one day in May 1957 and was immediately attracted to the boy because he liked to read and he had a spirit of adventure. As their friendship developed, Still came to know his family. When Still went to Morehead, James, who was in high school, maintained communication through letters.[45] He was interested in things that teenage mountain boys like: getting a driver's license, going hunting and swimming, having a part-time summer job, hanging out with his friend Lausie, and going out on dates. His only atypical interest was reading books. In April 1964 he sent a graduation invitation to Still and included a short letter saying that he had been measured for his cap and gown, that he had listed Still as a character reference in his college applications, and that he was applying to Morehead State and to Alice Lloyd.[46] The following summer, young Perry was working in Florida and suggested "Jim" meet him there. He reported that his car was doing well and thanked Still for helping him with it.

Their strongest connection was their common roots in Hindman, but that would change dramatically one summer day in 1966. The young man moved to Morehead sometime after returning from Florida. By then he was married and employed. Still related the story of James Perry's accident:[47]

> He had some kind of job on the road above Morehead. A North American Van Lines truck pulled out in front of him. When the truck driver tried to avoid another car, he jack-knifed over onto the car James was driving.
>
> I had just come home from summer school and had all this corn ready to eat. So I filled the back end of the car—old Ford of mine—and went to the Perry house to give them some. While I was there they got a message that their son was in the hospital. They didn't have money or anything.

James Sr. had taken out insurance with Chris Offutt's daddy and it went into effect the day of the accident. And Chris's daddy was at the hospital when we got there. James was broken up terrible. He had a tracheotomy and sometimes he would begin to drown in fluid. Somebody had to be there at all times.

I turned my apartment over to his young wife. She spent the day at the hospital and then I was there every night. When school started I was teaching too. Dr. Thomas had a pull-out bed and I slept on it when I could. I slept on benches when I was in the hospital. That went on into December.

North American Van Lines told [the hospital and family] not to spare any expense. . . . They put him on a breathing machine. I was in charge of it in a way. Even when they had the lawyer. The lawyer was married to a friend of mine, postmaster at Sandy Hook. . . . The $5,000 they first offered would only begin to pay [expenses]. The lawyer sued North American. . . . Two years and one day after the accident, our lawyer said North American Van Lines had hired a local lawyer who had cancer. As long as he was sick, they could put off the case. He advised us to settle for $100,000. The final settlement [dated September 11, 1967] gave James and [his wife] Judy $82,500.

They interviewed me. Before I saw their lawyers, my lawyer told me to tell the truth but not give them any information they didn't ask for. They asked about my relations with this boy. They asked if I had him in class. "Yes, in library science." "What was his grade?" "I don't know—I had hundreds. Truth is, I don't know this boy very well, but I know his family." Anyway, I was giving them such answers that they were chuckling. So they settled.

At the time of the trial, Still had known Perry and his family for at least ten years. But this near-tragic event brought them much closer. The year of the settlement, Teresa Lynn was born to James and Melzinia Perry, and she, along with her brothers and sister, would play a big role in Still's life when he returned to Hindman. For Teresa that role would eventually be formalized when Still officially adopted her as his daughter in 1998. Before that happened, she would grow up, and he would grow old. They supported each other along the way.

Still's last year at Morehead State ended in June 1970. He was ready to leave, but he did not make a complete break. He kept up with friends there and visited his dentist regularly. The university stayed connected by presenting him with honors and awards.[48] He continued corresponding with staff and administrators, particularly the directors of the Camden-Carroll Library, Jack Ellis and Larry Besant, and the librarians directly responsible for the James Still Room.[49] His legacy lives on through that special room, The James Still Room, now housed on the fifth floor of the library tower.

While on the campus, Still spent much time in that room, where his mark on the institution is enshrined. There are dog tags from his army days, gold weights from the Ashanti Kingdom, two dulcimers made by Jethro Amburgey, the pocket watch given to him by Guy Loomis, a portrait made by Sam McKinney in 1987, books, photographs, awards, manuscripts, letters, and memorabilia. Grace Paul, a 1964 writers' workshop participant, wrote a description of the room and its effect on people who visit: "To some it becomes almost a shrine; the magazines which are beginning to yellow with age reveal the generosity and sympathetic understanding of James Still. Students and admirers will revere everything from the yearbooks to the utilitarian filing cabinet. Historians will find much in the magazines besides his writings, but no matter what the guests see, the theme of the room will always be James Still."[50]

The negotiations of President Doran, Albert Stewart, and James Still to bring the writer and his collection to Morehead had been lengthy and complicated, but the result was positive. The institution acquired both—Still was a full-time member of the English faculty for seven years; his collection has remained for more than half a century.

21

Then-what Days

After you have clothing, food, and shelter—then what?
> —James Still

James Still's practical reason for taking a full-time position at Morehead State in 1963 had been to increase his income in order to help support his family. By the time he left in 1970, only three of his siblings were still alive: his sisters Elloree and Inez and his brother Comer. Married with adult children, they did not require the kind of attention Still had given Alfred.[1] Allowing for income to cover nursing-home bills, funeral costs, and his own generous nature, Still was financially stable by 1967. After working at Morehead for seven years, he had gained some security, but money was never a major goal—he was not a man with large needs nor a clear strategy for meeting them. He did not, for example, plan for retirement. Turning sixty-four in 1970, he was short of being eligible for a full pension. But he never thought of himself as retiring; he was resigning.

The timing of his decision is less obvious than the reason. Though a good teacher, Still was not inspired to follow teaching as a career. He had made some friends in Morehead, but leaving the place did not mean he would lose them. The weekly commute from Hindman was a strain and required him to maintain a reliable vehicle, but that was a minor frustration. Though he found no particular fault with the administration of his department, the internal politics of an expanding institution was a source of concern for him and his close colleagues.

All was not well at Morehead, at least in the opinion of Albert Stewart, who had resigned in March 1965. His letter to President Doran conveyed the message that it would be best for everyone if he remained at Pippa Passes (in Knott County) instead of returning to Morehead. He offered no explanation.[2] Gary Harmon, chair of the Department of Language and Literature, was also experiencing difficulty with the institution in 1967. On July 13 Harmon ended a letter to Dean Cadle with a story of a young man who was going to UNC-Asheville because he had been treated "most unfairly" at Morehead. Harmon added that he himself was leaving, as were several others.[3]

Still never spoke about particular problems or difficult people at Morehead, but he did write to Cadle on September 3, 1969, to let him know that he was preparing for another year of teaching and hoped that it would be his last.[4] It was. On March 4 Still submitted his formal letter of resignation to J. E. Duncan, dean of the School of Humanities: "Kindly accept my resignation effective June 6, 1970."[5] The responses were equally brief, except for one from the chair of the Division of Language and Literature, Dr. Joseph Price, who felt partly responsible for Still's dissatisfaction: "It is with a great measure of regret that I received your resignation. Although I am aware there may be other circumstances involved in your decision, the temptation is very great to me to take some responsibility for not making your situation here more pleasant and satisfactory."[6]

There was never a conversation exploring Still's resignation. Likewise, there was no special event to mark his departure, except for a tea hosted by the library. In addition to continuing correspondence with personal friends like M. K. Thomas, he stayed in touch with the library staff, in particular Larry Besant, who was very interested in maintaining a strong relationship between Still and the university.[7] In 1987 and again in 1993 Besant wrote memos to the university president, Nelson Grote and Ron Eaglin in those respective years, using the subject line "Mending Fences with James Still." His observation that mending was needed meant that Still's ongoing connection with the institution required frequent attention. As the years passed, some administrators saw value in maintaining a link with Still.

In 1970, however, maintaining an association with Morehead State was not important to Still. His resignation meant a clean break. He returned to Wolfpen but within the next few years established his primary residence in Hindman on the Settlement School property. The Hindman house that became his permanent residence was on the hillside above the school. Still continued to spend time at the log house on Dead Mare in warm weather. When he referred to "his house," that is the place he meant.[8]

During his years in Morehead, the Appalachian region had undergone great change, especially in the nation's eyes. At the beginning of the 1960s journalists were increasingly using Appalachia to illustrate the disparity between the nation's poverty and its affluence. The region's land was portrayed as rich and the people as poor. In 1963 Still's friend Harry Caudill, in nearby Whitesburg, published his landmark book *Night Comes to the Cumberland: A Biography of a Depressed Area*. President and Mrs. Lyndon Johnson visited Martin County, Kentucky, in 1964, a visit that provided background for the creation of the Appalachian Regional Commission in 1965. In 1968 Senator Robert Kennedy toured a coal camp in the region. Such attention transposed the region into a "media commodity" that would, according to Ronald Eller in *Uneven Ground,* sustain the image of Appalachia as a problem area for years to come.[9]

While in Morehead, Still had taken a small step toward political activism. The July 21, 1967, issue of *Time* magazine had published a letter to Mrs. Lyndon Johnson as part of an advertisement paid for by the strip-mining industry. Still was offended by the industry's claim that they agreed "wholeheartedly with [her] desire to beautify our land." On July 24 Still wrote to the first lady declaring those words to be "as cynical a statement as had been made in this century." Then he invited her to visit eastern Kentucky to understand the full impact of the devastation of strip mining. If she were to come, he predicted, she would see that "the damage already done to our home land our pride, our rightful heritage is forever."

A week later he received a personal letter from Mrs. Johnson's social secretary, addressing his points sympathetically and saying that Johnson appreciated his comments and shared his concern. "It is her hope that private industry will cooperate with efforts to restore ravaged lands."[10] Still was not becoming an activist or even a writer primarily concerned with environmental issues or policies, but this venture shows that he was ready to make public his views about coal mining and the environment. His experiences at Morehead were having some effect on his willingness to move beyond Wolfpen to a regional or national stage.

He had been concerned about the natural and social changes invading his neighborhood for some time, but he complained about it to friends more often than he did to public figures. His friend the Amherst poet Robert Francis made several trips to Morehead in the mid-1960s, but he had not visited Still at Wolfpen for twenty years. A frequent theme in their correspondence had been the change in the places where they lived. Still's frustration was evident in one letter when he tried to explain to Francis his return address as a box number in Hindman: "I give you my long-time Hindman address [because] Bath post-office is no more; Littcarr will shortly be discontinued." This was due to the building of "Carrs Fork Dam(n) which has uprooted seventeen miles of people. Many picked up their houses and set them down at the mouth of Wolfpen—in my very face. I became an instant townsman."[11] In August 1971 Still wrote again about changes, in stronger language. He had come home to Dead Mare Branch after retiring in 1970, but, he said, "Except for house and grounds the place as you knew it is no more." Still then painted a picture of the environmental devastation in his holler: "Above us the mountains have been ravaged by strip-mining; acid from the coal face destroyed all aquatic life in the streams. The Lemuel swamp has been tiled, drained, filled, built on. We can't even grow a mosquito. Foreseeing a little of this I stuck-in a double row of Lombardy poplars between my place and 'too much' . . . I let the wild growth of bush, vine, and tree do its best and now live in a jungle of sorts."[12] The response from Francis offered little consolation: "I rejoice that your home, in spite of all the dislocation close around you, holds out and remains where it was and is."[13]

Still lamented the changes near Wolfpen and Dead Mare Branch, but he could not ignore the transformations that had taken place in Hindman since he had left his job there in 1963. Upon his return, he became acutely aware of the challenges the county faced. Lyndon Johnson's War on Poverty had impacted the area. For example, a summer recreation program was funded at the school in 1966 and employed twenty local workers. A little later the government supported an initiative to help school dropouts. But some people were skeptical that the War on Poverty could solve the problems. Raymond McLain, the director of Hindman Settlement School from 1956 to 1971, stopped applying for federal funds because he believed that the resources invested in the projects were not worthwhile when the programs were too short-lived to bring significant improvement.[14]

Knott County and the school had critical needs in the 1970s. The area had been losing population since 1940. Of the people who did not leave, nearly half had not finished eighth grade, and only one in ten had completed high school. More distressing for Still personally was that the county and state had taken over the public library, which the Settlement School had maintained since 1902. Then after a few years the state withdrew funds, and the library closed. As a result, Knott County was one of only two counties in Kentucky without a library. The Settlement School responded by proposing to reinstate a two-year library project. That, however, added more cost, which the school could not afford.[15]

Even though Still had no direct link to the Settlement School when he first returned to Hindman, he found the administrative situation unstable. McLain had taken over as director from Elizabeth Watts in 1956 and, during his tenure, had struggled with deteriorating buildings and lack of funding. When McLain resigned at the end of 1970 to go to Berea, his replacement was Lionel Duff. He and his wife, Frankie, had been students at the Settlement School in the 1930s, and Duff served on the board of trustees for two years before becoming director. But that experience did not make his job easier. The school continued a decline in programming, and Duff experienced a strained relationship with his board.

Finally, the board members asked Duff to resign. Their rational was that he had not done anything positive for the school. His counter was that they had not given him the funds to do anything. One positive result of Duff's tenure was a stronger bond between Still and the school. According to Bob Young, when Still left Morehead, it was Duff who asked him to come live at the Settlement School and who fixed up the house, Oak Ledge, for him. Duff was friendly with Still, but the arrangement that he made was more than a nice gesture; it was mutually beneficial. This relationship continued and even expanded under the guidance of the next director, Mike Mullins, who came to the school in December 1977.[16]

Another project launched by Duff and expanded by Mullins was the annual Appalachian Writers' Workshop. Founded by Albert Stewart, it was related to the summer workshops he had directed at Morehead in the 1950s and 1960s. Stewart reshaped the workshop when he went to Alice Lloyd, then moved the program to Hindman in 1977, which was Duff's last summer as director.[17] When Mike Mullins arrived at the Settlement School, he immediately recognized the value and potential of the workshop and made it one of the school's flagship programs. The Appalachian Writers' Workshop has been flourishing for more than thirty-nine summers, and Still was a principal staff member for twenty-three of those. But when Still came back to Hindman from Morehead in 1970, he did not imagine that future. He did not even know the next turn his life would take. He was living his "then-what days."

His return to Knott County brought about no abrupt changes, except that Still was no longer employed by Morehead, nor was he living there during the week. He could have picked up where he had left off a decade earlier by moving back to Dead Mare Branch to garden, write, and hang out with neighbors. Instead, he spent time in transition, phasing out of teaching and a salaried job while increasing his emphasis on public life and publication. At the university, though, Still had experienced the taste of being a known person. He had also found people like Cadle and Stewart who wanted to promote his writing career. He had become more comfortable in public settings. The 1968 reissue of *River of Earth*, although as a cheap paperback copy, had given him a professional and personal boost. He often said that a great book is "one that won't go away." A revival of the novel meant it was worthy, and that spurred his interest in publishing more. He enjoyed knowing that people wanted to read his works. Though still not outgoing or gregarious, he was beginning to realize that he was good with an audience, and he could talk to groups without much preparation. The college classroom had been a key to that emerging talent.

Now that he was not on a tight teaching schedule, Still had free time to revise unpublished manuscripts and create new ones. Ironically, this less stressful phase in Still's life was neither relaxed nor creative. The itineraries and requests of others soon came to drive his life, a situation that he had avoided before going to Morehead. His network of professional acquaintances was expanding rapidly, which meant he had more opportunities and invitations to give talks or teach classes. He liked to travel, and a variety of venues gave him the excuse to go to different places. Gradually, he learned that he could do what others wanted him to do on his own terms. He continued to keep his own time so would frequently arrive at the last minute; sometimes he would change plans once he arrived. When he was establishing this more public persona, he was feeling his way rather than following a strategy.

As soon as it was known that he was leaving Morehead, he began receiving invitations from other institutions.[18] That first summer Still took a short-term teaching position at Ohio University in Portsmouth. There he received $1,200 for teaching one course of English 201 to eighteen students.[19] Why he chose Portsmouth is uncertain, but the fact that Temple Baker lived and worked there was probably a factor. The summer session's final exam was on July 23, but Still left early in order to participate in a workshop at Pikeville College, which began on July 20.[20] He was already overbooking.

After that first summer, Still accepted fewer engagements and public appearances. During 1971 he was more involved with his friends around Hindman and his property at Wolfpen. Jethro Amburgey's wife had died in 1969, and Jethro remarried in March 1971.[21] That summer Still was busy with his garden, which he described in a letter to his sister Elloree:

> All through July we had frequent downpours. . . . Not being able to do any hoeing, my garden got out of hand. Crabgrass, pigweed and foxtail have taken over. First, the tendercrop came in, then, last week, the white half-runners. I am drying about a half-bushels of the tendercrops, and Jethro and new wife Florence have put a bushel or more of the half-runners into the freezer. Plenty of squash, and they fairly grow while you are looking at them. I've hauled them around to neighbors who had furnished me garden sass before my own came in. Last week, on a rare dry day, I planted more beans and more squash. Had the first mess of blackeyed peas last night, and I note okra will be along in a day or two. Also had the first fried corn yesterday.[22]

Still was doing what he loved in the summer and what he had done every summer he could—growing, eating, and putting up food with his neighbors.

Amburgey died in the fall, which was a great loss for Still because Jethro had been his friend and helper since he first arrived in Hindman. Still sent the following message to all the people who had recently submitted requests for dulcimers. The message also served as a eulogy: "I regret to announce that Jethro Amburgey, the dulcimer maker, passed away on November 25, 1971. He is buried in the Rest Haven Cemetery on the mountain overlooking Jeff, Kentucky. His log book lists a dulcimer completed that very day. He was 76. Jethro passed into the Great Silence none of us understand or quite accept. He was my friend. A unique personality. A great man."[23]

Thirty-two years earlier, Amburgey had "given" Still his house on Dead Mare Branch to live in as long as he wished, but there had been no legal transfer. In fact, he had deeded it to his only son, Morris, in January 1962. Now the future of the house was uncertain. Still was the executor of Jethro's will, but the property belonged to Morris and his

wife. They honored Jethro's wishes two months after he died by deed-
ing the property to James Still for his lifetime.[24] Still was not then living at the log house year-round, but he spent much of his time there
and enjoyed the upkeep of the place as well as the gardening. To Still,
his neighbors, his garden, and his house on Dead Mare represented the
essence of Knott County life.

In the late summer of 1971 Still returned to teaching and took part
in four seminars at Alice Lloyd College. In a letter to his sister Elloree
on August 1, he listed the topics: "The effect of welfare and unemployment on family life," "'Cultural Colonialism' and indigenous culture,"
"Localism and kinship," and "Literature of Appalachia." He described
it as a government-sponsored institute on Appalachia serving primarily
young professors at colleges and universities from Maine to Alabama.[25]
The next year, these seminars expanded into a full institute organized
by Bill Weinberg, then director of the Appalachian Learning Laboratory. Weinberg tried hard to accommodate Still's schedule and arranged
for him to teach the first six weeks of the fall semester, from September 21 to November 1. And he would not have to be in Pippa Passes
until 10:30 in the morning.[26] Still's course, according to Weinberg, had
an impact on the students who would be "future leaders of Eastern
Kentucky." But Still also benefited by making contacts that would be
important to him later, especially Weinberg himself and Mike Mullins.

Still's most significant activity of this transition period was to establish a network of contacts. His primary goal was not self-promotion.
He was simply responding to letters and requests and, in some cases,
renewing old friendships. Still had sent copies of the paperback *River of
Earth* to people he thought would be interested. The responses ranged
from a thank-you from old friend Dare Redmond in October 1970 to a
letter of praise from poet and critic Allen Tate in June 1971. Tate told
Still that it was one of the few novels he had read in the last ten years,
and he regretted not having read it earlier. He ended that he had long
wanted to meet Still and regretted their paths had never crossed.[27] Of
course, the two men had been closer than Tate realized since Still had
been a student at Vanderbilt in 1930 when Tate was there participating
in the Southern Agrarian movement.

Another renewed contact was Cratis Williams, who was dean of the
Graduate School at Appalachian State University in Boone.[28] Williams,
who was five years younger than Still, had established a reputation by
1970 that led to his title "Father of Appalachian Studies." Williams was
from Lawrence County, Kentucky, north of Knott County, so would

have been familiar with Still's territory, but he lived and worked most of his professional life in western North Carolina. Still had also sent him an autographed copy of *River of Earth*.[29] Williams responded with thanks on June 23, 1972, calling the book a powerful and marvelously controlled novel. He added, "With all these programs in Appalachian Studies appearing here and there, your book will be read again, and by a younger audience interested in Appalachia in a new way." He reminded Still that the two of them had met on a bus from Morehead to Lexington sometime in the late 1930s, then closed, "Perhaps our paths shall cross again."[30] They did. Appalachian State University was attempting to connect with Still in a concrete way; for example, Charlotte Ross, the director of the Appalachian Room, had sent Still excerpts from Williams's dissertation. Still responded with appreciation to her and admiration for Williams's scholarly work, saying, "Most of those things of mine were written such a devil of a long time ago. By now I feel totally disconnected from them."[31]

Still must have felt distant from the writings that Williams had discussed in his classic study *The Mountaineer in Fact and Fiction*. The world of eastern Kentucky that had inspired those stories was different now, and Still's writing interest had changed. In fact, Still was publishing little. Aside from the paperback reissue of *River of Earth,* he published only five poems and one story between 1968 and 1973. The best known of those were the poems "Man O' War" (1969), honoring a racehorse, and "On Being Drafted into the U.S. Army from My Log Home" (1972). In each case, the world of the poem differed from his daily surroundings and had little connection to his earlier work.

Still's "then-what" transition moved him closer to the public persona that he would assume in his later years. Two factors were at work. The first one he initiated—establishing and renewing personal connections. The second was the increased attention being given to the Appalachian region. Both helped raise Still's visibility as a writer and as a long-term resident. Williams had observed that a new social and academic focus was emerging under the umbrella term "Appalachian Studies." While Still did not promote the scholarly inspection of Appalachia or its literature, he did establish friendships and strengthen ties to a number of people who were actively involved in the new field.[32]

One of the most important teaching engagements Still accepted at this time was at Berea College. He taught a one-month course in prose composition during the 1972 January term and lived in a furnished apartment on campus. The president's wife, Anne Weatherford, greeted him and walked him to class. While there he met several people who would become important to him, strong admirers and supporters. One was Loyal Jones, who had been the associate executive secretary of the Council of the Southern Mountains in the 1960s. Early in 1972 he became the director of the Appalachian Center at Berea and was instrumental in bringing Still to Berea.[33] Another person he met was Al Perrin, a retiree who was volunteering at the college library. Still and Perrin were friends from 1972 until Perrin's death twenty-three years later. Soon after Still left Berea, Perrin wrote to thank him for the gift of *Hounds on the Mountain* and to pass on the campus's reaction to Still's visit:[34] "So many have spoken enthusiastically about your month here. You were an eagle feather in the Appalachian Center bonnet. Expect you've slipped back gratefully content into your old house, neighbors and typewriter routine."[35]

Some of his engagements during the 1970s were for talks or lectures rather than full classes, and Cadle arranged or aided many of those. For example, in April 1972 Still made a trip to North Carolina—first to Asheville where he stayed with the Cadles, then to Chapel Hill to give a reading at UNC.[36] There he met Max Steele, who had arranged for the visit and reserved rooms at the Carolina Inn. It did not take long for Steele to send an official thank-you, noting that he had heard compliments from students and faculty. The more interesting content of Steele's letter was the follow up on a private talk between himself and Still about the slow or negative responses Still was getting from publishers. Steele had suggested Still contact Phyllis Jackson, a literary agent in New York, and added that it was time Still "let someone else handle the business part of [his] writing."[37] A month later Still responded with a formal but genuine letter thanking Steele for inviting him to Chapel Hill, for his hospitality, and for introducing him to Jackson at International Famous Agency. "We have swapped letters, conversed by telephone. If anything can be done for me, I'm convinced she will do it."[38]

Still's less-formal follow up to his North Carolina visit was his note to the Cadles, thanking them for taking good care of him "at home and abroad." Most of the letter, however, illustrates his underlying concern—the demands of the growing season and changes to his place.

Spring is not so far advanced here as in middle North Carolina. However, my pair of flowering crabapples are in full flounce, as are the primroses at their toes. . . . Salad peas are up an inch. Cabbage plants are trying hard, gaining two inches in four weeks. Young onions almost ready for the table. The mustard bolted while I was away.

And I might mention that the sky fell DURING MY ABSENCE: an automobile body shop is being erected one hundred and fifty yards from my house. My deciduous lombary [*sic*] poplars will no longer serve as a wall against *too much*. A row of pines?[39]

Like many of Still's letters, this one juxtaposes his own garden sanctuary with the encroachment of "progress" on Wolfpen. His typical image is a road expansion or a new building, and his reaction is to contemplate ways to wall himself off.

An alternative response to change is to change with it. To some extent, Still did that. He was creating a role for himself as a preserver, if not champion, of the old ways. He inscribed Perrin's first edition of *On Troublesome Creek* with the words "Tales of a lost time and place and folk." His early writings recorded and kept alive a life that was no more. In the 1970s he was offering through his books a reminder of what had been lost and its value. Though not making a conscious effort to become a spokesperson, Still was beginning to develop a complex persona that would eventually earn him the title "Dean of Appalachian Literature." Several colleges in the region recognized Still's emerging importance by granting him honorary degrees. Berea was the first, making him a Doctor of Literature on May 27, 1973. LMU, at the urging of Jesse Stuart, followed the next year on June 2 by awarding him a Doctor of Humane Letters. Institutions drew attention to themselves and to Appalachia by honoring writers and scholars who had immortalized the region.

One source of Still's expanding reputation came from interest in new anthologies of the region's literature. In early July 1972 Robert Higgs, associate professor of English at East Tennessee State University, wrote Still to thank him for the copy of *River of Earth*. He explained that he was teaching the book regularly in his courses. His students gave it high praise, he said, then he passed on one student's comment that Still surely found gratifying: "I want to thank you [Dr. Higgs] for introducing me to such southern writers as James Still and Cormac McCarthy. Their art helps to restore in me a pride in this region."[40]

A year later Still received a letter from Higgs and his collaborator, Ambrose Manning, requesting a representative work of Still's choice to be included in their comprehensive collection of Appalachian literature and criticism, which was to be published by Frederick Ungar

with the endorsement of the Appalachian Consortium. They were planning the classic collection *Voices from the Hills* that was published in
1975. Their request, sent to all writers being solicited, concluded with
this paragraph: "Owing to the growing interest in this subject we feel
that this project will be a successful one and a distinctive contribution to a better understanding of a fascinating region of America. Your
cooperation is appreciated and will help to make these the high quality
books which we hope to produce."[41] The project was successful, and
the anthology helped establish the study of Appalachia. Still's story "A
Master Time" represented his early writings in the anthology.

The changes in the region along with the attention being paid to its
problems and cultural heritage would have inspired some people in Still's
position to take up the banner, attach themselves to a major university,
and become part of the movement. While Still participated on the fringes
of different programs, he did not fully align himself with any one. He
was a gardener and writer, not a professor, not a public leader, nor even
a politically motivated citizen. The extent of his activism was the occasional letter, like the one to Ladybird Johnson in 1967. In September
1974 he wrote another letter to express himself, this time to President
Gerald Ford: "In pardoning Richard M. Nixon you have sullied a bright
beginning. I had counted on you not to mire yourself and the Republican
party in the crimes of Watergate. . . . I had hopes for honor and integrity
again in the White House, but you have now dashed any expectations.
What a giant pity for the United States of America which has been fairly
aching for faith in the highest office in the land."[42] Still was a liberal
and an idealist, but he rarely involved himself in politics or policy at the
national level. If he kept up with the Watergate trials on a daily basis,
it was not by watching television. He learned the news of the nation by
reading and the concerns of his neighbors by paying attention.

The first few years after his time at Morehead gave Still a taste of
the nation's emerging interest in the region, but he would participate by
being the person he had always been, by remaining in Knott County
and traveling whenever and wherever he chose. He did, of course, travel
extensively over the next two decades. Some of his adventures were
on international soil, but many were in the vicinity. In the summer of
1973 he turned sixty-seven years old, and he was staying close to home.
He had two places to live, an adequate living, and plenty to keep him
busy. When he needed to supplement his income or feel more useful or
involved, he worked on special projects for Hindman Settlement School.
In 1973, for example, he was the school's Appalachian librarian and did

archival research as well as student tutoring. From his base in town he could easily get to his log house, and he could drive to any locations in the region that might offer him an opportunity for short-term teaching or reading and lecturing.

He was becoming known. In the winter of 1973, in the first issue of *Appalachian Heritage,* Albert Stewart published his article "At Home with James Still," which he had written ten years earlier. Stewart added a postscript to point out how much Still's Knott County had changed since he first wrote the piece:

> Destroyers have come even more fierce and malicious than ever under the name of economy, patriotism, public need, energy crisis, and numerous other self-seeking disguises. While a projected government Carr Creek Dam moves slowly under government management, stripminers work frantically chewing at the guts, bones, and bloodstream of the landscape to provide adequate acid pollution and sedimentation for the lake if the dam gets finished and water impounded. Enormous (and enormously expensive) highways, cuts, bridges, have already obliterated all familiarity of landscape. . . . As Jim says, 'You can't even grow a respectable mosquito.' Above Jim's home the stripminers gouged out a vicious slanting road, and the big trucks disturbed the earth with dust, rocks, and noise for ages. But his small acreage retains its integrity and remains intact.[43]

In spite of the changes happening around him, Still felt at home. His most important asset was secured with the deed to his log house. He also derived security and appreciation from the Settlement School. Another detail on his mind was his will, which he signed on February 2, 1973. The people that he wished to inherit were Morris Amburgey and his long-time friend Monroe Amburgey, his brother Comer, his sisters Elloree Sharpe and Inez Barnes, and two children of the Perry family, Teresa Lynn (age six) and Michael (age fifteen). Cadle and the Hindman Settlement School were to be his literary executors and the executors of the will.[44]

Writing a will showed that he was thinking of the future, that he was fully engaged in asking the question "What next?" It would be a long time before the will would be executed. In the 1970s he still had an active life ahead of him. His planning at the beginning of the decade was not so much about writing. He was, however, poised to become fully engaged in publishing.

22

Making Friends and Keeping Them

> . . . it was unusual for [James Still] to ever patch up a friend-
> ship gone awry.
>
> —Jonathan Greene

James Still's work in Hindman during the 1950s then in Morehead during the 1960s meant that he was less isolated than he had been on Dead
Mare Branch. He was never a complete hermit, but in this time of his
life, friendships became more numerous and important to him: some
were social, others professional, a few were both. For example, at the
1955 Morehead Writers' Workshop he met Harriette Arnow, fellow
Kentucky writer; they remained friends until her death in 1986.[1] He
established a similar relationship with Temple Baker, who wanted to be
a writer. She began as his student then became a vocal supporter. Both
Arnow and Baker were married. Still always included their husbands in
his greetings or plans, but it was the women he befriended. Still was also
close to the writing couple James Stokely and Wilma Dykeman. From
1939 on, they followed his writing career, as he did theirs. Still wrote
a recommendation to the Guggenheim Foundation for Wilma, and she
wrote reviews in the Knoxville paper, reminding readers of the magic of
River of Earth. Their friendship was steady and long-lasting.[2]

In these cases, Still sustained trouble-free and mutually enriching
friendships. In others, he established associations with people whom he
had known a long time, who shared his passion for reading and writing,

or who had a special interest in his writing. How those alliances thrived or failed reveals Still's practical and personal need for other people but also his penchant for taking offense or holding grudges. His relationships with three people deserve a closer look: Jesse Stuart, Dean Cadle, and Albert Stewart.

The similarities between Still and Jesse Stuart (1906–1984) were notable, yet their personalities and general outlook were different.[3] Still was private, understated, introverted, and shy, while Stuart was boisterous, competitive, extroverted, and impulsive. Glory, publicity, even notoriety seemed to motivate Stuart. Still was happiest working privately in peaceful surroundings. They also differed physically; as young men, Still was small and compact while Stuart was large and athletic. As the years progressed, though, Still's health served him well while Stuart's more energetic personality brought on a heart attack in middle age and two strokes toward the end of his life.[4] After leaving college, Still and Stuart rarely saw each other even though they lived less than one hundred miles apart. Their forty-five–year friendship was based mainly on correspondence. The major topics of that interchange were their days at LMU, their writing and publications, and their mutual friend, Don West.[5]

Early on the two young men were competitive and even agreed that one must publish something before writing a letter to the other. This rivalry created a restriction even they did not observe for long, but they did follow each other's careers. Still, for example, saved a 1935 negative review by Theodore Morrison of *Man with a Bull-tongue Plow* that declared that this novice poet "needs to study art and modesty."[6]

In their early exchange of letters, Stuart frequently reminded Still of how much he himself had accomplished and encouraged him to raise his productivity. He also offered advice on his friend's appearance: "You should let your hair grow longer. It always stuck so close your head. I've heard people remark you had very prominent ears. If your hair was out just a little longer you will note the difference."[7] From such comments, it might seem that the two were very close friends. More likely, it exemplifies Stuart's lack of restraint; Still's sense of privacy probably read the suggestion as tactless if not offensive.

Like their personalities, their writing was quite different, as Dayton Kohler made clear in his 1942 critical study in *College English*. To him, Still's quality trumped Stuart's quantity. Still's writing was realistic and poetic while Stuart's was melodramatic and sentimental. Kohler summarized Stuart's strength as "much power poorly controlled." The man, he said, was not a writer but "a conversationalist with a quick eye and ear and a lively gift of expression." Still, on the other hand, was a serious writer, according to Kohler, and exhibited the qualities that Stuart lacked: precision, restraint, literary discipline, humility. His poetry conveyed meaning through quiet tones and sharp imagery; his style recorded "sensory impressions with poetic finality."[8]

Their mutual friend Don West made an even earlier comparison of the two men at a lecture on Kentucky writers. In a letter to Still, West summarized what he had conveyed about the would-be mountain realists. Stuart, he said, in his hunger for a career was "exploiting the old romantic sentimentalism," and as a result, his writing would not endure. Still, according to West, was a "very confused young guy" who wanted to paint a sincere picture of the mountains. But so far he had failed to "get into the vital stream of present day life."[9] West was critical of both and not shy about voicing his opinion. Still's reaction to this critique was to share it with Stuart, who responded, "Don West will continue to fight you long as you let him fight. It always made me sore the way he tried to dominate people who would be his friends. He just double dares to ever make an attack on me. . . . He knows I'm a better man physically now than he is. I weigh 202 and I believe I can double West up in a knot."[10] Stuart's tendency to reduce disagreements to physical contests dramatized his anger.

If Still's writing goal was perfection, Stuart's was publication. But one thing they agreed on was exasperation with West. Stuart wanted to like West and to interact with him, but usually their exchanges ended with antagonism. Yet Stuart thought of their future lives as grand: "Jimmie, did you realize, you, Don, and I are grown-up men now—occupying a place in a world of men. We are printing our images in the album of Destiny whether it be books or a farm or just a plain grave."[11]

One stop on their way to destiny was World War II. Stuart postponed his enlistment for the arrival of his baby daughter in 1942, then entered the navy in 1944 and was sent to Washington, D.C. to write training materials.[12] After returning to Kentucky at the war's end, Stuart, like Still, endured months of malaise, once declaring, "Never a day passes but what I think I'm through as a writer."[13] Yet Stuart's return to publishing was quicker than Still's. In 1951 Still nominated Stuart's piece "What America Means to Me" for an award. This gesture marked a shift in their relationship. During the 1950s their correspondence was mutually supportive and cordial.

In 1952 at the initial writers' workshop, the men saw each other for the first time in twenty-three years on the porch of the house of More-head president Dr. Charles Spain. In his journal, Stuart wrote that he was shocked at seeing Still, who "came and went shyly as in the days at LMU."[14] In a follow-up letter to Still, Stuart made their reunion seem the high point of his workshop experience. It made him relive the world of LMU, and he graciously extended an invitation for Still to visit any-time. He complimented his friend with statements like "You are James Still and no one else. You have produced a literature of your own. An author can write fifty books and not do this."[15] During the 1950s Stuart encouraged Still to teach at Morehead. He consulted him on running for political office; he sympathized with him on the death of his father. Their relationship was friendlier and gentler than it had been, but not intimate or confessional. While Still was quietly working at Hindman, Stuart was churning out publications, collecting awards and honors, but also suffering from the health issues that would ultimately lead to his death. Stuart suffered his first heart attack in 1954.[16]

In the 1960s their correspondence was less friendly and supportive, for no clear reason. When corresponding with Stuart in 1969, H. R. Stoneback asked about his friendship with Still. Everything in Stuart's response was dismissive or negative. He acknowledged that they had graduated from the same college class, but they had gone their separate ways:

> I thought of him [Still] as being a very odd person, never too friendly and a little distant. He once said, which came to me reliably that: "Stuart can't write a good sentence."[17] I tried for all the literary prizes that LMU offered and never won any. Still won these. . . . I had no contact with James Still while at Vanderbilt. . . . I doubt that James Still has ever corresponded with anyone more than a postcard. . . . There is, perhaps, a rea-son why James Still likes seclusion and found it in the moun-tains of Kentucky.[18]

When questioned by Stoneback, Still confirmed that he and Stuart "did not run together." Neither did they hold a common view of writ-ing.[19] This sort of public bickering interfered with everything positive they had enjoyed in the peaceful decade before. For example, Still was incensed at an incident that Stuart related to journalist Shirley Williams about their LMU days. According to Stuart, an enormous snake came into the dormitory and fell onto Still while he was sleeping. "He broke the bedslats," Stuart said to be funny. Still denied the story and was offended that Stuart had made it up.[20] If Stuart was too brazen, Still was too sensitive. So went their relationship for years.

By the middle of the 1970s, they seemed to be on good terms again. Stuart suggested to LMU that James Still be given an honorary doctorate. That gesture impressed Still, who drafted an appreciative response: "I am deeply moved by your wish to have our Alma Mater confer an honor on me. . . . that campus is sacred ground. They owe me nothing. I owe them my heart. I have driven onto the campus many times during the past twenty years and never without deep emotion. . . . all my nerves were exposed in those [LMU] days."[21] The next letter from Stuart, written a year later, exhibits his characteristic exuberance: "By-hell, we [Stuart and his wife] like you! You know I mean this! You're the real McCoy. . . . We love you, Jimmy! You looked wonderful [in Paintsville] and you're great! You're a somebody."[22] Sometime in 1975 Still sent Stuart a copy of On Troublesome Creek inscribed with these words: "If Jesse Stuart had not existed I would have invented him."[23]

According to James Gifford, Stuart was a man given to "extremes of hostility and generosity." He could be thoughtless or unkind.[24] Still, on the other hand, was noncombative and always appeared self-controlled. But he could definitely hold a grudge. While Stuart and Still sustained a career-long competition, Still never completely broke with his friend. Every rift they ever had could eventually be patched or ignored. In the 1980s Still wrote in his private notebook, "[Stuart's] works are a phenomenon of time and place. Yet all his books are about Jesse Stuart. He had no other subject. . . . No writer in Appalachia ever inspired such a 'following' among average readers. . . . His literary efforts actually paid-off financially. . . . I always admired his ability to crank out a new book every new moon, a further elaboration of himself. You have to tip your hat to such progress. He was a cracker-jack!"[25] Still concluded with this blunt realization: "In the world of creative activity there are no friends and no enemies." Stuart was not his enemy but was probably his friend only because time and circumstance put them together. In May 1980 Stuart suffered a serious stroke. When he visited in August 1982, Still found him uncommunicative. When Stuart died in 1984, Still went to the funeral in Greenup County. That was one of the few times he had ever gone to Stuart's special place in Kentucky.[26] Stuart never visited Still in Knott County.

Dean Cadle (1920–1998) was fourteen years younger than Still and is better described as Still's advocate than as his peer. For more than twenty-five years they worked together professionally and as friends, but their ultimate separation was so complete that it is hard to imagine they ever had a warm personal connection. Cadle had an interest in literary people and a desire to be a writer himself. His profession was that of librarian, but he kept writing, eventually publishing a number of poems in *Appalachian Heritage*.[27] His strength, however, was his critical ability, and his most significant accomplishment was his collection of material concerning James Still, including his own essays and photographs.[28] From the 1950s through the 1970s he was known officially as Still's bio-bibliographer and privately as his personal photographer.

Cadle's attachment to the region began with his childhood in Middlesboro, Kentucky. While attending Berea College, he worked at the press, which gave him a close view of regional manuscripts.[29] In the summer of 1941 Cadle proofread Still's short story "The Stir-Off" for the fall issue of *Mountain Life and Work*. He immediately recognized the story's "naturalness," a quality he found missing from other writings on the Appalachian region.[30] Cadle left Kentucky to serve in World War II. After returning to Berea, he sent the first of many letters to Still. "If it wouldn't interfere too much with your work," he wrote, "I'd like to see you for about an hour on any day that would be most convenient with you."[31] When arrangements were made, Cadle and a fellow student, Willard Arnett, hitchhiked from Middlesboro to Littcarr.[32]

In the draft of one unpublished essay, Cadle described his first meeting with Still, which took place not long after Still returned to Knott County from the military:[33]

> At the time I first met him, a green and shimmering afternoon in June, 1946, I think that past and future had become so tightly telescoped into the present that he was squeezed to a halt, paralyzed as a writer. For I found him sitting in the doorway of his house, between Dead Mare Branch and Wolfpen Creek, where he had sat for nearly a year after his return from World War II, mesmerized, gazing out onto the landscape and the people that had gone into his book.
>
> As we walked to the mouth of Wolfpen Creek, he enumerated the blatant changes that kept him glued to his doorway. . . . Blacktopped highways, which had been inching toward him for fifteen years, now passed within two miles of him. Entire families had gone North or to Indiana to work in the war plants; their sons had been round the world and weren't about to mine

coal or till farmland. Everybody had money; no one wanted
to work. . . . And then as we watched minnows dart in a pond
formed against a grassy bank, he said, "Despite all the changes,
I think [*River of Earth* is] a true book."[34]

Cadle also thought *River of Earth* was true and worth reviving.
He thought of Still as a man worth making known. Cadle's essay spent
eleven pages describing Still as a man who cherished his privacy and a
writer who welcomed obscurity.[35] Yet what Cadle set out to do was to
make *River of Earth* known to a wider readership and to portray its
author as an intriguing personage—in other words, to promote both
the writer and his work.

In the 1950s Cadle was busy with his education, career, and family,
but he stayed in touch with Still. As the decade ended, he began to put
together a bibliography of Still's writings. Creason's article in the Louisville *Courier-Journal* inspired him to intensify his own efforts and to
aim higher than a Kentucky newspaper. Cadle wanted to publish something about Still in *The Atlantic* or *Life*.[36] In the meantime, his project
was to pull together and publish a combined bibliography, biography,
and collection of commentary. The proposed title was "Pattern of a
Writer," and the rough outline included an introduction; a chronology;
a biographical article; representative quotations from reviews, correspondence, and newspapers; an interview with Still; and the bibliography compiled by Cadle.[37]

That plan remained constant in the years that followed, but the list
of contributors varied. Cadle invited writers and professional acquaintances of Still to submit essays, remarks, or memories. A few did, but
just as many politely declined or never responded. For example, Wilma
Dykeman and James Stokely turned Cadle down in 1961 and again
in 1965.[38] In January 1962 Cadle requested an essay from Harriette
Arnow. She declined, saying that she was neither poet nor critic and
that the dedication speech she gave at the opening of the James Still
Room at Morehead would not be appropriate. In March, Cadle wrote
to Edward Weeks at *The Atlantic Monthly*, asking for his opinion of
Still as a writer. Weeks did not respond. Yet Cadle was persistent. He
was committed to the collection and pushed ahead with his part—the
bibliography and chronology.

The level of cooperation Cadle got from Still is unclear, but he
would not have had access to many of the people he approached without help from Still. By the mid-1960s he had revised the plans. The title

would be *Man on Troublesome: James Still and His Work*. The opening essay would be "At Home with James Still on Dead Mare" by Albert Stewart, followed by a critical essay by John Napier. The chronology and bibliography would follow. A letter dated February 16, 1965, shows his determination: "I have decided to get it published if I have to reduce it to the bare bibliography and pay all the expenses myself."[39] He proposed they send it first to the University Press of Kentucky (UPK). A second choice would be the Council of the Southern Mountains. Third could be Alice Lloyd College in Knott County. They decided to go with Kentucky, which turned out to be the wrong choice. In January 1966 Cadle received a letter from Jerome Crouch at the press, rejecting the manuscript because it was simply too "light-weight."[40] The only section that was well received was Cadle's essay, leading Crouch to conclude that perhaps Cadle should do his own book on Still.

Cadle then shifted his efforts from the collection to a critical study of Still's writing that he had first submitted to the *Yale Review* in 1965. Paul Pickrel, managing editor of the review, responded that the editors were "much impressed"; his essay was a "fine piece of work."[41] Cadle promptly submitted the required changes, including a longer biographical section. In the last months of 1967 "Man on Troublesome" finally appeared. Once work on the article itself was complete, Cadle put energy into its distribution. He had already requested a large number of copies be sent to him and to people he knew.[42]

Still also mailed out copies of the article and typed excerpts from responses he received. He sent a compilation of these to Cadle with a margin note admitting it was "wicked" of him to send it. He must have considered such self-promotion inappropriate for a private, unassuming person. The glowing comments illustrated that the article had accomplished its goal of drawing attention to the personality of the man and his accomplishments as a writer. The article's more important goal was to provide an explication of Still's best prose. Roland Carter, a friend from LMU, wrote, "I now feel that I know you better than ever." Stewart grudgingly approved the essay but concluded in the words of Huck Finn, "He told the truth mainly." Of the quotes that Still selected to retype, the most notable was a short one from Marshall Best at Viking. Best found the article a "discerning piece" that renewed his eagerness to want more new work from Still.[43]

Positive reactions reenergized Cadle. His work had made Still more accessible and appealing. Stuart Forth, director of libraries at the University of Kentucky, responded with sincere thanks for the article, saying he had met Still once at a tea in Lexington but found him "almost completely uncommunicative."[44] He was not the only reader who felt that "Man on Troublesome" had provided insight into an impenetrable person. Rebecca Caudill Ayars praised the article and recounted a story of her first encounter with James Still sometime in the late 1940s. She and her husband had stopped by Hindman and called on Still in the library. He received them "less than enthusiastically" and suggested they come back some other time.

For all that Cadle was attempting to do for Still, their relationship seemed to be compatible and professional rather than close. Letters between them do not exhibit memories of the past, such as those Still shared with Stuart, or a special personal connection, like the one he had enjoyed with Dare Redmond. Cadle was more like a personal secretary. Still did appreciate his efforts, but there was little fun in their correspondence, no special fondness. One letter exhibits a negative, even surly tone, not directed toward Cadle but openly expressed:

> My car was "totaled" August 2. I expected you all of that torrid month. Where were you? This is my last vegetable week before I go back to the Rowan county feud at Morehead. The summer has been the snap of a finger long.
>
> The novel is being, or has been reprinted. The August statement from Viking had a check, plus the notation: "*River of Earth*, Reprint Edition, Popular Library." Paperback, I judge. Never heard of 'em. And "Popular" sounds ominous. Can you locate their address for me? Humn! . . . now must gird my girth for another classroom year. May it be my last![45]

This grouchy attitude was less evident after Still retired from Morehead. His frame of mind improved in the 1970s. In October 1973 Still wrote that he had recommended Cadle for the position of librarian at Berea College. This letter was colorful, almost playful, as shown in this excerpt:

> This is the opportunity to return to Kaintuck. . . . There's the job, that's all. Yours to leave or take. I don't know that it would be good change considering this and that and the t'other. But where else are you going to find a Library with elevators? And plug-in vacuum cleaners—dust container plug-ins. Awful sleepy, that old town. Lot of professor's widows

around. The president and his wife you'll love. Weatherford is a North Carolina gent, as you may know. Awful slow campus. Even the autumn leaves take five minutes to drift from limbs to ground.[46]

Cadle did not take the job in Berea but remained at UNC in Asheville.[47] Yet he continued to imagine and pursue Still-related projects. His next idea was to write a book about Still for the Twayne series on American writers.[48] That was sidelined when Still decided to allow UPK to republish *River of Earth*. A major question was who should write the foreword. After approaching Allen Tate, then considering Cleanth Brooks, Dykeman, Max Steele, and Arnow, Still and Crouch decided that the obvious person to do it was Cadle.[49] The actual writing of the foreword took months because Still read and commented on every draft.

When Cadle sent him one of the early versions, Still responded with a one-paragraph sample of what he thought appropriate, then followed with "What I had hoped for was merely an introduction [giving] background to the story, not the author. Not a critique probing into mechanisms of narration and into the psyche of the author. . . . Write it for my sister and brother, not some graduate student grubbing away in a dusty library stack. The story is simple; the intro should be the same."[50] Cadle reworked it until finally in December 1977 Still was satisfied.[51] That was the last of their accomplishments that satisfied both men.

Their correspondence began to show a strained relationship. In July 1978 Cadle wrote Still that he was concerned about an article Shirley Williams had published in the Louisville newspaper because it gave no credit to him.[52] She noted a revival of interest in Still's work but did not mention his *Yale Review* article as inspiration. She talked about Still's friends but did not name Cadle. She referred to him only in passing as a "North Carolina college librarian." When Still's interview with Jerry Williamson was published in *Appalachian Journal,* the rift between Still and Cadle was too wide to ignore.[53]

The friendship and working relationship that had begun in 1946 and lasted thirty years was doomed, but Cadle refused to allow it a natural death. He struggled to patch it up for more than five years. There were good reasons why he wanted to maintain this friendship. First, he admired Still's writing and was invested in reviving his reputation. Second, Cadle was a tenacious man and a hard worker. Finally, he wanted more than anything to be a writer, and much of the writing he had done was related to Still. For these reasons, and possibly others, he continued to feel insulted by comments, retractions, and omissions that he perceived Still made when talking to a wider circle of interviewers.

As Still gained prominence, Cadle felt less appreciated. Perhaps he was jealous of Still's rise in visibility—something that he had worked to make happen. More likely, he was jealous of other people whom Still admired and befriended. As the 1970s came to a close, an advocate and companion entered Still's world and displaced Cadle. Jim Wayne Miller was a more creative and successful manager of the man and his image. As Miller began to assume the role that Cadle had filled, Still practiced avoidance, an effective weapon against Cadle, who was resentful and showing signs of paranoia. In 1986 Miller wrote a scathing review of *The History of Southern Literature* titled, ". . . And Ladies of the Club," in which he called Cadle by name. Though a minor point in Miller's article, Cadle took offense. His rebuttal was titled ". . . And Members of the Pack." There he explored offenses he had suffered at the hands of Still. The liveliest paragraph gave rise to the mean-spirited "throne" comment Cadle attributed to his former friend:

> During those early years—1946–1960—there were relatively few attendants in the throne room, and I should have read a warning in Still's off-hand remark that those standing closest to the throne are the first to lose their heads. But I let it pass, and during the ensuing years the room became so crowded with aides and extollers, praise mongers and minions, counselors and consultants, envoys from other kingdoms, foolish clowns and clowning fools, and bevies of big-asted biddies that there was grave danger of being smothered upright or of being squeezed out a castle window.[54]

In 1987 Cadle decided to give his papers to the Appalachian collection at the University of Kentucky library. Before turning them over, he requested permission from Still to include material related to him. That letter concluded with a summary of his complaints and the cause of his heartache: "One of the more stimulating and enjoyable aspects of my life has been my friendship with you. . . . I thought we had a relationship of respect for each other as persons and of appreciation for each other's abilities and accomplishments. But my view of your interpretation changed with the publication of the *Appalachian Journal* interview, and I have found the attitudes you expressed there reinforced by the three recent instances in which you misused or permitted the misuse of my photographs."[55] Still responded with a formal permission statement to include his material in the library collection, but he did not address the overt accusations or the subliminal plea for understanding.

Cadle tried one last time to play the part of supporter when he published "Pattern of a Writer" in the Winter 1988 edition of *Appalachian Journal*. Editor Jerry Williamson was delighted to have the piece from Cadle because he had conducted and published the controversial interview to which Cadle referred. The piece is long because Cadle wanted to be sure that it was "right and truthful."[56] He wrote to Williamson in August 1987 that Still was a "complicated person," and he feared his responses. "I have carried these notes with me for almost thirty years without making an effort to publish them because I knew he would object strongly, if for no other reason than to illustrate his dictum: 'Be hard to pin down.'"[57] If Still had adverse reactions to the article that finally appeared, he did not publicize them.

Still was hard to pin down, but so was Cadle. The dissolution of their friendship and working partnership is inexplicable. In one sense, Still appeared disloyal and unappreciative. But Cadle seemed overreaching and emotionally unstable. When in 1994 Still was visiting western North Carolina, he called Cadle, who was living in Hendersonville. His wife, Jo, answered and, while surprised to hear from Still, was cordial in calling her husband to the phone. He refused to talk. Still appeared to be temporarily set back, but he claimed he had come to expect extreme behavior from Cadle.

Albert Stewart (1914—2001) first came to know Still as a teacher and librarian at Hindman Settlement School in the 1930s. The school was Stewart's home from the age of four until he left for Berea College. After earning a graduate degree at the University of Kentucky and serving as a naval officer in the South Pacific during the war, he returned to Knott County.[58] After his return, he and Still became well acquainted. Stewart's article that was to be included in Cadle's collection, "At Home with James Still on Dead Mare," contains details of their early friendship. He began by describing his summer of 1940 visit to Dead Mare as a seventeen-mile walk across the county.[59] When he finally got to the house, Still was not there. Tired and discouraged, the young man headed back home. Still came up behind him in a hired car, a kind of rural taxi, and took him back to the log house, where he spent the night.

Stewart's description of the house and Still's choice to live there sets the stage for their ensuing relationship. Although Stewart had grown up in the county, he found Littcarr and Dead Mare remote. Still's attraction to the house, in his view, was a sign that he was seeking isolation, a safe burrow in nature, an escape to a simpler life. Stewart saw Still as wanting to reverse the work that people had done to control nature, and it seemed strange. The article continues in this vein, with Stewart attempting to explain Still's choices, and at the same time trying to endorse them. The article ends with a collage of tidbits. For example, Stewart pictured Still as a wry individual with a comic sense when he told the story of why Still quit smoking: "I refuse to work for the R.J. Reynolds Tobacco Company. . . . It took me a long hard time to learn to smoke. . . . Anyone who takes the trouble to learn deserves the habit. . . . It got so I wasn't doing anything else. I wasn't smoking, they were smoking me. When I put one in my mouth and found one already there, I thought it was time to quit." Stewart was doing with Still what Still often did with his neighbors—listening and repeating the best stories and anecdotes. [60]

When he wrote the article in 1963, Stewart was one of Still's strongest advocates. He never took on the man as a project as Cadle did, but he wanted to be his friend, to help and support him, and to draw him out of the isolation of Knott County into the literary limelight or at least the educational arena. He did that, as we have seen, by encouraging Still to apply for a teaching position at Morehead and by negotiating on his behalf to get him hired as a writer-in-residence in 1961. [61] Stewart was ambivalent about Still's quiet lifestyle. Being a resident of Knott County himself, he could appreciate Still's connection to the place, but Stewart was not a man to retreat to the woods. He was a family man, which meant he had obligations; at heart he was a teacher and mentor of younger writers, and he enjoyed being part of projects, especially in planning and implementing them. Yet when he went to work at Morehead, he became frustrated at his lack of time to write or even live. He closed one letter to Still, "There is too little time to be spent at home. When is it that I shall be able to live quietly and deliberately rather than hectically and spasmodically?" [62] He envied Still's quiet, unencumbered life even though such a life was not possible for him, a man who liked to be active and involved.

One unsolved mystery of James Still's friendships is the rift that grew between himself and Stewart over the years. It began when they were both at Morehead, but the cause is unclear. Anyone who knew Still during his last twenty-five years was aware that he did not speak to or publicly acknowledge Stewart, a man who lived in Knott County and spent much of his time in Hindman at the Settlement School. If Still saw

Stewart walking toward him on the sidewalk, he would cross the road to avoid the possibility of a greeting. Sidney Farr, who followed Stewart as editor of *Appalachian Heritage,* touched on the estrangement between the two men when she said, "I was often amused in talking to Mr. Stewart or Mr. Still. Each acted like a prima donna at Hindman. They often spoke of one another critically and sarcastically, along with a few words of praise sprinkled in here and there."[63]

They shared a past and many friends, at one time the same employer; they both felt a commitment to heritage, to literature, to travel, and especially to Knott County. Although people close to them knew when they were no longer friends, no one seemed to know why. Mullins successfully interacted with them by simply refusing to get involved in their spat.[64] Loyal Jones, director of the Appalachian Center at Berea College, acknowledged that he liked both men but that they "couldn't stand each other." They may have retained a trace of mutual respect but certainly no affection. Stewart died a few weeks before Still. Still went to the funeral and sat in the front row, next to Jones. Still said to him that he was sorry for what happened between himself and Stewart but that it could not be helped.[65]

The problems must have begun at Morehead. When Still came there, they were good friends; Stewart was being helpful to Still. Shirley Williams, Stewart's cousin, remembered when the two men were talking to each other. Their friendship went back a long time before the falling out, she said. Still had implied to people in the community that Stewart tried to get him fired at Morehead. Williams was not sure of that, but she was aware that Stewart had stumbled on something upsetting at Morehead that he would talk about only peripherally. Whatever it was made him mad. As the years passed, irritation became normal, and even small things would aggravate one man or the other. For example, Stewart complained that Still would crow about every new honor he received. While Stewart was editor of *Appalachian Heritage* (1973– 1985), Still submitted poems. Some were rejected. Still kept those in a file, and when Stewart gave the magazine to Berea, Still sent Farr those poems, all of which she published in the very first issue. This infuriated Stewart. In spite of their bickering, Stewart and Still cared something about each other. Williams said that when Still had gallbladder surgery, Stewart went immediately to the hospital and stayed at his bedside until it was clear he was all right; then he left.[66]

There must be a reason why two friends would refuse to mend their friendship or even to be civil to each other. Did the problem stem from rivalry, competition, or jealousy, or was it an insurmountable conflict of personalities? Perhaps the break arose from a particular incident. At one time a vague rumor circulated that Stewart believed he had seen Still approaching some man in Morehead in a sexual or romantic way. If this issue divided them, reaching an understanding would have been difficult if not impossible.[67] Whatever the problem or its cause, the result was a permanent break and irreparable hard feelings. Perhaps it is enough to say that they were both "independent cusses," as Mullins acknowledged with respect and affection in his Hindman workshop talk of 2002, the year after both men had died.

Still was ambivalent about his need for and enjoyment of friends. On the one hand, he seemed to be a loner, yet over the years he had many friends; a few of them were very close, supportive, helpful, and loyal. In even fewer cases, he reciprocated, and the result was a lasting bond that he incorporated into his very existence. He "stuck" with Jesse Stuart, but they were never really close. He broke with Albert Stewart over something that "could not be helped." He appreciated Dean Cadle as long as Cadle was cooperative, predictable, and accommodating.

Part 6

Later Work

*Being a Writer, Becoming a Legend,
1974–2001*

23

Pattern of a Writer in Pursuit of Publication

It will take a little while to find him.
He may be in some unlikely place
Lying beneath a haw, lost in leafy sleep,
Or atop a high field digging his keep.
He is somewhere around. Go and look.
                    —James Still, from "Of the Wild Man"

These lines from a 1978 poem suggest a self-portrait; Still had always been somewhat elusive. The trait was natural to the person and necessary to his writing. While wanting to be "a wild man"—mysterious, unknowable, and hard to pin down—he also invited people to look and wonder. But did he welcome people to get to know him? Sometimes, somewhat. During the 1970s when the Appalachian region was in the public eye, so was Still. As he became better known though speaking appearances, he became more aware of his image and realized he could influence it.

Late in 1967 Dean Cadle's *Yale Review* article "Man on Troublesome" helped establish Still's position in the literary landscape, but it was more interpretive than personal. Cadle wanted to know all aspects of Still but hesitated to ask his permission to publish a biographical account.[1] Still was not ready to be revealed or exposed to readers. He had even responded to one of Cadle's essay drafts by asserting that he wanted an introduction to the book, not a probing into the author. The notes Cadle had made from their conversations in the 1950s remained in journal form for years. He wanted to publish them in an article that would receive Still's blessings. The first version, "The Act of Writing," surfaced in October 1974, and Cadle sent a copy to Loyal Jones. Jones mentioned the piece to Still, who responded that he could "refute everything that [was] said in it." This reaction stopped Cadle temporarily, but he tried again in 1977, calling this manuscript "Attitudes Toward Writing." Still did not even respond to this one; he was more concerned with the introduction Cadle was writing for the upcoming edition of *River of Earth*.[2]

Cadle finally publish his article a decade later. By then, so much had happened to sour their relationship that he had nothing to lose. The result was a long piece, "Pattern of a Writer," which appeared in the Winter 1988 issue of *Appalachian Journal*. In spite of their personal estrangement, the article is fair minded, even respectful and generous. It is also helpful in exploring Still's views on creativity in the late 1950s during a time he claimed to be writing many stories but publishing few. When it appeared thirty years later, much of what the article said was already part of Still's complex image.[3] Its value was in illustrating how difficult it was to capture Still's essence. The message Cadle conveyed is that James Still was "wild" and hard to find but definitely worth looking for.

"Pattern of a Writer" is constructed around the conversations of the two men in 1959.[4] The entries have no thematic order; taken together, however, they give an overall impression. For example, when Cadle asked about teachers who influenced him, Still responded, "A writer must . . . stay wild. He shouldn't be trained." Cadle tried to convey Still's creative process through comments about his writing habits. For example, Still claimed that he built his day around writing and fit in everything else as he could. He made a work chart to keep track of the number of hours he wrote. If at the end of a month the total came up short, he would work overtime the next month. This systematic approach seems to contradict Still's later claim that he never forced himself: "I've got to live with a story until it's ready to be written. I don't push it . . . [just] play around with it until I know it's right, sometimes for years."[5]

Another theme in "Pattern of a Writer" concerns the need to write versus the drive to publish. At the time of the interviews, Still was, by his own account, writing a lot but publishing little. He claimed that the publication process "has nothing whatever to do with writing." Cadle endorsed Still's approach by describing him as a dedicated artist who saw publication and popularity as "enemies of the act of writing." Still openly criticized writers who confuse salesmanship with writing, and he called public appearances, lecture tours, and autograph parties "the foe." When writers spend time "telling us how great they are, it is difficult for readers to know how good their writing is." Still told Cadle that he had no urge to publish. Writing for him was a privilege because he could live many lives while creating a book, and that brought him satisfaction. He thought he had "gotten a few things exactly right" and would be content, he said, if he wrote "one book of enduring merit."[6]

These excerpts from Cadle's article reveal Still's values and reflect his attitudes when they first knew each other. Between 1935 and 1941, Still wrote much and published with relative ease. Then came World War II, during and after which he wrote little and published even less. During the 1950s, when Cadle was interviewing Still, he was writing but not publishing. Later, when he needed to make a living, Still worked at Hindman then at Morehead, and he spent less time writing. He made friends, enjoyed travel, read books, gave lectures, taught classes. Still was never an extrovert, but he did become more sociable, and he began to find satisfaction in being a man of mystery.

Besides, he had already gotten a few things "exactly right." He had written at least one book that seemed to have enduring merit, but for a book to survive, it needs to be in print. By the 1970s when he was no longer tied to a salaried job, Still began to focus on reprinting books and submitting manuscripts he had been storing. The next few years showed him fulfilling his own prophecy: by working to publish and publicize, he did less writing. Still's interest in publication awakened in the mid 1960s. Between 1965 and 1978, he published or reprinted eight titles with five different publishers—an impressive accomplishment, considering that before 1965 he had published only three books, all of them with Viking.[7] A key element in this renaissance was the help of friends, especially Cadle and Jonathan Greene.

In September 1960 Cadle mentioned to Still that he had met a woman, Carolyn Hammer, who was interested in *Hounds on the Mountain*. This connection would eventually lead to the reissue of that first volume of poetry in a limited edition created on a hand press in Kentucky. The project took several years to complete. Hammer and her husband, Victor, began the edition after meeting Still in Lexington in early 1961; after two years, Wayne Williams took over its printing. In October 1965 Anvil Press finally completed the work, which Still dedicated to his brother Alfred. The launch was a small affair, a tea in Lexington, but it gained him attention and readers. Frances Shine, for example, at the University of Kentucky wrote a follow-up letter to Still, indicating that the Margaret King Library was interested in his manuscript collection. As with many of the publications to come, Still asked that copies of the poetry book be sent to friends and contacts.[8] He intended to use this small volume to reignite his publication efforts.

One recipient was Stokely, who had gone with Dykeman to Morehead in the spring of 1965 to participate in the visiting-writers series arranged by Still. That visit inspired Dykeman to try to rekindle interest in Still's work. On returning home, she wrote about Still's first novel in her Knoxville newspaper column:

> It seems impossible that a quarter-century can have passed since [River of Earth] was written, for it is as vivid and fresh and meaningful at this moment as it was the day it appeared. In fact, anyone who wants to have more than a superficial glimpse of what family life in the shut-down coal villages is like should read this excellent novel, which has both pathos and humor. As is true of all art, River of Earth is significant today no less than yesterday—and it is an utter delight to read because James Still is a writer, a magician with words.[9]

Dykeman expressed dismay that the novel was out of print and urged Viking Press to publish a paperback edition. In case the staff at Viking were not reading the Knoxville News-Sentinel, David Harkness, director of library services at the University of Tennessee, sent a copy of the column to Viking's editorial office with these words: "The enclosed column by the novelist Wilma Dykeman expresses the way many people all over the country feel about James Still's excellent novel River of Earth. With the current interest in Appalachia, a paperback edition would be most welcome."[10] Harkness was correct in predicting that interest in the region would add to the appeal of a reissue. Publishers sought to capitalize on that interest. The exact negotiations of the reissue are unclear, but Viking did make arrangements for the book to be brought out as a Popular Library paperback. The copyright was renewed in 1968, and the edition appeared in early 1970.[11]

Still was skeptical: it was a paperback, he had never heard of Popular Library, and he disliked the word "popular." He was disappointed when it was released, describing the book as a small cheap volume like those found on sleazy bookracks in drugstores.[12] The 245 pages of the Viking hardback had been reduced to 127 pages in the paperback; smaller print and smaller margins on thin paper helped keep the size and the price down. The book sold for only sixty cents, but buyers would have been disappointed in spite of the bargain price. If they liked the book, they would regret having it fall apart in their hands. Most buyers probably abandoned the book before the pages fell out because the alluring picture on the cover did not fit the text within. The sexy, barefoot woman might belong in an Erskine Caldwell novel or on a Tennessee Williams stage; she does not appear anywhere in *River of Earth*, even in a reader's imagination.

The reprint did not sell well, but it did serve an important purpose—to reintroduce the book and Still to readers. Still himself helped with the advertising. The thank-you letters he received show that he mailed copies to a long list of people, including but not limited to Cratis Williams, Robert J. Higgs, Anne and Harry Caudill, Carter Martin, and Allen Tate, whose response would have been especially gratifying to Still because Tate described *River of Earth* as "a brilliant and moving novel," "a masterpiece of style."[13] The availability of the novel along with Cadle's "Man on Troublesome" awakened the interest of critics, teachers, and scholars. Several master's theses on Still were written in the late 1960s, and journal articles began to appear in the early 1970s. Max Steele, who was reading sections of *River of Earth* to his college classes at UNC, wrote Still, asking if enough copies existed for him to order forty for his contemporary literature class.[14]

Still sent Best at Viking Press periodic progress reports. In January 1968 Still indicated that one manuscript of poems was on the way, he would soon send a set of short stories, and he was completing a novel. Best was receptive and, on February 8, responded that he looked forward to receiving the poetry manuscript; the short stories would be last on their prospect list; the novel was what they really wanted.[15] At the same time, other publishers were approaching Still about possible material. Regina Ryan, editor with Alfred Knopf, heard of Still through Loyal Jones in 1969 and wrote him about the possibility of reissuing "RIVERS OF EARTH." Her spelling error was understandable—she had not read the book because she could not get a copy. By her next letter Ryan had read it, plus a collection of his poems and one of his stories. She was complimentary of all, but Knopf wanted to publish a new novel first. That, she said, "would stir the attention of reviewers and bring [Still's] name before the book-buying public again—as a sort of re-introduction. Then the others could follow in its wake."[16] The pattern was clear: publishers were receptive to Still and would consider his work, but they really wanted a new novel. Still was busy writing and trying to publish as the decade of the 1970s began, but he did not have a novel.

He once again became occupied with publishing children's books. In 1956 he had approached Houghton Mifflin with a collection of riddles but had received a negative response, which Viking and Atlantic Monthly Press had echoed. That was when he connected with the agent Toni Strassman, who sent *Way Down Yonder* out seventeen times with no positive results. Still was so dissatisfied with Strassman's report that he decided to take Max Steele's advice and sign with a new agent, Phyllis Jackson. By June 1972, she was successful at getting Viking Press to acknowledge that the rights to the Popular Library edition of *River of Earth* would not expire until 1975, but that Viking would try to make a deal to relinquish the hardcover reprint rights. Jackson also set about to distribute the manuscript *Way Down Yonder*. She found a publisher by the end of the year, and Still began corresponding with Charles Mercer, senior editor of the Juvenile Department at G. P. Putnam's Sons (now known as Putnam). Over the next several years, Putnam published two of Still's books for children, both illustrated with woodcuts by Janet McCaffery. The first was *Way Down Yonder on Troublesome Creek: Appalachian Riddles and Rusties* (1974), and the second was *The Wolfpen Rusties: Appalachian Riddles and Gee-haw Whimmy-Diddles* (1975).

Still entered the world of juvenile literature. He had collected much of the material for these first two books over the years he had lived in Knott County. His task for publication was to select, edit, and present it in a way that a wider audience could enjoy. His first letter to Mercer at Putnam provided background on the project. He had collected the riddles and rusties, he said, while on the staff at the Settlement School. He held "riddle sessions with the children and recorded those handed down by oral tradition through parents and grandparents. Some came literally from the milk teeth of tadwhackers (small boys)."[17] Like his earlier works, these books contained elements of storytelling and poetry; they also depended on accurate, understandable use of dialect and cultural setting. The difference was the lack of a connecting story and the age of the intended reader. Several years after *Way Down Yonder* appeared, Still emphatically stated that he did not write for children, at least "not for children alone." But, he added, "I'd rather light up a child's eyes than earn a grunt of approval from a dozen of their elders."[18]

The riddle books did get approval and lots of bright eyes, but the big winner that followed two years later was *Jack and the Wonder Beans,* his classic Jack tale set in eastern Kentucky and told in mountain dialect. The book was beautifully illustrated by Margaret Tomes and was named the *New York Times Book Review* Judges' Choice for Best Illustrated Children's Book of 1977. To hear Still tell it, *Jack* was the quickest, easiest book he had ever written. He woke up early one morning in his log house with the idea in his head. He made himself a cup of coffee, sat in bed, and handwrote the whole story on a legal pad. Pleased with the published version, Still acknowledged that it had a good chance for a long life. "All my powers and my gifts, such as they are, came together in those few pages. The news that some children are sleeping with this book and that their elders are reading it with some delight tickles me in a spot that is hard to get to, to scratch—as the saying goes."[19]

The fourth of Still's books published by Putnam was *Sporty Creek,* a mix between his traditional stories and his writing for young readers. It is sometimes described as a sequel to *River of Earth;* they do have much in common. Both are told by young boy narrators—cousins growing up in the same time and place. Both are built around chapters that can function as self-contained stories.[20] Children's literature specialist Tina Hanlon notes that in spite of the obvious similarities, *Sporty Creek* is lighter and more optimistic than *River of Earth,* and it places more emphasis on humorous childhood experiences.[21] Other obvious differences are its length, its wonderful illustrations by Paul Brett Johnson, and its publisher, Putnam.

In the 1970s when Still was turning out these small books at Putnam, his editor Charles Mercer was loyal and supportive. To Mitch Douglas, a movie agent interested in Still's work, Mercer wrote, "[Still is] my favorite writer of all I've dealt with in my time as an editor at Putnam's. Wish we could sell his work better—and wish he'd come up with another book for us."[22] In spite of these kind words, the books were not impressive sellers, and Still did not send another. He was more interested in printing a collection of stories. Jonathan Greene at Gnomon Press obliged in 1976 by publishing Still's sixth book, *Pattern of a Man.*

Greene first learned about James Still through their mutual friend Carolyn Hammer when she was working on *Hounds on the Mountain* in 1965. Thinking of Still as overlooked and writing for children, Greene did not get to know him until 1974. In "A Memoir of James Still," Greene described his first encounter with Still's work. He had taken *River of Earth* and *On Troublesome Creek* with him when vacationing in the Bahamas and found them "eye-openers." He asked Still immediately if Gnomon could publish something of his. The result was *Pattern of a Man*. This collection, Greene noted, "ended a drought of 35 years in which [Still] had published no book of fiction for adults." *Pattern* included eleven stories—three of which had been published before the war and eight after. *Pattern* was important not only for ending the "drought" but also because it established a relationship between Still and a small, quality press in Kentucky.[23] The connection with Greene and Gnomon showed Still that people close to home were interested in making his earlier works available. It also gave him a friend who was less doting but more helpful than Cadle.[24]

Greene described the seventy-year-old Still as an intense and difficult man; he was "shy but yearned for friendship and discussion of good books and writers."[25] Greene provided both. Beginning in the summer of 1976, the correspondence between them showed how professional but also personal and helpful an editor could be. Once Still became involved in revising the manuscript, he was eager to see the final product in print. In August, Greene requested photographs from Cadle to use on the cover. Before the end of the year, the book was out in paperback and cloth. On receiving his copy on December 4, Still sent a postcard with this message: "Jon, Pattern of a Man arrived. Truly a handsome book. Physically a work of bookmaking art. My cup runneth over!"[26]

A prize quote for *Pattern of a Man* came to Still and Greene from Martha Foley, editor of *Best American Short Stories 1941–1977*. Though arriving too late for the book jacket publication, it appeared in subsequent advertising: "A delight to read are James Still's warm-hearted stories of his Kentucky neighbors whom he depicts in an English language as unspoiled as when Chaucer and the Elizabethans first made it into glorious literature. Anyone who loves words will love this book."[27] Still treasured her letter. When the collection was reissued in 2001, it included Wendell Berry's afterword, which also complimented Still's use of words. Berry's "A Master Language" ended with praise for Still's story "A Master Time," which Berry found "almost a miracle. It is absolutely lovely, quick and alight with shifting tones. It is a little globe, a world called into existence, reality and joy by a master workman." Discerning and influential readers recognized the artistry of the collection. Still must have realized with this publication that while children's books were fun and important, his strength lay in poetry and stories for adults. Years later, when Still gave Greene a copy of *The*

Wolfpen Notebooks, he inscribed it, "For Jonathan Greene, who with *Pattern of a Man*, rousted me out of the wilderness."

Their relationship continued when Greene took over distribution of the languishing Anvil Press edition of *Hounds of the Mountain*, and the remaining copies sold out quickly. *Pattern* received good reviews, but sales were modest.[28] The plan all along, as Greene remembered, was that Gnomon would bring out *Pattern* then republish *River of Earth* in a quality format. Still was interested in that prospect but did not feel bound to an agreement. Greene received disappointing news from Still in October (1976)—that UPK was seriously considering taking on *River of Earth*. Even while saying no to Greene, Still asked him to be involved in the book's design.

> Jon, The negotiations by persons, groups, institutions, departments, librarians over to [*sic*] years to get River of Earth reprinted came to nothing until my Madison County friends came into the picture. I had not expected them to succeed either. It has been in their hands about two years. How they brought it off, I do not know. I could not withdraw it from their hands until they threw them up. Their hands, I mean. I hope you'll design the book for UK if they do finally decide to undertake it. I understand and sympathize with your frustrations. I did not say No to you because I had no idea how the negotiations were going. If at all. I was not in the position to ask. And even now everything is tentative. Jim[29]

Still had been corresponding with the UKP about *River of Earth* since the summer of 1976. The two-year negotiations he referred to were the efforts to acquire the rights from Viking and Popular Library. By "Madison County friends," he meant people at Berea: Al Perrin, Loyal Jones, possibly even President Weatherford and his wife, Anne, who was now the chair of the Hindman Settlement School Board of Directors.[30] He was befriending people throughout the region. Cadle was a strong personal ally, and Greene was a professional advocate. Still's circle of influential acquaintances was expanding everywhere.

Still was also developing a relationship with people at the University of Kentucky, especially Gurney Norman, who had first met Still on that legendary trip from Hazard to Hindman in 1958. Much had happened to Norman in the interim. In November 1975 he wrote Still a long letter from California.[31] It was an effort to reconnect, a memoir of how he had gotten there and why he was coming back. Early in 1977 Norman, who was then in Lexington, invited Still to visit his class at the University of Kentucky.[32] Still went. Soon afterward, Norman visited Knott County, and Still's report to Greene showed how impressed the old writer was with the young one: "If all Gurney Norman's energy could be harnessed there'd be enough electricity to light up Hazard for six months. Was a pleasure and privilege to talk with him."[33] Still took it as a compliment that talented people wanted his time and attention. He had always resented that people in his own community did not appear to read or know about his writing. Now he was being sought out as a mentor to Norman and his students.

The need for Still to leave home in order to be fully appreciated was beginning to change. Hindman was becoming a center that attracted practicing writers and students. In the summer of 1977 the first writers' workshop at Hindman Settlement School had a staff of Stewart, Arnow, Billy Clark, Cadle, Shirley Williams, and Still.[34] The following year, the list looked like the "Who's Who" of Appalachian literature: Stewart, Arnow, Norman, Dykeman, Jim Wayne Miller, Cratis Williams, Jones, Verna Mae Slone, Caudill, Shirley Williams, and Still.[35] The establishment of the Writers' Workshop meant that Hindman was going to be a hub—a place where people would come, especially if they had an interest in the region and its literature.

The late 1970s were good years for Still. His publication was picking up. His circle of friends was growing, as were opportunities for exposure and professional connections. Awards and honors were coming his way. In the spring of 1978 he was honored with the Special Weatherford award.[36] That celebration in Berea occurred the same week that Morehead gave Still an honorary doctorate, his third. A month later, on August 21, 1978, he received a letter from John Stephenson, dean of undergraduate studies at the University of Kentucky, declaring that the university needed Still's presence and friendship. He was "somewhat chagrined" to realize how little attention the university had paid to Still; the letter concluded with an invitation to the campus for two weeks in the fall. After that visit, President Otis Singletary sent a gracious thank-you letter on November 17, 1978. At commencement the following spring, the University of Kentucky heaped another honor on James Still, his fourth honorary doctorate.[37]

For James Still, these honors and invitations were extras, definitely valuable and appreciated, but extras. The most important accomplishment of the 1970s was the reissue of *River of Earth*. That event initiated much of the attention he would receive throughout the region over the next decade. Such an important part of his later life and career deserves closer attention.

By the middle of the decade, the five-year lease on paperback rights from Viking to Popular Library had expired, and Still became the sole owner of *River of Earth*. His July 6, 1976, response letter to Crouch, editor at UPK, marked the critical point in his search for a publisher. Crouch had approached Still with a proposition, and Still's reply was positive: "It is pleasant to learn the University Press of Kentucky is considering reprinting various out-of-print books about Kentucky or by Kentucky authors and that my novel RIVER OF EARTH may be one of them."[38] The arrangement was positive for both parties. Still could have his novel brought back in a reputable, attractive format that would be available to schools and libraries as well as the general reader. UPK could reprint, at a critical time, a novel that had been lost but not forgotten. In addition, the revival of Still's reputation and his increasing production would help promote the book.

UPK made a practice of reprinting Kentucky material, a policy with a philosophical and a practical basis. In the early 1960s most university presses were small and oriented toward serving a scholarly community. Later in the decade, they began to grow and increase their offerings; successful ones began to solicit manuscripts and make decisions that would keep production costs down. Reprints were an important part of an overall plan because they were cheaper and easier to produce than new books, and their market was more predictable. UPK solicited out-of-print books that were germane to its interests and, in turn, provided a service to authors in the state and readers nationwide.[39] Director Kenneth Cherry made a statement about this policy to Don Edwards of the *Herald-Leader* when acknowledging his review of *River of Earth*: "We are very pleased to be able to bring Mr. Still's work before the public again. In fact, we are undertaking a reprint series of just such Kentucky books. . . . Kentuckians deserve to have these strong pieces of their history and culture widely available to them."[40]

The agreement between Still and Crouch, which began in 1976, progressed smoothly. Only three minor problems surfaced. The first was who would write the introduction. Allen Tate was approached because of his reputation as a critic and because of his positive response to the paperback edition in 1971. Being ill at the time, he declined, but his words to Crouch were supportive: "James Still is a star in the Kentucky galaxy." Still suggested other names: Cleanth Brooks, Dykeman, Max Steele, and Arnow. Eight months after beginning the reprint plans, both Still and Crouch realized that Cadle was the *"right* person to write the introduction."[41] Of course, Cadle knew Still personally and his work thoroughly. And this being a small world, Cadle had been roommates with Crouch at Berea. The fact that the three were closely connected may have been one reason why neither man thought of Cadle first. The actual writing of the introduction took months, possibly because Still read and commented on the drafts. At the end of October 1977 Cadle wrote Crouch with further revisions. Finally, in early December, Still expressed satisfaction that the introduction "could not have been better done" but added one last request that a quote from Delmore Schwartz—"River of Earth is a symphony"—be included somewhere. Cadle obliged.

The second problem came with Still's late realization that the book would be a paperback edition. In a letter to Cadle dated June 21, 1977, Still expressed concern that UPK intended to reprint *River of Earth* only in paperback. For two years he had expected a hardcover edition or a cloth and a paper edition, his major concern being that libraries did not buy paperbacks.[42] No doubt, the disappointment of the earlier reprint was also on his mind. Crouch and Still never discussed the hardcover edition directly, but Cadle did bring it up. Crouch promised to look into it, but the plans did not change, and relations among the men remained cordial.

The final problem was finding a satisfactory cover. Crouch flatly rejected one that looked like a rock wall left from a strip-mining operation.[43] The solution was to tap the talent and experience of Greene. Still had hoped Greene would do the design when he first told him that UPK would be the publisher. Greene obliged.

The press received copies on the last day of May 1978. Willis Popenoe, the sales manager, made arrangements with Shirley Williams of the *Courier-Journal* to follow the release with a long feature article to provide publicity beyond the scope of a review. Additional promotion included sending brochures to individuals listed by Cadle as "possible RIVER OF EARTH enthusiasts."[44] After the release, Crouch was satisfied and looked forward to the book's success. His only question was whether their efforts would create national interest. Two months later Crouch acknowledged to Jerry Williamson that the book was doing well, but he feared that it was held back by the regional label.[45] The book was priced at $4.95, and the first year's sales reached a total of 3,111 copies.

At least eighteen different papers or journals ran reviews of the book, but confirming Crouch's fears that national attention would be scant, all of them were local or regional periodicals. Reviewers and critics praised the book for its faithful portrayal of the area and the people who lived there, for its compassionate but unsentimental view. They praised Still's poetic use of language and realistic dialect, his spare style and simple story. However, they were most interested in its universal qualities. Rather than focusing on how Still had made the life of the Kentucky mountaineer seem different, they pointed out how the novel reflected general patterns and human characteristics. The story was described as timeless, the theme familiar, the problem contemporary, the characters archetypal. Art Jester's review in the *Anniston Star* (Alabama) summarized the strengths by saying that *River of Earth* is more than an outstanding rendering of mountain life: "The story of a single family scratching out their existence in eastern Kentucky becomes a universal tale of life and death, of all the feelings and occurrences among humans everywhere."[46]

In the minds of reviewers, Still was keeping excellent literary company. Cadle led the way in his foreword by quoting the comments of Marjorie Kinnan Rawlings and Schwartz, by comparing *River of Earth* to *The Grapes of Wrath,* and by alluding to stories by Katherine Anne Porter and Bernard Malamud. Some reviewers went further and expanded the literary circle. *Mountain Review* talked of the novel's theme of migration, a subject familiar to Arnow and Norman but also to William Faulkner and John Steinbeck. *Panorama* put Still beside great writers steeped in the culture of their places: Herman Melville, Mark Twain, and Faulkner. The *Tennessee Historical Quarterly* claimed that Still deserved to be placed with Steinbeck, Faulkner, Ernest Hemingway, and Wolfe. Ruel Foster moved beyond national boundaries to compare Still to James Joyce. The critics and reviews in 1978 placed the novel in a broader context than readers could have foreseen in 1940.

The book had not changed; the difference was the attitude toward regionalism and the Appalachian region. Dykeman began her review with an argument for a new look at the role of literature. It can, she said, recreate the specific from the general, separate the individual and mass experience so that the small and the large reality become more comprehensible. In spite of the efforts of writers and critics like Warren and Tate to update it, the regional or "local color" label of the past had been pejorative and limiting rather than descriptive of cultural diversity.

But this narrow view had begun changing in the late 1970s, and Dykeman claimed that the reappearance of *River of Earth* was evidence of that change.[47]

Since *River of Earth* first appeared in 1940, Still's world had changed. The attitudes of people, especially those interested in Appalachia, were evolving. In the intervening thirty-eight years, Still himself had changed. Ironically, the element of the man that appealed most to his growing regional audience was his constancy. He embodied an enduring connection to the past and to his place. That kind of commitment and permanence had become known only because Still was opening up and getting out. He was a more public person, interested in being involved, in going places, and in republishing books, writing new ones, and talking about them. As he entered the eighth decade of his life, Still was remaking himself.

Shirley Williams published her lengthy *Courier-Journal Magazine* article on July 9, 1978, just after *River of Earth* was released. Her idea, evident from her title "Still Writing after All These Years," was that the man lived and wrote in Knott County, almost half a century after he first moved there, but he was no longer forgotten or ignored—he was being rediscovered. Williams consulted her colleague Rena Niles, who had written about Still forty years earlier in the *Courier-Journal*. Niles had described him then as a shy, reticent person who had put down roots and stayed. He had "literally stood still," she said. While it is easy to see what she meant, Niles was wrong. Still had not stood still. He was not the same person that he had been in 1939 or even when Cadle met him in 1959. In his poems and his behavior, Still was now inviting people to know him, the "wild man." But when they "came inside," they found what Don Edwards of the *Herald-Leader* called "an elusive paradox of a man."[48] The qualities of paradox and intrigue became hallmarks of his later career.

24

Still the Explorer, 1972–1990

"If you take the job as town clerk,
you may not spend the winter
in Tierra del Fuego."—Thoreau, *Walden*

Grant me passage to Tierra del Fuego
So that I may go
See the glacial mountains
And the whale-spout fountains,
. . . .
Haste me to the "Lade of Fire"
Despite weather icily dire.
As Clerk-dom I deplore
The wherewithal
And I'm out the door.
                    —James Still, from "Midwinter Doldrums"

One paradox Still exhibited throughout his later years was a strong commitment to his place coupled with an urge to get away. From the time he wrote "Heritage" in 1935, he had been associated with the inability to leave his hills—"I cannot pass beyond." Yet like the transient character Walking John Gay in *River of Earth,* Still wanted to go "traipsing and trafficking, looking the world over." If mountains are the icon of stability in Still's writing, then roads suggest mobility. In "White Highways," roads take the speaker away, but they always bring him home again. Still's idea of exploration was the complete excursion—the going out and the coming back. As conveyed in "Apple Trip," the journey itself was "a worldly wonder." Between 1972 and 1990 Still encountered many wonders of travel; a few excursions were close to home, but most involved trips to Central America or Europe and England.[1]

His adventures were not always pleasant. One example was his short expedition to a nearby coal mine. In May 1976 Berea College awarded an honorary doctorate to Robert Penn Warren. As part of the weekend, Anne Weatherford, wife of Berea's president, arranged for Warren and his wife, Eleanor Clark, to visit an eastern Kentucky coal mine. She also invited Still and Jones to accompany them. Still knew he would not like the expedition because he suffered from mild claustrophobia. But he went. Everyone dressed out in mining gear and toured the tunnels of the Southeast Coal Company mine in Letcher County.[2] Though Still had lived near coal mines much of his life, he had never been in one. He liked walking on top of the ground. Like his young narrator in *River of Earth*, Still preferred exploring the earth as a "dream dreamt," not finding himself "buried down [under it] like a johnny-humpback."[3]

Most of his adventures were farther afield and in the open. His love of travel had begun with his love of reading. He first became interested in primitive peoples, he told Shirley Williams, when his sister read him a book about Alaska. As he got old enough to read himself, he read all he could find about arctic exploration. Then he became fascinated with Tibet, then the Aboriginal people of Australia—"And Tierra del Fuego, anything with primitive people." That interest led him to research the Mayan civilization in Central America. When telling about one dangerous experience in San Salvador in 1977, he ended the story, "You can't imagine what was going through my head."[4] But Williams could imagine because Still had a gift for taking listeners with him to a different time and place.

Still had first experienced long-distance travel in the military. His voyage to Africa was not only a way to get to his post; it was his initiation into travel as adventure. One reason he took *Walden* to Africa was to help him remember his own "pond," Dead Mare Branch, but he used its pages to record his experience of leaving home. Later ventures out from the base at Accra were his way of escaping routine personnel work in order to encounter history. His military experience taught him how much he needed journeying to find himself and be himself. His life in Hindman and especially his work at Morehead limited his opportunity to get away and explore. The Thoreau quote that inspired "Midwinter Doldrums" explains something of what he sought in travel after his retirement. Having given up his job "as town clerk," so to speak, he wanted to spend the winters where he wished, and that place for a number of years was Central America.[5]

For years, Still had tried to escape Kentucky's coldest months by going to Florida, usually to stay with his sister in Bushnell. In 1972 he went farther south, to the Yucatán Peninsula. What inspired him to pursue this adventure at age sixty-six was a book. In 1971 he read *Gods, Graves, and Scholars: The Story of Archaeology* (1951) by C. W. Ceram. The last section includes two chapters on Mayan cities; the most interesting to Still was about Edward Thompson's work at Chichén Itza. This led to his first trip to Yucatán. The decision was bold: he went alone, he knew no one there, and he was unfamiliar with the geography and the language. That quest made him want to go back.

Still did not keep specific travel plans or a journal for that first trip, but he did send postcards to friends. The one to Temple and Charles Baker on March 5, 1972, said only, "Chichen-Itza and Uxmal are more wonderful than I imagined. But I have language problems. Just barely making it." By April he was back home and followed with a longer letter to the Bakers about Yucatán: "It was more primitive than I could have dreamed. . . . I expected Mexicans and found a pure race of ancient Indians—small bird-like people, few taller than five feet. The poorest people in the world and the cleanest. I shall surely return." To Regina Ryan, editor at Albert Knopf, he wrote that it had been the "most memorable journey" of his life. To Perrin at Berea, he declared that he would return and stay longer.[6] He did return many times.

The following year, he wrote a letter from Mérida to the Bakers. His list of place names looks like a travel brochure in need of a spellchecker. The spirited description reveals details of his stay as well as his eager anticipation of returning home.

Within a couple of hours I'll be heading for the airport—and home. No child waiting for Santa Claus was ever more anxious. No Americano should ever stay in Yucatan more than 4 days. The heat is absolutely withering, blistering, overpowering, brain sickening. But I returned to Chichen Itza, Uxmal and Dzibilchaltun. And added other places—Mayapan, the third city (now ruins) in the Mayan confederation before the Spanish conquest—plus others: Kanasun, San Antaino Tertz, Tipch,

Peptenich, Acaneh, Tecoh, Techquito and other places I can't spell. I also went to Progreso for a day on the forsaken beaches. And, foremost, I went into the *Gruta de Balakanchen* which finished me off physically for this trip. . . .

Well, I've been here nearly 2 weeks. It seems 2 years. In a little while I'll hoist my suitcase, go down to my waiting driver who will take me first to the museum, then to the airport. He will bow so deeply his chin will almost touch his knees. I'll shake hands with him, a gesture he does not expect, and then we'll be off through the searing streets of Merida to the museum, and then to a good old Pan-American clipper-ship.[7]

In 1974 Still returned to Yucatán; in 1975 he was in Guatemala and Honduras; and in 1976 he spent two months in the region. His April 1976 letter to Mrs. Doran, wife of the former president of Morehead, is more formal, making him sound like a visiting professor rather than an adventuresome tourist.

The past five winters I have spent time visiting the ruined cities of ancient Mayan civilization in Yucatan (Mex.), Guatemala and Honduras. Last February I attempted to return to Tikal, in the Petén-Itza jungle, but on landing in Guatemala City from Mexico City shortly after the earthquake was not allowed to disembark. I flew on to Tegucigalpa, Honduras and made my way with difficulty to the fabled ruins of Copan ten miles from the Guatemala border. Honduras suffered from the earthquake, but not to the extent of Guatemala. . . . While I remain the complete amateur, my interest and studies and explorations have earned me the acquaintance of authorities in the field, in particular, Dr. Robert S. Chamberlain of the Carnegie Institute, and workers in the Anthropological Museum in Mexico City.[8]

Each trip to Central America held its own challenges and thrills, but one that stands out for danger occurred in 1977 when he confronted both a lost civilization and a troubled modern world. He described a miraculous escape from major unrest following an election in El Salvador.[9] He told the story more than once, each time adding details. His account to Shirley Williams ended with the declaration that he had "every chance of being killed."[10] His description to Perrin after returning home was also dramatic:

A quick word to let you know I escaped without a scratch from the riot—(political disturbance following the election of a new president) in San Salvador, February 28. I was suddenly caught up in the well-organized mob, pressed to the wall, practically forced to join. I refused. I was either saved by women who shielded me, or by the arrival of the army. Soldiers fired into the crowd. Some were killed, many wounded. All was confusion. Buses were burned by men with gasoline in bottles, cars over-turned and set afire. At one point I was pulled through a metal door, the door barred, and huddled there with a group. When we came out all was not over. Somewhere a man appeared at a corner and said, "Come into the American house." I went in and they kept me for 24 hours and fed me 3 meals. Firing was heard all night. By morning the army was in command, I got back to my hotel, grabbed bag, grabbed taxi, and headed for the airport. The greatest danger might have been the wild ride to the airport, through soldiers and tanks. Now that it's over, I wouldn't have missed it for the world.[11]

This urgent report evokes the perils he had survived in the plane crash in Egypt years before.[12] Still was not a man to put himself deliberately in harm's way, but when it did happen, he enjoyed the thrill. Most of all, he liked surviving to tell the tale. What he did not tell in this account or in any other was that he was not alone in the streets of San Salvador. He had made this 1977 trip with a friend, Carlyle Cross.[13] Yet throughout his description Still seldom used the pronoun "we"; he seemed to be the only American in the street that day.

When recounting his adventures, Still rarely referred to travel companions, though he was usually accompanied. For example, he went with Cross in 1977; he went with Jim Bergman in the early 1980s, with Jim Wayne Miller in 1986, and with Sam McKinney and John Quillen on his last trip in 1989. It is reasonable that a man in his seventies and eighties would want to travel with friends. But his reluctance to acknowledge those cohorts is noteworthy.[14] Perhaps he wanted to project the image of the lone wanderer, an independent and self-sufficient explorer.

Another example of potential danger in Central America came at Still's own hands. In 1981 he visited Belize, the one quiet spot in the region. While there he went to the Mayan ruins Xunantunich, on the Western Road very close to the border. Looking out from a high pyramid, he could easily see Guatemala, a country not on good terms with its neighbor. Daring to put himself at risk, Still hired a driver to take him into Guatemala without permission. The journey was tense, but his description is more intriguing than frightening: "We [he and Jim Bergman] were stopped several times by soldiers guarding the road, and once at a machine gun nest. They regarded us for a moment, then nodded us on. Well, it was a conscious folly, and one not recommended."[15] His travels showed a kind of boldness, perhaps even foolishness, that cannot be associated with his quiet life in Hindman.

In addition to the tense political situations that Still experienced in Central America, he had one profound spiritual experience, which he called an "epiphany." It was a terribly hot day at one of the sites; he had stopped under a tree. Then, when he walked into the ruins, the place took his breath away. He suddenly had an absolute sense of stillness. He felt as though he could stay there the rest of his life and be perfectly satisfied, as if he belonged there. He recalled "a peace" he had never felt anywhere. He kept going back, hoping the epiphany would happen again. "It never did."[16]

What was Still's fascination with Central America that took him the first time? What kept him going back year after year? He said himself that he wanted to feel that special experience again, but the epiphany occurred in his ninth or tenth visit so cannot explain his early attraction. Certainly Mayan culture and its ancient history fascinated him. Another draw was the excitement of being in a foreign land, one that spoke languages he could not understand and that was politically unstable. Central America was relatively close to home, yet far away and different, exotic even. Miller was curious about Still's repeated visits to Mayan sites and asked him in a 1984 interview about the connection between his love for his own part of the world, eastern Kentucky, and his avid interest in Central America. Still responded that he had always been interested in primitive peoples, then quickly pointed out that his neighbors were not primitive. Mayan civilization and especially the mystery of its disappearance fascinated him. Miller concluded that the similarity might be Still's interest in the passing way of life in eastern Kentucky and a similar passing of a different lifestyle in Central America. When Miller presented that idea, Still responded, "Yes, I think so."[17]

As always, Still resisted statements he thought might simplify and explain his motivations. Yet he agreed that the affinity he felt for the ancient Mayan world was not unlike the bond he had formed with rural

Appalachian culture. He was becoming uneasy about being labeled a writer who was too focused on one region. In 1975, as Cadle was drafting the introduction to *River of Earth,* Still suggested he make the case that his writing transcends the regional and local and illustrate that transcendence by mentioning his interest in Mayan civilization and his winters in Central America studying this culture. He did not want the introduction to present him as a "stuffy local with tunnel vision."[18] Cadle did not insert the suggestions into the text, but Still's thoughts show that even then, just a few years after he had begun his trips to Central America, he was concerned with his image as a man stuck in one place.

Different aspects of Still's personality emerged through his journeying: the budding archaeologist; the historian delving into the past; the adventurer seeking a new experience; the wanderer who, like the boy in *River of Earth,* contemplates his trip down Redbird River as a chance to "look the world over"; the perceptive writer who absorbed the surroundings and recreated them. Yet he rarely wrote about his travel adventures except in letters and the occasional newspaper report. His only published poem about Central America was "Yesterday in Belize," which appeared in the *Kentucky Poetry Review* in 1988.

Still made his final trip to Central America in March 1989 at the age of eighty-two. Friends from Morehead, McKinney and John Quillen, accompanied him.[19] The stated purpose of the trip was to make the video *Voyage to the Sun.* When recalling their travels, McKinney commented that he and Still were kindred spirits from their first meeting. Still had suggested they travel together. They first went to Mérida in 1987; the second time was in 1989. McKinney drove Still's car to St. Petersburg, then they went to Progreso. While there, they saw a banner advertising a tour to Cuba. They went. According to McKinney, Still blended into crowds easily. He was observant and absorbed everything going on around him. He was like an excited and curious child when in Cuba, but a bit apprehensive. Still kept a diary of that trip. The following excerpts exemplify his powers of observation while revealing the tone of his experience:

Still's Travel Diary 1989[20]

> *March 1 (Wednesday)* Miami to Merida, Mexico
> Photographed the sun rising from my window in the Merida Mission Hotel—the moment of human sacrifice during the

day of the Mayan priesthood. To bus station early afternoon, stuffed ourselves on the vehicle for Progreso. Fare .50 (equivalent). Taxi fare quoted $24.00. Rented suite in Tropical Suites, facing the beach. John and Sam have loaded the ice box with beer. My room #13.

September storm which devastated Cancun also damaged Progreso. First floor of hotel under repair. Knocking and hammering the day long. More masonry than carpentry. Extensive destruction along beach front where we are. . . .

March 2 (Thursday)

Yesterday, in Merida, before departing, noted an offer posted by a travel agent: "Cuba—7 days, $192 U.S." We signed up for the flight to Havana next Wednesday without hassle. . . .

This building is a drum, all sounds drifting up a central shaft—hammering, knocking, kitchen sounds, unceasing conversation, radio music, the mynah. The empty beach, sands white as a panama hat stretching out of sight, the waves breaking. . . .

March 3 (Friday)

Since my visit 3 years ago Luxmal has added a visitors center, a turnstile, theatre, toilet facilities not dreamed of in the past. Blistering hot in the sun, cool in the shade. . . . Climbed up into the ruins farther than I should. Two roving policemen drove up in a car, climbed up to me and helped me down some 100 feet. I could have made it alone—precariously. Returning stopped at the Altemira Restaurant in Ticul. Rested a while in ancient church where Mary is represented by a life-size doll. . . .

March 6 (Monday)

Coming here as I have for now fourteen years I seem to shift the burden of "civilization" from my shoulders. Introduced to "Neptune" the Canadian beach-comber. Said he was 69, young enough to be my son. Appears as a character invented by Hemingway. . . .

Rain in the night. High winds, rough waves. . . . "Neptune" came by to say, "By going to Cuba you are violating the laws of your country. You're required to have permission of the U.S. State Department." "Not by going from Mexico," was our reply. In the night wind and rain. Supper at the Montezuma, crowded, roaring with laughter and conversation. . . .

March 9 (Thursday) to Cuba

Up before daylight. Group for Havana, including several Americans, assembled. One hour flight to Havana, arriving in driving rain at José Marti airport of hijack fame. Soldiers reminded we were in a police state. Herded aboard bus for downtown Capri Hotel. My room, 915, overlooking Havana harbor. Luxury appointments. Organizational meeting for tour group on 17th floor. In Spanish, with interpreter. Much new construction. Cranes dot the horizon. Took a walk with S. & J. several blocks. Rain hurried us back to the Capri. TV features exploits and training of women soldiers in the Cuban army. . . . Sumptuous supper, the buffet would put Shoney's to shame.

March 10 (Friday)

Rain and wind battered the giant window all night and wind struggled with door. Montezuma had his delayed revenge in the night. Shirt and skivvies washed last evening, dry by morning. The postage stamp celebrating the Cuban Revolution has the Russian flag (red) spread across a map of Cuba. There would be another Revolution of sorts if the U.S. lifted its embargo on autos and other goods. Old car buffs would be ecstatic to see the ancient vehicles along the street nowadays. . . .

First impression—and doubt they'll change. People along the street lethargic, sort of wandering. No pep. Workers just doing a job. Friendly, yes, when appealed to. The people are of all colors, from jade to ultra blond, and all shades between. The dead hand of communism has sapped initiative. Or is it the climate, the geographical location? . . .

March 11 (Saturday)

Scheduled 2:30 tour of Havana today . . . "A Day in the Country" with tour group, swelled to twenty. 45 minutes out of Havana. A farm-show farm, Cuban banners flying, chicken with biddies. Several of us milked a cow. A man climbed a coconut tree using a rope sling, threw down nuts. I tried (for the film), managed 3 feet. Horses for riding. Into the saddle. Stage show under palm thatch. 10 musicians, 4 dancers (2 black 2 white.) Joined dancers on stage in finale and the "congo" line. Audacity is the ticket? Sumptuous lunch. In Havana, breadline. Stores empty.

At dinner we joined a retired Canadian and swapped information and anecdotes. When J.&S. inquired if it was safe for them to be on the streets at night—to take an evening stroll he said, "No. There are hungry people out there." J.&S. a bit anxious about being here. We've been told we are the first Americans seen here. Are we the first tourists?

My great window facing bay of Havana always smeared over by salt. . . . On TV continued communist propaganda. All phases of life—schools, recreation, social services, ballet. The scenes so beautiful on screen so grey in reality. Baseball seems an obsession. . . . We look forward to escape back to the Yucatan next Monday. We are calling Progreso home. Home compared to Havana. The endless futility of life here almost palpable. . . . This desperate country without hope. We came here with trepidation, stayed in apprehension, will leave in sadness for the people.

March 11 Saturday [continued]

Full sun at last. Would that these saline-smeared windows would open and I could photograph the bay where about once an hour a ship enters and slowly draws into harbor out of my sight. . . . I walked a distance to a park where a rounded black monument honored Chinese who fought and died as statue reads, to give Cuba its freedom in 1931. I sat long observing Havana folk go about their daily to-and-fro. A city without joy. A city without hope illustrated by passersby more wandering than going somewhere. . . . (So much I am "thinking" and not writing!) . . .

March 12 (Sunday)

This is the day we liberate Cuba—of our presence. John's apprehension has been great, and growing. I've had not a moment of unease. . . . The sun is shining, the trade winds are blowing.

This revealing diary of his last trip to Central America shows that he heard, saw, and smelled his surroundings. He met and talked with people on the street or at cafés and described some as he would characters in his writings. Still noted oddities, such as the doll of Mary in the church, and changes since his earlier visits. He appreciated the improvements, but they diluted the mystery of the place. His entries about Yucatán were not as full as those about Cuba. Even when the sun was shining, Havana seemed joyless to him; life there emitted futility. He wanted a clearer view through his hotel window and a more complete understanding of the place. In spite of their luxury hotel and the opportunity for adventure, Still longed for a return to his second home, Progreso—a place that he knew. As the March 6 entry states, making so many trips shifted "the burden of civilization" off his shoulders. Going to Central America was for Still an opportunity to delve into the mystery of the past and to escape the civilization, the culture, the "clerkdom" of his everyday existence. He did not have the same feeling or motivation when visiting Europe.

Traveling to Europe allowed Still to immerse himself in the recent history of Western culture. There he explored people and events he had encountered in books. He attended plays, visited the homes of writers, strolled through British gardens, walked over battlefields and cemeteries.[21] In Central America he was a "gringo" but otherwise an unknown person. During one trip to Rome he was an invited guest with modest celebrity status, an American writer from Appalachia. In all of his five trips to Europe and Britain, one or more friends accompanied him: Miller, Judi Jennings, Randy Wilson, or his British friend George Alexander.

The first trip occurred in August 1986. He and Miller flew Icelandic Air out of Chicago on Sunday, August 10. They spent a day in Luxembourg; one in Verdun, France; one in Trier, Germany. They visited the Diekirch War Museum and the Natzweiler-Struthof concentration camp; went to Bastogne, then Belgium, and finally to the Maginot Line in Lorraine. After a full week, they headed back and stopped in Iceland.[22] When introducing an article about Still for the *Vanderbilt Magazine,* Miller described their adventure as "skylarking" across Europe in a rented car, visiting battlefields, cemeteries, museums, and other public attractions. To their surprise they loved Iceland and spent four days there instead of one as planned. Miller called Still a wonderful traveling companion, adding his age "doesn't hold him back."[23]

On these trips to Europe, Still was in his eighties but Miller was not yet fifty. Jennings was still in her thirties. No doubt, Still could be a demanding travel companion. He was largely dependent while wanting everyone to believe that he was completely independent. He was sometimes pouty, and he always expected to set the pace at museums and public sites. An exchange of letters after their return shows that Miller was meticulous about ensuring that the expenses were shared. Still was always willing to put charges on his credit card, but he never paid the way of his guide or friend. So there had to be a reckoning when they returned home.

In the late 1980s Jennings traveled to England, Italy, and France with Still. They had met when Still became a member of the Kentucky Humanities Council, where Jennings began working in 1981. Before that she had lived in England for a year, so that was the destination of their first trip. She was fonder of the country than Still was, but as Jennings points out, they showed each other new things. For example, she took him places he wanted to go and would not have gone without her. He gave her an appreciation for World War I battlefields—one of his many passions, but until their trips a topic of little concern to her. He also taught her patience and how to coexist with an ornery man and maybe, in a small way, how to assert herself. She taught him how to interact even when he did not want to, how to go along "for the ride," and how to apologize. A few anecdotes show some of what they did and what they learned.

Jennings and Still joined Anne Campbell Ritchie and her husband, Don, to attend the 1987 International Oral History Conference at St. John's College in Oxford.[24] After the conference, Still told Jennings that he wanted to visit the home of one of his favorite writers, Richard Jefferies, which he thought was in Swindon. She knew the place to be a medium-sized railroad town, not far from Oxford. One Sunday morning they drove there. Jennings recounts their adventure:

> Mr. Still said Richard Jefferies lived on a farm, perhaps one of the very farms we were driving past just then. I was concentrating on staying in the left lane. I wondered how we would know Richard Jefferies' farm if we did drive right past it.
>
> When we got to Swindon, I went to the city centre to look for an information office. It was closed. We drove around Swindon for awhile on the off chance that we might just stumble upon Richard Jefferies' house. We didn't. I enquired in two petrol stations and one grocery store. No one I asked had ever heard of Richard Jefferies. . . .
>
> I found a city park and stopped. I suggested that Mr. Still wait for me while I looked for lunch and directions to the Richard Jefferies house. Since it was Sunday morning, few food places were open. I finally found a family-owned shop and brought some sandwiches. They had never heard of Richard Jefferies.
>
> When I returned to the park, Mr. Still was nowhere to be found. I walked round and round the park and finally spotted Mr. Still on a side street. He was sitting in a yard next to a severely disabled young man in a wheelchair. Mr. Still

was admiring two cats the young man had with him in his wheelchair.

I gave Mr. Still his lunch and told him I couldn't find anyone who knew anything about Richard Jefferies. Mr. Still wondered how I could have a Ph.D. in British History and have never heard of Richard Jefferies. We ate our sandwiches and left Swindon.[25]

Still rarely lost interest in a topic. Several years later he was again traveling with Jennings. This time they were driving from Yorkshire to Devon when Still asked if they could again go to Swindon and look for the Jefferies house. Always accommodating, Jennings agreed but made sure they would get there when the town's visitors center was open. They told her the house was near town at a round-about on a busy road. Jennings described their success this way: "Circling a busy British round-about is not the best way for an American driver to look for a tourist spot. I went round once, twice, three times. Neither Mr. Still nor I saw anything that looked remotely like the Richard Jefferies house. Finally, in desperation, I pulled the car off the road. I began to walk around the circular road. Sure enough. A small sign on a nondescript gate read: 'Entrance to Coate Farm, home of Richard Jefferies.'"[26]

On another trip, Still and Jennings were traveling with Still's friend Alexander.[27] Being an avid student of World War I military history, Still wanted to visit the battlefields at Verdun. The three of them took the ferry from Dover to Calais and then drove east past villages and fields until they began to see cemeteries. Still had them stop at each one so he could look around and sign the visitors book. At Verdun, Alexander and Still explored the bunkers and trenches while Jennings wandered through the woods and found the site of a charming village, which "had been pounded into oblivion." Before they left, Still asked to drive around the battlefield area and soon wanted to get out of the car and explore a site where he thought some maneuvers had taken place. Meanwhile, Jennings walked around, wondering what the place would have been like sixty years before. After fifteen minutes she returned to where she had left Still but found only Alexander looking around in bewilderment. "He was here five minutes ago, and now I can't find him," he said. "Where could he have gone?"

George and I searched the battlefield site for nearly two hours. I kept running back to the car thinking that Mr. Still might be waiting for us there. Finally, near 6:00 o'clock, as the dusk was gathering, I saw Mr. Still walking toward us.

Mr. Still explained completely unapologetically that he had found a foxhole and had crawled into it to see what it would feel like to have been a soldier. He lay down in the foxhole and stared up at the summer sky thinking about all the history he had read about the battles at Verdun. And then he fell asleep for nearly two hours. Refreshed after his nap, he asked me if it wasn't time for us to be looking for some place to eat dinner.[28]

Jennings was Still's patient and accommodating saint. She always seemed to follow the British motto "Keep Calm and Carry On."

Early in their travels she learned that his orneriness would temper itself, given time. Their first trip driving through the English countryside toward Devon gives an example:

It was spectacular country, which I was very wedded to. And I said things like "Oh, look over there. See that? Oh my." When he didn't respond, I said "You're not really saying anything. Do you not like the scenery?" He responded, "Yes, I like it, but if I was going to talk about it I would have a descriptive phrase and not an exclamation."

I was mad. He knew I was mad but he didn't apologize until hours later. He was dozing and he looked angelic, and I got over it.

We are driving when he wakes up. Dorsett has cows and some of them are laying down. I said "I guess it's gonna rain because my grandfather always said when the cows are laying down it's gonna rain." And he said, "Oh, I never heard that before. That's really good. I'm gonna put that in my notebook."

I took that as an apology.[29]

The last time Still traveled with Jennings was in 1989 when they went to Rome. This trip illustrates Still's appreciation for travel companions who cared about and assisted him. The specific problem Still had was crossing the busy streets of the city. As Jennings tells it: "[He] would stand on the curb, waiting for the cars to stop. The cars never do stop in Rome. After a few days, I got so I would take his arm, and the two of us would wade out into the traffic. I was pretty sure the cars wouldn't hit an older man like him." Later, Still sent Jennings yellow roses with a note saying that he "never would have gotten across the streets without [her]."[30]

The excursion to Rome was the final trip Jennings made with Still, but the first for Wilson, who had met Still in 1985 at the Settlement School. The young man had read Still's work and found it moving and real, especially Sim Mobberly's sermon in *River of Earth*. Wilson described himself as shy around Still, but Still noticed him, as he did many of the children and staff members. Wilson was working on a funny rendition of Appalachian ballad collector Bascom Lamar Lunsford and practiced in the cafeteria. Still asked if he would be willing to dramatize a section from *River of Earth*. They began collaborating, with Wilson choosing the music and the instrumentation and Still choosing the readings. Their joint performance, which became a hallmark of Still's later career, was originally put together for the trip to Rome where Alessandro Portelli, festival organizer, had invited Still to speak at the 1989 Appalachian Festival.[31]

Still was one of a group that Portelli had arranged. Writers Jo Carson and Gurney Norman were also on the program. They appeared at two venues: the University of Rome and the Center for American Studies. The audience was made up primarily of Portelli's American studies class and some faculty involved with the "Appalachian Project." Still and Wilson began with the sermon in *River of Earth*, then transitioned into other poems and musical selections. They were a great success, even though the audience did not understand everything they heard. They seemed especially baffled by the connection between the spiritual music and the social issues. Wilson later recalled the performance: "We went into a very old building. One of the landmarks of the Renaissance. . . . We were nervous. I asked the master of ceremonies to warn the audience that I would be shouting. He was nervous too and forgot to say anything. So I just went on and did the show as we had practiced it. They didn't understand the words even though their English was good."[32]

Still's memory of the event was entwined with its venue, a Roman villa where Henry James had once lived. The entire Rome trip was connected to experiences in special places. Jennings recalled, for example, one crystal clear, January day when the three of them went to the Uffizi Gallery in Florence. It was beautiful outside but too cold—a good day to walk through the gallery or sit in the café and look out the windows. Still sat a while then walked a while. He did not share his thoughts; he just took everything in. It was one of the shining moments in Still's travels with Jennings.[33] Still and Wilson had shared their place in eastern Kentucky with the Italian audience; in turn, they were learning about Rome and Italians by being in their place and experiencing their history. Still recorded his reactions to the Rome trip in a letter to Miller after arriving back in Hindman:

> The Roman experience was too unexpected, hurried, disorganized for early appraisal. The dust will have to settle a bit. . . . Rome is a city of sights: Vatican, Circus Maximus, etc. The traffic unbelievable. At colosseum [*sic*] a trinket salesman, when you decline to buy always says, "May your piss be yellow." A compliment, I'm told. We were entertained all-to-pieces. Sometimes, away from the ruins, I thought I was in Brooklyn. Visited the room where Keats died, beside the Spanish steps, and later to his grave in the protestant cemetery; to the grave of Shelly also—the only peaceful spot in that frenetic city called Eternal. Photos taken will view me embracing some great men (statues) as Moses. To the Vatican twice. What an enterprise! What evidence of entrenched wealth. In a Vatican restroom there was this piece of graffiti: "If the Vatican is so holy, why are there so many homeless sleeping on the streets of Rome?"[34]

Still did not return to Rome the next summer as Portelli had thought he would. Portelli was unsuccessful in having *River of Earth* translated into Italian. But Still had made an impression on the University of Rome. Professor Agostino Lombardo, the head of the department and founder of American studies in Italy, thought the book was a masterpiece.[35] The Italian audience found Still and Wilson's performance memorable, even if not understandable. In later years Still rarely talked about his European travels. As with his travels to Central America, he did not write stories or poems about them. He simply took in the experiences. At the age of eighty, Still was as curious about the world as was the young narrator and the odd man, Walking John Gay, in *River of Earth;* both wanted to traipse to "the scrag end of creation." They wanted to see it all before they came back home.

25

Jolly and Godey

People with rough corners and scratchy surfaces ultimately are the most interesting, and enduring.

—James Still to Jim Wayne Miller

During his travels, Still depended on companionship. His needs increased as he aged, but he kept on going, enlarging his horizons. His friend Perrin once commented that most people age by shrinking into smaller and smaller pieces, but Still, as he approached eighty, was expanding and transforming.[1] One impetus for personal change was Shirley Williams's *Courier-Journal* article that accompanied the reissue of *River of Earth*. Still jokingly complained that he got five proposals of marriage out of it: "You'd think if they saw that I had been a bachelor for 72 years, they would know it was hopeless." On a more serious note, he believed the article spearheaded a renewal of interest in his work.[2]

The article, however, was not entirely flattering. Williams captured the anomaly of the man. She noted his reputation for shyness but quickly pointed out that he loved to talk. He was, she noted, slightly overweight and a little bald; his eyes were filled with mischief. When he could not change an unpleasant circumstance, he simply dismissed it. But he could hold a grudge and be contradictory, sometimes on purpose. She included an observation made by Loyal Jones: "If Still thinks you've got his number, he will deliberately do something to convince you that you're wrong."

Williams never claimed to have Still's "number," but her article did a good job of catching his spirit. Another article of that time was perhaps less successful and certainly more frustrating to the interviewer, Jerry Williamson. Williamson had founded *The Appalachian Journal* in 1972; five years later the journal began publishing a series of interviews of the region's writers. The Still interview was the second in the series but the first that Williamson himself conducted. Early in July 1978 Cadle told him that Still was in Asheville and would like to meet him. Happy to have the chance, Williamson quickly did some reading to prepare. Years later, he recounted the interview experience:

> The first question I asked [Still] was about politics. He just bowed up like a puff toad at me. I mean, it just offended him to no end, what I had asked him. I never could figure out what I had said. Then it got worse. I said, "In nineteen so-and-so, somebody wrote about *River of Earth,* that it was such-and-such." And he said, "I don't believe anybody ever said any such of a thing." He was just antagonistic like that from the beginning. It was worse than pulling impacted wisdom teeth.[3]

Feeling discouraged, Williamson transcribed the "damn thing" and sent it to Still, who called him at home the next week. Still began, "I guess you noticed that the interview didn't go very well." When Williamson agreed, Still offered to "touch it up a little bit." Williamson agreed to that, too. What Still sent back to him three months later was, in Williamson's words, "a complete fabrication from the ground up. He kept most of my original questions and composed answers for himself that skillfully parried my thrusts and created this *persona* which was not at all the man I had sat down with in the library [on July 12, 1978] in Asheville. He's a very clever guy . . . manipulative in a wonderful way."[4]

Williamson responded graciously to the revision, complimenting Still for transforming the manuscript into a worthy document. Still's last request had been that they remove a sentence mentioning "the solid gold liar's license" because it might jeopardize all his statements.[5] Williamson strongly resisted, saying that it would not put everything in doubt, but even if it did, Still should appreciate that effect. Williamson had sensed the "Uncle Jolly" part of Still throughout their exchange. The "liar's license" comment did appear in the published interview. To give context: Still was responding to a question about the boy narrator in *River of Earth* and maintaining that he did not choose him. The boy "grabbed the reins from the start. If this is not the way it happened, it is nevertheless the way I want to tell it. (I should have warned you in the beginning that I am the possessor of a solid gold liar's license. I won it—The Rush Strong Medal—as a college senior for an essay whose assigned subject was 'The Value of Truth.' Uncle Jolly is at work here.)"[6] Still had irritated yet fascinated Williamson, and he wanted to discover the personal qualities that could elicit such conflicting reactions. Maybe Uncle Jolly was at work.

In *River of Earth,* Uncle Jolly is a lovable, exasperating character, always playing tricks on the Baldridge children. Jolly has a deceptive nature; for example, he was released early from jail because he heroically put out a fire that he later reveals he himself had set. Jolly is devilish but joyful, a likable troublemaker whose actions are never mean. His free spirit and touch of wildness connect him to the earth. Jolly's serious side emerges at the end of the novel in his conversation with the boy's father, who is preparing to move his family in search of work in the coal mines. Jolly invites Brack to come live with him; he plans to settle down, have a place, and raise a family. Jolly's commitment to the future is a continuation of the past way of life; he is a simple farmer who will succeed through his wit, experience, and good humor.

Toward the end of the interview, Williamson asked Still if Jolly was the center for the novel. Not wanting to be pinned down, Still responded, "A major character, not the center." Jolly is "free of the petty concerns that control the others. He has a solid base, a home. He'll live there to the day of his death. . . . Nobody can hem up Uncle Jolly because he never gets himself into a corner. His life has a roundness, a wholeness. He's one of the rare people who can't cry for laughing."[7] That description also applies to Still: he had a solid base and a home; he was whole and resisted change; he never wanted to be hemmed in; and he appreciated a good trick, especially one he pulled. Still rarely laughed out loud, but he enjoyed hearing others laugh, particularly at something he had said or done.

Still did not fashion his fictional characters around his own personality, but they shared traits—they are kinfolk. If Jolly is jolly and steady, what about Still's younger but less kind character, Godey? Perhaps Still was also showing Williamson his troublemaker side, his Godey Spurlock. Godey's best-known story, "Run for the Elbertas," was to accompany the published interview.[8] When asking Still about his memorable characters, Williamson suggested that Godey was the embodiment of an Appalachian folk hero. Still responded that he was not a folk hero but a product of his community and reflected young people in that community. In short, Godey is always cocky, has a clever reply to everything, and is a thorn in everyone's side. It is easy to see the Jolly qualities that are part of Still. It is harder to see Godey in Still, but Williamson was feeling goaded throughout the interview.

Williamson ended their project by saying they should have become acquainted before attempting the interview. "If we are going to dance our dance together, we ought to hear the same music at least."[9] As the years passed Still and Williamson did not "dance" together often. While Williamson was editor (1972–2000), Still published only one poem in the *Appalachian Journal*.[10] Williamson may have harbored some resentment, but their first meeting was educational for both men. The resulting interview also revealed the public persona that Still continued to fashion for himself during the 1980s.

Still did not share Williamson's interest in the politics of the Appalachian region. He was, however, always concerned with changes in the county, and he compared life there with life in other regions he was getting to know through his travels. For example, when Still wrote to Cadle in response to the draft of a biographical sketch, he disagreed with Cadle's description of his place as "the bleak-beautiful, poverty-stricken landscape of a two-mile creek and a few ridges in eastern Kentucky":

> Poverty is here, mental poverty the most grossly noted, but it is difficult to see or note in our Appalachian spring of dogwood, redbud, trillium and the hills struggling to reclaim their primitive vigor. After a winter in Yucatan and Honduras where primitive living is not even thought of as poverty I find it difficult to continue to empathize immediately with neighbors who live on food stamps (I'm in favor of them somewhat) and spend their lives sitting in front of a TV. Where they used to be grubbing sprouts on hillsides this time of year to put in a patch of corn, they are now planting Scott's grass seed in their yards and riding over it weekly with their riding lawnmowers. Troublesome Creek is now a sewer, the willows along it festooned with toilet tissue like a Lindberg parade along Fifth Avenue. A respectable mosquito could not be raised on Dead Mare Branch due to the acid runoff from the strip mines that circle us. The garbage along the roadsides bespeaks the living attitudes, the lives lived. What was here once is not here now. Except in spots.

In a few families. While I agree that poverty often brutalizes, unearned prosperity corrupts.[11]

He blamed mining for the pollution that was altering the country he loved, but he was equally concerned with the change in people's attitudes and priorities. Still was always aware of changes and challenges, but he did not actively confront them head on.

When Williamson asked Still if he had ever done any overtly political writing, Still answered, "Not a whet," then identified himself as a "liberal in the old-fashioned sense." His job was "to report life, not to pass judgment . . . only [wanting] people to have the chance to live the best life possible, to be their own best selves."[12] Still purposefully avoided getting mixed up in local politics, which he described as conflicts of personality, not issues. Nor did he show much concern with national politics. He was an observer, not a participant. Occasionally he wrote letters to politicians, for example, the one he sent Ford criticizing his pardon of Nixon in 1974.[13]

Still's reactions to the Watergate scandal are not recorded, but he had enough curiosity about Nixon to go to an event four years later in Hyden, Kentucky, the seat of Leslie County. The occasion was the dedication of the county's newest building—the Richard M. Nixon Recreation Center. It was Nixon's first public appearance since his resignation. As a result, tiny Hyden (population five hundred) expected to be "put on the map." More than four hundred reporters requested press passes to see and hear Nixon and to witness the public reaction. James Reston was there to cover the occasion for *The New Yorker*.[14] For forty minutes Nixon delivered a general message something like this: millions across this land have not lost faith in America and believe we should be strong and have the kind of leadership that will not fail, and so on. Reston summed up his Hyden experience:

I lounged outside on the sod, listening under booming loud-speakers that were intended to bring the speech to as many as twenty thousand people . . . but reached only about a thousand. I sat next to the eastern-Kentucky poet James Still, who had come over from his home, on Wolfpen Creek in Knott county to the northeast to watch the event. At this point he felt no particular emotions toward Nixon, positive or negative, and in that, I judged, he reflected the general American attitude.

Nixon has probably lost his power to engage the country emotionally on any level.

Reston and Still sympathized with the reporters who had traveled great distances to witness what turned out to be a nonevent. When the speech ended, Still remarked, "I defy you to find one person in this crowd who can repeat one sentence that Nixon uttered." Then he added, "Well, maybe somebody will remember the last one." It was, Reston recalls, "God bless America."

In the weeks following the dedication and his chance meeting with Still, Reston read *River of Earth*. On July 22 he wrote his new friend, "I could not have been in a more perfect mood to appreciate [the book's] riches, after just scratching the surface of your earth and after meeting you, and it has provided me with such pleasure. I envy you for the wealth of your language, the sharpness of the characters, the clarity of your images."[15] Years later, Reston remembered his first impression of Still on that summer day—a man worth remembering, one who made quite a figure in that remote place. Reston thought Still was pleased to be noticed. Though he never said so, Still must have enjoyed being quoted in *The New Yorker*.[16]

An honor that came to Still about this time—one he did talk about—was his induction into Phi Beta Kappa. John Stephenson, dean of Undergraduate Studies at the University of Kentucky, wanted to get Still to campus for an extended stay. Stephenson's neighbor, Linc Fisch, was president of the local chapter of the national honor society. When Fisch asked about bringing a visiting scholar to campus, Stephenson suggested Phi Beta Kappa cosponsor an invitation to Still. On August 21, 1979, Stephenson invited Still to visit the campus, meet with students, and read for the public. The university would cover his expenses and pay an honorarium.[17] Still accepted the invitation, specifying that he would not make speeches but would talk "off-the-cuff" or read for small groups. The details were worked out to everyone's satisfaction.

Anne Campbell, special collections librarian, managed the campus visit, which took place in November. On the last night Still attended a special Phi Beta Kappa event, a potluck supper followed by the induction of new members. After Still read several poems, Fisch began the initiation ceremony. Not expecting to be part of the remaining activities, Still sat quietly in the audience, but he soon became aware that the atmosphere had shifted. It took him a minute to realize that the words were directed toward him—Still was being inducted as the first honorary member of the Phi Beta Kappa chapter. Later, Still told Fisch that it was the finest honor he had ever received and recounted the story of his passing up the opportunity to read the Phi Beta Kappa poem for the Columbia chapter in 1940.[18] One reason Still had not accepted that invitation was his reluctance to speak to large groups of people. In the thirty-eight years between Still's two Phi Beta Kappa invitations, he had changed. He still preferred a small audience and informal venue. However, at the age of seventy-four he was less shy, more outgoing, and increasingly comfortable in a public arena.[19]

Still's circle of friends and list of admirers continued to expand in the 1980s, as did his public appearances and recognitions. At the end of the 1970s he visited Wade Hall's literature class at Bellarmine College in Louisville; he had been the featured writer of the *Kentucky Poetry Review* in the spring of 1978; in 1979 he received an honorary doctorate from the University of Kentucky and was awarded the Marjorie Peabody Waite Award in New York City. In February that same year he taped a conversation with James Farrell that aired on Kentucky Educational Television (KET); in July he spoke at a creative-writing workshop at East Tennessee State University; in August he participated in *Literature in Appalachia,* a series organized by Stokely at the public library of Oak Ridge, Tennessee. Throughout this period, he was on the staff of the Hindman Writers' Workshop every summer. This abbreviated list of awards and appearances reveals how busy and omnipresent Still was as the 1980s began. Sometimes he seemed not to believe it was all happening to him. On June 8, 1979, he wrote Hall, who had congratulated him on the Peabody Waite: "This 'honors-garnering,' as you call it, is a strange thing and I don't think it has anything to do with the man who was yesterday transplanting a row of wild strawberries and planting-in-corn a pint of 800-year-old red beans from plants that came from seed dug up in a New Mexico Indian mound several years ago." Perrin wrote him these words in December: "You've been popping-up in writers' groups all around the state as the *new* James Still. I'm all for it!"[20] At the stage in life when most people are slowing down, Still was ramping up, becoming revitalized.

His 1980s renaissance was revealing the "new" Still for a new decade. Without changing his inner essence, he transformed himself from a private to a public person. For example, he began serving on the Kentucky Humanities Council.[21] He was a member of the Honorable Order of Kentucky Colonels from 1984 to 1988.[22] He spoke at the opening of Appalshop in Whitesburg in 1982. He participated in a salute to Congressman Carl D. Perkins held at Morehead in 1983 and read "Heritage" at Perkins's funeral in August 1984.[23] In turn, he received greater appreciation and more honors. For example, the Andrew Mellon Foundation funded an endowment of $224,000 for faculty members from Appalachian area colleges to pursue research and named the award the James Still Fellowship.[24] The celebration of Still's birthday became a mid-July occasion in Kentucky, especially in Lexington and Hindman. On Still's seventy-sixth birthday, the governor, John Brown, proclaimed July 16, 1982, as "James Still Day." At that celebration, Edward Prichard, a Frankfort attorney known for humor and wisdom, gave an insightful tribute comparing Still to two giant modern poets: "With Pound and Frost, I thought that the person was less than the poet. With Still the person, if possible is greater than the poet. His personality and what it means is bigger than what he has written."[25]

Still's personality was becoming well known. In 1980 *River of Earth* celebrated its fortieth anniversary. Still's reputation was related to his writings, but his works were increasingly tied to the legend he was becoming. Prichard helped perpetuate that legend. Another Kentuckian, Charles House, who visited Still in the summer of 1983, shared his insight into the real Still in a perceptive, witty article that appeared in two small Kentucky newspapers.[26] The "interview" revolved around House's visit to Hindman and a drive to the log house, during which Still was driving, talking, and sometimes singing along with Kenny Rogers. Like Norman years earlier, House had come to interview a writer he would feature in the local paper, but he left with vivid memories of the man. The Still he found was no recluse: "There is nothing obscure or hermit-like, or even legendary, about the man. He is instead, sharply current, easily accessible, and damn near wildly exuberant about the world around him. (And likes his music loud.)" House appropriately titled his article "Hanging around with an unobscure James Still."

A few months later, Still was honored at the annual Emory & Henry three-day literary festival in Virginia.[27] The article describing the festival attributed the revival of Still's work to UPK's publications of *River of Earth* (1978) and the story collection *The Run for the Elbertas* (1980). Those books largely accounted for interest in Still as a writer, but the success of the festival was more directly related to the fact that younger writers and critics from the region were paying attention to his emerging persona.[28]

Beyond the Appalachian region, Still was less well known, but he did appear on a larger stage through an hour-long radio program that aired nationwide on his seventy-fourth birthday. His brief report to his nephew about the program shows Still's pride and tempered excitement: "I took up a third or more [of the hour with] reading and rambling talk. I have a tape of it and I'll bring it along to White Plains early August [for the family reunion]."[29] After that event he became a guest commentator for National Public Radio (NPR). Between 1981 and 1984 he recorded eighteen two-minute spots for NPR. The lead-in described his voice as "Southern without the syrup." But voice was not his only distinguishing feature. During each segment, he told a story or read a poem about his everyday life and surroundings.[30]

Still's public appearances were becoming so numerous that he often sought the privacy of his log house on Dead Mare Branch. But that too was becoming a place of attraction. In 1980 John Stephenson, now director of the Appalachian Center at the University of Kentucky, brought a group from the university to the house.[31] In July twenty-one students from Berea College came to visit and "filled the place to bursting." In 1983 KET did a five-part series ("At Home in Kentucky") on notable homes and the people who lived in them. Still's was featured on November 30.[32] The log house had become an icon. The man, meanwhile, needed a manager; Mullins, director of Hindman Settlement School, assumed the role of Still's unofficial agent and unpaid publicist and, as Perrin called him, Still's "side-kick." By this time, Mullins was in full charge of organizing the summer writers' workshop at Hindman. Still was always a staff member, even though his major contribution was being a presence rather than performing a service. To emphasize the camaraderie of the gathering, Mullins bragged that "James Still would occasionally even help with the dishes just to show that he could do it." By "gentlemen's agreement," Still participated in the workshop in exchange for all that Hindman Settlement School and Mullins did for him.[33]

Still's private experiences were sometimes more notable and less explainable than his public appearances. An example was his lack of church affiliation. As a child in Alabama, Still had attended two different Baptist churches with his family. When he lived in Knott County, he rarely went to church and never belonged to a particular congregation. Yet, one sanctuary he visited three times in the 1980s was the Abbey of Our Lady of Gethsemani, the monastic home of Thomas Merton, south of Louisville.[34] What he did at the abbey is unknown, but he did not spend time writing. Here is a simple thank-you he sent to Brothers Richard, Paul, and Harold: "I want to express my deep appreciation for your kindness and hospitality at Gethsemani last weekend. And in particular for the solemn privilege of being present at Mass last Sunday. May God will that we meet again. Your dedications have touched my heart."[35] The experience provided Still time for retreat and reflection. Herb E. Smith, a neighbor on Dead Mare Branch, once described Still as monklike. "How many people read at least four hours every day? . . . He does not live a cloistered life, but he has insights that can only be attained through contemplation." And, Smith added, his writings evoke revelations.[36]

Still wrote a poem after he hit a fox while driving one night in December 1982. The incident bothered him, and when something bothered him, he wrote about it to find relief. The result was "Death of a Fox."

> Last night I ran a fox over.
> A sudden brilliant flash of gold,
> A setting sun of gilded fur
> Appeared in my car's beam,
> And then the fatal thump.
>
> I asked the fox to forgive me.
> He spat as he died.
> I asked God to forgive me.
> I don't believe He will.
> Is there no pardon anywhere?[37]

The poem expresses spiritual questions rather than revelations. It is not the work of a monk but of a man trying to cope with the small tragedies of everyday life. Even so, these are not the sentiments of Uncle Jolly or Godey Spurlock. Still had many sides, a variety of interests and concerns.[38] His need to find respite from his new frenetic lifestyle led him to Gethsemani on occasion, but it also brought out his lifelong habit of reading for hours and writing poetry. One activity of the 1980s provided him the opportunity to blend his private writing life with his emerging public persona—a return to Yaddo, where he could contemplate and write in a pleasant setting.

Still went to Yaddo three years in a row during the 1980s. The first trip, in 1982, was harrowing. He drove himself, something he never did again, and lived to describe the experience in a letter to Temple and Charles Baker:

> Here I am, at Yaddo, despite all odds. It was so far, so much far-
> ther than I had imagined, and it rained all day after I left your
> house [in Ohio], and while the Pennsylvania Turnpike was not
> so crowded as expected, the New Jersey Turnpike and the Gar-
> den State Turnpike [sic] was madness itself. Well, I almost lost
> heart and wished I had the nerve and the guts to turn back. But,
> as you now see, I didn't. As I skirted NY City on the Hudson's
> west bank, I tried my damnedest to stay out of The City, but
> The Big Apple beckoned, every road, every twenty-lane high-
> way, tried to take me across some bridge or other into that great
> cancer of a metropolis, and in my striving I ended up in Hack-
> ensack, New Jersey.[39]

Once he arrived in Saratoga Springs, he spent much of his writing time
constructing entertaining letters. He wrote a tamer but very long one
to his friends at Hindman Settlement School. This excerpt conveys his
routine as well as his impression of the facilities and hospitality:

> I start work in my studio at nine o'clock . . . it's time to jump
> into my most commodious bath tub and soak my sins away,
> and then to repair to the Mansion (the Castle-house), for supper
> in a totally fantastic dining room, at the 18-foot table. . . . And
> off to the Great Hall—and when I say GREAT HALL, brother,
> I mean *Great*. What was a drawing room is now referred to as
> the Cocktail Room. All serious drinking is supposed to be done
> there. . . .
>
> Happy to be in West House. No stairs to climb, for I'm in
> suite number one. Had it once before, winter 1951. Then, as I
> recall I had five beds of choice. Now, dog-gone-it, there are only
> three. I try to make out. Chairs of many nationalities, includ-
> ing 2 rocking chairs. Hasn't occurred to me to sit in one of
> them yet. My bedroom is about the size of my entire house at
> Hindman.[40]

Still tailored this description to his readers, focusing on the large house
and grounds, the signs of wealth and class. The log entries from August
13 to 28, which recorded his 1983 stay at Yaddo, presented a different
experience. There he noted what he was reading (Aleksandr Solzhenit-
syn and Joan Didion), how he was entertaining himself (going to con-
certs and to the races), and whom he was meeting (Sally Bingham and

Jane Mayhall). The August 22 entry was typical: "I invited Sally B., JWM, Jane Mayhall, and Delmore Schwartz's 2nd wife for 'drinks' at the Adelphi. An hour of literary chat." The entries suggest a social calendar of a genial, outgoing man.

His favorite story from Yaddo in 1983 centered on his luck at the racetrack. He was with Miller in Saratoga Springs that year. One day after they went to the races, Still described his winning streak in his log:

> Aug. 17. Colonists turned out *en masse* for the race track—to view "The Yaddo," eighth race on the ticket. I bet on 5 races "To Win,"–won 4 of them. Considered sensational by those who have knowledge of such things. . . .
>
> Aug. 22. Again to races, altogether winning 10 races out of 12.—JWM [Miller] sent dispatches to 4 KY newspapers about my betting record.

If Still's description was understated, Miller's was embellished. Titled "Still still beating the odds," the article in *Troublesome Creek Times* on August 24, 1983, spanned two columns. A shortened version conveys the flavor:

> This year Still attended the 114th running of the Travers, a race first run here back in 1864. Deciding that when in Rome he should do as the Romans do—this once—Still placed a $2 bet in the race. The favorite in the Travers was the winner of the Belmont, but Still had heard that the Travers was "the graveyard of reputations." So he bet on another horse—and won. . . . I went with him to the track again on the following Wednesday, Aug. 17. The program consisted of nine races. We arrived in time for the fifth race, and Still bet $2 to win on horses in the fifth, sixth, seventh, eighth and ninth races—and won in every race except one. . . .
>
> I couldn't believe what I was witnessing. With one exception, each time a race concluded and the winning number appeared on an electronic board in the center of the track, Still held up a ticket with the winning number—and headed for the window to claim his winnings!
>
> But that is not the whole story by any means.
>
> The next day Still returned to the track, again placed $2 bets on five horses, and again won four out of five times.

This performance has not gone unnoticed here, though Saratoga Springs is a city in which the horse is king and where racetrack aficionados abound. Some found Still's feat almost past believing—including an editor of Vanity Fair magazine who is visiting Yaddo. But I was present on both days and can attest to the string of wins. . . .

The highlight of his 1984 season at Yaddo was not his wild success with the horses. It was a small incident that he made into a humorous encounter and enjoyed retelling. A young attendee named Cleopatra Mathis lost an item of clothing in the laundry room and wrote to Still, asking if he had picked it up by mistake. Here is her request typed on Dartmouth College letterhead, dated September 13, 1984:

Dear James Still,

I tried to find you the night before you left Yaddo, but couldn't. Apparently, you did your laundry after I did mine that evening, and could have taken my black leotard, which I had inadvertently left in the dryer. If you do have it, I would really appreciate it if you would mail it to me. It's cotton and therefore hard for me to replace. Thanks for your trouble.
Sincerely
Cleopatra Mathis

His response letter, dated four days later, was clever and slightly off-color.

Dear Cleopatria [sic]:

Ye gods! (Both Greek and Roman.)
Under no circumstances will I consider returning the beautiful leotards I purloined from the Yaddo laundry the night of September 4, 1984. How unconsciousably [sic], ungenerous and inhospitable of you to ask! Finders keepers. They are now thumbtacked spread-eagle to my bedroom wall where the old goat in me can rejoice at first morning light. And at nap time. Bedtime.
Sorry, dear girl. After all of my seventy-eight years it took a pair of black (ah, black) leotards (cotton as you say) to bring

out the larceny and carnality which were in my soul and loins all along.

Truly

Godey Spurlock (Alias James Still)

Still followed with a serious postscript explaining that it was the Mark Twain in him that caused him to jest and suggesting that the missing leotards were probably still in the laundry room with the "orphan socks lying about."[41] The point is that Still did not hesitate to write a bold, playful response to a person he hardly knew. His pseudonym, Godey Spurlock, allowed him to be someone he was not and to say things he would censor from his own conversation. Godey was Still's mischief-maker, his alter ego.

In 1983 Still began a column that appeared now and then in the *Troublesome Creek Times* under the name "Godey Spurlock's Note-book." Most submissions included a few sayings or simple quotes that Still had collected around Knott County. For example:

"When I was sixteen I thought I was in love, but come to find out it was just worms."

"He's got pretty good sense but he acts the fool so much you can't tell it."

Q: "That pistol you're packing, what's it for?"

A: "Hit's for making people like you attend to their own business."

Sometimes the column included quotes from writers or philosophers, such as William Blake's "I must create a System of my own or be enslaved by another man's." Such thinking hardly sounds like authentic Godey. Still was using the column to present ideas he found intriguing. Occasionally, he included a short prose piece or a travel memoir. The August 1986 feature was a report on the experience that he and Miller had in Luxembourg:

Godey Spurlock's Notebook
From Luxembourg
James Still and Jim Wayne Miller

Among the 5,100 Americans buried at the American Mil-itary Cemetery here (soldiers who died in the Battle of the

Bulge in the winter of 1944–45), we counted many Kentuckians. . . .

General George Patton is buried here, with troops who fought under him in the battle of the Bulge. General Patton and his troops are also remembered in a monument to the men of the American 4th Infantry, which stands in front of our hotel here within sight of the Luxembourg airport. The 4th Infantry saved the city of Luxembourg from the invasion of the Germans, and the people of Luxembourg erected this monument in gratitude for their valor. Perhaps because the people of Luxembourg remember well the help they had from America in World War II, they are friendly toward Americans.

At the American Military Cemetery, a sign says: Silence. Respect. Every American should visit the European battlefields where, in two wars in this century, our heroes fought and died. But don't wait until you are 80—as one of us did! (*Troublesome Creek Times* August 20, 1986)

As 1986 approached, and along with it Still's eightieth birthday, Mullins began preparing a celebration that would be remembered. He named a planning committee in the fall of 1985, which by January was inviting a list of impressive speakers.[42] Mullins gave the welcome; Jones moderated. Stephenson spoke first, followed by Hall, then Miller right before lunch. After a large picnic—box lunches for everyone—Norman spoke; then Bill Weinberg read his version of a Godey Spurlock letter to James Still; another break was followed by Dykeman's reading her witty version of "The Pattern of a Man," then, finally, Albert Smith. Last on the program was Still himself, but his remarks were prefaced by Governor Martha Layne Collins's official proclamation that July 16, 1986, was James Still Day in Kentucky. The whole affair lasted from 9:00 a.m. to 4:00 p.m. and was appropriately called "A Master Time."[43]

The day included lots of laughter and plenty of good-humored "roasting" of the man turning eighty. A side benefit was positive advertising for Hindman and the school. The event was an overwhelming success, with four hundred guests attending; newspaper articles followed, including one by Tom Eblen in the Sunday *Atlanta Journal*; and KET produced a video called *A Master's Time*. The sentiment was correct: Mullins had pulled the party together, but the time belonged to the master.

Still's final comments of the afternoon gave the right flavor to the accolades that came before. He sounded unruffled when he delivered his remarks in a calm voice. Still had expected a roasting and had participated in it by quoting from Joe Glaser's article "Slick as a Dogwood Hoe Handle." Glaser had a weakness for "scofflaws and scamps—fellows whose profession and amusement it is to confound the unwary." No one fit this category better than Still, "a supremely artful man who mixes misdirection into everything he does. In his public statements about his work, there is a large element of recreational flimflam . . . [for Still] guile is a prime ingredient of art."[44] Still must have enjoyed piling on himself those delightful insults that contained kernels of truth. He was using his artistic powers to manipulate his own image, and on his eightieth birthday that image was Jolly. When asked how he accounted for his longevity, he said, "People with big ears live longer than most."

Mullins wrote a note to Miller a week after the party, saying, "Mr. Still was very pleased with the entire day. He really hasn't 'come down to earth' yet." The thank-you from Still that the school sent to everyone who attended read simply,

> To express my thanks for the pleasure of your presence at my 80th birthday celebration. Mike Mullins, who "threw the party," joins me in appreciation.
>   Come again—for the 100th. Sincerely, James Still.[45]

The party had fulfilled its stated purpose—to celebrate the long life of a remarkable man and valued writer—but another goal had been to explain the master. Was he Jolly, was he Godey, was he Still? Miller, in his birthday remarks, concluded that opinions differed as to what kind of "fellar" he actually was. People supposed a lot of different things about Still and enjoyed the mystery of the man. Still certainly enjoyed keeping them guessing—perhaps it was the mischief-maker in him.[46]

26

Jim Wayne and Anson

I ride off in all directions at once, on wild horses, without rein
or saddle—looking for someone in the wilderness of the world
who understands my vision, my joys, my losses.

—James Still

During the 1980s James Still's public persona was emerging through
articles and interviews, as well as public appearances. He shared traits
with his own fictional characters Uncle Jolly and Godey Spurlock. His
voice reached a national audience through NPR. This "public" Still was
requiring a good deal of his creative energy. Yet behind the scenes in the
1980s and 1990s was another James Still—a private, searching man.
The quotation that begins this chapter captures his mission—to find a
person who could ground him, someone in the wilderness who could
understand. He did find such a person, his own "Boswell"—Jim Wayne
Miller—who became his right arm, generating articles and introduc-
tions, smoothing the way to publication.[1]

Miller, himself an Appalachian with wide-ranging interests, was a
spokesperson for the role of Appalachian studies and for the region's
literature. His academic affiliation was the German department of
Western Kentucky University, but his passion was the life and writing of Appalachia. From his 1974 essay "A Mirror for Appalachia" to
his 1987 "Anytime the Ground is Uneven," Miller made the case that
looking at a region is compatible with a global view. He claimed that

"regional approaches are lively entrees to many disciplines as well as a valid bridge to the great tradition." They help students see their own circumstances as reflections of the human condition.[2] In a memorial edition of *Appalachian Heritage,* George Brosi described Miller as "an icon in the field of Appalachian Literature—one of its earliest and most ardent supporters." Fred Chappell noted that "if it were not for Miller, the Appal-lit movement might have foundered before it got started."[3] As part of his commitment, Miller promoted Still and his work; he saw Still as a living example of an artist whose vision was both local and universal.

Miller acted as a literary scholar and an agent to help project the image that Still was cultivating. Often he would pass along "the master's" exact words. For example, in his article "Jim Dandy," Miller included quotes from Still to reveal who he was and how he wrote: "I'm a classical humanist. I don't know exactly what that means, but it sounds good." "Never use a word of two syllables until you have exhausted the possibilities for a word of one syllable." "There is simply nothing to match an Appalachian spring. It makes me feel new, reborn, shriven of all my sins. I have a new rototiller. My cup is running over." Miller also included anecdotes related to Still's life in Knott County:

> Once Still was leaving the house when the branch was in flood, and had to cross a footlog with both suitcase and his typewriter, also in its case. A neighbor, seeing the crossing would be precarious, took the typewriter and said: "You go on, I'll bring your wife."
>
> Another time he passed some neighbors who were chopping trees. They asked him to chop one down. Never much of a hand with an ax, Still nevertheless tried. His neighbors laughed at his efforts. They seemed to enjoy themselves so much, Still clowned for them, never striking anywhere near the same place twice. His neighbors roared with laughter.

The article ends with a comment one local resident made to Still: "I've lived here all my life, but until I read your novel, I'd never really seen the place." Miller's point was that when we turn from Still's stories and poems and look back at the world, we "see it as if for the first time." Something similar might be said of Miller. Still had been around for many years, but when people read what Miller said about him, they saw him for the first time. Of course, Miller was not the first to write about

Still, but only Cadle had set his sights on making Still known. Cadle's timing was off; when he was working hardest to promote Still, Still did not want to be promoted, nor was his audience receptive. Miller, on the other hand, discovered Still at a time when he wanted to be found. Plus, Still fit well into Miller's overall plan of writing about the literature and life of Appalachia. Miller enjoyed the mystery of the man and described his literary gifts in a way that was understandable to the general reader, to Appalachian scholars, and to people of the region.

Another part of Miller's success was his personality. He was the kind of friend Still needed—a man who was respectful but not adoring, helpful but not intrusive, intelligent but not erudite, ambitious but not unrealistic. They first met in 1979, and gradually Miller replaced Cadle, who was becoming disenchanted with Still's prickly side. The two men traveled together, visited often, and corresponded regularly. Miller was not only a capable associate but also a friend. He was a good listener, an enthusiastic responder, and generous with his time, in spite of always being busy writing his own poetry, fiction, and scholarly articles. He was perfect for Still.

The more than two hundred letters between Still and Miller that are housed in their respective collections in Lexington and Bowling Green document many of their interactions, beginning with their meeting in 1979 and tapering off in 1993.[4] Their initial exchange occurred after a conversation at Alice Lloyd College. Miller was forty-three years old and Still seventy-three. The two already knew each other because both had taken part in the writers' workshop at Hindman in 1978. The younger man must have been flattered when the well-known writer asked his advice about what poems to read at an upcoming celebration. Miller followed their exchange on October 30, 1979, with a short business-friendly letter in which he confessed that he had not been able to recall all the titles of Still's poems, so he had refreshed his memory later with a look at *Hounds on the Mountain* and could now suggest four. Still handwrote the titles at the bottom of the letter, showing how he valued Miller's opinion.[5] So began their friendship.

By the next year, Still was encouraging Miller to spend more time writing his own stories. Miller responded that he was beginning a novel that would not have progressed as far as it had if Still had not encouraged him. The frequency of their exchanges picked up during the 1980s. Usually they reported on their writing and offered mutual support. Most of the specific help was directed from Miller to Still when Miller began to take on projects related to Still's work. For example, Miller's

January 1982 letter opened with thanks for the inscribed copy of *Jack and the Wonder Beans* before launching into the business at hand, an essay on Still for the *Critical Survey of Poetry*. This letter ended with a rare reference to his own family: "You say I have the 'courage' to do this critical essay. Temerity is the word I would use. When my daughter was younger, I played a game with her: I typed up a bunch of sayings and proverbs, left blanks, and asked her to fill them in. I wrote: _____ rush in where angels fear to tread. In the blank she wrote 'Dads.'"[6]

Courage and temerity were his characteristics. And he never stopped working. Still was one of his many projects, an important one. He could not have realized in the early 1980s how challenging and time consuming it would be to involve himself in Still's world. He respected Still's writing and saw the opportunity to perpetuate Still's legacy. Also, Still inspired him to reach higher for himself. For example, in 1982 he encouraged Miller to apply to Yaddo. The next two seasons Miller and Still were there together. Their first important joint writing-publication project followed from the essay Miller had written for the *Critical Survey of Poetry*. The plan was to publish a complete collection of Still's poetry. The project took different forms over the years and finally appeared as *The Wolfpen Poems*, published by Berea College Press in 1986 just in time for Still's eightieth birthday celebration. Miller did most of the preparation for the edition. Still provided advice and guidance.

The publication story of *The Wolfpen Poems* began fifteen years earlier with a series of letters between Still and Best. Still's renewal of the copyright to *River of Earth* in 1968 followed the publication of Cadle's "Man on Troublesome" in the *Yale Review;* those two events encouraged Still to reconnect with the press that had published his first three books. He sent a small manuscript of poems to Best at Viking to see if the publisher might be interested in reprinting the poems. Best wrote a note thanking Still for the progress report on his writing. He was more interested in a new novel, but he would consider the poems when the manuscript arrived.[7] Still sent it.

On April 9 Best responded that he had passed the poems on to Malcolm Cowley. Their joint decision was simple: this is not the book for you to publish now. Best quoted Cowley: "Still is a serious and engaging poet and I think we should publish another book of his. This one, however, isn't well calculated for the present stage in his career. . . . THE WOLFPEN POEMS is essentially the earlier volume rearranged and not greatly improved. . . . [A collection] would gather some force if it gave us some notion of the destructive changes in the Troublesome Creek country since the strip mines came into it, a subject about which he has strong feelings." [8]

Still answered on May 1. He was respectful and seemed encouraged. Cowley, after all, was fifteen years older than Still and one of the most prolific editors, writers, and critics in the country. Still resubmitted, adding ten more poems. He did not contradict Cowley's statement about destructive changes but did include a response to the suggestion that he write poetry about strip mines, which he believed were a symptom rather than the cause of the region's problems: "Such poems as 'On Redbird Creek,' 'Spring,' 'When the Dulcimers Are Gone,' 'The Trees in the Road,' and 'The Broken Ibis' further suggest the passing of a way of life, of an era. I sensed the canker in the rose in the middle thirties. My area of these mountains was thrown headlong from a pioneer existence into the twentieth century. We did not survive the experience as a social unit. We were already *lost* when the bulldozers arrived." Another letter followed from Best (May 16, 1968) in which he complimented the additional poems but stood by the decision not to publish because even an expanded edition would fail "to give us the kind of possibilities for critical attention and publicity that we need to re-launch you as a writer after so many years."[9]

With that, Still put the poetry project aside. Yet this rejection marked a positive turn in the road. In 1968 he stopped submitting to Viking or any New York publisher and moved toward juvenile and regional publishers: Putnam, Gnomon, Berea College Press, and UPK. Fourteen years passed before Still again submitted his poetry manuscript. It was Miller who assumed the role as editor and agent.

In March 1982 Miller sent Still the draft of his essay for the *Survey of Poetry* and asked about his uncollected poems.[10] Gradually, Miller aroused Still's interest. The persistent attention to detail was a quality that Still lacked but one that was needed in this case. By October 14, Miller wrote that the manuscript was being typed. They had planned it together: Miller would write an introduction, based on the essay he had published in the *Survey;* they would solicit from Robert Francis a short appreciation and from Alexis Rannit a foreword or afterword.[11]

By March 22, 1983, Miller wrote that he had seen Crouch, editor at UPK, and updated him on the status of the poetry collection.[12] When Rannit's essay arrived, Miller planned to send the manuscript to Crouch. Miller had also seen Stephenson and asked him to use his influence with Crouch and Ken Cherry, the director of UPK.[13] By mid-

May, Miller had the whole package together: Rannit's revised essay, Francis's appreciation, Miller's own introduction, and the poems. Off it went to Crouch. The response was not what Miller wanted. On August 10 Crouch wrote to Still with guarded compliments, but the final decision was an echo of what Best had said years earlier: they had decided against accepting the poems for publication because they saw the manuscript as essentially a reprint of *Hounds on the Mountain*.[14]

Crouch suggested other university presses that might be interested, but Miller followed his own instincts. He sent it to Louisiana State University Press because it had published the poetry of Robert Morgan and Fred Chappell. He also followed a lead through Wendell Berry to North Point Press.[15] Berry was captured by the idea and suggested to Miller that Still consider bringing out a collected works. Jack Shoemaker, publisher of North Point Press, would be interested in publishing a collection of short stories first, then later a collection of poems. Miller had reservations because their project was to collect the poems.[16] At the end of 1983 Miller closed a lengthy letter to Still with this resolution: "I have several lines set, each one baited with The Wolfpen Poems, and in January and February I'm going to concentrate on finding the right publisher for these poems. I shall leave no press unqueried."[17] By September 1984 he had heard from Greene that Gnomon would not undertake the project, but he would design the book and serve as a distributor in a copublishing arrangement with either LMU Press or the Appalachian Consortium Press. Financial help could come from the Kentucky Arts Council and the National Endowment for the Arts.[18] A month later Perrin became involved and suggested that a Kentucky institution could serve as fiscal agent. Since Stephenson was president of Berea College, that was a logical choice. Also, Jones was the publisher for Berea College Press at the time.

Miller followed with a memo to Perrin, estimating that one thousand copies could be produced for $5,000. Jonathan Greene would be paid $500 for the design and production. Berea College Press took on the project with help from a range of people and foundations. Miller did not discuss the book again until November 1985, when he reported that Greene would have it produced and ready to distribute by June if he received the final copy by the end of the year.[19] The poetry book, titled *The Wolfpen Poems,* had been a long time in the making but was ready by the eightieth birthday celebration in July 1986. Fifty years earlier, Viking had published Still's first book, *Hounds on the Mountain*. Now, the New York publisher was not interested, nor was UPK. The project came together because of the efforts of a group of people, a small college committed to the mountain culture of eastern Kentucky, two funding agencies in the state, and several friends and supporters, primarily Greene, Perrin, Stephenson, Jones, and Miller.

Still expressed his attitude toward the completed process in his comment to Perrin: "Have seen galleys . . . [and] have recalled Don Marquis' warning: To publish a book of poems is like dropping a butterfly's wing into the Grand Canyon and listening for the echo."[20] Is that Still's way of dismissing the complications of bringing the project to fruition? Or is he simply saying, "Thanks, I hope you don't regret it." In any case, the question remains, how much effort did Still make, and how much came from the people around him? Miller, it seems, had been the key. There was a small echo when a year later *The Wolfpen Poems* was named Book of the Year by an Appalachian Writer.[21]

This is the longest story of a publication effort that paid off, but it is not the only one of Still's books in the 1980s with a story attached. At the beginning of the decade, about the time Miller and Still were becoming friends, Still had aggravated Greene. Miller was not involved, but he knew about their disagreement and saw it as a reason not to try publishing a full collection of Still's works. Getting the necessary permissions would be difficult. After UPK's successful release of *River of Earth,* Still casually mentioned in a letter to Greene that he had signed a contract with UPK to reprint *On Troublesome Creek.* The news surprised Greene, who had fully expected Gnomon to bring out Still's next book after *Pattern of a Man;* he responded with a formal letter that, in turn, drew a rejoinder from Still.[22] The result was a hiatus in their relationship.

Greene wrote Still, objecting to the proposed reprint because so many of the stories had appeared in *Pattern of a Man,* and Still's contract prevented their use elsewhere. A mutual friend, Herb E. Smith, told Greene that Still was angry because of the formality of the letter. Greene claimed that, in his view, a disagreement between friends required a clear statement to set the record straight; he had been intentionally formal in order to be "objective."[23] UPK did look over the Gnomon contract for *Pattern of a Man,* and Crouch determined that Greene was right: there was no way out of its provisions. Instead, UPK would bring out a new collection titled *The Run for the Elbertas.* Still wrote his short, huffy response to Greene on a postcard dated October 30, 1979: "As I have a contract with you which covers the short stories in PATTERN OF A MAN, I would have thought it unnecessary to mention that none of the narratives therein would be included in any book of mine the University Press of Kentucky proposes to publish. Over a period of forty-three years and a matter of nine contracts I have never violated an agreement. A question from you while you were here in late summer would have cleared up any uncertainty."[24]

Still was miffed at Greene's formal letter, but also at his own inability to achieve what he wanted. Such a disagreement could have easily resulted in a permanent schism. Greene, however, refused to be annoyed or to give in. The result was that Still tried to avoid him. One time, for example, Greene was talking to Josephine Richardson in the Cozy Corner bookstore in Whitesburg. Still entered the shop but, seeing Greene there, quickly retreated.[25] Greene never confronted Still about the difficulty; he did not acknowledge that their friendship had ended or had even been tested. Finally, Still let it all pass. And between the origin of the problem in 1979 and the group effort on *The Wolfpen Poems* in 1984, Greene was again "working" for Still. The person who helped bring them back together for the poetry project was Miller.

Still may not have gotten the exact book that he wanted from UPK in 1980, but he did get something of value—a publisher that would stay with him for the rest of his writing life. The bond had begun with *River of Earth* in 1978. This new collection of old stories, *The Run for the Elbertas,* followed in 1980. Nine years later, the press rereleased the two riddle books under one title, *Rusties and Riddles & Gee-Haw Whimmy-Diddles* (1989). During the years between, King Library Press published Still's special volume *River of Earth: A Poem and Other Poems* (1982), with a foreword by Kentuckian Edward Prichard.[26] Berea College Press published *The Wolfpen Poems* in 1986. About the time the poetry book was completed, Still became involved with a long-term project that would yield a different type of publication, a folklore collection.

Still had gathered the raw material forty years earlier. The first stage of the project was released in *The Foxfire Magazine* in the fall of 1988, and it was finally released in 1991 as *The Wolfpen Notebooks,* published by UPK. The work began in 1986 when Eliot Wigginton, as a new member of the Settlement School's board of directors, visited Hindman. He was a revolutionary English teacher who had been collaborating with students in northeastern Georgia to produce *The Foxfire Magazine* for twenty years.[27] While at Hindman, Wigginton gave Still a copy of his autobiography, *Once a Shining Moment,* and talked with him about Still's collection of folk material that he had jotted in notebooks over the years. On April 7, 1986, Still wrote the news of Wigginton's visit to Miller, but neither man had time to think about another venture since they were planning the eightieth birthday and would follow that celebration with a trip to Europe. Five months later, however, Still was sending Wigginton the materials in installments and referring to them as "The Man in the Bushes."

For *Foxfire,* the project involved the folklore but also a student interview of Still. In mid-October, Still and twelve others from Hindman made a three-day visit to Georgia. Still's follow-up handwritten note thanked the students for an excellent visit and invited them to Kentucky. The project's lead student was high school senior Laura Lee. She responded to Still's note with a typed letter on *Foxfire* stationary, accepting the invitation to Hindman. The second interview took place there on November 23–24, 1986. Eight students came with Wigginton. Lee gave an excellent account of the visit in the published introduction. The students concluded, "There is nothing artificial about Still."[28]

The interview became the first of several extensive autobiographical statements from Still, a mixture of facts about his life and words of wisdom from his experience. Still himself spent time refashioning this one to present the correct image, but he started with the text the students sent to him. He remarked to Miller in a letter dated April 24, 1987, that the transcript from Wigginton "looked thin—lacked substance." He set about to give the piece his stamp, his personality. The result is more essay than interview. Still also reshaped the text for the notebook or folklore section. He kept adding material. Finally, the manuscript was in a form that they could send to publishers by the end of July 1987.

In a letter dated July 23, Still informed Miller that three publishers had shown interest. The two he preferred were UNC Press and UPK. On that same day David Perry, editor at UNC, wrote to Wigginton with a response that was less than positive, but the press was willing to work with Wigginton and Still. Still responded to Perry that his conditions were acceptable, implying that he would sign a contract with UNC.[29] Four days later, Wigginton received word from Cherry that UPK would be very happy to have the book and would also be interested in reissuing *Sporty Creek.* To follow up, Cherry and Crouch wanted to meet with Still in Lexington on September 8. This change of plan surprised Miller, who began his response to Still, "I received your letter dated August 26 this morning. The tables have, indeed, turned!" He proceeded to outline the altered arrangement then concluded his letter, "The change to UK doesn't change my essential task."[30]

The plans had been to have the students conduct an interview for *Foxfire* and to have Miller write a biographical introduction for the printed version. There is no evidence that Miller actually met with Crouch and Cherry when they were in Lexington, but Still continued to consult with Miller about material for the introduction. He wrote a long, meditative letter in the early fall. Unlike the newsy, detail-heavy correspondence of recent weeks, this letter was serene and imaginative, a web of loosely connected thoughts. The first two paragraphs and the last convey the tone:

> Butterfly weather though it is a bit too cool for them this early in the morning. My neighbor across the branch is already up and busy with his saw and hammer, despite it being Sunday, despite his having worked in the mines all the other six days of the week, often in water shoe-mouth deep, as he tells me, and in spite of there not being a plank requiring sawing or a nail needing driving in. He must be doing something, creating something just as I might here propped up by pillows, on the poster bed Jethro Amburgey long ago built for me. I find I've created seven pages in a notebook—extraneous matter, hardly any page belonging in subject to any other, pages looking toward books or manuscripts partially written, or only projected to a number I could not possibly complete given my age and biological life span.
>
> The lady who once asked me, "Do you do your own writing?" has lately inquired, "Where do you get your ideas?" Where indeed! From the clouds overhead. For me ideas are hanging from limbs like pears, from fences like gourds. They rise up like birds from any field I glance across. They spring out of minor reports in *The Troublesome Creek Times,* from something said in a country store, something dreamed. Often they come to mind from an experience in childhood, then wondered about, now somewhat understood. . . .
>
> [Five pages later] My neighbor is still hammering and sawing. He has apparently decided on something to build and will not halt until it is accomplished. It is his poem for today.
> Anson

Still wrote that letter on September 27.[31] A more businesslike letter followed on October 2, one in which Still informed Miller that Wigginton had talked with Cherry, who had his own ideas about the introductory material to the manuscript, which would be titled *The Wolfpen Notebooks*. So Miller should "hold everything" until Cherry gave directions. The role that Miller played in the publication from there on is unclear, but he continued to write to Still and write about him. His visits and support did not waver.

The excerpt above gives two clues about other writing projects that were occupying Still at the time. Like the neighbor who simply had to create something with his hammer and saw, Still was compelled to write, and he got his material as well as his inspiration from the life around him. His mention of "something dreamed" refers to his poem "In My Dreaming," which would soon appear in *Kentucky Poetry Review*. A more telling hint was his reference to "an experience in childhood" and his signed name, "Anson."

With help from friends and supporters, Still was once again publishing, but most of what was appearing was old material refashioned. Occasionally a new poem would appear, but what about longer prose projects? According to Smith, Still was writing a novel about revenge that had an enormous number of characters, but Still did not talk about that to anyone else, and nothing came of it. The draft that obsessed him was the Texas story. A collection of material that came to be called the "Texas manuscript" consisted of bits and pieces—full and partial chapters, miscellaneous notes, and research material. From all of this, his undertaking emerged: a story about an Alabama boy going to East Texas with some workers to pick cotton and while there becoming "nearly" adopted by a man named Anson Winters and his lovely wife, Lurie.[32] The thirteen-year-old is small for his age, and the man, a wealthy rancher and farmer, has recently lost his son. He and Lurie have no children of their own, so Anson takes the boy in and gives him attention and affection. Any plans for adopting him are dropped when the couple discover that Lurie is pregnant. The boy returns home to Alabama.

Still's family did have connections with Texas; several of his father's siblings lived there, and possibly he visited them as a child. But it is certain that as a young man, Still made a two-week trip to Texas during the time he took off from LMU.[33] Fifty years later he was refashioning his memory of that trip. The result was pieces of half-written narratives, with which he played for years. The Texas material provides a rare glimpse into how he went about casting a long piece, at least this long piece, something that he had not done since 1940. Still told versions of the story to many of the people he knew. Frequently, he told and retold parts to the same person, pushing the narrative forward each time.[34] Perhaps he was trying it out on his listeners as he was writing, or maybe he was simply using them as a sounding board to search his own memory and create a story. While telling others about the experience, he was conducting extensive research.

One listener helped him with that research. From Fort Worth, Juanita McCulloh was volunteering her efforts with dyslexic children in Kentucky during the summer of 1984. The work brought her to the Hindman Settlement School where, at the evening meal, she met Still, whose attraction to her might have been her Texas address. After returning home, she sent Still a book that would help prod his memory and "set the exact county." What Still had told her made a deep impression. The story, she said, "grips the heart. I hope the material and data are helpful and you will write the beautiful story as you told it to me." Six months later she sent him more material about an area that is bisected by the black lands and prairies. And she recalled his tale as "haunting," "strong," and "vivid."[35]

Still's process for creating the Texas manuscript generated many scraps of paper and full pages—some in longhand, others typed; some containing large sections of what became the final book, others filled with notes and quotes of interest to him; and still others merely listing words and phrases. Direct connections between those pages and the emerging story would be unclear had he not marked each piece "TX" in the upper left corner. Some offer a psychological context for the story, such as the definition of adolescence—"Period of transition from the dependence and immaturity of childhood to the psychological, physical and social maturity of adulthood . . . from 13 to 21 in boys"—followed by fragments of thought. He typed another provocative comment: "Could it have happened this way. It was long ago, and I was thirteen, and since have indulged in fiction as a way of life."

During the time Still was working with the Texas story, Miller was his most trusted friend and correspondent. Many of Still's letters to him were signed, "Anson," "Anson Winters," "AW," or "Anson Winters Chastain," "AWC." Miller knew the allusion because he had seen the Texas material in 1985. It is not clear why Still referred to himself as Anson. If he were remembering something that had really happened to him, he would have associated himself with the young narrator, not the older man. Was his use of the name Anson a private joke, or was Still somehow entering into his own story as the man who wished for a son?

Perhaps he was thinking of himself as the adopted son, now grown old. Whatever his motivation, Still immersed his private self in the character of Anson Winters, the adult male—father figure—of the Texas story.[36] Few people at the time knew of Still's involvement with this identity or even his experimentation with the manuscript.[37]

Miller knew of Still's multiple identities and personality traits. He ended one of his long letters to Still with this comment: "You are the only person I know who is Jim, Jack, Anson and Godey all at the same time!"[38] Much of the magnetism that attracted Miller was the mystery of the man, these many identities. In an undated page of notes labeled "for JWM," Still wrote, "The collection of facts does not add up to a man, considering I metamorphose every seven years like a locust. As for honors and awards, I shed them like a snake its skin every year."[39] Still must have been reacting to a biographical description that someone had written, perhaps Miller himself. Still tried to veil his private self even from those who were closest to him.

In one letter, Still explained to Miller his attitude toward this continual reinvention by applying his comments to Katherine Anne Porter. Miller was writing an article about Porter (née Callie Russell Porter) in which he had quoted Still as saying, "Porter's version of her childhood was *just another one of her inventions*." Still responded, "This [statement] sounds critical on my part—those six words—I am not at all adverse to Callie Russell Porter changing her name to one that pleased her ears and view of herself, or to her 'inventing' a childhood that never was. The greatest reward for being an artist is that if there is something they want with all their heart and cannot have in reality, they may possess it in fantasy. In Porter's case, this was necessary for her happiness, her relating to her world, in the last analysis, her art."[40] This letter, like most others to Miller in the 1980s, was signed, "Anson." A similar sort of fantasy was necessary for Still's happiness and for his art.

Although the height of their friendship, if judged by the volume of their correspondence, occurred between 1985 and 1987, "Anson" and Jim Wayne continued to correspond until 1993. The stack of letters provides a record of the last decade of Still's active life and reveals a complex connection between the two. It also shows how attentive and helpful Miller was in matters unrelated to scholarship or publication. For example, he nominated Still for a senior fellowship for literature from the National Endowment for the Humanities. He arranged for Still to visit the Stokely Institute at the University of Tennessee at Knoxville and took care of all arrangements. He sent Still small, thoughtful packages, such as new file folders and small bottles of rosewater to give as gifts. When they returned from their visit to the Yucatán in February 1986, he sent photos and a menu from their favorite restaurant.[41] After their trip to Europe in the summer of 1986, Miller meticulously accounted for their individual expenses.

One important gift Miller gave his friend was the knowledge that Still was quoted in *Webster's Third New International Dictionary*: "The 6th meaning of mort runs: 'a great quantity or number, a great deal.–Had a mort of things to be thankful for—Ellen Glasgow.–After the mort of trouble I took.—James Still.' Did you know you were in there?"[42] Still had not known, but he became very proud of the fact and repeated it often, without crediting Miller with the discovery. Another special service that Miller offered was help with the repair of Still's electric typewriters, his essential writing tool.[43] One time he even took measurements for a windowpane that was out in the log house and brought the materials needed to repair it all the way from Bowling Green.

As Still grew older, he became more needy. Miller was occasionally frustrated with the amount of time he had to spend accomplishing tasks that were unrelated to his goals. For example, he made handwritten notes about one visit to Still in June 1994. He showed up in Hindman with the intent of taking Still to the house on Dead Mare Branch to tape an interview. Still took half an hour to get everything ready to go. When they arrived, starting up the air conditioner blew a fuse. So they drove to the shopping center to get a new one, but while Miller was in one store, Still disappeared into another and could not be found. After finally taping one side of one tape, Still went to take a nap. For a hardworking man like Miller, such a relaxed attitude had to be exasperating.[44] Yet they continued cooperating even when their time together was less productive.

The parallels between Still and Miller in real life and Anson and the narrator in the Texas story are suggestive; like the young boy who is under the spell of Anson Winters, Miller was attentive and open to the experience offered by the older man. But he was not obedient, not to be controlled or adopted. He had a life of his own. Still was a large part of Miller's professional commitment and a close friend, but when the man began to "own" him, Miller gently and gradually backed away. By 1994 Miller was less involved in Still's life and career. But in 1996—ten years after Still's eightieth birthday, which had been a monumental occasion for both men—Miller spoke at his ninetieth.

His words were profoundly moving to the entire audience because just a short time before, Miller had been diagnosed with cancer. He made a courageous effort to prepare his talk and to be present and deliver it in person. His treatments had led to the loss of hair, but he covered his head with a stylish beret. His voice was quiet, his message was clear—he was devoted and grateful to Still for all that he had created for literature and contributed to Appalachia. He concluded:

> [James Still] is compassionate—to man and beast. Once when he was airing a suit jacket on a bush above his quarters, he forgot the jacket and by the time he returned for it, a bird had begun building her nest in one of the pockets. He would not move the jacket, but instead left it hanging there for the bird to lay her eggs and raise her babies. . . .
>
> James Still is not a scholar or an academic—he was destined to be something more—an original source that scholars and academics go to when they want to understand the politics, the economics, the speech, the social arrangements—in short the culture of the place, Southern Appalachia, that he has written about almost exclusively—and beyond that he is the source for a vision of the human experience, most notably found in *River of Earth,* a vision both particular and concrete and at the same time overarchingly universal. James Still's life and his work blend to make the pattern of the man he is, a pattern no one of us could do wrong by emulating.[45]

A month after Miller delivered this moving tribute at the ninetieth birthday celebration in Hindman, he died at the age of sixty. Still went to Bowling Green for the funeral. His public statement there included heartfelt and true words ending with "There's no one in my life to take his place."

27

At Home in This World

There ain't no sense trying to see afar off . . . it's better to keep your eyeballs on things nigh, and let the rest come according to law and prophecy.

—Brack Baldridge to his son in *River of Earth*

In a 1991 review Miller observed that *The Wolfpen Notebooks* reflected universal experience through "the particulars of local life."[1] In other words, Still kept his "eyeballs on things nigh"—the world around him. Miller had first come to know him as an older writer, a retired professor, a private person. Still changed over the next twenty years, and Miller played a major role in that change. He promoted Still as a standard-bearer for the literature of the entire region, which was gaining attention on a larger stage. Surprisingly, the "man in the bushes" felt at home in this wider world. Still once wrote on a scrap of paper, "Being old has few rewards. Not many; come to think of it, not any."[2] To the contrary, aging brought Still many rewards. In his last decade he was maintaining old friendships and making new ones, appearing at schools and on college campuses, presenting readings, winning literary awards, transferring his papers to library archives, republishing much of his former writing, and fitting himself to the title others were giving him— "Dean of Appalachian Literature."

Still turned eighty-four in 1990, the year *River of Earth* celebrated its fiftieth anniversary. Over that half century, the novel had gone from short-lived success on the national stage, through a period of invisibility, to its stature as a classic in the Appalachian literary canon. Still acknowledged the novel's success in a roundabout way when he posed this question: "Will someone kindly tell me why this low-key, 'hillbilly,' sans sex, violence, and with unlettered characters living an 'ordinary' existence, keeps a-going?"[3] When later asked that same question, he hesitated a moment then said, "Because it's used in schools, it covers a part of the country that nobody has been writing about and gives an idea of the depression in Southeastern Kentucky, and there is no substitute for it, apparently. It's seen to be accurate about that day and time. That's one thing. But then, it was used at Indiana University in folklore. You could read it for, let's say, history of Kentucky. You could read it for literature: Appalachian lit, Southern lit. . . . I personally like to think that it was art."[4] Regardless of the reason, *River of Earth* was thriving. Ted Olson described the book's anniversary party at the University of Kentucky as "one of those literary wingdings attended by virtually 'everybody who was anybody' in Kentucky letters."[5]

Like his masterpiece, Still had had early success, then fell into obscurity, eventually to reemerge and approach celebrity status in the region. The following excerpt from a 1990 letter to Miller reveals Still's attitude toward being in a Fletcher County parade. "Rode in a 1931 Cadillac behind two fire trucks crying havoc. Behind the Cadillac a mile-long reach of high school bands, clowns, American legion, Shriners, etc. etc.—and somewhere among them a U.S. Senator riding in utter anonymity. I'm having my hat bands stretched. Emblazoned on the sides of my conveyance in gold glitter: James Still, Kentucky Author, Grand Marshal. My 14 minutes in the sun."[6] His cheerful sarcasm implies that all this is of no consequence, "no matter," to use his trademark expression. Though he would have lived happily without such recognition, he enjoyed the experiences and enjoyed retelling them. His attitude toward scholarly recognition was more ambivalent. In a letter to Greene dated February 16, 1990, Still commented that the Appalachian Studies Conference to be held in Helen, Georgia, in March was advertising many sessions about writers of the region, but not one was about him or his work. His comment to Greene: "I can only conclude that I'm low on the totem pole amongst the academics. That's OK. But what I don't understand is that I'm happy about it. A curious reversion of normal reactions."[7] His reaction four years later to a Still session at the South Atlantic Modern Language Association (SAMLA) conference held in Baltimore was very different. His work was a major topic of discussion.

He was pleased with the scholarly attention and enjoyed entertaining the large audience with the help of Randy Wilson.

In the 1990s Still was not publishing much "new" fiction, but only the publishers and literary scholars seemed to mind. His admiring public was satisfied with his folk notebooks, the reissue of his stories and poems, the occasional new poem, and his talk of memories of a life now passed. He delivered all that in live readings, lectures, and festival appearances; in videos and recorded interviews; and through autobiographical writing.

Being a well-read and widely traveled elderly man with an excellent memory and sharp wit was enough to make people listen. But why did they love him so much? He could be self-centered and sometimes curmudgeonly. He was known to agree to other's arrangements while following his own schedule. One close friend good-naturedly declared that Still's watch was always set on "Still Standard Time."[8] He was a humorous, surprising man who often displayed a mix of caring and indifference. Some people found him exasperating, yet they listened. For example, Williamson recalled Still's routine for storytelling at Hindman. Still would come late to lunch, make an entrance, then remain at the table as people finished eating and gathered around:

> He liked to hold court. I remember him telling a story for the truth that struck me as a total fiction. But he said that while he was at his cabin one day, his neighbors across the creek, husband and wife, were having this ferocious fight. They came out of their house into the yard. They were screaming and yelling and threatening to kill one another. In the middle of this, a huge limb broke off this oak tree and came crashing down to the ground in between them and stopped the fight. I thought, "that is the most improbable story I have ever heard" . . . But to hear him tell it was an indelible experience.[9]

"Mr. Still," as most people called him, had a habit of holding court.[10] Like Samuel Taylor Coleridge's ancient mariner, Still captivated listeners with his voice. He was a natural-born storyteller who believed one could only "tell the truth through fiction, and, stay alive."[11] In the last decade of his life, Still stayed alive through public appearances. His audiences yearned for that indelible experience. As time went on, he moved from storyteller to entertainer. Still's comic timing, for example, was noteworthy. At a reading in Big Stone Gap, Still sat quietly through the long introduction, which was a glowing tribute to him. When his moment finally arrived, the ninety-two-year-old walked to the podium. Instead of beginning with a nod to the audience and a gracious "thank you" to his hostess, he just stood there looking down. The extended silence was apparent to everyone in the room; soon it became uncomfortable, then alarming. Finally, Still said, "Thought I would give you a minute to lower your expectations."[12]

This was one of Still's last public appearances, and by then he was a master. His showmanship relied on understatement and a genuine "mountain eloquence."[13] His performances outside Hindman had begun about ten years before. Being both wordsmith and music fan, Still had recognized early that his reading would be more effective if accompanied by music. The partner he found came from home—Randy Wilson. In a note to Still's niece, Wilson told how he and Still got together: "One day we were all in line to eat at the Settlement School and I launched into a parody of some preaching I had heard just for fun. Jim said to me, 'I need you to do Brother Sim's sermon in my book.' . . . And we've been taking our dog and pony show around ever since."[14] In addition to musical talent, Wilson's gifts included patience, humor, a calm temperament, and knowledge of the life that Still's work evoked.

Their debut Kentucky performance was in April 1990 at the University of Kentucky's King Library.[15] This fiftieth anniversary celebration of *River of Earth* included remarks by Norman, Mary Bingham, and Miller, all leading up to the Still and Wilson show. Five days later, Still received an invitation from Jennings at Appalshop to come "do their thing" in Whitesburg. The collaboration of Jennings, Wilson, and Still led to the creation of *Heritage*, a cassette tape that introduced Still and his works to a wider audience.[16]

Still's public appearances in the 1990s were numerous and varied. He sometimes performed with Wilson, sometimes alone. He would read from his works or simply talk, and often he carried along a few books and tapes to sign and sell. He visited public schools, college campuses, Elderhostel events, bookstores, book fairs, state fairs, libraries, conferences, dedications, and celebrations. By 1994, when he had become a very busy man, he wrote to a friend that he always distrusted "busy" people—including himself. But then he explained, "I don't rush about. I do everything leisurely, not given much to worrying. While I'm often on platforms and in classrooms it's no hassle as I'm used to it. I speak without notes. When I leave home I'm on vacation."[17] He was not really on vacation, but once at a place, he tended to set his own pace and did not concern himself with the arrangements. Mullins at Hindman Settlement School or the Faculty Scholars Program at the University of Kentucky would make the plans with the host institution and work out an itinerary. When Still arrived, someone on site would be his guide.

Many of these visits were to colleges in Appalachia and were funded by the University of Kentucky Appalachian Center, which Stephenson directed from 1979 to 1984. Stephenson acquired a grant from the Andrew W. Mellon Foundation in 1980 to set up a fellowship program that would support research for visiting faculty members. He named the program for Still because of the writer's attachment to the region and because he wanted to strengthen the university's connection with the man.[18] By 1990 Still's name was associated with unprecedented opportunities for faculty members, particularly those from private colleges in Appalachia. One requirement of the fellowship was spending time on the campus of the University of Kentucky, and since Alice Brown, the director of the Faculty Scholars Program, had the fellows meet Still personally, the word spread through the academic community: Still Fellowships fund research, and James Still is alive and well-worth knowing.

For the first ten years, the Mellon Foundation provided support; in 1989 Mary and Barry Bingham endowed the fellowship. Over a twelve-year period, the Faculty Scholars Program provided research support for 155 fellows from 56 different institutions.[19] Brown remembers fondly one interaction Still had with the 1993 summer fellows when the University of Kentucky media center made a video outside the library. "He was talking about how he liked teaching but knew it was time to quit when he woke up one morning thinking it wasn't fun anymore. He said to them 'What I really needed was a James Still Fellowship so I could get away for a while. But nobody ever offered me a James Still Fellowship.'"[20]

By 1995 Brown had moved to Berea to direct the newly formed Appalachian College Association (ACA), a consortium of thirty-five private four-year liberal-arts institutions in the region. The administration of the Still Fellowships remained at the University of Kentucky, but the ACA was invested in keeping Still connected to the vibrant spirit of the Appalachian studies initiative. A year after Brown began, she acquired a gift from Eleanor Bingham Miller to assist colleges in paying a small honorarium to Still when he visited their campuses. This financial and logistical cooperation helped him become a sought-after writer and speaker. From 1990 through 1996 he appeared on thirty different college campuses, some more than once.

Public and private memories of Still's visits lingered long after he had returned to Hindman. Each visit put him in touch with another institution in the region and ensured that more students would come to know him. His individual hosts got a glimpse into his sometimes quirky habits and always generous heart. In April 1996, for example, he spent a week at Mars Hill College, near Asheville, North Carolina. He usually preferred to stay in a guesthouse or hotel so as not to impose on families. But in this case he stayed with Edwin Cheek and his wife, Pauline, whom he had met three years earlier. Ed reminded him of his good friend Dare Redmond. And their house had a room that he could use as his private suite.[21]

Pauline recalls two minor upsets that began the visit. First, he locked the keys in his car. After having a mechanic open the door, he discovered he had forgotten his suitcase. Ed took him to the local Roses to buy some basic supplies—socks, underwear, pajamas. Finally, they went to campus, where he dined with students in the college cafeteria. His first full day began at ten o'clock when Pauline drove him to the nearby elementary school where he would talk to a fifth-grade class. The school was in a state of minor chaos because the roof was leaking in the classroom where he was to speak. The children were excited, naturally, and the teacher was nervous about having a guest under such circumstances. She herded everyone to a dry room and tried to settle them. The only person who was unperturbed was Still. He calmly got the attention of the children by reading them *Jack and the Wonder Beans,* then followed by having them draw pictures of Jack.

When he was not with students, Still talked to the Cheeks about his travels in Central America and his World War II experiences. The last day of his visit, he lingered; perhaps he was hesitant to get on the road, or maybe he did not want to leave his new friends. Ed Cheek, English professor, and Betty Jolly, history professor, were retiring at the end of the semester, so the college was hosting a reception to honor them. Still was invited to join in, which he gladly did after borrowing a tie from Ed. In spite of knowing only three or four people in the crowded room, he was comfortable. He talked with history professor Tracy Campbell and a former James Still Scholar Noel Kinnamon. He even chatted with the president's wife. She must have told the president that a well-known writer was in the room. When Max Lennon called the crowd together to hear a tribute for the retirees, he introduced Still. He did not know the people; they had not come to hear him; he was thoroughly unprepared; yet when in his slow Southern voice he recited from memory

"Those I Want in Heaven with Me Should There Be Such a Place," the effect was profound—all the characters in the poem and all the people in the room were with him there. When Still finally got on the road to Hindman, Ed and Pauline returned home to discover his gift to them, a miniature rose.

In 1998 the ACA awarded the ninety-two-year-old a check for $10,000, along with a plaque that recognized "his many years of service to the private colleges of central Appalachia as a writer-in-residence and teacher of the future writers of the region."[22] Two days after the celebration, Still wrote Brown, "Blessings on you for your glorious presentation on Wolfpen Creek last Saturday. And the awesome gift bearing a figure never before beheld by me. Forever grateful." Most of all, Still appreciated the opportunity to be involved in the world of students, faculty, and audiences made possible through the program.

Still's attitude and behavior had changed dramatically since his retirement from Morehead. In a 1977 letter to Hall, he had been emphatic: "I don't give readings to general audiences. I don't consider myself an entertainer."[23] Yet two decades later he was reading, lecturing, making front-porch appearances, and holding court in the dining hall. His ability to touch so many different people was one reason patrons were willing to support his outreach. Lines of a poem he wrote in 1997 describe his situation: "Mine is a wide estate . . . I am possessor and possessed."[24] He had a greater sphere of influence than he had ever had; he owned the world, but it also owned him. Though never a slave to his public persona, he directed his attention away from writing and spent more time reconstructing his life from memory. People were interested in that life partly because it embodied the history of the place and served as a reminder of a different, a slower time.[25] Still represented a world that was disappearing.

People who missed his live appearances could listen to tapes or purchase videos. Three video productions in the 1990s were made available through KET: *James Still: Man on Troublesome, Meet Me at the Forks,* and *James Still's* River of Earth. Also, Appalshop released the audiotape *Heritage* and, soon after, produced a radio interview that Wilson did for WMMT in the series "Century of Summers: 100 Years of Childhood Memories in the Mountains." In 1995 Noah Adams interviewed Still on NPR's *All Things Considered*. Most of his writing and much of his speaking at this time was autobiographical. The interview with *Foxfire* students, rewritten as a biographical introduction for *The Wolfpen Notebooks*, set the stage. In 1993 *Contemporary Authors Autobi-*

ography series published an eighteen-page piece written by Still, which became the basis for "A Man Singing," the introduction to his 2001 poetry collection.

While thinking and writing about his life, Still was combing through his large collection of papers, letters, and mementos. He had always been a collector, but in the last years of his life his boxes and trunks full of material became a source of his personal history. As he used the papers to reconstruct moments in his own life, he became more conscious of the future home for the collection. The James Still Room at Morehead was one important repository, but in the 1990s Still began donating papers to the special collections library at the University of Kentucky in Lexington. He would copy individual pieces, occasionally mailing them to interested people or filing them in the office at Hindman. Periodically, he would fill a cardboard box and take it to the library or send it with trusted people going to Lexington. On occasion, Kate Black, the archivist in charge of the collection, would come to Hindman to consult with him. He recognized the value of the materials and ultimately wanted to share them with future researchers.

Was this process of self-reflection and -preservation a natural consequence of his growing old, or was it his deliberate attempt to shape his image for posterity? A quote he jotted on a scrap of paper implies the latter: "When you die others who think they know you will concoct things about you. . . . Better pick up a pen and write it yourself, for you know yourself best."[26] In some cases, he did not actually write the article, but he did supervise the process. One piece about his life, by George Zachry, was titled, "James Still: Biographical Sketch of Native of LaFayette, Alabama and the Chattahoochee Valley." Another was by Hall, who drove Still to Alabama in 1993 then created a short oral biography called *James Still: Portrait of the Artist as a Boy in Alabama.* As Still became more comfortable with his public self, he seemed to enjoy interviews. The one Elisabeth Beattie published in 1996 as part of the Kentucky Oral History Project is more a friendly conversation than a formal interview.[27]

Still liked talking about his own experiences. As he passed ninety, fewer bits of his private life were off-limits, and he was less likely to deny having made a statement or to object to a comment as out-of-context. While showing off his remarkable memory, he could talk for hours about his exploits, supplying people and place-names, sometimes even dates, though accurate chronology rarely concerned him.[28] He had no need for a questioner; he could simply land on a topic and begin the story that transported himself and his listeners. Yet even while talking, he remained aware of his surroundings.

During that same visit to Mars Hill in 1996, Still stayed with my family for several nights. The kitchen is the heart of our farmhouse—the place to cook, eat, visit, and relax. After one evening meal, the grown-ups sat at the table listening to Still tell tales of his days in the army. We were fascinated, not just because Still was talking but because people in our families who had served in World War II rarely talked about their experiences. Our ten-year-old son was more interested in the bowl of homemade ice cream that had been stuck in the freezer after supper than he was in hearing adventure stories from Africa. He kept sneaking to the fridge and on tiptoe reaching his spoon into the bowl. I noticed but thought the worst that could happen was a stomachache. Besides, Still's back was to the fridge, and he was somewhere in Egypt. Finally, when bedtime was the best option for all, he asked, "Where's the ice cream, boy?"[29] Still was the quintessential observer of the world around him even as he was weaving another world with his words.

His powers of observation and storytelling plus his facility with language did not diminish as he aged, but he directed his efforts to being in the real world—past and present—rather than creating new fictional worlds. The decade was a time for consolidation. Between 1990 and just after his death, UPK published five of Still's works, three of which had been published before:

1991   *Wolfpen Notebooks,* a folklife collection
1996   *Jack and the Wonder Beans,* illustrated by Margo Tomes, reprint arranged with Putnam
1998   *Appalachian Mother Goose,* illustrated by Paul Brett Johnson[30]
1999   *Sporty Creek,* reprint arranged with Putnam
2001   *From the Mountain, From the Valley: New and Collected Poems,* edited by Ted Olson

He had unpublished manuscripts in various stages of development—the Texas story was one—but he was not actively working to complete them.

Meanwhile, he continued receiving honors and awards through-out the decade.[31] An important one was the Medallion for Intellectual Excellence Award presented in 1994 at the Singletary Center in Lexington.[32] On April 25, 1995, the governor, Brereton C. Jones, named

Still Poet Laureate of Kentucky. In April 1997 he received the Fellow-ship of Southern Writers' Special Achievement Award, presented by Wendell Berry. Honors were coming from his hometowns as well: in 1997 he was Knott County Citizen of the Year, and July 16, 1999, was declared James Still Day in Lanett, Alabama. It is impossible to say which tributes he valued most—his seven honorary doctorates, a gen-erous donation to Hindman Settlement School made in his honor, a standing ovation at the conclusion of the Lexington Children's Theatre production of *Jack and the Wonder Beans* (February 1997), an invita-tion to a formal dinner at the Kentucky governor's mansion (Novem-ber 1995), or a weekend stay at the estate of wealthy Kentucky socialite Anita Madden (November 1991).[33] All of this was part of being alive in his widening world.

Still's status as a literary personality meant that scholars and writ-ers sought him out as subject or mentor. He talked with graduate stu-dents who wanted to study his life and work; a good example is Rhonda England, who interviewed him for her master's thesis at Morehead in 1984. He appreciated the attention of scholars as well as students. For example, he cooperated with H. R. Stoneback who in 1990 was writ-ing an article on the Southern Agrarians at Vanderbilt. Throughout the 1990s he endorsed his friend Linc Fisch and graduate student Tawny Acker Hogg in their efforts to collect materials for a book, which would serve as both a tribute to the man and an introduction to his writing.[34] Their goal was not unlike the long-term project that Cadle had begun thirty years before. The person who ultimately accomplished that task and put together two collections was Ted Olson.

When a student at the University of Kentucky in 1990, Olson first met Still at the fiftieth anniversary celebration of *River of Earth*. Eight years later he began teaching at Union College, not far from Hindman. One summer he assigned the novel to his Upward Bound students, who, after reading it, wanted to meet the author. Olson phoned Still and invited him to come to campus. He accepted, and that visit initiated a personal friendship and lasting professional connection between the two men.[35] While talking with the class, Still had said that all his writ-ing was in print except for a few poems. The claim interested Olson who, after some research, concluded that a number of poems were unavailable. He approached UPK and found the editors would be inter-ested in another Still publication.

Late in 1999, when Still was ninety-three, Olson wrote him a let-ter suggesting that they work together on a complete collection of his poetry. As Olson told Jeff Biggers for the *Bloomsbury Review,* Still "agreed to the project immediately, and he eventually participated in nearly every phase of the books' production."[36] In April 2000 Olson visited Still and found that the poems were chosen and drafts were ready; together they made editorial decisions quickly and without disagreements. The introductory piece, "A Man Singing to Himself," was a variation of the essay Still had written for the Contemporary Authors Autobiography series. Olson provided the preface, bibliography, and indices. The first page displayed the simple, heartfelt dedication "To my loved ones: Teresa Lynn, Kaila Ann, Jacob Alexander, and Hiram," followed by Still's classic signature. In 2001, a month after Still's death, UPK released *From the Mountain, From the Valley: New and Collected Poems,* a chronologically arranged collection of 123 poems that span sixty-four years. Olson's goal throughout the process had been to create an aesthetic, accurate volume while honoring the requests of Still himself. The process was smooth and satisfying, especially when compared to the complicated publication history of *The Wolfpen Poems,* which simmered for twenty years. This book took only two years. By the end of his life, Still had inadvertently established the reputation and the personality that could make things happen. But the project would not have come to fruition without Olson. Later, Olson edited Still's short stories, but this first collection was special because it was the only one that allowed Olson to collaborate with Still himself.

Still once said to Miller, "In 25 years I'll be a footnote."[37] The prediction shows his concern with approaching obscurity. Still was pleased at the thought that his work might endure. He also began to think of himself as part of a continuum and found satisfaction in connecting with and encouraging younger writers. The Appalachian Writers' Workshop, where Still was a presence more than a teacher, attracted aspiring writers each summer.[38] He freely admitted that he did not know how people learn to write, so he made no pronouncements about how to do it. But he shared aphorisms on what constitutes good writing: "I'm interested in perspiring authors not aspiring authors"; "Every sentence ought to be loaded"; "Life is not logical but fiction has to be"; "A great book is one I can't forget." Even without directly attempting to influence young writers, he made an impact on the next generation.

One person in that group was Wendell Berry. Still first met Berry at the writers' conference at MSC in 1954. Berry was twenty at the time, and Still was approaching fifty. On reading the young man's manuscript, Still realized his gift. No one could instruct him, thought Still, so he did not try. But he did talk with him and pass on practical advice. More than twenty years later, Berry ended a letter to Still, "I have not forgotten your generosity to me many years ago at Morehead. I have always hoped to see you again."[39] In 1965 Berry and Norman had gone to the log house on Dead Mare Branch, but Still was not at home. Thirty years later, the two men returned. This time Still was at home in Hindman, and I was there as well. The visit was too special to linger in the dining hall at the Settlement School. Instead, we drove to his log house on Dead Mare. After we walked over the grounds and settled inside, Still offered refreshments, a clear liquid from an unlabeled quart jar, then began several hours of conversation. His theme was his army days. We listened attentively as the evening moved on, inserting questions or comments now and then. He did most of the talking, but we all participated in the story. The place was filled with words and unspoken memories. It was in that room where fifty-five years earlier the solitary young Still had completed his masterpiece. As darkness settled, we said goodbye, locked the house, and headed for Hindman in separate cars. I was driving Still. He was unusually quiet. Tired, I assumed. Then his surprise comment: "I think I talked too much; I wish I'd listened more."

Their correspondence was infrequent and their meetings rare, but Still and Berry understood and appreciated each other. Still never talked to him about writing talent or secrets to success. Instead, he passed on simple advice: "Writers need to work and to work they need time"—practical guidance that Berry took to heart. Still was especially gratified when Berry presented him the Fellowship of Southern Writers award in 1997, concluding his tribute, "For a long time, James Still has been showing us how precious things are preserved and cultures made."[40] But as Berry noted in his afterword to *Pattern of a Man,* Still's stories were not the work of a collector, researcher, sociologist, folklorist, or anthropologist. They were created by "a surpassing artist." That night on Wolfpen was a small miracle, a moment that further bonded the three Kentucky writers—Still, Norman, and Berry. Still could have talked less, but why should he have? We were there to hear the master.

Another writer of Berry's generation that Still listened to was Lee Smith, who had learned an important lesson about writing from Still. She described that discovery in "The Terrain of the Heart."[41] She began telling stories as soon as she began to talk, but it was not until she read *River of Earth* at Hollins College that she found her setting and subject matter. The novel ends with the family moving to Grundy, Virginia, which happened to be Smith's childhood home. "I read this passage over and over. I simply could not believe that Grundy was in a novel! In print! Published! . . . Never had I been so moved by a book. In fact it didn't seem like a book at all. *River of Earth* was as real to me as the chair I sat on, as the hollers I'd grown up among, as the voices of my kinfolk." Reading that book transformed her storytelling. Knowing Still enriched her life. Smith and Still were lucky to find each other. They became friends in the 1970s when she joined the staff of the Appalachian Writers' Workshop in Hindman. One of their favorite pastimes of the workshop was "running around together," which meant driving over the countryside in Still's car. They enjoyed sipping a little moonshine from paper cups before heading out to his favorite steak restaurant in Hazard.

Though thirty years apart in age, they were friends. He gave her a model of a real writer from her part of the world, and she gave him help and advice. She assisted him with one of his last publications, *Appalachian Mother Goose*. They first sent the manuscript to UPK but were slow to get a response. In the meantime, UNC Press and the University of Tennessee Press rejected it but with kind words to Smith. In June 1997 the Alabama publisher Crane Hill accepted the manuscript. Smith trusted them but was hesitant to take the offer before hearing from Kentucky. On July 8 Cherry responded to her prodding with a yes to this "charming, wise volume." On July 17 she faxed Still and Mullins, saying that they should decide between Kentucky and Crane Hill, then concluded that she had "enjoyed being his 'agent.'"[42] The friendship between Smith and Still was mutually beneficial; Smith provided practical assistance while Still offered inspiration. More importantly, he gave her what he offered a number of younger writers from Appalachia—a model, a guide, and a friend.

Another writer Still met at the Hindman workshop was George Ella Lyon, who first attended in 1980. Her commitment to the annual event is evident in her work as joint editor of the two collections celebrating the writers and the spirit of the workshop. The second volume included an entire section honoring Still as a landmark.[43] Lyon's own memories of Still center around his prophetlike presence and his natural talent for making people feel selected and honored to be there. He had a special way, she remembered, of both keeping his distance and crossing it to connect, sometimes unexpectedly. After one memorable meal, he told her the Texas story, leaving her with the impression that it was the whole truth and that he was sharing it only with her. He frequently encouraged her writing by asking where she was publishing, then making suggestions. His praise was rarely direct and never effusive, but the element of surprise made it memorable. For example, when they were together at the Kentucky book fair in Frankfort, he signed her copy of *The Wolfpen Poems* with this inscription: "—to the best poet in Kentucky."

Lyon, like many writers, never knew quite how to relate to Still, who was already a living legend when she was just beginning. As she planned her workshop class on writing for children, she invited him to come. Naturally, she prepared a long list of thoughtful questions. But the strategy failed because he answered everything with a simple yes or no. When she finally asked, "What would you like to talk about?" off they went into the world he wove with words. His ability to create through voice and sound was what Lyon admired most in his writing. And while he did not teach her how to do it, he showed her it could be done. The mystery of the man, in Lyon's view, was an inspiration to workshop participants. A brief mention of his long-ago sweetheart (Mayme Brown), for example, inspired Lyon's friend Ann Olson to do some research and later publish her findings in "Before Saying Yes."[44] Another sort of inspiration shows in Jan Cook's tribute "Green Peppers and a Straw Hat." Still gave her the courage to write when one August day he came into the dining room with peppers from his garden and sat next to her. Not sure how to break the silence, she finally asked, "Is it the hot kind?" That led to the subject of gardening, a passion they shared. Cook learned from that conversation that revered writers are human beings, like herself.[45] Still did not need to teach, lecture, or respond to manuscripts in order to affect participants at the Appalachian Writers' Workshop. He needed only to be there. Lyon compared Still to a stone worn down to its essence. "When you hold it in your hand, you know this is a piece of the world."[46]

Many people sent Still copies of their poems or writing samples, most of which he ignored or returned with a note that he did not read unpublished manuscripts. But a number of his friends were writers, and some occasionally included in their letters poems, which he did read. One such correspondent was Jane Mayhall, whom he had first met at Yaddo in 1951. They corresponded from the 1950s until the late 1990s.[47] Though born in Louisville, Mayhall spent most of her life in Manhattan with her husband, Leslie Katz. Like Still, Mayhall wrote in a variety of genres. Over the years she sent Still copies of her poems and essays. She had first made contact with Still because Schwartz had told her to read this man who is "a good writer and an unusual person."

Years later, when they were both teaching at Morehead, she went home with him to the log house. Though his lifestyle did not appeal to her, she admired his talent. In 1998 she published a long article in *Shenandoah*, "James Still: Quality of Life, Quality of Art"—a perceptive study of Still's life and writing.[48]

Closer to home, Harry Brown at Eastern Kentucky University (EKU) began a correspondence with Still in 1990.[49] Their attempts to arrange a visit to Richmond became the basis of their friendship. Brown invited Still to do a reading at EKU and to stay at his family farm in nearby Paint Lick. They worked out the visit but not until 1992. In the meantime, Brown and Still shared all sorts of ideas and information, much of it about what they were reading and writing, as well as some poems in process. Brown wrote a long review of *The Wolfpen Notebooks* in 1991 for the *Filson Historical Quarterly* and sent a draft to Still, who responded with thanks for the trouble and a brief report on spending the weekend at Anita Madden's estate. This sort of friendly exchange led Brown to seek Still's help in applying to a writers' colony. By January 1994, Still congratulated him on receiving a residency at the Mary Anderson Center for the Arts in Indiana, then followed with a two-page discussion of books he was reading.[50]

There is no evidence that Still directly influenced the writing of Brown or Mayhall or Lyon, but his interest and support provided inspiration and increased their confidence. That is the type of endorsement that the elderly Still gave most freely. Claude Crum's book *River of Words: James Still's Literary Legacy* (2007) fully explores Still's influence on the next generation of Kentucky and Appalachian writers. A brief look at the relationships he had with several younger writers shows that while he never coddled or groomed, he was available and supportive. Still rarely gave specific advice, but he told one story when he did: a clerk in a Minit Mart asked him for help late one night in London, Kentucky. The man explained, "Jesus has told me to write a book. But I can't spell. And I don't know any grammar." He wanted Still to tell him how to go about writing this book. Still responded something, then forgot about it. Several months later he stopped at the same place and enquired how the book was going. The man cheerfully responded that he had followed Still's advice, which he quoted: "You said 'to hell with the spelling and the grammar. Full speed ahead!'"[51]

Most of Still's hints to writers were less direct but no less powerful. He did not seek out protégés, but he was receptive to promising individuals who approached him. The prose writer Chris Offutt was one. He had grown up in northeastern Kentucky, in the small town of Haldeman. Like Still, he was an avid reader and liked to travel.[52] Along with his initial letter to Still in December 1992 he included a copy of his first book, *Kentucky Straight,* plus acknowledgment of Still's influence on his work. In the description of his childhood home as an extension of the dying towns in eastern Kentucky, Offutt showed his complicated attitude toward the region: "By the time I was growing up, the town was down to a post office and a school. The school is closing next year. The post office is sustained by the amount of money orders it sells to people who have no checking accounts. There's less than 200 people there now." The younger man respected Still's determination to stay in eastern Kentucky because he himself could not.[53] Six months later Offutt wrote again, opening with this tribute: "I've read your work for twenty years. I learned from your writing. You showed me how to make my perceptions of the land come alive through language. Also to focus on characters and place, again through language." The point of this note was to say that he would attend the Appalachian Celebration simply because Still would be there, and "it would be worth it to meet a mentor." Though Still was more than fifty years older than Offutt, they shared much. When they first met in 1993, Offutt did not find a recluse living alone in the wilderness. Instead, he "met a man as conversant about contemporary literature as he was about the surrounding trees; a man who has traveled in twenty-six countries; a man who has received two Guggenheim fellowships and six honorary doctoral degrees." He met a man with whom he was comfortable: "We talked easily and at length, and I left his home that evening in a euphoric state. I had met the master."[54]

Only a few years younger than Offutt is Chris Holbrook. He too was born in Kentucky, in the heart of Still's territory—Soft Shell in Knott County. Perhaps Still knew him as a bagboy at the IGA. Holbrook knew Still as an elderly man in the county. He did not know him as a writer until he took classes with Norman and James Baker Hall at the University of Kentucky. After graduation, Holbrook earned a master of fine arts degree at the University of Iowa. By 1989 he was back teaching at Alice Lloyd College.[55] His correspondence with Still usually concerned arrangements for visits to the college. Holbrook thought of Still as a mentor from home. He appreciated Still's craft and admired his restraint. While teaching *River of Earth* in his Appalachian literature classes, he studied Still's use of narrative language as an enhancement of the characters and setting.

When Crystal Wilkinson interviewed Holbrook in 2009, his comment about writing could have come from Still in 1960. The two were cut from the same mold, except that Holbrook was gentler with his interviewer. Like Still, he tries to reflect accurately what is going on in the world of his stories. Writing for him is a process of discovery, and he dwells on the region in which he is writing. The hills are his playground, and he cares; but he is not political, does not march or carry banners of protest. Like Still, he presents his vision of the region's complexity and beauty. His response to Wilkinson's request for advice to writers echoes Still's own: "Be patient. Learn to recognize what you instinctively know to be right. Keep at it. Try to live a long time." Though not a clone, Holbrook extends the attitudes and style of Still.

Still also connected with young poets. One association was with Maurice Manning, a man sixty years his junior. Manning grew up in Danville but had family roots in eastern Kentucky. As a teenager, he knew a bit about Still's writing and had heard him perform with Wilson at Shakertown. When an undergraduate at Earlham, Manning arranged an independent study on *River of Earth.* His first personal encounter with Still was in October 1991 when Manning was only twenty. Art Jester, book review editor for the *Lexington Herald-Leader,* was covering the third annual Southern Festival of Books in Nashville, where Still was to read. One reason Jester invited the young man was to have someone to accompany Still. For Manning, it was a magical time.[56]

Manning describes many facets of Still over the weekend, beginning with his frown and tremulous voice the morning they picked him up in Lexington. Then there was his animated response to NPR's report on Anita Hill's graphic testimony at the Clarence Thomas hearings; and his surprise reaction when finding he was expected to read at the festival, but he had not brought any of his works. The most special feature for Manning was walking through Nashville with Still and hearing about his life as a graduate student at Vanderbilt sixty years earlier. After a leisurely breakfast on the second day of the festival, Still signed some books and talked with old friends. That evening, he and Manning reconvened for supper. Still was dressed casually in work boots and ball cap. He had obviously decided not to attend the reception for visiting writers. But when they passed the Tennessee Museum of History, where people were gathering, Still paused to think about whether they really should make an appearance. His final decision required a return to the hotel for a change of clothes, definitely worthwhile in the end because Jack Daniel's sponsored the reception.

The next day, the young man's festival experience culminated with Still's reading. Still came into the room, carrying his books in a paper bag. After Jester introduced him, Still read from *The Wolfpen Notebooks* and *The Run for the Elbertas*, mixing in unrehearsed anecdotes and tales. Manning remembered: "His voice was cleared of its morning gruffness, resonating through the room, leaving [the audience] silent and listening. I thought that if we are ever to believe in the literature and poetry born in Kentucky, we must thank this grandfather of a man who has gone before us and cleared a path."[57]

Manning's follow-up letter to Still expressed genuine appreciation: "The weekend left me with many fond memories. . . . I felt comfortable around you, undaunted by your notoriety and accomplishments, and unashamed of my lack of both. It reassured me that one needn't be an ass about making one's ideas public through the written word. I tire of people who are so completely self-involved. Thank you again for your honesty and friendship, and for teaching me." Attached was his poem "My Dog Is Half Coyote" with a note that it reminded him of Still's poetry. In the years that followed, Manning met Still several times for breakfast at the Springs Inn in Lexington and more than once at the house of their mutual friends Molly and Vernon Bundy.[58]

Silas House was a young prose writer who published his first book in 2001. Born in Lily, Kentucky, House had grown up hearing about the "great writer" who lived three counties away, but they did not meet until House attended the workshop at Hindman. He described himself as creeping "about the edges of [Still's] conversation, too in awe to ever have a real exchange." When they finally did talk, young House managed to ask Still for his advice on how to be a better writer. "He didn't answer for a long minute, gazing off at the hills as if ignoring me. But then he spoke, and I realized that he had taken that moment for quiet thought. 'Discover something new every day,' he said." House admitted that those words changed him and his writing. Discovery was more than advice to aspiring writers; it was, according to House, the belief or practice that allowed Still to lead a long and happy life.[59] The urge to be quiet and listen, to observe and learn, to be part of the place around him—all this contributed to his contentment as a human being and his success as a writer.

In old age Still acknowledged to Elisabeth Beattie that he had been happy with his life because he had no unrealistic expectations. Then he added, "There are a lot of good surprises in the world." One was "networking"—"You can hardly go it alone."[60] Still was at home in his world, supported by an extensive network of admirers, helpers, editors, fellow writers, and friends. He was a man who kept his eyes on things nigh, and people kept their eyes on him.

28

Invitation to the Eternal

I knew at last I had achieved something long sought;
. . . an invitation to the eternal.

—From "Dove"

By the mid-1990s, Still had become accustomed to his public life of being noticed and appreciated, and he remained an active writer. Even after the age of ninety, he continued to work with Smith, Olson, and UPK to publish *Appalachian Mother Goose* (1998), *Sporty Creek* (1999), and *From the Mountain, From the Valley* (2001). Yet as time passed he was slowing down and returning to his more private life. He increasingly appreciated attention from people with whom he had a personal connection. Still was especially gratified when an older man from his hometown, George Zachry, began corresponding. Still's letters to Zachry often recounted his frenetic schedule. One described a welcome respite: "Spent the past two weekends on the farm. Alone. Perfect silence. The telephone didn't ring. It's as near to heaven as I'll probably ever get. Picked up walnuts from three trees."[1] In spite of his role as a public figure, Still remained essentially a private man surrounded by a circle of close friends.

With stoic humor, he once said to his friend Molly Bundy, "Every day I get out of bed's a victory."[2] He did have health problems, but they were relatively minor for a man approaching ninety. He had little contact with hospitals until December 1992 when he was scheduled for outpatient prostate surgery in Hazard. The procedure was not complicated, but the flu kept him in the hospital a few days. Miller joked about the news event: "I saw the [*Courier Journal*] notice about your going into the hospital, and thought it must be a slow news day when journalists have nothing better to do than check the hospital records."[3] His next medical challenge was the removal of cataracts in 1993. He went to an ophthalmologist in Louisville and stayed with friends while recovering. In 1995 he burned his hand while on a college visit in Virginia. As the burn was being dressed, he was discovered to have pneumonia, but he chose to drive himself back to Hindman for treatment.[4] Another procedure, the unblocking of a carotid artery, drew his simple response: "The world got brighter." In the fall of 1999 he reported to Zachry that his three broken toes had kept him down. He had stayed in the hospital so long that he had begun "to wonder if out-there was still there." He had problems walking that ultimately made him less active in the last eight months of his life. Though he gradually lost physical vigor, a friend noted that "he never lost his passionate mind and his rage for life."[5]

Being old has its rewards, and people as healthy as Still can afford to joke about them. Still once said to Hall, "If you live long enough, you'll be honored because there's nobody your age left to be honored in the same way."[6] Revisiting his long life brought Still joy as well as sorrow. He had outlived many friends and his generation of family members. He had few people to talk with about times that had been important to him. His contemporaries who had passed away between 1984 and 1987 included Edward F. Prichard Jr., Carl Perkins, Jesse Stuart, Cratis Williams, and Harriette Arnow. Edward Weeks, his editor at *The Atlantic,* died in 1989. His most personal losses were his friend Robert Francis (1987), in Massachusetts, and his closest friend in Knott County, Monroe Amburgey (1988). His college roommate, Dare Redmond, died in 1991.

In the early1990s the Appalachian region lost two major spokesmen, both friends of Still: Don West at the age of eighty-six, and Harry Caudill at the age of sixty-eight. Still read "Heritage" at Caudill's funeral in Whitesburg on December 2, 1990, and jotted this on his program: "Harry Caudill was a great man who lived in our time—here, among us, a neighbor, a friend. A man of courage, historian of note. . . . He will be in our minds and hearts forever."[7] Hindman Settlement School lost a giant of its own when Elizabeth Watts died at the age of 102 in the spring of 1993.[8] April 18, 1995, was a sad day for all of Kentucky when Mary Bingham suddenly died while attending a banquet in her honor. Other losses Still felt deeply included the passing of Al Perrin, Temple Baker, and his close friend and confidant Jim Wayne Miller. Still created "On the Passing of My Good Friend John" when John Stephenson died in December 1994.[9] The poem affirms that losing friends would make it easier for him to "pass beyond." Such sincerity and eloquence was characteristic of Still's response to the death of friends, but humor was the more common response to his own aging. He felt like what a neighbor once called him—"the last possum up the tree."

He was not quite the oldest, as Thomas Clark reminded everyone at Still's ninetieth birthday party by addressing him as "junior." Clark was three years his senior, and the two men shared much: both were children of cotton farmers and had left the South to get their education; both had adopted Kentucky as home and wrote about the place and people throughout their long careers. Clark had met Still when they were young men. In preparing for his study of Kentucky in the 1930s, Clark visited Knott County at the invitation of Anna Moore of Hindman. He spent a weekend there with Moore's family and went to a square dance where he met a young fellow from Alabama who was writing. When he first read *River of Earth,* Clark recognized that Still had captured the place and the people.[10] He appreciated Still's ability to "talk with people in their vernacular. [Still] understood and communicated with them. They understood him. A kind of meeting of souls. He was a man who could go to dances and singings and funeralizings . . . a man who created a seminal book to define that vague and furtive thing called Appalachian personality or psyche."[11]

In spite of shared interests, their friendship did not begin in earnest until the 1980s, when Clark approached Still about serving with him as an advisor to the Kentucky Archives in Frankfort. The men stayed in touch. Fourteen letters from Clark to Still explore their common past, the century of changes in Kentucky, the books they were reading, and their occasional meetings. In 1994 Clark wrote to Still about having read his autobiographical material: "Many times I have thought how well you sounded the emotional and spiritual depths of the time and place where you chose to live. You did it with that magic seminal quality which has given literary permanence to place, way of life, and people caught in the inextricable web of circumstance. You surely must look back from the perspective of ninety years with the kind of inner satisfaction which puts one at peace and harmony with his talents, dreams, and the age in which he has lived."[12]

Being the next-to-oldest man around gave Still license to live how he wanted. He had always been his own master. Yet as he passed ninety he became more selective about public appearances and settled comfortably into his private life, living above the Settlement School in the Lucy Furman house, Oak Ledge. Though his pace was slowing, he continued to enjoy the people around him, especially Teresa Bradley and her family, and his pastimes. At the top of the list was reading anytime and anything he pleased. He typically read four or more hours a day and had eclectic taste, with a preference for nonfiction. Another favorite pastime was gardening. Though he did not keep a large garden in Hindman, he enjoyed growing hot peppers on the Settlement School campus. He often picked one on his way to the dining hall to spice up his food. He started flowers in the box outside the May Stone building and even transplanted some wild violets there that he intended to be on his grave some day.

For TV entertainment, he regularly watched British comedies and the game show *Jeopardy!* and was pleased to know more answers than the contestants. Another enjoyable activity was riding around Knott County in his car, especially when a friend would drive. The road from Hindman to Dead Mare Branch was his well-traveled path. Connected to that satisfaction was owning new cars and paying cash for them. His 1984 Chrysler LeBaron was replaced with a black Taurus 1988, then a Mercury Sable 1993, and finally a Lincoln Town Car 2000. When once asked how he liked his new car, Still responded, "Well, we keep going together, but we're not married yet."[13]

To follow news and events, he depended on the mail. After he stopped driving the short distance from his house to the post office, he patiently waited every day until someone, usually Teresa, brought him his stack of letters. Occasionally he would enter sweepstakes and sometimes won. His most impressive win was the grand prize in the OXY "Shop In Style" sweepstakes: a three-day trip for two to New York City plus $3,000 to buy fashionable clothes on Fifth Avenue. He chose cash instead and received a check for $4,600 on July 26, 1990.[14]

He liked cats, country music—especially Kenny Rogers—and chicken-and-dumplings. He loved trees more than people. He even became the honorary chair of the committee for the yellow poplar to be officially named the state tree of Kentucky by the general assembly in 1993.[15] Most of all, he loved children. Mullins once said that if Still had his way, "there would be only children in this world." A few stole his heart. One was Christopher [Piers] Thompson, a ten-month-old baby he described to Miller as "THE BABY . . . who is wise, self-contained, and only endures his infancy because he must."[16] The young child who finally stole his heart was Teresa and Hiram's boy Jacob Bradley, the child who would become his grandson when he adopted Teresa in 1998.

He also had his share of idiosyncrasies and pet peeves. He routinely boiled his socks, to sterilize them, he claimed, and sometimes would forget them on the stove until someone came with the mail. Neighbors urged him to abandon the practice for their comfort and his safety, but he persisted. Chief among his complaints were tobacco use and coal trucks. Both he saw as dangerous to public health and detrimental to the general well-being. He expressed his attitude about chewing in a letter to sports writer Chuck Culpepper: "We know who won the baseball championship: Atlanta. But who won the spitting contest? The moment a TV camera picked up a player, he spat. . . . If the spectators had indulged in the act of spitting to a like degree, the playing field would have flooded and both teams drowned."[17] Coal trucks that hogged the winding roads in Knott County were, in Still's view, a great threat to public safety, and he frequently reminded his friendly driver to beware.

Still's final years in Hindman were quiet. Though healthy and mentally alert, he became less mobile. He lived alone just above the Settlement School, and the staff members were attentive to his needs. As he had told Tom Eblen of the *Lexington Herald Leader* on his eightieth birthday, "I've lived with families all my life." Families of all sorts—from the Hindman Settlement School community, to his Alabama nieces and nephews, to the Bradley family that he made his own—became even more important to him as he aged.

Although he never lived in Alabama after leaving for college, Still stayed in touch with his family over the years. Only two of his siblings were alive as he approached eighty. His sister Elloree Sharpe resided in Bushnell, Florida, but had a cabin on Sharpe Lake near White Plains, Alabama, where until her death in 1985 she hosted an annual Still family reunion that kept James connected.[18] His brother William Comer, two years younger than Still, was his last sibling to die. Comer's daughter told of the bond and the differences between the brothers. Comer worked at Goodyear for thirty years and was a man adept at telling stories and jokes but with no interest in writing. He rarely spoke of his brother's literary accomplishments, yet he kept all of Still's books in his china cabinet. When Comer became very ill in 1988, Still made the six-hour drive to Akron, Ohio, to visit him. As soon as he returned to Hindman, he heard that Comer had died, so he turned around and went back again.[19] Still wrote to Greene shortly after Comer died, "There were ten of us. I am now the last leaf on the tree, a bare family tree, spinning in the wind, held by the thread of a spider's web."[20]

Barbara Sue Barnes Harris, another niece, reported that Still was shaken at Comer's funeral and kept repeating to her, "Don't leave me." In the summer of 1993 Still made a trip to Gadsden to visit as many of the family as Harris could pull together. His way of replacing his brothers and sisters was to build stronger ties with their children, especially Elloree's son Hervey Sharpe; Comer's oldest daughter, Rosemarie Livings; and Inez's daughter Harris. When the family reunions at Sharpe Lake ended, he invited nieces and nephews to Hindman, especially for his birthday celebrations; frequently they came. They related better to the open personality of the public Still than they had to the shy uncle they had known while growing up.[21]

Another family important to Still was the Amburgeys. The newsletter for the July 1987 Amburgey reunion carried the announcement that Still had been made an honorary Amburgey: "James has been in our midst for many years and is a part of the family. Without his presence, and loving care, the old AMBROSE AMBURGEY log home may well have decayed and be lost to us. His books oft relate tales about our ancestors and the land upon which they lived. For 'us' he has kept the past alive. We owe him so much, love him, and felt we had to tell him he belonged to 'us.'"[22] Still appreciated the honor, but it had little effect on his daily life after he moved from Wolfpen back to Hindman.

For practical purposes, Hindman Settlement School had been Still's extended family for many years. He lived in the school's housing, ate in the common dining room, and had strong friendships there. A very important family for him was that of Mike and Frieda Mullins and their children, Cassie, Nathan, and Brenda. When they moved to Hindman in 1977, Mike and Frieda crossed paths with Still every day and lived in adjacent houses on the hill. Soon after they settled, Still began to visit often, largely to see Cassie, who was a year old. Nathan was born three years later. One day when he was not yet two, Nathan toddled over to Still's back door. He entered, looked around; went into the kitchen, to the bedroom, then back out the door while Still just watched.[23] He loved being around these children and especially enjoyed picking at Cassie, who was not afraid to pick back. Still would tease, "Cassie, you look like you washed your hair in Troublesome Creek this morning." And she would goad him, "Well, at least I have hair."

Still had a special relationship with Frieda, who told a story of their first meeting. Before coming to Hindman, she and Mike had lived at

Alice Lloyd College without a washer and dryer, so she took her clothes to a laundromat in Hindman. On one trip, she saw an old man just sitting, partly watching her while reading a book. Finally, he asked, "You're gonna put that [piece of clothing] in there too?" implying it was a bad idea. She responded, "Yes, I don't want to sit here all day," then introduced herself. "I'm Frieda Mullins. What's your name?" He answered, "Jim Still." When she related the incident that night, Mike said, "That was James Still, the author." Frieda was embarrassed that she was not more reverential but had to smile that, while doing her laundry, she had met the author of *River of Earth*—a book that had "blown her away."

After they became well acquainted, she respected and loved him, but "reverence" was never the point. They were genuine friends for twenty-five years. They were "family." He would talk with her and bring her children small gifts from nature that he picked up on his walks. He liked her cooking and called her chicken and dumplings "nectar of the Gods." He would sometimes invite the whole Mullins family to Wolfpen Creek and cook for them. The last five years of his life, Frieda and Mike invited him to their house for Thanksgiving dinners. An even longer tradition was the Christmas party they hosted every year for the staff. They did not serve alcohol, with one exception: Still would sit in a comfortable chair, sipping his glass of eggnog-with-bourbon.[24]

If the Settlement School functioned like an extended family, Still was the esteemed elder, and, as a sign of respect, was addressed as Mr. Still. Older people in the community were always treated with respect, but according to Mullins, Still had special status; because he was a treasure, he was humored. The Mullins motto became "Even when Mr. Still is wrong he is right." Their personalities would sometimes clash since both were strong-willed men. When he arrived in Hindman, Still had expected to be asked to leave, but Mullins's philosophy was that the school takes care of people who have contributed much. A savvy manager, he quickly realized that Still made an important contribution and eventually admitted that Still's "very presence contributed more to this school than all the others combined."[25] Far from turning Still out, Mullins befriended him. They "clicked," even if both men had, as Mullins admitted, an ornery streak. Neither held a grudge for long. They could disagree, but Mullins was always there when Still needed something. They counted on each other.

Still's eightieth birthday celebration at Hindman was a big to-do. Mike was the principal agent in making it happen. As a thank-you, Still quietly put on his desk a first edition of *Hounds on the Mountain* with a note saying that someday he would write in it. More than two years passed before Still wrote this message: "One fine pretty day Mike Mullins came to the Hindman Settlement School and gave it new life, direction, goals—and honor."[26]

There must have been many times in the last years of Still's life when Mullins worried about Hindman's special charge. Even at the age of ninety-two, Still was driving. His house was on the side of the mountain. A winding half-mile driveway was the only way to reach it. The road just fit the car, so everyone who lived there knew to take great care. In February 1998 Still was going down the drive when, as he told it, the asphalt broke off under the weight of his tires and threw the car over the bank. A big rock stripped the underside of his car but prevented him from barreling down the mountainside. The neighbors heard the noise and came running; then the whole town showed up. It was not the first such incident. He had run off two times before and had to be pulled out.[27] As Mullins would say, "Mr. Still had his moments." This was a big one. Another had to do with the parking lot at the top of the hill. The space was small, and several houses, including Still's, used it. He would park right in the middle of the lot so no other cars could fit. People would not approach Still, but they would complain to Mullins. Whether confronting major concerns or minor headaches, Mike Mullins was Still's go-to man: his advocate, his unofficial agent, his friend.

One lesson Still passed on to him was the value of personal peace. Mullins was a driven man who worked hard and expected much of himself. When he came to his office early every morning, he would look out his window up to Still's bedroom window. Frequently, the light would be on, then would soon go off. Frieda explained this routine: Still would wake up and read in the night. When Mike got to the office at 6:30, it would usually be dark. Still would look out his window and see Mike's light. Feeling safe, he would go back to sleep until ten or eleven. Later in the day he would call Mike so they could exchange their customary greeting, never effusive. Still: "I saw your light on this morning." Mullins: "Yeah, I saw yours on too." Still was keeping an eye on him, and he was keeping an eye on Mr. Still. Even after Still died, Mullins would come to his office and glance up at that hill, looking for the light.[28]

The Hindman family fed him and entertained him, cleaned and maintained his house in town, and helped keep up the log house on Dead Mare. Other supportive members of the Settlement School's staff included Rebecca Ware and Doris Miller in the office, and Jim Phelps, the county's extension officer in charge of the 4-H program.[29] Phelps also lived on the campus and took his meals in the dining hall. Often, the two men would talk at dinner. Likely, Still did most of the talking and Phelps the listening, but the younger man appreciated the older's experience and knowledge and especially appreciated the slower pace of dining that was disappearing with the busy lifestyle invading even a place like Hindman.[30]

The Settlement School's staff member who was most helpful to Still in his last years was Sam Linkous, the program coordinator. Sam and his wife, Peggy, became Still's neighbors on the hill in June 1999. Sam, nicknamed "Sam Houston" by Still, quickly became a close friend. He was a natural-born storyteller who could match Still's own wit. One of his favorite stories about Still recounted their daily phone call on a morning in November 2000 when George W. Bush had been named winner of the close and controversial presidential election. Still reported, "I had a BM this morning. It's a good day for me and a bad day for the country."[31]

Sam would visit Still, drive him places, assist him in many ways. One of their most enjoyable outings was a trip to Dead Mare Branch. On their last visit, Still began to talk about the man who lived here. At first, Linkous thought he was referring to Jethro Amburgey but soon realized the man he meant was himself. Moved by the experience, Linkous wrote "The Man Who Used to Live Here," a poem to preserve the moment. "When that walnut was just a sprig, that was before I left for the war. Used to plant corn in that field over there. Now it's all grown over . . . planted grape vines right there, roses up here. Wild trilliums, wisteria, violets flourished. No road then. Sure was quiet." But Linkous could hear hoeing, and the water bucket being lifted from the well, friends talking, contentment, and sighs. The poem is a lasting tribute to the man, the log house, and their friendship.

Having a house on the Settlement School's property provided Still ready access to people in the town. Bob Young, for example, was his friend for years. Young grew up in Hindman and in high school had "followed Still around like a little pup." He moved away for college but returned in 1975. One day, as he told it, he ran into Still at the Ben Franklin store. They went to Garner's restaurant for a piece of pie, the first of many "meals" they would share. As time passed, Young took a variety of church music jobs in the region, then in the 1980s settled back in Hindman. For a short time, when Still's house was being repaired, the two lived next to each other in the Catherine Pettit building on campus, and they were, in Young's words, almost "inseparable." Eventually, they fell into the habit of sharing a meal once a week, usually on Friday nights and most often at the Ponderosa Steakhouse in Hazard. On the way home they would sometimes stop by the "Vitamin Shop," Still's nickname for the liquor store. Their meals were always cordial. Still would say, "We don't fuss and argue." That was because when they did not agree, Young would keep his mouth shut. Still, he added, was not a man to argue with because he always won anyway. Young cared for Still, but he cared even more for Gail, the woman he would marry in 2000. When Still heard they planned to marry he was unhappy, not because he disliked Gail but because he thought their union would mean the loss of his regular dinner partner. Instead, Still gained a friend.[32]

Another Hindman couple with ties to the school were the Weinbergs.[33] Bill Weinberg was a lawyer, politician, husband, father, and aspiring writer. Still lent encouragement by reading and commenting on his manuscripts and by writing a letter of recommendation to support his application for a visiting fellowship at Harvard. Still's writing process and style rubbed off on him. Its clarity and sparseness inspired him to eliminate unnecessary words. He rivaled Still's dialect and playfulness in the letter from Godey Spurlock to Still that he read at Still's eightieth birthday.[34] His piece "The Power of Still" reveals the man in a way that few could. Take, for example, his explanation of Still's simple trademark phrase—"No matter." Still, he said, used it to "curb digressions, to punctuate a thought, to express tolerance for a failing, to end a story. When you heard it, you knew the conversation was usually moving on to another subject. But it also underlined what each of us felt— that Mr. Still's friendship was eternal and lasting and not subject to the whims of our actions or the insensitivity of our words."[35]

A special person in the Hindman circle was Bill's wife, Lois Combs Weinberg.[36] Lois became active on the Settlement School's board in 1980 and was instrumental in the school's establishment of the dyslexia program, which officially opened in 1991. When she took children to the dining room every day for lunch, Still was there. She often had them sit with him because of his nonverbal way of commanding good behavior. They sensed that he was "at the head" of the table. Their response was positive and calm even when he teased them. For example, he would bring a hot pepper in, put it on his plate, slice it, then pass the plate around, offering the children a taste. A few brave ones took a bite, but all of them took note. In the four years that Lois directed the program, she came to know Still well. They were "regulars," to use her word. At first she was in awe of him. Then the awe turned to true affection.

Still and her father, Bert Combs, were contemporaries. They knew each other as professional friends. When Still sent him a copy of *The Wolfpen Notebooks,* Combs responded with a gracious thank-you note, calling Still "one of the country's great writers" and adding, "I'm glad that you and my daughter are friends. You are an inspiration to her."[37] Although no longer governor of Kentucky, Combs was an active, busy man. Still was more present in Lois's daily life than her father was. The last time she saw her dad was at a small dinner party at his cabin in Powell County on November 29, 1991. She drove from Lexington; Bill drove Still from Hindman. Mary Bingham was present, as were a few other guests from Louisville. After dinner, Lois drove Still back to Hindman through miserable rain and sleet. Four days later, Combs was caught in a flash flood while driving home from his law office; his body was recovered from the Red River.[38]

That incident enhanced Lois's relationship with Still who, during the 1990s, became a regular guest at the Weinberg home. One winter evening he played with her son's lovable bulldog and her litter of pups. Another time when she invited him to join them, he agreed, saying he was just sitting around with no plans. When Bill picked him up on his way home from football practice, Still had on his new brogans, blue jeans, a neat blue and white striped shirt, and a jean jacket. Bill offered him a glass of red wine, which he took, saying, "I guess I can tolerate it."[39] February 1996 brought a blizzard to Hindman. Again, arrangements were made to bring Still to their house, where he could sit by the fire and talk while waiting for the supper of corned beef and vegetables, sweet potatoes, and spinach with horseradish. He also had a little bourbon, which encouraged his "talky" self. They traded comments about the books they were reading.[40]

On November 22, 1997, the Kiwanis of Hindman honored Still with a dinner. The speakers included Offutt, Mullins, and Lois Weinberg. After the tributes, Still, age ninety-one, rose to read a poem, his signature "Heritage," and tell stories, one of which Lois recounted in her diary. "He had driven in a blizzard to Cincinnati, parked, dragged his suitcase into a building and told the man he had a reservation. The man said 'Do you know where you are?' Still responded, 'I hope I'm at the Holiday Inn.' The man said, 'Sir, you are at the Cincinnati Jail.'"[41]

To Lois, Still was an affirming person, warm and cordial. But he did not like to be hugged. Once when leaving for an extended vacation, she met him in the parking lot between the library and the James Still Center. When she tried to hug him goodbye, he froze. The reaction seemed strange to her, but "no matter." Several years later, when they visited him in the hospital, he allowed her to rub his feet as they chatted; the contact comforted him. His body was closing down, but his mind was clear. When he told her life was not exciting anymore, she knew the end was close.

Still attached himself to couples. Examples include Iris and Frank Grannis in the 1930s; Jethro and Ranie Amburgey in the 1940s and 1950s; Temple Baker and her husband, Charles, in the 1960s and 1970s; and in Hindman, Frieda and Mike Mullins as well as Lois and Bill Weinberg. From the late 1980s until his death, one couple he depended on greatly was Molly and Vernon Bundy who lived in New Albany, near Louisville.[42] Both had roots in rural Appalachia—Vernon had grown up in a farming family in eastern Kentucky, and Molly had grown up on Sewell Mountain, West Virginia, then graduated from Berea.[43] By the time Still met them, Vernon was a surgeon, practicing in Louisville and in New Albany. They had two daughters, one a physician and the other a student at Earlham College. Still's connection to the Bundy family was unique—they were neither neighbors nor caretakers. They had no ties to the Settlement School, nor could he visit them in Hindman. His time with them had to be arranged, and that was a job at which Molly excelled.

The friendship began through Molly's connection with Shirley Williams. They had been classmates at Berea and had stayed in touch over the years. Molly clipped and saved Williams's 1978 article for the *Courier-Journal*. Years later, when she came upon it, she read *River of Earth* and was "stunned by the eloquent writing, the accurate portrayal of the people, the respect for them, the beauty and the truth in his depictions. The writing was so poetic and so perfect."[44] The next time Molly saw her friend, she asked if Still might come to dinner at her house. Williams extended the invitation, and his first visit took place on November 13, 1988.

Molly enjoyed books, people, and conversation. The quintessential hostess of small dinner parties, she loved to cook, laugh, and make people comfortable. She also liked growing flowers that she could arrange and vegetables that everyone could eat. She enjoyed reading and was an excellent correspondent. She liked riding around Louisville, going to movies, shopping at specialty markets, picking through yard sales. With two doctors in the family, she was connected to the health-care system and aware of good practices for staying well and treating illness. She was the perfect friend for Still, and her house the perfect abode. The Bundy home, just across the Ohio River from Louisville, was very different from Still's log house on Dead Mare Branch. Theirs was a turn-of-the-century, three-story Queen Anne house with tall windows and a big screened front porch; it was filled with interesting artwork, books, and papers. The view through the windows was of trees, shrubs and bushes, flowering perennials, and an informal English garden. New Albany was not Wolfpen, but Still felt at home there because of the growing plants, the established neighborhood, the books on the shelves, and the gracious hospitality. During the last years of his life, the Bundy house, called Ridgeway, became his home away from home.

Still stayed with the Bundys at least a dozen times between 1988 and 1998. Some of those visits were connected with readings at Hawley-Cooke bookstore or literary festivals in Louisville, such as the Kentucky Authors Dinner in 1990. An extended visit in 1994 was associated with his eye surgery, which they had helped arrange. In 1997 he celebrated his ninety-first birthday there. Other friends in the area who would visit with him at the Bundy house included Anne Caudill, wife of the late Harry Caudill; Wade Hall and his partner, Gregg Swem; Judi Jennings; and Shirley Williams.

When Still came to Louisville, Molly was available. As time went on, she could predict what he might like to do, besides eating excellent food and talking to intelligent, willing listeners. He liked to go with her to yard sales, which he called "garbage sales." Since he was never an early riser, they would arrive around ten, when the best stuff was long gone. Still would usually buy one or two small items to take to children in Hindman, and he would always search through the old books. He also liked poking around cemeteries, so she took him to Cave Hill, the burial place of his friend and patron Mary Bingham. He did not cherish having his picture taken, but she convinced him to be photographed by Wayland Photography in Jeffersonville, Indiana.

One pastime he did like was watching movies. In 1994 he saw three in Louisville. Anne Caudill took him to *Schindler's List,* which Still described as "an *event.*" Another film that he wanted to see was *The Piano.* Molly was hesitant because of its R rating, but he insisted. As the "adult" scenes began, Still said, out loud in the small theater with an even smaller audience, "Well, I didn't expect it to be like *this.*" When it finally ended and they were driving home, Molly reminded him, "This was your idea." Later, he complained to Vernon, "We were spared

nothing. I kept thinking Molly would get up and leave, but she didn't."
His favorite movie of that year was *Shadowlands,* more because of his
personal connection than its artistic qualities. It tells the story of the
marriage between C. S. Lewis (Anthony Hopkins) and Joy Davidman
(Debra Winger), who had been Still's friend at MacDowell Colony in
1938. Though Winger was nominated for an Oscar for her role, Still
was disappointed because he remembered the real Joy as feisty and
more sophisticated.

Between visits to Louisville, Still had long phone conversations with
Molly, telling her stories that he did not share at book talks. One reveals
a private aspect of Still, his sensitivity to strangers and his gratitude
for their help. One November afternoon in 1995 he was driving from
Winchester to Lexington when he got sleepy. He pulled off in an empty
churchyard to have a nap and accidentally forgot to turn off his head-
lights. When he awoke, the battery was dead and the car was cold. With
no help in sight, he started walking and finally came to a little white
cottage. His knock brought a young woman carrying a small infant,
maybe three weeks old. She was wary, so they talked through the storm
door. She agreed to call AAA for him. After he walked back to the
church and waited a long while, help arrived. A new battery got him
back home, but he was shaken by the experience and could not get the
young woman out of his mind. He went to the grocery store, bought a
variety of fresh fruit, and drove it back to her house. He put the bag on
the porch with a note attached: "Thanks for making the call for me."
That incident did not mark the end of his solo driving trips, but it did
encourage Mullins to purchase a cell phone and install it in Still's car.

Still shared much of his life with Molly: his adventures on the road,
his favorite books and TV shows, his account of his trip with the Weinbergs to the Kentucky governor's party, his visit to the estate of Anita
Madden, his sadness at the death of his Whitesburg friend Terry Cornett, his dream of going to Tahiti, and especially his joy in welcoming
baby Jacob Bradley into the world. She listened patiently, sympathized
always, offered suggestions to improve his health, told him simple ways
to liven up his food. And she tried to get him to Louisville for visits.
When he came, she made good things happen.

One was introducing him to Jim Chatham, the minister at their
church in Louisville: Highland Presbyterian. Chatham was the right
kind of preacher for Still: thoughtful, perceptive, and spiritual. Chatham later speculated on Still's attitude toward organized religion by
saying that he must have "found much religious proclamation to be

verbal overkill, too much of the standard God, sin, and salvation talk and too little of the genuine quests of the human spirit, too many pat answers and not enough unanswerable questions."[45] After all, Chatham observed, Brother Sim Mobberly, the preacher in *River of Earth*, did not proclaim our destination; he challenged his congregation to think about where we are all going.

By invitation, Still would sometimes read a poem or scripture in the Sunday service at Highland. Chatham described these contributions as mesmerizing: "a time to sense down deep that you were in the presence of a master. . . . [Mr. Still's] capacity to know intimately the human heart, its struggles, its unanswered questions, its great joys, and its profound frustrations, was his genius. . . . To know him was to join a much larger universe, moving endlessly at the river's pace." In March 1994 Still sent Molly a print of his poem "Artist" with a request to pass it to "the preacher."[46] A month later Chatham wrote Still, thanking him for the treasured possession, which he had hung on his office wall. To him, the poem expressed the attribute of God that the contemporary world often forgets, "transcendence." Chatham recognized that Still's ability to transcend relied on his penetrating observation of the world and people around him. Chatham understood Still's spirituality.[47] But he also appreciated Still as a simple man of the hills, a playful fellow. Chatham liked to repeat a story that Still told of a meal he once shared with a man at a truck stop in Somerset, Kentucky. As they parted, the man said to Still, "Mister, you talk smart, but you got hillbilly wrote all over you." That, claimed Chatham, gave a clear picture of the man.

Another late poem that explores the link between everyday life and spiritual transcendence is "Dove." Still's inspiration was an actual moment in a real place—Molly Bundy's garden, in the late summer of 1992. Molly recounted the incident in her diary: "In our neighborhood there was a young, wild dove that was not afraid of people. It would alight on your head when you bent down to weed or set a tomato plant. When you went out the back door it would fly from nowhere and eat sunflower seeds from your hand. It perched on James Still's arm—an amazing experience." One night while there, he awoke and wrote:

Dove

When a wild bird, a dove, a mourning dove
Flew from a tree and plucked a seed from my fingers,
I knew at last I had achieved something long sought;

A oneness with earth, plant, animal, cloud, water,
Fowls of the air, denizens of the deep
The mist at morning, the sun at setting,
Wind song, hail pelt, thunder clap—
An invitation to the eternal,
The great meadow of the hereafter.
Peace.
Forever. [48]

Making connections, achieving oneness, being at peace—all were goals for Still as he passed the age of ninety, but he never pursued ephemeral ideals at the expense of living life in the real world. He did think about his literary legacy. He spent hours going through his papers and letters, all of which would eventually be in the James Still Room at Morehead State or in the Margaret King Library at the University of Kentucky.[49] He worked with Olson to prepare the collection of poems that UPK would release in 2001 just after his death. He was always pleased to get a report from the press about sales of River of Earth, not because of the royalties but because he believed that a great book was one that would not go away. He embraced the idea of permanence in his poetry and his selfhood. He thought about his own past and his childhood days; for example, a well-known poem from his later period, "Those I Want in Heaven with Me Should There Be Such a Place," catalogs a host of people from his youth with whom he longs to be reunited. As he approached "the great meadow of the hereafter," he was not concerned about sins of his past (he had always been able to forgive himself) or the future pleasures of paradise. But he was concerned about his personal legacy, a kind of continued permanence. He wanted an heir.

Still had many admirers and friends. He had been adopted by families in Knott County; he had strengthened connections with his extended family in Alabama; and he had been "taken in" by the Bundys in New Albany. Yet he did not have a family of his own. He had godchildren but no grandchildren. He never wrote about his religious beliefs, nor did he discuss his desire for descendants. But the idea of continuing himself into the next generation was on his mind. Though he could no longer father children, he could adopt them. And that is what he did. His decision was not arbitrary or sudden.

Still showed generosity and loyalty to several families in Knott County, but among the most important to him through the years was that of James and Melzinia Perry. James was a coal miner, and the couple had five children—the oldest, James Jr., and the youngest, Teresa Lynn.[50] Still first got to know them through "Junior," who was a frequent visitor to the library where Still worked. By the time the young man attended high school in the early 1960s, Still was teaching at Morehead. After graduation, Junior married and was working near Morehead when he suffered a serious auto accident.[51] Still was very helpful to Junior and his wife in Morehead where the young man was in the hospital from early August to November 1966. He was also helpful to the Perry family in Hindman; the crisis brought them closer.

Not long after Junior's accident, Teresa Lynn was born. One of her earliest memories of Still was a Christmas when, because her father could not afford gifts, nothing was under their tree. Still went to Cody Hardware in Hindman and came back with presents for them all, plus a story for the young ones. He had been uptown, he said, and Santa's sled had overturned. Santa had asked him to bring the gifts on to their house. Teresa Lynn may have been the only one who believed his story, but it worked for her. Was that when the little girl first won his heart, or was it the time she, as a four-year-old, insisted, "Learn me to read"?[52] Still "learned" Teresa many good lessons. When she was nine, she called him "Still" and sent him cards and letters. His habit was to give her little gifts. Before he went to Florida one year, she wrote him a letter, in her best childish cursive, politely asking him for five dollars. She promised to spend only one dollar a week before he came back, then closed, "Love ya, Teresa."

Tragedy struck the family again in 1973 when James Sr. died of black lung disease. Teresa was only six, but she remembers the night well. Still came to their house to help out; he quickly realized the child needed more help than the grown-ups did. He sat with her and reassured her that everything would be all right. After that loss, she thought of him as a surrogate father. When her mother died of cancer in 1989, Teresa relied even more on Still. When her first child, Kaila, was born, Teresa strengthened the family ties by having the baby call him "Papaw Still." In a letter detailing some expenses he had covered, she followed with a touching thank-you: "I want you to know that I never really say what is on my mind. I really appreciate what you do for Kaila and me. I really love you a lot, though I never tell you. You are the father that I never had. I'm really proud that you are someone that I can count on. Thank you for being there for me, and thanks for the money too."[53]

Still was not a man to declare his love openly. It was the small gifts he brought to Teresa as a girl and to her family as she grew older that provided evidence of his commitment. Even more valuable was his contribution to her education. Teresa attended Hindman grade school then Hindman Central High School for two years, then earned her GED in nearby Hazard. Still began supporting her education when she entered Alice Lloyd College, where she studied for one year. He was pleased when she transferred to Morehead to pursue a degree in special education and early elementary education. Having a young daughter made commuting stressful, so she took what courses she could at Hazard Community College. With her own perseverance and help from Still, she graduated in 1993 and, after securing a job, earned a fifth year at the University of Kentucky, again taking advantage of community college distance learning. He supported her throughout.

Immediately after graduation, Teresa got a job as a special-education teacher. Still received that news one evening in the dining hall at Hindman Settlement School. He sat talking after the meal; as was his custom, he was mentally wandering through his life and meditating aloud about this and that. A staff person came to tell him he had a phone call, one that he seemed to be expecting. With as much urgency as he could muster he left the table and returned a few minutes later, displaying pleasure and pride. Teresa, he reported, had landed a job with the Knott County school system. Although he never openly bragged about what this meant to him or how involved he had been in supporting her efforts, his satisfaction with her accomplishment was evident.[54]

The beginning of her Hindman teaching career brought more than a professional change to Teresa's life. Not long after she joined the faculty of the high school, she and the principal, Hiram Bradley, married. On November 12, 1994, she gave birth to a baby boy—Jacob Alexander Bradley. Their shared middle name indicated the connection between the child and James Alexander Still, but the bond from the start was stronger than a name. With the birth of Jake, Still was permanently attached to the young family. He had been fond of Kaila for years; now the baby boy became the love of his later life.

Still was not a touching person, and he rarely expressed affection directly. Some of his friends thought he avoided physical contact. He was more outwardly affection with children than with others, but even among children, Jake stood out. The video that KET made to celebrate Still's ninetieth birthday includes a joyful scene when Still arrived at Teresa's house and the toddler ran toward him to be embraced.[55] Once he reported with pride to Molly that Jake was growing, active, and trying to hold a pencil. And, he reported, "When he sees me, he sticks out his arms and runs to me . . . and when I leave, he cries."[56] Jake Bradley was a happy baby, and theirs was a magical bond.

On May 28, 1998, when Still was ninety-two, he made the family connection legal; on that day he officially adopted Teresa Perry Bradley as his daughter. Jake and Kaila became his grandchildren. The change in their relationship was not obvious. They were already close; Teresa was a daily helper and a source of pride for him. Teresa said that although he never introduced her to anyone as his "daughter," he did describe her to Zachry as his "heir." He did not publicly announce the adoption, but he did tell key people, including among others his niece in Alabama and the Bundys in Louisville. His exact reason for restraint is unknown, as is his precise motivation for the action. Why adopt this woman whom he had supported and nurtured for years? Or a better question: Why now, instead of earlier? Teresa already appeared in his will and had been there since 1973.[57] His last will and testament was signed July 21, 1999, in Whitesburg. It differed from the one signed a quarter century before largely because some of the people named earlier had died and others, like Teresa, had grown up. For example, the 1973 version bequeathed to Monroe Amburgey all royalties and income from his literary works. In the final version, Teresa was his literary heir. This later version also designated his literary advisors as writer Lee Smith; William Marshall, archivist at the University of Kentucky; and William Weinberg, lawyer and friend in Hindman. Throughout this last will, Teresa Bradley was the principal beneficiary, though she was not referred to as his "daughter." It could be that Still adopted Teresa not specifically to gain an heir but to make their personal bond more official and legal. It was a way he could formalize his connection to her family and to future generations, a symbol that helped ensure he would not "go away." Teresa and her children, and now her grandchildren, remain in the hills of Kentucky to this day.

As Still began his ninety-third year, his world was contracting; he was somewhat like the Baldridge family in *River of Earth,* "tying himself into a knot" so tight that few people could get in. His declining health mandated his need for more help. Mike and Frieda Mullins were always on call, as were Doris Miller and Rebecca Ware, but filling that daily caretaker role for the Hindman Settlement School was his neighbor on the hill, Sam Linkous. Other friends would drop in and help out: Bob Young, Jim Phelps, Bill and Lois Weinberg. Molly Bundy became his reliable telephone contact. But the day-to-day contact was left to people closest to home—Sam, Hiram, and Teresa.

After Still's hospital stay in January 2000, the school made adjustments to his house so he could return there. Teresa sorted papers and books to clear a pathway through the rooms. Much of that year he stayed mobile, and frequently Sam would take him for rides and occasionally local appearances. When he could not leave the house so freely, a pattern was established: Hiram would go by in the mornings and prepare his breakfast. Teresa would bring the mail in the afternoons. He spent much of his day reading. Most of the work he did was collaborating with Olson on the poetry collection. Frequently, he called Molly, who would encourage him to get out of the house, but he refused to go anywhere in a wheelchair. If he could not walk, he said, he would not go. Occasionally, he did.

One of his last excursions was to attend the funeral of his one-time friend Al Stewart, who died in April 2001. The animosity between them had been smoldering for years. When Stewart died, Still first told Mullins he did not want to go to the funeral, but that morning he changed his mind. Mullins took him to the church and placed him in the front row, next to Loyal Jones. Still said to Jones, "I'm sorry for what happened between me and Al, but it started a long time ago and it couldn't be helped. It was a matter of ego." To Mullins, he explained his change of heart by saying, "You reach a point when it's time to let things go."[58]

Soon after that, Still was back in the hospital in Hazard.[59] Perhaps he expected this stay to be his last. He had prepared carefully, making sure that Teresa knew his wishes in detail. She recalled that one day he awoke from a nap, sat up in his hospital bed, and instructed her to get a pen. Then for two hours he talked about what she should do— go through every piece of paper, choose this sort of stone, request that these people be part of whatever memorial service there might be. He had tried to tell her his wishes before, but the firm urgency of his voice convinced her to listen carefully this time, even though she wanted to believe that he would go home again.

During these last weeks he was having trouble recovering from pneumonia and had suffered several episodes of congestive heart failure, but he was showing signs of improvement. The hospital was preparing to move him to a rehabilitation facility on April 28. Molly Bundy had set up an email list to keep a small network of people informed of his condition. On April 25, a Thursday, I felt for some inexplicable reason that I needed to make a trip to Hazard to visit him. It had been a while since I had last seen him, and my only excuse was the crunch of spring semester at the college and the three-and-a-half-hour trip from my western North Carolina home to his in eastern Kentucky. I called Teresa to ask if he would feel like a visit. She said, "Yes, come."

April 28 was a good day for a drive. My son William (the "ice-cream boy"), then fifteen, decided to join me, probably to get practice with his new learner's permit. We arrived in Hazard around eleven but were delayed in finding the hospital. Once there, I remember passing by the room that the central desk had told me was Still's, but the door was closed with a hospital cart in front of it. Not wanting to wake him with a knock, I stood by the door and waited. When a nurse came out with a look of urgent concern on her face, I knew that something more and something less than James Still was in that room. She told me in health-care language that I could not enter because the patient was experiencing cardiac arrest and a team of medical professionals was with him. Teresa had been notified and was on her way.

The wait seemed to suspend time, but somehow events moved on: Still died; Teresa and Hiram arrived; the doctor was talked to; the body was seen to; the effects were removed from the room. Then we went to Hindman. William occupied Jake while Teresa talked with Mullins; I stood by for support. The funeral required little planning because Still himself had made detailed notes concerning his wishes. Mullins and Teresa calmly and respectfully worked through all the plans. The "celebration" would be on May 1.

As we concluded the grown-up business, I left Mullins's office to find William and begin the trip home, knowing that I would return in a few days. There he was with young Jake—they were talking together beside the swinging bridge that crosses Troublesome Creek. William urged Jake to chase after a beautiful butterfly, and off he went, running with joy.

Epilogue

On Tuesday, May 1, 2001, people came to Hindman from far and wide to bid farewell to James Still. The previous night at the Hindman Funeral Services chapel, the solemn visitation had shifted into an impromptu program of song and story. By noon on Tuesday, the memorial gathering had expanded to three hundred guests. It was a genuine celebration, a get-together that Still would have enjoyed. Everyone there felt the personal sorrow of losing this remarkable person. But the occasion was also filled with kind words, spiritual comfort, sincere tributes, consoling music, and good humor. The man's spirit filled up and spilled over the formality of his funeral.

Mike Mullins opened the program. Teresa gave a special welcome to all and shared personal stories of her life with Still. Then followed tributes from Gurney Norman and Loyal Jones, Herb E. Smith of Appalshop, fellow-traveler Jim Bergman of Alice Lloyd College, friend and writer Lee Smith, and long-time friend Wilma Dykeman, who reminded us that not all his contemporaries were dead. Robert Young, his Hindman comrade, provided the music. Reverend James Chatham from Louisville offered words of wisdom and comfort, reminding us that Still was one with the forest, the mountains, and the living creatures there. "The oneness was his deep connection with all else being carried forward in the river's flow."[1] Mullins concluded by reading "Heritage," ending with these prophetic lines: "Being one with death rising to bloom again, I cannot go. Being of these hills I cannot pass beyond."

After the service, people made their way to the Settlement School a few miles down the road. There the pallbearers slowly carried the coffin up the hill above the May Stone building. Bob Saylor played taps, and the burial closed with a solemn graveside salute. Then came fellowship in the dining hall. For years, Still's birthdays had brought people together in Hindman. His death had done something similar in creating an occasion for friends and family to gather and celebrate the life that had passed and the spirit that remained. It was fitting that Still should be buried on the hill above the Hindman Settlement School on May 1, a day that commemorates the return of spring. There his modest shrine would remain, the gravesite eventually covered by wild violets and marked at the base with a large craggy stone inscribed with a verse: "The range of the mountains is his pasture, and he searcheth after every green thing" (Job 39:8). Later, his daughter would add a bench that listed the titles of Still's books—a place for quiet meditation or private reading.

The news of his death and reflections on his life were not limited to Knott County. Between April 29 and May 2, newspapers across Kentucky carried long articles recounting the occasion. Two days before the funeral, the Sunday *Lexington Herald-Leader* quoted Mullins's declaration "The death of Mr. Still is the loss of a giant." Norman called him "the most influential Kentucky writer of the last 50 years . . . the parent of the present generation of writers."[2] On May 1, NPR's *Morning Edition* announced the event to the nation when Bob Edwards interviewed Ted Olson. Edwards began by identifying Still as "one of Appalachia's most eloquent . . . the best writer you've never heard of." The tribute intended to let people hear of Still and to encourage their interest in the poetry collection that would soon be available. The closing words came from Still himself reading "Heritage," a sound bite excerpted from a 1979 NPR interview, echoing the line: "Being of these hills, I cannot pass beyond."[3]

Soon memorials began to appear in journals. *Appalachian Journal* carried Norman's "Remembering James Still." Charles May, a professor at California State University, wrote a tribute for the pages of *Appalachian Heritage*. The summer edition of the *Louisville Review* included the elegy poem "Protection" by Jane Mayhall. *The Oxford American* carried Hal Crowther's "A Man of the World" in the fall of 2001, and the winter issue of *Arts Across Kentucky* included "Remembering James Still" by Silas House.[4]

During the next year, homages to his life and writing continued. One notable project was an exhibition called "Still Moments," compiled and displayed by Judith Hensley, Rhonda Robinson, and Jennifer McDaniels. More than fifty people contributed prose pieces, poems, photographs, and art. The brochure accompanying the exhibit described Still's writings as "vivid snapshots of Appalachia" that revealed the "creative soul of the celebrated Appalachian author."[5] The purpose of the display was to show mountain people, especially youth, that Still lived among them, wrote about them, and would be remembered. The contributors wanted to preserve their memories of this man who had amused, perplexed, and inspired them. A similar tribute was included in the 2002 publication *Crossing Troublesome* that celebrated twenty-five years of the writers' workshop at Hindman. The section devoted to Still began with his poem "I Shall Go Singing," then followed with four poems and twelve prose pieces by other writers, all inspired by Still. Eight years later, the fall issue of *Appalachian Heritage* featured Still by devoting fifty pages of essays and tributes to the man and his writing.[6]

In 2003 KET released "James Still's Legacy," hosted by Bill Goodman, an hour-long program in their Bookclub series. Like several KET productions featuring Still, the film opened at Hindman Settlement School with Goodman talking to Mullins. The backdrop was Still's burial site, next to which the school had built an outdoor chapel. Mullins's reverence for the place matched his profound admiration for Still's influence and intellect. From there, Goodman took viewers to a roundtable where panelists discussed *River of Earth*. Then he shifted to elicit reactions to the novel from high-school students across Kentucky. The program concluded back in Hindman with Goodman talking to a group of Kentucky writers: Silas House, Chris Holbrook, Crystal Wilkinson, Frank X Walker, and Leatha Kendrick.

The general question for these writers was "What did James Still teach you; how has he influenced your writing?" Though a summary cannot do justice to the responses, it can show Still's impact on this younger generation. His writing, they agreed, captured the soul of the hills and the dignity of the people. It embodied a passion for heritage and connection to place that inspired them to write about what they knew and where they were from. Still encouraged them, through example, to be patient because a piece of writing is a work of art, not a product. They all agreed that "the master" was an observer, a listener and learner. House recalled Still's early advice: "Learn something new every day." Walker recalled Still's powerful encouragement when, after a poetry reading, the old mentor passed by the young man and quietly said, "Good stuff." The conversation involving the five writers illustrated the profound importance of community to the solitary act of writing. Kendrick concluded that the younger writers in the community always carry something of Still within them.[7]

Public acknowledgments continued. In 2002 the Downtown Lexington Corporation named James Still along with Rosemary Clooney, Loretta Lynn, Bobbie Ann Mason, and three others as Kentucky Stars, with a ceremony in the Lexington Theatre on October 22. A decade later, he was inducted into the Kentucky Writers Hall of Fame.[8] Another sort of honor was bestowed closer to home when on July 28, 2003, the section of Kentucky Highway 160, from Hindman to Carr Fork Lake near Wolfpen, was officially named the James Still Highway. It is a road that he traveled often and knew intimately. In 2005 the Appalachian College Association, with funding from the Mellon Foundation, sponsored a two-day James Still workshop at Hindman for thirty participants—librarians and English faculty from colleges in the region. By that time, ownership of the log house at Wolfpen had returned to the Amburgey family, so the Still "place" that the group explored was the house on the hill in Hindman, the school itself, and the hill where he was buried. I led the workshop discussions centering around the man's life; Olson, the discussions about Still's literary achievements; and Claude Crum, those on Still's impact and influence.[9]

A year later, the Settlement School invited people to Hindman for a memorial celebration of Still's one hundredth birthday. Crowther's address began, "If anyone I ever knew seemed as permanent and indestructible as a granite boulder, it was Mr. Still. . . . If any personality ever haunted a place entirely, before and after the formality of his death, it was Mr. Still at Hindman."[10] Still's continuing gift to the school was what his life and work embodied, a permanent link to the past, the people, and the place. Being of these particular hills, he had chosen not to pass beyond, and the school was keeping his memory alive. Other institutions in the region also marked the centennial. The Mountain Heritage Literary Festival at LMU featured Mullins, who on June 24, 2006, delivered his talk "My Friend, Mr. Still." A month later, the James Still Room in the library at MSU held a five-day event called "The River Eternal: James Still Centennial Celebration."[11]

The memorials and honors bestowed after his death and the occasions for remembering his life show how much his town and state valued Still. He seemed to haunt the place, as Crowther had said. Celebrating his birthday, naming a highway for him, and electing him to a hall of fame helped solidify the Still legend. His charismatic personality was remembered, and his influence as a cultural figure was ongoing. But such occasions and honors do little to enhance a literary legacy. What matters for that is whether the writings survive and are read, whether new works are published posthumously, how much critical attention is shown the works, and the degree of influence they have on future generations of readers and writers.

Less obvious to the general public but an important gift to historians, students, and scholars are the collections of letters, manuscripts, and memorabilia that Still left behind. In the 1960s as his tenure at MSU began, Still donated a large amount of material to what would become the James Still Room. In the early 1990s he began to give additional materials to the library at the University of Kentucky. After his death, his daughter and literary heir, Teresa Bradley Reynolds, assumed the task of sending the remaining papers to the two collections, most going to Lexington. The Margaret King Library continued to process the papers under the direction of Manuscript Archivist Kate Black and with the support of the Director of Special Collection and Archives William Marshall. The enormous task was completed, and the dedication of the Still papers took place on October 21, 2007, an event that brought together scholars, writers, friends, family, and staff members of the library.[12] The collection preserves a valuable record of Still's interests and work and provides an in-depth picture of the twentieth century as experienced by this careful observer and meticulous collector.

Still's papers are vital and irreplaceable. His charismatic personality is memorable for those who knew him. His influence as a cultural figure of the twentieth century is valued. But critical to a literary legacy is having books available to readers. At his death, eight of Still's books were in print. The most recent ones—*Jack and the Wonder Beans* (1996), *Appalachian Mother Goose* (1998), and *Sporty Creek* (1999)— were for children and young adults. Of all of his works, the book with the best chance for a long life is his 1940 masterpiece *River of Earth* (reprinted by UPK in 1978). The key to his entire writing career, this novel illustrates his strengths in multiple genres—short story, folklore, poetry—while exploring themes of a child's journey of discovery, the effects of modernization on traditional culture, and the nature of human endurance in the face of hardship. The story is realistic, the language is authentic, the setting is specific, yet the human situation within that setting is everywhere and everlasting. *River of Earth*'s most notable influence on the twentieth-century American literary canon may be its contribution to the demise of the Appalachian stereotype perpetuated by earlier local-color writers. *River of Earth* helped awaken a vibrant literary community within the region, the effects of which are recognized throughout the nation.[13] Still's classic has been read widely by students of American literature, especially those in Appalachia.

Olson was one of those students. In a graduate class at the University of Kentucky, he read the novel and was attracted to its "vivid evocations of life in Appalachia." Soon after, he discovered *The Wolfpen Poems.* When Still came to Lexington to celebrate the novel's fiftieth anniversary, Olson took along a copy of the poetry book to be signed. "The book was my excuse to meet Mr. Still," he said. When his turn came, Still took his book "and uttered quietly, Ah, my verses."[14] Eight years later, when Olson had Still speak to his class at Union College, one student asked if he planned to publish any more books. Still responded that he had some pieces no one had yet read. Olson followed up with an offer to help him publish some of that material.[15]

It was natural to begin with the poetry. Still had been writing poems and submitting them to magazines since 1930, but he had published only three small volumes, *Hounds on the Mountain* (Viking, 1937), *River of Earth: A Poem and Other Poems* (King Library Press, 1982), and *The Wolfpen Poems* (Berea College Press, 1986). Olson's aim was to bring all Still's poems together into one collection. *From the Mountain, From the Valley: New and Collected Poems* (UPK, 2001) was the result of their collaboration. The book was completed before and released just after Still's death. A sample of reviews shows appreciation for the poet and the book:

> "The work of a man accomplished in gentleness, humorousness,
>   compassion, and clarity." —Wendell Berry
> "The true value of this book is to reintroduce a modern readership
>   to Still's poetry on its own terms." —*Kentucky Monthly*
> "This volume . . . will appeal to general readers and provide
>   material for students and scholars, memories for friends
>   and admirers, and meaningful echoes for all residents of
>   Appalachia." —*Appalachian Journal*

Essayist Crowther did more than praise this latest publication. In "A Man of the World," he appealed to readers to look at the man and his whole body of work:

> Though Still outlived all the rest [of America's "Greatest Generation" of writers], he was not prolific; his pursuit was perfection, not saturation. If you read the classic Appalachian novel *River of Earth,* the new collected poems *From the Mountain,*

From the Valley, and the story collection *Pattern of a Man,* you haven't covered James Still by a long shot, but you've measured him fairly. If you're not impressed—if you're new to Still and you're not astonished—then possibly literature isn't your strong suit after all.[16]

The challenge issued by Crowther is one kind of compliment. Another came in the words of poet Manning, whose review reveals the perception and use of language that he shared with his mentor:

Reading any one of these poems is like holding an old pocket-knife. It feels good in the hand; you trust it, you are familiar with it, and when you open the blade—when you carefully read the poem—you know with certainty that it is well-honed and razor sharp. And then you realize it is also beautiful, which might make you thankful, and might make you want to cry. . . . It is a book about us, who we were and who we are, and a book about the dark and lovely place where we live.[17]

While Olson was working with Still on the poetry, the topic of his short stories came up. *Pattern of a Man* (Gnomon, 1976) and *The Run for the Elbertas* (UPK, 1980) together supplied a generous sampling of his stories, but there was no complete collection. Still seemed interested in the project but hesitant. He died before Olson could discover the source of his hesitation. Olson explained in a 2013 blog that Still was right, the task was complex.[18] There were copyright problems, manuscript challenges, and cataloging issues, but Olson persisted. In 2012 UPK released *The Hills Remember: The Complete Short Stories of James Still.* A sample of reviews from the press's webpage conveys the reaction:

"Bravo to Ted Olson and University Press of Kentucky for this valuable addition to James Still's legacy."—Ron Rash

"These stories affirm Still's art as a master story teller."—Loyal Jones

"Mr. Still is more than the master. He is our grandfather, our great-grandfather, our godfather—the revered elder of the tribe of Appalachian writers."—Chris Offutt

"The hills do remember James Still, and so should readers everywhere."—*Appalachian Journal*

The book was well done and well received, but it did not seem to reach a large audience beyond the region.[19]

Between completing the poetry collection in 2001 and submitting the story collection in 2012, Olson solicited and edited two useful volumes of essays and memories: *James Still: Critical Essays on the Dean of Appalachian Literature* (2007) and *James Still in Interviews, Oral Histories and Memoirs* (2009). McFarland published these books as part of the Southern Appalachian Studies series. Altogether, forty-eight people contributed fifty-nine different entries—some as short as two pages, others as long as twenty. Many of the articles were reprinted from earlier publications, but a number were written at the specific invitation of Olson. The books inform readers, writers, and scholars about Still's work, accomplishments, and influence.[20] With two collections of Still's writing and two volumes of scholarly essays and personal responses, Olson had taken a major step toward ensuring Still's literary legacy. But a decade after his death, the question remained: being of these hills, could Still pass beyond? Would his writing reach a broader audience? Could his reputation be local and limitless at the same time?

On the flyleaf of the poetry collection, Lee Smith praised Still's ability to capture "the spirit and language of the Appalachian South—his own beloved patch of ground in eastern Kentucky—like no other." Gurney Norman had a similar observation for the story collection: "In his stories drawn from local life and speech in the Kentucky mountains, James Still finds timeless beauty and universal meaning." Wendell Berry's forecast on the cover of *James Still in Interviews, Oral Histories and Memoirs* looks forward to the day when Still "will not be identified quite so invariably as 'an Appalachian writer.'" He sees the association between this writer and his region as inevitable and positive, but it does not have to be restrictive because "the value of good regional writing extends far beyond its region." Berry concludes, "James Still, by any standard, is a supreme writer."

The Hills Remember is a display case for Still's long career as a writer of short stories. It is the value of his prose rather than the memory of the man that won the book the 2012 Thomas D. Clark Medallion Book Award. The celebration took place on August 15 at the Carnegie Center for Literacy and Learning in Lexington. Bill Goodman of KET moderated. Olson spoke about the project. Other speakers were old-timer Norman and young writer Crystal Wilkinson. Her contribution illustrated that Still had inspired the newest generation of Appalachian writers even if they had never met the man. Wilkinson was the director of the creative-writing program at MSU, the school's first writer-in-residence since Still in the 1970s. Knowledge of Still, she said, came to her through his words on the page. She learned from him what it meant to live the life of a writer. He was her model for writing about ordinary people, for capturing the melodic voice of the mountains, and for creating child characters who are both simple and complex. The years following Still's death extended his legacy. The younger generation, including Wilkinson, were learning from Still and passing his works along to their students.[21] Claude Lafie Crum at Alice Lloyd College is an example of a teacher/literary scholar whose 2007 book *River of Words* explored Still's influence. Writers, scholars, KET, and UPK were doing their part to keep his name and his works available to the reading public.[22]

The last story in *The Hills Remember,* "From the Morgue," is a humorous dialogue between two old men on the topic of being remembered. An older poet (Still himself) gets a call from a newspaperman who specializes in writing obituaries ("obits") for paying customers long before they are needed. The calls persist even after the poet says he is not interested. But, asserts the obit writer, "It's all in your behalf. What was it T. S. Eliot said? Something about going out with a bang not a whimper. That's what I'm trying to help you with. . . . You were somebody once. . . . You may be again." The poet responds, "All I am is a tinkerer—a tinkerer with words. As for recognition, the little I had, that will be all." The story concludes when the obit writer gets from the poet a revelation he can use, one he describes as a firecracker rather than dynamite. "It'll have to do. . . . Good for one hundred bucks!"[23]

If there was a firecracker in Still's later career it was the publication of *Chinaberry,* a story he had worked on for years, especially during the 1980s.[24] In the last years of his life, when Smith was helping with the publication of *An Appalachian Mother Goose,* Still gave her the Texas manuscript, a hodgepodge of pages stuffed into an old briefcase. She read it with great interest and in April 2001 sent him a letter offering suggestions about how to proceed with editing.[25] Perhaps his consideration of those suggestions explains why he had the manuscript near him the month before he died. There is no evidence that Still made a final decision about publishing the Texas story. That would be left to his literary executors: Smith, Bill Marshall from the University of Kentucky Archives, and Bill Weinburg, his friend and lawyer in Hindman. Teresa Reynolds also had a voice in the decision. In July 2004 the literary advisors met in Hindman and decided to approach Silas House about the task of editing.

In 2011 UPK published *Chinaberry,* the narrative that resulted when House took on the Texas manuscript. In the book's introduction, House tells how it all came to be. When, in 2004, Still's literary advisors asked him to edit the material, House quickly agreed, feeling both "daunted and blessed" to be able to work on something left by one of his "literary heroes." Two years later he got an old briefcase from Smith filled with an assortment of pages, notes, chapters, and a list of chapter titles. Working with the manuscript showed him that "every single sentence in any book has to be fretted over, polished, pruned . . . the best writing has to be packed tight with emotion."[26] House tried to stay true to Still's creation. We cannot know what Still would have thought of *Chinaberry.* He had ambivalent feelings about the manuscript, tinkering with it for at least fifteen years without getting it close to publication. But he would have approved of House, whose main goal was to "stay completely true to Mr. Still's intentions."[27] House approached the work with skill, dedication, and love. The resulting book represents a collaboration in the process of creation.

Chinaberry may not be the proverbial "dynamite" that the obit writer was seeking, but it is an important addition to Still's work, one that has generated a variety of reactions. Its publication led to a number of reviews and articles, most of them appearing in Kentucky newspapers and regional journals. On the book's jacket the press featured comments from known Appalachian writers: Ron Rash stated that the publication confirms Still as "not only a great Appalachian writer but a great American writer." Robert Morgan predicted that Still's "fans will be excited to have this new work . . . new readers will be thrilled to discover the range and depth of this classic master." Smith described it as "the capstone of Still's extraordinary career . . . perhaps the most original coming-of-age story ever written with a mystery lodged right in the heart of it."[28]

Chinaberry is the story of a thirteen-year-old boy who goes with family friends from Alabama to Texas, where they plan to pick cotton for the summer. The boy is quickly discovered by the wealthy farmer Anson Winters, who owns a ranch called Chinaberry. A three-way relationship develops between the boy, Anson, and his young wife, Lurie. Anson babies the boy and plans to adopt him to replace his own young son whose death he is grieving. When Lurie becomes pregnant and the boy's parents send word for him to come back, the cotton-pickers return to Alabama. The last words Anson utters are "Go home, Jim." The narrator then closes, "I never saw them again. I grew up; I remembered."[29]

In the story's protagonist, readers can recognize traces of the young boy from *River of Earth* and of the troublemakers from "A Run for the Elbertas." Familiar Still motifs thread throughout the work: the family under stress, the journey of discovery, the exploration of a simpler time and place, the strong evocation of landscape. The style illustrates Still's masterful prose, the narrator who speaks in a simple voice, and descriptions that come alive on the page. Although *Chinaberry* has much in common with Still's earlier work, the differences are important. This boy is not a six-year-old but a small thirteen-year-old who is treated as if he were six. The setting is not the hills and coalfields of eastern Kentucky but the ranchlands and cotton fields of central Texas. Unlike anything else Still wrote, this story seems to be told by the author himself about his own childhood experience—a memory of an event long past but not entirely forgotten.

The way *Chinaberry* mingles fiction and autobiography raises questions about how the story relates to Still's life experiences. The publisher describes the work as "a combination of truth, imagination and fiction," but it is difficult to know how much of the narrative is based on Still's own childhood. He was always interested in Texas and had relatives there. He made several trips to the state, one time to pick cotton with members of his family and again after he joined the army. But there is nothing to suggest that the situation in this story of a young teenager being taken in and nearly adopted by a man desperate to replace the child he had lost is anything other than fiction. Regardless, Still uses the story to explore the development of a pubescent child who leaves his family home to venture into unknown territory. Does the boy feel frightened and vulnerable or does he embrace this strange new experience, coming to love this troubled man and his beautiful wife? There is never a moment of overt sexuality on the page, but readers may get a sense of something beneath the surface. Is there an inkling of desire between the man and boy or a budding physical attraction between the boy and woman? Is this Still's exploration of puberty in general? Or does it reflect something of his own development?

There are no clear answers to these questions, but several quotes included in the box with the Texas manuscript provide hints about how Still thought of the work. On one page, Still handwrote a textbook definition of adolescence. On another he described any remembered event as a compression of memory and emotion. The most provocative scribble was a question that Still appeared to be asking himself: "Could it have happened this way? It was long ago and I was thirteen, and since have indulged in fiction as a way of life." Though it is unlikely that the events of *Chinaberry* happened as they are written, the book may be a personal account of experiences and thoughts that he had never before revealed. The intensely private nature of the work may be one reason he never chose to complete it during his lifetime.

The mystery of Still's posthumous work will never be solved, just as the man was never fully comprehended in his lifetime. Recall the jovial but fruitless effort his friends made on his eightieth birthday to explain "what made the master tick." At one point in *Chinaberry*, when Lurie is telling him about Anson's complicated background, the boy responds, "We can never get plumb to the bottom of anybody, not all the way down to what is dark and hidden and cannot bear the light of recognition." That simple truth applies to Still the man as well as to this final publication. *Chinaberry* is like the master's own life: simple on the surface but complicated beneath. One thing we can know is that Still wrote words and stories that deserve the light of recognition. To know the essence of the man, read the full range of his work. The last entry in *From the Mountain* is this lighthearted verse, a fitting end to this story of his life.

My Days

Those, those were my days,
My thoughts and my ways.
How did I stand the times?
Read my tales, spin my rhymes.

Acknowledgments

While researching and writing this biography, I have received help and support from many individuals and institutions. Mars Hill University (MHU), its faculty committee for enrichment and renewal, and the Kinnamon travel grant sponsored research trips and provided three semesters of sabbatical support. The Appalachian College Association (ACA), with funding from the Mellon Foundation and from the John B. Stephenson Fellowship for Faculty in the Arts and Sciences, matched two of the major gifts awarded by MHU. I owe a special debt of gratitude to Alice Brown at the ACA and to my MHU colleagues in the Division of Humanities, in Renfro Library, and in the Liston B. Ramsey Center for Regional Studies. Several students participated in the research and interviews over the years, including Amy Payne Whitehead, Mike Dollar, and Ashley Blackford. Many colleagues have given me the confidence and courage to complete the project even when it seemed overwhelming. My special thanks for their personal support go to President Dan Lunsford, to my colleague Brandon Johnson, to Kathryn Newfont at the University of Kentucky, and to my great mentor and friend, Noel Kinnamon.

For many years James Still saved letters, manuscripts, journals, photos, and other materials related to his life and career. After his death and before the collections were fully established, Teresa Reynolds allowed me to explore papers that had not yet been given to the libraries. Between Still and his daughter, the bulk of his papers have been donated to key archives in the state of Kentucky, collections that I have been fortunate to research. The James Still Papers at the University of Kentucky are a treasure for the region and the nation. My most valuable contact there was archivist Kate Black. The James Still Room at Morehead State University was helpful throughout the project, and I am indebted especially to Donna Baker and Rob Sammons. Hindman Settlement School was generous in offering their Still files and photos. I am grateful to the staff and to Mike Mullins and then Brent Hutchinson. Liz Lamont was helpful in guiding me through the library collection at Lincoln Memorial University. Mary Ellen Miller encouraged my explorations of the Jim Wayne Miller Collection at Western Kentucky University.

As his life story shows, Still had many friends and followers. This venture has provided me the opportunity to know a number of them, and I am grateful for their cooperation and encouragement, and for their generous sharing of memories, stories, photos, letters, and good wishes. Still's daughter, Teresa, and his close friend Molly Bundy have been supportive and helpful throughout. His Alabama friends and family, especially his niece Barbara Sue Barnes Harris and his friend George Zachry, willingly answered questions and supplied materials. A list of those interviewed follows in the Sources, but let me recognize here some individuals with whom my interactions were particularly productive and memorable: Wilma Dykeman, Jim Wayne Miller, Alfred Perrin, Thomas Clark, Wade Hall, and Mike Mullins. Also Sandra Ballard, Sam Linkous, Loyal Jones, Jonathan Greene, Gurney Norman, Tom Eblen, Bob Young, Lois Weinberg, Shirley Williams, Judi Jennings, George Ella Lyon, Sam McKinney, Pauline Cheek, Jim Chatham, and Randy Wilson. All of these and many more contributed to my knowledge and understanding of James Still, the man and the writer.

Readers everywhere should be grateful to UPK for keeping James Still, the writer, alive in our literature. Ted Olson, Silas House, Lee Smith, Bill Marshall, Bill Weinberg, and Teresa Reynolds have aided the press in making Still's writing available to present and future generations. No book is created and published by one person. Without the help of many, this work would not have been completed. The project has been a long one, but the directors and editors of the university press have been patient, encouraging, and helpful. Thank you to Jennifer Peckinpaugh, Laura Sutton, Ashley Runyon, to David Cobb, Patrick O'Dowd, Anthony Chiffolo, and especially to Leila Salisbury, and Stephen Wrinn.

Many friends have also stood by me. Whether providing lodging in Kentucky, building bookshelves for a massive research collection, helping decipher cryptic handwriting, reading multiple drafts and offering revisions, talking about perplexing incidents, or simply being there with an encouraging word, friends like Randolph Hollingsworth and Richard Greissman, Robert Allen, Karen Paar, Elizabeth Boggess, and Sylvia Lindman have been essential to the process.

Finally, this book would not have happened without my own family and our place in the hills. When Still visited us in Yancey County, North Carolina, he seemed at home on our farm. Just as he did in Knott County, I find inspiration and strength in the landscape. That setting has been a key to this project. And the people who have been key are my family. William, now an editor himself, has helped with the writing. My husband, Sam, and daughter, Laura, have listened and laughed, pondered and advised, sympathized and celebrated at every stage of this adventure. It is to them and to the past and future readers of James Still that I dedicate this work.

Notes

Abbreviations

CAA	Contemporary Authors Autobiography Series
HSS	Hindman Settlement School
JWM	Jim Wayne Miller Collection at Western Kentucky University
KET	Kentucky Educational Television
LMU	Lincoln Memorial University
MSC	Morehead State College
MSU	Morehead State University
NPR	National Public Radio
UK	University of Kentucky
UPK	University Press of Kentucky

"Still Storage" refers to the papers that Teresa Reynolds had in a storage unit in Hindman after Still's death and before sorting and moving most of them to the libraries at UK and MSU.

Preface

1. Wilma Dykeman, "Mock Letters," in *A Gathering at the Forks*, eds. George Ella Lyon, Jim Wayne Miller, Gurney Norman (Wise, VA: Vision Books, 1993), 119.

2. Still scratched out this poem in 1977 while waiting for a tardy breakfast of limp pancakes at a hotel in Athens, Tennessee. Collected in Still, *From the Mountain, From the Valley*, 118.

1. A Place to Begin

Epigraph: James Still, quoted in Wade Hall, *Portrait of the Artist as a Boy in Alabama* (Lexington, KY: The King Library Press, 1998), ii.

1. Hall, *Portrait*, ii. A relative, Dr. Gaines, attended the mother.

2. "James Still," Contemporary Authors Autobiography Series, 17 (Detroit: Gale, 1993), 232.

3. Dean Cadle Coll. Box 12 #8. This short article appeared in the *Chambers County News* in 1939 to commend James Still for an early publication but was an appreciation of the father more than the son.

4. James Still Room, Camden-Carroll Library, MSU, Box 23 #8. Handwritten love letter from J. A. Still to his future wife. Spelling and punctuation have been altered to facilitate reading.

5. James Still, interview by Laura Lee, in *The Wolfpen Notebooks: A Record of Appalachian Life* (Lexington: UPK, 1991), 11.

6. James Still, *Chinaberry*, ed. Silas House (Lexington: UPK, 2012), 85–86.

7. For one version of the story, see *The Wolfpen Notebooks* interview, 10. Family members of Still's two oldest sisters could not recall any mention of their mother's ever living in Texas. Still's nephew Hervey Sharpe recalled that his birth certificate listed his mother as being from Texas, but he had no knowledge of the connection. The 1900 census listed the family as having three girls, all born in Alabama.

8. Hall, *Portrait*, 1.

9. James Still, "A Man Singing to Himself: An Autobiographical Essay by James Still," in *From the Mountain, From the Valley: New and Collected Poems*, ed. Ted Olson (Lexington: UPK, 2001), 6.

10. Hall, *Portrait*, 3–4.

11. "Still," CAA, 232.

12. James Still, interview by author, July 10, 1997.

13. "Still," CAA, 232.

14. Still, "A Man Singing," 5.

15. Still's niece Barbara Sue Barnes Harris followed up by saving records supplied by Simpkins. In 1999 Chambers County published *The Heritage of Chambers County Alabama*, which included brief biographies of longtime residents and explored family connections. George Zachry submitted the entry on James Still, 273–74. Nina Still Langley, Martha Still Rogers, and Martha Still submitted the entry on the Still Family, 271–72.

16. Andrew Taylor Still was born in Lee County, Virginia, in 1828. The family origins in Virginia were important because they allowed Still to complete a "genealogical circle" when he moved from Alabama to attend college in the Cumberland Gap area of Tennessee, not far from Jonesville. See Still, "A Man Singing," 5.

17. Still to Zachry, September 7, 1998. Cobb Memorial Archives (Valley Archives), F 38. Still's response to the Still Family report that questioned the Tennessee connection: "I was depending on another source—my cousin Marvin Still. When I attended Lincoln Memorial there were students from Virginia named Still. We addressed each other as cousin. And Park Lanier at Radford University (VA) calls me cousin. And once a visitor at Morehead State University said she had traced me to the Georgia Laniers." In 1996 Mary Lois Howard Harrison compiled the early Still Family Ancestry, including the Quattlebaum Ancestry (contributed in part by Paul Quattlebaum), which was made available through Barbara Sue Barnes Harris.

18. A description of the Abner Still Family appears in *The Heritage of Chambers County Alabama*, 271–72. The couple made the trip along the widely used Traveler's Road that followed the Federal Road from the South Carolina–Georgia line to the Alabama line near Mobile. Three of Abner's

sons fought for the Confederacy. One family registry records William Watson's name as William Willis; census records refer to him as William W.; his obituary identifies him W. W. Still.

19. James Still Room, Camden-Carroll Library, MSU, Box 12 #14. Letter from Still to Faye Belcher, the librarian at MSU, written in 1986.

20. In the Alabama state audit in 1900, William was listed as a Class A disabled veteran of the war and received pension checks at his address in Buffalo. The old man must have felt a camaraderie and nostalgia when talking about the war because he regularly attended Old Soldiers' conventions in places like Montgomery, South Carolina, and Florida. Evidence of W. W. Still's service in the Confederate Army is limited. Still, in personal interviews, reported the incidents described here. The state audit was found in the LaFayette library in Bobby L. Lindsey, *The Reason for the Tears: A History of Chambers 1832–1900* (West Point, GA: Hester Print., 1971), 148.

21. The children of William and Anna were Willie A. (b. 1862), Martha (b. 1865), Enore (b. 1866, d. 1952), John Willis McKnight (b. 1868, d. 1951), Mary Elizabeth (b. 1871, d. 1963), James Alexander (b. 1872, d. 1957), and Ada (b. 1874).

22. What is known of the Lindsey family is compiled from Still's memories together with genealogical work done by Marguerite Lindsey Brock in 1985 and provided by Still's niece Barbara Sue Barnes Harris. The child of Melissa Carrie Jackson and her first husband, Green, was a girl named Tommy. The children of Carrie and James Lindsey were Mary Ann (b. ?), Joseph J. (b. 1869), Elizabeth (b. ?), Lonie (1875–1930), Luther, Benjamin Franklin (b. 1880), Carrie (b. 1882), John (b. 1884), and Eddie Boozer (b. 1889). James Still interviews by author, June 25 and July 11, 1997.

23. Marguerite Lindsey Brock letter to Barbara Harris, April 2, 1985. Harris papers.

24. Still, *From the Mountain*, 146. The same story was recounted in a Still interview by author, July 11, 1997.

25. JWM Coll. In a letter from Still to Eliot Wigginton, when the interview for *Wolfpen Notebooks* was being edited (January 15, 1988): "My Uncle Edd once said to me, 'Did you know that when your mother was a girl the kitchen floor was beaten earth?'" The comment was abbreviated for the final draft. See Still, *Wolfpen Notebooks*, 10.

26. JWM Coll. From a letter dated January 15, 1988, to Eliot Wigginton, while preparing the introductory interview for *Wolfpen Notebooks*. The entire paragraph was edited out of the published version.

27. James Still, interview by author, June 26, 1997.

28. Jim Wayne Miller, "Madly to Learn: James Still, the Teacher," in *From the Fort to the Future: Educating the Children of Kentucky*, ed. Edwina Doyle, Ruby Layson, and Anne Thompson (Lexington: Kentucky Images, 1987), 231.

29. Hall, *Portrait*, 4.

30. James Still, interview by Randy Wilson, "A Century of Summers: 100 Years of Childhood Memories Right Here in the Mountains," Kid's

Radio WMMT, August 19, 1998. Church attendance was so important that when Grandma Lindsey was unable to leave the house because of her rheumatism, the preacher would go to her. Similar to his uncle's having to apologize for laughing, his father had to apologize to the congregation for missing a service. His excuse was that he was a doctor and had been called to an emergency case.

31. James Still, interview by author, July 11, 1997.

32. "James Still on His Life and Work," interview by Judi Jennings, *Heritage,* June Appal Recordings (Whitesburg, KY: Appalshop, 1992). Jennings provided the author with the full unedited transcript of the interview.

33. For information about the churches, see *The Heritage of Chambers County, Alabama.* James Still never spoke of his baptism, but if one did occur, it would have taken place in the baptismal pool built around the spring issuing from a rock and surrounded by a natural amphitheater.

34. "Still," CAA, 232–33.

35. James Still, interview by Randy Wilson.

36. Still, *From the Mountain,* 150.

37. Still, *From the Mountain,* 79.

38. Hall, *Portrait,* 5.

39. Still, "A Man Singing," 7–8.

40. See "Blunt Arrow," chapter 11, *Chinaberry.*

41. "Still," CAA, 233.

42. James Still, interview by Elisabeth Beattie, *Conversations with Kentucky Writers,* ed. Elisabeth Beattie (August 2, 1991): 358.

43. James Still, *Sporty Creek* (Lexington: UPK, 1999), 118–119.

2. Old Enough to Go Traipsing

Epigraph: James Still, *The Hills Remember,* 152.

1. Still, *Wolfpen Notebooks,* 11.

2. Still told the story of meeting Miss Porterfield years later, when he was a student at Vanderbilt. She was taking classes at Peabody College. She remembered him. But, she confessed, she had never thought "he would be the one" to continue his education through graduate school. Miss Porterfield had no knowledge that she was the one who started James Still on his lifelong journey of learning. Jim Wayne Miller retold the story in "Madly to Learn," 232.

3. Jim Wayne Miller, "Happy Man on Troublesome Creek," *Vanderbilt Magazine* (Summer 1987): 18.

4. Beattie, *Conversations,* 358.

5. Still, *Wolfpen Notebooks,* 11.

6. "First Reading" rough transcript projected for NPR project, summer 1984. Still Storage.

7. Hall, *Portrait,* 8. This indirect contact with the Civil War eventually led Still to a long research project in preparation for writing a novel about the prison at Andersonville, Georgia. He abandoned the work when MacKinlay Kantor published his novel *Andersonville* in the mid-1950s.

Still kept materials concerning Andersonville, including a small notebook filled with tiny writing that includes chapter-by-chapter notes probably on a book by John McElroy called *Andersonville: A Story of Rebel Military Prisons . . .*, published in 1879. Notes found in Still Storage.

8. Transcript of an interview by Jim Wayne Miller, November 15, 1986. JWM Coll. Also found in UK Coll. Box 98 #2.

9. James Still, interview by author, July 10, 1997. Still did not remember the boy's name but recalled that he was killed in a cyclone some years later.

10. Hall, *Portrait,* 10.

11. There is no evidence, other than Still's comment, that Mun Barrow worked as a janitor. The Joe Lewis website indicates he was a cotton farmer. *The Lafayette Sun,* October 28, 1998, called him a "fairly prosperous cotton farmer and landowner."

12. This connection between work and socializing occurs as a motif in Still's short stories. For example, work and play are intermingled in "A Master Time": young couples gather for a hog killing and, after the work, engage in a glorious snowball fight. In "The Stir-Off" there is more tomfoolery than work, but somehow the gathering produces seventeen gallons of molasses.

13. Still, *Wolfpen Notebooks,* 10.

14. James Still, interview by Randy Wilson.

15. This handwritten story was prepared as a possible text for the 1980s NPR project. There is no evidence that the spot was recorded. Still Storage. Still also told the story on the radio interview by Randy Wilson in 1998.

16. James Still, interview by Randy Wilson. Still was interested in World War I and years later went to France to visit battlefields. See chapter 24.

17. Hall, *Portrait,* 10.

18. Beattie, *Conversations,* 358.

19. James Still, interview by Randy Wilson.

20. This section was part of the original Texas manuscript. It does not appear in *Chinaberry.*

21. "Still," CAA, 233.

22. Still, "A Man Singing," 11.

23. "Still," CAA, 234.

24. James Still, interview by Randy Wilson.

25. James Still, interview by author, June 25, 1997.

26. Still *Chinaberry,* 87.

27. Beattie, *Conversations,* 360.

28. Still, *Chinaberry,* 32–33.

29. Still, *Wolfpen Notebooks,* 12.

30. The article was titled "The Valley of Ten Thousand Smokes" by Robert F. Griggs, who also led Mount Katmai expeditions in 1915 and 1916. The volcano had erupted in June 1912 when Still was six. The article that he read appeared in *National Geographic* (January 1917): 13–68.

31. Still, *Wolfpen Notebooks,* 12.

32. James Still, interview by author, March 29, 1994. Quoting Still: "Growing up I never thought of writing as a profession. . . . I did write—

I still have it too—it was on a tablet. I wrote a little novel . . . with a hard pencil . . . I don't know how old I was. Maybe 8 or 9. . . . It was called 'The Gold Nugget.' It came from an idea [in a story] that the teacher read to us."

33. Beattie, *Conversations,* 359.

34. James Still, interview by author, July 11, 1997.

3. The Model Scout

Epigraph: James Still, quoted in Hall, *Portrait,* 12.

1. Still, "A Man Singing," 9.

2. Gradually, he established a small-animal practice and became a rabies inspector for Georgia and Alabama.

3. The area has changed dramatically since 1918—what used to be independent mill villages spread and blended to make one urban area called Valley. Lanier Avenue still exists but is located in Lanett, not in the area currently known as Shawmut. The street is near the Chattahoochee River, which Still enjoyed as a boy.

4. "Huge Growth in the Valley Is Surprising," *Chattahoochee Valley Times,* August 17, 1921; *Valley Times,* January 28, 1921; *Valley Times,* March 18, 1921.

5. "Still," CAA, 235.

6. Edith Johnson—married to Still's first cousin—tells of a Julia Murphy who kept the library in the town when she lived there in the 1940s (twenty-plus years after Still moved to Shawmut). This may not be the same person if the woman was elderly when Still knew her. Johnson remembered the attention that Murphy paid to everything Still published in the late 1930s and early 1940s.

7. Jim Wayne Miller, "Daring to Look in the Well," *The Iron Mountain Review* 2 (1984): 3.

8. Hall, *Portrait,* 11.

9. James Still, interview by Randy Wilson.

10. Still, *Wolfpen Noteooks,* 13.

11. Hall, *Portrait,* 11.

12. His diary entry on July 22, shortly after his sixteenth birthday, showed his reaction to seeing the news of the prize: "Arose at 6.10 and began to clean up. Saw an article I had written in Birmingham News. I was so supprized [*sic*]. I like to have fainted. I had won second prize. Good luck! Eh!" Diary found in Still Storage.

13. James Still, interview by author, July 10, 1997.

14. Beattie, *Conversations,* 359.

15. James Still Papers, UK Libraries, Box 24 #1. Thomas E. Watson was a politician that the family admired; Still's brother, born in 1911, was named Thomas Watson Still.

16. James Still, interview by Judi Jennings for the *Heritage* tape.

17. James Still, interview by author, August 10, 1998.

18. James Still Papers, UK Libraries, Box 5.

19. James Still, interview by author, August 10, 1998; Miller, "Daring to Look in the Well," 3.

20. Walter R. Marsh, *Elementary Algebra* (New York: Scribner's, 1907). Found in the James Still Room, Camden-Carroll Library, MSU.

21. The two people on the list with whom he stayed friends were Henry Johnson and Forrest Word. The list appears not in the book but in notes he made for an NPR spot about algebra.

22. Information provided by *Scout News* in *Chattahoochee Valley Times*, January 17, March 23, April 4, 1923, and January 30, 1924: the scoutmaster was L. L. Scales; assistant scoutmaster was Clyde McKinty. Brother Comer was in Troop 2, and brother Thomas Watson was in Troop 3.

23. James Still, *Heritage* interview by Judi Jennings, *Chattahoochee Valley Times*, November 5, 1924. The emblem is a pair of Scout Signal Flags enclosed in a circle of red. It is an honor to win because the requirements are hard.

24. Diary of James Still kept at age sixteen from May 29 to September 9, 1922. Still Storage.

25. *Chattahoochee Valley Times*. Later, Still commented that he did not know anything the Laniers had done for the Valley: "Except for furnishing low-pay wages in the cotton mills. . . . Yet the name is on everything: hospitals, schools, statues, etc." Either Still had forgotten this contribution in the intervening years, or he no longer considered a gift to the Boy Scouts as helping Valley. James Still, interview by author, June 25, 1997.

26. *Chattahoochee Valley Times*, April 30, 1924.

27. Lyrics from camp booklet. James Still Room, Camden-Carroll Library, MSU.

28. February 22, 1928, James Still Room, Camden-Carroll Library, MSU, Box 19 #11.

29. NPR draft of "On Becoming a Poet." Notes and transcriptions of NPR spots provided courtesy of Linc Fisch.

30. "bull dog quote" written on a page labeled "For *Foxfire*" and placed in a folder called "Sticking It Out on Dead Mare Branch," Still Storage; "expectations of society" written on a page of notes in Still's handwriting, Still Storage.

4. Working His Way

Epigraph: James Still, *The Hills Remember*, 108.

1. James Still, "Journey to the Forks," in *The Hills Remember*, ed. Ted Olson (Lexington: UPK, 2012), 133.

2. Still, "A Man Singing," 12.

3. James Still, *Heritage* interview by Judi Jennings, full transcript.

4. From the foreword to the 1925 LMU catalog.

5. LMU catalog, 13.

6. Still, "Mountain College," 1–2, James Still Papers, UK Libraries, Box 68 #8.

7. Miller, "Daring to Look," 4.

8. Tuition $16 per quarter; room and laundry $20 per quarter; board $3.50 per week, as stated in 1927 LMU catalog, 26.

9. Still, "Mountain College," 2.

10. LMU catalog, 25.

11. Still, "A Man Singing," 12.

12. Still, "Mountain College," 3.

13. November 8, 1925, James Still Room, Camden-Carroll Library, MSU, Box 1 #1.

14. October 17, 1927, James Still Papers, UK Libraries, Box 24 #1, and January 24, 1928, Box 24 #2.

15. Robert Kincaid, "Hill-Life to the Poet," *The Lincoln Herald* 41, no. 1 (October 1938): 9.

16. Beattie, *Conversations,* 361.

17. James Still, interview by Laura Lee, 16. Still claimed that LMU was forced to economize because of its own financial difficulties, and that accounted for the "spartan diet."

18. Still, "Mountain College," 4.

19. Still, "A Man Singing," 12.

20. Still, "Mountain College," 8. One interesting story tells of Jesse Stuart's going through the "barrels" when he returned to Harrogate in 1927 after working all summer in the steel mills at Ashland. He and his friend did not find anything: "We decided if we had to wear clothes like what was in those barrels, we'd go back to the steel mills." Quoted in Edward Richardson, *Jesse: The Biography of an American Writer, Jesse Hilton Stuart* (New York: McGraw-Hill, 1984), 88.

21. "Autobiography of Dare Vincent Redmond," courtesy of Alan Redmond.

22. 1926 *Railsplitter* (LMU Yearbook), 81.

23. James Still Papers, UK Libraries, "Lincoln Memorial 1924–29" contains two essays from Still's English courses: "The Advantages of a Literary Society," November 6, 1924, no grade, and a two-page essay "History of Language," December 5, 1925, in English One, grade C, no comments. Also a program shows he was part of the Annual Oratorical Contest on May 11 at 7:00 p.m. and spoke on the topic "Youth of America."

24. James Still Papers, UK Libraries. This was the last math course Still ever took. UK Coll., LMU file, contains material from the algebra course. Professor Sarrett was the instructor. First lesson A; second A; third B; fourth A; fifth C- with comment "What is wrong. Bring your work up"; another C-; A-; B; A-; C-; C; and B+.

25. James Still rarely spoke of Mayme Brown, but her appearance as a mystery person in one version of his well-known poem "Those I Want in Heaven with Me (Should There Be Such a Place)" invites speculation that, at the least, she was his first sweetheart and, at most, the love of his life. See Ann Olson, "Before Saying Yes: Discovering James Still's 'Sweetheart,'" in *Interviews, Oral Histories and Memoirs,* ed. Ted Olson (Jefferson, NC: McFarland, 2009), 201–04.

26. Quoted in Ann Olson, 203.

27. *Railsplitter,* 41.

28. Still, *Wolfpen Notebooks,* 16.

29. Letter from C. P. Williams, May 30, 1925, James Still Room, Camden-Carroll Library, MSU, Box 1 #1.

30. Letters from James Still to Dare Redmond, courtesy of Alan Redmond.

31. Ibid.

32. After his death, in a box of Still's disorganized papers, a memento was found without date or comment: a place card from a party or dinner with a watercolor daffodil in the upper left corner and a neatly handwritten name on the card: Mattie Brown. Mattie also sent a Christmas card (date unknown) to Still with the inscription "Christmas greetings Love Mattie in remembrance of Brownie [her nickname for Mayme]." LMU Coll.

33. September 15, 1926, Private collection of Alan Redmond (hereafter Redmond Coll.).

34. Ibid.

35. The younger Still reported that "the office was bought once again. There were seven in the race and Papa received more votes than the other five put together, yet not quite enough to strip the present incumbent." September 15, 1926, Redmond Coll.

36. In the full transcript of the *Heritage* interview with Judi Jennings, Still talks about visiting Texas when he was twenty with his father and brothers.

37. Letter to Redmond, September 27, 1926, Redmond Coll. Note the place-names Anson and Winters, names he chose for his adult character in the Texas manuscripts, which later became the posthumous work, *Chinaberry*.

38. In the full transcript of the *Heritage* interview.

39. September 27, 1926, Redmond Coll.

40. A fellow apprentice was Joe Lanier, who became a superintendent and made his career in the cotton mills. Another friend began a stimulating career in textiles. His letter to Still in December 1928 expressed his enjoyment of learning the business at Buck Creek Cotton Mills in Siluria, Alabama, south of Birmingham. Letter to Still from Henry Johnson, December 4, 1928, James Still Papers, UK Libraries, Box 24 #2. Johnson was the brother of Still's brother-in-law. In the July 10, 1997, interview, Still described him as "the smartest boy, keenest mind I ever encountered. He was the superintendent of a cotton mill. He never went to college."

41. March 28, 1927, Redmond Coll.

5. Mentors, Friends, and Patron

1. Beattie, *Conversations*, 361.

2. Letter to "Folks," dated "Thursday 9:15," probably written in October 1927, James Still Room, Camden-Carroll Library, MSU, Box 1 #3. Still enrolled in Classical Literature for three quarters and earned a B in two of those. One quarter he earned a D, with the explanation on his transcript that the second quarter grades [were] cut for having more than six absences following the holidays.

3. One letter he dated "Monday 10:30 a. m." (1927 or 1928) describes a packed weekend and conveys his intense involvement and high spirits, James Still Room, Camden-Carroll Library, MSU, Box 1 #3.

4. Undated letter to his "Folks," probably written in October of his junior year (1927–1928), found in Still Storage, now in James Still Papers, UK Libraries, Box 24.

5. James Still, interview by Judi Jennings, *Heritage;* Dr. Lucia Danforth, the French instructor, was the only faculty member at the time who held a doctorate. Soon after Still graduated, Danforth took a position at Iowa Wesleyan College but maintained contact with her LMU students. From Danforth to Still, November 1, 1931, James Still Room, Camden-Carroll Library, MSU, Box 16 #1.

6. Letters from Redmond to Still over the years include twenty-seven in the UK Coll., twenty-nine in the MSU Coll., with little overlap between them. Alan Redmond graciously made available his father's collection of letters from Still, which includes twenty-eight letters from Still to Red between 1926 and 1938.

7. "Autobiography of Dare Vincent Redmond," 15, Redmond Coll.

8. Beattie, *Conversations*, 361.

9. George Zachry, "James Still: Biographical Sketch of a Native of LaFayette, Alabama," *Chronicles of the Chattahoochee Valley*, 1995, 153. The name of the journal at this time was *The Atlantic Monthly*. Beginning in 2007, the official name became *The Atlantic*. The names are written as they appear in quotations but are essentially interchangeable.

10. Elizabeth Lamont, "An Unsung Appalachian Literary Heritage: The Significance of James Still's Undergraduate Experience," *Appalachian Heritage* (Fall 2010): 36.

11. James Still, interview by author, July 13, 1994. *Mountain Herald* (campus magazine) reports on the visits of the Fords to LMU in 1927.

12. The pedigree name for the dog was Reigh Count Grannis. Frank Grannis is listed as the breeder. AKC paper are in James Still Room, Camden-Carroll Library, MSU, Box 23 #23.

13. Undated letter typed on Nancy Hanks Memorial Association letterhead. Note that "Mrs. Frank Grannis" was secretary of the association.

14. Perhaps unloading Grannis on his parents was Still's way of replacing the dog Jack that had disappeared twelve years earlier. His mother did not seem to mind the responsibility. By April 27 she reported that the dog had adjusted to his new home: "Grannis is getting along fine we all think a lot of him he keeps the chickens out of the garden." James Still Papers, UK Libraries, Box 24 #2.

15. Richardson, *Jesse*, 67.

16. Quoted in Richardson, *Jesse*, 76.

17. Kroll quoted in Richard Saunders, *Never Been Rich: Life and Work of a Southern Ruralist Writer, Harry Harrison Kroll* (Knoxville: University of Tennessee Press, 2011), 79.

18. Richardson, *Jesse*, 78. Also see Saunders, *Never Been Rich*, 79–80.

19. Saunders, *Never Been Rich*, 79.

20. Ibid., 70–71.

21. Lamont, "Literary Heritage," 35.

22. Ibid.

23. *Mountain Herald* (September 1927), quoted in Saunders, *Never Been Rich*, 79, footnote 73.

24. Saunders, *Never Been Rich*, 83–84.

25. James Still, interview by Judi Jennings, *Heritage*. Still added that many years after leaving LMU, he got to know Kroll and liked him very much. That reconnection was most likely in 1959 when Kroll took part in the Morehead Writers' Workshop along with Still and Stuart.

26. The class numbered thirty-eight graduates.

27. Richardson, *Jesse*, 67.

28. Still had either $40 or $60 depending on the account. Stuart had $29.30 according to Richardson ($65), and West had only $1.65 in his pocket according to Jeff Biggers in his introduction to Don West, *No Lonesome Road: Selected Prose and Poems,* ed. Jeff Biggers and George Brosi (Urbana: University of Illinois, 2004), xv.

29. James Lorence, *A Hard Journey: The Life of Don West* (Urbana: University of Illinois Press, 2007), 11.

30. Stuart also complained of the small rations. According to David Dick, Stuart claimed he almost starved his first two months at LMU. David Dick, *Jesse Stuart: The Heritage, A Biograph,* (North Middleton, KY: Plum Lick Publishing, 2005), 69.

31. Ibid.

32. Richardson, *Jesse*, 84.

33. Ibid., 69, 71. In his freshman year, Jesse published three poems in *The Blue and Gray*. The next year, after becoming editor, he published another, "The Cumberland Call." During the summer after graduation, Stuart signed a contract that would lead to the publication in August 1930 of his first book of poetry, *Harvest of Youth.*

34. Lamont, "Literary Heritage," 32. Note that Still came in third and Stuart fourth.

35. Lorence, *Hard Journey*, 15. While there, he composed many of the poems that would appear in his first collection, *Crab-Grass,* published in 1931.

36. 1929 *Railsplitter* (LMU Yearbook). Even the quotes each chose to accompany his description show contrast: Still's "Men at some time are masters of their fates"; Stuart's "What price glory?" LMU Archives.

37. *The Mountain Herald,* June-July (1928): 41, LMU Archives.

38. *Blue and Gray,* December 12, 1928, LMU Archives.

39. Though not published, "Nancy Hanks: A Playlet in Three Acts" was staged in Lexington and Middlesboro, Kentucky, and Harrogate, Tennessee, in the summer of 1929.

40. Stuart to Still, May 24, 1933, from Greenup, KY, to Fairfax, AL, James Still Room, Camden-Carroll Library, MSU, Box 2 #2.

41. Still to Redmond, November 21, 1932, Redmond Coll.

42. Loomis is listed in the 1927 LMU catalog as financing a number of ten-dollar prizes to girls who kept the neatest rooms in the dormitories.

43. Still's success at essay contests could have been motivated by a course he took with Harry Harrison Kroll. He never credited Kroll with

influencing him, but he did take two of Kroll's classes. In the *Heritage* interview transcript, he noted, "One was poetry which amounted to nothing and one was the teaching of composition [in summer 1928]. . . . we did write compositions everyday. . . . He would choose one and read it to the class." It is not known if Still wrote any of his prize-winning compositions for Kroll, but the course must have developed his skills; "A Man Singing," 13; *Wolfpen Notebooks,* 17.

44. Later referred to as his "solid gold liar's license."

45. Loomis to Still, James Still Papers, UK Libraries, Box 24 #3.

46. Still to parents, September 14, 1929, James Still Room, Camden-Carroll Library, MSU, Box 1 #8.

47. Letter to his family, written "Thursday 9:15 pm." Handwritten date on the back "1928" but probably mailed in October 1927. Found in Still Storage.

48. Mother to Still, January 21, 1929, James Still Papers, UK Libraries, Box 24 #3.

49. Ibid., May 19, 1929.

50. Undated letter from Still to Tom, probably written in the summer of 1928, James Still Room, Camden-Carroll Library, MSU, Box 1 #4.

6. The Scholar's Tale

Epigraph: Jerry Williamson, "An Interview with James Still," *Appalachian Journal* 6 (Winter 1979): 134.

1. On August 30, 1929, Still received a letter from Illinois saying he had been conditionally admitted but was denied full enrollment because the library school did not recognize all the courses he had taken at LMU, presumably because the institution lacked accreditation. Still could enter as an "unclassified student." If his first semester's grades were good enough, he would be fully admitted in the second. He would be charged an additional $7.50/semester for unclassified status. From Phineas Windsor, Still Storage.

2. Several years later, Iris Grannis wrote a letter to Still in which she referred to a scandal involving scholarship money. The letter implied that LMU had received money for a student (Still) to attend Duke. When he went to Vanderbilt, Grannis had the money paid directly to him. By 1932 she was no longer at LMU, but the finance officer must have questioned the decision. She offered to repay the scholarship money herself. Letter dated September 16, 1932, James Still Papers, UK Libraries, Box 24 #6.

3. James Still, interview by author, 1997.

4. James Still, conversation/interview by author, 1994, 1997.

5. Letters, James Still Room, Camden-Carroll Library, MSU, Box 14 #12. His comment in the *Heritage* interview with Judi Jennings: "They [Frank and Iris Grannis] made every effort to get me into Yale. The problem was they [Yale] required . . . four years of Latin and I had only two. . . . I regret I didn't have those four years."

6. Still to Shanks, n.d. Redmond to Still, October 6, 1929: "You seem to have quite an LMU club at Nashville," James Still Room, Camden-Carroll

Library, MSU, Box 1 #9; Still to Stoneback, January 20, 1985, James Still Papers, UK Libraries, Box 33 #1. Also see H. R. Stoneback, "Rivers of Earth and Troublesome Creeks: The Agrarianism of James Still," *Kentucky Review* 10, no. 3 (1990): 3–26.

7. His Alabama classmate and friend Henry Johnson [brother of Still's brother-in-law Allen Johnson] wrote to him on September 18, 1929, and referenced a card that he had received from Still a few days earlier from "somewhere in the East."

8. James Still, interview by Judi Jennings, *Heritage*. He was there in the summers of 1929 and 1930, as illustrated by a photo taken at Cape Cod.

9. Still to parents, James Still Room, Camden-Carroll Library, MSU, Box 19 #6.

10. September 20, 1929, James Still Room, Camden-Carroll Library, MSU, Box 1 #8; October 6, 1929, James Still Room, Camden-Carroll Library, MSU, Box 1 #9.

11. James Still Room, Camden-Carroll Library, MSU, Box 1 #8.

12. Still to Stoneback, January 20, 1985, James Still Papers, UK Libraries, Box 33 #1. For a more dramatic version of his living situation, see Still, "A Man Singing," 15.

13. Still's comments to Molly Bundy, February 9, 1996.

14. Little is known about the history course or the professor. Still does comment in his letter to Stoneback that he wrote his history term paper on Gustavus Adolphus, and "Dr. Walker suggested that I stay on at VU for a doctorate in history."

15. Vanderbilt U. Special Collection: www.library.vanderbilt.edu/speccol/urr/biographybiblio.shtml.

16. James Still, interview by author, June 25, 1997.

17. The letter continues, "Mim's [*sic*] recently published THE ADVANCING SOUTH was held in considerable disregard by some faculty members. And that was the year of I'LL TAKE MY STAND. Ransom and Wade read their chapters to us. R. Penn Warren was, I believe, in Oxford. Andrew Lytle was at Sewanee and came to read a play of his to us, but not from this book"; James Still Papers, UK Libraries, Box 35 #1.

18. Ransom's first collection of essays, *God without Thunder,* was published in 1930. *The World's Body* followed in 1938, and *The New Criticism* in 1941.

19. Edwin Mims, *History of Vanderbilt University* (Nashville: Vanderbilt University Press, 1946), 414.

20. James Still, interview by author, June 25, 1997.

21. James Still, interview by author, August 1, 1994. Still had just read Ransom's biography *Gentleman in a Dustcoat,* written by Thomas Daniel Young (1976), and by then had decided that Ransom deserved consideration as one of the most important and influential men of letters of the twentieth century.

22. Essays from Ransom's class are in James Still Papers, UK Libraries, Box 20 #10.

23. James Still, interview by Judi Jennings, *Heritage*.

24. Wade and Ransom both contributed essays to the agrarian collection *I'll Take My Stand* (1930). Ransom's "Reconstructed and Unregenerate" leads the collection; Wade's is "The Life and Death of Cousin Lucius."

25. James Still, interview by Judi Jennings, *Heritage*.

26. Manuscript is in UK collection; it is unclear if this is the actual essay or a draft. The manuscript is twenty-two single-spaced typed pages. It divides Cotton Mather's life into sections: 1–12; College Days; A Young Minister; Witchcraft; Middle Age; and Later Period.

27. Transcript (grade reports) for Vanderbilt, December 14, 1929, and March 15, 1930, James Still Room, Camden-Carroll Library, MSU, Box 19 #10.

28. Mims, *Vanderbilt*, 412.

29. Still to Stoneback, January 20, 1985, James Still Papers, UK Libraries, Box 33 #1.

30. James Still, interview by Judi Jennings, *Heritage*. In a conversation with the author, Still identified the humor and sarcasm he shared with Chaucer.

31. Ibid.

32. To describe the scope of the work: it was eighty-one pages, had eighty footnotes, dealt with seventeen primary sources, and consulted ten secondary sources. The Still Coll. at UK contains a stack of approximately one hundred note cards related to the project, all neatly typed back and front, and tied with string.

33. Beattie, *Conversations*, 361. He claimed he wrote two articles (for *American Speech*) when he was a sophomore. Later, when H. L. Mencken wrote *The American Language*, he used both those articles and credited Still. Elizabeth Lamont states that the essays were written in History of the English Language, a course taught by Vryling Buffum. Lamont, "Literary Heritage," 35.

34. Lucia Danforth held the doctorate. Harry Harrison Kroll published *Mountainy Singer* in 1928 but left LMU shortly after the publication.

35. James Still's talk to a class at Hindman on August 3, 1994. A major effect these teachers had on Still was their influence on what and how he would read. Still kept from Ransom's class a "Reference List of American and British Critics," which summarizes faculty members' attitudes toward the type and value of critical responses. For example, Davidson called T. S. Eliot "the best of the 'intellectual' set" and "less radical as a critic than would be thought." Wade found him "extremely modern" and his poetry "erratic and painfully self-conscious." Ransom found his criticism in *The Sacred Wood* "very learned, original, and modernistic." About Mencken, who had written the critical essay about the South only twelve years earlier ("Sahara of the Bozart"), they were less gracious. Davidson called him "professionally impressionistic. A public performer and moralist." Wade called him a "gad-fly," and Ransom labeled him "a critic of great violence." UK Coll: Vanderbilt.

36. Still to Stoneback, January 20, 1985, James Still Papers, UK Librar-

ies, Box 33 #1. There is no record of what Still paid the boardinghouse for lodging. But in a letter dated October 6, 1929, Redmond commented that living expenses were higher in Nashville because in Chapel Hill he was paying only eleven dollars per month for his dorm room.

37. James Still, interview by Judi Jennings, *Heritage*.

38. "Still," CAA, 237.

39. James Still Room, Camden-Carroll Library, MSU, Box 1 #11.

40. May 20, 1930. James Still Room, Camden-Carroll Library, MSU, Box 1 #12.

41. Ibid.

42. Undated, James Still Room, Camden-Carroll Library, MSU, Box 1 #13.

43. June 7, 1930, James Still Room, Camden-Carroll Library, MSU, Box 1 #12.

7. A Practical Degree

Epigraph: James Still, *From the Mountain, From the Valley*, 27.

1. Still had no interest in pursuing a doctorate, though he said that his history professor at Vanderbilt (Wilfred Walker), after reading his paper on Gustavus Adolphus, suggested that he work on a doctorate in history. Beattie, *Conversations*, 364.

2. May 3, 1930, James Still Room, Camden-Carroll Library, MSU, Box 1 #6; May 22, 1930, James Still Room, Camden-Carroll Library, MSU, Box 1 #12; July 16, 1930, James Still Papers, UK Libraries, Box 24 #4.

3. Reproduced verbatim. June 25, 1929, James Still Papers, UK Libraries, Box 24 #3.

4. June 25, 1930, James Still Room, Camden-Carroll Library, MSU, Box 1 #12.

5. James Still, interview by author, June 25, 1997.

6. The original 1930 film was *With Byrd at the South Pole*. One of the most popular heroes in the 1920s, Byrd was the first to fly over the South Pole in what became a media expedition for publicity as well as science.

7. Reproduced verbatim. July 1, 1930, James Still Room, Camden-Carroll Library, MSU, Box 1 #12. This was the last letter that Still's mother wrote to him. She died three months later.

8. July 3, 1930, James Still Room, Camden-Carroll Library, MSU, Box 1 #12. Ralph Williams's father owned a Sheet Metal Contracting Company in Harlan. Ralph recovered from this episode and continued to write Still until 1955. A letter from his father to Still in 1931 showed that the young man was continuing to experience serious mental-health issues.

9. August 19, 1930, James Still Papers, UK Libraries, Box 24 #4.

10. Undated (ca. 1930), James Still Room, Camden-Carroll Library, MSU, Box 1 #11; August 20, 1930, James Still Room, Camden-Carroll Library, MSU, Box 1 #12.

11. August 19, 1930, James Still Papers, UK Libraries, Box 24 #4.

12. September 4, 1930, James Still Room, Camden-Carroll Library,

MSU, Box 1 #13; September 12, 1930, James Still Room, Camden-Carroll Library, MSU, Box 1 #13.

13. September 17, 1930, James Still Room, Camden-Carroll Library, MSU, Box 1 #13.

14. Telegram from father to "JS" in Champaign, James Still Papers, UK Libraries, Box 24 #4.

15. He sent his brothers books for Christmas and cigars to his dad. Alfred, his youngest brother, was making plans to live with their sister Inez, letter in James Still Papers, UK Libraries, Box 24 #5.

16. March 19, 1928, James Still Papers UK Libraries Box 24 #2; December 9, 1929, James Still Papers, UK Libraries Box 24 #4.

17. November 7, 1929, James Still Papers, UK Libraries, Box 24 #3.

18. Ibid.

19. October 25, 1930, James Still Room, Camden-Carroll Library, MSU, Box 1 #13. A month later, West wrote that he was sending Still an old musical instrument, a dulcimer made by J. D. Thomas. In December, Still reciprocated with a book, James Still Room, Camden-Carroll Library, MSU, Box 1 #14.

20. See receipt dated November 24, 1930, James Still Room, MSU.

21. James Still, interview by author, June 25, 1997. One famous band that Still remembered was Paul Whiteman.

22. Ibid.

23. Ibid. When Still visited Williams at Tuskegee, he also met Booker T. Washington's son. Still admitted, "I lived in Alabama and yet I had never really talked to black people."

24. Redmond's autobiography, 16, Redmond Coll.

25. Excerpt from a paper written as part of a course at the University of Illinois, James Still Papers, UK Libraries, Box 19 #16.

26. For a discussion of the difficulties, see chapters 7 and 8 of Earl Hess, *Lincoln Memorial University and the Shaping of Appalachia* (Knoxville: University of Tennessee Press, 2011).

27. Manuscript "Mountain College," James Still Papers, UK Libraries, Box 68 #8.

28. Still, "A Man Singing," 15.

29. Rena Niles, "Obscurity Begins at Home for Kentucky's James Still," *Louisville Courier-Journal Magazine,* April 30, 1939, n.p.

30. His first printed poem, "Dreams," appeared in *Arcadian Magazine,* April 1931. Poems were published regularly in 1935; a few stories appeared as early as 1936, but by 1938, Still was publishing more stories than poems.

31. Still, *From the Mountain,* 27.

8. "19-Dirty-one"

Epigraph: Letter from Still to Redmond, January 23, 1932, Redmond Coll.

1. May 24, 1931, James Still Papers, UK Libraries, Box 24 #5.

2. In a letter dated November 10, 1931, Still reminded Red not to share news of the trip Still made to Florida because Loomis had asked "why he

was running about so much, and didn't it cost money, and please explain"; Redmond Coll.

3. June 30, 1931, Redmond Coll.

4. Iris Grannis at Lake Lure, NC, to Still, winter 1931, James Still Room, Camden-Carroll Library, MSU, Box 1 #15.

5. In an informal conversation, Still remembered the projected title of the book as *God's Green Acre*, and its topic to be tourists in the mountains. It was never published. It's an odd coincidence that Viking published Erskine Caldwell's popular, controversial novel *God's Little Acre,* set in Georgia, in 1933.

6. July 19, 1931, Redmond Coll.

7. Throughout his life, James Still appreciated a reading light next to his bed. One example was in Mars Hill, NC, in 1993 when he became quite irritated because a woman managing the guesthouse where he was staying had objected to his moving a lamp so that he could read in bed.

8. July 24, 1931, Redmond Coll. This typed letter contains many proper nouns beginning with small letters. The typewriter could have been at fault, but the shift did work occasionally. One side effect of this unconventional typing is a tone of hopelessness.

9. The trip he describes could be considered a precursor to or inspiration for later stories about journeys of mishap and adventure, like "The Run for the Elbertas."

10. July 31, 1931, Redmond Coll.

11. August 13, 1931, and August 14, 1931, James Still Papers, UK Libraries, Box 49 #5.

12. Still to Redmond, August 16, 1931, Redmond Coll; James Still Papers, UK Libraries, Box 24 #5. The reason for rejection was stated: "question ref. military or naval service."

13. November 10, 1931, Redmond Coll.

14. The agency he refers to is most likely The Albert Teachers' Agency. A contract signed by Still indicates that he was registered with this organization and was seeking employment as a librarian. He lists as references Lucia Danforth, Francis Simpson (assistant director of the Library School at the University of Illinois), Iris Grannis, and Harry Harrison Kroll (at Peabody College). Still Storage.

15. Reference letter from Grannis on Austin Peay Normal School letterhead, Still Storage.

16. James Still Room, Camden-Carroll Library, MSU, Box 16 #1.

17. Comer to James Still, August 31, 1931, James Still Papers, UK Libraries, Box 24 #5.

18. James Still, interview by author, June 26, 1997.

19. Austin Peay Normal School, which opened on September 23, 1929, offered a two-year curriculum that prepared graduates to pass the state certification requirements for elementary school teachers. For more information, see *Tennessee Encyclopedia of History and Culture* online https:// tennesseeencyclopedia.net/.

20. Estimated date January 22, 1932, Redmond Coll.

21. Scrap of paper in James Still Room, Camden-Carroll Library, MSU.
22. James Still, interview by author, August 1, 1994.
23. January 23, 1932, Redmond Coll.

9. To the Jumping-off Place

Epigraph: James Still, interview by author, March 29, 1994.
1. James Still Room, Camden-Carroll Library, MSU, Box 10 #21.
2. February 5, 1932, Redmond Coll.
3. November 10, 1931, Redmond Coll.
4. Loomis from Phoenix, Arizona, to Still, February 15, 1932, Still Storage.
5. Saturday, late February 1932, Redmond Coll.
6. October 25, 1930, James Still Room, Camden-Carroll Library, MSU, Box 1 #13.
7. Letter dated December 23. Sometime that month West had sent Still a dulcimer made in Knott County.
8. James Still Room, Camden-Carroll Library, MSU, Box 2 #1.
9. James Still Papers, UK Libraries, Box 24 #4.
10. James Still, interview by author, March 29, 1994.
11. The original invitation was to help him, his wife, Connie, and her brother Jack Adams. In the biography of West, James Lorence does not mention West as being or working in Hindman during the summer of 1932. He was helping establish the Highlander Folk School with Myles Horton in Monteagle, TN; *A Hard Journey,* 28.
12. James Still Papers, UK Libraries, Box 24 #6.
13. June 28, 1932, Redmond Coll.
14. James Still Papers, UK Libraries, Box 24 # 6.
15. Jess Stoddart, *Challenge and Change in Appalachia: The Story of Hindman Settlement School* (Lexington: UPK, 2002), 12. Katherine Pettit and May Stone, "quintessential Progressive leaders, the kind of women who founded social settlement institutions and then successfully led them," founded the school in 1902.
16. James Still Papers, UK Libraries, Box 24 #6.
17. July 23, 1932, James Still Papers, UK Libraries, Box 24 #6; letter to Bowdon College, no date, James Still Papers, UK Libraries, Box 24 #6.
18. Ralph Williams was the son of W. A. Williams, who owned W. A. Williams Sheet Metal Contractors in Harlan, KY. He had had "a break-up" in 1924 and was in a sanitarium in Louisville in October of 1931, according to a letter from his father to Still, who had written to inquire; James Still Papers, UK Libraries, Box 24 #5.
19. James Still Papers, UK Libraries, Box 24 # 6.
20. August 8, 1932, James Still Room, Camden-Carroll Library, MSU, Box 1 #2.
21. James Lorence's biography of West does not mention West's correspondence with Alice Lloyd or any interest in taking a position at Caney Creek. Between the summer of 1932 and the spring of 1933, West was concerned with the plight of the coal miners in Wilder and was involved,

along with other volunteers, in taking supplies there on weekends. James J. Lorence, *A Hard Journey: The Life of Don West* (Urbana: University of Illinois Press, 2007), 26. West was becoming active in so many social issues that taking a position as chair of the English department at Caney Creek is unlikely.

22. James Still Papers, UK Libraries, Box 24 #6.

23. For example, a woman with whom he had begun a correspondence during the summer, Marguerite Davison, wrote him on October 6 and began by saying that West had told her that Still was teaching at Caney Creek. Davison was in charge of the southeast branch of the Congregational Church Extension Board, the organization that sponsored the summer work in Hindman. She had met Still there, but the extent of their friendship is unknown except for a handful of personal and philosophical letters she wrote to him in the 1930s.

24. The job offer from Alice Lloyd occurred in the summer of 1932, but Lucy Furman did not hear of it and respond to Still until August 1933, just before Still was to join the staff at HSS, hence the date of this letter; James Still Room, Camden-Carroll Library, MSU, Box 2.

25. Lucy Furman, a friend of Katherine Pettit, arrived in Hindman in 1907. She became a housemother for the little boys at the school and wrote several novels about working with them. *Mothering on Perilous* (1913) and *The Quare Women* (ca. 1924) are the best known. As stated by Stoddart, in *Story of Hindman Settlement School* (66), "Furman's importance in helping to create a nationwide support network for the Settlement cannot be overestimated."

26. For a discussion of the conflict between the Settlement and Lloyd, see Stoddart, 103–4 and footnote 37.

27. September 16, 1932, James Still Papers, UK Libraries, Box 24 #6.

28. Ibid.

29. October 16, 1932, James Still Room, Camden-Carroll Library, MSU, Box 2 #1.

30. Telegram, James Still Papers, UK Libraries, Box 24 #6.

31. November 21, 1932, Redmond Coll.

32. Mr. Wheeler from Austin Peay had recommended both of them to Mr. Alden at the Goodlettsville, Tennessee, high school.

33. Still received a note, dated November 2, 1932, from the Massachusetts Society for the Prevention of Cruelty to Animals with a check for $1.75 for the article "Horse Swapping Court"; James Still Papers, UK Libraries, Box 24 # 6.

34. James Still Papers, UK Libraries, Box 24 #6. This article was published sometime before June 1926 and is referred to by Jesse Stuart.

35. November 26, 1932, James Still Room, Camden-Carroll Library, MSU, Box 2 #1.

36. December 6, 1932, James Still Papers, UK Libraries, Box 24 #6.

37. James Still Papers, UK Libraries, Box 24 #7.

38. May 9, 1933, Redmond Coll.

39. Still to Red, May 9, 1933, Redmond Coll.

40. Ibid.

41. Ibid.

42. This period was very unstable for West. He was to leave Highlander Folk School in 1933 and go to Georgia to set up his own school. See Lorence, *A Hard Journey,* 22–44.

43. He is referring to the collection published in 1934 as "Man with the Bull-Tongued Plow"; James Still Papers, UK Libraries, Box 24 #7.

44. James Still Room, Camden-Carroll Library, MSU, Box 2 #2.

10. Hindman Becomes a Haven

Epigraph: James Still, *From the Mountain, From the Valley,* 50.

1. Still quoted in Miller, "Madly to Learn," 233–34.

2. *History and Families of Knott County, Kentucky* (Paducah, Kentucky: Turner Pub., 1995), 129.

3. See Vicky Hayes, "The 1930's: Farming Was Subsistence," in *History and Families of Knott County,* 130–31.

4. Stoddart, *Story of Hindman Settlement School,* 28.

5. Mission statement on the historical marker at the school. Stoddart, *Story of Hindman Settlement School,* 3.

6. Miller, "Madly to Learn," 238.

7. Stoddart, *Story of Hindman Settlement School,* 94.

8. Ibid., 99, 91.

9. This claim is exaggerated. Still probably received a salary beginning in his third rather than his fourth year, and the amount could have been seventy-five dollars per month. See letter from Clara Standish, September 15, 1935, James Still Room, Camden-Carroll Library, MSU, Box 2 #6.

10. Still, *Wolfpen Notebooks,* 18.

11. James Still, interview by author, March 29, 1994.

12. Robert Miller from Manuel, KY, wrote Still on August 26, 1932, and again on April 16, 1933. Sid Nickles from Raven, KY, wrote him on October 6, 1933; and James Gayheart from Vest, KY, on July 20, 1934. James Still Papers, UK Libraries, Box 24 #6, 7.

13. James Still, interview by Judi Jennings, *Heritage.*

14. Jethro was married to Lurania "Rania"; they had one child, Morris, born in July 1926. While teaching at HSS, Jethro continued his own education at Berea College and Eastern State Teachers College, finally graduating from MSC in 1937. *History and Families of Knott County,* 215. He is best known for his skills as a dulcimer maker, a craft he had learned from the master Ed'ud Thomas. Still once said that Thomas was so proficient at making dulcimers that "we used to think [he'd] invented them." James Still, interview by Laura Lee, *Wolfpen Notebooks,* 19.

15. A travel souvenir dates his visit to May 28; Still Room, MSU.

16. June 14, 1934, James Still Papers, UK Libraries, Box 24 #7.

17. Still to Amburgey, June 18, 1934. Ibid. Stone to Still, July 13, 1934, Still Room, MSU.

18. There is no evidence of correspondence with *The Atlantic Monthly* in 1934; however, during the first half of the year, Still had received rejec-

tion letters from *Sewanee Review, The Virginia Quarterly Review,* and *The Saturday Evening Post.* James Still Room, Camden-Carroll Library, MSU, Box 2 #3.

19. Draft letter from Still to Stone, July 1934, James Still Papers, UK Libraries, Box 24 #7. Stone to Still, July 26, 1934, Still Room, MSU.

20. Several of the acceptances were for short stories and included small checks. For example, *The Atlantic Monthly* paid him $150 for "Job's Tears," published in March 1937; it later became a chapter in *River of Earth.*

21. In spite of the encouraging events, November was sad for his family in Alabama. His young half-brother, Don, died of dengue fever. The two-year-old was living with Still's sister in Shawmut. Still served as a pallbearer at the funeral. The grave remained unmarked until 2000, when Still had a gravestone put there.

22. The poem appears second in the 1937 collection *Hounds on the Mountain* and eleventh in *From the Mountain, From the Valley,* under the title "Dulcimer." Chris Green calls it Still's first major publication because it was built around the symbol of Appalachia, the dulcimer, and because it "illustrates the contradictions and tensions of outsiders' beliefs about seeing Appalachia as a premodern space where contemporary Americans felt that people still lived in vital proximity to nature." Chris Green, "Headwaters: The Early Poetics of James Still, Don West, and Jesse Stuart," in *James Still: Critical Essays on the Dean of Appalachian Literature,* eds. Ted Olson and Kathy H. Olson (Jefferson, NC: McFarland, 2009), 27.

23. April 12, 1935, Redmond Coll. The poem was probably "Horse Swapping," published by *Saturday Review* in July.

24. Still's incentive to publish poems came partly from the old competition between himself and Stuart. Toward the end of 1934, Stuart published his second book, *Man with a Bull-Tongue Plow,* which included 703 poems. In Still's papers was the copy of a review of the collection in the April 1935 issue of *The Atlantic Monthly,* 20. Interestingly, this review was not torn out of the magazine but retyped, complete with several typos. Still had gone out of his way to type every word of Theodore Morrison's negative review. HSS Still files.

25. September 5, 1935, James Still Room, Camden-Carroll Library, MSU, Box 2 #6.

26. "Living through the Great Depression," *History and Families of Knott County,* 134–35.

27. For a discussion of the economy of Appalachia in the 1930s, see John Alexander Williams, *Appalachia: A History* (Chapel Hill: University of North Carolina Press, 2002), 312–17.

28. The Federal Emergency Relief Act, passed by Congress on May 12, 1933, created the Federal Emergency Relief Administration, which had a start-up fund of $500 million to help the needy and unemployed. Direct aid was given to the states, and they funneled it through local agencies. The funds, intended to help those hurt most by the Depression, paid for work completed, cash outlays, food, and clothes.

29. This summer job for FERA marked the beginning of Still's lifelong

habit of keeping notebooks and journals about the life of his place. He recorded speech patterns, interesting anecdotes, memorable events. Rarely do the notebooks include commentary or analysis; rather, they record a life that was quickly passing away. In 1991 he was persuaded to publish one collection of this treasure in what became *The Wolfpen Notebooks: A Record of Appalachian Life.*

30. James Still, *Wolfpen Notebooks,* 18.

31. In the CAA sketch, he claims to have spent one day a week carrying children's books from school to school, and he could serve only four schools (239). In *The Wolfpen Notebooks,* he says he delivered boxes of books on foot to eight schools (18). The most dramatic description was published on the flyleaf to *Hounds on the Mountain* (1937) in an autobiographical note: "Last year, besides my work in the Settlement, I delivered traveling libraries on foot to nineteen schools having no books. I carried twenty books in a carton on my shoulder, often walking fifteen to seventeen miles."

32. June 9, 1936, James Still Room, Camden-Carroll Library, MSU, Box 2 #13.

33. Miller, "Jim Dandy," 17.

34. James Still, interview by Judi Jennings, *Heritage.*

35. For example, "Mrs. Razor" and "The Nest."

36. James Still, interview by Judi Jennings, *Heritage.* Parks sent Still a postcard on June 3, 1936, James Still Papers, UK Libraries, Box 24 #8.

37. In 1935 and 1936 he published thirty poems and only five short stories.

38. August 1, 1935, Redmond Coll.

39. James Still, interview by Williamson, *Appalachian Journal* 6 (1979): 126.

11. Beyond the Hills

First stanza. Still's poem was accepted by *The Yale Review* on December 23, 1935, and published in the Autumn 1936 issue.

1. Perhaps he gave it such status because it was his first poem accepted by that prestigious journal and the letter opened with a subtle but profound compliment: "There is a calm, quiet beauty in your 'Child in the Hills' which has gone home to us all in this office . . . we look forward to reading more of your work." Letter from Edward Weeks, September 5, 1935, James Still Room, Camden-Carroll Library, MSU, Box 2 #6.

2. Letter to Red, written August 1, postmarked August 12, 1935, Redmond Coll.

3. Still did not talk or write about details of his regular trips to New Orleans, but in a letter to Red three years later (July 13, 1938), he commented that he went to New Orleans before going to MacDowell Colony and that he had been there four summers in a row.

4. Frances Grover joined the Hindman staff in the fall of 1935. Clara Standish described her to Still: "While [Frances] is not a young woman whom men as a rule care about, I have a notion that you will overlook some things for you should have much in common. She will be much interested

in your writing"; September 15, 1935, James Still Room, Camden-Carroll Library, MSU, Box 2 #6. Grover's aunt, Eulalie Osgood Grover, was the creator of the "Sunbonnet Babies" and "Overall Boys," a series of popular children's books. Blowing Rock School of English, a joint venture between Duke University and Rollins College, began in the summer of 1935. Still attended the second season.

5. Letters from Loomis to Still dated October 31, 1935, and November 9, 1935, refer to his meetings with Kenyon; Edwin Grover to Frances, December 17, 1935, James Still Room, Camden-Carroll Library, MSU, Box 2 #7.

6. The amount settled on was fifty dollars, sent by money order. Loomis to Still, December 15, 1935, James Still Room, Camden-Carroll Library, MSU, Box 2 #7.

7. January 14, 1936, Redmond Coll.

8. An advertising flyer for the summer program indicated that Margaret Mitchell spent a week in Banner Elk in 1936; Still Storage. Still had left before her arrival.

9. Grover to Carol Hill, April 20, 1936, James Still Papers, UK Libraries, Box 24 #8.

10. This "Letter from Mrs. Roosevelt," a rough manuscript written on a scrap of paper, is a semifictional description of the summer of 1936. The letter from Mrs. Roosevelt he planned to quote is alluded to but not included; Still Storage. The 1936 session was held in Banner Elk; later it was moved to nearby Blowing Rock and the name changed.

11. Born in 1896, Marjorie Kinnan Rawlings was the age of Still's second-oldest sister and ten years older than Still himself. When Still met her that summer in North Carolina, she was beginning work on *The Yearling*. In 1928 Rawlings and her husband purchased a seventy-two–acre orange grove in rural Florida; after their divorce in 1933, she continued to live on the farm and manage it. Her first vignettes, published in *Scribner Magazine* in 1930, showed that her material would be the place and the people of her Cross Creek area. By 1935 she had published two novels. Her best-known novel, *The Yearling,* won the Pulitzer Prize in 1939.

12. July 13, 1936, Dean Cadle Coll., UK Libraries, Box 14 #4.

13. July 31, 1936, Marjorie Kinnan Rawlings Collection at the University of Florida, the Department of Special Collections, Smathers Library.

14. Ibid., February 24, 1937.

15. The estimated date of the letter is early March 1937, James Still Papers, UK Libraries, Box 24 #8.

16. March 16, 1937, Rawlings Coll.

17. May 30, 1938, James Still Papers, UK Libraries, Box 24 #8.

18. Still to Grover, March 3, 1937, James Still Papers, UK Libraries, Box 24 #8.

19. Robert Francis, *The Trouble with Francis: An Autobiography* (Amherst: University of Massachusetts Press, 1971), 18.

20. *Stand Here with Me,* published 1936.

21. Francis, *Trouble with Francis,* 19–20.

22. For information on Bread Loaf, see David Howard Bain, *Whose Woods These Are: A History of the Bread Loaf Writers' Conference 1926–1992* (Hopewell, NJ: Ecco Press, 1993).

23. James Still Papers, UK Libraries, Box 24 #8. The story was "Bat Flight," published September 2, 1938. The acceptance letter for "Bat Flight" from *The Saturday Evening Post* is dated May 26, 1938, James Still Room, Camden-Carroll Library, MSU, Box 3 #10.

24. See the letter from Mrs. MacDowell dated May 4, 1939, James Still Room, Camden-Carroll Library, MSU, Box 3 #10.

25. July 1938, James Still Papers, UK Libraries, Box 24 #8.

26. In a handwritten marginal note, Still comments on the last sentence with the phrase "no sarcasm meant here."

27. Undated, probably August 1939, James Still Papers, UK Libraries, Box 24 #8.

28. Still Storage.

29. Francis, *Trouble with Francis*, 20. Before Still went back south, he spent a night with Francis.

30. Story retold by Linc Fisch, "In Remembrance of James Still," in *James Still in Interviews, Oral Histories and Memoirs,* ed. Ted Olson (Jefferson, NC: McFarland, 2009), 273.

31. September 1, 1938, James Still Papers, UK Libraries, Box 24 #8.

32. October 2, 1938, James Still Papers, UK Libraries, Box 24 #8. If Still did apply for the Guggenheim, his application was not successful.

33. MacDowell Colony closed the 1939 series because the hurricane had rendered studios unsafe and roads impassable. See the McDowell Colony timeline online at www.macdowellcolony.org/timeline.html.

34. Elizabeth Ames was the executive director.

35. Evidence suggests he left sometime before September 15.

36. In 1935 Schwartz had published a short story that gripped the literary establishment, "In Dreams Begin Responsibilities." The year before they met, he had collected poems and stories in a volume with the same title.

37. September 16, 1939. Collected in *Letters of Delmore Schwartz,* ed. Robert Phillips (Ontario Review Press, 1984). Still copied this page, James Still Room, Camden-Carroll Library, MSU, Box 2 #4.

38. James Still Room, Camden-Carroll Library, MSU, Box 2 #4.

39. January 27, 1940, James Still Room, Camden-Carroll Library, MSU, Box 5 #4.

40. She was married four times; her last husband was twenty-two years her junior. While Porter began publishing individual stories in the 1920s, her first collection, *Flowering Judas,* did not appear until 1930. Her second, *Pale Horse, Pale Rider,* was published in 1939. Five years later came *Leaning Tower and Other Stories,* and in 1964 she won the Pulitzer Prize and the National Book Award for her collected stories.

41. Still to Porter, October 28, 1940, Katherine Anne Porter Collection, Special Collections, University of Maryland.

42. Porter to Still, October 5, 1940, James Still Papers, UK Libraries, Box 24 #9.

43. Still to Porter, October 28, 1940, Katherine Anne Porter Papers.

44. Porter to Still, January 31, 1941, James Still Papers, UK Libraries, Box 24 #9.

45. Still to Porter, February 4, 1941 (mistakenly dated February 4, 1940), Katherine Anne Porter Papers.

46. Still to Grover, undated, ca. June 1937, James Still Papers, UK Libraries, Box 24 #8.

47. Roberts to Still, June 23, 1937, James Still Papers, UK Libraries, Box 24 #8; Roberts to Still, August 15, 1938, James Still Papers, UK Libraries, Box 24 #8.

48. This reference to Roberts appears in an early draft of a 1978 interview that Williamson conducted for *Appalachian Journal*. Williamson had asked if Still was in the "school" of Roberts. Still snapped back, "I reject the assumption that I belong to anyone's school."

49. The 1940 listing of releases from Viking Press features *River of Earth* as an exciting new book announcement, 9. Roberts is referenced in the description of Still's novel and in the comment about its projected market: "Perhaps the best way to indicate its special quality is to prophesy that Elizabeth Madox Roberts, John Steinbeck, and Marjorie Rawlings should all have a fellow-feeling for its author." An ad for Roberts's *Song in the Meadow* appears in the same brochure, 15, and predicts that it will be an outstanding literary event of the spring. In the world of Viking books, Roberts had a reputation, while Still was a newcomer, but in their personal worlds of rural Kentucky, they were peers. Viking Press 1940 promotional material, James Still Room, Camden-Carroll Library, MSU.

50. It is unclear where and when Still met Stokely, but their earliest exchange of letters was dated October 1939.

51. October 9, 1939, James Still Room, Camden-Carroll Library, MSU, Box 4 #2. September 27, 1940, James Still Room, Camden-Carroll Library, MSU, Box 4 #17.

12. A Man Singing to Himself

Epigraph: James Still, quoted in Williamson's interview for *Appalachian Journal*, 134.

1. "We're all homing pigeons. . . . I feel like homing to a place that doesn't exist anymore." Quoted in Beattie, *Conversations*, 371.

2. Based on the bibliography complied by William Terrell Cornett, in *The Wolfpen Notebooks*. The periodicals are listed here in order of the volume published: *Mountain Life and Work* (9), *Kaleidograph* (8), *Atlantic* (6), *Sewanee Review* (6), *Household* (6), *Frontier and Midland* (6), *Poetry* (5), *Saturday Evening Post* (5), *New York Times* (3), *Saturday Review of Literature* (3), *Better Homes* (3), *Arcadian Life* (3), *Fantasy* (3), *North Georgia Review* (3), *New Republic* (2), *Yale Review* (2), *Virginia Quarterly Review* (2). Each of the following published one work by Still: *New York Herald Tribune*, *Poetry Society of Florida*, *Skyline*, *Esquire*, *Nation*, *Story*, *Lyric*, *Prairie Schooner*, *American Mercury*, and *Time*.

3. September 10, 1935, Redmond Coll.

4. Still, "A Man Singing," 17.

5. Redmond Coll.

6. Quoted in Stoddart, *Story of Hindman Settlement School,* 131.

7. James Still, interview by Laura Lee, *Wolfpen Notebooks,* 18. Still says that in the fourth year, he was paid fifteen dollars per month (slightly more the fifth and sixth years). He was so rich he retired.

8. Loomis to Still, James Still Room, Camden-Carroll Library, MSU, Box 2 #6; Standish to Still, September 15, 1935, James Still Room, Camden-Carroll Library, MSU, Box 2 #6. The offer of the room is confirmed by a letter Elizabeth Watts wrote to Still on August 3; for the coming year, she and Stone "thought that [he] might like to have Miss Standish's old room, as it is vacant."

9. An online inflation calculator shows that $675 in 1935 would have had the buying power of $11,700 in 2015.

10. December 3, 1936, Redmond Coll.

11. Stoddart, *Story of Hindman Settlement School,* 131.

12. For example, on May 6, 1936, the MSU Coll. has six letters dated or postmarked to Still. On February 5, 1940, there were nine letters; February 6, seven letters; February 7, five letters.

13. James Still, interview by Laura Lee, *Wolfpen Notebooks,* 34.

14. James Still Room, Camden-Carroll Library, MSU, Box 2.

15. A typescript draft is available in James Still Papers, UK Libraries, Box 62 #5; a copy of *The Atlantic Monthly* publication, James Still Papers, UK Libraries, Box 83 #3. The poem, which Still called his first major publication, appeared the following February and earned him twenty-five dollars.

16. Grover to Still, January 25, 1936; Still to Grover, James Still Papers, UK Libraries, Box 24 #8.

17. Maxeda Hess had been a student at Rollins College and had published a book titled *Young Dawn* in 1935. Grover was the editor. Grover to Still, February 7, 1936, James Still Papers, UK Libraries, Box 24, #8.

18. Apparently, Still had, on his own, sent it to *Frontier and Midland* (magazine of the West), which accepted and published it the winter of 1936–37. Later, the title of the story was changed to "The Scrape."

19. April 23, 1936, James Still Room, Camden-Carroll Library, MSU, Box 2 #11; April 24, 1936, James Still Room, Camden-Carroll Library, MSU, Box 2 #11.

20. Still had written an enquiry to the publisher Covici Friede several months earlier, but Grover was not enthusiastic about that possibility. Still did meet Theda Kenyon.

21. August 25, 1936, James Still Room, Camden-Carroll Library, MSU, Box 2 #15. This story was included in the O. Henry collection for 1937.

22. The poems and payments were "Child in the Hills," $25; "Graveyard in the Hills," $20. The stories were "All Their Ways Are Dark," $75; "Job's Tears," $150; "Mole Bane," $75; "Uncle Jolly," $100; and "The Plowing," $75. All these stories later appeared with some revision as chapters in *River of Earth.*

23. December 11, 1936, James Still Room, Camden-Carroll Library, MSU, Box 2 #16.

24. July 7, 1936, James Still Room, Camden-Carroll Library, MSU, Box 2 #14; February 9, 1937, James Still Room, Camden-Carroll Library, MSU, Box 3 #1.

25. Undated draft, mailed between February 9 and 24, James Still Room, Camden-Carroll Library, MSU, Box 2 #5.

26. February 24, 1937, James Still Room, Camden-Carroll Library, MSU, Box 3 #1.

27. March 29, 1937, James Still Room, Camden-Carroll Library, MSU, Box 3 #2.

28. April 13, 1937, James Still Papers, UK Libraries, Box 24 #8.

29. Undated letter, James Still Papers, UK Libraries, Box 24 #8.

30. Still's letter to Red from Blowing Rock on June 25, 1937, summarizes the reviews of *Hounds on the Mountain;* Redmond Coll. Also see UK: Book reviews, Brickell and Kirkusreviews.com; letter August 4, 1937, James Still Room, Camden-Carroll Library, MSU, Box 3 #6; November 20, 1937, James Still Room, Camden-Carroll Library, MSU, Box 3 #7. The proceeds from the sale of *Hounds on the Mountain* totaled $84. Still to Robert Francis, no date, James Still Papers, UK Libraries, Box 24 #8. He claims he used it to buy a marble slab for his mother's grave in the Rock Creek Church Cemetery on June 20, 1938 ($80 for the slab, $1.60 for tax, and the remainder to install it).

31. Between June 1937 and December 1939, Still published fifteen poems and thirteen stories.

32. James Still Room, Camden-Carroll Library, MSU, Box 3 #9.

33. February 24, 1939, James Still Room, Camden-Carroll Library, MSU, Box 3 #15.

34. June 7, 1939, James Still Room, Camden-Carroll Library, MSU, Box 3 #17.

35. F. Scott Fitzgerald earned $150,000 more from magazine fiction than from his novels between 1919 and 1936. Theodore Dreiser relied heavily on magazine fees for day-to-day expenses, and Edith Wharton sought profitable arrangements for serializing her novels in magazines. "Serial money, collected in advance, could make it possible to complete a book," James West, *American Authors and the Literary Marketplace since 1900* (Philadelphia: University of Pennsylvania Press, 1988), 107.

36. Still, "A Man Singing," 17–18.

37. James Still, interview by Laura Lee, *Wolfpen Notebooks,* 35.

38. Miller, "Daring to Look," 5.

39. A copy of the original Viking contract signed by Still on December 28, 1939, is held in the editorial file on *River of Earth* at UPK. He was paid an advance of $250; the terms stated that Still would receive royalties of 15 percent of the publisher's charge on the first five thousand copies sold, 20 percent on the next five thousand, and 25 percent on any further sales. This was the first of three optioned novels mentioned in the contract for *Hounds on the Mountain* signed March 5, 1937.

40. November 20, 1929, James Still Room, Camden-Carroll Library, MSU, Box 4 #2.

41. "Still," CAA, 241.

42. This letter found in James Still Papers, UK Libraries, Box 24 #8 is dated 1938, but the date was 1939.

43. October 4, 1939, James Still Room, Camden-Carroll Library, MSU, Box 4 #2.

44. Watts to Still, August 3, 1939, James Still Room, Camden-Carroll Library, MSU, Box 4 #1.

45. May 16, 1940, James Still Room, Camden-Carroll Library, MSU, Box 4 #12.

46. James Still, interview by Laura Lee, *Wolfpen Notebooks,* 49; Amburgey did not give him the house outright. An arrangement was finalized later when Amburgey gave him the use of it for his lifetime.

47. The James Still Collection at MSU contains 165 items from Jethro Amburgey to James Still between 1929 and 1946. Many are undated casual notes, while others are longer business or personal letters.

48. Joe Creason, "Some Things a Man Does Just for Himself," *Louisville Courier-Journal Magazine,* February 14, 1960, 9; Still, "Man Singing," 18.

49. "Still," CAA, 241.

50. Some of Still's most animated and detailed conversations in personal interviews have concerned the Amburgey family: Jethro and his wife, Ranie; his twin brother, Woodrow, and two other brothers Melvin and Marion; and a nephew, Monroe. Still was closer to this family, both physically and emotionally, than to any other people in Knott County. Jethro died in 1971, and Monroe died in 1987; Still outlived an entire generation of the family.

51. Rena Niles, "Obscurity Begins Back Home," April 30, 1939; January 1, 1938, James Still Room, Camden-Carroll Library, MSU, Box 3 #8.

52. James Still, interview by Jerry Williamson, 126.

53. Still, *River of Earth,* 6, 245.

54. James Still, "Bloody Breathitt," Letters to the Editor, *Time,* February 26, 1940, 2.

55. "Still," CAA, 241–42.

56. December 5, 1939, James Still Papers, UK Libraries, Box 24 #8.

57. Viking published a bulletin for the Preview Associates (edited by Aeth C. Browne), and Still was featured in a three-page article in vol. 3, no. 3. Apparently, amateur reviews were awarded a prize, but in this case the editors could not choose one review so seven people received complimentary copies of *Hounds on the Mountain* as a prize for submitting reviews of *River of Earth. Previews and Reviews: A Bulletin for the Preview Associates.*

58. April 1, 1940, James Still Room, Camden-Carroll Library, MSU, Viking.

59. For a background discussion of regionalism in the late nineteenth and early twentieth centuries, see James M. Cox, "Regionalism: A Diminished Thing," in *Columbia Literary History of the United States,* ed. Emory Elliott (New York: Columbia University Press, 1988), 761–84.

60. February 5, 1940. Granberry cared little for accurate detail; he erroneously set the book in the Carolina hills, possibly because he associated Still with Blowing Rock School of English in western North Carolina. A copy of this review in the *New York Sun* is in the Dean Cadle Coll. Box 12.

61. Dayton Kohler, review of *River of Earth,* by James Still, *The Southern Literary Messenger* (March 1940): 205.

62. Dayton Kohler, "Jesse Stuart and James Still Mountain Regionalists," *College English* 3 (1942): 531.

63. April 1, 1940, James Still Room, Camden-Carroll Library, MSU, Box 14 #15.

64. Linc Fisch reported that Still told him Robert Lowell was given the award that year because Still did not accept the invitation. "In Remembrance of James Still," 266. This circumstance seems unlikely because Lowell's first book of poetry was not published by 1940. He did win the Pulitzer Prize for poetry in 1947.

65. He was made an honorary member of Phi Beta Kappa in 1978. See chapter 25.

66. Telegrams sent January 13 and January 18, 1941, James Still Room, Camden-Carroll Library, MSU, Box 5 #4.

67. January 26, 1941, Sunday *New York Times,* Dean Cadle Coll. Box 12.

68. James Still, interview by author, June 25, 1997.

69. Wilma Dykeman's lecture at the Hindman Writers' Workshop, July 30, 2002.

70. June 14, 1940, James Still Room, Camden-Carroll Library, MSU, Box 4 #14.

71. December 23, 1940, James Still Room, Camden-Carroll Library, MSU, Box 5 #3.

72. November 27, 1941, James Still Room, Camden-Carroll Library, MSU, Box 5 #15.

73. Marjorie K. Rawlings, "An Epic of Kentucky," review of *On Troublesome Creek,* by James Still, *Chicago Daily News,* n.d. For a typed version of the review, see Dean Cadle Coll. Box 8. For Sterling North's letter to Rawlings, thanking her for the review, see James Still Papers, UK Libraries, Box 114 #2.

74. December 11, 1941, Rawlings Papers.

75. These stories were included in the respective volumes of the annual O. Henry story collections: "Job's Tears," 1937; "So Large a Thing as Seven," 1938; "Bat Flight," 1939; and "The Proud Walkers," 1941. "Bat Flight," which had been published in *The Saturday Evening Post,* won second prize—the first-prize story that year was William Faulkner's "Barn Burning."

76. James Still, interview by Laura Lee, *Wolfpen Notebooks,* 18.

77. Still, *From the Mountain,* 19.

13. Jolly in a Courting Mood

Epigraph: James Still, *River of Earth,* 242.

1. For research into the mystery of Mayme Woodson Brown, the girl

referred to in the poem, see Ann Olson, "Before Saying Yes," 201–4. Also see chapter 4.

2. August 23, 1938, James Still Room, Camden-Carroll Library, MSU, Box 3 #11.

3. Still, *River of Earth,* 241–42.

4. Codey was a writer and chair of the English Department of Bennett Junior College in upstate New York. Francis to Still, November 28, 1937, Still Room, Camden-Carroll Library, MSU, Box 3 #7. Still to Grover, April 17, 1939, James Still Papers, UK Libraries, Box 24 #8.

5. September 1, 1938, James Still Room, Camden-Carroll Library, MSU, Box 3 #12.

6. July 18, 1939, Still Room, Camden-Carroll Library, MSU, Box 4 #1.

7. February 15, 1940, James Still Papers, UK Libraries, Box 24 #9.

8. It seems that he was writing "Mrs. Razor" in 1941, though it was not published until July 1945. Pan Sterling's letters are held in the MSU Coll.

9. Christine Pappas has a brief biography of Dorothy Thomas in the archives of the Lincoln City Libraries. See also her article "Singers of Life: The Literary Relationship of Dorothy Thomas and Loren Eiseley," *News-letter of the Friends of Loren Eiseley* 15, no. 1 (2001): 7.

10. Harold Ross, first editor of *The New Yorker,* said "The Getaway" was "the best damn story ever in *The New Yorker.*"

11. July 30, 1940, James Still Room, Camden-Carroll Library, MSU, Box 4 #15.

12. May 19, 1941, James Still Room, Camden-Carroll Library, MSU, Box 5 #8.

13. Letter identified only as "Friday afternoon," James Still Room, Camden-Carroll Library, MSU, Box 5 #4.

14. July 7, 1941, James Still Room, Camden-Carroll Library, MSU, Box 5 #10.

15. "Saturday evening," Still Room, Camden-Carroll Library, MSU Box 5 #4.

16. May 8, 1941, Katherine Anne Porter Papers.

17. "Saturday evening." As she wrote more frequently, Thomas did not date her letters. The season was the spring of 1941.

18. "Sunday morning," before June 24, 1941, James Still Room, Camden-Carroll Library, MSU, Box 5 #10.

19. "Sunday night" (probably July 12, 1941), Still Room, MSU.

20. November 19, 1941, James Still Room, Camden-Carroll Library, MSU, Box 5 #15.

21. Still's letters to Thomas are not available. See the Guide to the Dorothy Thomas Archive in the Lincoln City Libraries (www.lincolnlibraries .org). The following short biography is adapted from that website: Thomas was born in August 1898 in Kansas, the sixth of ten children. When she was seven, the family moved to Alberta, Canada, where they homesteaded near a logging company for five years. They moved back to Kansas. Beginning in 1918, she taught school in Nebraska for ten years. Selling a story to *Scribners* in 1928 gave Thomas the confidence to quit teaching in order

to write full-time. Throughout the 1930s she supported her family with her writings. By 1975, she had sold more than 150 stories, many appearing in *American Mercury, The New Yorker, Harper's,* and other literary magazines. After the 1940s her stories mainly appeared in women's magazines such as *Red Book* and *Good Housekeeping.* Knopf published her two novels: *Ma Jeeter's Girls* (1931) and *The Home Place* (1934). In the summer of 1935 Thomas attended Yaddo and fell in love with prominent writer Leonard Ehrlich—a relationship that, she said, "pulled a ligament in my personality." Twenty-five years later, while in New Jersey, she met and married retired machinist John Buickerood. They lived happily, reading, writing, and gardening together until his death in 1990. She had two foster children in the 1950s. She loved clothes almost as much as she loved books, and many of her letters contain drawings and descriptions of the newest article of clothing. She died of a stroke in 1990. She wanted her grave marker to say, "She told an enjoyable story."

22. When researching in the MSU correspondence collection in 1993, I found the letters from Dorothy Thomas and asked James Still about them and about the trip. It took him a moment to register what I was asking, but once he did, he seemed surprised and a little pleased that he had kept the letters. He offered no commentary on the trip or his travel companion.

14. Joining Up and Shipping Out

Epigraph: James Still, "On Being Drafted," *From the Mountain, From the Valley,* 115.

1. August 27, 1941, James Still Papers, UK Libraries, Box 24 #9.

2. April 18, 1941, Porter Papers.

3. November 15, 1941, James Still Room, Camden-Carroll Library, MSU, Box 5 #14.

4. Beattie, *Conversations,* 370.

5. January 10, 1942, James Still Room, Camden-Carroll Library, MSU, Box 6 #10. Tom had participated in the Citizens Military Training Camp in the summer of 1929, making it easier for him to join the infantry in 1942 and earn his status as a noncommissioned officer (91st Division; 363rd Regiment).

6. One early mention of Still's joining the army occurred in the letter that Marguerite wrote to Dorothy after their trip had dissolved. "Don't you wonder what the army will do to Jim? I can't imagine his being at all happy or reconciled to army life. It is so difficult for very sensitive and very conscientious people." July 11, 1941, James Still Room, Camden-Carroll Library, MSU, Box 5 #10.

7. Beattie, *Conversations,* 369.

8. A scrap saved from this time indicates that the Local Board #94 of Knott County classified James Still as 1-A on January 27, 1942; Still Storage.

9. Zachry, "Biographical Sketch," 164.

10. James Still, interview by author, August 11, 1998.

11. Beattie, *Conversations,* 370.

12. The correspondence collections include many letters he received and a few that he wrote while in Africa. His war experiences can be gleaned from the rudiments of a diary, a couple of existing notebooks, plus odd bits of paper. Still's most enduring war stories are the ones he told in the 1990s.

13. January 10, 1943, James Still Room, Camden-Carroll Library, MSU, Box 6 #10.

14. He described himself as "5'7" weighing 150 pounds"; however, his army discharge papers listed his height as 5'8½" and his weight as 165 pounds.

15. January 10, 1943, James Still Room, Camden-Carroll Library, MSU, Box 6 #10.

16. His place was amidships, port side, A Deck, boat station 8. In a notebook that Still kept the first year he was in Africa, he tells of a dream about having the gun in the bunk with him. The entry is dated January 6, 1943: "Dreamed I died last night. The grave was dug. Coffin sat beside it, with lid off. I said, 'I want my gun buried with me.' A gun was brought. I checked the Rifle no. 'No,' I said, 'I want the gun I lost coming over on the boat.' I gave the number, and it was found. 'Put it in so the bolt won't stick in my back,' I said recalling how this had happened when I bunked with my gun on the Aquatania [sic]."

17. The *Aquitania* was a steam-turbine ship of 45,647 tons gross weight, capable of 23–24 knots average speed. *Time* magazine, December 1949.

18. Zachry, "Biographical Sketch," 164. This account of leaving New York is almost identical to a piece that Still published in the Louisville *Courier-Journal* on June 29, 1986, under the heading "What the Statue of Liberty Means to Me."

19. The handwriting is difficult to read; the formatting is impossible to represent—thus the editing. The book is available in the James Still Room at MSU.

20. Whether true or not, Still relates an intriguing tidbit about the harbormaster at Cape Town, who "turned out to be a German spy which accounted for the sinkings of numerous merchant vessels in the area." Zachry, "Biographical Sketch," 164.

21. Still identifies the *Antenor* as a Norwegian ship and as French. In fact, the SS *Antenor* (1924) was British.

22. Zachry, "Biographical Sketch," 164.

15. Somewhere in Africa

Epigraph: Katherine Anne Porter to James Still, Christmas Day 1942.

1. Katherine Anne Porter Papers, Special Collections, University of Maryland Libraries.

2. December 25, 1942, James Still Papers, UK Libraries, Box 24 #10.

3. Pan Am built runways in Florida, Trinidad, Brazil, and Ascension Island. Landing fields already existed at Khartoum, Sudan, and Cairo.

4. Information from the website WNET NY "New York War Stories" www.thirteen.org/newyorkwarstories/story, and from a clipping of the

article "Wings Over Africa" by Sgt. Jack Denton Scott in *YANK,* James Still Room, Camden-Carroll Library, MSU, Box 22 #11.

5. Still to his father, January 10, 1943, James Still Room, Camden-Carroll Library, MSU, Box 6 #10.

6. For the complete interview of Wade Johnson, see the oral history preservation project sponsored by the University of North Carolina–Wilmington. Johnson was interviewed by Paul Zarbock on November 15, 2002, Transcript 251, library.uncw.edu/capefearww2/voices/251bio.html.

7. Ibid.

8. September 9, 1944, James Still Room, Camden-Carroll Library, MSU, Box 7 #4.

9. July 19, 1943, Marjorie Kinnan Rawlings Papers, University of Florida Smathers Library, Gainesville, FL.

10. April 14, 1944, James Still Room, Camden-Carroll Library, MSU, Box 7 #20.

11. James Still, conversation with author, July 13, 1994. The canaries are mentioned in a letter to Rawlings, July 19, 1943, Rawlings Papers.

12. James Still, interview by author, August 10, 1998.

13. October 6, 1944, James Still Room, Camden-Carroll Library, MSU, Box 7 #4.

14. September 9, 1944, James Still Room, Camden-Carroll Library, MSU, Box 7 #4.

15. This copy of *YANK* (the army's weekly paper) is available in James Still Room, Camden-Carroll Library, MSU, Box 22 file 11. Still saved this issue and sent it to Amburgey in September 1944. CAFW is the acronym for Central African Flight Wing.

16. Army separation record: Honorable Discharge from the Army of the United States. On file in Book 5 page 75, Rowan County, KY. Copy available in Still Storage.

17. James Still, interview by Randy Wilson, James Still Papers, UK Libraries, Box 3, folder 7.

18. Still, conversation with Gurney Norman and Wendell Berry at the log house on Dead Mare Branch, June 26, 1997.

19. September 9, 1944, James Still Room, Camden-Carroll Library, MSU, Box 7 #4.

20. July 19, 1943, Rawlings Papers.

21. The book is an autobiographical account of Lawrence of Arabia's experiences while serving with the rebel forces during the Arab revolt against the Ottoman Turks, 1916–1918.

22. Newspaper clipping from an Alabama paper, no date, Dean Cadle Coll. Box 12.

23. A letter dated January 31, 1945, from Guy Loomis indicates that his secretary had sent Still a Christmas box. He also attaches an article from Robert Kincaid, president of LMU, that talks about Still's visit to the Holy Land.

24. James Still, interview by the author, August 10, 1998 (edited to remove sidetracks). He was talking about his trip to Egypt and the Holy Land.

25. Ibid.

26. "Sgt. Still Is Commended," clipping from *Hindman Herald,* January 26, 1945, James Still Room, MSU Folder of Military Material.

27. James Still Papers, UK Libraries, Box 24 #10.

28. James Still, interview by author, August 10, 1998.

29. Ibid.

30. *On Troublesome Creek* was published in October 1941; the poem "Drought on Troublesome" was published in *The Virginia Quarterly Review* (Spring 1945).

31. The boy was William Lee Parks, a former student at HSS.

32. Published April 19, 1942, which means that he probably sent it to the paper before he enlisted on March 10.

33. At MSU are personnel forms that he recycled by typing short pieces on the back. For example, he created one paragraph describing the lab where he worked for Frank Grannis at Austin Peay in 1931.

34. "Drought on Troublesome" was one of the poems rejected. It was published in the Spring 1945 issue of *The Virginia Quarterly Review.*

35. August 11, 1943, Rawlings Papers. In her letter of January 1945, Rawlings is still offering to send books, but she had not yet found the poem he wanted.

36. February 1, 1943, James Still Room, Camden-Carroll Library, MSU, Box 6 #11.

37. January 11, 1944, James Still Room, Camden-Carroll Library, MSU, Box 6 #17. "School Butter" was published in the Autumn 1946 issue of *The Virginia Quarterly Review.*

38. Weeks to Still and Still to Morton at *The Atlantic Monthly;* both located in the display case, Still Room, Camden-Carroll Library, MSU.

39. Letters from Pan Sterling indicate that "Mrs. Razor" was a real girl and that he was writing a story about her from October 1940 to July 1942. See MSU Box 5.

40. June 1, 1943, James Still Room, Camden-Carroll Library, MSU, Box 6 #13.

16. Coming Home Again

Epigraph: James Still to George Zachry, September 7, 1998, Valley Archives.

1. He saved many letters and periodically would send packets of them and other memorabilia to Jethro Amburgey.

2. James Still Papers, UK Libraries, Box 24 #10.

3. January 10, 1943, James Still Room, Camden-Carroll Library, MSU, Box 6 #10.

4. A clipping attached to a letter from Thomas saved by Still. The headline is "Fairfax, Shawmut soldiers fight with famous 363rd," James Still Room, Camden-Carroll Library, MSU, Box 7 #8.

5. October 18, 1944, James Still Room, Camden-Carroll Library, MSU, Box 7 #4.

6. July 27, 1945, James Still Room, Camden-Carroll Library, MSU, Box 7 #4.

7. The story of having been sent to Miami was recounted in a 1998 interview. A letter from his brother Thomas, who was serving in Italy, was addressed to Still at the President Madison Hotel in Miami on August 15, 1945.

8. James Still, interview by author, August 11, 1998.

9. James Still, conversation with author, July 13, 1994.

10. Ibid.

11. Still did not give specific dates for his work at Plattsburgh Barracks or his training in New York City, but letters written to him at this time indicate that he was in upstate New York and in New York City during August 1945.

12. Story told by James Still to Randy Wilson. He does not identify the warden, but it was probably Lewis Laws who was warden there from 1920 to 1940 and who wrote several books: his most famous was *Twenty Thousand Years in Sing Sing* (1932).

13. Still gives the address of the office as Park Avenue. Correspondence to him was addressed to the U.S. Personnel School, Capital Hotel, 8th Ave. and 51st Street, New York, New York.

14. The watch is in the locked case of the James Still Room at MSU.

15. Dorothy Mount sent Still a telegram informing him that Loomis had passed away on the morning of November 11, 1946, James Still Room, Camden-Carroll Library, MSU, Box 7.

16. James Still, interview by author, August 11, 1998.

17. From a letter dated August 12, 1945, Jones seems to be a genuine guy, not highly educated, married to Ruby, to whom he was devoted. He signs the letter, "Alway a Buddy, Charles." This is interesting because Still claimed that he had no buddies in the army—but of the men he knew, he seemed to think Charles was special.

18. James Still, interview by author, August 11, 1998.

19. April 17, 1945, James Still Room, Camden-Carroll Library, MSU, Box 7 #8.

20. October 15, 1945, Porter Papers.

21. James Still Papers, UK Libraries, Box 24 #10.

22. In spite of having little time, he had managed to write, he says, "a poem and two short stories in Egypt. Virginia Quarterly Review published the poem ["Drought on Troublesome"] last Spring, *Atlantic Monthly* printed a story in July ["Mrs. Razor"], and *Yale Review* expects to print the other story ["Pattern of a Man"] in a forthcoming issue."

23. James Still, interview by author, August 11, 1998.

24. Miller, "Jim Dandy," 18.

25. Notes in Still Storage: application made, presumably to the Veterans Administration in September 1947.

26. Studs Terkel, *"The Good War": An Oral History of World War Two* (New York: New Press, 1984), 6–7.

27. Knott County had suffered seventy-seven casualties during World War II, which is a significant number in an area with a total population of only twenty thousand; Terkel, *"The Good War,"* 8.

28. Still ended the story by saying that a year later the doctor came to his house on Dead Mare Branch for a visit. Information related in conversation with Wendell Berry and Gurney Norman, July 1997.

29. These numbers are based on existing correspondence from editors. The numbers portray not the writing he was doing, only the responses he was receiving.

30. In 1956 Still wrote to Temple Baker about "The Nest" (MSU display case) and reported that the story was based on a real little girl in the Cornett family, on Big Branch, who would walk through the woods to visit the Nickles family. One winter day she became lost, and the family took two days to find her. She lived, unlike the girl in the story. Still tells Baker not to send the story to Edward Weeks because he had already read and rejected it.

31. Letters requesting permission to publish "Mrs. Razor" can be found at MSU in Boxes 7 and 8.

17. On Dead Mare Branch

Epigraph: James Still, note on a list of supplies needed for the house (Still Storage).

1. April 11, 1946, James Still Room, Camden-Carroll Library, MSU, Box 7 #16.

2. The two versions of the story vary in the language and expressions as well as character and place-names. In "Cedars of Lebanon" the preacher is Gath Crownover from Old Sarum, TN, and the soldier is Talt Sorrels from Thoms Reach, TN. In "The Sharpe Tack" the preacher, Jerb Powell, is from Standing Rock, KY, and Talt Evarts is from Wiley, KY.

3. *American Mercury* publication, 294.

4. The line ending "whispers of the foe" appears only in the revised version, "The Sharp Tack," included in *Pattern of a Man*. The irony of the final sentence could not have been anticipated even by its creator in 1946. "A country named for the heavenly one ought to be a pattern for folks living everywhere." This is one month before the United States and Britain drew up plans to separate Palestine into Jewish and Arab states.

5. March 13, 1946, James Still Room, Camden-Carroll Library, MSU, Box 7 #15.

6. March 2, 1946, James Still Room, Camden-Carroll Library, MSU, Box 7 #15.

7. March 14, 1946, James Still Room, Camden-Carroll Library, MSU, Box 7 #15.

8. Albert Stewart, "At Home with James Still on Dead Mare" (written in 1963 but describing the house in the 1940s), *Appalachian Heritage* 1, no. 1 (1973): 41.

9. Dean Cadle, "Pattern of a Writer," *Appalachian Journal* 15, no. 2 (1988): 113.

10. James Still Papers, UK Libraries, Box 83 #3.

11. He worked for hours on the chapter called "Master Occasion," which was the story published in the January 1949 *Atlantic Monthly*. And

he wrote a letter to Marshall Best at Viking thanking him for *The Red Pony*, a Christmas gift. Also gave him an interim report on the "Green Project, which was never completed.

12. From mid-January through the first week in March, Still was in Alabama and did not write in his journal.

13. He is considering an alternative title for TWM—"The World Is Big," which comes from Elizabeth Madox Roberts's sentence in *The Time of Man* "The world is big and all you do is set in it and that's all there is."

14. The final section of *Chinaberry*, edited by Silas House and published in 2011, was titled "Alabama, Alabama," but there is no indication that the project he referenced here was connected to that chapter.

15. Andersonville was a Civil War prison in Sumter County, Georgia, which opened in 1864 and, at one time, held 33,000 Union prisoners. Still intended to write this novel but did not get his project completed before MacKinlay Kantor published his Pulitzer Prize–winning novel *Andersonville* in 1955.

16. Although he received the award, he did not go to the ceremony in New York.

17. Daughter of Marion and Mattie Amburgey, Jethro's oldest brother. She was born in 1923 and married in 1954.

18. January 19, 1949, James Still Room, Camden-Carroll Library, MSU, Box 8 #20.

19. February 28, 1945, James Still Room, Camden-Carroll Library, MSU, Box 7 #7; May 19, 1949, James Still Room, Camden-Carroll Library, MSU, Box #20.

20. January 11, 1948, James Still Room, Camden-Carroll Library, MSU, Box 8 #10.

21. This picture contrasted sharply with Still's own house, which was becoming surrounded by vegetation, most of it deliberately planted and tended.

22. James Still Room, Camden-Carroll Library, MSU, Box 8 #16.

23. Coincidentally, Santa Monica, where Still visited Hakes, was where Katherine Anne Porter was living when she invited Still to come to California in 1945. She was not there in 1949, but Still sent her a postcard encouraging her to come.

24. March 4 and 11, 1949, James Still Room, Camden-Carroll Library, MSU, Box 8 #19. Hakes did send Still a box of books including a copy of the out-of-print book *Palaces of Sin*, which he had found at Still's special request.

25. Performed in New York City on February 15, 1950; see postcard from Ethel Glenn Hier announcing "Mountain Preacher," a poem by Still, to be broadcast on WNYC; James Still Papers, UK Libraries, Box 24 #11.

26. November 1950, James Still Papers, UK Libraries, Box 24 #11

27. Elizabeth Bishop was a poet whose first book of poems, *North and South*, was published a year before Still's *Hounds on the Mountain*. Eleanor Clark was a travel writer who married novelist Robert Penn Warren in 1952. Alexei Haieff was a composer; William Goyen was best known for

his novel begun during World War II. Kit Parker was a painter and Ilse a writer; they were friends with Bishop. Calvin Kentfield was a young writer whose first novel, *The Alchemist's Voyage,* appeared in 1955.

28. James Still Papers, UK Libraries, Box 29 #1, copy attached to her January 23, 1980, letter to Still.

29. James Still Papers, UK Libraries, Box 24 #11.

30. Miller, "Daring to Look," 8.

31. It is likely that he met Jane Mayhall in Saratoga during the Yaddo visits of 1950 or 1951, and she did remain a friend. However, there is no mention of her at the time. See her 1998 article in *Shenandoah.*

18. Back to Hindman

Epigraph: James Still, quoted in "Daring to Look in the Well," interview by Jim Wayne Miller, 9.

1. James Still, interview by Laura Lee, *Wolfpen Notebooks,* 19.

2. James Still, interview by author, June 25, 1997.

3. James Still, interview by Laura Lee, *Wolfpen Notebooks,* 20.

4. Jethro and Woodrow Amburgey were the twin sons of Wiley J. Amburgey and Surilda Madden. They had several other brothers in the area when Still lived there in the 1950s: Marion and Melvin lived closest to Still. Monroe Amburgey's parents were Jasper Amburgey and Tina Madden. Little is known about his extended family.

5. Notes in Still Storage.

6. The second child and oldest son, Stanley, continued to live in the family home for years after everyone else had died or left. Even after Monroe's death in 1988, Still often spent Thanksgiving with Stanley at the house on Big Doubles, according to Bob Young.

7. Still, *Wolfpen Notebooks,* 60.

8. His obituary in 1988 reports that he was supervisor for the building of Pioneer Village at Red Fox.

9. Mike Mullins, "I Call Him Mr. Still," *A Gathering at the Forks,* 290.

10. The first letter from McConkey to Still was dated January 26, 1952.

11. Bob Young explained that before the roads were improved and passable, the people in the outer reaches of the county would have their mules pull sleds to go from place to place. The sleds moved more easily on rocky creek beds than did wheeled vehicles.

12. Email from James McConkey to author, October 14, 2012.

13. The workshop was to be held on the campus of MSC July 14–25 and the cost was ten dollars for tuition and twenty-five dollars for room and board. In addition to Still, writers and teachers included Jesse Stuart, Collister Hutchison (poetry collection *Toward Daybreak*), and Hollis Summers (professor of creative writing at UK).

14. James Still Room, Camden-Carroll Library, MSU, Box 9 #11.

15. One example is the handwritten letter dated August 8, 1952, from Emma Lee Orr, whose favorite part of the workshop was Still and Stuart. She found the people at Morehead very friendly. See James Still Papers, UK Libraries, Box 24 #11.

16. Baker to Still, January 1953, James Still Papers, UK Libraries Box 24 #11.

17. The pageant was titled "From Where the Pattern Grew" by 1920 graduate Una Ritchie. According to the *Hindman News,* two thousand people came to the celebration.

18. Stoddart, *Story of Hindman Settlement School,* 141. Still also wrote words for the plaque that would honor May Stone: "Her achievement was to give the people of the mountains the opportunity to be their own best selves." Letter from Watts to Still, James Still Room, Camden-Carroll Library, MSU, Box 9 #11.

19. Stoddart, *Story of Hindman Settlement School,* 27.

20. This library building is the same one that was renamed the James Still Learning Center in the early 1990s when the school began a program to teach dyslexic children.

21. $150 in 1953 would be the equivalent of approximately $1,200 in 2010.

22. $1,700 in 1952 would be valued at approximately $14,000 in 2010, and $4,800 in 1960 would be equivalent to $35,000 in 2010.

23. *Courier-Journal,* August 14, 1957.

24. Bob Young and Hiram Bradley, interviews by author, August 2012.

25. James Perry is the older brother of Teresa Lynn Perry who became Still's adopted daughter in 1998.

26. Notes dated Sunday, May 5, 1957, Still Storage.

27. Gurney Norman, "I Write Because I'm Unhappy When Not Writing," *Hazard Herald,* October 2, 1958.

28. James Still, "This Is My Best" introduction, *Mountain Life and Work* 30, no. 3 (1954): 33.

29. That year, Still was at the workshop during the fiction week, from July 29 to August 3.

30. July 16, 1956, James Still Papers, UK Libraries, Box 25 #2.

31. James Still Papers, UK Libraries, Box 25 #3. The quote is the first line of Edna St. Vincent Millay's poem "God's World."

32. James Still, "Apple Trip," *From the Mountain,* 109.

19. Family Loss and Brotherly Love

Epigraph: James Still, *From the Mountain, From the Valley,* 111.

1. Box 12 #8, Dean Cadle Coll.

2. Barbara Sue Barnes Harris, interview by author, September 11, 2002.

3. James Still, interview by author, June 25, 1997.

4. Still evokes this lively family atmosphere in the first stanza of "Those I Want in Heaven" when he reminisces about childhood; his visits to his Alabama family throughout his life retained that spirit.

5. James Still, interview by author, July 10, 1997.

6. James Still Room, Camden-Carroll Library, MSU, Box 20 #9.

7. Reproduced verbatim. May 31, 1957, James Still Papers, UK Libraries, Box 25 #3.

8. Reproduced verbatim. James Still Papers, UK Libraries, Box 25 #3.

9. James Still, interview by author, July 6, 1994.

10. James Still Papers, UK Libraries, Box 25 #3.

11. Barbara Sue Barnes Harris, interview by author, September 11, 2002.

12. December 17, 1957, Still Storage.

13. June 30, 1958, James Still Papers, UK Libraries, Box 25 #4.

14. James Still, interview by author, July 10, 1997. This is one of two "epiphanies" that Still experienced in his life. The second was in Guatemala at the Mayan ruins.

15. The poem by that title was first published in the 1968 winter issue of *Appalachian Review.* A poem by the title "Woods in the Road" was sent to and rejected by several publications in 1959 and 1960.

16. In transcript of "Conversation with James Still," November 1986; project directed by Michael Lasater at Western Kentucky University, JWM Coll.

17. James Still Room, Camden-Carroll Library, MSU, Box 10 #3. A note from his wife, Mae, written August 30, 1958, told Still of the heart attack that put his brother in the hospital. He died three days later.

18. James Still, interview by author, July 11, 1997.

19. Ibid., July 6, 1994.

20. James Still Room, Camden-Carroll Library, MSU, Box 10 #2.

21. Ibid.

22. Friday, June 13, 1958, James Still Room, Camden-Carroll Library, MSU, Box 10 #3.

23. June 23, 1958, James Still Papers, UK Libraries, Box 25 #4.

24. February 9, 1959, James Still Papers, UK Libraries, Box 25 #5.

25. February 13, 1959, James Still Papers, UK Libraries, Box 25 #5.

26. April 11, 1960, James Still Room, Camden-Carroll Library, MSU, Box 10 #7.

27. August 4, 1960, James Still Room, Camden-Carroll Library, MSU, Box 10 #8.

28. August 13, no year, James Still Room, Camden-Carroll Library, MSU, Box 10 #8.

29. December 2, 1960, James Still Room, Camden-Carroll Library, MSU, Box 10 #10.

30. January 26, 1961, James Still Room, Camden-Carroll Library, MSU, Box 10 #11.

31. January 20, 1961, James Still Papers, UK Libraries, Box 25 #7.

32. $2,500 in 1961 was equal to more than $18,000 in 2011. Still mentions this novel more than once in his letters to Alfred, but the title is unknown. He does not publish another novel until 1977's *Sporty Creek.*

33. February 8, 1962, James Still Papers, UK Libraries, Box 25 #8.

34. March 9, 1962, James Still Papers, UK Libraries, Box 25 #8.

35. May 4, 1962, James Still Papers, UK Libraries, Box 25 #9.

36. November 6, 1962, James Still Papers, UK Libraries, Box 25 #9.

37. November 28, 1962; December 21, 1962; James Still Papers, UK Libraries, Box 25 #9.

38. Later in the letter he spells out his health situation: "For the past six

weeks my own medical bill is $67.00 due to three sieges with an infected ear. . . . Also, a partial plate (dental) which suddenly came necessary will cost no less than $50."

39. September 17, 1962, James Still Room, Camden-Carroll Library, MSU, Box 10 #16. The draft letter was addressed to Drs. Cook and Clark at the Lineville Clinic. Still also included a copy when he wrote to Paula Dick, the administrator of the Linville Nursing Home.

40. January 17, 1963 (corrected to 1964), James Still Papers, UK Libraries, Box 25 #10.

41. This summary comes from a rough transcription of a taped conversation between Jim Wayne Miller and Still on November 15, 1986. A typed copy is in the JWM Coll.

42. Audiotape in the James Still Room at MSU.

43. Not published until the fall of 1984 in the *Kentucky Poetry Review*. Republished under the title "On the Passing of My Good Friend John" in *Appalachian Heritage* (Winter 1995), for John Stephenson who died on December 6, 1994. It did not appear in *The Wolfpen Poems* in 1986.

20. On to Morehead

Epigraph: James Still, quoted in Donna J. Baker, "Keeper at 'The Light to the Mountains': James Still at Morehead State University," *Appalachian Heritage* 38, no. 4 (2010): 39.

1. Creason to Still, October 22, 1959, James Still Papers, UK Libraries, Box 25 #5.

2. Creason, "Some things a man does," 8.

3. James Still Papers, UK Libraries, Box 25 #6.

4. Cadle first approached Still in a letter dated May 25, 1946. He was a student at Berea College, a little older than the typical undergraduate because he had been a soldier.

5. February 15, 1960, James Still Papers, UK Libraries, Box 25 #6.

6. James Still Papers, UK Libraries, Box 25 #2.

7. Strassman to Still, May 7, 1956, James Still Papers, UK Libraries, Box 25 #2.

8. Strassman to Still, James Still Papers, UK Libraries, Box 25 #5. This manuscript eventually became *The Wolfpen Rusties*, published by Putnam in 1975, almost twenty years after it was first submitted.

9. May 22, 1959, James Still Papers, UK Libraries, Box 25 #5; June 13, 1959, James Still Papers, UK Libraries, Box 25 #5.

10. James Still Papers, UK Libraries, Box 25 #5.

11. February 7, 1961, James Still Papers, UK Libraries, Box 25 #7; February 8, 1968, James Still Papers, UK Libraries, Box 26 #4.

12. Log available in James Still Papers, UK Libraries.

13. James Still, interview by author, March 29, 1994.

14. It was the third year that Albert Stewart had been director of the workshop.

15. August 18, 1959, office files of Larry Besant, director of the library at MSU.

16. August 25, 1959, office files of Larry Besant.

17. August 31, 1959, office files of Larry Besant.

18. Baker, "Keeper," 40.

19. Stewart to Doran, October 9, 1960, quoted in Baker, "Keeper," 40.

20. Still to Doran, November 29, 1960, James Still Room, Camden-Carroll Library, MSU, Box 10 #10; Doran to Still, December 1, 1960, James Still Papers, UK Libraries, Box 25 #6.

21. October 5, 1961, office files of Larry Besant.

22. According to Donna Baker, the library dedicated the James Still Room with a program featuring a reading by Harriette Arnow in the morning and a small reception later in the afternoon. Despite missing the dedication, Still always enjoyed his room, first located in the main part of the library and later relocated to the fifth floor of the library tower. When he returned to MSC in the summer of 1962, Still held office hours there. Baker, "Keeper," 42.

23. October 16, 1961; October 21, 1961; November 10, 1961; James Still Papers, UK Libraries, Box 25 #7.

24. March 15, 1962, James Still Papers, UK Libraries, Box 25 #8.

25. James Still Papers, UK Libraries, Box 19 #11.

26. Contract letter for 1965–1966, April 14, 1965, MSU Besant file.

27. James Still Papers, UK Libraries, biography file.

28. July 3, 1963, James Still Papers, UK Libraries, Box 25 #10.

29. Morehead State College (MSC) became Morehead State University (MSU) in 1966. Still usually referred to the institution simply as "Morehead." James Still, interview by author, July 11, 1997.

30. Other faculty friends of Still at MSU included Fran Helpingstein, Charles Pelphrey, and Sam McKinney.

31. He lived at Lakewood most of the time he was at Morehead. However, a contract for apartment #5 indicates that he first lived at Vansant Hall, paying $50.85 per month from September 9 through May 30, 1964.

32. M. K. Thomas, telephone interview by author, February 25, 2003.

33. Still received a memo from J. E. Price in February 1970 that presented to the faculty of Languages and Literature information about grade distribution for the past five years. Still had awarded As and Bs to 38 percent of his students and Ds and Es (failing grade) to 17 percent. Compared to other professors in the department, Still would have been a moderately hard grader. James Still Papers, UK Libraries, Box 16 #4.

34. James Still, interview by author, July 10, 1997.

35. Letters from Mrs. Stephen Bailey to Still and from Gary Harmon to Mrs. Bailey, James Still Papers, UK Libraries, Box 8 #15.

36. James Still Papers, UK Libraries, Box 25 #11.

37. March 17, 1969, James Still Papers, UK Libraries, Box 26 #6.

38. One is a five-page typed letter from a woman named Pat that was sent to Still's fellow teacher at Morehead, Betty Jean Wells, in 1962; a second is a short essay submitted by an unnamed student to Wells as part of a freshman essay assignment in 1964; the third is a thirteen-page piece written by J. Marshall Porter in 1964.

39. Still became acquainted with Fred's sister, Mabel Wolfe Wheaton, in New York City when he received the Southern Author Award in 1940 and had visited her in Asheville in 1956.

40. James Still, interview by author, June 25, 1997.

41. James Still Papers, UK Libraries, Box 26 #2.

42. An interesting outcome of the Farrell visit was a personal letter written to Still in May 1967. To read the nearly illegible handwriting, Still typed it. Because Still had not written promptly, Farrell assumed something was wrong—he was ill or angry. Farrell begged Still to explain what he had done to offend him. He included a sixteen-line handwritten poem, also cryptic, which Still rewrote in his own neat handwriting. Still's response is unknown, but the next letter from Farrell was direct and related only to the reimbursement. May 15, 1957, James Still Papers, UK Libraries, Box 27 #2. On August 2, 1978, Farrell wrote again to Still, thanking him for sending the review of his newest book *The Death of Nora Ryan*. He recalled the time at Morehead as happy. James Still Papers, UK Libraries, Box 28 #5.

43. Letter to Dr. J. E. Duncan, October 27, 1967, James Still Papers, UK Libraries, Box 26 #2.

44. For example, Monroe Amburgey's youngest son, Earl, suffered from a heart problem. Beginning in 1956, Still set up appointments for Earl to be seen by a specialist in Louisville and drove the boy there several times over a three-year period. Letters from the Kentucky Crippled Children Commission, James Still Papers, UK Libraries, Box 25 #2, #3, #4.

45. See chapter 18: "Back to Hindman." James was the oldest of five children born to Melzenia and James Perry Sr. James, also known as Junior, was born in 1946, Mark in 1948, Sharon Kay in 1953, Mike in 1958, and Teresa in 1967. James Still legally adopted Teresa Lynn Perry in 1998.

46. James Still Room, Camden-Carroll Library, MSU, Box 10 #19.

47. James Still, interview by author, June 25, 1997. Though his memory of the event and its aftermath was excellent, a few details can be added. James Perry was twenty years old. His father was a coal miner. According to Perry (interview by author, March 2006), the accident happened on Highway 60 north of Morehead on August 8, 1966. He was in the Morehead hospital for ten days then transferred to Lexington, then back to Morehead, finally to Lexington for speech therapy. He was home by Thanksgiving 1966. The settlement letter (James Still Room, Camden-Carroll Library, MSU, Box 11 #4) dated September 11, 1967, indicates that the attorneys for Perry were John Keck of Grayson, KY, and Stanley Preiser. Still was called the "next friend." The settlement check for $82,500 was to be made payable to James Perry Jr. and his wife, Judy.

48. MSU awarded him an honorary doctorate in 1978, the Special Service Award for Literature in 1982, and the Thomas and Lillie D. Chaffin Award for Appalachian Writing in 1996.

49. When Still was on campus, the library was called the Johnson Camden Library. Jack Ellis was director 1966–1986 (twenty years younger than Still; a graduate of Vanderbilt and a World War II veteran). Larry Besant (graduate of the library school at the University of Illinois) was direc-

tor from 1986 to 2006. Special Collections librarians have included Faye Belcher, 1971–1985; Clara Keyes, 1987–2009; and Clay Howard, Donna Baker, and Robert Sammons.

50. James Still Papers, UK Libraries, Box 16 #4. An essay with a margin note by Grace Paul at the writers' workshop at MSU in 1964.

21. Then-what Days

Epigraph: James Still, quoted in Miller, "Madly to Learn," 232.

1. Soon after Alfred's death, Still transferred his caretaking to James Perry's family. The same year of the Van Line accident, the baby, Teresa, was born, making five children altogether. Six years after the accident, the father, a coal miner, died of black lung, leaving the mother and at least two of the children to be cared for at home.

2. James Still Papers, UK Libraries, Box 25 #12. Stewart had received a "highly critical letter" from Doran the previous November, which helped push him to resign, but he never offered a full explanation for his decision.

3. Dean Cadle Coll. Box 15.

4. Dean Cadle Coll. Box 14 #6.

5. James Still Papers, UK Libraries, Box 26 #8. He copied it to Adron Doran, president, and Dr. Joseph Price, chair of the Division of Languages and Literature.

6. February 27, 1970, James Still Papers, UK Libraries, Box 26 #8.

7. Faye Belcher was the associate director of Libraries 1971–1985. Clara Keyes Potter was the head of Special Collections and Archives but later became associate director of Libraries, 1987–2009; Larry Besant was dean of Libraries 1986–2006. See chapter 20, footnote 49.

8. Beginning in 1970, his correspondence went to different Kentucky addresses: Box 703 Morehead; Wolfpen Creek Mallie; and Box 361 Hindman.

9. Ronald Eller, *Uneven Ground: Appalachia Since 1945* (Lexington: UPK, 2008), 89. See chapter 2, "The Politics of Poverty," for a discussion of the period.

10. Still to Johnson and the White House to Still, August 2, 1967. James Still Papers, UK Libraries, Box 26 #3.

11. July 9, 1969, Robert Francis Papers, University of Massachusetts.

12. August 4, 1971, Robert Francis Papers, University of Massachusetts.

13. August 15, 1971, James Still Papers, UK Libraries, Box 26 #13.

14. Stoddart, *Story of Hindman Settlement School,* 167.

15. Ibid., 170–73.

16. Bob Young, interview by author, December 9, 2002.

17. Mike Mullins, in his introduction to *25 Years of the Appalachian Writers Workshop* (xvii), notes that the staff of the first workshop included Al Stewart, James Still, Harriette Arnow, Billy Clark, Dean Cadle, and Shirley Williams.

18. For example, Raymond McLain Sr., father of the director of the Settlement School and former president of Transylvania College in Lexington, was then president of the University of Alabama. He wrote Still early

in 1970, inviting him to come to Alabama; March 1970, James Still Papers, UK Libraries, Box 26 #8. There is no indication that Still would have taken the offer even if it had been officially extended.

19. In the 1970s Portsmouth was home to Ohio University Southern Campus; ten years later that branch of the state system moved to Ironton, and the former university buildings became home to Shawnee State Community College, which in 1986 became Shawnee State University; James Still Papers, UK Libraries, Box 16 #14.

20. Bruce Brown, codirector of the Appalachian Studies Center, had arranged for Harriette Arnow, Hollis Summers, David Madden, and James Still to staff the workshop; James Still Papers, UK Libraries, Box 26 #8.

21. Still was at the marriage and reported very simply to Temple Baker that Jethro had taken "the fateful step so matter-of-factly, so unemotionally"; James Still Papers, UK Libraries, Box 27 #2.

22. August 1, 1971, James Still Papers, UK Libraries, Box 26 #3.

23. He died November 25, 1971; James Still Papers, UK Libraries, Box 26 #1.

24. On January 7, 1972, Morris and Gertrude Amburgey deeded the property to James Still for his lifetime. (Book 95 page 24 Knott County Clerk's office). When surveyed in 1982, the size of the property was listed as 34.8 acres.

25. August 1, 1971, James Still Papers, UK Libraries, Box 26 #13.

26. Total compensation would be $1,500; letters August 2 and 22, 1972, James Still Papers, UK Libraries, Box 27 #4.

27. June 2, 1971, James Still Papers, UK Libraries, Box 26 #12. Allen Tate was a native of Kentucky and had attended Vanderbilt in the 1920s, where he became a member of the group known first as the Fugitive Poets and later as the Southern Agrarians. Still knew the woman Tate married in 1925, Carolina Gordon, through one of the New England workshops.

28. Cratis Williams had written a monumental dissertation titled "The Southern Mountaineer in Fact and Fiction" to earn his doctorate in 1961. It included a section on *River of Earth*. The study at New York University was researched in the 1950s and published in 1961. The original dissertation was 1,600 pages, 34 of which were devoted to Still's early work.

29. The inscription that Still wrote in the copy he sent to Cratis Williams read, "For Cratis Williams—this thirty-year-old tale of a lost time, a vanished place, a vanquished people. [signed] James Still."

30. Dean Cadle Coll. Box 14 #6. Also in the Cratis D. Williams Papers of the Belk Library at Appalachian State University in Boone, NC.

31. November 20, 1972, Cratis Williams Papers.

32. In 1972, for example, Still renewed his connections with Loyal Jones at Berea College in Kentucky, with Max Steele at the University of North Carolina, and with Robert Higgs and Ambrose Manning at East Tennessee State University.

33. Jones sent Still a thank-you note with reference to several students, dated February 14, 1972, James Still Papers, UK Libraries, Box 27 #2.

34. This limited edition of *Hounds on the Mountain* that Still gave to Al

Perrin and his wife is number 430 out of 750 numbered copies. The inscription reads, "For Alfred and Jean Perin [sic]—These verses from my head and heart, with affection. James Still," dated January 26, 1972.

35. February 5, 1972, James Still Papers, UK Libraries, Box 27 #2.

36. Max Steele, director of the University of North Carolina's creative-writing program 1967–1986, was a published writer, a professor of English, and a strong mentor to younger writers. Originally from South Carolina, he attended Furman University, then Vanderbilt. He was six years younger than Still.

37. April 14, 1972, Dean Cadle Coll. Box 14 #6.

38. May 8, 1972, James Still Papers, UK Libraries, Box 27 #3.

39. April 18, 1972, Dean Cadle Coll. Box 14.

40. July 5, 1972, Dean Cadle Coll. Box 14 #6.

41. This 562-page anthology became the most widely used textbook on Appalachian writing in the nation's schools and colleges and was the basis of the two-volume collection *Appalachia Inside Out,* edited by Robert J. Higgs, Ambrose N. Manning, and Jim Wayne Miller and published in 1995; September 27, 1973, Dean Cadle Coll. Box 14 #6.

42. September 9, 1974, James Still Papers, UK Libraries, Box 27 #8.

43. Stewart, "At Home with James Still on Dead Mare," *Appalachian Heritage* 1, no. 1 (1973): 14.

44. A codicil attached in 1978 made an adjustment concerning his sister Inez, who had died in 1977. A more important change covered in the codicil was the naming of Teresa Lynn Perry (then age eleven) to receive all royalties and income from his literary works, and following her death, all income was to go to her heirs.

22. Making Friends and Keeping Them

Epigraph: From Jonathan Greene, "A Memoir of James Still," in *James Still in Interviews, Oral Histories and Memoirs,* ed. Ted Olson (Jefferson, NC: McFarland, 2009), 261.

1. Still and Arnow worked together at several writers' workshops in Morehead and at Hindman. He traced her hand in 1961 and kept the paper. She spoke at the James Still Room dedication in October 1961, and Still participated with her in a July 1964 workshop on Urban Adjustment of Southern Appalachian Migrants organized by the Council of Southern Mountains and Loyal Jones.

2. Still attended the wedding of Dykeman and Stokely in 1940; Dykeman, "Mountain Story Keeps Its Magic." Stokely died in 1977, but Dykeman outlived Still and was the only member of his generation to speak at his funeral in 2001.

3. Thomas Clark, interview by author, October 22, 2002. Tom Clark, friend to both Still and Stuart, contrasted them in this way: "Jesse was an incessant talker, Still you would have to drag things out of."

4. Still outlived Stuart by seventeen years.

5. The letters from Stuart to Still number more than one hundred, written between 1933 and 1975. They are held in the MSU Coll. in the James

Still Room. Extant letters from Still to Stuart are in private collections. For an analysis of their correspondence, see James M. Gifford and Erin Kazee, "Both Ends of a Walnut Log: The Correspondence of James Still and Jesse Stuart," in *James Still in Interviews, Oral Histories and Memoirs,* ed. Ted Olson (Jefferson, NC: McFarland, 2009), 219–32.

6. Theodore Morrison, review of *Man with a Bull-Tongue Plow,* by Jesse Stuart, *The Atlantic Monthly* 155, no. 4 (April 1935): 30. After labeling the 703 sonnets a travesty of true nature poetry, Morrison qualified his criticism: "Mr. Stuart now and again produces a naively charming piece of natural description."

7. Stuart to Still, May 24, 1933, James Still Room, Camden-Carroll Library, MSU, Box 2 folder 2.

8. Kohler, "Jesse Stuart and James Still," 528, 533. See also chapter 12: "A Man Singing to Himself."

9. West (at Kentucky Workers' Alliance in Lexington) to Still, November 6, 1936, James Still Room, Camden-Carroll Library, MSU, Box 2 #16.

10. Stuart to Still, estimated date December 1936, from Fullerton, KY, James Still Room, Camden-Carroll Library, MSU, Box 2.

11. May 6, 1939, James Still Room, Camden-Carroll Library, MSU, Box 3 #4.

12. See Lorence, *A Hard Journey,* 107; and Richardson, *Jesse: The Biography of an American Writer,* 310.

13. Quoted in Richardson, 331.

14. Ibid., 345.

15. July 6, 1952, James Still Room, Camden-Carroll Library, MSU, Box 9 #11.

16. Stuart enjoyed Jesse Stuart Day in 1955. In November 1960 Murray State University opened the Jesse Stuart Room. Joe Creason published an article about Stuart for the *Courier-Journal* in 1950, "The Author Who Writes So True." For the purposes of comparison, Creason's article on Still appeared ten years later. James Still Day in Kentucky was not celebrated until 1982; the James Still Room at MSC was not opened until 1961.

17. The source is unclear. This statement became controversial when *History of Southern Literature* quoted Cadle, who attributed it to Still. Jim Wayne Miller denied it in his review (". . . And Ladies of the Club"). Cadle denied he ever said it in ". . . And Members of the Pack," a typed manuscript in the Dean Cadle Coll.

18. June 14, 1969, letter from Stuart to Stoneback in H. R. Stoneback, "Roberts, Still, Stuart, and Warren," *Kentucky Humanities* (2001): 30.

19. Ibid., 31.

20. Shirley Williams, interview by author, December 10, 2002.

21. Drafted 1974, James Still Papers, UK Libraries, Box 29 #1.

22. October 11, 1975, James Still Room, Camden-Carroll Library, MSU, Box 11 #16.

23. James M. Gifford and Erin R. Kazee, *Jesse Stuart: An Extraordinary Life* (Ashland, KY: Jesse Stuart Foundation), 254.

24. Ibid., 262.

25. Notebook in James Still Room, Camden-Carroll Library, MSU.

26. The only record of Still's visiting Stuart is in a memoir of William Henry Young, "Personal Memories of Jesse Stuart and James Still," *Kentucky Explorer* (November 2001), 14. He claims he was visiting Still soon after he got out of the army, and Still suggested they go to Greenup in the young man's car. "I was game for the trip, and a pleasant visit with the two men became one of my treasured memories."

27. Cadle's statement on writing: "However rewarding the living of my own life may be, writing about it and out of it gives me an assurance of belonging, an impression of completeness, that otherwise would be lacking. Writing is the only thing I do that affords me any lasting satisfaction and any compensation for the world's inanities, deceptions and inequities over which I have no control. It doesn't answer the questions of why, but it helps me identify the people, the attitudes, the acts I'm running from and those toward which I'm moving. Everything else I have done seems to be a substitute for writing or an excuse for not writing. I have disturbing dreams and a continually waking sense of guilt and anxiety because I'm unable to perform a small miracle such as James Still's *Mrs. Razor* or James Joyce's *The Dead* or Katherine Anne Porter's *Flowering Judas*." Dean Cadle in Southern Appalachian Writers Coll., D. H. Ramsey Library, University of North Carolina at Asheville.

28. Dean Cadle Coll. 1919–1997, Special Collections and Digital Programs, UK Libraries, 15 boxes.

29. Other biographical highlights of Cadle: recipient of the Wallace Stegner creative-writing fellowship at Stanford; degrees from UK and the State University of Iowa; a librarian and teacher in Kentucky and North Carolina; advising editor of *Appalachian Heritage* from 1972 to 1984.

30. Preface to the collection *Man on Troublesome*, Dean Cadle Coll. Box 8.

31. May 25, 1946, James Still Room, Camden-Carroll Library, MSU, Box 7 #17.

32. June 19, 1946, James Still Room, Camden-Carroll Library, MSU, Box 7 #18.

33. From an early version of the introduction to the 1978 edition of *River of Earth*. Found in the Dean Cadle Coll. and the Cratis D. Williams Papers.

34. Dean Cadle Coll. Box 10 #1.

35. This motif is nothing new. Rena Niles ("Obscurity Begins at Home," 1939), Gurney Norman ("I Write Because I'm Unhappy When I'm not Writing," 1958), and Joe Creason ("Something a Man Does Just for Himself," 1960) had picked up on Still's tendency to value writing over publishing and to resist a public life.

36. February 15, 1960, James Still Papers, UK Libraries, Box 25 #6.

37. Letter to James Gribble at UK Library, the Anvil Press. Dean Cadle Coll. Box 14.

38. May 25, 1961, and March 10, 1965, letters in Dean Cadle Coll.

39. James Still Papers, UK Libraries, Box 25 #12. The book was never

published, but these articles by Stewart and Napier ("Melody of the Spoken Word") appeared later in *Appalachian Heritage*. Letter from Cadle to Still, February 16, 1965, James Still Papers, UK Libraries, Box 25 #12.

40. February 16, 1965, James Still Papers, UK Libraries, Box 25 #12; James Still Papers, UK Libraries, Box 26 #1.

41. August 19, 1965, James Still Papers, UK Libraries, Box 25 #13. The only possible slight that Cadle might have felt from the letter was that Pickrel confused him with Harry Caudill, author of *Night Comes to the Cumberlands* (1962).

42. Cadle mailed the review to a list of thirty people that he and Still wanted to receive copies, and he requested for himself eighty copies of the magazine and an additional fifty offprints of the article.

43. Reactions to "Man on Troublesome" collected by Still and sent to Cadle, Dean Cadle Coll. Box 14.

44. Letter from Stuart Forth to Cadle, January 25, 1968, Dean Cadle Coll. Box 15.

45. September 3, 1969, Dean Cadle Coll. Box 14.

46. October 11, 1973, Dean Cadle Coll. Box 14.

47. Cadle had gone to the University of North Carolina–Asheville in 1966 as the circulation-reference librarian. Still had written a reference letter dated June 1, 1966, James Still Papers, UK Libraries, Box 26 #1.

48. January 14, 1977, James Still Papers, UK Libraries, Box 27 #14.

49. Letter to Crouch from Still, October 25, 1976, James Still Papers, UK Libraries, Box 27 #12.

50. Dean Cadle Coll. Box 14.

51. A letter from Crouch to Cadle sympathizes with the difficulty Cadle was having in satisfying Still with the introduction, July 27, 1977, Dean Cadle Coll. Box 15.

52. July 25, 1978, James Still Papers, UK Libraries, Box 28 #4. Shirley Williams, "Still Writing after All These Years."

53. Cadle to Still, March 31, 1979, James Still Papers, UK Libraries, Box 29 #3; Jerry Williamson, "An Interview with James Still," *Appalachian Journal* (1979):

54. A typed version (seven pages double-spaced, dated April 1987) of ". . . And Members of the Pack" is available in the Dean Cadle Coll.

55. December 11, 1986, James Still Papers, UK Libraries, Box 35 #3.

56. Thirty-nine pages built loosely on journal entries that Cadle had written in 1959. Still was shown the manuscript and asked to comment or approve. Most of his comments were ignored. Notes on the manuscript said that the comments were given to John Stephenson on April 31, 1981.

57. Dean Cadle Coll, Box 15.

58. Other information concerning Al Stewart: He taught in several high schools, at Caney Junior College, at MSC, and at Alice Lloyd College. While at MSC he took over as director of the writers' workshop in 1957. When he went from MSC to Alice Lloyd in 1965, he moved the workshop there and then on to Hindman. In 1972 he established *Appalachian Heritage* and was editor until 1984. Two of his own collections

of poems are *Untoward Hills* (1962) and *The Holy Season: Walking in the Wild* (1994).

59. Though written in 1963, it did not appear until the first issue of *Appalachian Heritage* 1, no. 1 (Winter, 1973); to date their first meeting, see letter May 12, 1940, James Still Room, Camden-Carroll Library, MSU, Box 12 #4.

60. Stewart, "At Home," 41–42.

61. See chapter 20: "On to Morehead."

62. November 11, 1957, James Still Papers, UK Libraries, Box 25 #3.

63. Sidney Faar, "I'm Always Writing," *Appalachian Heritage* 35, no. 3 (2007): 22.

64. Words of tribute to Still and Stewart at Hindman, July 31, 2002.

65. See Loyal Jones, "Remarks at James Still's Funeral (May 1, 2001)," in *Interviews*, 283–84.

66. Shirley Williams, interview by author, December 10, 2002.

67. If Still had homosexual interests or tendencies, he never admitted it. Once he emphatically denied it, while not giving the topic credence of a name. At one of his readings/conversations in the 1990s, a young man asked Still about his sexuality. Still would not repeat the question when recounting the incident, but he was upset and emphatically restated his answer—"No, I do not believe in that." The young man had raised a taboo topic and had asked a question that was boldly inappropriate and insulting to the old gentleman and would have been so for most people of his generation. Why did Still tell this incident? I was not present at the session and had no knowledge of or curiosity about the topic. At that time I was not his biographer but was merely driving him from place to place. Did he tell me this in veiled hints and angrily deny it because the insult was so great, or was he taking the opportunity to give me a definitive answer to a question I had not asked?

23. Pattern of a Writer in Pursuit of Publication

Epigraph: James Still, first stanza "Of the Wild Man," *From the Mountain, From the Valley*, 119.

1. See chapter 22 for more on the relationship between Still and Cadle.

2. Jones to Perrin, October 31, 1974, Dean Cadle Coll.; Cadle to Still, January 14, 1977, includes a copy of "Attitudes Towards Writing," James Still Room, Camden-Carroll Library, MSU, Box 11 #18.

3. Even Cadle's "Man on Troublesome" (1968) article uses some key Still quotes that appear later in "Pattern of a Writer;" for example, "A writer has to stay wild" (252) and "It would be enough if I were to write one book of enduring merit in my lifetime" (254).

4. The article is thirty-nine pages long and includes nine photographs that Cadle made of Still. The title echoes Still's short story "Pattern of a Man," which was published in the *Yale Review* in 1946.

5. Ibid., 134, 110, 139, 142.

6. Ibid., 114, 133, 116, 106, 143.

7. *Hounds on the Mountain*, Anvil Press, 1965; *River of Earth*, paper-

back, Popular Library, 1969; *Way Down Yonder*, Putnam, 1974; *Wolfpen Rusties*, Putnam, 1975; *Pattern of a Man*, Gnomon, 1976; *Jack and the Wonder Beans* and *Sporty Creek*, Putnam, 1977; *River of Earth*, UPK, 1978. Published earlier by Viking: *Hounds on the Mountain*, 1937; *River of Earth*, 1940; and *On Troublesome Creek*, 1941.

8. Shine to Still, November 24, 1965, James Still Papers, UK Libraries; for a print run of only 250 copies, Still's request for 50 seems large.

9. Dykeman, "Mountain Story," *Knoxville News-Sentinel*, November 7, 1965.

10. November 8, 1965, James Still Papers, UK Libraries, Box 25 #13.

11. Popular Library is now an imprint of Warner Books. The publisher answered a letter of inquiry regarding the paperback edition of *River of Earth* with the comment that the company's files have no history of this book, June 28, 1994.

12. Still wrote of the reprint in a letter to Cadle on September 3, 1969: "The August statement from Viking had a check, plus the notation: '*River of Earth*, Reprint Edition, Popular Library. . . . Never heard of 'em. And 'Popular' sounds ominous." James Still, interview by author, March 29, 1994.

13. Williams was dean of the Graduate School at Appalachian State and an Appalachian scholar; Higgs was professor of English at Tennessee State and coeditor of *Voices from the Hills*; Harry Caudill was author of *Night Comes to the Cumberland*, 1962; Martin was a professor at the University of Alabama in Huntsville. Allen Tate (1899–1979) was a native of Kentucky and a graduate of Vanderbilt before Still entered the English program. His early connections to the Fugitive Poets and the Southern Agrarians plus his later positions at Princeton and *The Sewanee Review* made him a high-profile reviewer and critic. See Tate to Still, June 2, 1971, Dean Cadle Coll. Box 14 #6.

14. January 8, 1975, James Still Papers, UK Libraries, Box 27 #9. The following year, Steele asked Still to help him track down more copies and suggested that he talk to Phyllis Jackson, a literary agent, about submitting it for republication.

15. James Still Papers, UK Libraries, Box 26 #4.

16. November 17, 1971, James Still Papers, UK Libraries, Box 26 #14.

17. November 30, 1972, James Still Papers, UK Libraries, Box 29 #4.

18. James Still, "An Interview," by Williamson, 124.

19. Ibid.

20. *Sporty Creek* borrows two chapters from *River of Earth*, the first, "Simon Brawl," and the fifth, "The Force Put."

21. Tina Hanlon, "'Read my tales, spin my rhymes': The Books for Children," in *James Still: Critical Essays on the Dean of Appalachian Literature*, eds. Ted Olson and Kathy H. Olson (Jefferson, NC: MacFarland, 2007), 179. Twenty years later, the UPK published one more of Still's books for children, *An Appalachian Mother Goose*, also illustrated by Johnson. Still actually had that manuscript completed in 1976 and presented it to Putnam, which refused it on the grounds that it might be perceived

as tampering with the traditional Mother Goose rhymes. After receiving less-than-enthusiastic responses from several other publishers, he put the collection to rest until later when UPK was reissuing the whole group of children's books.

22. August 18, 1978, James Still Papers, UK Libraries, Box 28 #5.

23. Greene, "A Memoir," 261–62; Greene started Gnomon Press in 1965; in his own words, the press was "dedicated to publishing quality literary and photographic books in handsome trade edition." Jonathan Greene, interview by author, August 1, 2002.

24. As early as April 1975, Still was thinking about having Gnomon publish his stories. In a letter to Cadle, he floated the idea: "Instead of reprinting On Troublesome Creek, I think I'll agree (with Gnomen [sic] Press) that a book of stories would be best that haven't seen book-light. Jonathan Greene used to be with UK Press. He's published Wendell Berry. . . . He gets NEA money for some of his projects." Dean Cadle Coll. Box 14 #6.

25. Greene, "A Memoir," 262.

26. Postcard from Still to Greene, Greene's papers. Still dedicated the book to Dean and his wife, Jo.

27. December 29, 1976, HSS Still files.

28. One letter from Greene to Still in January 1978 and one in August 1978 show that approximately fifty copies were sold every six months. Gross receipts were about $700, which means at 10 percent Still received roughly $70 in each royalty check. James Still Papers, UK Libraries, Box 28 #1 and #5.

29. Still to Greene, October 8, 1976, Greene's papers.

30. Still had taught several short courses at Berea in the 1970s and was awarded an honorary doctorate in 1973.

31. Divine Rights Trip, published in 1972, can provide the flavor if not all the details; James Still Room, Camden-Carroll Library, MSU, Box 11 #16.

32. The English Department chairman, J. A. Bryant, was supportive of Norman's proposal and came up with a $500 honorarium. But, as Norman explained, Still would need to do an evening session for the public, and that would involve an overnight stay. James Still Papers, UK Libraries, Box 27 #15.

33. May 28, 1977, Greene's papers.

34. Introduction to Crossing Troublesome.

35. Stoddart, Story of Hindman Settlement School, 180.

36. Awards were made on May 9 at Boone Tavern in Berea. Gurney Norman won the annual fiction award for Kinfolks. See letter from Tom Parrish, April 3, 1978, James Still Papers, UK Libraries, Box 28 #2.

37. Stephenson to Still, James Still Room, Camden-Carroll Library, MSU, Box 28 #5. August 21, 1978, James Still Papers, UK Libraries, Box 28 #5; April 4, 1979, James Still Papers, UK Libraries, Box 28 #11. Still received an Honorary Doctorate of Letters on May 12, 1979. After the commencement exercises, Still's company was requested at the buffet supper at the president's home on Maxwell Place.

38. *River of Earth* editorial file, UPK.

39. This summary of the policy toward reprinting Kentucky-related books is based on comments made by Jerome Crouch in a personal interview, June 15, 1994. Titles that were reprinted with new forewords include Roberts' *The Time of Man* (originally published by Viking in 1926; UPK edition 1982), John Fox's *The Little Shepherd of Kingdom Come* (Scribner's 1903, UPK edition 1987), Janice Holt Giles's *The Kentuckians* (Houghton-Mifflin 1953, UPK edition 1987), Jesse Stuart's *Trees of Heaven* (Dutton 1940, UPK edition 1980).

40. *River of Earth* editorial file, June 23, 1978.

41. Ibid., August 10, 1976, October 25, 1976, and April 5, 1977.

42. Dean Cadle Coll. Box 14. There is no evidence that Still complained directly to Crouch, but Cadle did mention it. Crouch responded that he would bring up the point when making production plans. Meanwhile, Still had written to Greene about the problem. Greene's proposal was to let UPK print the paperback and Gnomon the cloth edition. That suggestion got no further because, as Greene recognized, it would be "too confusing to bookbuyers and sellers." June 23, 1977, James Still Papers, UK Libraries, Box 27 #16.

43. Jerome Crouch, interview by author, June 15, 1994.

44. July 28, 1978, Dean Cadle Coll. Box 15.

45. *River of Earth* editorial file, Crouch to Still, July 28, 1978; Crouch to Williamson, September 15, 1978.

46. Art Jester's review in *The Anniston Star,* Alabama, September 28, 1980(?), no page; Dean Cadle Coll. Box 12.

47. *Knoxville Lifestyle*'s monthly book review, 59. All reviews listed here are available in James Still Papers, UK Libraries. For a full discussion and a complete list of reviews of the 1940 and 1978 editions, see Carol Boggess, "Following *River of Earth* from Source to Destination" (PhD diss., UK, 1995).

48. November 12, 1978, JWM Coll.

24. Still the Explorer

Epigraph: James Still, "Midwinter Doldrums." This poem is not included in Still's collected poems. Still sent it to Jonathan Greene, December 31, 1995, along with a letter to support Greene's application to Yaddo. Greene later published the poem as part of a portfolio of broadsides hand-printed at the King Library Press in the spring of 2006 to mark the fortieth anniversary of Gnomon Press.

1. Still, *From the Mountain,* 43, 77, 109; *River of Earth,* 52. Between 1972 and 1989, Still made fourteen trips to Central America. Between 1986 and 1990 he made five trips to Europe or England. The final trip to England is not well documented, but he does refer to it in a letter on September 14, 1990: "On the eve of my 84th birthday I wended my way to Canterbury, a true pilgrimage as Chaucer is about the only writer I feel a one-ness with." James Still Papers, UK Libraries, Box 38 #9.

2. Still and Warren were acquaintances and shared connections to

Vanderbilt. Still also knew Warren's wife, Eleanor Clark, from summer workshops in New England; Weatherford interview, August 10, 2008. Photos provided by Loyal Jones, May 27, 2002.

3. *River of Earth*, 172–73.

4. Shirley Williams, "Still Writing," 31.

5. Still made numerous trips to Central America between 1972 and 1989. He said later that his first was in 1971, but the earliest that can be verified was 1972. Letters, interviews, notes, journals, as well as the writings of fellow travelers document his adventures.

6. Cards, letters to Bakers and Ryan, James Still Papers, UK Libraries, Box 27; to Perrin, Berea Coll. Box 1, April 1972.

7. March 10, 1973, James Still Papers, UK Libraries, Box 27 #5.

8. James Still Room, Camden-Carroll Library, MSU, Box 11 #17. Still did exchange letters with Chamberlain in 1974, but there is no indication that his interest in anthropology or archaeology was more than casual.

9. The February demonstration was against General Carlos Romero of El Salvador, who had been chosen to succeed President Arturo Armando Molina. According to an April 14, 1977, article in *The Whitley Republican* of Williamsburg, KY, the demonstrations were a reaction by Romero's opponents, who believed the elections were fraudulent. The article tells of the trip that Still made with his friend Carlyle Cross.

10. Williams, "Still Writing," 31.

11. March 2, 1977. James Still Coll., Berea College, Box 1, Correspondence.

12. For another, longer version of the event in San Salvador, see Still's account to Jim Wayne Miller in the conversation "Daring to Look," 6–7.

13. Cross was associate professor of English and director of the libraries at Cumberland College.

14. In the diary he kept during his 1989 trip, he expresses some frustration at the traveling friends he has chosen over the years: "Can I pick companions for travel! . . . Three's a crowd. Two is a crowd. Sometimes one."

15. James Still, interview by author, July 11, 1997.

16. Ibid. Ceram describes Thompson's similar experience one hundred years earlier at Chichén Itza: "Thompson stood where he was, immobile and enchanted. The jungle melted away before his gaze. Wide spaces opened up, processions crept up to the temple site, music sounded, palaces became filled with reveling, the temples hummed with religious adjuration. . . . Then suddenly he was no longer bemused." C. W. Ceram, *Gods, Graves, and Scholars; The Story of Archaeology* (New York: Knopf, 1951), 376.

17. Miller, "Daring to Look," 8.

18. Dean Cadle Coll, Box 14 #6.

19. Sam McKinney was an artist who had grown up in Letcher County and was residing in Morehead when he first met Still; he was commissioned to paint Still's portrait in 1986. McKinney is quoted on the website of Northern Kentucky University (accessed February 25, 2013): "James was in his mid-80s, so I was fortunate to spend quite a bit of time at Dead Mare Branch in Knott County, not only as an artist, but as an invited friend

and travel companion. . . . One cannot help but evolve as a person when in the company of such an intellectual and mature soul." Observations here are from the author's interview of McKinney in 2003.

20. Still recorded the 1989 trip to Cuba in a handwritten diary. Entries for twelve days are available in James Still Papers, UK Libraries, Box 83 #7; the last pages are missing.

21. Still wrote to Forest Cain (a British friend from his military days) that he had seen the plays *A Man for all Seasons, King Lear, Zeigfield,* and *Much Ado About Nothing.* But his main interest in Britain was Kew Gardens and Castle Howard, where *Brideshead Revisited* was filmed.

22. Mary Ellen Miller, interview by author, August 17, 2012. She remembered that Still had not been happy about going to Iceland, but once they got there, it became one of his favorite parts of the trip. Still's handwritten itinerary provides the list of places visited, James Still Papers, UK Libraries, Box 19 #1.

23. Miller, "James Still: Happy Man," 17.

24. Ann Campbell was the Appalachian librarian at UK when Still began talking about depositing his papers there. She and her husband, Don Ritchie, had since moved to Washington, D.C., where he was in the U.S. Senate history office and she was archivist at the National Gallery of Art.

25. Judi Jennings, "Travels with Mr. Still: In Search of Richard Jefferies," in *James Still in Interviews, Oral Histories and Memoirs,* ed. Ted Olson (Jefferson, NC: McFarland, 2009), 243, 245.

26. Ibid., 246. Richard Jefferies was born at Coate Farm on November 6, 1848, and died in 1887. He was a well-known nature writer who wrote one astonishing book, *The Story of My Heart,* in which he tried to explain his vision of nature and life. His writings, according to Jenning's guidebook, "reveal an intense absorption in such details as would escape a casual rambler, the ascent of a caterpillar upon an almost invisible thread; a speckled trout immobile in the shadow of a bridge, the subtle differences in colouring in a tuft of grass." His writing became a nineteenth-century standard for the close examination of nature.

27. George Alexander had grown up in a Catholic orphanage in England. He wrote children's stories and music and had a fondness for Appalachian folklore. He lived in Epsom, England. Alexander and Still had met at Hindman; they corresponded for years and saw each other when they could. Jennings described their friendship: "He worshipped Mr. Still and Mr. Still liked people who worshiped him."

28. Jennings, "Travels," 245–46.

29. Judi Jennings, interview by author, September 19, 2002.

30. Ibid.

31. Alessandro Portelli began his academic career at the University of Siena, where he taught American literature. In 1981 he moved to the University of Rome La Sapienza. A meeting between Portelli and UK sociologist David Walls in 1973 led to his visiting Harlan County. Portelli returned as a James Still Fellow at the UK Appalachian Center in the fall of 1983 and began developing extensive oral-history work in Harlan County. He

also began an exchange program, involving graduate students and faculty, between the Appalachian Center and La Sapienza. His *They Say in Harlan County,* which tells the story of a coal-mining community between 1964 and 2009, won the W. D. Weatherford Award for the best nonfiction book on Appalachia published in 2010.

    32. Randy Wilson, interview by author, December 12, 2002.

    33. Judi Jennings, interview by author, September 19, 2002.

    34. February 7, 1989, JWM Coll. Box 163 #3.

    35. Alessandro Portelli, email to author, May 31, 2013.

25. Jolly and Godey

Epigraph: James Still to Jim Wayne Miller, December 31, 1985, James Still Papers, UK Libraries, Box 33 #11.

    1. Shirley Williams quoted Al Perrin in "Still Writing."

    2. Shirley Williams, interview by author, December 10, 2002. A year after the *Courier-Journal* article, when Still got the Peabody Waite Award, he asked Williams to go with him to New York, saying, "You're the reason I got this."

    3. Jerry Williamson, "A Cold Day in Hell: An Interview with Jerry Williamson," by Pat Beaver and Helen Lewis, *Appalachian Journal* 28, no. 1 (2000): 97.

    4. Ibid., 98. Williamson was describing this incident in the journal issue that accompanied his retirement, more than twenty years after the Still interview. In recounting an early challenge as editor, he was showing traits of a storyteller himself. Comparing the first transcript with Still's revision does reveal changes, but to call it a "complete fabrication" is an exaggeration. The final version makes better sense, is more readable, and shows both men in a more favorable light.

    5. September 30, 1978, James Still Papers, UK Libraries, Box 28 #6.

    6. James Still, "An Interview with James Still," by Williamson, *Appalachian Journal* 6 (Winter 1979): 134.

    7. Ibid., 140.

    8. The interview was first published in the Winter 1979 issue of *Appalachian Journal:* 120–41. It was modified and republished in *Interviewing Appalachia: The Appalachian Journal Interviews, 1978–1992* (1994): 49–66.

    9. October 4, 1978, James Still Papers, UK Libraries, Box 28 #7.

    10. "Those I Want in Heaven with Me (Should There Be Such a Place)" (1991). *Appalachian Journal* also published the long work of Cadle, "Pattern of a Writer" (1988), and one critical article about Still by Fred Chappell, "The Seamless Vision of James Still" (1981).

    11. April 22, 1975, Dean Cadle Coll, Box 14 #6.

    12. James Still, "An Interview," 130.

    13. James Still Papers, UK Libraries, Box 27 #8.

    14. The column was "Our Far-Flung Correspondents," August 21, 1978, 73.

    15. James Still Papers, UK Libraries, Box 28 #4.

16. James Reston, telephone interview by author, September 28, 2012.

17. James Still Papers, UK Libraries, Box 28 #5. The cosponsors of the visit would be the Appalachian Studies Program, the Margaret King Library, the dean of Undergraduate Studies Office, and Phi Beta Kappa.

18. Linc Fisch, "In Remembrance," 266; Erwin Edman of Columbia's Philosophy Department sent the invitation, March 28, 1940, Dean Cadle Coll. Box 14 #6.

19. Miller, "Jim Dandy," 17. Miller quoted Still as saying, "I am proud of my Phi Beta Kappa key. When I feel especially ignorant, I wear it (out of sight)."

20. Still to Wade Hall, June 8, 1979, Hall Coll.; Perrin to Still, December 1989, James Still Papers, UK Libraries, Box 28 #16.

21. James Still Papers, UK Libraries, Box 6 #3. He was on the council 1980–1983, then 1984–1986. He served on the speakers bureau 1988–1989. On a scrap of paper at one of the meetings in Lexington, he scratched out, "Kentucky is a place where everybody is somebody." HSS Still files.

22. James Still Papers, UK Libraries, Box 6 #5.

23. "I think of myself as a story-teller. That's the only way you can tell the truth—through fiction, and, stay alive. Alive, to this point," from the notes for Still's tribute to Carl Perkins at MSU, July 3, 1983.

24. John Stephenson established the James Still Fellowship in 1983 or 1984—the first year it supported eleven professors. In later years, the funds were shifted to support James Still scholarships for graduate students.

25. James Still Papers, UK Libraries, Box 2 #1.

26. *Sentinel Echo*, London, KY, June 16, 1983; *Troublesome Creek Times*, Hindman, July 13, 1983. James Still Papers, UK Libraries, Box 2 #14. The article was published as "Dealing with fame in folkie heaven" in Charles House, *One With the Fox* (Sarasota, FL: Pub This Press, 2005), 7–12.

27. October 1983. Still was the first living writer to be honored. As the years continued, the festival became a landmark event in the celebration and study of Appalachian literature. More than thirty writers have been honored at Emory & Henry. It opened with a documentary film, followed by a conversation, described as a dialogue lecture, between Still and Jim Wayne Miller. On Thursday an Appalshop film was aired; then there were lectures on Still's poetry by Jeff Daniel Marion and on his fiction by Fred Chappell. The final day featured a discussion on literary themes by Miller, Marion, and Terry Cornett, presented a documentary produced by Sally Jackson of KET in Lexington, and culminated with an evening reading by Still himself.

28. *Smith County News* in Marion, VA, October 18, 1983, James Still Room, Camden-Carroll Library, MSU.

29. Still to Hervey and Gladys Sharpe, July 21, 1980, James Still Papers, UK Libraries, Box 29 #5.

30. Titles of the NPR spots are listed in the collection of Linc Fisch: Crows, Winter Tree, Child in the Hills, No work in the Depression, Visiting Man O' War, Studs Terkel, Hushpuppies, Family disappointments,

Unsavory characters, Bluebird on Endangered list. Herb E. Smith recorded Still reading the scripts at Appalshop then sent tapes to NPR. Herb E. Smith, interview by author, December 10, 2002.

31. Stephenson was interested in having the house and land of Dead Mare Branch under the protection of the state, specifically UK, and had pursued that idea. On March 2, 1981, he wrote to Still that budget restrictions meant the university was not able to make the commitment. June 23, 1981, James Still Papers, UK Libraries, Box 29 #13.

32. By 1984 a photo of his house was on the cover of the "Appalachian Simple Lifestyle Calendar."

33. "'It's Not a Job To Me': Mike Mullins and the Hindman Settlement School," *Appalachian Journal* (Spring/Summer 2006): 330. Mike Mullins, interview by author, December 12, 2002.

34. May 1980, May 1984, June 1987. The website tells visitors they can expect solitude, stillness, and an emptiness while attending to the Spirit. Silence is fundamental to the experience.

35. May 7, 1980, James Still Papers, UK Libraries, Box 29 #4.

36. Herb E. Smith, "A Gentleman and a Scholar," available in the materials collected by Linc Fisch.

37. Still, *From the Mountain*, 132.

38. Miller refers to the incident in his letter of December 10, 1982, and speaks of the poem in "Jim Dandy."

39. James Still Papers, UK Libraries, Box 30 #8.

40. Still to Frieda [Mullins] and staff, August 1983, HSS Still files.

41. James Still Papers, UK Libraries, Box 32 #6. When asked in 2013 if she remembered James Still, Mathis responded that she did, and she remembered his short letter to her. In 1984 she had laughed when reading it because he seemed so old. When she read it to her daughter, at age thirty-four in 2013, her response was more extreme—finding the note weird and the writer a possible pervert. Cleopatra's response: "I guess times really have changed." Email exchange with Cleopatra Mathis, July 2013.

42. The committee members were John Stephenson, president of Berea College; Jim Wayne Miller, professor at Western Kentucky; Ronald Eller, director of the Appalachian Center at UK; M. K. Thomas, Still's colleague and friend at MSU; and Mike Mullins, director of HSS.

43. The title of a Still story first published in *The Atlantic Monthly* in 1949. The occasion is a fun-filled hog kill. The narrator receives the invitation with these words: "Hit's to be a quiet affair, a picked crowd. . . . [They] will treat you clever. You'll have a master time."

44. Joe Glaser, "Slick as a Dogwood Hoe Handle," *Appalachian Heritage* (Summer, 1983): 4–9.

45. Mullins, the Settlement School, and many of Still's friends and admirers did celebrate the one hundredth birthday, but the master was present only in spirit. He was, however, very much involved in his ninetieth birthday party, also held in Hindman. His alternative personality, Godey Spurlock, sent out the invitations and thanks.

46. Miller's words at the party were extended in the article that he published in the fall issue of *Appalachian Heritage* called "Jim Dandy: James Still at Eighty."

26. Jim Wayne and Anson

Epigraph: James Still, quoted in Jim Wayne Miller, "Jim Dandy: James Still at Eighty," 19.

1. Here is a partial chronological listing of Miller's published writings concerning Still and his work: James Still entry, *Critical Survey of Poetry*, ed. Frank Magill (1982). "Daring to Look in The Well" and "Appalachian Literature: At Home in this World," *Iron Mountain Review* (1984). "Jim Dandy: James Still at Eighty," *Appalachian Heritage* (1986). "A Mountain Still," *Courier-Journal Magazine* (1986). Introduction to *The Wolfpen Poems* (1986). "James Still: A Good Writer A Good Man," *The Mountain Spirit* (1987). "James Still: Happy Man on Troublesome Creek," *Vanderbilt Magazine* (1987). "Madly to Learn," *From the Fort to the Future* (1987). "*The Wolfpen Notebooks*: James Still's Record of Appalachian Life," *Appalachian Heritage* (1991).

2. "Preface," *Geography and Literature*, xii.

3. George Brosi, "Jim Wayne Miller," *Appalachian Heritage* 37, no. 3 (2009): 11.

4. These letters are held in the UK correspondence collection, which also has sixty-five letters from Still to Miller; copies of the original letters are held in the JWM Coll. at Western Kentucky University.

5. James Still Papers, UK Libraries, Box 28 #15.

6. James Still Papers, UK Libraries, Box 30 #1.

7. James Still Papers, UK Libraries, Box 26 #4. See chapter 23: "Pattern of a Writer in Pursuit of Publication".

8. There is a short series of correspondence between Best and Still. The letters are available only in the JWM Coll. at Western Kentucky University. Still must have sent the exchange to Miller without keeping copies.

9. JWM Coll.

10. James Still Papers, UK Libraries, Box 30 #2. Terry Cornett was preparing a chronological bibliography of Still's published works, which indicated that thirteen poems appeared between 1968 and 1980. Cornett was a doctoral candidate at Vanderbilt who was teaching at Hazard Community College. The bibliography was eventually published in the *Iron Mountain Review* (Summer 1984) and later revised and reprinted in *The Wolfpen Notebooks*, 1991.

11. Aleksis Rannit was a professor emeritus from Yale. He described himself as a specialist in comparative aesthetics. He had met Still at Yaddo and greatly admired his poetry, using the definition of true poetry from Boris Pasternak to describe Still's achievement as "the grain of pure prose." See letter from Rannit to Miller, November 16, 1982, included in Miller's letter to Still, James Still Papers, UK Libraries, Box 30 #13.

12. HSS Still files.

13. For Miller to approach Crouch and Stephenson at the conference

would have been influential. In 1983 Miller was president of the Appalachian Studies Association.

14. James Still Papers, UK Libraries, Box 31 #9.

15. North Point Press, an independent book publisher from 1980 to 1990, published more than 280 books, including titles by Evan S. Connell, Beryl Markham, James Salter, Guy Davenport, Wendell Berry, and M. F. K. Fisher. The editor was Jack Shoemaker.

16. James Still Papers, UK Libraries, Box 31 #12. His reservations concerned the possible difficulty of acquiring permission to reprint the stories.

17. James Still Papers, UK Libraries, Box 31 #15.

18. James Still Papers, UK Libraries, Box 32 #7.

19. In the published volume, the color photograph of Still at the log house was by Earl Palmer. The blurb on the back cover was from James Dickey. The essay by Rannit and the tribute by Francis did not appear, but Miller's introduction did.

20. March 26, 1985, James Still Coll., Berea College.

21. Clipping in a letter from Miller, August 9, 1987. Award given by the Appalachian Writers Association at a conference at Western Carolina University in Cullowhee, NC.

22. Still's first letter to Greene was dated August 20, 1979. Still did not donate Greene's "formal" letter to the library collection.

23. Greene, "A Memoir," 263.

24. James Still Papers, UK Libraries, Box 28 #15.

25. Greene, "A Memoir," 263.

26. Tracy Campbell appropriately called Prichard's contribution a "masterful introduction" in *Short of the Glory: The Fall and Redemption of Edward F. Prichard Jr.* (Lexington: UPK, 1998), 272. Campbell also pointed out (footnote 14) that unfortunately Prichard did not receive the credit he deserved as a literary critic; even his name was misspelled by the King Library Press.

27. The Foxfire website states its mission: "Foxfire is a not-for-profit, educational and literary organization based in Rabun County, Georgia. Founded in 1966, Foxfire's learner-centered, community-based educational approach is advocated through both a regional demonstration site grounded in the Southern Appalachian culture that gave rise to Foxfire, and a national program of teacher training and support that promotes a sense of place and appreciation of local people, community, and culture as essential educational tools" (http://www.foxfirefund.org/mission-statement.html). Eliot Wigginton was essential to the establishment of Foxfire from its origins in 1966 until 1992, when he admitted to a charge of child molestation. James Still wrote this note to Wigginton on September 22, 1992, less than a month before Wigginton confessed: "Eliot, You are on my mind and heart. With you all the way. This, given time, will pass. Foxfire will gain in fiber and resolve from this ordeal. Jim"; HSS Still files.

28. Laura Lee, "Introduction," *The Wolfpen Notebooks*, 1.

29. Perry to Wigginton, July 23, 1987, James Still Papers, UK Libraries,

Box 80 #4; Still to Perry, August 17, 1987, James Still Papers, UK Libraries, Box 35 #11.

30. Cherry to Wigginton, August 21, 1987, James Still Papers, UK Libraries, Box 80 #5; Crouch to Wigginton, August 28, 1987; Miller to Still, August 28, 1987, JWM Coll.

31. Still to Miller, September 27, 1987, JWM Coll. This letter was adapted to be Part V of the "James Still" entry in CAA in 1993. Still changed it to be a letter to his brother William Comer.

32. The first section of the manuscript that became the opening chapter of *Chinaberry* was dated and titled GTT [Gone to Texas]; Still Storage. That unfinished material was what Silas House edited into Still's posthumous work, *Chinaberry*, published by UPK in 2011.

33. See chapter 4: "Working His Way." Also see Still, *Wolfpen Notebooks*, 16.

34. In an interview on December 10, 2002, Smith told the author that Still frequently wanted to talk about the Texas story, and when he did it seemed as though he were recounting a dream. Those conversations probably took place in the late 1970s when Smith and his wife lived near Still's log house. Smith remembered that Still seemed to be wrestling with the book because it was different both geographically and in subject matter. He toyed with the idea of publishing it under a different name. Another person he told and retold the story to in bits and pieces was Sidney Farr; interview by author, March 30, 2003.

35. The book was *Black Land Heritage* by Troy Crenshaw; McCulloh's letter was dated July 31, 1984. McCulloh to Still, January 21, 1985, Still Storage, with the Texas manuscript.

36. Still much later shared the rough manuscript with Lee Smith, who encouraged him to revise and publish it. Still never completed the task though it would seem that he continued to consider the possibility. His literary executors arranged for the manuscript to be edited and completed by Silas House and published as *Chinaberry* in 2011.

37. Still wrote to Miller on May 29, 1987, that he would have to reveal the secret identity to Ann Campbell at the UK Special Collections because, as he was giving his correspondence to the collection, she would discover his alter ego, "Anson."

38. Miller to Still, January 17, 1984, James Still Papers, UK Libraries, Box 32 #1. Miller mentioned the names again in a letter to Still dated December 31, 1985, when he suggested including in his article the fact that Still had several names (Godey, Anson, Lucky, Jack, etc.). Cover letter for the article "Still Making Things Happen," James Still Papers, UK Libraries, Box 33 #12. The article remained unpublished.

39. James Still Papers, UK Libraries, Box 71 #1.

40. December 30, 1985, James Still Papers, UK Libraries, Box 33 #12 .

41. Nomination, February 19, 1985, James Still Papers, UK Libraries, Box 33 #2; visit to the Stokely Institute, June 5, 1985, James Still Papers, UK Libraries, Box 33 #6; letter with menu, March 4, 1986, James Still Papers, UK Libraries, Box 34 #3.

42. March 16, 1987, James Still Papers, UK Libraries, Box 35 #6.

43. See letter from September 2, 1987, JWM Coll.

44. Notes from Miller, collection folder: Interviewing JS June 15–17, 1994. For a fictional account by Miller, see "Truth and Fiction," in *Every Leaf a Mirror: A Jim Wayne Miller Reader,* eds. Morris Grubbs and Mary Ellen Miller (Lexington: UPK, 2014), 117–24. It is an account of a European trip that the narrator (Miller) made with Still (named McLean in the story) in 1986. The narrator's frustration is balanced by his ultimate realization that by being with the vain, needy, and demanding old man, he was "in the presence of genius" (124).

45. JWM Coll. Box 163 #7.

27. At Home in This World

Epigraph: James Still, *River of Earth,* 25.

1. Miller, "*The Wolfpen Notebooks:* James Still's Record," 20–24.

2. Notes for BH (a manuscript project titled Bad Hair), James Still Papers, UK Libraries, Box 57 #15.

3. March 9, 1992, JWM Coll. 163 #3.

4. James Still, interview by author, August 1, 1994.

5. Jeff Biggers, "His Side of the Mountains: The Enduring Legacy of Southern Poet James Still, Interview with Ted Olson," in *James Still in Interviews, Oral Histories and Memoirs,* ed. Ted Olson (Jefferson, NC: McFarland, 2009), 287.

6. October 4, 1990, JWM Coll.

7. Letter from Jonathan Greene's personal collection.

8. Sam Linkous, comment to author.

9. Williamson, "A Cold Day in Hell," 99.

10. Bill Weinberg explained why he called James Still "Mr. Still." It was "an unarticulated respect for his intellect and his writing ability. Though we were friends, we were not peers. It was a distinction not to his liking. Hal Crowther posits (in "A Man of the World") that 'You called him "Mr." Still unless you were a writer he admired, a woman he fancied, or his rare equal in years.' Though it's good prose, I suspect that even that select company most often called him Mr. Still." From Bill Weinberg, "The Power of James Still," *Appalachian Journal* 36, no. 3–4 (2009): 225.

11. Margin note on the draft of his tribute to Carl Perkins, July 3, 1983, James Still Room, Camden-Carroll Library, MSU.

12. Story reported by Sam Linkous, interview by author, March 2003.

13. Wade Hall interview by author, September 18, 2002.

14. Undated letter (ca. 1990) from Randy Wilson to Barbara Sue Barnes Harris (Still's niece), courtesy of Harris.

15. Alice Brown, interview by author, October 21, 2002. She recalled the day (April 3): "I'll never forget—it was raining. We were in one place for lunch and then somewhere else for the presentation. Security came to pick up Mrs. Bingham and took her to the auditorium. Wendell Berry was behind me and he said, 'What do I have to do to get limousine service on this campus?' And I said, 'You have to give us half a million dollars.'"

16. James Still Papers, UK Libraries, Box 38 #4. *Heritage* was produced by June Appal Recordings, a part of Appalshop. The tape was created in 1991 but released in 1992; the project was funded by the Kentucky Humanities Council and directed by Herb E. Smith. Produced and edited by Rich Kirby. Recorded and mixed by Doug Dorschug.

17. Letters to George Zachry dated June 25, 1994, and October 27, 1994. Zachry was from Alabama and had written a letter to Still in 1988. Still wrote back in 1994 and began an exchange that lasted until 2000, with most of the correspondence in 1994 when Zachry was writing an extensive biographical article on Still. The James Still Papers, UK Libraries holds fifty-one letters from Zachry. Zachry contributed letters from Still for this research.

18. Another factor was to enhance the university's efforts to bring the remainder of his papers to the UK library.

19. On Still's eighty-third birthday (July 1989), notice was made that Mary Bingham had given $500,000 to UK to endow the James Still Fellowships for the Appalachian Scholars Program. The gift would allow faculty member from thirty-eight colleges in the Appalachian region to receive stipends of $3,000 each to come to UK to do research in the library. Pamela Mitchell, "Appalachian Program given $500,000," *Kentucky Kernel,* July 13, 1989; James Still Papers, UK Libraries, Bingham file. Of the fifty-six institutions, forty-four were from the region; nine were in other states including Massachusetts, New York, Kansas, Missouri, Wisconsin, Washington, and California; three were from other countries—Italy, Scotland, Wales.

20. Alice Brown, interview by author, October 21, 2002.

21. His first visit to Mars Hill College was for two weeks in 1993. Although the college provided a room in the guesthouse, Still left after one night because he felt the caretaker had chastised him for moving a lamp to his bed so he could read. He went to Ed and Pauline Cheek's house for the remainder of his visit. Pauline Cheek shared the story of his 1996 visit in a note to the author, March 2016.

22. The money was a gift from Eleanor Bingham Miller.

23. Still to Hall, May 10, 1977, courtesy of Wade Hall.

24. *Appalachian Heritage* 25, no 2 (Spring 1997): 3. Also in Still, *From the Mountain,* 145.

25. In April 1994 a film crew came to his Wolfpen house and stayed four days to include him in the PBS series on the nation's poetry. When the film was released two years later, Still, the oldest of the sixty featured poets, appeared reading "Heritage" in a quiet, idyllic setting. The crew later wrote him a personal letter remembering that spring day with "awe and tenderness." *The United States of Poetry* was a production of Washington Square films for the Independent Television Service and PBS. It premiered in February 1996; Still appeared in the first program "The Land and the People" (James Still Papers, UK Libraries, Box 3). A version can be viewed at: archive.org/details/TheUnitedStatesOfPoetry.

26. A quotation of Sholom Aleichem in Still TX manuscript notes, James Still Papers, UK Libraries.

27. For example, in 1985 *Limestone* published an interview conducted by Tom and Carol French-Corbett and Lois Kleffman, and in 1986 Frank Edward Bourne had a less-formal interview, which was published in *Appalachian Heritage* in 2002. The Beattie interview, dated August 2, 1991, appeared in *Conversations with Kentucky Writers* in 1996. Joyce LeMaster (associate professor of English at MSU) and Mont Whitson (professor of Sociology at MSU) did a joint interview of Still early in 1994, "The Genesis of *River of Earth*." They intended to publish it in one of the region's journals. A typed copy can be found in the James Still Room, Camden-Carroll Library, at MSU and in the James Still Papers, UK Libraries. Also in the early 1990s Linc Fisch and Tawny Acker Hogg interviewed Still. The transcript (courtesy of Fisch) remains in rough-draft form.

28. Jane Mayhall observes in her 1998 article "James Still: Quality of Life, Quality of Art" that his memory "flows in a clear progression"; however, he "never tries to force the accuracy of his material [written or oral] into a specified time frame." *Shenandoah: The Washington and Lee University Review* 48, no. 2 (1998): 56–73, 56–57.

29. He did not forget this nickname and months later signed a copy of *Jack and the Wonder Beans*, "For William, the ice cream boy."

30. Still wrote to Zachry on September 7, 1998, that this work was "evidence of his second childhood." Lee Smith played a major role in urging UPK to publish *Appalachian Mother Goose*, which had the manuscript title "The Blab School."

31. In 1991: the Award for Educational Service to Appalachia from Carson Newman College; the DAR Medal of Honor awarded in Hindman; and the proposal to establish the James Still Chair in Writing at Pikeville College. In 1992: the dedication of James Still Learning Center at HSS; and named Honorary Citizen of Louisville. In 1994: commissioned as Honorary John Adair General in Columbia, KY; Hazard Community College established the James Still Scholarship. In 1996: named the first recipient of the MSU Thomas & Lillie Chaffin Award for Appalachian Writing. He also received his sixth and seventh honorary doctorates from Cumberland College in 1996 and Kentucky Wesleyan College in 1998.

32. Awarded by UK Libraries. Still was in good company with former medallion holders: Thomas Clark, historian; O. Leonard Press, founder of KET; Wendell Berry, Kentucky writer; and Bert T. Combs, former governor.

33. Three governors were present: Brereton Jones (then current), Julian Carroll, and Ned Breathit.

34. Rhonda England, "A Literary Biography of James Still: A Beginning" (unpublished master's thesis, MSU, 1984). H. R. Stoneback, "Rivers of Earth and Troublesome Creeks: The Agrarianism of James Still," *The Kentucky Review* 10, no. 3 (1990): 3–26. Collection planned by Linc Fisch and Tawny Acker: *The Legacy of James Still: Turning Words into Windows*. An alternative title for their collection was *Still Life: Reflections on the Man, the Muse, and the Mountains* (letter from Hogg, James Still Papers, UK Libraries, Box 41 #1).

35. Ted Olson, "His Side of the Mountains: The Enduring Legacy of

Southern Poet James Still," interview by Jeff Biggers, *Bloomsbury Review* (July/August 2002). Volumes of works by or about Still edited by Ted Olson: *From the Mountain, From the Valley: New and Collected Poems* (2001) and *The Hills Remember: The Complete Short Stories of James Still* (2012) published by UPK; *James Still: Collected Essays on the Dean of Appalachian Literature* (2008) and *James Still in Interviews, Oral Histories and Memoirs* (2009) published by McFarland.

36. Ted Olson, interviewed by Jeff Biggers, "His Side of the Mountain," 18.

37. In transcript of "Conversations with James Still," project directed by Michael Lasater at Western Kentucky University, November 1986, JWM Coll.

38. Still referred to himself as a "manuscript consultant" rather than a teacher of writing: "Interview with James Still," by Jerry Williamson (1979), 135.

39. Berry to Still, March 22, 1977, James Still Room, Camden-Carroll Library, MSU, Box 18 #11.

40. Wendell Berry, "In Memory: James Still," *Imagination in Place* (Berkeley, CA: Counterpoint, 2010), 73, 75.

41. First published in the Raleigh *News and Observer,* October 10, 1993. For a more recent version, see Smith's essay "Marble Cake and Moonshine," in *Dimestore: A Writer's Life* (Chapel Hill, NC: Algonquin, 2016), 63–75.

42. James Still Papers, UK Libraries, Box 46 #6–8. Still did have an agent in 1980 at International Creative Management, Mitch Douglas, but there is little evidence that he was active. In August 1997 Smith sent Still a thank-you note for sending her *Max Perkins: Editor of Genius.*

43. *A Gathering at the Forks* celebrated the fifteenth anniversary. *Crossing Troublesome* celebrated the twenty-fifth. Selections in the second that mention Still were by Chris Offutt, Jim Hinsdale, Elaine Cavanaugh, David Todd, Charles Simpson, Irene Mosvold, Betty Barger Pace, Alan MacKellar, Linda Caldwell, Jane Hicks, Linda Parsons Marion, Virginia Dulworth, Jeff Daniel Marion, Jan Walters Cook, Laura Weddle, and Lee Smith.

44. Ann Olson, "Before Saying Yes," 201–4.

45. Jan Cook, "Green Peppers and a Straw Hat," *Crossing Troublesome,* 114–15.

46. George Ella Lyon, interview by author, October 7, 2014.

47. Jane Mayhall was born in Louisville, Kentucky, in 1918 and attended Black Mountain College in North Carolina. She taught at the New School for Social Research, Hofstra University, MSU, and the Summer Writers' Workshop at HSS in Kentucky. Her fiction and poems appeared in *The Yale Review, The New Yorker,* and *The Paris Review.* Mayhall lived in New York City until her death in 2009. (See author biography on Random House website). There are sixty-seven letters from Mayhall to Still in the James Still Papers, UK Libraries.

48. Jane Mayhall, phone interview by author, February 23, 2003.

49. Harry Brown earned a doctorate from Ohio University and had been on the English faculty at Eastern Kentucky University since 1970. He lived with his wife and children on a farm at Paint Lick, between Richmond and Berea. His avocation of farming and writing poetry appealed to Still. Also Harry's wife, Alice, director of the Appalachian College Association, was a connection for Still. By 2011 Brown had published five collections of poems. Most of the publication occurred after he met Still. Still letters courtesy of Harry Brown.

50. Still was an avid reader and talked often about his reading. Titles listed in this letter include Howard Kissel's *David Merrick: The Abominable Snow Man;* Frank McShane's *Into Eternity: The Life of James Jones* (he had once attempted Jones's *From Here to Eternity* but found that the "nasty words seemed entirely gratuitous and the prose pedestrian"); a biography of John Marquand by Stephen Birmingham. He reread *All Quiet on the Western Front* and was currently rereading W. H. Hudson's *Little Boy Lost.*

51. Story repeated from Papers by Guest Speakers KPA (Kentucky Philological Association), Murray, KY, 1984.

52. Chris Offutt had gotten Still's address from his friend Sam McKinney at MSU.

53. Offutt to Still, December 7, 1992, HSS Still files.

54. Quoted from "Meeting the Master" submitted to the collection of Linc Fisch, James Still Papers, UK Libraries, Box 96 #2.

55. In 1995 Gnomon Press published his first story collection, *Hell and Ohio.* In 2003, two years after Still's death, Chris Holbrook joined the English faculty at MSU.

56. Maurice Manning, phone conversation with author, July 2014. See "Travels with the Wolfpen Poet," published in *Writer's Bloc* (an English Club newsletter at UK).

57. "Travels with the Wolfpen Poet," 4.

58. Manning to Still, January 30, 1992, James Still Papers, UK Libraries, Box 40 #7; Manning refers to one of those visits in a letter dated July 27, 1993. He includes his poem "Prayer for a Country Flower"; James Still Papers, UK Libraries, Box 41 #13.

59. Introduction to *Chinaberry,* ix–x; Silas House, "The Art of Being Still," *New York Times* online opinion page, December 1, 2012; "The Legacy," *Arts Across Kentucky,* Winter 2001.

60. Beattie, *Conversations,* 372.

28. Invitation to the Eternal

Epigraph: James Still, *From the Mountain, From the Valley,* 143.

1. Still to Zachry, October 27, 1994, James Still Papers, Cobb Memorial (Valley) Archives, AL.

2. Molly Bundy, telephone conversation with author, April 13, 1996.

3. At Appalachian Regional Hospital. Miller to Still, December 10, 1992, James Still Papers, UK Libraries, Box 41 #5.

4. Molly Bundy to Still, April 17, 1995, James Still Papers, UK Libraries, Box 44 #4.

5. Still to Zachry, September 23, 1999, and May 17, 2000, James Still Papers, Cobb Memorial (Valley) Archives.

6. Wade Hall, interview by author, September 18, 2002.

7. The poem with notes in Still's handwriting was enclosed in a letter from Anne Caudill, April 1, 1994, James Still Papers, UK Libraries, Box 43 #1.

8. Elizabeth Watts (1891–1993) went to HSS in 1909. She retired in 1956 but continued to serve on the board of directors; her service amounted to eighty-four years. HSS did a fund-raiser to pay for her ledger stone, and Still contributed twenty-five dollars, which Mike Mullins acknowledged with a form letter dated March 12, 1997; James Still Papers, UK Libraries, Box 46 #3. Still is buried near Watts on a hill above the school.

9. The poem was originally a memorial for his brother Alfred, but Still renamed it for John Stephenson. See the poem at the end of chapter 19: "Family Loss and Brotherly Love."

10. Clark's book, *The Kentucky,* was published two years after *River of Earth,* and his chapter on mountain life has much in common with Still's work.

11. Thomas Clark, interview by author, October 22, 2002.

12. Clark to Still, August 1, 1994, James Still Papers, UK Libraries, Box 43 #5.

13. A dark green Comet was first; then a silver Cougar. The Town Car was purchased at Paul Miller Ford in Lexington. Still's response to the questions appeared in a short piece by Jeff Daniel Marion in *Crossing Troublesome,* 110.

14. Award letters are in James Still Papers, UK Libraries, Boxes 37 and 38. Other winnings include first place in Visine's 1989 "View of the World Sweepstakes," the prize a pair of Bushnell binoculars; fifth-place prize in 1990 (sunglasses) in the Champion Spark Plug "We Race, You Win" Give-away; and a nonstick steel wok in the "Use Your Noodle" sweepstakes.

15. James Still Papers, UK Libraries, Box 42 #3.

16. August 15, 1988. Still visited Mr. and Mrs. Paul Thompson, who had worked at HSS before moving to Mayfield, KY. Their baby was his godson, and he was sad to be separated from him. He lists all his official and unofficial godsons in the dedication of *An Appalachian Mother Goose;* even more impressive was his dedication of the 1996 edition of *Jack and the Wonder Beans* "To the Children of my Heart: Namesakes, Godchildren, Playfellows, Friends," followed by a list of forty names.

17. October 30, 1995, James Still Papers, UK Libraries, Box 44 #9.

18. Elloree Still Sharpe died on May 31, 1985, at the age of eighty-nine. She is buried in Lebanon Cemetery in Lafayette, AL.

19. Mary Beth Edelen (Comer's daughter by second marriage), telephone interview by author, September 25, 2002.

20. January 5, 1990, Greene's papers.

21. Barbara Sue Barnes Harris, interview by author, September 6, 2002.

22. Amburgey newsletter, 1987, James Still Papers, UK Libraries, Boxes 5 and 100, Amburgey Family.

23. Story of baby Nathan told by Frieda Mullins, interview by author, July 30, 2008.

24. Ibid.

25. Mike Mullins, interview by author, December 12, 2002.

26. Written by Still in December 1989; story and inscription quoted in Bill Weinberg, "Power of James Still," 219.

27. Story told to Molly Bundy in a phone conversation by Still in February 1998.

28. Mike Mullins, interview by author, December 12, 2002. Also remarks by Mullins in tributes to Still and Stewart at Hindman workshop, July 31, 2002.

29. Another friend was Helen Earp, who had been school bookkeeper from the 1960s until her retirement; she and Still maintained their correspondence until her death in 2000.

30. Jim Phelps, interview by author, April 3, 2003. In the summer of 2000, Helen visited the school, and Phelps drove the "two old timers" to the log house for a last visit.

31. Sam Linkous, comment to author.

32. Bob Young, interviews by author, December 9, 2002, and September 21–22, 2012.

33. The law firm was Weinberg, Campbell, Slone and Slone. Bill grew up in Roanoke, VA. After he and Lois married, he earned a master's at the Johns Hopkins School of Advanced International Studies; his thesis compared the economic development of Appalachia to areas in other countries. He took a job at Alice Lloyd College in order to live in the region. In 1975 he went into law practice in Hindman and served as Kentucky state representative from 1978 to 1982.

34. Bill Weinberg, interview by author, July 29, 2008. Also see June 21, 1996, Weinberg to Still, saying he has been accepted as a visiting fellow for 1996–1997 at Harvard Graduate School. James Still Papers, UK Libraries, Box 45 #6. Transcript of "A Letter from Godey" is in the HSS Still files.

35. Bill Weinberg, "The Power of James Still." This essay was originally a lecture Weinberg delivered at the LMU Mountain Heritage Literature Festival in 2008.

36. Lois Weinberg is the daughter of Kentucky governor (1959–1963) Bert T. Combs, a native of Clay County. Her mother, Mabel Hall, was from Knott County. Lois grew up in Prestonburg, then Frankfort. She met Bill in Virginia, and after marrying, they moved back to Knott County. She was founder and first director of the James Still Learning Center, the dyslexia program at HSS.

37. May 11, 1989, James Still Papers, UK Libraries, Box 37 #5.

38. Lois Weinberg, interview by author, July 29, 2008.

39. From Lois Weinberg's journal, October 17, 1995.

40. When Bill asked him his five favorite authors, Still acknowledged three Frenchmen: Alphonse Daudet for *Le Petit Chose,* Gustave Flaubert for *Madame Bovary,* and Jean Giono for *Horseman on the Roof.* A more recent title mentioned was *An Island Unto Oneself* (1990) by Tom Neale,

and he included an old favorite, *Little Boy Lost* (1920) by W. H. Hudson. Still liked anything by Richard Jefferies (1848–1887), the English nature writer.

41. For another version of the story, see Teresa Reynolds, "Reflections on Pappy Still," in *James Still in Interviews, Oral Histories and Memoirs,* ed. Ted Olson (Jefferson, NC: McFarland, 2009), 294.

42. Information and stories concerning James Still and the Bundy family were found in the correspondence of the James Still Papers, UK Libraries or provided by Molly Bundy through records of Still's visits and phone conversations from 1988 to 2001.

43. Molly also earned a master's degree at UK in Classics.

44. Molly Bundy, email to author, June 23, 2014.

45. James Chatham, "Rest My Soul," *Matching and Dispatching: Wedding and Funeral Stories of a Battle-Toughened Pastor* (Eugene, OR: Wipf and Stock Publishers, 2011), 146.

46. Ibid., 149, 151–52. "Artist" was first published in *Kentucky Poetry Review* 25, no. 2 (1989–90): 102.

47. Comments based on Jim Chatham's personal reflections following Still's funeral and on his public reflections drawn from his essay "Rest, My Soul."

48. First published in *Appalachian Heritage* 21, no. 2 (Spring 1993): 3. Also in Still, *From the Mountain,* 143.

49. After his death, his daughter and literary heir Teresa Reynolds made final arrangements for the UK library to remove the remainder of the materials to Lexington, where they were sorted and cataloged by Kate Black and her staff. The opening and dedication of the collection took place in 2007.

50. James Jr., born in 1946; Mark, 1948; Sharon Kay, 1953; Michael, 1958; and Teresa, 1967.

51. See chapter 20: "On to Morehead."

52. Still, *Wolfpen Notebooks,* 51.

53. January 20, 1986, James Still Papers, UK Libraries, Box 34 #1.

54. Estimated date of the conversation in the dining hall: August 3 or 4, 1993, during the sixteenth annual Appalachian Writers' Workshop.

55. *James Still's River of Earth,* made by KET to celebrate his ninetieth birthday.

56. James Still, phone conversation with Molly Bundy, February 9, 1996.

57. Teresa and her brother Michael had been named in his 1973 will to share the value of a small trust for their education. Five years later Still added a codicil that made Teresa rather than Monroe Amburgey the heir to all royalties and income from his literary works; and following her death, that income should go to her children. (Still Storage). A third will, written in Still's own distinctive cursive and dated 1993, named his literary executors as Jim Wayne Miller and Kate Black and the general executors as Mike Mullins and Lois Weinberg. His car, book royalties, and the remainder of his estate would be divided between Teresa and her daughter, Kaila. In his final will (signed July 1999), Teresa Bradley as principal was designated as

the recipient of his car and all his personal effects at his Hindman house and Wolfpen house. If there were items she did not want, they would go to HSS. The income from royalties as well as money in accounts was willed to Teresa. Insurance proceeds from his policies plus CDs at the Bank of Whitesburg were to benefit Kaila and Jacob. (Copies of James Still's wills are available in James Still Room, Camden-Carroll Library, MSU; James Still Papers, UK Libraries; and HSS Still files.)

58. Mike Mullins, interview by author, December 12, 2002, and Loyal Jones, interview by author, October 23, 2002.

59. Still was put in the same room that Teresa's mother had occupied twelve years before, when she died of cancer.

Epilogue

1. James Chatham, "Rest, My Soul," *Matching and Dispatching: Wedding and Funeral Stories of a Battle-Toughened Pastor* (Eugene, OR: Wipf and Stock Publishers, 2011), 147–48. For Loyal Jones's "Remarks at James Still's Funeral," see *Interviews*, 283–84.

2. Jennifer Hewlett and Art Jester, "James Still, Appalachian writer, dies: Former Kentucky poet laureate inspired generations of writers," *Lexington Herald-Leader*, April 29, 2001.

3. Bob Edwards interviewed Ted Olson on NPR's *Morning Edition*, May 1, 2001. The spot also included segments from a 1979 interview that Edwards did when he visited Still in Kentucky. The transcript was provided by NPR Audience and Community Relations.

4. Gurney Norman, "In Memoriam: Remembering James Still," *Appalachian Journal* 16, no. 1, 2 (2001): 6–9. Charles May, "Tribute to Jim Still," *Appalachian Heritage* 29, no. 4 (2001): 7–9. Jane Mayhall, "Protection: Elegy for James Still," *The Louisville Review* 49 (2001): 22. Hal Crowther, "A Man of the World," *The Oxford American* 41 (2001): 11–13. Silas House, "Remembering James Still," *Arts Across Kentucky* (Winter 2001): 10–15.

5. The exhibit first appeared in Hindman in the Kentucky Appalachian Artisan Center in the spring and summer of 2002. It was also displayed at LMU that fall.

6. *Crossing Troublesome* featured four landmark writers: Harriette Arnow, Jim Wayne Miller, Albert Stewart, and James Still; *Appalachian Heritage* 38, no. 4 (2010): 10–65.

7. This KET documentary is part of the bookclub@ket series and is available through the KET website www.ket.org/series/KBKCL. It first aired in November 2003 then appeared three more times in 2008 and twice in 2009.

8. Other writers inducted were Harriette Arnow, William Wells Brown, Harry Caudill, Elizabeth Madox Roberts, and Robert Penn Warren. The Kentucky Writers Hall of Fame recognizes Kentucky writers whose work reflects the character and culture of Kentucky and educates people about the state's literary heritage.

9. Boggess from Mars Hill College; Olson from East Tennessee State

University; and Crum from Alice Lloyd College. Participants in the workshop came from fifteen different institutions in Appalachia.

10. Hal Crowther, "On the Occasion of James Still's 100th Birthday," *Appalachian Journal* (Winter 2007): 186.

11. The address by Mike Mullins was published in *Appalachian Heritage* 38, no. 4 (2010). Donna Baker, head of Special Collections and Archives at MSU, organized the series, which took place July 17–21, 2006.

12. Gurney Norman moderated a panel discussion, Ted Olson gave a lecture, Randy Wilson performed music, Teresa Reynolds delivered comments, and William Marshall conducted the formal dedication. The collection, which comprises more than sixty cubic feet and covers a period of 120 years, includes published works, manuscripts, diaries, biographical material, personal and professional correspondence, financial records, interviews, book reviews, photographs, and memorabilia.

13. For a detailed study of *River of Earth*, its publication history, and its effects on the region and the nation, see chapters 3–5 in the author's dissertation "Following *River of Earth* from Source to Destination" (UK, 1995).

14. Ted Olson, interviewed by Jeff Biggers in "His Side of the Mountains," 17.

15. Ted Olson, "Behind the Scenes with Appalachian Writer James Still," *Appalachian History: Stories, Quotes and Anecdotes* (blog), posted by Dave Tabler, April 23, 2013; accessed October 20, 2015, www.appalachianhistory.net/20,3/04/behind-the-scenes-with-appalachian-writer-james-still.html.

16. The article appeared in *The Oxford American* in the fall of 2001 and is reprinted in *Critical Essays*, 242.

17. Maurice Manning, "Still's Lifework," *Lexington Herald-Leader*, May 27, 2001, quoted in Bill Weinberg, "The Power of James Still."

18. Ted Olson, "Behind the Scenes with Appalachian Writer James Still," *Appalachian History: Stories, Quotes*, April 23, 2013.

19. In 2016 a quick survey of responses on Amazon and Goodreads revealed that readers rated the book highly, but fewer than twenty total ratings appeared on the two popular websites.

20. Dean Cadle had tried to make such a contribution in the 1960s; Jim Wayne Miller was on his way to doing the same in the 1980s; Linc Fisch and Tawny Acker made an effort between 1985 and 1995; but no one before Olson had successfully published a collection of critical and personal responses to Still or his work.

21. One example of the influence across generations is the poem that was arranged by Frank X Walker to honor Danny Miller (1949–2008). Walker blended Wilkinson's poem "Terrain" (first published in *Appalachian Heritage*, 2008) and Still's "Heritage" (first published in *New Republic*, 1935), and "Voices from the Hills: A Celebration of Appalachian Writers in Honor of Danny Miller" provided it as a keepsake. It was published by Larkspur Press in 2009.

22. In 2016 UPK reported that their total net sales of all James Still works since 2001 numbered 32,370.

23. James Still, "From the Morgue," *The Hills Remember,* 397, 398–99.

24. See chapter 26: "Jim Wayne and Anson" for a discussion of the "Texas manuscript."

25. Smith to Still, April 5, 2001, Still Storage.

26. Silas House, introduction to *Chinaberry* by James Still, x.

27. Ibid., xi

28. Book flap of James Still, *Chinaberry,* ed. Silas House (Lexington: UPK, 2011).

29. Still, *Chinaberry,* 141. Erik Reece, "The Book in the Briefcase: James Still's Lost Literary Masterpiece," *Oxford American* no. 73 (September 2011): 129. Erik Reece points out that not until this penultimate line is the boy called "Jim." Reece called Silas House to ask about the naming of the character, and House responded that Still had written several conclusions to the book, and he had chosen to use the one that contained the line with the name.

Bibliography

Books by James Still (in order of publication date)

Hounds on the Mountain. New York: Viking, 1937.

River of Earth. New York: Viking, 1940.

On Troublesome Creek. New York: Viking, 1941.

Hounds on the Mountain. Edited by Victor and Carolyn Hammer. Lexington, Kentucky: Anvil Press, 1965.

River of Earth. New York: Popular Library paperback edition, copyright renewed 1968. Estimated printing date 1970.

Way Down Yonder on Troublesome Creek: Appalachian Riddles and Rusties. New York: Putnam, 1974.

Wolfpen Rusties: Appalachian Riddles & Gee-Haw Whimmy-Diddles. Illustrated by Janet McCaffery. New York: Putnam, 1975.

Pattern of a Man and Other Stories. Frankfort, KY: Gnomon, 1976.

Jack and the Wonder Beans. New York: Putnam, 1976.

Sporty Creek: A Novel about an Appalachian Boyhood. New York: Putnam, 1977.

River of Earth. Lexington: University Press of Kentucky, 1978.

The Run for the Elbertas. Lexington: University Press of Kentucky, 1980.

River of Earth: A Poem and Other Poems. Foreword by Edward Prichard. Lexington, KY: King Library Press, 1982.

Wolfpen Poems. Berea, KY: Berea College Press, 1986.

Rusties, Riddles, & Gee-Haw Whimmy-Diddles. Illustrated by Janet McCaffery. Lexington: University Press of Kentucky, 1989.

The Wolfpen Notebooks: A Record of Appalachian Life. Lexington: University Press of Kentucky, 1991.

Jack and the Wonder Beans. Illustrated by Margo Tomes. Lexington: University Press of Kentucky, 1996.

Appalachian Mother Goose. Illustrated by Paul Brett Johnson. Lexington: University Press of Kentucky, 1998.

Sporty Creek. Illustrated by Paul Brett Johnson. Lexington: University Press of Kentucky, 1999.

From the Mountain, From the Valley: New and Collected Poems. Edited by Ted Olson. Lexington: University Press of Kentucky, 2001.

Chinaberry. Edited by Silas House. Lexington: University Press of Kentucky, 2011.

The Hills Remember: The Complete Short Stories of James Still. Edited by Ted Olson. Lexington: University Press of Kentucky, 2012.

Major Collections

James Still Papers, 1885–2007. 87M12, Special Collections and Digital Programs, University of Kentucky Libraries, Lexington, KY.

The James Still Room. Special Collections section of Camden-Carroll Library, Morehead State University, Morehead, KY. Also letters and memos from the office files of Larry Besant, director of the library 1986–2003.

James Still files. Hindman Settlement School office, Hindman, KY.

Jim Wayne Miller Collection. Special Collections Library, Western Kentucky University, Bowling Green, KY.

Still Storage, Hindman, KY. At Still's death, the letters and papers in his Hindman house and his log house were temporarily stored near Hindman, under the supervision of his daughter, Teresa Reynolds. Research for this biography conducted at that location is cited as "Still Storage." A large portion of those papers has since been moved to the collections at the University of Kentucky or the James Still Room at Morehead State University.

Other Collections

Cratis D. Williams Papers, 1783–1986. Appalachian State University, Belk Library, Boone, NC.

Dean Cadle Collection, 1919–1997. Special Collections and Digital Programs, University of Kentucky Libraries, Lexington, KY.

Dean Cadle, in Southern Appalachian Writers Collection, D. H. Ramsey Library, Special Collections, University of North Carolina–Asheville, Asheville, NC.

Dorothy Thomas Archive. Lincoln City Library, Lincoln, NE.

James Still Collection. Berea College Special Collections & Archives, Berea, KY.

James Still Papers. Archives and Special Collections of Lincoln Memorial University, Carnegie-Vincent Library, Harrogate, TN.

James Still Papers. Cobb Memorial (Valley) Archives, Shawmut and Valley, AL.

James Still publication files. University Press of Kentucky, Lexington, KY.

Katherine Anne Porter Papers. Special Collections, University of Maryland Libraries, Hornbake Library, College Park, MD.

Marjorie Kinnan Rawlings Papers. University of Florida Smathers Library, Special and Area Studies Collections, Gainesville, FL.

Robert Francis Papers (MS 403). Special Collections and University Archives, University of Massachusetts–Amherst Libraries, Amherst, MA.

Vanderbilt U. Special Collection: www.library.vanderbilt.edu/speccol/urr/
biographybiblio.shtml.

Private Collections

Correspondence and photos drawn from the collections of Dobree Adams,
Alice Brown, Harry Brown, Walter Brunner, Molly Bundy, Ed and Pauline Cheek, Tom Eblen, Linc Fisch, Marita Garin, Jonathan Greene,
Wade Hall, Barbara Sue Barnes Harris, Loyal Jones, Elizabeth Lamont,
Maurice Manning, Sam McKinney, Alfred Perrin, Dare Redmond
(courtesy of Alan Redmond), Teresa Perry Reynolds, Anne Weatherford, Lois Weinberg, and Bob Young.

Interviews of James Still

The author's unpublished interviews and conversations with James Still are
transcribed or noted.
1993 ACA visit to Mars Hill College, September 20–October 1.
Conversations.
1994 March 29 interview in Lexington; June 4 telephone conversation; July
6 and 13 conversations at Springs Inn in Lexington; August 1 conversations at Hindman Writers' Workshop; November 12 meeting in Baltimore for SAMLA.
1995 May 7 meeting in Berea for Al Perrin's memorial service.
1996 Visit to Mars Hill College, April 25–30.
1997 Interviews at Still's house in Hindman: June 25 and 26; July 10 and
11. Conversation at the log house with Gurney Norman, Wendell Berry,
James Still, Amy Payne (student researcher), and Carol Boggess.
1998 August 10 interview at log house. Still visited North Carolina October 8–11.

Interviews and Communications with James Still's Family and Friends

Alabama: Mary Beth Edelen, Barbara Sue Barnes Harris, Edith Johnson,
Nina Still Langley, Rosemarie Livings, Hervey and Gladys Sharpe,
George Zachry, Mary Zatezelo
Berea: George Brosi, Alice Brown, Warren Brunner, Sidney Farr, Loyal
Jones
Bowling Green/Frankfort: Jim Wayne Miller, Mary Ellen Miller, Jonathan
Greene
Hindman: Hiram Bradley, Chris Holbrook, James Hurt, Sam Linkous,
Mason Moore, Frieda Mullins, Mike Mullins, James Perry, Jim Phelps,
Teresa Lynn Perry Reynolds, Barbara Smith, Herb E. Smith, Shirley
Williams, Randy Wilson, Bill Weinberg, Lois Combs Weinberg, Bob
Young
Lexington: Kate Black, Thomas Clark, Jerome Crouch, Tom Eblen, Linc
Fisch, Morris Grubbs, Sally Jackson, Bill Marshall, Gurney Norman,
Laura Sutton

Louisville: Molly Bundy, Jim Chatham, Wade Hall, Judi Jennings, Greg Swem

Morehead: Larry Besant, Wilma Crawford, Jack Ellis, Fran Helpingstein, Claudia Hicks, Sam McKinney, Ann Olson, M. K. Thomas

Western North Carolina/East Tennessee: Sandra Ballard, Rhonda England Breedlove, Ed and Pauline Cheek, Wilma Dykeman, Elizabeth Lamont, George Ella Lyon, Ted Olson, Alfred Perrin, Tom Perrin, Anne Weatherford

Email/telephone: Harry Brown, James Gifford, James McConkey, Maurice Manning, Cleopatra Mathis, Jane Mayhall, Chris Offutt, Alessandro Portelli, James Reston, Richard Saunders

Books and Articles

Bain, David Howard. *Whose Woods These Are: A History of the Bread Loaf Writers' Conference 1926–1992.* Hopewell, NJ: Ecco Press, 1993.

Baker, Donna J. "Keeper at 'The Light to the Mountains': James Still at Morehead State University." *Appalachian Heritage* 38, no. 4 (2010): 39–43.

Beattie, L. Elisabeth. "James Still: Conversation with a Kentucky Writer." In *Conversations with Kentucky Writers,* 356–74. Lexington: University Press of Kentucky, 1996.

Berry, Wendell. "In Memory: James Still," "A Master Language." In *Imagination in Place,* 73–82. Berkeley, CA: Counterpoint, 2010.

Biggers, Jeff. "His Side of the Mountains: The Enduring Legacy of Southern Poet James Still: An Interview with Editor Ted Olson." *The Bloomsbury Review,* July/August 2002, 17–18. Reprinted in Olson, Ted, ed. *James Still in Interviews, Oral Histories, and Memoirs.* Southern Appalachian Studies vol. 23. Jefferson, NC: McFarland, 2009.

Biggers, Jeff. "Introduction." In *No Lonesome Road: Selected Prose and Poems by Don West,* edited by Jeff Biggers and George Brosi, xiii-lviii. Urbana: University of Illinois Press, 2004.

Boggess, Carol. "Following *River of Earth* from Source to Destination." PhD diss., University of Kentucky, 1995.

Brosi, George. "Jim Wayne Miller." *Appalachian Heritage* 37, no. 3 (2009): 11–15.

Burns, Ken, and Lynn Novik, directors. *The War.* PBS, 2007. DVD.

Cadle, Dean. "Man on Troublesome." *Yale Review* 57 (1968): 236–55.

Cadle, Dean. "Pattern of a Writer: Attitudes of James Still." *Appalachian Journal* 15, no. 2 (1988): 104–43.

Campbell, Tracy. *Short of the Glory: The Fall and Redemption of Edward F. Prichard, Jr.* Lexington: University Press of Kentucky, 1998.

Ceram, C. W. *Gods, Graves, and Scholars; The Story of Archaeology.* New York: Knopf, 1951.

Chatham, James O. *Matching and Dispatching: Wedding and Funeral Stories of a Battle-toughened Pastor.* Eugene, OR: Wipf & Stock Publishers, 2011.

Clark, Thomas D., and John A. Spelman. *The Kentucky*. New York: Farrar & Rinehart, 1942.

Cook, Jan Walters. "Green Peppers and a Straw Hat." In *Crossing Troublesome: 25 Years of the Appalachian Writers Workshop*, edited by Leatha Kendrick and George Ella Lyon, 114–15. Nicholasville, KY: Wind Publications, 2002. Reprinted in *Interviews*.

Cornett, Terry. "A James Still Bibliography." In *The Iron Mountain Review: James Still Issue*, edited by John M. Coward and Robert D. Dunham, 29–33. vol. 2 (Summer). Emory, VA: Emory & Henry College, 1984. Revised and reprinted in *The Wolfpen Notebooks*, 1991.

Coward, John M., and Robert D. Denham, eds. *The Iron Mountain Review: James Still Issue*, vol. 2. Emory, VA: Emory & Henry College, 1984.

Cox, James M. "Regionalism: A Diminished Thing." In *Columbia Literary History of the United States*, edited by Emory Elliott, 761–84. New York: Columbia University Press, 1988.

Creason, Joe. "Some Things a Man Does Just for Himself." *Louisville Courier-Journal Magazine*, February 14, 1960. Reprinted in *Interviews*.

Crowther, Hal. "A Man of the World." *Oxford American* 41 (2001): 11–13.

Crowther, Hal. "On the Occasion of James Still's 100th Birthday." *Appalachian Journal* (Winter 2001): 189–90. Reprinted in *Interviews*.

Crum, Claude Lafie. *River of Words: James Still's Literary Legacy*. Nicholasville, KY: Wind Publications, 2007.

Dick, David. *Jesse Stuart: The Heritage, A Biography*. North Middletown, KY: Plum Lick Pub., 2005.

Dykeman, Wilma. "Mock Letters." In *A Gathering at the Forks*, edited by George Ella Lyon, Jim Wayne Miller, and Gurney Norman, 118–19. Wise, VA: Vision Books, 1993.

Dykeman, Wilma. "Mountain Story Keeps Its Magic." *Knoxville News-Sentinel*, November 7, 1965.

Dykeman, Wilma. Untitled lecture. (Writers' Workshop, Hindman Settlement School, Hindman, KY, July 30, 2002.

Edwards, Bob. NPR *Morning Edition*. May 1, 2001, interview of Ted Olson and clips from 1979 interview of James Still.

Eller, Ronald D. *Uneven Ground: Appalachia since 1945*. Lexington: University Press of Kentucky, 2008.

England, Rhonda George. "Literary Biography of James Still: A Beginning." MA thesis, Morehead State University, 1984.

Farr, Sidney. "I'm Always Writing." *Appalachian Heritage* 35, no. 3 (2007): 22–23.

Fisch, Linc. "In Remembrance of James Still." In *James Still in Interviews, Oral Histories and Memoirs*, edited by Ted Olson, 265–75. Jefferson, NC: McFarland, 2009.

Francis, Robert. *The Trouble with Francis: An Autobiography*. Amherst: University of Massachusetts Press, 1971.

Gifford, James M., and Erin R. Kazee. "Both Ends of a Walnut Log: The Correspondence of James Still and Jesse Stuart." In *James Still in Inter-*

views, Oral Histories and Memoirs, edited by Ted Olson, 212–32. Jefferson, NC: McFarland, 2009.

Gifford, James M., and Erin R. Kazee. *Jesse Stuart: An Extraordinary Life.* Ashland, KY: Jesse Stuart Foundation, 2010.

Glaser, Joe. "Slick as a Dogwood Hoe Handle." *Appalachian Journal* 11, no. 3 (1983): 4–9. Reprinted in Olson, Ted, and Kathy H. Olson, eds. *James Still: Critical Essays on the Dean of Appalachian Literature.* Southern Appalachian Studies vol. 17. Jefferson, NC: McFarland, 2007.

Goodman, Bill, host. "James Still's Legacy." Kentucky Educational Television. November 25, 2003. Available at http://www.ket.org/bookclub/.

Green, Chris. "Headwaters: The Early Poetics of James Still, Don West, and Jesse Stuart." In *James Still: Critical Essays on the Dean of Appalachian Literature,* edited by Ted Olson and Kathy H. Olson, 261–64. Jefferson, NC: McFarland, 2009.

Greene, Jonathan. "A Memoir of James Still." In *James Still in Interviews, Oral Histories and Memoirs,* edited by Ted Olson, 261–64. Jefferson, NC: McFarland, 2009.

Griggs, Robert. "Valley of Ten Thousand Smokes, The." *National Geographic,* January 1917, 33–68.

Hall, Wade. *James Still: Portrait of the Artist as a Boy in Alabama.* Lexington, KY: King Library Press, 1998.

Hanlon, Tina. "'Read My Tales, Spin My Rhymes': The Books for Children." In *James Still: Critical Essays on the Dean of Appalachian Literature,* edited by Ted Olson and Kathy H. Olson, 174–89. Jefferson, NC: McFarland, 2007.

The Heritage of Chambers County, Alabama vol. 9. Clanton, AL: Heritage Pub. Consultants, 1999.

Hess, Earl J. *Lincoln Memorial University and the Shaping of Appalachia.* Knoxville: University of Tennessee Press, 2011.

History and Families, Knott County, Kentucky. Paducah, KY: Turner Pub., 1995.

House, Charles. *One with the Fox.* Sarasota, FL: Pub This Press, 2005.

House, Silas. "Introduction." In *Chinaberry,* by James Still, edited by Silas House, ix-xviii. Lexington: University Press of Kentucky, 2011.

House, Silas. "Remembering James Still." *Arts Across Kentucky,* Winter 2001, 10–13. Reprinted in *Interviews.*

House, Silas. "The Art of Being Still." *New York Times* online opinion page. December 1, 2012.

Hudock, Sandy. James Still Homepage. http://faculty.csupueblo.edu/sandy.hudock/ jshome.html.

Jennings, Judi. "Travels with Mr. Still." In *James Still in Interviews, Oral Histories and Memoirs,* edited by Ted Olson, 242–47. Jefferson, NC: McFarland, 2009.

Johnson, Wade. "World War II through the eyes of the Cape Fear," interview by Paul Zarbock, November 15, 2002. http://capefearww2.uncwil.edu/voices/wade_johnson251.html.

Jones, Loyal. "Remarks at James Still's Funeral (May 1, 2001)." In *James*

Still in Interviews, Oral Histories and Memoirs, edited by Ted Olson, 283–84. Jefferson, NC: McFarland, 2009.

Kendrick, Leatha, and George Ella Lyon, eds. *Crossing Troublesome: 25 Years of the Appalachian Writers Workshop.* Nicholasville, KY: Wind, 2002.

Kohler, Dayton. "Jesse Stuart and James Still Mountain Regionalists." *College English* 3 (1942): 523–33.

Kohler, Dayton. "River of Earth." Review of *River of Earth. The Southern Literary Messenger,* March 1940, 205.

Kroll, Harry Harrison. *The Mountainy Singer.* New York: W. Morrow, 1928.

Lamont, Elizabeth. "An Unsung Appalachian Literary Heritage: The Significance of James Still's Undergraduate Experience." *Appalachian Heritage* 38, no. 4 (2010): 32–37.

Lee, Laura. Introduction to *The Wolfpen Notebooks: A Record of Appalachian Life,* by James Still, 1–8. Lexington: University Press of Kentucky, 1991.

Lindsey, Bobby L. *The Reason for the Tears: A History of Chambers County, Alabama, 1832–1900.* West Point, GA: Hester Print., 1971.

Lorence, James J. *A Hard Journey: The Life of Don West.* Urbana: University of Illinois Press, 2007.

Lyon, George Ella, Jim Wayne Miller, and Gurney Norman, eds. *A Gathering at the Forks: Fifteen Years of the Hindman Settlement School Appalachian Writers Workshop.* Wise, VA: Vision Books, 1993.

Manning, Maurice. "Still's Lifework." Review of *From the Mountain, From the Valley. Lexington Herald-Leader,* May 27, 2001.

Manning, Maurice. "Travels with the Wolfpen Poet." *Writer's Bloc: English Club Newsletter.* This text was made available by Manning.

Marion, Jeff Daniel. "A Hindman Recipe." In *Crossing Troublesome: 25 Years of the Appalachian Writers Workshop,* edited by Leatha Kendrick and George Ella Lyon, 110–11. Nicholasville, KY: Wind Publications, 2002.

Marsh, Walter R. *Elementary Algebra.* New York: Charles Scribner's Sons, 1907.

May, Charles. "Tribute to James Still." *Appalachian Heritage* 29, no. 4 (2001): 7–9.

Mayhall, Jane. "James Still: Quality of Life, Quality of Art." *Shenandoah: The Washington and Lee University Review* 48, no. 2 (1998): 56–73. Reprinted in *Critical Essays.*

Mayhall, Jane. "Protection: Elegy for James Still." *The Louisville Review* 49 (2001): 22.

Miller, Jim Wayne. " . . . And Ladies of the Club." Review of *The History of Southern Literature,* edited by Louis Rubin. *Appalachian Journal* 14, no. 1 (1986): 64–69.

Miller, Jim Wayne. "A Mountain Still." *Louisville Courier-Journal Magazine,* July 13, 1986, 18–24.

Miller, Jim Wayne. "Daring to Look in the Well: A Conversation." In *The*

Iron Mountain Review: James Still Issue, edited by John M. Coward and Robert D. Denham, 3–10. Emory, VA: Emory & Henry College, 1984. Reprinted in *Interviews.*

Miller, Jim Wayne. *Every Leaf a Mirror: A Jim Wayne Miller Reader.* Edited by Morris Allen Grubbs and Mary Ellen Miller. Lexington: University Press of Kentucky, 2014.

Miller, Jim Wayne. "Happy Man on Troublesome Creek." *Vanderbilt Magazine,* Summer 1987, 17–18.

Miller, Jim Wayne. "Jim Dandy: James Still at Eighty." *Appalachian Heritage* 14, no. 4 (1986): 8–20. Reprinted in *Critical Essays.*

Miller, Jim Wayne. "Madly to Learn: James Still, the Teacher." In *From the Fort to the Future: Educating the Children of Kentucky,* edited by Edwina Ann Doyle, Ruby Layson, and Anne Armstrong Thompson, 230–43. Lexington, KY: Kentucky Images, 1987.

Mims, Edwin. *History of Vanderbilt University.* Nashville: Vanderbilt University Press, 1946.

Morrison, Theodore. Review of *Man with a Bull-Tongue Plow,* by Jesse Stuart. *The Atlantic Monthly* 155, no. 4 (1935).

Mullins, Mike, Geneva Smith, and Ron Daley, eds. *History and Families, Knott County, Kentucky.* Paducah, KY: Turner Pub., 1995.

Mullins, Mike. "'It's Not a Job to Me': Mike Mullins and the Hindman Settlement School." *Appalachian Journal* 33, no. 3/4 (2006): 310–42.

Mullins, Michael Lee. "I Call Him Mr. Still." In *A Gathering at the Forks,* edited by George Ella Lyon, Jim Wayne Miller, and Gurney Norman, 287–91. Wise, VA: Vision Books, 1993.

Mullins, Mike. "My Friend, Mr. Still." *Appalachian Heritage* 38, no. 4 (2010): 12–18.

Niles, Rena. "Obscurity Begins Back Home for Kentucky's James Still." *Louisville Courier-Journal Magazine,* April 30, 1939. Reprinted in *Interviews.*

Norman, Gurney. *Divine Right's Trip.* Frankfort, KY: Gnomon Press, 1990. First published in 1972.

Norman, Gurney. "I Write Because I'm Unhappy When Not Writing." *Hazard Herald,* October 2, 1958.

Norman, Gurney. "In Memoriam: Remembering James Still." *Appalachian Journal* 16, no. 2 (2001): 6–9.

Olson, Ann. "Before Saying Yes." In *James Still in Interviews, Oral Histories and Memoirs,* edited by Ted Olson, 201–4. Jefferson, NC: Wind Publications, 2009.

Olson, Ted. "Behind the Scenes with Appalachia Writer James Still," interview by Dave Tabler. *Appalachian History: Stories, Quotes and Anecdotes* (blog), April 23, 2013. Accessed October 20, 2015. www.appalachianhistory.net/2013/04/behind-the-scenes-with-appaachian-writer-james-still.html.

Olson, Ted, and Kathy H. Olson, eds. *James Still: Critical Essays on the Dean of Appalachian Literature.* Southern Appalachian Studies vol. 17. Jefferson, NC: McFarland, 2007.

Olson, Ted, ed. *James Still in Interviews, Oral Histories and Memoirs.* Southern Appalachian Studies vol. 23. Jefferson, NC: McFarland, 2009.

Pappas, Christine. "Singers of Life: The Literary Relationship of Dorothy Thomas and Loren Eiseley." *Newsletter of the Friends of Loren Eiseley* 15 (Spring 2001): 7.

Phillips, Robert, ed. *Letters of Delmore Schwartz.* Ontario Review Press, 1984.

Pictorial History of Knott County Kentucky. Morley, MO: Acclaim Press, 2010.

Reece, Erik. "The Book in the Briefcase: James Still's Lost Literary Masterpiece." *Oxford American* no. 73 (September 2011): 128–30.

Reynolds, Teresa Perry. "Reflections on Pappy Still." In *James Still in Interviews, Oral Histories and Memoirs,* edited by Ted Olson, 292–97. Jefferson, NC: Wind Publications, 2009.

Richardson, H. Edward. *Jesse: The Biography of an American Writer, Jesse Hilton Stuart.* New York: McGraw-Hill, 1984.

Saunders, Richard L. *Never Been Rich: The Life and Work of a Southern Ruralist Writer, Harry Harrison Kroll.* Knoxville: University of Tennessee Press, 2011.

Smith, Lee. "Marble Cake and Moonshine." In *Dimestore: A Writer's Life,* 63–75. Chapel Hill, NC: Algonquin, 2016.

Stewart, Albert. "At Home with James Still on Dead Mare." *Appalachian Heritage* 1, no. 1 (1973): 37–45.

Still, James. "A Century of Summers: 100 Years of Childhood Memories Right Here in the Mountains." Interview by Randy Wilson. *Kid's Radio.* WMMT. August 19, 1998.

Still, James. "An Interview with James Still" by Jerry Williamson. *Appalachian Journal* 6 (Winter 1979): 121–41. An edited form is available in *Interviewing Appalachia:* The Appalachian Journal *Interviews 1978–1992,* edited by J. W. Williamson and Edwin T. Arnold, 49–66. Knoxville: University of Tennessee Press, 1994.

Still, James. *A Master's Time: 80 Years for James Still.* Kentucky Educational Television, 1986. DVD. Can be accessed at https://vimeo.com/38946606.

Still, James. "Bloody Breathitt." *Time,* February 26, 1940.

Still, James. "James Still on His Life and Work." Interview by Judi Jennings. *Heritage.* June Appal Recordings, Whitesburg, KY: Appalshop. 1992 tape, 2011 CD. The full transcript was made available to the author by Jennings.

Still, James, and Randy Wilson, performers. *Heritage.* June Appal Recordings, 1992 tape, 2011 CD.

Still, James. *Conversations with James Still.* Directed by Michael Lasater. VIMEO. Adapted from a 1998 video recording. Accessed at https://vimeo.com/38946606. Transcript interview in JWM Coll.

Still, James. "A Man Singing to Himself: An Autobiographical Essay." In *From the Mountain, From the Valley: New and Collected Poems,* by James Still, edited by Ted Olson, 5–24. Lexington: University Press of Kentucky, 2001.

Still, James. "James Still 1906–." In Contemporary Authors Autobiography Series, vol. 17, 231–48. Detroit, MI: Gale, 1993.

Still, James. *James Still's River of Earth.* Kentucky Educational Television, 1997. DVD. Access through the KET website www.ket.org.

Still, James. "This Is My Best." *Mountain Life and Work: Magazine of the Southern Mountains,* 1954, 32–37.

Stoddart, Jess. *Challenge and Change in Appalachia: The Story of Hindman Settlement School.* Lexington: University Press of Kentucky, 2002.

Stoneback, H. R. "Rivers of Earth and Troublesome Creeks: The Agrarianism of James Still." *Kentucky Review* 10, no. 3 (1990): 3–26.

Stoneback, H. R. "Roberts, Still, Stuart, and Warren." *Kentucky Humanities* no. 1/2 (2001): 27–37.

Terkel, Studs. *"The Good War": An Oral History of World War Two.* New York: New Press, 1984.

The United States of Poetry. Washington Square Films for Independent Television Service and PBS. 1996.

Weinberg, Bill. "The Power of James Still." *Appalachian Journal* 36, no. 3/4 (2009): 218–27.

West, James L. W. *American Authors and the Literary Marketplace since 1900.* Philadelphia: University of Pennsylvania Press, 1988.

Williams, John Alexander. *Appalachia: A History.* Chapel Hill: University of North Carolina Press, 2002.

Williams, Shirley. "Still Writing after All These Years." *Louisville Courier-Journal Magazine,* July 9, 1978, 23–31. Reprinted in *Interviews.*

Williamson, Jerry. "A Cold Day in Hell: An Interview with Jerry Williamson" by Pat Beaver and Helen Lewis. *Appalachian Journal* 28, no. 1 (2000): 78–115.

Young, William Henry. "Personal Memories of Jesse Stuart and James Still." *Kentucky Explorer,* November 2001, 12–14. Reprinted in *Interviews.*

Zachry, George C. "James Still: A Biographical Sketch of a Native of LaFayette, Alabama and the Chattahoochee Valley." In *Chronicles of the Chattahoochee Valley,* 145–89. Valley, AL: Chattahoochee Valley Historical Society, 1995.

Index